Exam 70-220

MCSE

Windows® 2000
Network Security
Design

TRAINING GUIDE

New Riders

Roberta Bragg, MCSE, MCT

MCSE TRAINING GUIDE (70-220): DESIGNING SECURITY FOR A WINDOWS 2000 NETWORK

Copyright © 2000 by New Riders Publishing

FIRST EDITION: *August, 2000*

International Standard Book Number: 0-7357-0984-X

Library of Congress Catalog Card Number: 00-100503

04 03 02 01 00   7 6 5 4 3 2 1

Composed in Garamond and MCPdigital by New Riders Publishing

Printed in the United States of America

Trademarks

All terms mentioned in this book that are known to be trademarks or service marks have been appropriately capitalized. New Riders Publishing cannot attest to the accuracy of this information. Use of a term in this book should not be regarded as affecting the validity of any trademark or service mark.

Windows is a registered trademark of the Microsoft Corporation.

Warning and Disclaimer

This book is designed to provide information about the *Windows 2000 Network Security Design* exam. Every effort has been made to make this book as complete and as accurate as possible, but no warranty or fitness is implied.

Use of the Microsoft Approved Study Guide Logo on this product signifies that it has been independently reviewed and approved in complying with the following standards:

- Acceptable coverage of all content related to Microsoft exam number 70-220, entitled Designing Security for a Microsoft Windows 2000 Network
- Sufficient performance-based exercises that relate closely to all required content
- Technically accurate content, based on sampling of text

PUBLISHER
David Dwyer

EXECUTIVE EDITOR
Al Valvano

ACQUISITIONS EDITORS
Nancy Maragioglio
Ann Quinn

MANAGING EDITOR
Gina Brown

PRODUCT MARKETING MANAGER
Stephanie Layton

MANAGER OF PUBLICITY
Susan Petro

DEVELOPMENT EDITOR
Christopher Morris

PROJECT EDITOR
Lori A. Lyons

COPY EDITORS
Keith Cline
Krista Hansing

TECHNICAL REVIEWERS
Brian Komar
Grant Jones

SOFTWARE DEVELOPMENT SPECIALIST
Michael Hunter

INDEXER
Cheryl Lenser

PROOFREADER
Shanon Martin

COMPOSITION
Scan Communications Group, Inc.

MANUFACTURING COORDINATOR
Chris Moos

INTERIOR DESIGNER
Louisa Klucznik

COVER DESIGNER
Aren Howell

Contents at a Glance

Part V Designing a Security Solution for Access Between Networks

Part VI Final Review

Part VII Appendixes

Table of Contents

PART I: Analyzing Business Requirements

PART II: Analyzing Technical Requirements

PART III: Analyzing Security Requirements

PART IV: Designing a Windows 2000 Security Solution

PART V: Designing a Security Solution for Access Between Networks

PART VI: Final Review

PART VII: Appendixes

About the Author

A veteran of more than 20 years of information system experience, **Roberta Bragg** currently specializes in Windows (NT and Windows 2000) security issues. She is a columnist (Security Advisor) and contributing editor for *Microsoft Certified Professional Magazine.* In the past, she has developed curriculum on C, C++, Windows NT, Microsoft Exchange Server, VPNs, and firewalls. Her virtual company, Have Computer Will Travel, has her working across the world, lecturing, consulting, and training.

About the Technical Reviewers

These reviewers contributed their considerable hands-on expertise to the entire development process for *MCSE Training Guide: Windows 2000 Network Security Design.* As the book was being written, these dedicated professionals reviewed all the material for technical content, organization, and flow. Their feedback was critical to ensuring that *MCSE Training Guide: Windows 2000 Network Security Design* fits our reader's need for the highest-quality technical information.

Brian Komar

Brian Komar, MCSE+I, MCT, is an independent consultant currently doing lots of work with Microsoft Corporation. Tasks include acting as the technical lead for the Windows 2000 security course, reviewing published materials, delivering Windows 2000 MOC courses, consulting, and speaking at several conferences on Windows 2000 Active Directory and security design topics.

In his spare time, Brian enjoys travelling with his wife, Krista.

Grant Jones

Grant Jones has worked as a network engineer for the past five years, and is certified as an MCSE, MCP+I, MCT, CNE 3/4 (Certified NetWare Engineer versions 3 and 4), and CNI (Certified NetWare Instructor). For the past three years, Grant has been teaching the official Microsoft core classes along with IIS and TCP/IP. He currently is working for Prosoft I-Net Solutions, where he is creating courseware for CIW certifications. Grant has written courses on Internet security and IIS 4.0; the course he developed on IIS 4.0 was taught to Microsoft Visual Basic programmers in Redmond, Washington. In addition, Grant has spoken at trade shows, such as Internet World and Internet Commerce Expo on the topics of Internet security and electronic commerce.

Dedication

This book is for Lori, to whom I never gave a lion, and to Luke and Aaron, who never needed one.

To all of you responsible for the security of information systems everywhere:

"Illegitimus non-Carborendum."

Acknowledgments

Simple thanks are not enough, but they'll have to do for now. Thanks to all of you at New Riders who made this book possible. Special appreciation is due to Christopher Morris, who kept all the pieces together (especially my spirit), and to Brian Komar, whose knowledge of Windows 2000 and insistence on perfection makes this book.

Tell Us What You Think!

As the reader of this book, you are the most important critic and commentator. We value your opinion and want to know what we're doing right, what we could do better, what areas you'd like to see us publish in, and any other words of wisdom you're willing to pass our way.

As the Executive Editor for the Networking team at New Riders Publishing, I welcome your comments. You can fax, email, or write me directly to let me know what you did or didn't like about this book—as well as what we can do to make our books stronger.

Please note that I cannot help you with technical problems related to the topic of this book, and that due to the high volume of mail I receive, I might not be able to reply to every message.

When you write, please be sure to include this book's title and author as well as your name and phone or fax number. I will carefully review your comments and share them with the author and editors who worked on the book.

Fax: 317-581-4663

Email: nrfeedback@newriders.com

Mail: Al Valvano
          Executive Editor
          Certification
          New Riders Publishing
          201 West 103rd Street
          Indianapolis, IN 46290 USA

How to Use This Book

New Riders Publishing has made an effort in its *Training Guide* series to make the information as accessible as possible for the purposes of learning the certification material. Here, you have an opportunity to view the many instructional features that have been incorporated into the books to achieve that goal.

CHAPTER OPENER

Each chapter begins with a set of features designed to allow you to maximize study time for that material.

List of Objectives: Each chapter begins with a list of the objectives as stated by Microsoft.

Objective Explanations: Immediately following each objective is an explanation of it, providing context that defines it more meaningfully in relation to the exam. Because Microsoft can sometimes be vague in its objectives list, the objective explanations are designed to clarify any vagueness by relying on the authors' test-taking experience.

OBJECTIVES

This chapter covers the following Microsoft-specified objectives for the "Analyzing Technical Requirements" section of the Designing Security for a Microsoft Windows 2000 Network exam:

Evaluate the company's existing and planned technical environment.

- Analyze company size and user and resource distribution.
- Assess the available connectivity between the geographic location of work sites and remote sites.
- Assess the net available bandwidth.
- Analyze performance requirements.
- Analyze the method of accessing data and systems.
- Analyze network roles and responsibilities. Roles include administrative, user, service, resource ownership, and application.

▶ Security exists to protect the network. The network exists to support the business. The business is composed of people and activities. Before you can devise a security strategy, you need to know the business needs of the company, its people, its processes and locations, and its current information system and infrastructure. This objective addresses specific technical areas of the infrastructure.

Analyze the impact of the security design on the existing and planned technical environment.

- Assess existing systems and applications.
- Identify existing and planned upgrades and rollouts.
- Analyze technical support structure.
- Analyze existing and planned network and systems management.

CHAPTER 3

Analyzing Technical Environments

Chapter Outline: Learning always gets a boost when you can see both the forest and the trees. To give you a visual image of how the topics in a chapter fit together, you will find a chapter outline at the beginning of each chapter. You will also be able to use this for easy reference when looking for a particular topic.

STUDY STRATEGIES

▶ This is not material that you can learn while sitting at a computer and practicing the steps. Nor is this material that comes easily to many IT people. We are used more to analyzing why we can't reach a system over the network or how to set up a virtual private network (VPN) than to analyzing the business structure. Take heart, though. Although making a business the next Microsoft or Amazon.com may be difficult, understanding basic business structures and strategies is not.

▶ Most of the information that you seek is well documented and easy to interpret.

▶ Don't blow it off, though; understanding the structure, orientation, and scope of a business is critical if you are to secure it.

▶ Understanding your business practice requires understanding others. Use the examples in this book for reference, and then find others. You're lucky—the Internet makes this process so easy. Use it. A good place to start is with www.yahoo.com or www.altavista.com. Hoovers (www.hoovers.com) will provide you a synopsis and some financial information on most businesses. It also has an excellent search engine that will enable you to search by company name, stock index, keywords, or location. You can use this to identify businesses in a certain industry segment. You then can subscribe to this service to receive detailed information, but many services are free. Visit the Web sites of e-zines such as *New York Times*, *Newsweek*, *Business Weekly*, MSNBC, CNBC, and the *Wall Street Journal*. All these will reference the Web sites of businesses you may want to examine. While business information on a Web site can vary, you may be surprised at how much you can learn about a business—even yours—from looking there. You likely will find annual reports, locations of plants, history, chief officers, management philosophies, acquisition strategies, and expansion plans. You may find information that companies paid to learn about their competitors in the past. You may even learn first of some new technological development that is applicable to your particular needs. Soon you will feel comfortable with the terminology and strategies that businesses use.

▶ Remember—when you are analyzing your business, it is not an inconsequential exercise. You are gathering significant information that you will need later to design your security solution.

Study Strategies: Each topic presents its own learning challenge. To support you through this, New Riders has included strategies for how to best approach studying in order to retain the material in the chapter, particularly as it is addressed on the exam.

Instructional Features Within the Chapter

These books include a large amount and different kinds of information. The many different elements are designed to help you identify information by its purpose and importance to the exam and also to provide you with varied ways to learn the material. You will be able to determine how much attention to devote to certain elements, depending on what your goals are. By becoming familiar with the different presentations of information, you will know what information will be important to you as a test-taker and which information will be important to you as a practitioner.

EXAM TIP

Keep User Management Local
Create Domain Global groups and place users only in the domain controller groups that exist on that domain controller. To allow access to resources within that domain, create Universal groups or Domain Local groups. Access is granted to Universal groups or Domain Local groups, and then Domain Global groups from any domain can be included in the Universal group or Domain Local group.

Exam Tip: Exam Tips appear in the margins to provide specific exam-related advice. Such tips may address what material is covered (or not covered) on the exam, how it is covered, mnemonic devices, or particular quirks of that exam.

Objective Coverage Text: In the text before an exam objective is specifically addressed, you will notice the objective is listed to help call your attention to that particular material.

---

222   Part III   ANALYZING SECURITY REQUIREMENTS

Applying Security to File Systems

Identify the required level of security for each resource. Resources include printers, files, shares, Internet access, and dial-in access.

Windows 2000 supports the use of three file systems: NTFS, FAT, and FAT32. NTFS is recommended. FAT32 is similar to FAT except FAT32 supports large disks. These systems are supported primarily for compatibility with Windows 9x and Windows 2000 dual-boot systems. Windows 9x clients can access files over the network on NTFS partitions. FAT and FAT32 can be secured at the share level. They do not provide local file security.

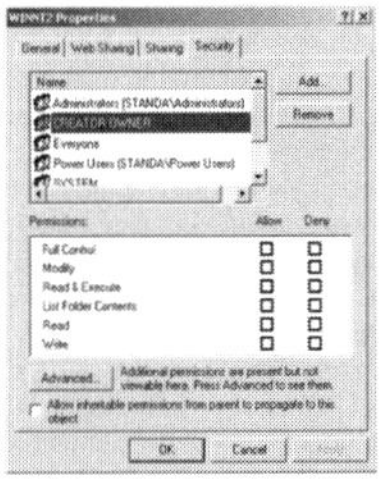

Examining NTFS Features

Windows 2000 offers a new version of NTFS that supports improved file and folder DACLS, Active Directory, domains, sparse files, remote storage, recovery logging of disk activities, disk quotas, better scalability to large drives, and file encryption. You cannot use these features unless you use NTFS as your file system.

Learning File System DACLs

The DACL for each file and folder can be set if you are using NTFS. Windows 2000 offers a refined list of permissions that can be set. The section in this chapter titled "Securing FAT and NTFS Shares" describes share permissions. In addition to allowing different types of access, Windows 2000 also enables you to deny any type of access. Windows NT just enabled you to deny access period.

Folder permissions are actually representative of a logical group of special permissions (see Figure 5.1). The section titled "Special Permissions" discusses folder permissions in detail. The following permissions can be set on each folder:

◆ **Modify.** A combination of List Folder Contents, Write, Delete, and Read Permissions, as follows:

• **List Folder Contents**—See which files and folders are within this folder.

Figure: To improve readability, the figures have been placed in the margins wherever possible so that they do not interrupt the main flow of text.

FIGURE 5.1
Folder permissions.

Note: Notes appear in the margins and contain various kinds of useful information, such as tips on the technology or administrative practices, historical background on terms and technologies, or side commentary on industry issues.

NOTE

Permission Gotcha #1 Peter has Full Control permission on the folder Stuff. He does not have any permissions on the files and folder within Stuff. Can he delete the file Stuff\johnie? Yes!

This seemingly contradictory situation results from the need to maintain compliance with POSIX.

STEP BY STEP

5.2 Creating a Share

1. Open the Shared Folders console and select Shares.

2. On the action menu, click New File Share.

3. Enter the folder path or use the Browse button to locate the folder.

4. Enter the share name and the share description in the boxes provided.

5. Select custom permissions such as All Users Have Full Control, Administrators Have Full Control, Other Users Have Read-Only Access, Administrators Have Full Control, Other Users Have No Access, or Customize and Folder Permission.

6. If you selected Customize, you can click the Custom button and add users and use permissions in the Customize Permission dialog box.

WARNING

WARNING! DACL Security   If you put the DHCP server in this group, modify the DACL of the DNS of the DHCP server so that it has security.

Warning: In using sophisticated information technology, there is always potential for mistakes or even catastrophes that can occur through improper application of the technology. Warnings appear in the margins to alert you to such potential problems.

Step by Step: Step by Steps are hands-on tutorial instructions that walk you through a particular task or function relevant to the exam objectives.

Chapter 1   GENERAL BUSINESS ANALYSIS   29

Is the management style bureaucratic and authoritarian? Does it stress accounting and close control? Is it democratic, encouraging initiative and enterprise? Does it follow the tried and true, or is it willing to take risks?

IN THE FIELD

GETTING WORK DONE DESPITE AN AUTOCRATIC MANAGEMENT STYLE

I once worked in a medium-sized company that the owners had sold but then had agreed to stay on to run. The former owners maintained close control while pretending to encourage initiative and discussion. Weekly management meetings were held in which each manager was required to discuss progress in meeting rigid goals and to offer suggestions for improving the business. Managers learned to sit to the right of the CEO because he always started to his left. Time constraints usually did not allow for everyone to speak. Any manager who had not met his or her goals was castigated. Managers whose ideas were considered to be frivolous, impossible, or undesirable were belittled and mocked—sometimes it did not even seem to matter if the new idea reduced cost, increased productivity, or created new markets. Initiates soon learned to offer up only ideas that reflected the thought of the CEO or his cronies. It became a contest in presenting old ideas as if they were new. Others spent time seeding the field, or somehow introducing ideas in short segments outside the meeting, and then bringing them up as something the CEO had mentioned. This was the classic psychology developed by the old-fashioned wife: To get what you want, make him think it was his idea.

Nevertheless, progress was made in introducing new ways of doing things. The trick was to balance something radical with something only slightly variant from the norm. This, of course, was the desired step. The radical item was ranted about, while the other was ignored but not turned down. The second part of the process was to keep introducing the desired change from other directions—and to be in the right place at the right time.

Company Organization

How is the company organized? Is it organized around products, as with Philip Morris or Hines Horticulture? Is it organized by international regions, as with Kraft Foods International? Or is it organized by customer groups, as with Microsoft?

In the Field Sidebar: These more extensive discussions cover material that perhaps is not as directly relevant to the exam, but which is useful as reference material or in everyday practice. In the Field may also provide useful background or contextual information necessary for understanding the larger topic under consideration.

CASE STUDIES

Case Studies are presented throughout the book to provide you with another, more conceptual opportunity to apply the knowledge you are developing. They also reflect the "real-world" experiences of the authors in ways that prepare you not only for the exam but for actual network administration as well. In each Case Study, you will find similar elements: a Background of the Case, a Problem Statement, and an Analysis.

CASE STUDY: ITS

BACKGROUND

ITS sells products to truck stops around the country. The company carries a large inventory of everything from antennas, blankets, and coffee pots that plug into truck cigarette lighters, to chips and salsa. A sales force of 200 travels to the truck stops to sell and to introduce new product lines to truck stop managers. ITS also markets an inventory control service called FullStock. Bar code readers are used for inventory counts, and ITS maintains the customers inventory on computers in Akron, Ohio. This allows ITS to recommend order quantities and dates to the customer, which gains them a lot of repeat business. Inventory counts are transmitted to Akron by connecting the scanner to the Akron computer via a phone.

PROBLEM STATEMENT

Data security is the single most pressing issue.

impact the servers they connect to as well. Just the other day, Joe, our sales manager, accidentally deleted the entire contents of the D drive on the sales department server.

Sales Manager
Our customer inventory information is confidential. Imagine what would happen if our competitors could get at our information. It hasn't happened, yet but I hear a lot about disgruntled employees destroying information, or spying on their own company and selling information to its competitors. I need to know that this can't happen here.

Help Desk Staff
I spend most of my time repairing PEBKAC errors, you know, "problem exists between keyboard and chair." Users just don't get it. They shouldn't touch their system. They load games and other "productivity utilities" and then wonder

---

Background: Lists the key problems or issues that need to be addressed in the Case Study.

Problem Statement: A few paragraphs describing a situation that professional practitioners in the field might face. A Problem Statement will deal with an issue relating to the objectives covered in the chapter, and it includes the kinds of details that make a difference.

Analysis: This is a description of the best way to handle the problems listed in the Case. In this section, you might find a table summarizing the solutions, a worded example, or both.

CASE STUDY: TREMAIN POLSON PKI
continued

ANALYSIS

A carefully planned and implemented PKI can have a number of benefits for Tremain Polson, including smart card logon, control over EFS recovery agents, and the availability of certificates for IPSec. One of their first steps is to plan the CA hierarchy.

Using several layers is good. A good place to start is to plan for a subordinate CA that issues server certificates to an intermediate layer of CAs only. The root CA need never be online and can be locked away and physically protected as well. The intermediate CA(s) can be restricted to the issuing of server certificates for the third layer. This third layer of CAs can be used to issue user certificates. The user certificate CAs can be restricted to just issuing user certificates and not be authorized to issue server certificates. Because these CAs get

TABLE 11.10

TREMAIN POLSON CA HIERARCHY

Role	On or Off	Level	Certificates Issued	Certificate Lifetime
Standalone root	Offline	1	Server	10 years
Standalone subordinate	Offline	2	Server	5 years
Enterprise subordinate	Online	3	EFS and IPSec	1 year
Enterprise subordinate	Online	3	Smart card	1 year

The control over EFS will also be good. Although some companies are uncomfortable with users

CHAPTER SUMMARY

KEY TERMS

- Group Policy
- security templates
- Security Configuration and Analysis Template
- security groups
- RAS server
- IAS server
- EAP

This chapter may have posed more questions than it answered. Just what are all those security options and user rights? What is recommended for an audit and password policy? What security groups exist, and what are their privileges? How are communications secured? Upcoming chapters will define these in detail. Your goal here was to baseline, not to fine-tune the process.

You learned about available security templates that can be selected as baselines for various platforms. You also learned how easy they are to modify and mix and match. In addition, you practiced working with the Security Configuration and Analysis console, and with the command-line tool secedit. The ITS case study defined a situation for you to begin your analysis process.

Key Terms: A list of key terms appears at the end of each chapter. These are terms that you should be sure you know and are comfortable defining and understanding when you go in to take the exam.

Chapter Summary: Before the Apply Your Knowledge section, you will find a chapter summary that wraps up the chapter and reviews what you should have learned.

EXTENSIVE REVIEW AND SELF-TEST OPTIONS

At the end of each chapter, along with some summary elements, you will find a section called "Apply Your Knowledge" that gives you several different methods with which to test your understanding of the material and review what you have learned.

---

556   Part IV   DESIGNING A WINDOWS 2000 SECURITY SOLUTION

APPLY YOUR KNOWLEDGE

Exercises

11.1 Establish Certificate Services

Estimated Time: 15 minutes

Use detailed steps from Step by Step 11.1 and 11.2 to assist you with this exercise.

1. Use Add, Remove Programs, Windows Components, and select Certificate Services.
2. Select Enterprise Root CA.
3. Select a key length of 2048 bits.
4. Name the CA and fill out other Identifying Information.
5. Use the Validity Duration box to specify a lifetime of five years.

11.2 Configure Certificate Services

Estimated Time: 15 minutes

1. Open the Certification Authority console (Start, Programs, Administrative Tools).
2. Right-click the CA node and click Properties.
3. Click Policy Module.
4. Click Add to add another distribution point for the CRL. Why might this be important?
5. Click Exit Module and examine the exit module listed. What does the exit module do?
6. Close the Properties page.
7. Right-click the Revoked Certificates node and change the CRL publish interval to six months. Why might you do this? When would you Disable Scheduled Publishing?

8. Right-click the Policy Settings node of the CA.
9. Click New and click Certificate to Issue. Add a certificate from the list.

11.3 Configure Public Key Policy

Estimated Time: 15 minutes

1. Open the Group Policy snap-in focused on the default domain policy.
2. Open the Computer Configuration, Security Settings, Public Key Policies node.
3. Right-click the Automatic Certificate Request Settings node.
4. Click New.
5. Select a computer certificate template and click Next. Computers within this scope are issued a certificate the next time the computer restarts and logs on.
6. Select your CA and click Next. (Multiple selections can be made, but only one CA will process.) What's good about multiple selections?

Review Questions

1. In a public/private key encryption system, the public key is available to anyone. How are messages kept secret if the key is known by all?
2. Explain how public/private key can be used for nonrepudiation.
3. What will happen if the CRL is not available?
4. If the root CA is placed offline, how can the PKI function?

Exercises: These activities provide an opportunity for you to master specific hands-on tasks. Our goal is to increase your proficiency with the product or technology. You must be able to conduct these tasks in order to pass the exam. When applicable, you can find solutions to exercises in the "Answers to Exercises" section, which follows the "Exam Questions."

Review Questions: These open-ended, short-answer questions allow you to quickly assess your comprehension of what you just read in the chapter. Instead of asking you to choose from a list of options, these questions require you to state the correct answers in your own words. Although you will not experience these kinds of questions on the exam, these questions will indeed test your level of comprehension of key concepts.

Exam Questions: These questions reflect the kinds of multiple-choice questions that appear on the Microsoft exams. Use them to become familiar with the exam question formats and to help you determine what you know and what you need to review or study more.

APPLY YOUR KNOWLEDGE

Fred thinks. "I'd better get that report on system security ready for him." Should Fred be so cool and collected?

6. Mary's project development program runs fine on her Windows 2000 Professional computer. When she installs it for other members of her department, they cannot run it. She has John, the network administrator, give these users Administrator accounts on their machines so that they can run the program. Is this the only way to get them access?

7. The auditors think Pete should audit access to the printer used to print checks. Pete finds the

Exam Questions

1. John Smith at Cote sets up a test network to study Windows 2000 auditing. He wants to ensure that events are audited on all domain controllers. Where does he do this? (Choose the best and most complete answer.)

   A. He uses the MMC snap-in Security Configuration Manager to turn on auditing in the Local Policies\ Audit Policy area.

   B. He uses the Domain Controller Security Policy and turns on auditing in the Local Policies\Audit Policy area.

Answers to Review Questions

1. ITS Windows 2000 Professional laptops should have NTFS loaded as their file system. Effective file protection can be implemented. This way data that is on the road can be better secured.

2. Tell the help desk manager that although there is no guarantee that Windows 2000 will totally protect Jane's computer from Jane, Windows File Protection will not allow any program that she loads to overwrite files needed to keep the operating system running.

3. Although it takes time to learn the ins and outs of securing his registry and file system to best suit his systems, both have many default settings that help protect the system right out-of-the-box. You can also tell him about the templates provided for system configuration.

6. ITS needs to develop a Windows 2000–compliant version of the product. In the interim, it may have to relax both access privileges and give users elevated rights so that they can run the application.

Answers to Exam Questions

1. **A.** Label printers are for printing labels, not for general use. You might think that people would realize that by themselves, but you'd be surprised how many labels would be wasted. (For more information, see the section "Controlling Printer Access.")

2. **C, D.** Although you cannot be 100% sure, even with all of this going for you, you do stand a reasonable chance. The Power Users group has backward compatibility with user permissions in Windows NT 4.0, and users can run the program in NT 4.0. The program itself isn't causing prob-

Answers and Explanations: For some of the exercises, and for each of the Review and Exam questions, you will find thorough explanations located at the end of the section.

Suggested Readings and Resources: The very last element in every chapter is a list of additional resources you can use if you want to go above and beyond certification-level material or if you need to spend more time on a particular subject that you are having trouble understanding.

Suggested Readings and Resources

1. *Windows 2000 Resource Kit: Windows 2000 Server Deployment Planning Guide.* Microsoft Press:
   • "Developing an Automated Installation"
   • "Developing an Automated Installation of Windows 2000 Professional"

2. Cone, Erick, Boggs, Jon, and Perez, Sergio. 1999. *Planning for Windows 2000.* Indianapolis: New Riders Publishing.
   • Chapter 1, "Windows 2000 Overview"
   • Chapter 3, "Implementing Standards"

3. Sheresh, Beth, and Doug Sheresh. 2000. *Understanding Directory Services.* Indianapolis: New Riders Publishing.
   • Chapter 7, "Lightweight Directory Access Protocol"
   • Chapter 9, "Active Directory"

Introduction

MCSE Training Guide: Windows 2000 Network Security Design is designed for advanced users, technicians, or system administrators with the goal of certification as a Microsoft Certified Systems Engineer (MCSE). It covers the Designing Security for a Microsoft Windows 2000 Network exam (70-220). This exam measures your ability to analyze the business requirements for security and to design a security solution that meets business requirements.

This book is your one-stop shop. Everything you need to know to pass the exam is in here, and Microsoft has approved it as study material. You do not have to take a class in addition to buying this book to pass the exam. However, depending on your personal study habits or learning style, you may benefit from buying this book *and* taking a class.

Microsoft assumes that the typical candidate for this exam will have a minimum of one year of experience implementing and administering network operating systems in medium to very large network environments.

Notes on This Book's Organization

It may seem strange to start with basic business analysis in a book that is supposed to help you prepare to pass an exam on designing security for Windows 2000. It may seem strange for Microsoft to list these requirements in its objectives for study. Yes, it may *seem* strange, but only until you realize that a sound understanding of your organization's makeup, business model, corporate culture, and current structure will allow you to best protect it.

Of what use is the most technologically advanced intrusion detection system, the tightest security policy, and the most hardened system platform if a simple phone call can produce a password? What value does your carefully constructed, choke-point defense provide if you aren't aware of other portals to your systems from dial-up desktop modems or leased lines to branches with unsecured servers?

If we are going to develop a security framework, we have to be able to rely on our understanding of the organizational infrastructure that we are to protect and must build upon. We must act a little like intelligence agents—that is, we must gather information about our organization and its individuals, and then analyze that information to produce an effective defense. Ira Winkler (in *Corporate Espionage*, Prima Publishing) and others describe four parts to this intelligence-gathering process. Their descriptions fit our process of designing a security solution.

1. **Define requirements**—What are the information patterns we must follow? First, we should define our requirements. What are we looking for? Should we blindly look for every scrap of information about our company, its business partners, and its customers? Alternatively, should we gather specific details? Part I, "Analyzing Business Requirements," details the questions to ask and specifies where you might look for the answers. Fortunately, we are information gatherers on the inside—we do not have to intrude from outside, nor do we risk anything by asking questions. We'll also point out the rationale behind the scrutiny.

2. **Collect information**—Although Part I specifies where you might look for the information you desire, it is not meant to prevent you from using

other sources. Train yourself to look for information important to your goals. The first step in intelligence gathering is to determine where the information is. As you collect information about the structure of your company, you should keep these points in mind:

- Is this information sensitive? Could it be exploited in any way?

- Does the information lead to the exposure of vulnerability? Alternatively, does it indicate an area that needs to be secured?

- What is the general attitude of people to your collection efforts?

- What about disinformation? In the real spy world, companies and governments try to mislead the competition by circulating large amounts of disinformation to mislead the intelligence gathers. Agents must learn to recognize gold from fool's gold. Fortunately, you shouldn't have to deal with this phenomenon, but it never hurts to verify information.

3. **Analyze the information**—Two types of intelligence information are gathered: general information and traffic. Traffic information produces information about people and companies by examining their patterns of movement, their mail and email, and other forms of communication. In Part II, "Analyzing Technical Requirements," we examine the communication information flows of the company, for similar reasons. We need to know what information is needed, what communications take place in what directions and by what media, so that we can protect them. Our goal here is not to change an organization's method, but to protect both what currently exists

and what may exist in the future. General information needs to be quantified, organized, *updated,* and verified. Check the dates on reports and sources of information to make sure that you have the latest information.

4. **Evaluate your results and recommend actions**—After the information is organized into reports and categorized, you will need to see how well it meets your requirements. You may find that you are missing information and must return to gather it. You may question the veracity of important information and must verify it from a second source or by revisiting the original. When you are sure of your information, you can begin to evaluate results and recommend actions. In Part III, "Analyzing Security Requirements," we design a security baseline for our Windows 2000 network.

When you have determined the structure of the organization and the status of security and technical infrastructure, you will need to evaluate and design the security infrastructure. Part IV, "Designing a Windows 2000 Security Solution," and Part V, "Designing a Security Solution for Access Between Networks," will complete your knowledge of the toolset you need to do so.

How This Book Helps You

This book takes you on a self-guided tour of all the areas covered by the Designing Security for a Microsoft Windows 2000 Network exam and teaches you the specific skills you'll need to achieve your MCSE certification. You'll also find helpful hints, tips, real-world examples, and exercises, as well as references to additional study materials. Specifically, this book is set up to help you in the following ways:

◆ **Organization**—The book is organized by individual exam objectives. Every objective you need to know for the Designing Security for a Microsoft Windows 2000 Network exam is covered in this book. We have attempted to present the objectives in an order that is as close as possible to that listed by Microsoft. However, we have not hesitated to reorganize the objectives where needed to make the material as easy as possible for you to learn. We also have attempted to make the information accessible in the following ways:

  • The full list of exam topics and objectives is included in this introduction.

  • Each chapter begins with a list of the objectives to be covered.

  • Each chapter also begins with an outline that provides you with an overview of the material and the page numbers where particular topics can be found.

  • The objectives are repeated where the material most directly relevant to it is covered (unless the whole chapter addresses a single objective).

  • The CD-ROM included with this book contains, in PDF format, a complete listing of the test objectives and where they are covered within the book.

◆ **Instructional features**—This book has been designed to provide you with multiple ways to learn and reinforce the exam material. Following are some of the helpful methods:

  • *Case studies.* Given the case study basis of the exam, we designed this *Training Guide* around them. Case studies appear in each chapter and

also serve as the basis for exam questions.

• *Objective explanations.* As mentioned previously, each chapter begins with a list of the objectives covered in the chapter. In addition, immediately following each objective is an explanation in a context that defines it more meaningfully.

• *Study strategies.* The beginning of the chapter also includes strategies for studying and retaining the material in the chapter, particularly as it is addressed on the exam.

• *Exam tips.* Exam tips appear in the margin to provide specific exam-related advice. Such tips may address what material is covered (or not covered) on the exam and how it is covered, and may discuss mnemonic devices or particular quirks of that exam.

• *Review breaks and summaries.* Crucial information is summarized at various points in the book in lists or tables. Each chapter ends with a summary as well.

• *Key terms.* A list of key terms appears at the end of each chapter.

• *Notes.* These appear in the margin and contain various kinds of useful information such as tips on technology or administrative practices, historical background on terms and technologies, or side commentary on industry issues.

• *Warnings.* When using sophisticated information technology, there is always the potential for mistakes or even catastrophes that can occur because of improper application of the technology. Warnings appear in the margin to alert you to such potential problems.

• *In the field.* These more extensive discussions cover material that may not be directly relevant to the exam but that is useful as reference material or in everyday practice. These tips may also provide useful background or contextual information necessary for understanding the larger topic under consideration.

- *Exercises.* Found at the end of the chapters in the "Apply Your Knowledge" section, exercises are performance-based opportunities for you to learn and assess your knowledge. Solutions to the exercises, when applicable, are provided later in a separate section titled "Answers to Exercises."

◆ **Extensive practice test options**—The book provides numerous opportunities for you to assess your knowledge and to practice for the exam. The practice options include the following:

- *Review Questions.* These open-ended questions appear in the "Apply Your Knowledge" section at the end of each chapter. They allow you to quickly assess your comprehension of what you just read in the chapter. Answers to the questions are provided later in a separate section titled "Answers to Review Questions."

- *Exam Questions.* These questions also appear in the "Apply Your Knowledge" section. Use them to help you determine what you know and what you need to review or study further. Answers and explanations for them are provided in a separate section titled "Answers to Exam Questions."

- *Practice Exam.* A Practice Exam is included in the "Final Review" section. The "Final Review" section and the Practice Exam are discussed later in this list.

- *ExamGear.* The special Training Guide version of the *ExamGear* software included on the CD-ROM provides further opportunities for you to assess how well you understood the material in this book.

> **NOTE**
> For a description of the New Riders *ExamGear, Training Guide* software, see Appendix D, "Using the ExamGear, Training Guide Edition Software."

◆ **Final Review**—This part of the book provides you with three valuable tools for preparing for the exam:

- *Fast Facts.* This condensed version of the information contained in the book will prove extremely useful for last-minute review.

- *Study and Exam Prep Tips.* Read this section early on to help you develop study strategies. This section also provides you with valuable exam-day tips and information on exam/question formats such as adaptive tests and case study-based questions.

- *Practice Exam.* A Practice Exam is included here. Questions are written in styles similar to those used on the actual exam. Use this to assess your understanding of the material in the book.

This book contains several other features, including a section titled "Suggested Readings and Resources" at the end of each chapter that directs you toward further information that could aid you in your exam preparation or your actual work. You'll find valuable appendixes as well, including a glossary (Appendix A), an overview of the Microsoft certification program (Appendix B), and a description of what is on the CD-ROM (Appendix C).

The Microsoft Designing Security for a Microsoft Windows 2000 Network exam is structured around case studies and is really more of a reading comprehension exam than any other Microsoft exam that you may have taken. All the book features mentioned previously will supply you with thorough exam preparation.

For more information about the exam or the certification process, contact Microsoft:

Microsoft Education: 1-800-636-7544
Internet:
`ftp://ftp.microsoft.com/Services/MSEdCert`
World Wide Web:
`http://www.microsoft.com/train_cert`
CompuServe Forum: GO MSEDCERT

WHAT THE DESIGNING SECURITY FOR A MICROSOFT WINDOWS 2000 NETWORK EXAM (70-220) COVERS

◆ Analyzing Business Requirements

◆ Analyzing Technical Requirements

◆ Analyzing Security Requirements

◆ Designing a Windows 2000 Security Solution

◆ Designing a Security Solution for Access Between Networks

◆ Designing Security for Communication Channels

Before taking the exam, you should be proficient in the job skills represented by the following units, objectives, and subobjectives.

Analyzing Business Requirements

Analyze the existing and planned business models.

◆ Analyze the company model and the geographical scope. Models include regional, national, international, subsidiary, and branch offices.

◆ Analyze company processes. Processes include information flow, communication flow, service and product life cycles, and decision-making.

Analyze the existing and planned organizational structures. Considerations include management model; company organization; vendor, partner, and customer relationships; and acquisition plans.

Analyze factors that influence company strategies.

◆ Identify company priorities.

◆ Identify the projected growth and growth strategy.

◆ Identify relevant laws and regulations.

◆ Identify the company's tolerance for risk.

◆ Identify the total cost of operations.

Analyze business and security requirements for the end user.

Analyze the structure of IT management. Considerations include type of administration, such as centralized or decentralized; funding model; outsourcing; decision-making process; and change-management process.

Analyze the current physical model and information security model.

◆ Analyze internal and external security risks.

Analyzing Technical Requirements

Evaluate the company's existing and planned technical environment.

◆ Analyze company size and user and resource distribution.

◆ Assess the available connectivity between the geographic location of work sites and remote sites.

◆ Assess the net available bandwidth.

◆ Analyze performance requirements.

◆ Analyze the method of accessing data and systems.

◆ Analyze network roles and responsibilities. Roles include administrative, user, service, resource ownership, and application.

Analyze the impact of the security design on the existing and planned technical environment.

◆ Assess existing systems and applications.

◆ Identify existing and planned upgrades and rollouts.

◆ Analyze technical support structure.

◆ Analyze existing and planned network and systems management.

Analyzing Security Requirements

Design a security baseline for a Windows 2000 network that includes domain controllers, operations masters, application servers, file and print servers, RAS servers, desktop computers, portable computers, and kiosks.

Identify the required level of security for each resource. Resources include printers, files, shares, Internet access, and dial-in access.

Designing a Windows 2000 Security Solution

Design an audit policy.

Design a delegation of authority strategy.

Design the placement and inheritance of security policies for sites, domains, and organizational units.

Design an Encrypting File System strategy.

Design an authentication strategy.

◆ Select authentication methods. Methods include certificate-based authentication, Kerberos authentication, clear-text passwords, digest authentication, smart cards, NTLM, RADIUS, and SSL.

◆ Design an authentication strategy for integration with other systems.

Design a security group strategy.

Design a Public Key Infrastructure.

◆ Design Certificate Authority (CA) hierarchies.

◆ Identify certificate server roles.

◆ Manage certificates.

◆ Integrate with third-party CAs.

◆ Map certificates.

Design Windows 2000 network services security.

◆ Design Windows 2000 DNS security.

◆ Design Windows 2000 Remote Installation Services (RIS) security.

◆ Design Windows 2000 SNMP security.

◆ Design Windows 2000 Terminal Services security.

Designing a Security Solution for Access Between Networks

Provide secure access to public networks from a private network.

Provide external users with secure access to private network resources.

Provide secure access between private networks.

- Provide secure access within a LAN.

- Provide secure access within a WAN.

- Provide secure access across a public network.

Design Windows 2000 security for remote access users.

Designing Security for Communication Channels

Design an SMB-signing solution.

Design an IPSec solution.

- Design an IPSec encryption scheme.

- Design an IPSec management strategy.

- Design negotiation policies.

- Design security policies.

- Design IP filters.

- Define security levels.

HARDWARE AND SOFTWARE YOU'LL NEED

As a self-paced study guide, *MCSE Training Guide: Windows 2000 Network Security Design* is meant to help you understand concepts that must be refined through hands-on experience. To make the most of your studying, you must have as much background on and experience with all versions of Windows 2000 (Professional, Server and Advanced Server) as possible. The best way to do this is to combine studying with

work on Windows 2000 version. This section gives you a description of the minimum computer requirements that you need to enjoy a solid practice environment.

- Windows 2000 Server and Professional

- A server and a workstation computer on the Microsoft Hardware Compatibility List

- Pentium 90MHz (or better) processor

- 600MB (or larger) hard disk

- VGA (or Super VGA) video adapter and monitor

- Mouse or equivalent pointing device

- CD-ROM drive

- Network interface card (NIC) or modem connection to Internet

- Presence on an existing network, or use of a two-port (or more) miniport hub to create a test network

- Internet access with Internet Explorer 4 (Service Pack 1) or later

- 24MB of RAM (32MB recommended)

- Windows NT Option Pack recommended

- Microsoft SQL Server 6.5 (or better) optional

- Microsoft SNA Server optional

It is fairly easy to obtain access to the necessary computer hardware and software in a corporate business environment. It can be difficult, however, to allocate enough time within the busy work day to complete a self-study program. Most of your study time will occur after normal working hours, away from the everyday interruptions and pressures of your regular job.

ADVICE ON TAKING THE EXAM

More extensive tips are found in the "Final Review" section titled "Study and Exam Prep Tips," but keep this advice in mind as you study:

◆ **Read all the material.** Microsoft has been known to include material not expressly specified in the objectives. This book has included additional information not reflected in the objectives in an effort to give you the best possible preparation for the examination—and for the real-world experiences to come.

◆ **Do the Step by Steps and complete the Exercises in each chapter.** They will help you gain experience using the specified methodology or approach. All Microsoft exams are task- and experienced-based and require you to have experience actually performing the tasks upon which you will be tested.

◆ **Use the questions to assess your knowledge.** Don't just read the chapter content; use the questions to find out what you know and what you don't. You also need the experience of analyzing case studies. If you are struggling at all, study some more, review, and then assess your knowledge again.

◆ **Review the exam objectives.** Develop your own questions and examples for each topic listed. If you can develop and answer several questions for each topic, you should not find it difficult to pass the exam.

> **NOTE**
>
> **Exam-taking Advice** Although this book is designed to prepare you to take and pass the Designing Security for a Microsoft Windows 2000 Network certification exam, there are no guarantees. Read this book, work through the questions and exercises, and when you feel confident, take the Assessment Exam and additional exams using the *ExamGear, Training Guide Edition* test software. This should tell you whether you are ready for the real thing.
>
> When taking the actual certification exam, make sure that you answer all the questions before your time limit expires. Do not spend too much time on any one question. If you are unsure, answer the questions as best as you can; then mark it for review when you have finished the rest of the questions. However, this advice will not apply if you are taking an adaptive exam. In that case, take your time on each question. There is no opportunity to go back to a question.

Remember, the primary object is not to pass the exam—it is to understand the material. After you understand the material, passing the exam should be simple. Knowledge is a pyramid; to build upward, you need a solid foundation. This book and the Microsoft Certified Professional programs are designed to ensure that you have that solid foundation.

Good luck!

NEW RIDERS PUBLISHING

The staff of New Riders Publishing is committed to bringing you the very best in computer reference material. Each New Riders book is the result of months of work by authors and staff who research and refine the information contained within its covers.

As part of this commitment to you, the NRP reader, New Riders invites your input. Please let us know if you enjoy this book, if you have trouble with the information or examples presented, or if you have a suggestion for the next edition.

Please note, however, that New Riders staff cannot serve as a technical resource during your preparation for the Microsoft certification exams or for questions about software- or hardware-related problems. Please refer instead to the documentation that accompanies the Microsoft products or to the applications' Help systems.

If you have a question or comment about any New Riders book, there are several ways to contact New Riders Publishing. We will respond to as many readers as we can. Your name, address, or phone number will never become part of a mailing list or be used for any purpose other than to help us continue to bring you the best books possible. You can write to us at the following address:

New Riders Publishing
Attn: Al Valvano
201 W. 103rd Street
Indianapolis, IN 46290

If you prefer, you can fax New Riders Publishing at 317-581-4663.

You also can send email to New Riders at the following Internet address:

nrfeedback@newriders.com

NRP is an imprint of Pearson Education. To obtain a catalog or information, contact us at nrmedia@newriders.com. To purchase a New Riders book, call 1-800-428-5331.

Thank you for selecting *MCSE Training Guide: Windows 2000 Network Security Design.*

ANALYZING BUSINESS REQUIREMENTS

This chapter covers the following Microsoft-specified objectives for the "Analyzing Business Requirements" section of the Designing Security for a Microsoft Windows 2000 Network exam:

Analyze the existing and planned business models.

- **Analyze the company model and the geographical scope. Models include regional, national, international, subsidiary, and branch offices.**

- **Analyze company processes. Processes include information flow, communications flow, service and product life cycles, and decision making.**

▶ It's important here to look at the big picture while collecting fine details. Here you are defining the business architecture. At the end of your study, you should have a firm understanding of the business.

▶ The more widespread the company is, the more important it is to take the time to place company locations on a map. It's very difficult to conceptualize communications and imagine threats if you are not aware of the extent of your exposure.

▶ A common complaint business managers have is that IT people do not understand the business part of business. A common complaint that IT has is that business managers do not understand IT. You must take the first step: Attempt to meet the business manager halfway.

▶ Relax. Stop concentrating on protecting the empire, and concentrate on getting to know it.

Analyze the existing and planned organizational structures. Considerations include the management model; company organization; vendor, partner, and customer relationships; and acquisitions plans.

CHAPTER 1

General Business Analysis

▶ You must scrutinize your corporate structure to help you plan not only for the present, but also for the future. Understanding the management model will point the way to whom to include in your design and in your implementation discussions. Knowledge of external relationships (customer, vendor, partner) will assist you in determining current and future communications directions, will help you determine how to protect your internal systems, and will aid in these conversations.

▶ Your IT infrastructure is like the highway system of a country. It provides routes for travelers across boundaries as well as within them. If you are to protect them on your journey, you will need advance knowledge of where they might need to go.

Analyze factors that influence company strategies.

- **Identify company priorities.**
- **Identify the projected growth and growth strategy.**
- **Identify relevant laws and regulations.**
- **Identify the company's tolerance of risk.**
- **Identify the total cost of operations.**

▶ Did you think you would design security in a vacuum? Ever propose a change and have it denied because of its cost? Although security may be identified as paramount, businesses may decide that the cost of protection outweighs any possible loss. You should determine this prior to presenting your proposal.

▶ Here, you will consider how to modify proposals based on legal requirements, how to hedge bets on future expansion, and even how to overprotect an asset, if the situation warrants.

- This is not material that you can learn while sitting at a computer and practicing the steps. Nor is this material that comes easily to many IT people. We are used more to analyzing why we can't reach a system over the network or how to set up a virtual private network (VPN) than to analyzing the business structure. Take heart, though. Although making a business the next Microsoft or Amazon.com may be difficult, understanding basic business structures and strategies is not.

- Most of the information that you seek is well documented and easy to interpret.

- Don't blow it off, though; understanding the structure, orientation, and scope of a business is critical if you are to secure it.

- Understanding your business practice requires understanding others. Use the examples in this book for reference, and then find others. You're lucky—the Internet makes this process so easy. Use it. A good place to start is with www.yahoo.com or www.altavista.com. Hoovers (www.hoovers.com) will provide you a synopsis and some financial information on most businesses. It also has an excellent search engine that will enable you to search by company name, stock index, keywords, or location. You can use this to identify businesses in a certain industry segment. You then can subscribe to this service to receive detailed information, but many services are free. Visit the Web sites of e-zines such as *New York Times*, *Newsweek, Business Weekly*, MSNBC, CNBC, and the *Wall Street Journal*. All these will reference the Web sites of businesses you may want to examine. While business information on a Web site can vary, you may be surprised at how much you can learn about a business—even yours—from looking there. You likely will find annual reports, locations of plants, history, chief officers, management philosophies, acquisition strategies, and expansion plans. You may find information that companies paid to learn about their competitors in the past. You may even learn first of some new technological development that is applicable to your particular needs. Soon you will feel comfortable with the terminology and strategies that businesses use.

- Remember—when you are analyzing your business, it is not an inconsequential exercise. You are gathering significant information that you will need later to design your security solution.

INTRODUCTION

"Would you tell me, please, which way I ought to go from here?" asks Alice.

"That depends a good deal on where you want to get to," said the Cat.

"I don't much care where," said Alice.

"Then it doesn't matter which way you go," said the Cat.

—*Alice in Wonderland*

Business management often sees IT the way Alice described Wonderland. Things are not as they seem. You have to go backward to make progress. You might find lots of instructions on things, but they make no sense ("this one will make you larger, this one will make you small"). There are illusive Queens, Mad Hatters, and white rabbits that are always late. It always seems as if you've not only arrived late for the tea party, but you also are very unaware of the protocol and therefore can't follow the conversation.

Business managers are looking for IT to tell them which way to go, but it often seems to IT as if business managers don't know where they want to be. Stop grinning like a Cheshire cat, and learn how to ask them questions they understand.

As IT professionals, you and I must take the time to learn the business side of business so that we can support that business with IT efforts and protect it with a security solution. If you encompass the organization's business drives, opportunities, processes, and goals in your IT proposals, you are more likely to succeed. If you recognize that investments in IT should be driven by business, not technical aspects, you may just realize, if not the most technically advanced security solution, surely the best security solution for the problem at hand.

This chapter is meant to help you ground yourself with a little business knowledge before you embark on your security design. You will analyze the business in general by looking at three business-related objectives: analyzing existing and planned business models, analyzing existing and planned organizational structures, and analyzing factors that influence company strategies. At the least, I hope that it gives you a better sense of direction to follow. At the best, perhaps it will give you enough insight to direct your IT proposals toward business goals. Either way, you and your company should benefit from your increased understanding.

ANALYZING EXISTING AND PLANNED BUSINESS MODELS

Companies often are defined by the answers to several questions. What are their products, and what industry are they in? What markets do they do business in, and how centralized is their control? Knowing these things about a company gives you a frame of reference. If you know other companies that follow this model, you will feel that you know something about how this new business functions, which in turn will make you feel more comfortable with it.

Companies with the same model often find similarities in their requirements for communications, financing, marketing, management, development, expansion, human resources, and technologies.

Another way to look at a business is to define the way it does business—the steps it takes to complete a business function. These functions, or business processes, also tell us much about the business.

So, how do you start your quest for business knowledge?

Today, knowing the geographical scope of a business often serves to define it and its IT infrastructure. An international corporation that produces laptop computers may have much more in common with an international corporation that produces luggage than with a local producer of PCs. A branch office of Allstate Insurance has more in common with a branch office of Arthur Anderson Consulting than it does with the national headquarters of Prudential. In these comparisons, many business processes and information technological needs are similar.

Analyzing Company Model and Geographical Scope

Analyze the company model and the geographical scope. Models include regional, national, international, subsidiary, and branch offices.

Just what is the geographical scope of the company for which you need to develop your security infrastructure? Is it the only office? Does it trade locally? Regionally? Nationally? Internationally? Is there a corporate headquarters? A main office? Branch offices? Are you a subsidiary of another business? Is your business in consumer products on the grand international scale like Philip Morris (Miller Beer, Kraft Foods, Philip Morris Tobacco), or is it primarily local but with international sales, as is tiny IMP, Inc., a manufacturer of analog integrated circuits in San Jose, California. Are you regional, like Southwestern Bell, or national, like Hines Horticulture, Inc.? Or, are you one of the new virtual corporations whose amorphous model is now small and contained, now spreading contagiously and consisting of partnerships and projects that span the globe and that yet are managed from a single building with a couple hundred employees?

How do you make these distinctions, and why?

Sometimes it is easy to peg a company model. You work there and are faced every day with the realities of its geographical scope. Every employee knows the story. Every manager can list the locations and tick off the brand names. Other times you find yourself visiting the corporate Web site to read the annual report. You also will want to know the geographical locations for manufacturing plants, warehouses, and sales offices.

The organization type, of course, will be local, regional, national, or international. But what does this mean? Companies with physical corporate locations in other countries mean additional complications for IT folks. These companies will face everything from different sources of power supply to different laws that impact what must be done to protect the information infrastructure. The geographical scope of the business also influences other aspects than IT. These things may influence IT decisions and needs in an indirect way. Some of these influences are things such as the corporate culture, management style, and perception of risk.

So, to use this information wisely, you must look first at the broad scope.

Even if the scope of your design does not incorporate all offices of the company—and even if you are given directives by someone else—you need to understand the big picture. If you know where the other pieces of the corporate infrastructure are located, you may

NOTE

A Business Snapshot Southwestern Bell offers telecommunications services to the states of Arkansas, Kansas, Missouri, Oklahoma, and Texas. SBC Technology Resources identifies and assesses emerging technology in broadband delivery, systems, intelligent networks, information technology, video networks, voices technology, and wireless networks. SBC Technology Resources is the research and development arm of SBC Communications, which is the parent of Southwestern Bell. Products include anonymous call rejection, area-wide networking ATM cell relay, ISDN, DSL, auto redial, autoconnection, automatic route selection, bill Plus, call notes, and 186,000 coin phones.

find ready sources of assistance, or at least knowledge. You also will be more prepared to design your piece of the infrastructure if you are fully aware of what already exists or has begun elsewhere. For example, I once did some work for a company that had just leased a line directly to its corporate headquarters in a distant city, only to discover that a recently acquired business nearby had lines already in place that it could have linked to. Such knowledge was recent, but it certainly was readily available if anyone had looked outside his or her area of control.

Obtain or develop a map of your company's business locations. Identify each location by type and functionality—that is, you should label all manufacturing plants, warehouses, branch offices, business offices, headquarters, and similar structures. You will use this proto-type to lay out the existing IT infrastructure and, later, a proposed security infrastructure. This is not the time to ask whether a location will be included in the plan; this is the time to simply prepare a profile that includes everything. Take a look at an example map in Figure 1.1.

1. Alantic
2. Pro Gro
3. Strong Life
4. Lakeland Peat Moss
5. Bryfogles
6. Pacific Color
7. Flynn
8. Iverson
9. Oregon Garden
10. Sun Grow

FIGURE 1.1
Hines Horticulture locations.

While you are finding all the locations of the business, you often will find information on its current IT structure. Although we will be examining that in the next chapter, don't neglect the collection of this information. Remember, you are looking for all the locations of the business, not just where IT currently exists—and certainly not only the places that are currently linked through public or private networks.

IT may have a map that identifies current locations and connectivity, but do not use this as your only resource. You must verify information with other sources. It is not that the IT map will be inaccurate, but it may not be up-to-date or show all locations. Some business locations may not have been considered for previous connectivity due to cost. Others may not have existed when the map was drawn, and some may be no longer relevant because of downsizing or divestiture. Therefore, you should use additional sources. Check with the marketing and public relations departments, and examine the annual report. A good reality check may be the corporate Web site. Many companies, such as Philip Morris International (www.philipmorris.com) and Applebee's International, Inc. (www.Applebees.com), post extensive information on their sites, including their annual reports online; perhaps yours does as well.

When you have compiled your map, identify the scope of your security design. Although security should be a corporate function and although all the smaller pieces should be developed to fit within the larger picture, sometimes you will be called upon to look at an area of smaller scope. You may not be able to influence corporate policy and protection, but you may be able to protect your regional or branch office. Your only concern could be the financials picture, and that may exist primarily at headquarters.

In either case, you will be concerned by things outside your scope because they may represent security vulnerabilities for you. Imagine the impact if plant managers have access to financial information and use unsecured dial-up access to transmit their daily reports. Consider how your road-warriors should be equipped to secure their traveling data and the company information that they access and transmit while on the road. In Chapter 2, "Analyzing IT," you will analyze these and other business and security needs, but it is good to keep this in mind at this point as well.

This is also a good time to identify whether control is centralized or decentralized, and to what degree. You will want to establish how, what, and by whom various functions of IT are managed. Questions to ask include these:

◆ Who manages user accounts?

◆ Who is in charge of DNS?

◆ Which area manages the routers and other network devices?

◆ Does one department manage PCs and another servers?

◆ Is administration divided by operating systems? By division? By location?

◆ Are central policies and procedures developed, but is actual administration done locally?

◆ Who determines whether new equipment is ordered? Who determines whether computers are upgraded?

In a highly centralized corporate structure, your decision-making capability greatly depends on your position in the hierarchy. Even if you have autonomy over some geographical section, you still need to work with others to develop a security strategy that best serves the entire business.

Also ask these questions: Is the control structure hierarchical or horizontal? Horizontal control structures may be based on a segment of the business or some process. Instead of a strict, hierarchical management structure, control could be based on a flatter management model. A centralized manager may supervise multiple administrators from a broad range of locations. For example, consider the relationships and similarities that exist among the database administrators in a company. Microsoft SQL Server database administrators certainly have more in common with each other than with IT infrastructure administrators. Whom should they report to? Should control be hierarchical, with these database administrators reporting to the IT administration of their geographical location? Or should control be horizontal, with all the database administrators reporting to an IT administrator at the main corporate location? You will need to understand these arrangements if you are to map your security architecture as closely as possible to your business system.

By contrast, the hierarchical control structure insulates the front-line worker from executive thought, contact, and direction. Decision making for the corporation is channeled from the executive office through layers.

Mapping any infrastructure is more difficult if you are trying to map a moving target—especially if you don't even know the target is moving. When you are gathering your information on current locations, don't forget to ask this important question: Are new locations planned? Be sure to find out the nature of the new location. The infrastructure and security needs of a branch office are different from those of a warehouse or a new corporate headquarters.

While you are seeking information about new locations, you should realize that this expansion information may be considered highly confidential, especially at certain stages. If you are not given access to concrete information, you might consider asking your questions in relative terms: Are there expansions planned over the next five years?

Analyzing Company Processes

Analyze company processes. Processes include information flow, communication flow, service and product life cycles, and decision-making.

All processes can be diagrammed as a series of steps that may branch. They can be documented with an ending and a beginning, but they essentially could be constantly in motion.

You will need to discover the nature of the business processes within your company. Flow charts and other diagrams are the maps here, and you may find them readily available within your company. If not, you can develop your own. You should be comfortable with reading and interpreting flow charts, and you should be able to construct simple ones. Although a detailed knowledge of every business process is not required, you should document several that are relevant to requirements for local area network (LAN) and wide area network (WAN) traffic, storage processing, and bandwidth. These processes include information flow, communication flow, service and product life cycles, and decision making.

Information Flow

Understanding and mapping information flow is not always easy, but if your business follows a particular organizational structure, the flow of information may be predictable. In a company with a typical hierarchical organization structure, information flow typically starts at the top and moves downward. Executives pass information to midlevel managers, who pass it on to supervisors, who give orders to workers. Workers are considered to have neither the ability nor the desire to make decisions. The flow of information from the bottom up may be negligible. Information might flow in both directions from one layer to the other, but it rarely moves in a lateral direction, and it almost never moves from the bottom directly to the top.

Information provided to the corporate customer is guarded and must be reviewed extensively before public access is allowed. You can recognize this structure easily by examining the respected large companies of 20 or more years ago. Many of them, including General Motors and IBM, still are operating in this manner today. Ask yourself what information is publicly available about corporate structure, goals, activities, and products. What information is available to employees, and at what level? How many layers of management are there? Are line employees empowered to make decisions?

The typical hierarchical management structure and the direction of information flow is represented in Figure 1.2.

Contrast this with the information flow from more recently organized companies. While it may sometimes be daunting to try to find a particular piece of information on Microsoft's Web site, no doubt a wealth of information can be found there by anyone who cares to look. A wealth of information also is brought directly to the public in the form of free seminars and discussions in cities across the country.

This ubiquitous flow of information is modeled in Figure 1.3.

NOTE

Pulling Teeth The concepts of support and information flow from the company to its customers are interesting to examine. Some companies choose to make lots of information freely available, while others seek to control their knowledge and provide it a drip at a time. These companies may share it with registered customers on a need-to-know basis while making information difficult to find for all others. Just try to find information on software and hardware products produced by IBM, for example. As an independent contractor, I provided services indirectly to IBM through an IBM business partner. Finding information on the products for which I was to assist IBM customers was difficult, and neither the partner nor IBM was responsive to requests without a large amount of persistence. Public access Web site locations had little information, and what they did have was obfuscated by difficult organization. Phone calls also met requests for support contract numbers. On the other hand, finding assistance and support for IBM products that I own as a business owner, or on products that companies I directly work for owned, has never been a problem. In that arena, IBM undoubtedly offers the best hardware support in the industry.

FIGURE 1.2
Hierarchical management structure and information flow.

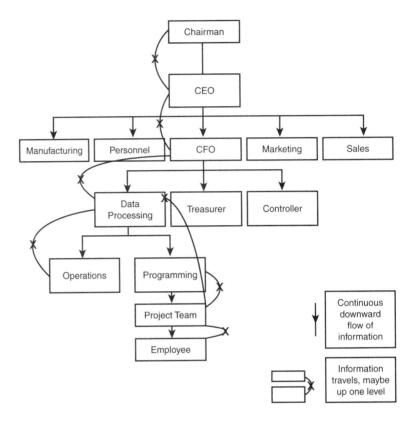

Communication Flow

Communication is different from information: It implies a request and a response. It implies a conversation. It does not imply acquiescence or compromise, but it does imply voice. Do you question whether there is communication in your business? Does your operation mimic the 1970s poster "They must think I'm a mushroom. They keep me in the dark, and they feed me fertilizer?"

What is the model for communication flow in your company? Who says what to whom? When? Who has a say? Is there true two-way communication? Communication flow includes conversations with partners and customers. How does this occur? Is the company responsive or silent? Layered with several levels?

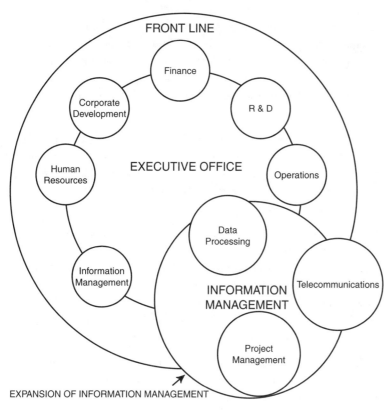

EXPANSION OF INFORMATION MANAGEMENT

FIGURE 1.3
Information-based management and information flow.

In your examination, you once again will be looking for channels that may need to be supported, protected, and somehow exposed to valid access.

Service and Product Life Cycles

Are products seasonal? Stable? Volatile? Consumer goods offer interesting examples of the extremes of product life cycle.

Ponder, if you will, the translation of products such as Tickle Me Elmo and Furbees into household words and Christmastime store riots. Then contemplate their relative obscurity just short weeks later.

Compare this to oatmeal and baking soda. Oatmeal has been around for centuries, and baking soda was created in the late nineteenth century. Each has passed from concept through maturity, but neither has reached obscurity. You might even say that baking soda has reached the stage of resurgence because new uses for it (as a deodorizer for the refrigerator and the cat box, and as a toothpaste substitute or additive) have given it new life. Marketers have different models for explaining the product life cycle. Two of them are pictured in Figure 1.4.

Often the relative time span, season, length, or staying power of a product determines the need for infrastructure to support it. A company producing the next Tickle Me Elmo or Furbee will have greater short-term infrastructure needs and possibly tighter security needs than a company producing oatmeal.

Does the product require service? The answer is clear when we are talking about automobiles or computers. However, what about food? Kraft Foods North America provides extended facilities for servicing customer needs with its innovative, interactive, virtual kitchen (www.kraftfoods.com), as well as its online cookbooks, recipes by email, "What's for dinner?" idea service, and private online "recipe box," where any customer can store up to 100 recipes.

Collect information for these types of questions: Is your business seasonal? Is service required? If so, of what type, and is it a profit center? Does your company have its own research and development department, or are you a reseller of other products? This information will aid you in later examination and design.

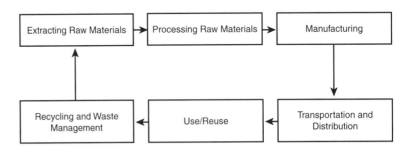

Environmentalist Product Life Cycle

FIGURE 1.4
Product life cycles.

Marketing Product Life Cycle

Decision Making

Who has the ability to make decisions? Are instructions handed down from above? Is there local autonomy? Are decisions the result of analysis, discussion, follow-up, and review? Take the time to chart the process. You may find an existing chart such as the one in Figure 1.5. First in the process is recognition that a decision must be made; then comes analysis of the problem and, if possible, a choice is made. Finally, the decision is implemented, follow-up and review take place, and the process starts up again.

Another way to speak about business organization is to define the organization as open or closed. A closed decision-making process was followed in the industrial era, and closed organizations consider decision making the province of a few. In an open organization, decision making is influenced by its impact on the total environment. Because of this, it is easier to write decision-making programs in a closed organization.

Your understanding of the decision-making process may be reflected not only in your desire to obtain a decision that parallels your needs, requirements, and belief for the system you are developing, but also in how you choose to implement that system.

For example, a closed decision-making process can be used to implement an intrusion-detection program. You may believe that all security threats can be defined; therefore, all intrusional activity can be programmatically detected with a high degree of accuracy.

NOTE

Know the Flow   Why is modeling business processes for communication flow and information flow important? IT infrastructure should support and nurture these flows. Security infrastructure should protect information and communication with relative strengths. You cannot protect what you do not know is occurring.

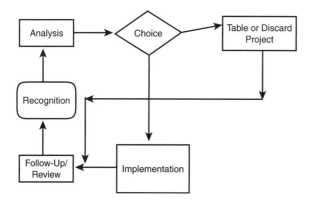

FIGURE 1.5
Decision-making process.

Certainly, much is to be said for this objective method, and many types of attacks can be detected in this manner. However, a first-time implementer of such an intrusion-detection system will see false positives. Any individual who has been around them long enough has witnessed an attack that the intrusion detection system missed.

ANALYZING EXISTING AND PLANNED ORGANIZATIONAL STRUCTURES

Analyze the existing and planned organizational structures. Considerations include the management model; company organization; vendor, partner, and customer relationships; and acquisition plans.

How is the company organized? Is it along product lines? Along regional locations? Is it focused on customer groups? What is the management model? Can you describe vendor and partner relationships and acquisition plans? Take the time to highlight your company's focus on each of these items.

Management Model

First, determine whether there is separation of ownership and control. That is, is there a board of directors, shareholders, and a chief executive officer? Alternatively, is this a family-run business? Is the CEO the founder and the primary stockholder?

The former model, separation of ownership and control, describes the majority of large American industries. Smaller businesses still might be owned and operated by the founders.

Even the large, publicly traded business or organization may be run as if the CEO were pursuing power, fame, or gratification. Many times this quest will mean success, recovery, or advancement, but it does require a charismatic individual who often maintains control by his very essence. Dissention is just not imagined.

Is the management style bureaucratic and authoritarian? Does it stress accounting and close control? Is it democratic, encouraging initiative and enterprise? Does it follow the tried and true, or is it willing to take risks?

IN THE FIELD

GETTING WORK DONE DESPITE AN AUTOCRATIC MANAGEMENT STYLE

I once worked in a medium-sized company that the owners had sold but then had agreed to stay on to run. The former owners maintained close control while pretending to encourage initiative and discussion. Weekly management meetings were held in which each manager was required to discuss progress in meeting rigid goals and to offer suggestions for improving the business. Managers learned to sit to the right of the CEO because he always started to his left. Time constraints usually did not allow for everyone to speak. Any manager who had not met his or her goals was castigated. Managers whose ideas were considered to be frivolous, impossible, or undesirable were belittled and mocked—sometimes it did not even seem to matter if the new idea reduced cost, increased productivity, or created new markets. Initiates soon learned to offer up only ideas that reflected the thought of the CEO or his cronies. It became a contest in presenting old ideas as if they were new. Others spent time seeding the field, or somehow introducing ideas in short segments outside the meeting, and then bringing them up as something the CEO had mentioned. This was the classic psychology developed by the old-fashioned wife: To get what you want, make him think it was his idea.

Nevertheless, progress was made in introducing new ways of doing things. The trick was to balance something radical with something only slightly variant from the norm. This, of course, was the desired step. The radical item was ranted about, while the other was ignored but not turned down. The second part of the process was to keep introducing the desired change from other directions—and to be in the right place at the right time.

Company Organization

How is the company organized? Is it organized around products, as with Philip Morris or Hines Horticulture? Is it organized by international regions, as with Kraft Foods International? Or is it organized by customer groups, as with Microsoft?

NOTE

MS Reorg   In March 1999, Microsoft changed the way it previously was organized. The company was restructured into customer-oriented business groups, and a new Business Leadership Team of executives from across the company now is the focus for senior–level decision making. The new groups and their orientation are listed in Table 1.1.

TABLE 1.1

MICROSOFT ORGANIZATIONAL STRUCTURE

Division	*Customers Served*
Business and Enterprise	Large organizations, IT
Consumer Windows	End users
Business Productivity	Road-warriors, knowledge-workers
Consumer and Commerce	Ease getting customers and companies together online
Developer	Software developers

NOTE

Warm Fuzzies   Microsoft has many different relationships with partners and customers. In addition to working groups with related industries (Microsoft is a member of many industry standard groups), Microsoft has a Certified Solution Providers (MCSP) partnering group and maintains the Direct Access program.

The Direct Access program allows small businesses to obtain not-for-resale copies of popular Microsoft software, to attend events that provide direct contact with Microsoft, and to participate in special promotions. A special Web site provides links to all activities, as well as special links to technical information.

The Microsoft Certified Solution Provider program is an annually renewable program that encourages the sale and promotion of Microsoft products. Companies that meet eligibility requirements pay an annual fee and receive both information from Microsoft and a monthly box of software for testing and training purposes. They also receive some software licenses, invitations to special events, and special promotional offers.

Philip Morris, International, is organized around product lines and includes Kraft Foods, Kraft Foods International, Miller Beer, Philip Morris Financial Products, and Philip Morris Tobacco.

Take the time to determine which way your company is organized, and note the impact this has on your information infrastructure. What differences would affect IT if the organizational structure changed? What would this mean to security?

Vendor, Partner, and Customer Relationships

Take time to list and explain current partner relationships and working groups. What are the contact points, such as Internet, extranet, retail, business-to-business, and wholesale, for these groups? Examine their technological sophistication. Do opportunities exist for connectivity that might benefit your company and its vendors, partners, or customers?

An example of a company maximizing vendor and partner relationships is Chemdex, a life science industry. Chemdex's entire business relies on connecting customers and vendors online. The company forms strategic alliances with vendors in its market so that it can present the best variety and deals to potential customers. Chemdex courts trade organizations and business divisions to build customer bases for itself and its vendor partners. Examine the Chemdex case study at the end of this chapter to learn more about this example of a business-to-business venture.

Acquisition Plans

Is your company vigorously pursuing acquisitions? Are you about to be acquired? Either action can considerably affect your responsibilities and efforts.

Where can you find such information? Although the details of a particular acquisition are kept confidential, the strategy is not, especially if planning is in the works to change company organization by diversification. Companies often freely broadcast their broad growth strategies.

If you visit the Web site of Applebee's International (`www.Applebees.com`), you will immediately learn that Applebee's is in constant flux as it acquires franchise sites to become company-run stores, sells an unprofitable acquisition, or broadcasts its desire to sell more franchises.

Follow news stories in the local business journal or the business pages of national papers and e-zines. I can still remember the day I learned of my company's proposed merger with another on the MSNBC Web site.

What will these changes mean to your connectivity and security requirements? What strain will they promote on your infrastructure?

ANALYZING FACTORS THAT INFLUENCE COMPANY STRATEGIES

Company strategies determine what happens when and where. Your company's priorities, total cost of operations, tolerance for risk, projected growth, and growth strategies have an enormous impact on the demand and justification for IT infrastructure improvement and security requirements. The relevant laws and regulations can have a dampening effect on company profit, can protect the privacy of employees and customers, and can lead to new opportunities and experiences in security.

Company Priorities

Identify company priorities.

It's easy to quip that company priorities are to make the most money that can be made at the least cost. Buy cheaply, sell dear. Well, that's true, of course, but that's a given. You must determine what steps the company will take, in which order, in pursuit of that goal. Look closely at the company's stated goals. You may need to start with the mission statement. Microsoft's previously was "A computer on every desktop." So, would you imagine that its priority might be to sell software at exorbitant prices and to reduce support to a minimum? Or was it to get its software running on as many computers as possible and to make it so easy that more would follow?

Review the case study at the end of the chapter. Is your company's priority to diversify by acquisition, as was the case at Hines Horticulture? Is it to improve the public's opinion of the company, as it is at Philip Morris Tobacco? Or, is it to improve the financial picture by reducing operating expenses (and the number of employees), as it was at IMP? Is your company ready to expand, and will it do this by increasing quotas, finding new markets, or developing new product lines? Will it restructure, reorganize, or reengineer? Is training employees or hiring skilled labor more important?

Priorities may change with the time of year. Seasonal businesses have learned to put off housecleaning, training, and new hires until after their peak season and to build sales staff and inventory beforehand.

Projected Growth

Identify the projected growth and growth strategy.

The growth strategy of a business may be rapid, moderate, or stable. The company may pursue that growth strategy via acquisition, franchise sales, or expansion. Expansion may be via increasing quotas, finding new markets, acquiring new businesses, or developing new product lines.

Chapter 1   GENERAL BUSINESS ANALYSIS   33

Growth may be directed by pursuing revenue to the detriment of assets acquirements and, ultimately, profit. For example, examine the many Internet companies that are experiencing rapid growth but are losing money. They hope to reap larger rewards sometime in the nebulous future—some of them actually may.

Applebee's International is an example of rapid and profitable growth. This company is the world's largest casual dining brand, with 1,064 restaurants (247 company-owned and 817 franchises). Its announced desire is to grow to 1,800 restaurants in the United States; the company experienced $2.07 billion in system sales in 1998. The Applebee's International division has locations in Canada, Holland, Germany, Sweden, Greece, Kuwait, Egypt, Mexico, Central America, and the Caribbean Islands. Until recently, it also owned the franchise for Rio Brava Cantina (66 company-owned stores and 26 franchises) and four other specialty restaurants. Franchise income is more than $66 million.

As for Amazon.com, let's just say that it sells a lot of books but doesn't have much to say for it.

Relevant Laws and Regulations

Identify relevant laws and regulations.

Understanding your business quite naturally leads to the investigation of laws that may impact the business. Some laws affect particular industries and may relate to the need for increased security or the handling of information within databases. For example, hospitals are required to maintain the privacy of patient information. When most test results, patient charts, and related items were hard copies, these copies were secured in locked rooms, vaults, and other storage areas when not under the control of medical staff. As hospitals move toward complete online information databases, their needs and legal requirements have increased as well.

In all businesses, certain laws refer specifically to the treatment of electronic data. Specifically, such laws are concerned with privacy, communication, encryption, digital signatures, wiretaps, access, junk–mail, and even bandwidth.

For many years, severe restrictions governed the export of encryption technology. Products that had encryption strengths of more than 40-bit keys could not be exported. The definition of export included even the transport of such software by an individual. I can remember attending a trainer prep (T-Prep) at Microsoft shortly before the release of Microsoft Exchange. Because Microsoft wanted trainers to practice with the product before teaching its first class, the company supplied copies of the beta product to each attendee. One of the trainers was from Germany and was quick to request an international version of the product with restricted encryption strength. He was well aware of laws that might put him in jeopardy during customs inspection upon his trip home.

Relaxation of encryption strength laws for financial instructions—and now proposed and passed U.S. (1999) legislation that will widely open up these restrictions—point out the need for IT staff to remain knowledgeable about laws that may impact security products. In addition to maintaining awareness of encryption export laws, IT staff must to be aware of the import laws of each country.

Another example concerning attention to encryption laws involves service packs and updates to software. Microsoft supplies service packs for its products. These packs are freely downloadable from the Internet, are available for purchase on CD-ROM at minimal cost, and are provided with Technet subscriptions. To obtain the higher encryption-strength version of the product, you must download it from a verifiable U.S. site or have the product shipped to a U.S. address.

If you are not in the business of software production and sale, consider this: Much open-source source code is freely given across international boundaries. For example, the Kerberos authentication software source code produced by the Massachusetts Institute of Technology for Kerberos cannot be downloaded to non-U.S. addresses. However, a version stripped of encryption code (e-bones) has been made available. Programmers in other countries then must supply their own implementation of the encryption algorithms.

All this may change as new laws are considered and Clinton administration objections are abandoned.

Information disclosure may also be limited: A recent law (Fuels Regulatory Relief Act, s. 880) limits the online disclosure of information on chemical plant risks (off-site consequence analysis) and imposes a $5,000 fine.

Be sure to ask yourself what additional laws affect your organization.

For information on current and pending legislation that impacts IT in general and the Internet specifically, visit the Center for Democracy and Technology online at `www.cdt.org/crypto`. To read the full text of any current legislation, or for online information on pending legislation and bill status, go to `http://thomas.loc.gov/`. To search for current laws by title, go to `http://www4.law.cornell.edu/uscode/`.

Tolerance of Risk

Identify the company's tolerance for risk.

To evaluate tolerance of risk, we need to look at three things: stated policies, actual practices, and perception of risk.

First, what are the stated policies? What policies exist on information security? What policies deal with tackling new ways of doing things? What are the directed investment practices? What statements have been made about current industry practices? Does the company insist on training and experience for its new hires and promotees?

Second, what are the actual practices that will help you determine where the company really stands? Ask the following questions:

◆ Does the company leap into new industries?

◆ Does the company embrace new technologies when they are in beta versions? Is the company an early adopter, or does it wait for first service packs or versions x.1?

◆ How long did it take the company to put up a Web site? What about an e-commerce site?

◆ How old are the managers who can make decisions?

◆ Are managers and line workers empowered with decision-making capability? Or are all hindered by strict sets of rules?

◆ Who is given access to corporate databases?

◆ Are security badges worn in the building?

◆ Are parts of the site off-limits, except to employees?

◆ Are keypad doors on data centers?

Third, what is the company's perception of risk? We might say that the company likes to live dangerously if we realize the risky actions it takes vis-á-vis unprotected servers, a lack of firewalls, and a laid-back attitude toward account passwords. But the company may not be aware that such practices are risky.

Does your company promote or avoid risk-seeking behavior? Is it a member of a high-risk group? High-risk groups include those that have invested heavily in unprofitable e-commerce sites.

Who trusts whom? Does your company form easy alliances and online associations with trading partners, vendors, and customers?

What is there to protect? Is your company a bank or other financial institution? Is it involved in weapons manufacture, high-tech inventions, or medical research and development?

Who is the company protecting itself from? Does your company see enemies only in strangers? It is an oft-reported fact that a large amount—perhaps up to 80 percent—of all computer crime involves inside help and information.

Risk tolerance refers to how much we tolerate the exposure to risk. To evaluate risk tolerance, we have to know what risk is. Risk has been defined as the following:

$$\text{risk} = \text{threat} \times \text{vulnerability} / \text{countermeasures} \times \text{value}$$

Value is the worth of information, monetary and otherwise.

Threat represents people or organizations out to get your organization.

Vulnerability stands for your weaknesses.

Countermeasures include your setup procedures, security devices, and operations.

Although only value can conceivably be quantified, we can assign relative worth to each item. That is, at least in most situations, the threat of a tornado completely destroying the data center is a much more serious threat than that of a contract worker's account not being disabled the minute he finishes a contract. Vulnerability, on the other hand, tells us how likely it is that a tornado will hit the data center. Countermeasures, of course, help to mitigate any risk. Off-site backups or replicated data might allow you to switch operations elsewhere without missing a beat when the tornado strikes.

You can use this equation to compare risks and determine those that may require your attention.

So, what you are trying to do here is not to determine whether the company is engaged in risky behavior, but whether it is engaged in what it perceives as risky behaviors for the industry.

For examples, consider IBM and eCommerce as two companies at opposite ends of the risk spectrum. IBM has been around for a long time and is considered by many as a staunchly conservative company. Change does not come quickly there. eCommerce, on the other hand, recently paid $7.5 million for the domain name business.com and did not even have the concept for the Web site/business at the time!

Cost of Operations

Identify the total cost of operations.

If you don't know how much it's worth, how can you ever figure out how much to spend to protect it? The value of many things is not judged by how much they cost, but by what it would cost to replace them. This is sometimes hard to determine, but we can determine the hard cost of operations. This is an important parameter in the risk/cost equation. Determining cost of operations helps you to determine how much to spend on security.

You should determine the cost of operations. Consider your business and each operation, and find the figures.

If you manufacture automobile tires, what does it cost you to produce a tire? What does it cost to produce tires annually, at all locations?

If you run a hospital, what does it cost to see a patient in the emergency room? What does it cost to perform an appendectomy?

What does it cost to provide email services to every employee?

Sometimes it is easy to determine cost; other times it is not. What really is a cost? The total cost of ownership (TCO) of a desktop PC is widely estimated from slightly over $3,000 to $13,000 annually. This includes maintenance, help desk support, software licenses, and so on. It also includes other soft costs, or costs that cannot be easily attributable to a particular product or action. For example, who can

NOTE   **What's in a Name?** eCommerce (www.ecommerce.com) was established in June 1999 as an Internet incubator. Its stated mission is to rapidly launch Internet start-ups. It provides funding, strategy, people, creative development, technology, business development, and marketing. On November 30, 1999, the company purchased the domain name business.com for $7.5 million from Marc Ostrofsky, former owner of MultiMedia Publishing Corp., a business-to-business magazine and conference company. The site www.business.com will host eCommerce's business-to-business Internet service.

determine the cost of reduced productivity because an end user uses less efficient methods within software products? Soft costs are the problem areas that cause wide discrepancies in estimates of TCO.

The fact that you cannot determine with any accuracy the soft costs of a particular area of the company is not a reason to abandon the attempt. You *can* determine hard costs. You *can* determine the impact of disasters that might result if basic security measurers are not in place.

A large insurance company once estimated that its systems, which currently run 24×7, could not ever be allowed to go down. The company's estimates show them that if these systems did go down for more than four hours, the company would never catch up and might as well shut the doors. This company has a lot of latitude for security spending.

CASE STUDY: CHEMDEX

Chemdex (www.chemdex.com) is an online business-to-business (B2B) marketplace for the life sciences industry. Its target customers are hospitals, research institutions, medical and other laboratories, physicians and other medical practitioners, and scientists and researchers.

The company was founded in 1997 and employs 202 people. Its 80,000-square-foot headquarters are located in Mountain View, California.

PRODUCTS

Chemdex offers electronic procurement, systems integration, interfaces with third-party and back office systems, service, and support. Its Science360™ product is touted as a one-stop shop for biological and chemical reagents, lab supplies, instruments, and equipment.

Chemdex offers management of product features, cost comparison, and order processing and tracking. A customer can search, order, approve, and track orders using software hosted by Chemdex. The software can handle negotiated discounts.

Another component, MarketLink™, can be accessed from existing procurement systems such as Ariba, Commerce One, SAP, JD Edwards, Oracle, Baan, and others.

The products offer support for contract or negotiated pricing and automated purchasing rules. They enforce preferred suppliers, spending limits, ordering guidelines, and approval requirements. They contain automated approval work flows, consolidated and automated ordering, shipping, tracking, and reorders. Summary billing and consolidated reporting are also part of the package. Shipping data is kept and can be reported by expenditures.

Chemdex's main catalog currently offers 240,000 products from 100 suppliers. A larger offering is available to some customers—550,000 products as part of the LabPoint product.

CASE STUDY: CHEMDEX

Chemdex received the Business on the Internet (BOT) award for best business-to-business electronic commerce and also the Upside Hot 100 award for electronic commerce.

In addition, the Massachusetts Biotechnology Council (MBO) selected Chemdex as its preferred e-commerce provider. MBO is a not-for-profit trade association that represents 264 members in Massachusetts. Roche Molecular systems, a business unit of the Diagnostic Division of the Roche Group, also chose Chemdex for its procurement partner. The Roche Group is a research-oriented health-care group involved in pharmaceuticals, diagnostics, vitamins, fragrances, and flavors.

Chemdex has formed an alliance with the IBM Global Services Division for resources and system integration.

The concept of B2B is simple: to transform purchasing dynamics by giving the commercial consumer access to far more information in one place, and to streamline purchasing operations. It replaces the old request-for-proposal model or the hunt-through-a-catalog model with a newer, bidding-related model.

Chemdex fits this model but is not simply a convenient replacement for the traditional purchasing model. Chemdex targets a purchasing segment that relies heavily on the labor of highly educated scientists whose time can be better spent. The ordering of lab supplies, reagents, chemicals, and other materials cannot be done entirely by typical purchasing employees. In many cases, the scientist cannot simply specify what is needed; he or she must examine a large number of mail-order catalogs to find the right product. Although repeat orders can be specified and maintained by clerical personnel and although large order contracts can be negotiated by procurement managers, businesses need different products, and the availability of products changes. The marketplace is crowded with many producers, and a large number of unique products are managed and produced by many suppliers. Any system that can reduce this nonproductive, labor-intensive process for scientists is a good thing.

Chemdex has formed strategic, symbiotic business relations with providers of processes and products that it needs (such as IBM for help with infrastructure) and has gained endorsements by major purchasing organizations. As Chemdex and the business-to-business marketplace matures, these associations and relationships should change because they are useful and profitable for both parties. Chemdex is a virtual organization.

CHEMDEX CUSTOMER BUSINESS PROCESS EXAMINATION

Scientists are highly involved in the purchase of life sciences research products. They must use a large number of paper catalogs and phone calls to locate and possibly order supplies. In a large research organization with a sophisticated purchasing organization, hundreds of hours are lost when a scientist is often needed to approve any change from standard orders or to determine what is needed and where it can be found.

continues

CASE STUDY: CHEMDEX

continued

Order tracking and follow-up is fragmented because of the large number of products and suppliers. Preferred purchasing plans are difficult to enforce because scientists are quick to demand their own selection. The purchasing process may resemble the flow chart in Figure 1.6.

Typical online purchasing can be arranged with a B2B company such as Chemdex. In this model, a services consultant reviews the organization's current rules, processes, and strategies and uses the information to configure a procurement solution. A solution that is noninvasive to current organization information systems is designed and implemented. Standard browsers can be used, and all the processing resides on the B2B Web site. An account manager provides adoption assistance (one-on-one or group training) and

ongoing support (monitoring frequently ordered products and producing a "favorites" page, in addition to other customization).

Integration with commercial procurement systems can be made at this point. XML, electronic data interchange (EDI), and other formats are accepted; see Figure 1.7 for potential linkage points.

Customer service provides a single point of contact for all order tracking, fulfillment, status updates, and order expediting—all online.

Products include the following:

MarketLink™ integrates with enterprise customer procurement and enterprise resource planning (ERP) systems.

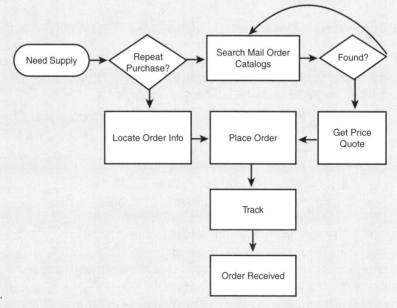

FIGURE 1.6
Life sciences supply-purchasing process.

CASE STUDY: CHEMDEX

Customer Systems   Chemdex Systems   Suppliers

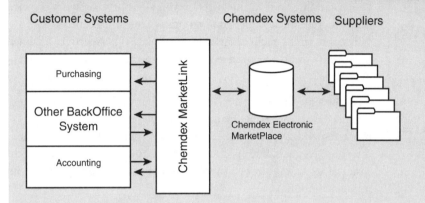

FIGURE 1.7
Chemdex and customer integration points.

Science360™ uses automated work flow approval and consolidated and automated ordering, invoicing, and billing to streamline the purchasing process.

LabPoint™ is Science360 on steroids. A larger set of products is available through a partnership with VWR Scientific Products to give LabPoint customer online access to VWR's catalog.

ANALYSIS

Online purchasing systems are not new; large companies have had them for a long time. Leased lines provided connectivity to their major suppliers and customers. Huge enterprise resource planning (ERP) systems support automated purchasing, among other things. With the widespread use of the Internet for everyday business communications, many of these systems have moved or now provide additional paths for these older services. What is new here is the arrangement by a company to host the entire operation, including the supplier catalog, customer work flow approval processes, order tracking, and reporting. Furthermore, this particular business-to-business solution is targeted at a market segment that will benefit immensely from a streamlining that reduces a labor-intensive purchasing operation that scientists, not clerks, participate in. The flow chart in Figure 1.6 maps the typical purchasing process.

In the new model, the customer recognizes a need for supplies and can use an automated search. Negotiated or standard orders can be accepted. The Chemdex system can obtain quotes for the customer and then return them. The customer still approves the quote, and the order is placed. Chemdex tracks the order, invoices the customer, and pays the supplier.

CHAPTER SUMMARY

KEY TERMS

- business process
- product life cycle
- business-to-business (B2B)
- soft cost

Understanding your business before you attempt to design a security infrastructure for it is just good common senses. It's time for IT to start approaching technology from the business perspective. It's time for security to be perceived as practical protection, not as paranoid projection.

Take the time to collect the facts about your business's locations, its organizational model, its management style, its priorities and processes, and its perceptions. Emphasize seeking knowledge of its direction, its goals, and its circumstances. You will be rewarded with easier progress in your security design, both in its approval and in its implementation.

APPLY YOUR KNOWLEDGE

Exercises

1.1 Analyze Existing and Planned Business Models

Background

Davison, Weidermyer, and West is an accounting firm. The three principal members are looking for new clients to whom they can pitch their security services. The firm specializes in analyzing the information security readiness of companies and proposing strategies that will improve it. The members are looking for companies that meet the following criteria:

- Are regional or national in scope

- Have a sustained growth rate

- Have an investment in, or are willing to invest in, a modern information systems infrastructure

- Have committed to Windows operating systems (a plus, but not a requirement)

> **NOTE**
> Information and statistics cited for corporations in this Exercise were obtained from information published on those corporations' Web sites.

Problem Statement

The new associates of the firm have gathered information on many interesting companies. Before approaching any of these companies, Davison, Weidermyer, and West want to see how closely the companies match the previous criteria and how easy they might be to approach and work with. They do not want to spend large amounts of time with a company and then not produce results.

The following companies are under consideration.

Hines Horticulture

Many factors can influence the selection of business priorities and the strategies they employ. Of course, one of the strongest motivators is falling sales or profit margins.

Hines Horticulture, Inc. (www.hineshorticulture.com), is the largest North American producer of ornamental container and field plants. It has two divisions: Hines Nurseries grows 4,100 varieties of ornamental shrubs and plants in eight nurseries in California, Oregon, Pennsylvania, South Carolina, and Texas. This division sells to home centers, mass merchandisers, and independent garden centers in the United States and Canada. Hines Sun Grow Horticulture sells sphagnum peat moss and other professional growing mixes.

Business is seasonal, and the early 1990s showed a decline in the company's traditional sales base and volume. Hines Horticulture responded by acquiring the 10 companies listed in Table 1.2. The company believes that sales have increased because it purchased 10 plant and plant mix companies during the 1990s and developed value-added marketing plans. Value-added plans include custom labeling, bar-coding, EDI, and technical support.

Hines Horticulture has added new products as well. The company has become a leading supplier of peat-based growing mixes for professionals. These mixes are used for seed germination, cutting propagation, and greenhouse crop production. These high-margin mixes have surpassed in volume the professional sales of sphagnum mosses.

In 1999, the company made significant investments in improved infrastructure, training, and expansion of sales forces.

APPLY YOUR KNOWLEDGE

TABLE 1.2

HINES HORTICULTURE ACQUISITIONS

Date	Company	Location	Products
September 1999	Atlantic Greenhouses, Inc.	New York and Pennsylvania	Potted flowering plants and color bedding plants
August 1999	Pro Gro	North and South Carolina	Bark-based mixes
August 1999	Strong Lite	Arkansas and Illinois	Bark-based mixes, perlite, and vermiculite
April 1998	Lakeland Peat Moss Ltd.	Canada, Oregon, and Utah	Sphagnum peat moss and mixes
December 1997	Bryfogle's Wholesale, Inc.	Pennsylvania	Color bedding plants
October 1997	Pacific Color	California	Color bedding plants
November 1996	Flynn Nurseries, Inc.	California	Ornamental plants and flowering bedding plants
August 1996	Iverson Perennial Gardens	South Carolina	Perennial flowers and plants
January 1995	Oregon Garden Products	Oregon	Ornamental, cold-tolerant plants and flowering color plants
June 1993	Sun Gro-U.S.	Canada, Michigan, Texas, and Washington	Sphagnum peat moss and peat-based mixes

Sun Gro products are sold directly and by distributors in the United States and Canada, and by distributors to Mexico, Japan, and other countries in Asia and South America.

As a grower and vendor of ornamental plants, Hines Horticulture previously was a seasonal, regional business dependent on a limited market and less capable of taking advantage of new product markets and geographical markets outside its region. The company's first major acquisition in the early 1990s, Sun Gro, allowed it to enter the peat moss market. This brought diversification and entry to the professional growers market. Purchases later that decade expanded the company's range of flowering plants and bedding plants. Both the peat moss and the bedding plant additions lengthened Hines Horticulture's major growing season and geographical market. A new crop of acquisitions of bark-based mixes in the late 1990s further solidified its lead in this market.

This expansion also allowed Hines Horticulture to develop new product lines and capitalize on an existing customer base.

The company is now capable of offering nationwide a large assortment in large volumes with a range of value-added services. Many of its competitors cannot offer the same record of accomplishment, product variety, or services.

Net sales in 1998 increased 17% to $235 million, up from $201.3 million in 1997. Gross margins improved by 0.5% to 51.1%. Because of increased efficiencies, operating expenses (as a percentage of sales) fell from 35.2% to 35.0%, even though general and administrative expenses increased 24%. This resulted in a 21% growth in operating income to $37.8 million. In addition, before recording extinguishing debt, net income grew by 81% to 10.5 million from $5.8 million.

APPLY YOUR KNOWLEDGE

Hines Horticulture appears to be taking steps to continue to develop an infrastructure that will support this expansion.

The Standard Register Company

The Standard Register Company (www.stdreg.com) of Dayton, Ohio, has 59 manufacturing facilities and 79 warehouses in the United States. It offers technology and consulting services to its associates in 29 countries. Of its 8,200 employees, 962 are involved in direct sales. The company's products include electronic and printed business forms, and smart cards. It also staffs 25 Stanfast centers that are available for print on demand. It maintains document security standards for businesses, including layered authentication systems, secure disbursement systems, controlled security paper, and printed security features. Its current catalog features 35,000 office supplies.

Bob's Valley Market

Bob's Valley Market is a 12,000-plus-square-foot minimarket with an attached ham-processing facility, deli, contract post office, diesel and automotive fuel service, fish and game license service, and pump service. This is a family-run business. Expansion has proceeded rapidly with small business loans; most of the building work has been done by family members. As they say, Pa built. Ma ran things. The local community has grown quite large over the last 30 years.

IMP

IMP, Inc. (www.impweb.com) is an analog-integrated circuit manufacturer in San Jose, California. Although in the past its primary business came from its wafer foundry and integrated circuit manufacturing services, today it offers its own analog and mixed-signal integrated circuits (ICs), which account for a third of sales. These products are data communications interface ICs (including SCSI terminators) and power management ICs (voltage regulators and lamp drivers) for communications, computer, and systems control industries.

IMP ended 1999 with sales of $33.4 million and a net income of $–7.9 million. Second quarter results in 1999 continue the downward trend (a net loss of $2.2 million).

The company has recently released new products, lower-power versions of devices offered by Dallas Semiconductor. It reduced staff by 14%, which helped reduce selling, general, and administrative expenses from 20% to 14%. Research and development expenses were also reduced from the preceding year.

IMP has announced an alliance with Teamasia, an Indian corporation that manufacturers and sells discrete semiconductor devices. Teamasia will invest in IMP (purchasing 16.7% of shares) and will use IMP's foundry.

IMP's CEO resigned and was replaced with an interim.

Prices on the company's SCSI terminators were reduced.

Philip Morris Companies, Inc.

Philip Morris Companies, Inc. (www.philipmorris.com) is an international conglomerate consisting of five subdivisions: Tobacco, Kraft Foods North America, Kraft Foods International, Miller Beer, and Philip Morris Financial Services.

Philip Morris Tobacco produces Marlboro cigarettes. Marlboro generates more than $1 billion in revenue. Kraft Foods generates $17.3 billion, Miller Beer brings in more than $4 billion, and Philip Morris Financial Services generates $275 million.

Kraft Foods North America (www.kraft.com/corporate) has 50 manufacturing facilities and 260 distribution

APPLY YOUR KNOWLEDGE

centers in the United States and 90 facilities in 35 other countries. Kraft and General Foods merged in the 1980s. Kraft has 37,500 of Philip Morris's 144,000 employees. Its stated vision is "to be the undisputed global food leader." It has nine divisions: beverages and desserts, Maxwell House and Post, Kraft Canada, Kraft cheese, Kraft food services, New Means, Oscar Mayer Foods, pizza, and e-commerce3000. With an annual earning growth rate of 8.8% and a tripling of its volume growth in North America in 1998, it is the largest packaged food company in the United States and the second-largest in the world.

Kraft Foods International has offices in Europe, Central and Eastern Europe, the Middle East and Africa, and the Asia Pacific Region.

Philip Morris claims that its continuing success is due to strong marketing, improved business skills, fine-tuning of its architecture, and new leadership development programs. Settlement charges from lawsuits have not crippled this behemoth.

Miller Brewing (www.millerbrewing.com), in business since 1855, is the second-largest brewer in the United States and the third-largest in the world. It was started by Frederick Miller, whose mission statement "Quality, uncompromising and unchanging" is still prominently displayed in its offices and plants. Miller has six breweries: one each in North Carolina, Georgia, Texas, California, Ohio, and Wisconsin. Forty-four million barrels of beer are brewed each year and sold in 100 countries around the world. Brand names include Miller Times, Miller Lite, Miller Genuine Draft, Miller High Life, Miller Beer, Meister Brau, and Milwaukee's Best. Plant Road Brewery is a division of Miller that produces the Icehouse and Red Dog brands. Miller acquired Henry Weinhards and gained Hamm's, Old English 9800, and Mickey's Malt Liquor. Miller also produces Sharp's, a nonalcoholic beer.

Philip Morris Tobacco is sold in 180 markets worldwide. One out of every six cigarettes sold is produced by Philip Morris. Philip Morris started as an English tobacco shop on Bond Street in London in the 1850s and incorporated in New York in the early 1900s. Twenty states are tobacco–growers, with Kentucky and North Carolina being the largest producers. The United States produces 1.68 billion pounds of tobacco leaf annual—this is a $3 billion industry, with 1.5 billion pounds of the leaf exported.

The Richmond plant consists of six connected buildings, which cover 43 acres: 1.6 million square feet under one roof. A total of 3,500 employees work in three shifts, 24 hours a day, five days a week. This plant ships 730 million cigarettes a day (3.6 million cartons). It pays $5.08 million in federal excise taxes a day.

Operations in Cabarrus County, North Carolina, reside on 2,100 acres, with 2.3 million square feet under one roof. There, 2,500 employees work in three shifts, 24 hours a day, five days a week. Each day the plant produces 600 million cigarettes, or 3 million cartons—that's 1.1 million pounds of tobacco daily.

The company is phasing out an old 23.7-acre facility in Louisville, Kentucky. The primary processing plant produces 322 million cigarettes a day; 500,000 to 600,000 pounds of cut filter per day are also produced.

Your Task

Help Davison, Weidermyer, and West evaluate these companies against their criteria by filling in the information in Table 1.3.

APPLY YOUR KNOWLEDGE

TABLE 1.3: EXERCISE 1.1

Company	Scope	Growth	IS Infrastructure	Windows
Standard Register				
Bob's Valley Market				
IMP				
Hines Horticulture				
Philip Morris				

1.2 Analyze Business Processes

Refer to the Chemdex case study. Examine the traditional purchasing operation. How would a flow chart of the new business process look?

Review Questions

1. Hines Horticulture (discussed previously) faced falling profits and reorganized. The company continues to be a successful business today. What did it do to accomplish this? What impact did this change in organizational structure have on IT?

2. Hines Horticulture has several geographic locations (the Northeast, the South, California, and the Northwest). It has two major product lines: plants and growing mixes. It even has two markets: retailers and professional growers. Of the following business models, pick the one that you think is the most accurate description of Hines Horticulture's IT infrastructure needs: geographical scope, industry, product. Why?

3. What is the relationship between risk, value, vulnerability, and countermeasures?

4. Examine the information on Philip Morris International given in Exercise 1.1. What is the growth strategy of this company?

5. What will be the impact of relaxing the export restrictions on encryption strengths?

6. Would you consider Chemdex to be local, regional, international, or something else?

7. IMP took steps to contain business losses. Like Hines Horticulture, this company needed to make changes. Compare IMP's strategy to that of Hines Horticulture.

8. Hines Horticulture acquired new business to diversify its operations. What IT operations did this company change that also improved its financial status?

9. What are two things that make the Chemdex offerings attractive to companies with an investment in ERP systems?

10. What special IT challenges are there for a company with the international scope of Philip Morris?

11. Imagine that your business has agreed to the development of an Internet-based extranet with several suppliers. Online quote, approval, purchasing, and invoicing systems will be developed. You will have lots of questions to ask the new business partners and their IT departments at your first meeting. What should some of these questions be?

Exam Questions

1. Seattle's Best Coffee was started in 1968 in Couperville, Washington, on Whidby Island as an ice cream and coffee shop. In 1969, its owner purchased a roaster from a peanut vendor, and the first pot of Wet Whisker Coffee was produced. In 1970, the firm was moved to Pier 70 on Seattle's Waterfront and was named Stewart Brothers Coffee. All the coffee was produced on the Pier until 1983. SBC, as it came to be known, was dubbed Seattle's Best Coffee in the late 1980s.

   Now the company's coffee is distributed nationally in supermarkets by Millstone coffee. It operates cafés in Seattle, Portland, Los Angeles, Chicago, and Boston, in addition to international wholesale operations. The coffee also is available in office service through Aramark.

   Which of the following correctly characterizes Seattle's Best Coffee?

   A. Seattle's Best Coffee is a local business.

   B. Seattle's Best Coffee is an international business.

   C. Seattle's Best Coffee is following a rapid expansion plan by acquiring new businesses to complement its niche market.

   D. Seattle's Best Coffee is not reaching its marketing goals.

2. Oreo Power and Light is headquartered in White River, Wisconsin. Power plant locations are spread along the Oreo River. Information on daily coal purchase quantities and quality is collected at the plant and uploaded to the database in Akron, Ohio. Weekly plant reports are generated, and information is returned to plant managers. Purchasing personnel in Akron use the information in negotiations with coal producers to ensure acquisition of high-quality coal at the best price.

   Which of the following is true of Oreo Power and Light? (Select all that apply.)

   A. Oreo Power and Light's information flows up from the power plants to headquarters.

   B. Oreo Power and Light's information flows down from headquarters to the power plants.

   C. Oreo Power and Light's coal purchasing information is restricted to plant managers and data processing personnel.

   D. Oreo Power and Light's coal purchasing information is used by the purchasing department and management.

3. Chute Industrial Supply is a wholesaler with divisions in the northeast, central, and southwestern regions of the United States. Each division is given wide discretion over the handling of customer relations, discounts, and promotions. The company must stock the same 3,000-plus products. A monthly meeting of division heads reviews marketing, sales, and inventory information and reviews proposed new products and recommended inventory levels. Which of the following statements is true?

   A. Chute company executives have autonomy at the branch level.

B. Chute uses the communal approach to decision making.

C. Chute company executives have autonomy at the division level.

D. Chute company executives have autonomy at the division level with respect to customers, promotions, and discounts.

4. Return to the case study on Chemdex to pick the correct answers from the following:

A. Chemdex provides an e-commerce presence and collection process for its vendor partners.

B. Chemdex offers its customers an automated, streamlined procurement system and automatic reduced costs on purchases.

C. Chemdex requires cooperation between purchasing and IT to integrate current ERP systems with its procurement system.

D. Chemdex cannot integrate with SAP.

5. Pointyhead Productions, Inc., provides technical training in its classrooms in every major city or at customer locations. Recently, National Tech acquired Pointyhead Productions and has plans to purchase all franchise locations within five years. National Tech correctly predicts a downturn in the rapidly growing technical training market. Training companies that are to survive, it feels, must consolidate. If there is going to be a shakeout, the company wants to come out on top. To do so, National Tech realizes that it must become more efficient and has plans to cut staff trainers at some locations and eliminate some locations. In essence, the company will be buying

up the competition to close it down. This should leave the company with few locations, but also few competitors. Because National Tech has more than adequate capital, it can then increase revenue by using national marketing efforts and maintaining locations only in profitable cities.

A. National Tech's growth strategy is one of acquisition.

B. Pointyhead Production's growth strategy is one of expansion.

C. National Tech's growth strategy is one of expansion.

D. Pointyhead Production's growth strategy is one of acquisition.

E. National Tech's growth strategy is a combination of acquisition, reduction, and reentry in a new market.

Read and study the following, and then answer the following two questions.

Fred Pumpkin Productions has recently entered the B2B market. The company offers one-stop shopping for information security products. Customers have the opportunity to compare features, interfaces, and costs in a virtual try-before-you-buy showplace that consists of simulations of products in different categories. As members or day-pass shoppers, customers can examine side by side products in the intrusion detection, firewall, VPN, biometric, smart card, and miscellaneous categories. They can examine feature comparison lists and see products in action. The customers fill out a requirements form so simulated software is configured to their specifications and

APPLY YOUR KNOWLEDGE

demos can be run. Simulated attacks run against simulated protective modules. Complicated scenarios can be devised with proper notice. The setup also can be used for preinstallation training or dry runs.

Vendors gain when their products are evaluated in a neutral manner. No vendor is allowed to advertise or pay for more virtual reality space than another. The list order of products is rotated so that no vendor is more likely to be chosen for examination over another. Vendors can purchase day passes to provide their prospective customers access to the site. Fred Pumpkin Productions provides elaborate site usage reports to its vendor partners, which gives vendors information on how many visitors spent how much time on their products and their competitors' products, and what features prospective buyers indicated a preference for. Although these reports do not list customer names, the names and activities of visitors using passes provided by vendors are reported to the vendor owners.

6. Fred Pumpkin Productions's lawyers had a fit when they saw the proposed business plan. What two items below concerned Fred Pumpkin Productions's lawyers?

    A. When selling a security product, Fred Pumpkin Productions needs to be concerned with laws that govern the strength of encryption exports.

    B. Security products cannot be sold over the Internet.

    C. Fred Pumpkin Productions must have a security structure in place to deal with privacy laws.

D. The simulations will require a large amount of processing power. The Web site might go down, and customers might sue, claiming false advertising because they couldn't run the simulations.

7. What is Fred Pumpkin Productions's risk tolerance level?

    A. Fred Pumpkin Productions has a low tolerance of risk.

    B. Fred Pumpkin Productions has a high tolerance of risk.

    C. Fred Pumpkin Productions is not in a risky business.

    D. Fred Pumpkin offsets its risk by sharing it with other companies.

Use the following description to answer the next two questions.

Fugee Denche Peaches purchases peaches and makes pies. The company's pies are produced only in Peoria, Illinois. Fugee Denche markets its pies internationally to the countries from which it purchases its peaches. Currently its pies are sold in 10 countries to grocery stores, restaurants, and hospitals. Fugee Denche recently opened peach-processing plants in South America. Peaches now will be skinned, sliced, cored, and preserved before shipping. This will reduce costs because of reduced labor costs and reduced spoilage. Fugee Denche has just announced plans to make peach preserves. It actively is searching for complementary fruits from which to make specialty jams and jellies.

APPLY YOUR KNOWLEDGE

8. What is the business model for Fugee Denche?

    A. Fugee Denche is a regional company.

    B. Fugee Denche is a local company.

    C. Fugee Denche is an international company.

    D. Fugee Denche is a virtual company.

9. What does Fugee Denche bases its growth strategy on?

    A. The company's growth strategy is based on acquisition.

    B. The company's growth strategy is based on expansion into new markets.

    C. The companies growth strategy is based on both changes to operations that will reduce costs and expansion into new markets.

    D. The company's growth strategy is based on reduction of operations, shrinking in revenue, and containment of markets.

Read and study the following description to answer the next question.

Aunt Eddie's Cakes is a home-based business located in Kansas City, Missouri. Its distinctive single-serving cakes are homemade, and a picture of Eddie is on the label. (It's not her real picture, her name's not Eddie, and she's nobody's aunt, but that's another story.) Aunt Eddie's Cakes are sold to consumers through grocery stores, bakeries, and convenience stores in the greater metropolitan Kansas City area. Eddie has no plans for expansion. "I can't bake no more cakes in a day nohow," says Eddie.

10. What is the business model for Aunt Eddie's Cakes:

    A. Aunt Eddie's Cakes is an international business.

    B. Aunt Eddie's Cakes is a local business.

    C. Aunt Eddie's Cakes is a virtual business.

    D. Aunt Eddie's Cakes is a regional business.

11. Why would an analysis of information and communication flow be important to the development of a security infrastructure? Select all that apply.

    A. Appropriate bandwidth and access points must be in place to support these flows within the corporation.

    B. Knowing the extent, breadth, and routes of information throughout the company allows proper privacy planning.

    C. Different types of communication will have different privacy needs and require different security structures to be in place.

    D. A determination can be made as to the need for internal and external email, discussion groups, and chat rooms.

Answers to Exercises

The solution to the Exercise 1.1 is presented in Table 1.4.

Figure 1.8 illustrates the solution to Exercise 1.2.

APPLY YOUR KNOWLEDGE

TABLE 1.4: EXERCISE 1.1 SOLUTION

Company	Scope	Growth	IS Infrastructure	Windows
Standard Register	International	Sustained	Heavily invested	Unknown
Bob's Valley Market	Local	Sustained	None	None
IMP	International	Not profitable	Unknown	Unknown
Hines Horticulture	National	Sustained	Heavily invested	Unknown
Philip Morris	International	Sustained	Heavily invested	Mixed infrastructure

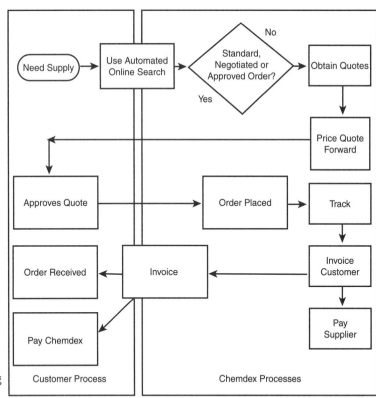

FIGURE 1.8
Exercise 1.2 Solution—Revised B2B Purchasing Process.

Answers to Review Questions

1. When sales of current products suffered, Hines Horticulture diversified to support sales year-round. The company acquired another company whose product complemented its current structure. The company also realized its need to update its IT infrastructure to support the new product lines. In addition to acquisition, Hines Horticulture built new products, including the added-value product, which increased the value of purchases to its wholesale companies. Customer services as well as increased computing support resulted in increased and repeat sales opportunities.

2. The major difference in Hines Horticulture's business is in market. Although all its products are sold to retailers, the growing mixes are also sold to professional growers. While added-value programs attract and keep retailers, professional growers are attracted by quality products. Therefore, the specialized added-value programs and services will continue to mean different IT programs and infrastructure for that market.

3. Risk = threat × vulnerability / countermeasures. Considering a threat alone gives you no information on how to handle it. Instead, if you are able to determine something about it, you can rank the risk that it poses to your business. Multiply a threat by your vulnerability to that threat (give the threat and your vulnerability a relative value). Next, divide that answer by the value of any steps that have already been taken to lessen the effect. The answer will be a number that, when compared to others, tells you which threats are your greatest risks and perhaps should be further examined to find out how to prevent them from happening. For example, if I have an e-commerce Web site, I might consider the threat of a hacker breaking in and stealing the credit card numbers of my customers to be a rather large threat. I might give it a number 10 out of 10 for a threat value. Next, to assign a vulnerability rating, I would consider things like the quality of my implementation and how large a target I might appear to be (how well known I am, how much activity I have daily). Am I using well-known products to produce my site? Am I protecting transactions with appropriate technology? Have I hired well-trained staff or hired a professional, experienced company to host my site? Perhaps I judge that my vulnerability is relatively high and that my staff and product are good, but I am a huge, well-known site dealing in high dollar volume. So, I give my vulnerability rating an 8. However, I also have the best firewalls and intrusion-detection systems, and I am constantly vigilant. Therefore, I give myself a figure of 7 for countermeasures. When I use the formula, I get a risk factor of 11.43. This risk factor is only meaningful when compared to other risk factors.

4. Philip Morris International's growth strategy is: New markets for current products, and new products to current markets.

5. Products with strong encryption strengths can be shipped to any country that does not support state-sponsored terrorism, but shipping also will be subject to the import laws of the other country.

6. Chemdex is a virtual company.

7. IPM reduced spending by cutting research. The company changed its top executives and merged with another company, which now appears to have major control. In contrast, Hines Horticulture developed new markets with new products and existing products.

APPLY YOUR KNOWLEDGE

8. Hines Horticulture developed a new value-added program for retailers. The company also made major modifications to its IT infrastructure. It added bar-coding labels to products and added the IT infrastructure (printers and programs) to support this. The company also acquired the infrastructure to support electronic data exchange, or the handling of monetary transactions electronically.

9. First, Chemdex provides an interface for companies that already have an investment in ERP systems. Second, Chemdex forms close relationships with its business partners and seems to be flexible in its approach. Hundreds of products are displayed in its general catalog. To bind with VWR and obtain rights to present its catalog to VWR customers, Chemdex built a new product that is not available to all customers. Chemdex provides invoicing services for its vendor partners and seeks trade organization relations to promote its product.

10. Philip Morris has several IT challenges, two of which are these: First, because of its international scope, it faces the problems inherent in interfacing disparate systems, working in multiple languages and with multiple cultures. Second, because Philip Morris is so large and because large physical distances separate its divisions, the process of linking all systems together and providing quick, error-free communications is not easy.

11. A. Are current ERP systems in place? Which ones?

    B. What is the infrastructure composed of? Which OS, border routers, and so on are involved?

    C. Is a virtual private network (VPN) infrastructure in place?

    D. What additional systems does the company feel will be involved, however peripherally?

    E. Who will be involved in the development process?

    F. Who are the other extranet partners?

Answers to Exam Questions

1. **B.** Although Seattle's Best Coffee started in Seattle, it now has national presence in shops and grocery stores around the country. In addition, its coffee is marketed internationally. (See the previous section "Analyzing Existing and Planned Business Models.")

2. **A, B, D.** Information does flow in both directions. Plant managers receive reports made from the data that they provide, so both answers A and B are correct. The purchasing department and management receive the information and can use it to their advantage, so answer D is correct. You have not been given any information that would tell you any restrictions on the data, but you have been told that purchasing personnel receive the information; so, answer C is incorrect. (See the previous section "Information Flow.")

3. **B, D.** Chute managers get together monthly to determine strategies for the coming month, so answer B is correct. The only mention of local decision making is for that affecting customers, promotions, and discounts. This makes answer D correct. The authority is placed at the division level, not the branch level, making answer A incorrect. You have been told only a few decision-making areas where division heads have autonomy, and you have specifically been told that they must stock the same products. This makes

APPLY YOUR KNOWLEDGE

answer D incorrect. (See the previous section "Analyzing Company Processes.")

4. **C, D.** Answer A is incorrect. Chemdex can integrate with SAO. Answer B is also incorrect. Chemdex does not mean automatic reduction in purchasing costs—it might, but this is not guaranteed. Answers C and D are correct. Chemdex does provide a Web presence for its vendor partners; to integrate with ERP systems, IT and the other companies purchasing must cooperate. (See the case study and the previous section "Analyzing Company Processes.")

5. **E.** Answers B and D are incorrect. Pointyhead Productions has been purchased and has no strategy. Although answers A and C appear to be correct, National Tech is growing by acquiring other companies and by expanding its operations, so neither answer is complete. National Tech is also changing the marketplace by closing down many of the offices of the company it acquired in an attempt to move its training operations to a few major cities. (See the section "Analyze Existing and Planned Organizational Structures.")

6. **A, C.** Laws govern the export of encryption products. The lawyers want to make sure that the company does not violate any of these laws. Individuals will be entering information, and some of that information will be reported back to vendors. This is a hot legal issue currently, concerning what type of information can be electronically collected and how it can be used. Therefore, answers A and C are correct. Although concerns about processing power are an issue, they are not a legal issue. Just because a product deals with security does not restrict its sale; it is the encryption strength of the product that may

limit its export or import. (See the section "Relevant Laws and Regulations.")

7. **D.** Starting this type of new e-business can be risky. Fred Pumpkin Productions is sharing the risk with other companies because they are allowed to show their products side by side with others. (See the section "Tolerance of Risk.")

8. **C.** Fugee Denche is an international company. It has processing plants in South America and markets its products internationally. (See "Analyzing Existing and Planned Business Models.")

9. **C.** By doing preproduction at the source of its products, Fugee Denche should be capable of reducing costs. It also is willing to expand into new markets. This makes answer C correct. There is no indication that Fugee Denche is acquiring any other company, so answer A is wrong. The company is expanding into other markets, but this answer, B, is incomplete. Answer D is wrong also—the company is expanding its operations, not reducing them. (See the section "Acquisition Plans.")

10. **B.** Aunt Eddie's Cakes supplies only the Kansas City market, so it is a local business. Answer B is correct. Answer A, therefore, is incorrect, as is D. There is no indication of any Web presence, making answer C wrong as well. (See the section "Analyzing Existing and Planned Business Models.")

11. **C.** Although answer A is important for communication and information flow, and although privacy (B) is important, answer C is the best answer because it speaks to the security needs and structures. Answer D deals with types of products, not security issues, and so it is incorrect. (See the section "Information Flow.")

APPLY YOUR KNOWLEDGE

Suggested Readings and Resources

1. Winkler, Ira. *Corporate Espionage.* Prima Publishing, 1997.

2. Morgan, Gareth. *Images of Organization, The Executive Edition.* Berrett-Koehler, 1998.

3. Vincent, David R. *The Information Based Corporation.* Dow-Jones Irwin, 1990.

4. Kaeo, Merike. *Designing Network Security.* Cisco Press, 1999.

5. Hammer, Michael, and James Champy. *Reengineering the Corporation.* Harper Business, 1993.

6. Web Sites:

   - www.hoovers.com

   - www.applebees.com (Annual Report for 1997)

   - http://thomas.loc.gov

   - www.cdt.org/crypto

   - www.fortune.com

   - www.businessweek.com

   - http://www4.law.cornell.edu/uscode

   - www.msnbc.com

This chapter covers the following Microsoft-specified objectives for the "Analyzing Business Requirements" section of the Designing Security for a Microsoft Windows 2000 Network exam:

Analyze business and security requirements for the end user.

▶ What good are elaborate intrusion-detection products, firewalls, and other devices if we don't protect our networks, our data at its weakest point? What good is super security if our users can't get to the data they need? The needs of the user and the security requirements of the organization must be reconciled. First you must understand them.

Analyze the structure of IT management.

- Type of Administration—Centralized or Decentralized
- Funding Model
- Outsourcing
- Decision-Making Process
- Change-Management Process

▶ Understanding the structure of IT management will assist security design by providing answers to these questions: Who makes the decision here? Where does the money come from (so, who would be interested in the decision on how to spend it)? What part of IT is outsourced and to whom? What is the process for managing change?

Analyze the current physical model and information security model.

▶ Although engineers, like artists, like to start with a clean canvas, engineers, unlike artists, must deal with elements already in place. You must examine the current structure and determine controls that are in place.

CHAPTER 2

Analyzing IT

Analyze internal and external security risks.

▶ Risks, actual and perceived, internal and external, cannot be eliminated, but they can be mitigated. Knowing what they are is a large part of the battle. This will become the focus against which to test your design.

STUDY STRATEGIES

▶ First examine your own IT structure; is it centralized or decentralized? Who controls its funding? Who does the Chief Information Officer (CIO) report to? What does the physical model look like? What risks do you perceive in your network?

▶ Read industry magazines and visit Internet sites; have discussions with the IT and business communities to learn about the IT management structure of other companies. How do they compare to yours?

▶ Find articles, join Web discussions, access internal records of intrusion, and then list the reasons why intrusions were able to occur and what was done about them.

INTRODUCTION

This chapter continues the theme of Chapter 1, "General Business Analysis." You must know about your business if you are to protect it. Here you study the makeup of your IT management. Is the CIO or Chief Technology Officer (CTO) down in the trenches or up in the boardroom? Are technology decisions made to support the business or to follow the latest technology direction? Have you ever looked at things from the end-users' perspective?

Finally, you list, examine, and quantify potential risks to your business.

END-USER REQUIREMENTS

Analyze business and security requirements for the end user.

Three security principles are authentication, authorization, and the integrity of data. Authentication is the practice of proving you are who you say you are. When you enter your ID and password at a logon screen, the system verifies that information. Authorization, sometimes referred to as access control, is the process of verifying that you have the right or permission to perform an act or access some data. Maintaining the integrity of data means that the data is not changed except by authorized individuals, and that it will not be corrupted.

It is not necessary at this point to examine in detail the infrastructure that supports the end user. Instead, look from the end-user perspective. To do their job, the end users need two things: access to resources (data and software), and the tools to get there. This describes their business needs. As for security needs, the end users also require assurance that only they can manipulate their data (authentication and authorization), that the data is accurate (integrity), and that the process will always work (reliability). You can categorize these concrete business and security needs of the end user into five subsets (see Figure 2.1).

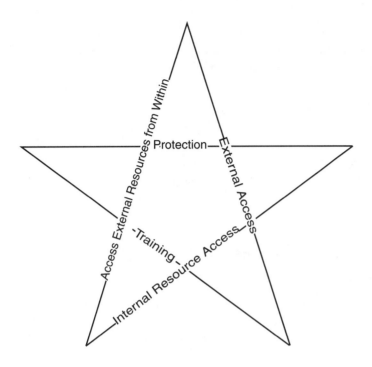

Protection

External Access

Access External Resources from Within

Training

Internal Resource Access

FIGURE 2.1
End-user information requirements.

◆ Access to local network-based resources from within the company

◆ Access to remote-based resources from within the company

◆ Access to company resources from external locations

◆ Protection of the organization's assets that the end user may carry away from the organization's buildings

◆ Training in systems and software use and security awareness

Local Network Resource Access

These resources may consist of user documents, whether based on a network file server or a desktop machine, databases, software—which consists of operating system, business productivity, data access, and others—and the desktop computer used by the end user.

In some cases, end users share computers. This may be due to multiple shifts, dedicated kiosk machines, or the relative minor computer needs of the end user.

You also need to consider the method of access. Is the user connected on a LAN or WAN segment? What protocols are necessary on the end-user computer? What physical devices and communications software must be present to enable this access?

Security usually consists of user ID and password access to the network and resource protection by authorization schemes. Authorization may be handled by the operating system in the form of file Discretionary Access Control Lists (DACLs) or by the server side of the software (database management systems often support their own security infrastructure) or by both.

Remote Resource Access from Organization Location

If the organization has remote locations, does the end user need access to these resources? Are there groups of end users who do not? To which physical resources, (dial-up modems, leased lines, public networks) does the end user need access to get to the remote resource?

Access to Organization Resources from Outside the Organization

Organizations increasingly staff large numbers of employees whose main location is offsite, or variable. These users may work at home or may be part of a staff of "road-warriors" who travel extensively, their business office consisting of a laptop computer and/or PDA. "I don't live out of a suitcase, I live out of a computer case," they quip.

These users need remote access. That access may be as previously mentioned—direct, leased lines, or the use of public networks including the Internet. In most cases, they need a high-speed modem and dial-up software. A Web browser, or other more specialized client software, completes the package.

Users working at home are usually issued company desktop machines and peripheral hardware, whereas traveling employees are often issued laptop computers. Appropriate hardware and software is supplied in both cases.

Protection of Traveling Company Assets

Computers not located within company offices require special security considerations. There are two items to protect: the computer, and the data and configuration information on the computer. Because laptop computers are easily stolen, they require special considerations. End users should be provided with some form of security device that can assist them.

Training and Security Awareness

Finally, end users require knowledge of the access systems that they need to use. They need to know where data and software is located, and where they should keep private files. They also need security-awareness education. Locking users down so that they can't ever get into trouble is impossible. Enforcing strict security guidelines is difficult without cooperation from the end user. Treating end users like two year olds, who will never realize that they shouldn't put small parts in their mouths, is not acceptable. End users must and can become responsible partners in IT's efforts to maintain accessibility and security.

IT MANAGEMENT

Analyze the structure of IT management. Considerations include type of administration, such as centralized or decentralized; funding model; outsourcing; decision-making process; and change-management process.

To understand IT, understand IT administration. Traditional MIS is conservative; the primary concern is to keep systems up and running at all times. Nontraditional IT administration may concern itself more with rapid deployment of new technologies than with putting the perfect system online the first time, every time. Each orientation has much to offer and can cause many problems. Which is yours?

Regardless of inclination, IT management can be examined in light of its funding model, its organization (centralized or decentralized), whether and to what degree it outsources its functions, and how it handles decision-making and change management processes.

Type of Administration—Centralized or Decentralized

In a highly centralized IT structure, the focus is on locating resources, administration, and control at a central location. Databases, staffing, and network infrastructure are primarily located at a central place and managed there. Remote access is provided via leased lines or, increasingly, over public networks. Even departments or divisions located at corporate headquarters do not have internal IT staff or servers. Large data centers house all resources.

More importantly, all IT decisions are made at the central location.

Decentralized IT structures place smaller, data-center sites at division, warehouse, or other major locations. Each data center houses its own equipment, management staff, systems and network administrators, as well as help desk and support technicians. Departmental servers may be the rule, because each can focus the use of resources on its respective business area (accounting, payroll, human resources, and so on).

It is possible to have mixtures of these systems. Many years ago when I made sales calls on Goodyear Tire and Rubber, its payroll department housed and managed its own minicomputer. Goodyear had a highly centralized IT environment at that time. However, payroll management was able to acquire and manage its own system because of its inherent specialized security needs as well as the Goodyear dictum "you can't miss a payroll." (Guess not, tens of thousands of union workers whose paychecks were late would be a bit hard to manage.)

Companies move from one organizational structure to another. They often decentralize because of rapid expansion (or because they anticipate the requirements of such expansion) or divestiture. The Ford Motor Company has spent the past year moving its parts department's operations to a separate division and gradually moving the required infrastructure from headquarters to the new division to decrease the new division's reliance on corporate data and structure. They have formed a joint venture with Oracle to create AutoXchange, a B2B business. *Playboy* magazine is shifting management resources to business units, attempting to make IT an integral part of the business effort rather than just a support role (see the following note).

IN THE FIELD

PLAYBOY PLAYS WITH IT

Playboy magazine made many changes to IT in 1999. IT personnel were transferred to business units where they are expected to become experts in that phase of the business and assist IT in basing technology direction on business needs.

Staff was increased by 30%. Plans were made to give each division a Chief Technology Officer, a manager with a background in that part of the business.

IT and "new-media technologies" were merged to blend the no-nonsense, conservative IT with the quick-acting, but less-prone-to-look-for-mistakes new-media technologies.

Web-site Netscape servers were replaced with Transact servers to handle catalog order-processing in real-time. Financial and catalog systems run on midrange IBM AS/400s. *Playboy*'s online sales reached $77.8 million in the third quarter of 1999.

Plans were made to return Sun Microsystems servers from distributed sites to decrease management costs. Management costs outweighed performance increases.

There are two themes here:

- *Playboy* is making good technology decisions. Moving a growing Web site to a platform that will handle orders more efficiently and moving servers from remote locations to reduce administration headaches will impact current operations.

- By insisting on a business motivation, not a technology motivation for IT, *Playboy* is looking to reap the benefits of putting technology to work building the business, not merely supporting it in some background role. (*Playboy* is not just draining its resources by purchasing new technology for technology's sake.)

continues

continued

Moving IT professionals to business units is not a new thing. It may be just the result of a decentralization process and still take old IT separatist values with it. However, *Playboy* is also seeking to reduce administrative costs and hassles by returning Sun Microsystems servers from distributed locations. Although the goal of decentralization may be to increase efficiency, or to plan for expansion, the stated rational here is to staff IT with business-knowledgeable managers. By giving each division a technology officer, by moving IT professionals out to learn the business side of the business, and by tempering enthusiasm with conservatism, *Playboy* is placing IT in a proactive role.

Movement of resources and personnel back to the corporate data center often results from attempts to reduce costs.

In a move similar to Goodyear's payroll manager, departments today are leading the decentralization of IT with their own departmental Web sites.

Funding Model

The CIO often reports to the Chief Financial Officer (CFO). Increased spending in IT has meant increased scrutiny and a demand for accountability. Funding for IT can come from three sources: money budgeted as expenses, money from charge back (accounting for the use of IT by other divisions), and outside funding or reduced costs.

Elaborate charge-back schemes are used corporatewide in an attempt to focus on this particular cost of doing business. IBM uses the expression "green money versus blue money," and its management keeps strict accountability of both. Green money, of course, is real; blue money is from usage of corporate assets by departments or divisions within IBM.

In most companies, IT is seen as an operating expense. That is, some money must be spent on IT just because the business is in business, and basic IT expenditures are not easily attributable to a particular operation, product, or project.

Many vendors offer reduced costs to early adopters of new technology. This provides a way to stretch budgets and the reach of technology to all parts of the corporation. Microsoft has an early-adopter program. A company can receive reduced licensing fees, training, and extensive support by agreeing to move to new products (or new versions of products). IBM has several partner programs that pay for development and promotion of products that use IBM hardware and software. Almost every major hardware and software vendor has some program in place.

Outsourcing

The outsourcing of IT, or the fulfillment of IT functions by outside companies, is often a part of the realities of modern information systems.

Outsourcing is chosen for many reasons including a shortage of skilled professionals, the need to complete a project quickly, requirements to reduce costs, and the search for the best-of-the-best.

If projects are international in scope, new challenges may require outsourcing. These challenges include the differences in network telecommunications from country to country and the need to gain efficiency and cost effectiveness by hiring local field-service personnel.

Outsourcing is especially useful when service is required at remote locations. Placing servers and desktops in every field office and warehouse, every division no matter how remote, may seem like the only way to go, but it is increasingly difficult to manage remote systems.

Decision-Making Process

How are IT decisions made? How does this process affect day-to-day operations, upgrading of hardware and software, new hires, promotions, and major reconstruction and realignment?

Understanding the decision-making process will help you in proposing changes and in getting designs approved, allowing projects to move forward more smoothly. Ignoring this process may mean that your projects won't move at all.

Who gets involved in the process? Is there a certain dollar limit beyond which even your CTO or CIO does not have authority? Are there review committees?

If you are not the only IT location, what impact does management at those other locations have on your ability to pursue your project?

Is IT a part of the business objectives or merely a support service (billing or custodial services, for example)?

Is the purchase of IT services or products even up for discussion? Several years ago, the state of Kansas adopted a preferred-vendor program. Annual bids for services and products were obtained, and one vendor in each area was given the contract. Everything from training to IT services and products was accounted for. No other vendor could be used for products or services without demonstrating how this would save the state money. Most departments just went with the preferred vendor. Decision making, in this respect, was not an option.

The decision to move forward on a project (the design of a security infrastructure, for example) is usually arrived at with management review. Assume, for example, that you may have been given the go ahead to create a security infrastructure's preliminary design. How can you ensure its completion?

When beginning such a project, there may be no real firm understanding of the final cost. The decision to do a design may be based on a rough estimate. By the time you have finished a preliminary design, you will have probably developed enough detail to estimate a final cost for the project. At this point, most organizations perform management review. Your project will be examined in light of its costs. Of almost equal importance, however, is whether the project meets the business needs of the organization. If the revised cost estimate is perceived as too high, the project may be delayed, reduced, or never implemented.

Keep this in mind as you gather data. Have a plan B! It is better to implement a less-than-ideal solution than no solution at all. Furthermore, if you can pin your security strategy to business objectives, you will stand a far better chance of a positive decision.

Change Management Process

Change means stress. Change means upgrading systems and replacing components. Change means getting systems and people to do things in unfamiliar ways. Your understanding of how change is managed in your organization, as well as how it can best be managed, can mean the difference between a successful project and employment at a fast-food establishment.

◆ Are new systems implemented without advanced warning to every possible user of the system? Are customers who access data systems considered in the process?

◆ Is training on new systems provided in a logical, just-in-time manner?

◆ Are upgrades and migrations done in a logical manner to minimize system downtime and user confusion?

People in general do not like change. We are all more comfortable with sitting in the same chair at the same desk, taking the same route to work, working with the same set of tools. Do you doubt this is the same for IT professionals? Don't we embrace change? Isn't technology changing at the speed of light?

Consider, for example, the high degree of sensitivity regarding operating systems. It has become an almost religious issue. NT administrators belittle Linux. UNIX operators disparage "big iron." Macintosh users can't imagine why anyone would use anything else. And everyone likes to complain about Microsoft. The operating system a person has "grown up" with definitely influences this sensitivity. Information professionals form their views about how an operating system should act based on the one they have spent the most time with. They can't imagine that any other OS could come even close.

Fortunately, more IT professionals are beginning to understand that large internetworked organizations (and that is all of us if we use the Internet) require the possibilities that a variety of operating systems and network hardware offers. We just don't want it crammed down our throats.

Your organization's employees feel the same way. They fear and distrust change, so your project must be implemented with grace and acuity.

NOTE

Change Management? Not This past spring, I could not receive email from my long-term MSN account. After several attempts failed, I tried to find out why. Checking local account settings proved all was okay. I could receive email from other accounts, so hardware and software on my end was in working order.

I visited the MSN Web site and entered the Customer Service area. Although there was not a phone number immediately in sight, there was a comforting Contact Us button. Unfortunately, when I sent them an email (through another account), the Web site response was that they would be contacting me via email, but at my MSN account! Of course, I would never get it. An hour later, I still could not locate a customer service phone number on the Web site. Finally, I found one on my credit card bill from the preceding month.

When I called, I found out that a new law required MSN to have current credit card expiration dates on file. Because my account was opened years before, the expiration date on file was not up to date and MSN had to deactivate my account.

"Couldn't you have sent me notice? Couldn't you have requested a new expiration date?" I asked. "We did," they said, "via email."

Unfortunately, the email had not been sent until after my account was deactivated.

MSN could have managed change a little better.

Your organization's existing infrastructure must also be considered. You must plan. Change management should also be a part of your design.

PHYSICAL AND INFORMATION SECURITY MODELS

Analyze the current physical model and information security model.

Before you get specific about your infrastructure and security requirements, before you detail your current technical environment, take a minute to consider the overall picture. You can model IT physical structure and security in several ways.

Physical Model

Physical models include the following:

- ◆ Mainframe/terminal
- ◆ Client/server
- ◆ Thin client
- ◆ LAN
- ◆ WAN
- ◆ Intranet/Internet/extranet

Years ago, the only IT physical model was a mainframe, upon which all applications and data rested. Amen. Users accessed the mainframe through "dumb" terminals. The terminals had no processing power. Keystrokes traveled to the mainframe and screens returned.

The PC revolution enabled users to lay claim to the ownership of data and how to processes it; midrange systems allowed the development of client/server-styled operation. In the client/server model, data is stored on the server or in special storage systems. Processing is shared between the client (desktop machine) and the server (back-end processor). In a multitiered client/server system, the server processes (business rules) may be separated from the data, as well as the client. Data, and data management systems, may reside on multiple systems in multiple locations. When Bill Gates talks about digital network architecture, he is talking about a multitiered client/server system.

As PC based networks spread, network and systems administrators became increasingly concerned with their lack of control over how the end user stored and used data and software. Multiple management problems, including the spread of virus programs and the use of PCs for nonbusiness purposes (game playing, personal email, and other projects), and the high cost of service and training brought a desire for tighter control. Short-lived diskless workstations proliferated for a while in the mid-1990s.

Soon after Windows NT penetrated corporate IT, Citrix negotiated with Microsoft to provide a multiuser version of Windows NT. In this model, software can be loaded to the Citrix server and independent sessions for multiple users are provided. User data can reside wherever it is dictated. Only keystrokes, mouse clicks, and screens pass across the network. Unlike the terminal/mainframe model, Citrix and, later, Microsoft's Terminal Server version of Windows NT enable users to utilize multiple Windows client operating systems (Windows 3.x., Windows 9x, Windows CE, and Windows NT.). Citrix and Terminal Server, as well as Citrix Metrafame, also support UNIX and Macintosh clients. This is similar to the touted "thin-client" solution. In a thin-client solution, clients need minimal hardware and software because all processing is done on the server. In the Citrix and Microsoft Terminal Services modified thin-client solution, the client systems can operate on their own as well (see Figure 2.2). It is possible to run a Terminal Server session while at the same time running a local software package. Data can be shared from client to server through the Windows Clipboard. Terminal Services is an optional Windows 2000 Server and Advanced Server component.

The LAN, WAN, and internetwork models look at IT physical structure from a network standpoint. Both the LAN and WAN, although covering different physical spaces, can be simple networks that are still under the same administrative control and can be operating with the same underlying transmission method. Therefore, combining corporate locations by building an X.25 network might still be considered a network, even though it uses a public network

NOTE

Control Versus Productivity I once taught a class in C programming to engineers at a factory in New York. Most PCs in the company, including those in the training room and on the factory floor, were diskless workstations. To run the class, the C compiler had to be loaded and run from the network (including separate data files for each student as well).

Twice during the class the network went down for many hours and students were unable to work on exercises. We finally moved the class to the students' respective offices, where each engineer had a hard drive and could load the software and complete exercises. I spent lab times roaming from one office to another. This was when I learned that the disruption was complete. When the network went down, we suffered an inconvenience. When it stayed down, the factory could not run either! Thousands of dollars in productivity was lost because of a desire to control end users.

FIGURE 2.2
Modified thin-client model.

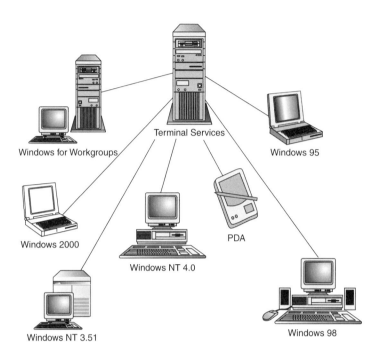

to connect many locations. The internetwork, however, no matter what geographical spaces it covers, combines multiple networks, some of them quite possibly under separate administrative control and using multiple different transmission technologies. Internetwork is media independent—that is, no one medium is everywhere. Technical obsolescence is less of a risk. Automated recovery is possible because multiple, alternative systems can exist. Let's face it, it is also a way of patching together the various networks that life has presented.

The Internet model can be thought of as just an extension of the client/server model, or as an extension to the corporate internetwork model. Users use a browser to access data and applications. It is also unique, because it allows data access to be through a familiar interface. Users can find data through easy links. File access over legacy networks is complicated by the need to know where data is located. A user has to know the name of the computer and the share name. In the Internet model, links can be listings on a page or buttons, and multiple search engines exist. Microsoft's Index server has been available since Windows NT 4.0 Service Pack 3. You can use the Index server to set up document searching on IIS-based machines.

Information Security Model

Security models are not as easily identified, but they do exist. The models are often classified by the type of security product used or the type of network that must be protected. Certain government standards, when applied, also become models. The following are some security models:

◆ Internet

◆ Public key infrastructure

◆ Local area network

◆ Remote access

◆ Road Warrior

◆ Single server

◆ Government standards

Internet

The Internet model provides protection for users accessing the Internet and also specifies how the Web site should be protected (see Figure 2.3).

Internet access protection includes the following:

◆ Proxy servers, which obtain Internet requests for the user and therefore protect internal addresses and assets

◆ Network address translation (NAT) services, which translate each internal address into a registered Internet address

◆ Configurable firewalls, which block access to ports and systems and from external systems by address

◆ Intrusion detection systems, which seek to alert network engineers to attacks

Web site protection includes the following:

◆ Firewalls

◆ Server authentication and other key technologies (secure sockets layer, public key infrastructure)

FIGURE 2.3
The Internet model.

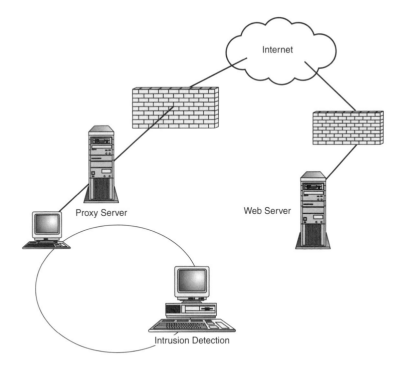

◆ Removal of unessential services

◆ Isolation from the rest of the internal network

Centralizing: Kerberos and Public Key Infrastructure

The single most identifiable security technique is to control access through point of entry by requiring a user identification and password. Two important, recognized algorithms for such protection are Kerberos and PKI. Older authentication protocols are NT LAN Manager (used in Windows NT) and LAN Manager (used in Windows 95). Kerberos uses single-key cryptography and a series of checks and balances to ensure the identity of a user and the resources he accesses. Chapter 10, "Designing an Authentication Strategy," discusses Kerberos in more detail.

A PKI describes a system that maintains two cryptographic keys, one public and the other private. These keys can be used for authentication, to obtain session encryption keys, and to produce digital signatures. For more information, see Chapter 11, "Designing a Public Key Infrastructure."

Local Area Network

Because local area networks are small in scope and usually have less diversity in hardware and software, a model for securing this network follows a similar pattern. The model should include specification for server and client security, physical access, and disaster recovery.

Single Server/Single Machine

It is often easiest to define a security model that hardens an operating system on one machine. Access external to the server is considered, but only as to authentication and authorization. This simple model fits the small and home office (SOHO) network model. Similar requirements are often appropriate for the home computer.

Road Warrior

Computers that travel with users require special treatment. They are vulnerable not just to attack, but also to theft. This model includes the provision for antitheft devices, data file encryption, personal firewalls, as well as antivirus and intrusion-detection products (see Chapter 14, "Designing Security for Access Between Networks").

Remote Access

Access from outside the corporate network (and therefore outside its control) is particularly troubling. This model includes the use of remote access servers, RADIUS servers for authentication, and virtual private network architectures (see Chapter 14).

Government Standards

One such government standards model is the Trusted Computer System Evaluation Criteria (TCSEC) developed by the National

Computer Security Center (NCSC), which is an arm of the U.S. government's National Security Agency (NSA). NCSC sponsors a security evaluation process Trusted Products Evaluation Process (TPEP), for operating systems. Vendors can submit their operating systems for evaluation and receive a rating. Third parties perform the tests.

The C2 level is defined as follows:

◆ **Mandatory identification and authentication of all users on the system.** The system can recognize authorized users and only allows them access.

◆ **Discretionary access control.** Users can protect data as they want to.

◆ **Accountability and auditing.** The system can audit user and system actions.

◆ **Object reuse.** The system can prevent users from obtaining information from resources that were used by others (released memory and deleted files, for example).

Another model, the U.K. government's ITSEC evaluation system, has similar requirements at the E3/F-C2 level.

Other levels in both systems specify different levels of security evaluation.

SECURITY RISKS

Analyze internal and external security risks.

Before you can determine the extent of your security design, you must ponder what you are protecting your systems against. Risk management is the determination and handling of corporate security measures. It is the how, when, where, and how much of security. The first step is to determine what risks exist. Risk assessment identifies critical assets, places a value on them, and determines whether they are likely to be attacked.

Risk assessment must be done for each organization. No list of valid risks exists that fits all.

To assess risk, follow these steps:

1. Determine network assets (hardware, software, data, people, and documentation).

2. Place a value on each asset. (What would be the replacement cost? What would be the result to the corporation if the asset were destroyed, stolen, damaged?)

3. Determine potential security threats.

4. Determine probability of risk occurring.

Threats are persons, objects, and events that can potentially damage any part of your information system. They can be accidental (file deletion) or malicious (the Melissa virus).

Vulnerabilities are weaknesses, such as weak passwords, or operating system holes that threats can exploit. Table 2.1 lists types of attacks that can occur.

TABLE 2.1

TYPES OF ATTACK

Type of Attack	How It Might Occur	Result
Data theft	Theft of backup tapes, unauthorized access, theft of physical machine	Loss of revenue, loss of information
Damaged integrity	Crashing a server that has inadequate backup, unauthorized access	Loss of revenue, out of business
Denial of service (DoS)	TCP/IP exploits across the internal network or from the external network, bad code, network failure	Loss of revenue, loss of information, loss of productivity, loss of visibility

continues

TABLE 2.1	*continued*

TYPES OF ATTACK

Type of Attack	*How It Might Occur*	*Result*
Annoyances	Unauthorized remote control, which merely shows off to resident user	Loss of productivity
Unauthorized access	Weak password, password written on notes near desk, leaving system logged on	Data theft, damage to data integrity

In all cases, one of the results of a successful attack may be loss of employee or customer confidence. After all, would you make an effort to shop online after finding that a hacker was just arrested and had thousands of stolen credit card numbers on his computer?

In Chapter 1, you learned that

Risk = Threat × Vulnerability / Countermeasures × Value

How can this be used to determine where to concentrate security efforts? Use Table 2.2 and the following instructions to assist you in estimating risk. For each range, the higher the number, the greater the value—that is, the bigger risk has a larger number.

STEP BY STEP

2.1 Calculating Risk

1. Fill in the Asset column.

2. Assign a number from 1 to 10 for each threat. Greater threats should have larger numbers. For example, a natural disaster, such as a tornado touching down on your data center, would be a 10.

3. Assign a number from 1 to 10 for each vulnerability. The less possibility something has of happening, the lower number it should have. So, for the tornado scenario? A 1, unless of course you are located in the infamous tornado alley, a region of the lower Midwest where multiple tornadoes touch down every year. Then the vulnerability level might be a little higher.

4. Assume no countermeasures in place.

5. Assign a value for the loss of each asset. The value may be in dollars, or some relative number. Just remember to be consistent and, of course, give larger numbers to the greater values. Dollars make impressive charts and graphs; just make sure your numbers are absolutely correct. Any presentation to management can lose its value if your dollar values are wrong.

6. Multiply threat × vulnerability × value.

TABLE 2.2

RISK CALCULATION

Asset	Risk =	Threat	Vulnerability	Value

This formula gives you a comparative risk value for each asset. You can use the values to determine where to first assign security measures.

CASE STUDY: NEXT CENTURY INDEPENDENT INSURANCE

END USERS

End users consist of three groups:

- Agents, who use Windows 2000 Professional laptops and have dial-up access to company databases

- Internal staff, who have a combination of Windows 2000 Professional, Windows 98, and Windows NT 4.0 Workstation

- Clients, who use their business and home computers to access information about their policies and claims via the Internet

BACKGROUND

Next Century Independent Insurance is an insurance co-op that provides services for independent agents. It primarily services the health care insurance field. Agent clients are considered members of the insurance co-op. There are now more than 8 million members. Last year, 13.4 million claims were filed. Next Century works with more than 25,000 employer groups and manages more than 750 unique benefit packages. Overall it has more than 1,000 unique contracts. It manages claims with more than 53,000 providers.

ADMINISTRATION

Each data center has its own IT staff. Corporate headquarters maintains a "technical help desk" responsible for assisting data-center technical staff with problem resolution.

Equipment Purchases

To maintain consistency, decisions on equipment purchase are managed by a corporate headquarters.

Training

When new equipment or processes are introduced, IT staff from each data center are brought together for training. Human Resources is in charge of providing nontechnical training for affected staff.

Policy

Policies and procedures are determined at corporate headquarters. All decisions are made here, the seat of legal and fiduciary responsibility.

CASE STUDY: NEXT CENTURY INDEPENDENT INSURANCE

DATA-CENTER PLANT

Around the country, 4,390 servers are located in 120 different data centers. Of these, 2,000 are Windows 2000 Servers; another 2,000 are Windows NT 4.0 Servers. The rest are a combination of UNIX, NetWare, and IBM AS400 (although only 2 of these). Within the year, 40% of all servers will be Windows 2000 Data Center Servers. The AS400 will be retired along with some of the Windows NT and NetWare servers.

SECURITY

Access to data centers is restricted to IT staff and screened service technicians. Wherever possible, equipment is moved to auxiliary rooms for servicing if it must be done by nonemployees.

A strict password policy is maintained. Complex passwords are required and changed every 45 days. Other strict guidelines for account policy are followed.

Backup tapes are protected by locked vaults (onsite and offsite storage).

OUTSOURCING

Remote access is outsourced. Agents can dial in from almost anywhere—even client homes—and access status of claims, update policy information, and so on.

PROBLEM STATEMENT

New laws and an increased awareness of privacy issues are changing the way all health insurers are required to do business.

Information Security Auditor

Laws are changing and there is a huge concern about the confidentiality of patient information. Every healthcare organization should be able to document how that information is protected. We have a huge investment in labor and equipment to make sure that data is secure in our data centers. However, we then have independent agents who can dial-up from anywhere in the country and access that same data.

We need a way to account for that access.

Vice President of Agent Relations

Our agents have been handling confidential data for years. They're not suddenly going to change that and make it available to anyone.

PROPOSED SOLUTION

Certificate Services will be deployed and agents will be required to use smart cards to obtain access.

Chapter Summary

IT management plays an important role in security design. Just as you must determine the physical model of IT and document security systems currently in place, you must also be aware of how it is managed. An IT department with a rigid, conservative modus operandi will be difficult to move to new technologies. One that likes to operate on the bleeding-edge of technology may require special handling to ensure security is given a nod, or may go overboard and adopt security structures that limit productivity. This chapter has introduced these issues and has provided direction on how to examine these areas.

APPLY YOUR KNOWLEDGE

Exercises

2.1   TSCED and ITSEC Evaluation Processes

Use your browser to access the U.S. or U.K. government site (www.radium.ncsc.mil/tpep, www.itsec.gov.uk) and read about the TSCED and ITSEC evaluation process. What other levels of evaluation are there?

Estimated Time: 20 minutes

1. Enter the URL in your browser.

2. Search the NCSC site for C2.

    or

3. Search the ITSEC site for E3.

4. Compare your understanding of the Windows NT evaluation to the one published by Microsoft at www.microsoft.com/security.

2.2   Calculating Internet Risks

Next Century Insurance stated a security concern regarding agents accessing confidential patient data via dial-up. What about clients accessing data over the Internet? Use Table 2.3 to calculate possible risks involved in providing client information in this way.

Estimated Time: 30 minutes

1. Enter the nature of the threat in the Threat Description column.

2. List assets in the first column.

3. Assign a relative value (1 to 10) to each asset. Place it in the value column. Higher numbers mean a more valuable asset.

4. Assign a value from 1 to 10 for vulnerability. How likely is this to occur? Lower values mean less possibility.

5. Apply the formula risk = value × vulnerability × threat.

6. Which asset should receive the most consideration?

TABLE 2.3

RISK CALCULATION

Asset	Threat Description		Risk =	Value	Vulnerability	Threat

APPLY YOUR KNOWLEDGE

Review Questions

1. Next Century was concerned about agents accessing patient data and are thinking of having agents use smart cards for _____ (*fill in the blank*). They also need to do something else to make sure the data is protected. They need to make sure the agent is _____ (*fill in the blank*).

2. Mark has health insurance with Next Century. On Tuesday he looks up a claim over the Internet and finds that it has not been evaluated yet. Claims are normally marked Not Evaluated, Rejected, or Paid. Claim information is available for 30 days. On Friday Mark looks again and the claim is gone. Moreover, in his profile his address has changed. (He hasn't moved.) What has happened?

3. Does Next Century have a centralized or decentralized IT administrative structure?

4. What is the difference between the mainframe/terminal IT model and the Terminal Server model?

5. What are three examples of threats to IT assets?

6. How are end-user security needs at Next Century being met?

7. What might be two reasons for IT staff being brought back to headquarters for training on new technologies?

8. How is change management handled at Next Century?

9. Johnson Consulting is a small consulting firm with 35 consultants who work at customer locations. Every night they use client software to dial in to a company-owned Windows 2000 Server and access a timesheet application. Multiple agents can connect simultaneously. John uses his Windows 98 system. Peter uses Windows NT 4.0, and Mary uses Windows 2000 Professional. No part of the application runs on their machines. This is an example of which kind of physical model? How do you know?

10. PepCap Industries just moved its main sales and customer information database from its mainframe to Microsoft Windows 2000 and Microsoft SQL Server 7.0 running on Compaq's eight-way Proliant Servers. Client software runs on Windows 2000 Professional. A separate Business Rules database, which runs on intermediary machines, filters all requests for data and activity. The requests then can go to the appropriate back-end database server and/or be fulfilled by multiple servers. Describe the physical model that this matches and relate the architecture of that model to the process just described.

Exam Questions

1. The following threats and vulnerabilities directly interfere with internal end-user business needs at Next Century Insurance:

    Check all that apply:

    A. Denial of service (DoS)

    B. Weak passwords

    C. Unauthorized access

    D. Lack of data backup

    E. House burglary

    F. Convenience store robbery

    G. Corrupt politicians

APPLY YOUR KNOWLEDGE

2. John receives an email with attachments. The attachments are a Word document that consists of some funny jokes, and a little game. He emails this to 10 other coworkers. The company has only 20 employees. What security issue does this present for his company?

   A. The attachment may contain a virus.

   B. His fellow workers won't get any work done today as they read the jokes and play the game.

   C. When users launch the game, they may unknowingly launch a program that gives remote control of their machine to another person.

   D. Some of his friends mail the attachments to their friends at other companies.

Use the following information to answer the next two questions.

The New Orleans Insurance Company has 4,000 insurance field agents. Each agent is provided with a company laptop, modem, and software. Agents can issue quotes and proposals to their clients and prospects. A browser connection is made to run specialized software at headquarters. Headquarters maintains a Terminal Server farm (a collection of Microsoft Terminal Servers). Processing occurs on the headquarters machines. Agents can download information about their clients, check commission calculations, and receive money and quarterly reports on their sales. They also use their computers for other parts of their job such as writing letters, accessing information on the Internet, and keeping their own prospect lists.

3. What is the physical model here?

   A. Mainframe/terminal

   B. Terminal Server/client

   C. LAN

   D. WAN

   E. Terminal Server/client/road warrior

4. What assets in this model need protection?

   A. Laptop, software

   B. Software, data on laptop, laptop

   C. Laptop, software, data on laptop, any peripheral equipment, communications between agent and headquarters

   D. Data, software, laptop and peripherals, communications between agent and headquarters, Terminal Server farm

5. Prior to the implementation of the previously mentioned model, New Orleans Insurance agents primarily used preprinted forms, calculators, and company reports to perform the same functions. Only a few agents had computers and used them in their business. Federal laws, a need to compete, and a way to more efficiently manage information prompted the redesign of this model.

Required Result:

The new system must meet all Federal stipulations for data presentation and collection.

Optional Desired Results:

Agents must perceive the change as a good thing. This should not be a disruption for them, but a way to ease their paperwork burden.

APPLY YOUR KNOWLEDGE

The system should efficiently and correctly handle all data.

Proposed Solution:

The system is provided as outlined in the previous notes. Laptops are issued and a server farm is established. The system is easy to use. The system was submitted for approval (as required) to the government and passed all tests for compliance to the new laws.

Evaluation of Proposed Solution:

Which result does the proposed solution produce?

A. The proposed solution produces the required results and both of the optional results.

B. The proposed solution produces the required results and one of the optional results.

C. The proposed solution produces the required result but neither of the optional results.

D. The proposed solution does not produce the required result.

6. The following reasons might cause a company to decentralize its IT operations and administration.

Choose all that apply:

A. The company wants to reduce expenditures.

B. The company wants to expand.

C. The company wants to more clearly align IT with business units.

D. The company wants to reduce administrative overhead.

7. Migration to Windows 2000 may mean a considerable expenditure as hardware and software is upgraded. There will also be other expenses related to training, implementation, and troubleshooting. TCO may be reduced, but the effect may not be seen immediately. What ways can IT mitigate its costs?

A. Charging back departments, no company sponsored training, setting up Terminal Services

B. Setting up Terminal Services, training key technical personnel, planning

C. Charging back departments, training key personnel, planning, setting up Terminal Services

D. Outsourcing parts of the migration effort, charging back departments, training key personnel, planning, setting up Terminal Services

8. Peter Pumpkin is the CIO for Midwest Manufacturing. Midwest Manufacturing has 10 locations. Of these locations, 7 are in the United States; the 3 others are in South America. Peter wants to provide each location with information systems and access to corporate headquarters. He wants real-time information from each location and expects to keep them updated with centralized inventory information. He has been talking with Johnson Consulting about designing and implementing his WAN, and the quotes have come back very high. Johnson Consulting also advises him that they will not be able to implement their solution for six months to a year. Peter has begun to consider alternatives. Of the following proposals, which is the best one for Midwest Manufacturing?

A. Go with Johnson Consulting.

B. Find a firm whose international locations align with his own.

C. Bring the development in-house.

D. Find a firm whose international locations align with his own and who also can manage any locations after implementation.

9. Mary has spent months designing a security solution that will protect patient data accessed over the Internet by New Century Insurance clients. Mary knows more about her company's IT structure, equipment, and locations than anyone else does. She also is a security expert. She is up on the most recent technologies and applications in her field. Mary's proposal includes charts and graphs that clearly explain all of this and the threats and vulnerabilities to the assets of the company are exposed. Mary is shocked to find out that her proposal is turned down because it is too costly. What did Mary forget about? What else should she have done?

A. Mary forgot about office politics.

B. Mary did not research the decision-making process in her company. Understanding here would have made the difference.

C. Mary was too technical in her design report. She should have dumbed it down.

D. Mary ignored or forgot about the decision-making process. She could have spent time determining what was important to her company and the financial climate and security-awareness level of the company executives.

10. Businesses are increasingly using the Internet to conduct business. When they do so, they are exposing their business to a completely new plethora of attacks. What are some of these threats?

A. Wire-born viruses

B. Trojan horses

C. Credit card fraud

D. Password cracking

E. Pornography

F. Data theft

G. Loss of data integrity

H. Misuse of company time

11. Windows NT 4.0 met the requirements for C2 evaluation. It will be some time before we know official results for Windows 2000. Which of the following features of Windows 2000 appear to support C2 requirements?

A. File ACLs for discretionary access control, Security Event log for accounting and audit ability, NTLM for mandatory identification, and kernel design for object reuse.

B. File DMZ for discretionary access control, Audit Event log for accounting and audit ability, NTLM for mandatory identification, and kernel design for object reuse.

C. File ACLs for discretionary access control, Security Event log for accounting and audit ability, LM for mandatory identification, and kernel design for object reuse.

D. File ACLs for discretionary access control, Security Event log for accounting and audit ability, Kerberos for mandatory identification, and kernel design for object reuse.

APPLY YOUR KNOWLEDGE

Answers to Exercises

The solution to the Exercise 2.2 is presented in Table 2.4.

Your answers may vary, be more extensive, or have different listings and values for each category.

Answers to Review Questions

1. Authentication is the proof that you are who you say you are. Authorization allows you access to data or the right to perform a function. Smart cards are used to authenticate the agents. New Century will have to make sure they are then authorized to access the appropriate files.

TABLE 2.4: SOLUTION TO EXERCISE 2.2

RISK CALCULATION

Asset	Threat Description	Risk =	Value	Vulnerability	Threat
Client data	Accidentally deleted/destroyed.	70	10	1	7
	Someone other than patient sees the data.	240	10	8	3
Goodwill, confidence in company	Data is captured and provided to client employer; client loses job, other financial harm.	172	9	2	9
	Web site defaced.	192	8	8	3
Company hardware and software	Damage to hardware/software as a result of attack on the system.	144	9	2	8
	Web site is defaced (damage to software).	72	3	8	3
	Web site defaced, loss of new business.	147	6	8	3

APPLY YOUR KNOWLEDGE

2. Somewhere there is a problem with data integrity. Data integrity can be destroyed by hard disk crashes, unauthorized access, and accidental deletion.

3. Next Century has centralized administration. Although their staff is distributed to data centers, decisions are made at corporate headquarters.

4. In the mainframe model, the terminals were just that, dumb machines that could never do anything on their own. All data processing, data storage, everything was kept on the mainframe. The Terminal Server model uses a client system. The system can process and store data. Moreover, by loading the client software and using the services of the Terminal Server, they receive the rich GUI environment of the host.

5. Threats to assets include weak passwords, physically unsecured servers, hostile workers, and former employees.

6. End-user security needs are met by a requirement for strong passwords and account policy and the proposed introduction of smart cards. Training on new systems helps to ensure correct practices are followed.

7. Bring IT staff back to headquarters for training on new technologies. This helps to ensure staff understanding of how the new technologies work, and allows the presentation of standards and enforcement of central control over implementation and practice.

8. Change management is handled by formal training of technical staff and others.

9. This is an example of a Terminal Server model. The giveaway here is the simultaneous use of a server-side application, which records different data from its clients, and the use of different clients.

10. The physical model used here is an n-tier model. The Windows 2000 Professional systems operate as the clients and the SQL servers as the back-end database. The Business Rules database runs in the middle on SQL server. The services provided by the Windows 2000 operating system family form the underlying system services component.

Answers to Exam Questions

1. **A, B, C, D, E, F, G.** Although the policies of Next Century seem to be strong, nevertheless it is still possible that some users might write down passwords or create passwords that are easier to crack. This is also true of backup. Every data center worth its salt has a backup plan, but something can always go wrong. DoS attacks are a threat to every system, as is unauthorized access. Fortunately, the internal users are working in a secured building, not at home or on laptops as they pick up milk at the convenience store. Conceivably these could be risks, if someone took his work home with him. A corrupt city building inspector might look the other way, overlooking a safety violation. Later when the ceiling collapses and water pores into the data center, damage is done to the data. Some of these threats are not likely to become reality—nevertheless, they do exist. (See the section "Security Risks.")

APPLY YOUR KNOWLEDGE

2. **A, B, C, D.** Every attachment could possibly contain a virus or Trojan horse program. (The unsuspecting user launches a game, unbeknownst to him, the game program launches a program which does some damage.) Although it's doubtful that all workers will not get any work done, there is a definite possibility of loss of productivity (depending on how funny the jokes are and how good the game is). The real problem here is that they will send it on and others will send them more, until it is possible to collapse a system with this overload of "harmless" jokes. (See the section "End-User Requirements.")

3. **B.** The agents obtain information from an application managed at headquarters, but they can also use their systems to do other things. (See the section "Physical and Information Security Models.")

4. **D.** Every part of the system must be protected from the agent's equipment and data, to the company systems and the communications between the two systems. (See the section "Physical and Information Security Models.")

5. **C.** It indicates that the system passed the federal law requirements. Although it does note that the system is easy to use, it doesn't indicate what, if any, steps were taken to address change management with the agents. What is their opinion of the system? Likewise, there is no information given that would enable you to judge how "efficiently" or "correctly" the system works. (See the section "Physical and Information Security Models.")

6. **B, C.** Because decentralization usually costs more, choice A is wrong. Likewise, more administrators at far-flung locations may increase administrative overhead. It will be easier for local administrators to understand and apply the needs of the business unit at which they are working, however, and the company can more easily

expand and support its data-processing needs if it doesn't have to locate all resources in a central place. (See the section "Type of Administration—Centralized or Decentralized.")

7. **D.** All the suggestions can work to reduce the cost of migration, but choice D is the most complete. (See the section "Change Management Process.")

8. **D.** Working with different international locations can be quite expensive and difficult. There are language and cultural difference as well as distances to be worked with and understood. New systems should not be delayed for several months unless all other alternatives are researched. Instead, other consulting firms should be inspected. An international consulting firm with offices in the countries that Midwest is also working in is a viable alternative. If this firm can also give service after the job is done, all the better. Remember that Johnson consulting is a small, Midwestern consulting firm. (See the section "IT Management.")

9. **D.** Office politics are important factors to consider; however, choice D covers that possibility. Likewise, the technical level of her presentation may have not been at the right level for her audience; but choice D considers that as well. (See the section "Decsion-Making Process.")

10. **A, B, C, D, F, G.** New types of attacks are occurring every day. All the mentioned attacks might threaten every business. Although pornography is present on the Internet, it is not an attack. (See the section "Security Risks.")

11. **D.** Kerberos is the new network authentication standard for Windows 2000. Although it could be argued that NTLM met the requirements for Windows NT 4.0, we are more aware of the vulnerabilities of this protocol now. (See the section "Government Standards.")

Suggested Readings and Resources

Web Sites:

- www.Outsourcing-networks.com

- www.informationweek.com

- http://www.rms.net/rc_analysis_main.htm

ANALYZING TECHNICAL REQUIREMENTS

This chapter covers the following Microsoft-specified objectives for the "Analyzing Technical Requirements" section of the Designing Security for a Microsoft Windows 2000 Network exam:

Evaluate the company's existing and planned technical environment.

- Analyze company size and user and resource distribution.

- Assess the available connectivity between the geographic location of work sites and remote sites.

- Assess the net available bandwidth.

- Analyze performance requirements.

- Analyze the method of accessing data and systems.

- Analyze network roles and responsibilities. Roles include administrative, user, service, resource ownership, and application.

▶ Security exists to protect the network. The network exists to support the business. The business is composed of people and activities. Before you can devise a security strategy, you need to know the business needs of the company, its people, its processes and locations, and its current information system and infrastructure. This objective addresses specific technical areas of the infrastructure.

Analyze the impact of the security design on the existing and planned technical environment.

- Assess existing systems and applications.

- Identify existing and planned upgrades and rollouts.

- Analyze technical support structure.

- Analyze existing and planned network and systems management.

CHAPTER 3

Analyzing Technical Environments

▶ As you formulate your security design, you must consider the impact on the systems and applications in your environment. Security structures are often at exact odds with ease of use. After all, the securest system is one that is unplugged from the network and locked away where no one can get to it. Your ability to lock down your system will be greatly enhanced in Windows 2000. If correctly designed, much of the increased security can be transparent to the user. If the design effort ignores the usability quotient, the effect can be disastrous.

▶ You may have already witnessed this as you have dealt with applications that disregarded the security structure of the Windows NT registry. These applications insisted on writing to areas of the registry that should be protected from normal user access. Running these applications in your environment often was challenging because you had to determine exactly what access users needed and then either relax your security or give elevated privileges to users so that they could run the applications or quickly find alternative applications.

▶ Creating a security design may mean major changes to the operation of your systems and applications within it. Do not create your design in a vacuum.

STUDY STRATEGIES

▶ Complete your studies of the current and planned information systems with a comprehensive understanding of the scope of your business and its IT needs. It's not just a matter of knowing how many users there are and where they are located. It's not just listing the databases and hardware and transport systems that make up the infrastructure. It's also not just who needs access to what when. It *is* how this organism comes together to function as a coherent entity.

▶ Take time to learn that, because you are about to change it.

▶ Take time to develop a close understanding of the factors that you will need to know. Dissect case studies, examples, and references until you can flash a company description up on a screen and tick off in an organized fashion the information present and the questions you'd need to ask.

Introduction

Are you surprised that it's taking so long to get to a discussion of Windows 2000? The process of security design is not so different from building a house. If you spend time understanding the current living arrangements, it will help you in planning the new house and will save money and heartache later.

In the first section of this book, you learned how to analyze business and IT management. This chapter completes your preliminary studies with a study of the current IT technology so that you can do requirements planning in the next. Here you will study the information resources, as well as their users and the connectivity technologies that permit access and communication, whether user to resource, user to user, across the network, and across the world. You will finish your study of your current network by examining the factors that currently provide security for business information assets.

Analyze Company Size and User and Resource Distribution

Analyze company size and user and resource distribution.

Grab those maps you made in Chapter 1, "General Business Analysis"—you're about to put some useful information in them. (You can use tables to hold detail if you want.) First, label each location with the number of users. Next, place markers to indicate the locations of all resources. Resources include printers, file servers, mail servers, databases, and similar items. Finally, map groups of users to resources they must access (see Figure 3.1).

A good source of information is the resource owner. Production management, for example, will have data on where production information is generated, who needs the information, who works with it from where, and where the information resides. If you have maps or network diagrams to assist you in your work, so much the better. If you are part of a Windows 2000 deployment team, some of this work may already be done. However, check for accuracy. Are there users in locations who should have access but do not? Are there resources not on the charts? Departmental servers and Web

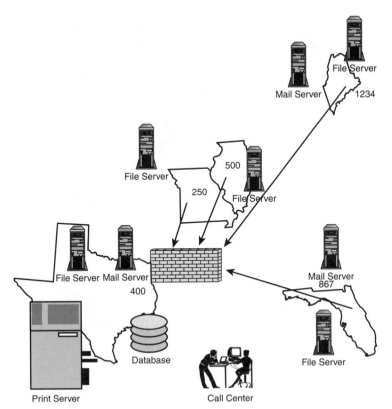

FIGURE 3.1
Mapping location resource data.

sites are resources that often are not included in IT charts and graphs. Don't be judgmental at this stage; your purpose is to sketch the current situation.

Collect or examine network design maps. You need a different kind of map here. A network design map should show all the details of hardware in your infrastructure, including each router, switch, server, and connection. Public networks can be identified by using a cloud configuration. Locate servers and IP addresses, and identify server role and domain membership. Indicate special server applications. Where is the location of the DHCP servers? DNS servers? WINS servers?

Create a physical network diagram (see Figure 3.2) and a logical network diagram (see Figure 3.3). Physical network diagrams include details of communication links; server name and special services; locations of printers hubs, switches, modems, routers, bridges, proxy servers, and communication links; and the available

FIGURE 3.2

Physical network diagram.

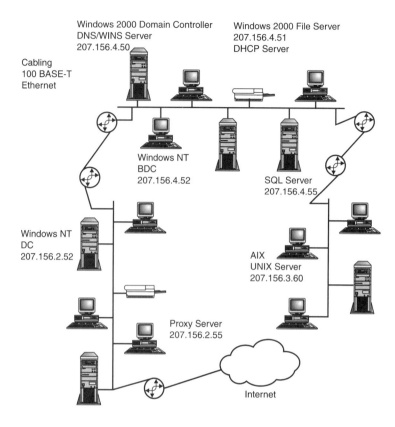

FIGURE 3.3

Logical network diagram.

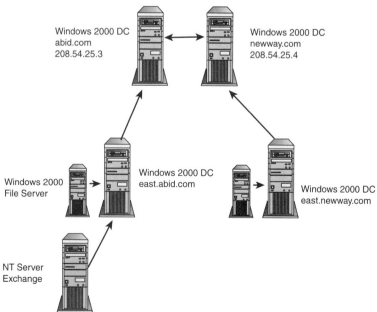

bandwidth between sites. A logical network diagram shows the domain architecture, including hierarchy, names and addressing scheme, server roles, and trust relationships.

If network diagrams are available, make sure that you understand them. Verify the existence of hardware. Make sure that the diagram is up to date.

If you need to develop your own diagram, you can follow these suggestions:

Determine the hierarchical structure of your network. Because routers work best if they have information only on immediate connections, and humans work best if they can break down information into small chunks, networks are usually designed in a hierarchical fashion. Layers beneath the backbone are often hidden, and you may find that existing diagrams lack the inner details. Or, you may need to create multiple diagrams to expose the architecture of your company's design.

Identify backbone locations. The backbone represents the shape of your network. Backbone locations often came about due to physical factors (room to house equipment, circuit mileage characteristics, and traffic patterns).

NOTE **Small Price/Easy Diagrams Title** If you do not have a diagramming tool you may be able to download a 30-day trial tool, Smart Draw, from `www.smartdraw.com`. This site has a library of more than 1,500 pictures of network hardware. Don't forget to purchase it if you feel that it will meet your needs. Pencil and paper are also adequate.

ASSESS AVAILABLE CONNECTIVITY

Assess the available connectivity between the geographic location of work sites and remote sites.

How is information getting from resources to users, and from server to server? While local users access LAN resources, users at other sites gain access across WAN connections. You should identify and record connectivity between sites. Add this information to your diagrams, and be sure to include the type of transmission technology. Transmission technologies include x.25, Frame Relay, ATM, and ISDN, among others. Table 3.1 lists common transmission technologies and their relative speed in kilobits per second (Kbps). Table 3.2 lists transmission technologies and the type used. You should identify speed wherever there may be confusion because many design decisions will depend on the transmission speed available between different locations.

TABLE 3.1

IDENTIFY MAJOR TRANSMISSION TECHNOLOGIES

Transmission Technology	Speed in Kbps	Notes
Copper leased lines	56–45,000	In the past, High Level Data Link Control (HDLC) was used to provide error detection; today, with more reliable circuits, Point-to-Point Protocol (PPP), which provides HDLC framing, is used.
SONET leased lines	51,000–2,488,000	Synchronous Optical Network.
		Synchronous transmission takes place over fiber optic cables. Transmission speed is reported in Optical Carrier (OC) rates from OC-1, at 51.85Mbps, up to OC 48, at 2.488Gbps.
		A similar international standard is Synchronous Digital Hierarchy (SDH).
Channelization	56–2,480,000	Aggregated circuits (combined or multiplexed circuits) are used.
Circuit switching	56–2,480,000	A circuit is routed through one location to reach another. Drop and insert, and/or add and drop multiplexes (ADMs)are used. Static assignments are made and changing is labor intensive.
Frame Relay	56–45,000	Virtual circuits are used. A logical path from one location in a network to another is made at the data link level of OSI. This option is best for multiple connections.
SMDS	56–155,000	A switched-multimegabit data service which involves high overhead, and is complex. Large frames are transmitted in ATM cells across the network. SMDS is connectionless.
ATM Asynchronous Transfer Mode	1,544 (T1) to 2,480,000 (fiber)	This option involves voice and video over a single network. Primarily is a WAN protocol that operates at the data link layer and operates at T3 or above. Transmission is by fixed-sized packets or cells instead of the larger, irregular packet size of other protocols. The fixed-sized cells allow transmission of voice as well as data over the same network and offers greater control of bandwidth.
POTS	56	Analog dial-up, dial-up terminal servers, and telephones are used.
ISDN BRI Basic Rate Interface	64–2* 64	Integrated Digital Services Network is used for transmission of voice, data, and video over standard telephone lines.
ISDN PRI Primary Rate Interface	64–23 * 64	This option provides digital access, transmitted on T1 lines.
Cable	128–10,000/home	Faster than POTS, this option offers stability and reliability. After this shared medium is up, it stays up.
ADSL	128–6,000	This asymmetric digital subscriber line was developed with interactive video services in mind; the higher speeds are reached during the downloading of data. Uploading is much slower.

Transmission Technology	Speed in Kbps	Notes
VDSL	20,000–155,000	A faster DSL, this option is a very high-speed digital subscriber line for voice, video, and high-definition TV.
IP tunneling	56–45,000	This operates over various networks, including the Internet and iVPN.
Wireless CDPD	19.2	This option uses normal analog cellular telephone channels and multiplexes them for greater bandwidth. CDPD is Cellular Digital Packet Data, which was developed for use on cellular phone frequencies. CDPD provides better error correction than regular analog lines. It uses unused cellular channels.
Public wireless		Public wireless uses normal cellular phones services.
T1	1,544,000	Dedicated 23 B channels are used for data, and 1 D channel is used for clocking, in addition to fractionalized T1 divides T! into separate. 64 Kbps segments.

TABLE 3.2

TRANSMISSION TECHNOLOGIES AND TYPE USED

Transmission Technology	Usage			
	Residential	Access Concentration	Backbone	Commercial
Copper leased lines		x	x	x
SONET leased lines		x	x	x
Channelization		x	x	x
Circuit Switching		x		
Frame Relay		x	x	x
SMDS		x		x
ATM		x	x	x
POTS	x			
ISDN BRI	x			x
ISDN PRI		x		
Cable	x			
ADSL	x			x
VDSL	x			x

continues

TABLE 3.2	*continued*		

TRANSMISSION TECHNOLOGIES AND TYPE USED

Transmission Technology	Usage			
	Residential	Access Concentration	Backbone	Commercial
IP tunneling	x	x	x	x
Wireless CDPD				x
Public wireless	x			x
T1				x

Note each transmission type used. Understanding something about each transmission type will enable you to consider the possible implications for your security design. You also will have a better chance to recognize the additional hardware that should be present. Knowing whether hardware should exist is useful in preventing rogue connections.

Implications for design include the following:

◆ Permanent virtual circuits (PVC), though created administratively, may remain active for years and may not be easy to move; switched virtual circuits (SVC) can be created dynamically when needed. Both SVC and PVC are possible with ATM and Frame Relay.

◆ The current implementation of L2TP is not capable of tunneling over ATM, Frame Relay, or X.25.

◆ Bandwidth will be affected by some security design decisions.

◆ Windows 2000 has limited support for ATM. There is an updated NDIS 5.0 miniport driver, limited support for the installation of ATM hardware adapters, and ARP/MARS service, which enables MS TCP/IP stack to resolve ATM addresses to hardware addresses. (The IP over ATM model meets RFC 2225, specifications for ARP over ATM.)

◆ ADSL is particularly suited for home and small business Internet access because it supports higher transmission speeds in one direction over the other, reducing crosstalk. It is possible to have 6Mbps downlink (outbound to the consumer from the ISP) and 600Kbps uplink (inbound), although carriers implement at lower speeds.

◆ Windows 2000 offers dial-up connection support for PPP over ATM, ATM over DSL, and ATM over cable modem.

Don't forget to locate any instances where the Internet is used as if it were a transmission medium. Here, I mean the creation of IP tunnels or virtual private networks (VPNs) (see Figure 3.4). Each IP tunnel can be though of as if was a Frame Relay or ATM PVC.

A VPN is a logically or virtually private internetwork that interconnects multiple locations that are under a common ownership or administration. Similar technology can be used in e-commerce (see Figure 3.5), but both points in a VPN are owned by the company; in e-commerce, the customer, whether commercial or consumer, owns half of the connection. A VPN creates multiple points of exposure for the network administrator or architect to secure.

What about the movement, transport or otherwise, of non-IP data? You should document this as well.

> **NOTE**
>
> **A B2B VPN** In Figure 3.5, The Tilapi Automotive company has a business-to-business (B2B) site set up for its parts suppliers to bid on orders and for plants to purchase parts at approved prices. A VPN provides security. In addition, dealerships can use the VPN to access inventory information, post their inventory, and learn about promotions. Customers and prospects can use the normal Internet channels to learn about the new car models, find a dealership, and contact a salesperson.

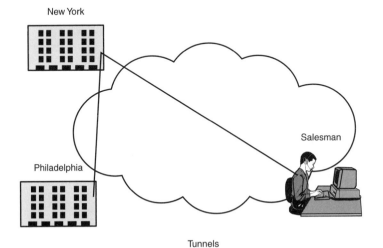

FIGURE 3.4
Virtual private network (VPN).

FIGURE 3.5
An e-commerce configuration.

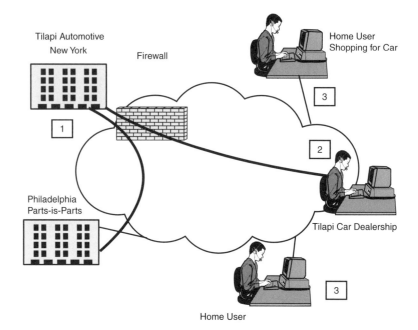

IDENTIFY NETWORK TOPOLOGY

Knowing network topology tells you about the connection points and the information flows. Knowing where information goes helps you to protect it. Knowing where the major connection points are enables you to look for security vulnerabilities.

A good example of examining information flow is the requirement of some sort of a gateway. For example, if the topology is a physical star and various mail servers are used, there must be a central gateway or mail hub; all mail travels to the center of the star and then back out again. Examine the Mid Ho Pharmaceuticals case study at the end of the chapter for an example of a mail hub/physical star topology. Connection points are points to check for security weaknesses.

FIGURE 3.6
Physical star.

Topology includes the following:

◆ **Physical star**—(See Figure 3.6.) This configuration may have resulted from the need for a hub at the greatest traffic intensity point. When leased lines were the only solution, the obvious choice was to end all lines at the center location. This was often the corporate headquarters. The center then can be accessed from any location in one hop, and any location is no more than two hops from any other.

◆ **Logical star**—(See Figure 3.7.) Leased lines create permanent circuits directly between company-owned points. Frame Relay, which creates virtual circuits between Telco-owned points, is better served by this architecture. There is no need to locate the hub at "the geographic center of gravity of network." Traffic concentration is important as distances becomes almost irrelevant. (Carrier service usually provides distance-insensitive tariffs.) Propagation delay, or the extra time it takes for data to travel longer distances, may be insignificant.

◆ **Full mesh**—(See Figure 3.8). Every location has direct connectivity to every other location. This is usually accomplished with leased lines. (This configuration is fairly rare because it is costly.)

FIGURE 3.7
Logical star.

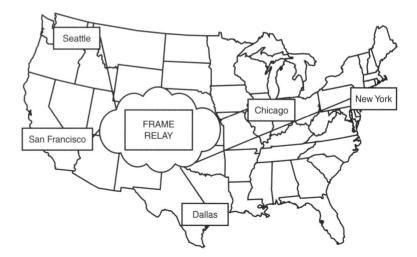

FIGURE 3.8
Full mesh.

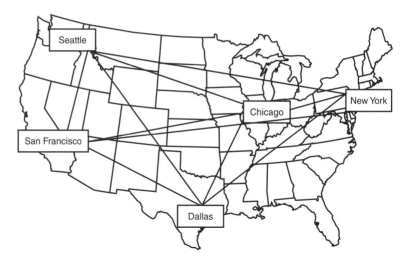

◆ **Partial mesh**—(See Figure 3.9.) This configuration provides good performance and vigorous recovery from failure at a more modest cost.

Continue to add detail to your network diagrams. Indicate the location of routers, especially Interior Gateway Protocol (IGPs within the organization) and Exterior Gateway Protocol routers that border your extremities and connect to the outside world.

Document security standards for routing configuration. Have default passwords been removed? Are routers remotely managed? Are routers used as packet filtering firewalls?

FIGURE 3.9
Partial mesh.

Document your addressing and naming standards. Is addressing assigned using DHCP? Are BOOTP-enabled routers used? What about DHCP relays? Do naming conventions follow DNS standards or NetBIOS standards? (The Internet standard character set for DNS host naming is defined in RFC 1123 and is composed of all uppercase and lowercase letters [A–Z and a–z], numbers [0–9], and the hyphen [–]). Microsoft DNS includes support for extended ASCII and Unicode characters, although this is useful only in pure Windows 2000 networks. Are your DNS servers Microsoft Windows 2000 DNS servers? Other DNS servers meet standards as well and may provide support for an extended character set. BIND 8.x (Berkell Internet Name Domain, a UNIX DNS server) supports an extended character set (" ") or underscore, but earlier versions may not.

If your naming standard does not meet the Internet standard, or if you use extended character sets that are not available elsewhere, you may find yourself battling connectivity issues.

ASSESS NET AVAILABLE BANDWIDTH

Assess the net available bandwidth.

Net available bandwidth is the bandwidth available after all current services and applications are accounted for. This seems logical, but how do we assess the bandwidth of the current services and applications, and why is this important to our security design?

Bandwidth, of course, is the number of bits that can be transmitted per second (the throughput) over a network medium. Many security features such as IPSec, encryption, and tunneling add demands to the network and can reduce throughput. It is important to develop a utilization baseline before implementing these new features. Knowing the raw capacity of communication resources on the LAN, between networks in your WAN, is not enough. You need to know how much of it is currently used. Before implementing new technologies, you need to determine if existing capacity will support, within performance requirements, the load that new features will demand.

You can use a number of Windows 2000 tools to obtain metrics for bytes and packets sent and received; transmit and received errors; and packets per second. Performance Monitor, Network Monitor, and the extended SMS Network Monitor have these capabilities. Network Monitor also reports the percentage of network utilization.

A number of existing third-party network and systems management tools also can be used in your network, for these purposes. More information can be found under the section "Analyze Existing and Planned Network and Systems Management," later in this chapter.

Document the existence location and administrative responsibility for these tools. Obtain current reports, and provide input to network engineers and deployment and planning teams on the additional requirements of security protocols and functions.

ANALYZE PERFORMANCE REQUIREMENTS

Analyze performance requirements.

What are the current performance requirements for your network? Performance requirements may be specified in response time and throughput, or the amount of data transferred per second or processed in a particular amount of time. Typical measurements are bandwidth, latency (wasted time and propagation delay), number of lost packets, and guarantee of connectivity. Database applications may be benchmarked at a number of transactions per second.

If you contract with an ISP for a VPN, or if you purchase line services directly from a Telco for Internet access, you may also have negotiated service agreements that specify the level of acceptable performance. These service level agreements (SLA) also specify your recourse if these are not met.

Record these SLAs. Although they reflect performance on transmission outside the scope of your organization, they do represent performance upon which your organization depends. As more organizations add increased demands on these external circuits, your need for SLA agreements will increase. Your benchmarks and performance requirements for communications between sites will be impacted by the delivery they offer.

It important to note that while pure movement of bits can be quantified, the actual level of performance required may vary depending on the application used. For example, VPN performance requirements may specify network backbone availability and server availability above throughput guarantees.

Conversely, major signs of network problems are these:

◆ **Peak utilization**—Greater than 70% on backbone circuits.

◆ **Frame or cell loss**—Greater than 2–3%.

◆ **Network latency**—Increase by more than 10%.

Additional signs of trouble are these:

◆ **Permanent virtual circuit flapping**—Routes between two nodes alternate rapidly between two paths because of intermittent failures.

◆ **Cyclic redundancy check**—Errors increase.

◆ **Data loss during peak periods**—The committed information rate (CRI) is substantially oversubscribed.

◆ **Applications**—Periodic timeouts occur.

◆ **Help desk**—A rapid increase in help desk calls occurs, or a gradual increase in related help desk calls is noticed over time, with no new upgrades or rollouts in process.

NOTE

The Ivory Soap Statistic Years ago, Ivory soap advertised that it was 99.99% pure, and this became a standard for all things—only the best was 99.99%. It is interesting to note that availability guarantees from AT&T, MCI, Sprint and Concentric Network have offered guarantee of 99.9% to 100% availability for Frame Relay, ATM services, and IP-based services. Average round-trip latency guarantees 80–85 milliseconds (ms), with a maximum latency of 120ms and a guarantee that packet loss will not exceed an average of 1% per month for dedicated connections.

Internet guarantees usually are at 99.9% availability as well.

Computer performance is also important. Baselines on important, widely used, or critical servers should be made because increased security may affect them as well. Performance Monitor can be used to develop this baseline. A good reference is the Windows 2000 Resource Kit. Both Windows 2000 Server and Windows 2000 Professional editions have extensive information on performance monitoring. For more information on computer performance evaluation, visit The Standard Performance Evaluation Corporation (www.spec.org).

ANALYZE DATA AND SYSTEMS ACCESS METHOD

Analyze the method of accessing data and systems.

As you know, one of the major areas of security concern involves the access points to your network, your systems, and your data. Your network diagrams identify physical connection points to your network from other parts of your corporation and from external networks. They should be evaluated for possible security issues. Are firewalls and intrusion-detection systems in place? Is management of routers secured? Is there a strict policy about modem location? Are remote access servers protected and protective?

Next, examine connection points on your internal network, both physical and programmatical. Physical access includes availability of both computers and connection points or ports. Programmatical access includes user authentication to systems and application access control, as well as restrictions possible at the file and/or folder level.

Are users required to log on? How are files protected? What granularity exists?

You can categorize your search and documentation efforts.

◆ Physical access to systems

◆ Authentication

◆ Authorization

◆ Handling of backups and other data stores

◆ External access

Physical Access

Are servers located in rooms where access is restricted? Note locations of all servers and their physical environment. Determine who has physical access and when. Are any security devices (key lock doors, biometrics, or badges) used to restrict access?

Are all access ports documented and accounted for? You should be especially concerned with those exposed ports—ports that may exist in lobbies, conference rooms, training rooms, or other areas open to more public access and potential abuse.

Authentication

Authentication is the process of proving that you are who you say you are. In computer networks, this usually is accomplished by the use of a user ID and password, and the confirmation of this information by some cryptographic algorithm. List all the authentication mechanisms used on your network. Windows networks, for example, use LM and/or NTLM to authenticate users. Windows 2000 offers significantly more secure authentication mechanisms, including Kerberos, certificate-based authentication, and Extensible Authentication Protocol (EAP). The algorithms and more details can be found in Chapter 10 "Designing an Authentication Strategy."

If your environment is more varied, how is authentication handled? Do users have multiple user IDs and passwords? Are accounts synchronized between systems? Are passwords passed in the clear across the network? Other systems already use algorithms such as Kerberos and RADIUS that Windows 2000 supports. Which of these will you need to plan integration with?

Applications in your enterprise may not rely on the OS for authentication, but they may use a security structure of their own. Investigate and document how they handle security. It may be a weak or strong point in your authentication scheme, but in designing a Windows 2000 authentication strategy, it is critical to understand so that you may determine how to deal with it. Database applications are one of the first applications to consider in searching for these alternative plans.

Are additional authentication mechanisms currently in place in your network? Are smart cards, tokens, and biometrics used? Document the existence of public key usage and architecture.

Authorization

Is there a carefully planned, granular design that controls user access to shares, files, and folders? Is this periodically reviewed for correctness? Who controls the access to sensitive files? Is it the owner? Who can delete files? Windows 2000 uses discretionary access control lists (DACLs) to set authentication privileges on files, folders, and shares.

Registry keys also use DACLs.

You should document the file and registry key DACLs for all servers. Useful, downloadable tools for this purpose are available from Somarsoft (www.somarsoft.com). The Windows 2000 Resource Kit also has utilities that might help, and other third-party tools may be used as well.

IN THE FIELD

MEANWHILE, AT THE CUSTOMER SITE

How many of you have been arrested for data destruction? One of my friends narrowly escaped.

Not too many years ago, I worked for a training firm that sent most of its trainers to customer sites to do training. This was at a time when the networking model was just beginning to spread across the business landscape. Most end-user trainers had little to no experience with operating systems, and no experience with networks.

My friend—I'll call her Amy—was an experienced trainer. She always arrived early, got along well with folks, and got excellent reviews. The curriculum she taught required her to place data files for the students on their PCs when she arrived. One day she arrived and found that the student computers were networked together. She asked if she might put her data files on the network to make that job easier.

She was given a user ID and a password, as well as a location to place the files. She copied the files to the network and then realized she had put them in the wrong folder. Amy had just learned this really cool DOS command deltree. Well you can guess what happened. She had been given administrative privilege on the network. She had placed her files at the root of the network file server. When she ran `deltree`, in the words of the network administrator, "she deleted everything on the server."

It took some pretty hard talking to convince that company that they really shouldn't have made it so easy for an outsider to destroy their file server.

Backups and Other Data Stores

Determining who has access to your backup data is as critical as determining access to your systems. Record backup management processes and the location of onsite and offsite copies.

Don't forget to check for emergency repair disks (ERDs). While Windows NT stores a copy of the Security Accounts Manager (SAM) (if it's small enough) on the ERD disk, Windows 2000 stores data that can be used during system recovery. (No registry data is stored on it.)

Both Windows NT and Windows 2000 use the %system root%\repair folder to store a copy of the SAM. This folder can be used during recovery. Windows 2000 systems include only local accounts in the SAM (domain accounts are in the Active Directory), but don't forget that for Windows 2000 Professional and Windows 2000 Server, that includes the local Administrator account. If a malicious individual obtains a copy of the SAM, he could use it in a dictionary attack on accounts and passwords. With knowledge of the local Administrator account or NT 4.0 domain Administrator account (in mixed-mode Windows 2000 networks), your attacker has significant power.

Windows NT discs were a great source for hackers, so Windows 2000 ERD disks cannot be used alone to recover the registry. Instead, they are used to repair system files, the partition book sector, and the startup environment. The registry is recovered using the Recovery Console and system state backups. System state backup tapes, like any form of backup, should be protected.

Security policy may dictate how ERD disks and repair folders are protected or managed. If written policy does not indicate this, be sure to record this information.

> **NOTE**
>
> **Dictionary Attacks** A dictionary attack is one in which a list of common words (or a dictionary) is encrypted with the same algorithm as the passwords the hacker wishes to crack. The encrypted passwords then are compared one by one with every word in the dictionary, hoping for a match. A match, of course, means that the hacker has cracked a password. Sadly, many people use common words as their passwords.

Windows 2000 systems also offer the opportunity to back up system state information only. System state backups include the following:

◆ Registry

◆ COM+ Class registration database

◆ Boot files

◆ Certificate Services Database

◆ Active Directory directory service

◆ SYSVOL directory

◆ Cluster service information

Another area to research is the status of recovery programs. Windows 2000 uses the Recovery Console, a set of command-line administrative commands that can be used to stop and start services, read and write data on local drives (including NTFS drives), repair master boot records, and format drives. The recovery console can be installed on the system or, if left off, requires the Windows 2000 CD-ROM. Only administrators can use the Recovery Console. Policy should dictate who can use the Recovery Console.

Gather similar significant information on other OSs in your project scope.

External Access

What are the entry points to your network? Dial-up servers? VPN endpoints? Border gateway routers? Internet Web sites? Any point at which authorized access can occur must be documented so that it can be protected. Be sure to look for dial-up modems on desktop machines. Also document wireless entry points. Modern computer systems are coming equipped with wireless ports, making every computer system a potential point of entry.

What is the policy on bringing software and data from outside the network? Who is traveling with corporate data and access software on a laptop? What is policy on protection of corporate data that travels? Is it followed? Are security devices, smart cards, tokens, and biometrics issued with laptops?

ANALYZE NETWORK ROLES AND RESPONSIBILITIES

Analyze network roles and responsibilities. Roles include administrative, user, service, resource ownership, and application.

For Windows networks, each domain, standalone server, and Professional workstation, has a list of users and groups. Non-Windows systems do as well.

Your job is two-fold: You must validate the roles of all the users and groups that exist, and you must determine whether there are additional roles that are not being addressed, or whether the current plan could or should be modified in some way. You can start by obtaining or making a list of current roles and responsibilities, or you can start with hypothetical roles and responsibilities based on your view of the network, the company, and its processes. If you have extensive background in these things, then you will realize that many of the roles and responsibilities will be the same on every network, but that each company will have special assignments of its own as well. An organization's business practice should not have to be forced into a preconceived notion of what users and groups it needs.

NOTE

Double-Loop Learning In all your documentation efforts, use the double-loop learning process. This process was first described by Gareth Morgan in *Images of Organization* (Berrett-Koehler Publishers, 1998, page 80) to define how errors that go against the norm should be handled. I adapt it here for documentation processing.

Single-loop learning is the process of documenting the system before upgrading it. You assume that the system works; you are just going to make it work faster or make it more secure.

Double-loop learning is the process of questioning whether the current system is the correct one (see Figure 3.10). Designing a secure system that doesn't work isn't a good thing. Users will do their job somehow and will look for ways around any security if it means getting the job done faster or easier.

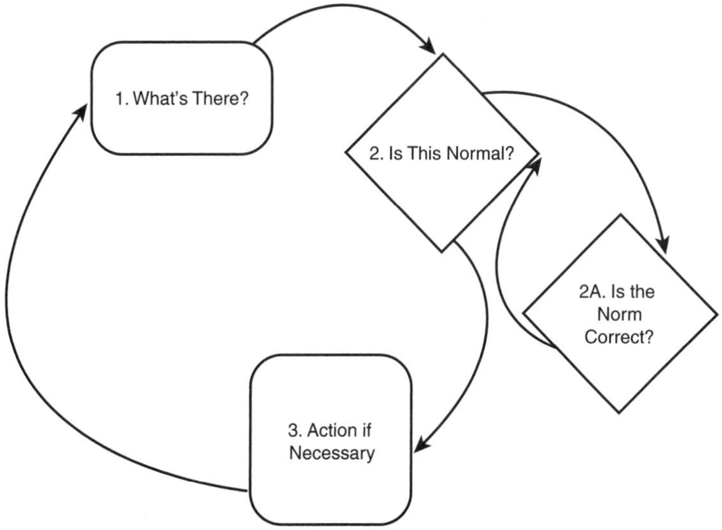

1. What's There?

2. Is This Normal?

2A. Is the Norm Correct?

3. Action if Necessary

FIGURE 3.10
Double-loop learning process.

Administrative

Administrative roles should be granular within any but the smallest organization. In many networks, administrative roles are broken down by job responsibilities and include things such as the following:

◆ Backup operator

◆ Account management

◆ Server operator

◆ Database management

◆ Security management

◆ Global management

◆ Audit management

◆ Domain name server management

Within this structure, there may be a need for further horizontal or vertical organization. Roles may need to be delegated for particular groups of servers.

Are there additional management groups? Look for network and OS and database management, not production or accounting; perhaps also look for network engineers, folks who need special access to systems and networks.

User

The standard definition of a user on most networks is that it represents the lowest common denominator. Users have the basic right to log on to the network or a system.

Other groups may be devised to denote resource ownership or additional responsibility beyond basic access to the network. Contractors who need the right to add Windows 2000 workstations to the domain come to mind. This group of individuals is hired to assist with installation, and they may need this one administrative right in the domain. While Windows 2000 users can add up to 10 computer accounts to the domain, these contractors may be responsible for making sure that hundreds or even thousands of systems are set up correctly. By creating a group and giving the group the added responsibility (and right), you have given these employees only what they need, and no additional administrative access to your systems.

Service

In a Windows 2000/NT system, all programs must run in the context of some authorized account (see Figure 3.11). When you use Microsoft Word, its processes use your account to access resources. The application can access resources and perform actions that you are authorized to do.

Many server-based applications, on the other hand, run processes internally that have nothing to do with user access. They need special rights and privileges similar to users. They need to be able to run, even if no real user is logged on, and they need to run consistently, no matter who accesses the data. These processes run whether or not the application is being used by users. Applications that use this approach are Microsoft Exchange, Microsoft SQL Server, IBM's

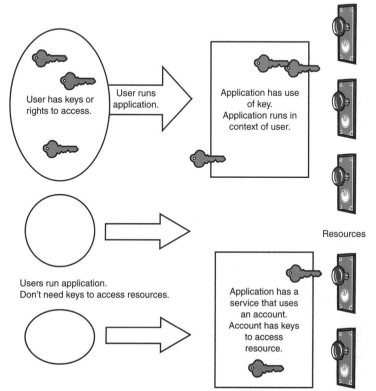

FIGURE 3.11
An application runs in the context of an account.

DB2 Universal Database, and the Windows 2000/NT operating systems itself. Other OSs have similar setups. UNIX calls these processes daemons. In Windows 2000/NT, these processes are called services. Because they are accessing resources on the system, they must have an account to use for authentication and authorization. Many can use the local system account, an account that represents the OS. Others need regular Windows 2000/NT user accounts, to which they have been given the right to log on as a service, in addition to perhaps other privileges.

Resource Ownership

Each resource on your system has an owner. The owner may be the user who created the object, or ownership may be in the hands of the Administrators group. Access to file objects is defined in Windows 2000/NT by the type of file system, whether access is interactive or across the network, and by permission placed on file system objects. Permissions are granted to users and/or groups. The right to grant permissions is also specified and belongs to the owner of the object and any group or user granted the Permission right.

Windows 2000 supports three basic file types: NTFS, FAT32, and FAT. (Windows NT 4.0 supports FAT and NTFS). Access to objects in the FAT file system cannot be controlled except through shares. Access through shares implies network access. Interactive users are not bound by permission specified on shares. NTFS, however, allows granular access on an object to be specified. DACLs are created for each file and folder.

Access to network printers and remote access servers is also controlled. Other server application access can be controlled through file permissions and through the application itself. The Windows 2000/NT registry is also controlled by ACLs set on registry keys.

Other operating systems in your enterprise may also have access permissions and definitions of resource ownership.

You will find multiple groups of users defined in Windows 2000/NT domains as well as on standalone and member servers, NT workstations, and Windows 2000 Professional systems. You should make a record of these groups, their purposes, and their rights. Record the resource ownership. When designing Windows 2000 security, you must not allow arbitrary changes to these permission sets.

You should also validate current arrangements.

Are groups given appropriate rights and not any extra? Are files and folders, printers, RAS services, and registry keys, appropriately assigned? Do appropriate shares exist? What compromises have been made to security because of improperly assigned permissions? What applications necessitate this arrangement? Are updated, Windows 2000-certified versions of these applications available?

Windows 2000 offers new possibilities for group assignment. Knowing current group arrangements and how well they fit your organization's needs will make for a smoother transition. More information on Windows 2000 groups can be found in Chapter 7, "Designing a Security Group Strategy."

Application

Applications also access resources and operate according to rules within the OS. When their processes are running under the context of service accounts, the resource DACLs must give them appropriate access. When they are not, these applications operate under context of the user who is using them.

Which folders and files and registry keys does the application require access to? Are there registry keys, files, or system files where that access is inappropriate and causes a relaxation in protection, or an elevation in user privileges, just so the user can run the program? These types of programs may also cause problems in Windows 2000. Windows 2000 gives users more innate privileges and system file and registry access than Windows NT does. However, Windows 2000 uses the Power Users groups as a replacement for the Users group. Those users who need to run poorly designed applications in Windows 2000 may need to be given membership in the Power Users group until replacement or upgraded applications can be found. More information on user groups, privileges, and authentication can be found in Chapter 7.

ANALYZE THE SECURITY DESIGN

Analyze the impact of the security design on the existing and planned technical environment.

Windows 2000 offers a plethora of new security features designed to provide high levels of security and ease of implementation and administration. These include IPSec, L2TP, Kerberos, an Encrypting Files system (EFS), public key infrastructure, RADIUS, smart card support, new security groups, and a higher level of default file and system access restrictions. What security features you implement, how easy implementation and administration will be, and the impact your design has, depend greatly on policy and current network physical and security structure. Now that you have documented this, you must round up documentation, ask for clarification, and examine company policy, needs, and requirements in light of this.

What systems does your Windows NT network interface with? Are you using Gateway Services for NetWare? Service for UNIX? Third-party integration strategies? The number of opportunities you have for interoperability with other OSs is widely expanded in Windows 2000. Kerberos, RADIUS, and IPSec all can be used in this effort. There are new versions of old tools, with enhanced capabilities and increased requirements. Will your third-party tools work with Windows 2000? Some of these features were written with interoperability in mind. Information on interoperation with external Kerberos realms (the administrative domains of MIT Kerberos v5) can be found in Chapter 10, "Designing an Authentication Strategy." If you are using third-party solutions involving smart cards, you may no longer need the server-side software to use them. You will need to contact third-party tool vendors for information on their interoperability with Windows 2000.

You must understand current server applications that may require service packs or patches, such as Proxy Server and Exchange Server. New versions of these products will take advantage of Windows 2000's additional directory and security services. You must plan time to study new and different security features that these upgrades will bring. At this point, you must document what you do have in the current environment.

Assess Existing Systems and Applications

Previously, you created current hardware and software inventories of server and client computers in your network—get them now. You listed all routers, modems, and remote access servers. Now include details: BIOS settings, peripheral device configurations, and driver versions.

Did you list all the applications found on all the computers with version numbers, date and time stamp data, dynamic link libraries, and service packs applied? Do you have network configuration documented for servers and client computers?

Use the results collected by any systems management programs, such as Microsoft's Systems Management Server.

If your security design team is a member of a greater deployment or migration effort, then much of this documentation may reside in this group's domain. Make sure that you have access to it. While migration and upgrade efforts need this data to enable efforts at basic hardware and software compatibility level, you need it to determine the best way to implement security policy in your design.

Pay particular attention to problem areas. If current hardware or software is not working well, is it related to security? Will new Windows 2000 security features resolve the issue or make it more complicated?

Examine non-Windows NT DNS servers for their implementation of dynamic registration and service (SRV) resource records. If they are not capable of these features, does an upgrade exist that would enable them? Windows 2000 uses these features, and you may want to have integration with non-Windows 2000 DNS servers. Some DNS servers, such as BIND 4.97 and BIND 8.x, support SRV resource records.

Does existing documentation include information on services running on all servers? Be sure to include services running on non-Microsoft servers, such as UNIX BIND, Service Advertising Protocol (SAP), and Routing Information Protocol (RIP).

Check details on servers, and look for configurations that should have been documented elsewhere. For example, servers may host banks of modems but not be identified as RAS servers, or servers may be multihomed (have multiple network adapters) (see Figure 3.12). This may mean that they are looking for the increased throughput that this arrangement might offer, or it may mean they are undocumented links to the outside world. Firewalls, routers, and proxy servers usually are multihomed. Note whether servers require or rely on special protocols. Do applications require residence on a domain controller? Domain controllers should have tighter security settings—in fact, Windows 2000 domain controllers do. If applications must run on a domain controller, they may require a loosening of these security settings to run.

Web and proxy servers require special security and bandwidth because of their nature and location. For more information, see Chapter 4, "Designing a Security Baseline," and Chapter 10.

Line of Business Applications

Line of business applications should also be considered for the impact of a new security design. You identified core applications such as database, email, and financial systems. If these are being migrated to Windows 2000 or have already been moved, basic compatibility studies may have been already completed. Are upgrades planned to make them compatible, or simply to provide necessary business features? Look for the "Certified for Windows" logo. Microsoft has implemented a new application certification program that has significant security requirements for approval. Applications that are certified will work more smoothly and

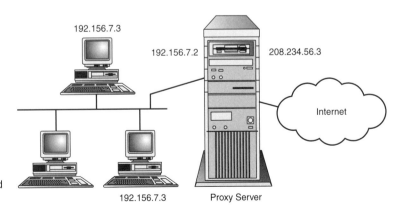

FIGURE 3.12
The presence of an undocumented multihomed computer may pose a security problem.

appropriately within your new security design. Understanding their appropriateness and functionality before requiring strict compliance can help. Whether only certified applications will reside in the upgraded network is a policy decision. Implementing the best and most workable security design, whatever the policy, is your job. To do so, you need to know application status.

What are the built-in security features of these applications? Do you integrate with Windows NT users and groups, or develop your own security structure? Do these applications require particular protocols for communication or authentication? How are passwords communicated across networks? Windows NT and Windows 2000, as well as many other OSs do not pass passwords in the clear across the network. However, applications that insist on their own security structure, and even many that integrate with Windows security architecture, may communicate passwords across the network form their client applications to the server in clear text. Before Version 6 of IBM's DB2-UDB for Windows NT, client passwords were transmitted in clear text. DB2UDB utilized Windows NT usernames and passwords to delegate authentication and authorization, but failed to integrate fully with the security architecture and thus exposed network passwords. I am told that DB2-UDB for Windows NT Version 6 corrects this problem.

Domain Structure

Are current domain structure and trusts adequate and appropriate? Why do they exist? Are they the result of corporate IT administration division politics? Do they stem from misunderstandings of domain structure?

Knowing how and why current structure exists can help you determine whether things can and should be changed in the administrative model. Doing so can reduce costs, make operation more efficient, and improve security. You may be the voice of reason. The trust structure in Windows 2000 is very different. Transitive trust relationships can be created automatically during configuration, and trust extends automatically to all servers in a tree. A tree is a logical grouping of Windows 2000 domains within a DNS namespace.

Identify Existing and Planned Upgrades and Rollouts

You cannot rely on things staying the same. At this point, you want a snapshot so that you can analyze the implication of your design; while you work, things are changing. Identify upgrades and rollouts that are currently in progress. Inquire about and document anything in a planning stage. While it may be true that it's difficult to hit a moving target, it doesn't make sense to pretend that the target hasn't moved or won't move.

You will need to coordinate your planning efforts with those of other systems.

Analyze Technical Support Structure

Knowing what kind of support is available, how it's managed, and what the level of support staff expertise is can be invaluable.

Document the location of support staff. Is support internal? Is it outsourced?

Determine what you can expect during your implementation phase. Your knowledge of other upgrade and planning efforts is critical here. If everyone is off working on that other project, where's your help going to come from? Is support organized by levels of expertise? Is there a budget for training in the new technologies? Who controls the assignment of support staff to projects?

Analyze Existing and Planned Network and Systems Management

How are the network and its systems managed? Who is in charge? Previously you examined the structure of IT management. Here you will look at security policy, and network and systems management tools.

Security Policy

Document existing policy and guidelines on security. Are there requirements for appropriate network usage? Is Internet access allowed? For what purpose? What constitutes prohibited or inappropriate access?

What are the policies in place regarding partner access to company networks? Are partners able to access the entire work as recognized users (or as anonymous users, such as Web site visitors)? What are your policies concerning their access to data and resources? Is their access to data read-only? Or are they allowed to change or add data on your network? How is their access to applications restricted?

Are encryption and security standards in place or planned? What permissions exist by user and user group? What are the domains and their trust relationships? What are your password standards? For Windows NT domains and computers, information can be found in User Manager for Domain Account Policy. Are there security protocols implemented on your network, such as Secure Sockets Layer (SSL), IP Security (IPSec), and Point-to-Point Tunneling Protocol (PPTP)? How are users from the Internet authenticated? How are dial-up users authenticated? What about users that cross WAN links?

Do multiple accounts exist for single users? Do these users require these multiple accounts due to their usage of multiple operating systems, due to separate user and administrative actions by the same person, or due to appropriate or inappropriate domain structure or resource management? By documenting users with multiple accounts, you may find ways to reduce this without compromising security. Tools exist for integration of passwords—are they in use on your network?

Network Management Tools and Systems

What tools are used for network management? Commercial tools exist that enable you to assess multiple network parameters and change remote server configurations. Some of them work with multiple OSs.

A useful resource on network management can be found at `netman.cit.buffalo.edu/index.html`.

Several categories of tools exist:

Network sniffers, or protocol analyzers, used to be the toys of the wealthy, or used only as a last resort. Network General produces general expert sniffers; agents are placed on network segments as routers block network utilization measurements.

Microsoft Network Monitor comes with Windows NT. Although this version can monitor packets only directed at it or of a broadcast nature, a more elaborate version is available with Systems Management Server.

Sophisticated devices dynamically allocate bandwidth as required for ATM switches and hubs.

Other Simple Network Management Protocol (SNMP) management tools can be used to control the tables of a router, bridge, or concentrator.

CyberGauge (from neon software, at `www.neon.com`) is a bandwidth measurement utility and monitor. It analyzes the throughput of a router and determines how much bandwidth is being used on various switches and hubs. It uses the Simple Network Management Protocol (SNMP). CyberGauge displays information on a real-time graph, saves information for review, and exports or prints on demand. You also can use this tool to find out your bandwidth utilization. It is often used to measure your link to the Internet.

LANsurveyor automatically maps networks, if computers have the LANsurveyor client responder on them.

Netcomsystems (`www.netcomsystems.com`) produces network measurement products. SmartBits Network Performance Analysis system is hardware and software that can be used to simulate network use.

Concord Communications, Inc. (`www.concord.com`), produces Network Health suite, which monitors your network and produces continuous graphical data on capacity and resource allocation.

Hewlett Packard (`www.hp.com`) and Radcom Ltd. (`www.radcom-inc.com`) also produce network management tools.

Systems Management Tools and Systems

Native Windows NT tools allow management of users' (User Manager for Domains) account policy, services, and servers. Microsoft's Systems Management Server brings remote control, push application installation, and software and hardware inventory. Various third-party tools allow broad and enterprise-wide management of systems and servers as well as management of multiple OSs.

CASE STUDY: MID-HO PHARMACEUTICALS

ESSENCE OF THE CASE

A good way to begin your approach to understanding any case study is to first summarize the key points. Don't forget to examine any exhibits.

· International company with six locations

· Oracle database in Paris and Boston; replication desired

· Diverse mail systems and mail hub in Boston

· Plans to migrate all to Exchange 2000

· Plans to put copies of database at other location.

· Apparently has a rogue Web site in Fort Myers

BACKGROUND

Mid-Ho Pharmaceuticals has five locations in the United States and one in Paris, France. The distribution of users and other details can be found in Figure 3.13; additional information is presented in Figures 3.14 and 3.15.

DATA CENTERS AND ADMINISTRATION

Mid-Ho has a corporate-wide multimaster Windows NT domain architecture.

Boston

Mid-Ho has an Oracle database that manages data on inventories and is located in Boston. Replication of the database to the Paris, France, location is online, and replication is planned for each of the other U.S. locations.

A mail hub in Boston allows communication between different mail systems.

Warehouses

Warehouses are located in Paris, Dallas, and Chicago. Each warehouse has a data center staffed by "first-level" technicians. First-level

continues

CASE STUDY: MID-HO PHARMACEUTICALS

continued

FIGURE 3.13
Used and asset distribution—Mid-Ho
Pharmaceuticals.

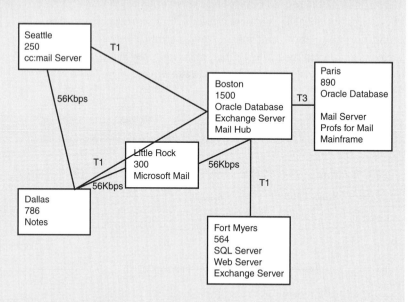

FIGURE 3.14
Domain structure.

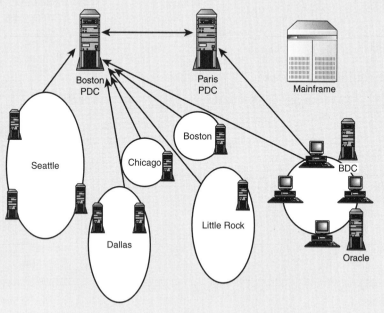

CASE STUDY: MID-HO PHARMACEUTICALS

Boston

Paris

FIGURE 3.15
User groups.

```
GROUPS
Administrators
Backup Operators
Server Operators
Account Operators
Print Operators
Domain Admins
Domain Users
Domain Guest
Guests
Domain Database Admins
Database Admins
Domain Mail Admins
Mail Admins
```

```
GROUPS
Administrators
Backup Operators
Server Operators
Account Operators
Print Operators
Domain Admins
Domain Users
Domain Guest
Guests
Domain Database Admins
Database Admins
Domain Mail Admins
Mail Admins
```

Each Location Domain

```
Mail Admins
Administrators
Users
Database Admins
```

technicians can repair and replace components that do not require manufacturer techs. They have received training in the normal operation of systems implemented and can call on expertise at corporate headquarters for assistance.

Future Plans

The company was planning migration to Microsoft Exchange, but plans have been tabled until after Windows 2000, service pack 1, has been released and until the next version of Exchange has been released.

The company plans to move to Windows 2000 within the year.

PROBLEM STATEMENT

A recently discovered Web site and SQL database in Fort Myers have caused increased attention to security. Because migration is in the planning stages, IT management has placed an increased emphasis on documentation of the existing system.

continues

CASE STUDY: MID-HO PHARMACEUTICALS

continued

ANALYSIS

Mid-Ho Pharmaceuticals has an interesting dispersion of employees. Several slow links will cause problems if the company continues with plans to place databases at all locations and to replicate content. Multiple mail servers complicate the traffic patterns, as mail must all travel to Boston, be converted and then travel out to all sites.

Knowing about these upgrade and deployment plans and communication links will assist planning a security design. Additional security issues include access to the database, planned rollout of the database to multiple locations, and the security of the replication traffic.

Special consideration must be taken to explore the security issues of the Web site located in Fort Myers.

CHAPTER SUMMARY

This chapter has moved the discussion away from business management and into the technical arrangement of the current infrastructure. It should be clear by now that time spent building a database of information on the current system is time well spent. As you learn more about Windows 2000 and its capabilities and shortcomings, you will return to these specifications again and again. Your job is not to repeat the mistakes of the past, nor is it to redo what works well. Your job is to secure the business operations of the company in the best manner possible, given the status of current technology and the policy of the corporation.

KEY TERMS

- net available bandwidth
- switched virtual circuits
- permanent virtual circuits
- DSL
- virtual private network
- IPSec
- tunneling
- latency
- propagational delay
- service level agreement
- EDI
- permanent virtual circuit flapping
- cyclic redundancy check
- authentication
- authorization
- SAM
- ERD
- domain controller
- standalone server
- service account
- access control list
- Kerberos
- RADIUS
- smart cards
- BIND
- SAP
- RIP

APPLY YOUR KNOWLEDGE

Exercises

3.1 Case Study: Associated Wholesale Grocers

Background

Associated Wholesale Grocers (AWG) is one of the largest supermarket cooperatives. Membership consists of more than 350 grocery store chains, representing 850 shops located in the Midwest and the southern United States. Among the membership are Co-op, Cash Saver, Apple Market, Country Mart, and Price Chopper. AWG also operates its own 30 Fraleys stores in Kansas.

AWG offers design and decor service, member service, real estate service, retail systems support, education and training, a print shop, reclamation, store engineering, and advertising assistance.

The company offers retail pricing support functions, including bulletin board hosting, price changes, unit cost changes, new items, discontinued items, exception reports, other information, deals and allowances, and preferred products.

AWG Retailers Connection offers member-only information over the Internet from its Web site at www.awginc.com.

AWG has been in business for more than 70 years.

Data Systems

The company has a modern Warehouse Management System (WMS), a material and resource management system. It receives an advanced shipping notice processing; cross docking; directed putaway; order processing; shipment assignment; wave management; picking, replenishment, and packing verification; and lot control. The design is platform-independent and is the result of open system design. It includes multiple computer databases and bar coding, radio frequency reports, paper-based accounting, bar coding, automatic identification, voice technology, portable RF terminals with bar code scanners, and receiving, picking, loading, and cycle-counting modules.

Problem Statement

The company would like to move toward paperless systems. Paperless systems surely have their own security considerations. When all data is stored online, is it more vulnerable to attack? How is data protected from origination to destruction?

Proposed Solution

To meet this goal, AWG is working with optical imaging. To reduce paper flow, the company uses bar codes in warehouse receiving. Orders are filled electronically, and AWG accepts electronic data interchange (EDI). EDI is the transfer of information between companies over a network. Many implementations concern billing or ordering in which the data exchanged is information about money owed or promised.

Analysis

AWG offers an opportunity to study a moderate-sized business with a wide range of equipment, infrastructure, and new technology. The company also has a pervasive attitude of cheerful acceptance, if not evangelism toward its new systems. While plentiful information is provided here, there is little hard detail on the location of resources, transmission media, and similar considerations.

APPLY YOUR KNOWLEDGE

Estimated Time: 60 minutes

1. Visit the AWG Web site at www.awginc.com.

2. Collect the following data (Table 3.3):

TABLE 3.3

EXERCISE 3.1

State	Warehouse/Data Centers	Store Locations

3. Map company locations.

   Use the information on the Web site to plot company locations on the map provided in Figure 3.16.

4. What additional information would you collect and plot on this or other maps or drawings?

3.2 Case Study: PeaceWeaver

Background

PeaceWeaver is an international weaving cooperative with members in 26 countries. It is a virtual organization founded to promote weaving arts and crafts. While its original intent was to foster weaving heritage, to keep old crafts from dying, and to rediscover ancient techniques, its scope has broadened to include modern weaving. A large number of its members use computer-driven looms, and PeaceWeaver has recently

FIGURE 3.16
Location map.

APPLY YOUR KNOWLEDGE

introduced its own software for these looms. Income from software sales and Web-zine advertising are used to promote research.

Information Systems

Headquartered in New Hampshire, PeaceWeaver is currently undergoing growth in all aspects. Information systems include the Web site, a Microsoft SQL Server database of weaving information and resource locations that is downloadable to members, the Web-zine *Spotted Recluse*, a separate development network, and a number of PC-driven looms and loom computers. The development network consists of 15 Windows 2000 Professional systems, a file server used to manage source code, a color printer, and a color plotter. Each development station is connected to a Dolby loom (a computer-driven weaving loom).

Current membership and locations are shown in Table 3.4.

TABLE 3.4

EXERCISE 3.2

Country	Number of Users
United States	432
South America	700
Russia	100
India	345
Australia	183
Africa	234
Canada	243

All connectivity between members and between members and the organization is through the Internet. While some members may have ISDN, DSL, or better connectivity to local Internet service providers, it should be assumed that most do not.

Three projects are in the planning or development stages:

- An Internet business-to-business project is in the works that, when completed, will offer a single-stop source for weaving and spinning supplies.

- An online shop is proposed, where artists may offer weaving and spinning projects for sale.

- Expansion of the database is planned to hold spinning information and data as well as weaving.

PeaceWeaver wants to build its information system to last into the future and has chosen Windows 2000 as the platform of choice.

Analysis

PeaceWeaver is a small organization, but it either has or is about to have as wide a variety in need for services and IT function as a much larger enterprise. This is the perfect size of security design project to begin with. Although you may not at first see any real reason for concern, the Internet exposure and the need for providing access to its expanding databases for members and the public are point to consider. The development of two e-commerce sites will bring additional risks.

Estimated Time: 20 minutes

1. Use the map in Figure 3.17, and plot the locations of users.

APPLY YOUR KNOWLEDGE

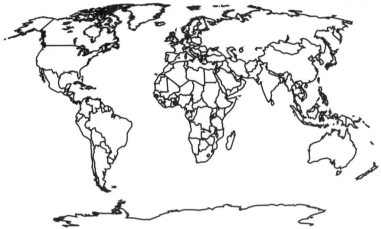

FIGURE 3.17
PeaceWeaver user distribution.

2. Use the space here to draw a network diagram of the Headquarters network.

3. What groups of users would you expect to find? Make a list and indicate the resources to which they need access in the network.

4. What do you think will be the impact of the expected upgrades and expansions?

5. What would be the questions that would need to be asked before proceeding on this strategy? What additional questions must be asked to determine the impact of a security design on the technical environment?

Review Questions

1. The AWG case study and Web site do not list user and resource distribution. If you were working for this company and developing a security design, where would you go and who would you ask to find this information?

2. Examine the diagrams in Figures 3.14 and 3.15 and review the case study on Mid-Ho Pharmaceuticals. Do the diagrams clearly model the information in the case study? Is information missing from the diagrams? Are pre-existing diagrams of networks good sources for your development work?

APPLY YOUR KNOWLEDGE

3. When you are creating a network diagram, what elements should you add first?

4. RPMB is a company that still relies on leased lines for communication between its divisions. What type of WAN topology is this company more likely to have?

5. John is charged with mapping Charleston Launch Metrics, Inc. (CLM) network. CLM has offices in 128 cities nationwide and 16 foreign countries. His map(s) will be part of a CLM-wide network redesign. A task force has been appointed to gather information. It has members from each location. The task force will coordinate activities via email. What should John use for the scope of his mapping?

6. Help John by making a list of the detailed information points that should be included on his diagrams.

7. Why is the gathering of information on network performance and performance requirements of importance to a security design?

8. If you have no special network and systems management tools, how can this task (network and systems management) be undertaken?

9. Dragon_Tongue is a hacker who delights in gaining entry into business networks. It is always possible that he might be able to obtain a user ID and password on your network by tricking a user, or finding where someone has written down a password. It is also possible that he might be able to sniff password data as it crosses your network, and perhaps determine what password was used. Is there another source of this data that Dragon_Tongue might find?

10. What is the difference between authentication and authorization?

11. Why is it important to consider the uses that people make of data when determining network roles?

12. Do you really need to identify ownership of all resources (down to folders and files) on your network?

13. What are two ways that applications can acquire access to resources?

14. A new design for the network and the introduction of a new operating system can mean changes to security settings. What are two reasons for this?

15. How can knowledge of existing and planned upgrades and rollouts assist you in your project?

16. Are technical support resources of interest to security design? Why?

Exam Questions

1. Figure 3.18 is a map of the Gergia, Smythe, and Underwood network. Which of the following statements is true?

   A. Gergia, Smythe, and Underwood have a central database in Mozambique that is accessed by some 10,000 users.

   B. Gergia, Smythe, and Underwood's database can be accessed locally by 5,000 employees and at three distribution points by 500, 2,000, and 500 users.

APPLY YOUR KNOWLEDGE

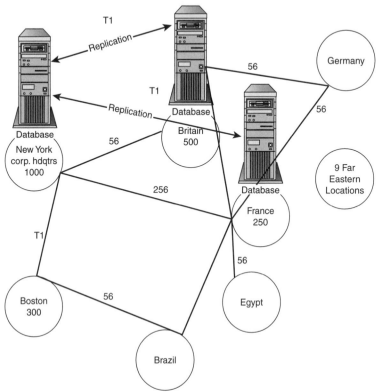

FIGURE 3.18
Gergia, Smythe, and Underwood network map.

C. Gergia, Smythe, and Underwood's database is accessed locally by 1000 employees and by 250, 500, and 300 users in France, Britain, and New York, respectively.

D. Gergia, Smythe, and Underwood's database is accessed locally by 1,000 employees.

2. Users that are not in a location with a local copy of the database can access it over a WAN connection, if they have one. Far Eastern locations do not currently have connection to any other point on the network. Which of the following is true?

A. Users at all 16 locations have adequate connectivity to corporate headquarters.

B. Users in France, Britain, and the United States have adequate connectivity to corporate headquarters.

C. Users in France, Britain, and Germany have adequate connectivity to corporate headquarters.

D. You should ask questions about the data needs of users in all locations.

3. Sally is presenting her security design to management for Mid-Ho Pharmaceuticals. She has included the use of IPSec for securing communications between branches of the company. IT questions her about the added bandwidth

requirements of IPSec, and she answers that while there may be some additional requirements, she feels that the connections between sites will be adequate. When asked reasons why IPSec should be used, she replies that it will encrypt the data traveling from branch to branch. That starts a discussion about how much extra CPU processing will be involved and how that will either slow things down or cause the company to purchase newer machines.

The use of IPSec in her design is turned down. What could Sally have done differently? Check the two best answers:

A. She should have done a better job explaining the benefits of IPSec.

B. She should have presented data that shows that the 56Kbps lines are underutilized now, in addition to industry guidelines on how much IPSec will add to the overhead.

C. Because a 56Kbps line will never be adequate for IPSec, Sally should have proposed the replacement of these slow lines with faster connections.

D. Sally should have been prepared to answer the questions on CPU by explaining the capability to offload processing onto special network interface cards. Replacing whole computers would not be necessary; just supplying different NICs.

4. You are on the Windows 2000 evaluation team for The Chicago Sheet Metal Company. The company has just made a major upgrade to ATM and wants to know whether Windows 2000

supports ATM, particularly if you can still do L2TP tunneling on the company's ATM network. You answer as follows:

A. Windows 2000 does not currently support ATM, but it will with the first service pack.

B. Windows 2000 provides support for ATM, including an updated ATM miniport drivers, limited support for ATM adapter hardware, ARP/MARS services, and support for tunneling.

C. Windows 2000 has support for ATM but cannot participate in a mixed IP and ATM environment.

D. Windows 2000 supports Layer 2 Tunneling Protocol (L2TP). L2TP is designed to run over IP networks.

E. Currently, this implementation of L2TP does not support native tunneling over X.25, Frame Relay, or ATM networks.

5. Peter Craven saved his company some money. He installed cable modems in three PCs in the main office. All employees can use the PCs when they need to access the Internet. What are the security issues here?

A. Users might be able to access each other's email.

B. Users might be able to see the files that the last user was looking at.

C. The PCs and modems create a back door into the network.

D. Users may leave sensitive documents in the PC area.

APPLY YOUR KNOWLEDGE

6. Which of the following show good matches of technology to required performance? Mark all that apply.

    A. Leased lines and business-to-business e-commerce

    B. DSL and Web browsing

    C. DSL and business-to-business e-commerce

    D. Email and POTS

7. George is charged with monitoring network performance and stability. At 3:45, he notices that utilization is over 80% on backbone circuits, that frame loss is 1–2 percent, and that there have been a number of help desk calls.

    A. George should immediately begin checking for problems on his network; these readings indicate severe issues.

    B. George should continue monitoring. He doesn't have enough historical information to make a judgment.

    C. George should not be concerned. These readings are normal.

    D. George needs to check other elements before determining whether there is a real problem to deal with.

8. George is watching as the network has been logging data over time. Utilization is staying about 69%, frame loss is 4%, latency has increased 20%, applications are timing out, and there is data loss during peak periods.

    A. George should immediately begin checking for problems on his network; these readings indicate severe issues.

    B. George should continue monitoring. He doesn't have enough historical information to make a judgment.

    C. George should not be concerned. These readings are normal.

    D. George needs to check other elements before determining whether there is a real problem to deal with.

9. The following techniques can be used for authentication in Windows 2000 networks:

    A. Kerberos, RADIUS, LM, NTLM, PKI, L2TP

    B. Kerberos LM, NTLM, RIS, PKI

    C. RADIUS, LM, L2TP, PKI, NTLM, NTLMv2

    D. Kerberos, PKI, RADIUS

10. If you have a strong password policy, which of the following is true?

    A. Applications will not be capable of implementing their own security mechanisms.

    B. Applications may implement security mechanisms that may weaken the security in your network.

    C. Kerberos is so secure that it will be impossible for anyone to crack passwords in your Windows 2000 network.

    D. You will still have the same problems you had in Windows NT because Windows 2000 must be backward-compatible.

11. Even though you have set up an intrusion-detection systems to monitor activity, and even though it can tell if someone is trying to guess passwords or run a password-cracking program against your

APPLY YOUR KNOWLEDGE

security database, there are other ways that your user passwords can be compromised. Check all that apply.

A. Users might pick easy-to-guess passwords.

B. Users might write down their passwords and tape the note to the underside of their keyboards.

C. A copy of the NT SAM might be found in the repair directory, and then be copied and fed into a password-cracking program.

D. The security algorithm for NTLM is so weak that anyone can figure out how to decode the password.

E. A copy of the SAM might be found on a backup tape and fed into a password-cracking program.

F. A copy of the SAM might be found on a Windows 98 boot disk and fed into a password-cracking program.

12. Peter will be defining user roles on the Mid-Ho network. He wants to know what users do so that he can determine which security groups he needs to create, as well as possible membership in OUs. A good resource Peter can use to determine the roles of users on the network is which of the following?

A. Examine user and groups lists on the OS

B. Examine the way people use the systems and applications that exist on the network.

C. Make a list from the list of approved users and groups for the network, available from Microsoft

D. A and B

E. B and C

F. A, B, and C

13. Peter and James share a computer. An application running on Windows NT runs perfectly when James, who is an administrator, runs it. When Peter, who is not an administrator, attempts to run the program, it crashes. The most likely problem is:

A. The program is not designed to run on Windows NT. Access to registry keys that the user does not have access to is needed.

B. Peter has too many other programs running.

C. Peter doesn't have enough disk space.

D. The amount of RAM Peter has is restricted by systems policy, and he doesn't have enough to run the program.

14. At Cannon, Inc., it is a fireable offense to have a connection to the Internet or a data connections to the outside world other than through the designated proxy server. Nevertheless, staff members occasionally create another connection. Cannon IT periodically does a sweep of the entire system looking for possible violations. To discover potential connections with remote sites, the Internet, or other companies, IT looks for which of the following? (Check all that apply).

A. Multihomed machines

B. People whose spouses work for other companies

C. Machines running Web servers

D. Modems

E. Undocumented routers, switches, or additional unexplained hardware

F. Disgruntled employees

G. All the people who did not get significant raises last year

15. You have learned that a planned rollout of the company's new payroll system is scheduled for six months from now. Which of the following is not important to ask?

    A. What parts of the program, if any will be placed on Windows 2000 machines?

    B. How will the rollout be impacted by the move to Windows 2000? Does it happen before or after the beginning or end of that effort?

    C. If part of the program will run on Windows 2000 machines, was it created with the Windows 2000 applications certification structure in mind? Is it certified?

    D. Whose pet project is this?

    E. Are the programmers MCSEs?

16. Network and systems managers at Algonquin have trained with multiple systems and components. They are not crosstrained with each other's jobs. There have been problems in IT management for a long time over who had the most authority. A lot of constant bickering and trick-playing takes place. Everyone knew that something was going to happen, and either one group or the other would not be around for long. During the Windows 2000 rollout, 75% of the network management staff quits. Your security design and its implementation will not suffer if you do which of the following?

    A. Were aware of this possibility and made lots of contacts and friends in the systems management area

    B. Made solid contacts and relationships in both areas

    C. Were aware of this potential conflict and avoided forging relationships with either area

    D. Were aware of this potential and made solid contacts and relationships in both areas but did not champion one over the other.

Answers to Exercises

3.1 The solution to item 2 (refer to Table 3.3) in Exercise 3.1 is presented in Table 3.5.

TABLE 3.5

SOLUTION TO TABLE 3.3 IN EXERCISE 3.1

State	Warehouse/Data Centers	Store Locations
Kansas	Kansas City, Fort Scott	X
Missouri	Springfield	X
Oklahoma	Oklahoma City	X
Arkansas		X
Iowa		X
Nebraska		X
Texas		X
Illinois		X
Tennessee		X
Kentucky		X

The solution to item 3 in Exercise 3.1 is presented in Figure 3.19.

3.2 The solution to item 1 in Exercise 3.2 is presented in Figure 3.20.

3.2 The solution to item 2 in Exercise 3.2 is presented in Figure 3.21.

APPLY YOUR KNOWLEDGE

FIGURE 3.19
AWG network map.
(Solution to item 3 in Exercise 3.1)

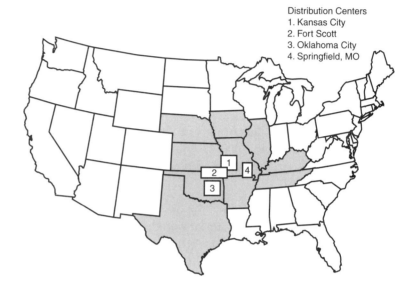

Distribution Centers
1. Kansas City
2. Fort Scott
3. Oklahoma City
4. Springfield, MO

FIGURE 3.20
PeaceWeaver user distribution answer.
(Solution to item 1 in Exercise 3.2)

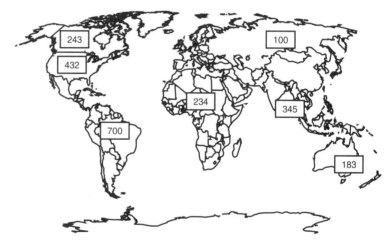

Groups of users (item 3) are these:

    Developers

    Administrators

    Users (local)

    Anonymous Internet users

    Members

Your response to item 4 should look something like the following:

The impact of upgrades and expansion will mean an increased need for security and changes in personnel. In the past, the company has been focused on information for free, but now they are moving into a sales-oriented function. New hires

APPLY YOUR KNOWLEDGE

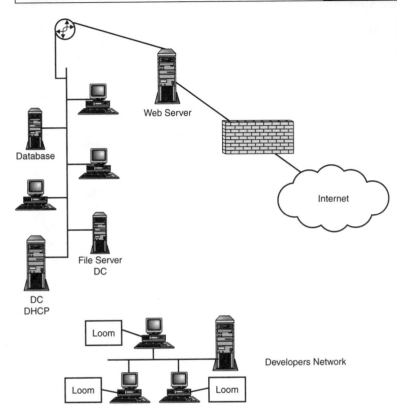

FIGURE 3.21
PeaceWeaver LAN.
(Solution to item 2 in Exercise 3.2)

likely will be experienced business-to-business people rather than designers and weavers. Because credit card transactions and products will be involved, the company will be looking at choices in new protocols, increased efforts in securing data in the database, and protecting the Web site. The internal design network is separate from the database and Web site, so security efforts may change little.

In responding to item 5, you might ask the following questions:

What is the estimated increase in traffic to the site?

How will the ordering of materials be handled? Will this be a portal to existing online merchants? Will products actually be bought and sold? How will transfer of funds happen? Should financial data and transactions be handled in-house or be outsourced? What additional hardware and software will need to be purchased? Will member receive discounts?

Answers to Review Questions

1. You would ask IT management, management staff of the resource owners, and database managers. You also would consult network maps.

2. One diagram does not have the Fort Myers site listed. If that was the only diagram you used, and if you didn't use other resources, you could have missed that. From the case study, someone did— or if that person knew there was a site, they may have considered it unimportant, until they discovered the Web site there. So, of course, you will want to check many resources to make sure that your diagrams are up to date.

3. You should add locations of sites, servers, and connectivity between sites.

4. Leased lines were more commonly arranged in a star topology.

5. While it might seem as if John should assume responsibility for mapping the entire international network, he may want to clarify his role. The scope of the design will determine the scope of the map. Here the text does talk about a network-wide redesign, but it also mentions members from each location working on the project. The map(s) will encompass the entire network, but it looks like they are still in the planning stage; John may be coordinating activities or simply merging together work done elsewhere.

6. Information points should include connectivity transmission types, bandwidth, number of users at sites, resources, and who needs access from where.

7. Many security practices can change processing and communication times. The impact on performance can be significant. You need to know whether there is adequate bandwidth and processing power to add these features, or whether additional network infrastructure is needed. Minimally, you need to know the current performance requirements and whether they are being met.

8. Windows NT provides systems management tools. Server Manager, User Manager, Systems Policy Editor, and Performance Manager may be adequate for smaller networks. Windows 2000 has a more extensive array of tools. Many standardized tools, Active Directory Users and Computers, Active Directory Sites and Services, Computer Management, Local Security Policy, as well as numerous snap-ins for The Microsoft Management Console provide a large number of tools that can be used for this process.

9. Backup copies still pose a security threat, as do emergency repair disks (Windows NT ERDs contain a copy of the registry, but Windows 2000 disks do not) and the Repair folder. All contain copies of the SAM. Backup copies contain sensitive data of other types as well. The issue is that they provide points of access, some of which do not require login. Copies of the SAM can be subjected to brute force attack. Although Windows 2000 domains store domain user account information in the Active Directory, not in the SAM, every Windows 2000 Professional and standalone server still must have a SAM for the storage of local accounts.

APPLY YOUR KNOWLEDGE

10. Authentication is the process of proving that you are who you say you are. This may give you the ability to logon, but it does not automatically give you the ability to perform tasks or manipulate data. Authorization is a set of permission to do things, such as use a printer, read a file, and create a backup.

11. You can create groups or use built-in groups that have appropriate access to resources, or rights to do tasks. You can then place people in those groups and give them only the access they need. It is also easier to manage access to resources and task permissions by a few groups than by thousands of users.

12. Yes. Fortunately, you can usually groups files and the need to control them under folders, giving yourself less to manage.

13. Applications can acquire access to resources because they are acting under the context of the user account running them. Their privileges with the resource are governed by the rights of the user. Applications can also gain access because they or some part of their processes is running under the context of a service account.

14. Two things may cause changes to current security settings. First, the new operating system has the potential for greater control over resources and actions. It possible to tighten security, or the desired security level can be set. Second, the close studying of resources and access opportunities can mean a change to policy.

15. Knowledge of existing and planned rollouts enables you to factor in the possible changes to the resources you have been studying. It allows possible changes to the schedule of these activities or to the implementation of your security design.

16. Technical support services are critical to the smooth rollout of any change in IT. Security is no exception. Treat support services as a resource that must be protected and utilized to promote security. Planning must also ensure their access to resources in the new design that they need.

Answers to Exam Questions

1. **C.** The only locations that have a local copy of the database are New York, France, and Britain. To determine the answer, all you must do is add the numbers at each site. (See the questions scenario.)

2. **D.** Three factors determine whether there is adequate connectivity between sites: line speed, available bandwidth, and usage patterns. Line speed and available bandwidth are documentable facts. Usage patterns can be recorded, but to really determine whether there are adequate resources, you must examine the needs of the users in each site. There may be little need for access to the database, or the needs may be occasional. In this case, even the slowest of line speeds may be perfectly adequate. On the other hand, users may require instant access to information. Consider the value of immediate access to current stock market information, or the capability to consult with a medical expert when a life is at stake. (See the section "Assess Available Connectivity.")

3. **B, D.** Sally's presentation lacks the facts that will answer management's concerns. It's not enough to present new technology as an answer to a security concern. Sally should have been prepared to document her answers to questions about line

APPLY YOUR KNOWLEDGE

speed, bandwidth, and processing power. The real issue for management here was not whether IPSec was a good fit technically, but how much it would cost them to add more bandwidth and to possible upgrade systems. Sally should have anticipated these types of questions and been prepared to answer them—or, better still, presented the answers before the questions were asked. (See the section "Assess Net Available Bandwidth.")

4. **E.** Windows 2000 does support ATM. The problem here is L2TP. In its current implementation, you must tunnel it over IP. (See the section "Assess Available Connectivity.")

5. **C.** The use of modems alone does not allow any user to instantly compromise security. Cable modems do have some interesting security issues of their own, but the real issue here has to do with the addition of modems. Placing a firewall and locking down access to networks is a good step, but it is ruined if you turn around and open new doors that can be used to access your network. (See the section "External Access.")

6. **B, D.** Leased lines are expensive but can provide a secure mechanism for two or more businesses to share confidential information. In some circumstances, this would provide the ideal way for the businesses to trade goods. If many businesses became involved, cost alone would get prohibitive. DSL is especially well suited for Web browsing because users will have high-speed downloads. This is not particularly well suited for business-to-business e-commerce, however, because the speed varies in both directions. Email over public telephone lines may be okay for home users. (See the section "Assess Available Connectivity.")

7. **B.** These numbers should make you take notice and begin to watch for a pattern, but occasional peaks in network activity are going to happen. They become significant only if they are sustained over time. (See the section "Assess Available Bandwidth.")

8. **A.** It looks like this information has been obtained over time. The 20% increase in latency would be enough of a warning sign. The other issues tell you that it's time to investigate. (See the section "Assess Available Bandwidth.")

9. **D.** L2TP is a tunneling protocol, not an authentication mechanism. Remote Installation Service (RIS), is a method for the rapid deployment and installation of operating systems. Answer D does not list all the authentication mechanisms, but it is the only list where all elements are correct. (See the section "Analyze Data and Systems Access Method.")

10. **B.** Applications will always be capable of adding their own layer of security. The question is whether this is a good idea. If security is strong in the operating system, it would be a good idea if applications use this security layer. Security is difficult to perfect, and it is easy to destroy. For example, if an application requires its own passwords and then allows them to be sent in clear text across the network, then the application has become a security risk. (See the section "Analyze Data and Systems Access Method.")

11. **A, B, C, E.** Users will usually do things to help them remember passwords—they may write them down or make they easy to guess. The Windows NT SAM may be found on a carelessly stored ERD or backup tape, and then be used to obtain passwords. Anyone can download a password-

cracking program from the Internet. A Windows 98 boot disk will not have a copy of the SAM. Reverse-engineering any protocol to write your own password-cracking utility, or to quickly determine passwords, is not an option for most people. (See the section "Backups and Other Data Stores.")

12. **D.** Peter can use information on the current operating system to begin his study, but he also should spend some time investigating how things really are used. The current system may not correctly model the best use of the system. (See the section "Analyze Network Roles and Responsibilities.")

13. **A.** The fact than an administrator can run the program while a user cannot is a dead giveaway that there is a file system or registry permission issue. This means that the program did not successfully follow guidelines for running on Windows NT. The same problems can occur with Windows 20000. (See the section "Resource Ownership.")

14. **A, C, D, E, F.** Just because someone's spouse works for another company is not reason to suspect foul play; you would have to suspect most of your workforce. Likewise, did anyone ever think that a raise was significant? However, the hardware and software mentioned in the other choices can be sources of security breeches in your network. (See the section "Analyze Data and Systems Access Method.")

15. **E.** The MCSE certification does not tell you anything about the programming ability of the person who has it. (See the section "Identify Existing and Planned Upgrades and Rollouts.")

16. **B.** In any company, there are politics. Although you may be astute in figuring out which way the wind is blowing, it is possible that you will be wrong. It is far better to understand the politics and still make sure that you are in the best possible position, no matter what happens. (See the section "Domain Structure.")

Suggested Readings and Resources

1. Technet Article: "Planning Your Implementation of MS Exchange Server."

2. Technet Article: "Designing the Active Directory Structure."

3. Marcus, J. Scott. *Designing Wide Area Networks and Internetworks, A Practical Guide.* Addison-Wesley, 1999.

4. www.networkmagazine.com

ANALYZING SECURITY REQUIREMENTS

This chapter covers the following Microsoft-specified objective for the "Analyzing Security Requirements" section of the Designing Security for a Microsoft Windows 2000 Network exam:

Design a security baseline for a Windows 2000 network that includes domain controllers, operations masters, application servers, file and print servers, RAS servers, desktop computers, portable computers, and kiosks.

▶ A security baseline is an important marker against which to judge a secured system. This is the combination of settings and hallmarks that should be in existence before the machine is placed into service on your network or as a standalone system. It is not enough to place external controls on your systems. Placing networks behind firewalls, locking server doors, and other physical techniques does not excuse hardening the operating system against known risks. The reality of risk is influenced by the use and usage patterns of each machine.

CHAPTER 4

Designing a Security Baseline

▶ This is a pretty tough area to swallow in one piece. Like any large meal, start with dessert. Fire up your test lab and start playing with the Security Configuration and Analysis console. Here are the things you should do to learn this material:

- If you are already familiar with these tools, or if you have used the Windows NT 4.0 version, proceed. If this is new to you, read the section "Understanding Security Templates and Computer Policy Introduction" in this chapter. An additional white paper is available at
  `www.microsoft.com/windows2000.`

- Make sure that the system you are testing on is isolated from any production system.

- Load the Security Configuration and Analysis snap-in and the Security Templates snap-in into a fresh MMC console. Don't forget to save the console so that you can bring it back later.

▶ Import a template into Security Configuration and Analysis, and analyze your system against it.

▶ Modify the security settings and run the analysis again.

▶ Examine each provided security template. Using the charts in this chapter, begin to compare and contrast them.

▶ Read the ITS case study at the beginning of this chapter. Where do you think each of the templates could be used to set security baselines for ITS systems?

▶ Proceed with studying the approach written in the chapter.

INTRODUCTION

Now that you are quite comfortable with the steps needed to evaluate the current system, you are ready to begin architecting your security design by planning a security structure for each specialized Windows 2000 computer in your network. This chapter examines the basics of doing so. If you are to maintain this security baseline and improve on it, you will want to learn more about Group Policies. Group Policies is a way to set and manage configuration settings for groups of computers and users. You will become skilled at using it in Chapter 8, "Designing Security Policy Inheritance."

You will also be seeing a lot of new areas: listings of user rights, security options, audit, and account policies. These areas are not explained in detail. Often it can seem as if you are making choices without knowing all the facts. Remember, this is a baseline; as you travel farther down the road in designing security for Windows 2000, you will learn to appreciate the statement in the introduction that this process is iterative and nondeterministic—that is, you will be coming back and visiting areas of your design more than once, and possibly in different orders. For now, concentrate on creating a baseline for each role that a Windows 2000 computer can play. You will need to examine each type separately. Later chapters will consider the specifics of resource protection, audit, authentication, and the securing of connections. You will first concentrate on the specifications for different types of computers.

This process can be defined in three steps:

STEP BY STEP

4.1 Three steps to Baselining Win2k Roles

1. Understand the context within which most Windows 2000 computers will work: Active Directory.

2. Learn where initial security settings are derived (templates) and how to change them.

3. Examine each computer role. Learn what it is used for, and then determine the level of security, or the baseline for this system.

CASE STUDY: ITS

BACKGROUND

ITS sells products to truck stops around the country. The company carries a large inventory of everything from antennas, blankets, and coffee pots that plug into truck cigarette lighters, to chips and salsa. A sales force of 200 travels to the truck stops to sell and to introduce new product lines to truck stop managers. ITS also markets an inventory control service called FullStock. Bar code readers are used for inventory counts, and ITS maintains the customers inventory on computers in Akron, Ohio. This allows ITS to recommend order quantities and dates to the customer, which gains them a lot of repeat business. Inventory counts are transmitted to Akron by connecting the scanner to the Akron computer via a phone.

PROBLEM STATEMENT

Data security is the single most pressing issue.

Information Systems Manager

We have a number of concerns with security on our current system. The first issue to us is to make sure that the inventory information is secured.

Systems Administrator

We keep the inventory data in a SQL database, and we feel that we've got it well protected. What I'm not comfortable with is the NT Workstations that our users have on their desktop. We have to give our users more permission than they should have to allow them to run the software. That can

impact the servers they connect to as well. Just the other day, Joe, our sales manager, accidentally deleted the entire contents of the D drive on the sales department server.

Sales Manager

Our customer inventory information is confidential. Imagine what would happen if our competitors could get at our information. It hasn't happened, yet but I hear a lot about disgruntled employees destroying information, or spying on their own company and selling information to its competitors. I need to know that this can't happen here.

Help Desk Staff

I spend most of my time repairing PEBKAC errors, you know, "problem exists between keyboard and chair." Users just don't get it. They shouldn't touch their system. They load games and other "productivity utilities" and then wonder why the system doesn't work. Other times they delete files that they don't recognize. This usually turns out to be something important like a system file, or the client software for the FullStock program. This morning our office manager removed Network Neighborhood. It seems he'd been up on some Web site that told him he was making his system vulnerable to hackers on the Internet and then told him how to remove it. Of course, then I got a call from him that the network was down.

CURRENT SYSTEM

The process is currently automated.

continues

CASE STUDY: ITS

continued

Sales Manager

Our sales reps use a handheld bar code scanner to scan shelf labels at the stores. They enter inventory counts at that time. Each rep is expected to visit each of his customers to take monthly inventory. When the count is complete, the information is transmitted via phone lines back to Akron, and the inventory database gets updated. At night we run inventory reports that are Fed Ex'd to the customer. The reports show inventory status, recommended orders, and our price quotes. Order quantities are automatically adjusted—quick-selling product order size is increased, and slow-moving merchandise is decreased. Seasonal adjustments are also accounted for. Our sales reps can dial into our system in the morning and see the same reports. He then calls the customer to get order approval. Many customers accept our suggestions without discussion; they just tell us to keep their bins full. For them we don't send the reports, and the sales rep does not contact them via phone. When the sales rep next visits them, they can go over the reports and decide to drop a product that's not selling, or adjust other order quantities.

Accounting Manager

We enter the invoice information into our accounting program and can keep track of customer information. We invoice the customer when we ship and have the data to use to follow up on payments.

Warehouse Manager

The system generates pick lists, and my staff fills the orders. UPS picks up twice a day, and we can handle overnight as well as same-day deliveries in some areas. The system does a good job of giving me forecast reports so that I can keep my inventory current. We are planning to open three warehouses this year in San Jose, Atlanta, and South Dakota.

ENVIRONMENT

Windows NT, SQL Server, and RAS servers serve as the platform for the inventory control system.

Information Technology Manager

The business side of the company runs on UNIX, and we have no plans to change. The FullStock program is on Windows NT. I wanted to move it to UNIX, but it's just too expensive.

System Admin

Our RS6000 is not involved in this process. We have two Windows NT 4.0 domains with 20 servers. Two RAS servers are available and can handle up to 400 simultaneous connections. Data from scanners is automatically uploaded into the SQL database. Reports are run at night but can be generated at any time. The SQL data is replicated to two other servers for redundancy and to help balance the load. Office staff can access reports and make queries against the database. Sales reps can dial in and look at reports, as well as transmit orders that they complete on their Windows 98 laptops. Invoices are generated by the system, and then the data is bulk-copied to a file that can be imported into our Accounts Receivable system.

We have 100 Windows NT Workstations and 50 Windows 98 machines here at the office. Our sales reps have Pentium laptops running

CASE STUDY: ITS

Windows 98. We will be replacing these laptops with Pentium IIIs and Windows 2000 Professional this spring.

ENVISIONED SYSTEM

Windows 2000 is envisioned as the new platform.

Sales Manager

Our reps are getting new laptops, and they'll be able to download customer inventory information to them. They can show the reports to their customers and enter orders, check payment history, and display new product catalog information. If Internet connectivity is possible, they'll be able to get current information and even place the order before leaving the store.

Information Systems Manager

We're migrating this system to Windows 2000 because I hear that it offers increased security. I'm skeptical, but I've approved a training budget for systems and help desk staff.

Systems Admin

We'll have domains in our new warehouses and will keep inventory information updated there as well. Gradually we'll upgrade all Windows NT Servers to Windows 2000 Advanced Server, but our budget will not allow the necessary hardware purchases to move all systems at once. There's going to be some Windows NT Servers around for some time to come. It's also going to take a while to upgrade our Windows NT Workstations and Windows 98 systems to Windows 2000

Professional. Where the hardware is compatible, we will do so right away. Others may have to wait. We'll purchase hardware for servers first. The sales reps will be getting new laptops with Windows 2000 Professional preloaded.

SECURITY

A new design created for efficiency and to maximize profit has generated increased security concerns.

Sales Manager

The sales reps are now going to have lots of confidential customer and company information on their laptops. What happens if the laptop is lost or stolen?

Warehouse Manager

If customers can place their own orders, how will I know whether an order is real? I don't want to see stock disappear. Could internal folks, or outsiders, divert stock to themselves and charge it to a nonexistent customer, or incorrectly to one of our customers?

Systems Admin

It has been hell to administer Windows NT security. I've heard that Windows 2000 is a lot more complicated, so I'm going to have a lot to learn. When I started here, we had one Windows NT Server, and I grew with the company. I can't afford that kind of time learning how to secure our new systems. I can't afford to make mistakes.

continues

CASE STUDY: ITS

continued

Accounting Manager

If sales reps have access to my customer files, how can I be sure that they aren't changing information?

Accounts Receivable Clerk

The last time they "fixed" the system, I couldn't do my job for a week. I guess if they want me to have all that time to surf the Internet, its okay by me.

PERFORMANCE

Every business now believes that it has to be capable of operating 24 × 7. The capability to do this puts an increased load on all systems, including users, help desk, and infrastructure.

Sales Manager

The reps are good salespeople, not computer nerds. The new laptops and system must not put any new pressure on them to learn new computer skills.

Systems Admin

A total of 250-plus users, including sales reps, customers, and internal folks, must be supported during our normal business day, which is 7 a.m. to 7 p.m. Peak times are mornings. We expect that our new capability of customer access will generate new requirements for access to information 24 × 7. The summer is a particularly busy time because the truck stops obtain significant business from people on vacation.

We feel that we have an excess of bandwidth internally, but we are a little concerned about increased external access.

Information Technology Manager

The system must protect itself and our information assets. It must be reliable and available 24 × 7.

MAINTAINABILITY

A commitment to long-term support is imperative.

Sales Manager

Change is good, but I'm worried about all this new technology out in the field.

Information Technology Manager

My people are the best. They will make this system work.

AVAILABILITY

As sales manager, I can tell you that sales folks often spend time with their customer reports while they are in their hotel rooms at night. They need to be able to check data online at any time. When they are at the customer site, it would be very embarrassing if they couldn't get to the customer's data. We also expect that customers may want to place orders at odd times. The system just has to be available any time they want it.

ANALYSIS

ITS has a number of security and work organization issues that may be answered with appropriate security structures present in Windows 2000. One of the company's challenges will be to secure laptops for sales reps, warehouse stations, and office worker PCs. This is the perfect opportunity for ITS to develop standard templates that it can use to configure any new system before it is distributed. As older systems are replaced, new systems will start out locked down appropriately for their use.

Problems with applications that require administrative access to run will need to be dealt with. Legacy applications will not run any better on Windows 2000. However, with the increased flexi-bility of the level of application, a policy for an OU of users could be created and used until the applications can be updated. This OU might have registry and file settings relaxed, or the primary PC issue could have the relaxed settings and an organizational unit (OU, explained later) of sales-people; other systems that need tighter security could be set up.

ACTIVE DIRECTORY INTRODUCTION

If you do not understand Active Directory, then you do not understand Windows 2000. How can you secure something that you don't understand?

Active Directory is an enterprise-class directory service that is scalable and fully integrated at the operating system level. It can simplify administration and make it easier for users to find resources. Some of its features include the following:

◆ Administrative privileges and security settings are controlled in hierarchical information structures.

◆ User and resource management is simplified.

◆ The same hierarchical structure that makes administration easy also helps users find printers and other resources.

◆ Administrators can create and assign policies over several Active Directory containers. These containers, sites, domains, or organizational units (OUs) contain users and computers (these are explained further throughout this chapter). Policies are applied to the container to control or administer it. Each policy is a collection of settings that can be automatically applied and refreshed.

◆ Support for Kerberos V5, Secure Sockets Layer v3. and Transport Layer Security authentication is provided.

◆ LDAP is spoken here. Lightweight Directory Access Protocol (LDAP) can be used to access and manage the information in the directory.

◆ If it can be networked, you may be able to manage and configure it with Active Directory.

◆ Active Directory Service Interfaces (ADSI) is available to aid developers.

Directory Service

The Active Directory Service is composed of the following:

◆ The directory store that stores the objects (servers, files, printers, network users, and computer accounts). The directory is stored in the %systemroot%\ntds\ntds.dit file on a domain controller. Although you do not have to use an NTFS partition, you should so that you may more easily protect it. (No Active Directory, no domain controller.) Private data is secured, and public data is stored on a shared system volume so that it can be replicated to other domain controllers. The following types of data are replicated:

- **Domain data**—Objects and configuration data.

- **Forest data**—Domain, trees, and location of domain controllers and global catalogs.

- **Schema data**—Definitions of the schema classes and attributes.

More on each of these items later.

◆ Directory data, which consists of these items:

- The set of rules (schema) that defines classes of objects and attributes

- The global catalog that contains some information on every object in the directory

- Objects

- Configuration data: forests, domain, trees, and locations

◆ Query and index mechanisms.

◆ Replication service.

◆ Integration with security subsystem.

To use the features of the Active Directory, a computer must be running the Active Directory client software. Active Directory Client software resides on every Windows 2000 computer and is available for Windows 9x on the Windows 2000 and Windows 2000 Advanced Server installation CD-ROMs. Active Directory client software for Windows NT systems should be available soon.

Active Directory and Security

Active Directory stores information on access control. The user who logs on to the network is authenticated with information stored in the Active Directory. Information required to authorize access to objects (the Discretionary Access Control List of DACL) also resides in Active Directory. The Security Accounts Manager (SAM) is not required but is present to provide compatibility where necessary with down-level clients. For more information on how SAM and Active Directory work to provide authentication, see Chapter 10, "Designing an Authentication Strategy."

Domain Trees and Forests

A domain in Active Directory is represented by a DNS domain name. It requires at least one domain controller. A forest is a collection of one or more domains that share a common schema, configuration, and Global Catalog. The Global Catalog is a collection of forest-wide data. Groups of domains within the forest that have contiguous DNS domain names (see Figure 4.1) are called trees. Many trees can exist within the forest (see Figure 4.2).

FIGURE 4.1
A forest with a single tree.

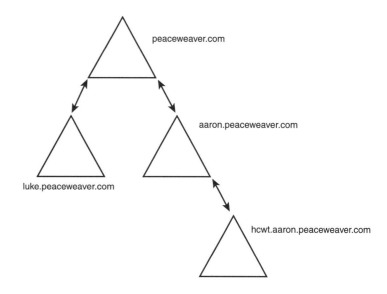

FIGURE 4.2
A multiple-tree forest.

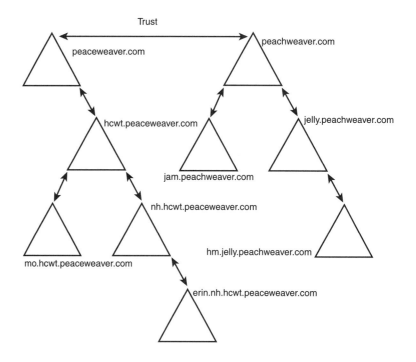

Trusts

Windows NT domains could share resources by creating one-way trusts between domains. Windows 2000 enables two-way transitive trusts based on Kerberos v5. Kerberos is an IETF standard (RFC 1510, RFC 1964) and is respected for its secure authentication services (see Chapter 10).

Trusts in Windows 2000 are automatically created between the forest root domain and the root domain of each domain tree added to the forest. Users and computers can be authenticated between any domains in the domain tree or in the forest. Authentication, therefore, allows them limited access to any domain. Resource access and other privileges must be extended for them to gain access or exercise privileges. We show this by a double-headed arrow placed between domains (see Figure 4.3). In this figure, because peaceweaver.com trusts aaron.peaceweaver.com, and aaron.peaceweaver.com trusts hcwt.aaron.peaceweaver.com, then peaceweaver.com trusts hcwt.aaron.peaceweaver.com. Users in peaceweaver.com can access (with permission) resources in hcwt.aaron.peaceweaver.com.

External trusts must be created with pre-Windows 2000 domains, if desired. Upgraded Windows NT domains maintain any one-way trusts that may already be established.

External trusts are one-way trusts that exist between a domain in your forest and another domain outside the forest.

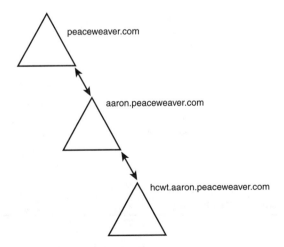

FIGURE 4.3
Transitive trusts.

More information on trusts, including shortcut trusts, explicit trusts, and trust paths, can be found in Chapter 10.

Organizational Units

OUs are Active Directory containers. They can be used to organize users, groups, computers, and other OUs. They cannot contain objects from other domains. OUs (see Figure 4.4) are the smallest scope to which a Group Policy can be defined and administrative authority can be delegated.

Sites

Sites map to the physical structure of your network. Sites may be defined by sets of computers in one or more IP subnets. Computers in a site must have good connectivity. WANs usually employ multiple sites for efficient replication of directory information.

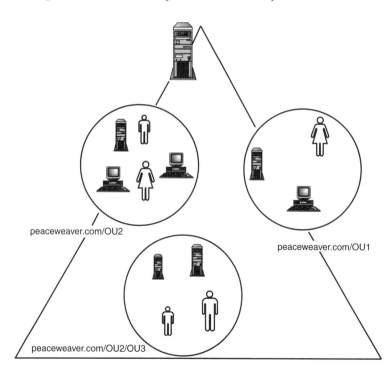

FIGURE 4.4
Organizational units.

Domains generally map the logical structure of your organization. No correlation must exist between the site structure (physical network) and the domain structure (logical network). Multiple domains can reside in a site, and multiple sites can make up one domain.

If you use the Active Directory Sites and Services console to specify site information, Active Directory will use this information to direct efficient use of network resources. Service requests from domain controllers will be directed to available services in the same site. Directory replication efforts can be reduced, thus also reducing the use of network bandwidth.

Clients dynamically determine which site they are in at boot. A domain controller's site is consistent; it is determined by the site its server object belongs to in the directory.

Domains

Domains, which are groups of network objects (users, groups, and computers), are security boundaries. Security policies and settings are maintained in one domain. Administrators in one domain do not have rights to set policies in any domain other than their own.

Windows NT domains were limited by the number of user accounts. Multiple domains often were created due to this fact, and management of these domains followed several models. Typically, domains were organized into master domains, which managed user and group accounts, and resource domains, which managed resources. If more than one master domain was needed, a multimaster domain model was followed. In this case, resource domains required multiple trust relationships, one with each master domain.

UNDERSTANDING SECURITY TEMPLATES AND COMPUTER POLICY INTRODUCTION

Although you may wish to develop your own rules, and although over time you may find a better way to implement your baseline, Microsoft has made it easy to begin. You can choose from a number of security policy templates available, all conveniently configured to fit major system types. Templates can be applied during installation or at any time. Applying new templates on existing systems may require additional planning, however, and should not be done on production systems without testing.

These templates represent Microsoft's design of baseline security. You need to understand your organization's security policy and the makeup of your infrastructure to determine which, if any, of these templates is correct for your systems.

Templates can be modified by working in the script file or by editing the template in the Security Templates snap-in. Security settings can be modified by setting Local Computer Policy. In a Windows 2000 Active Directory-based enterprise, templates can also be used to enforce security policy at the sites, domain, and organizational unit using Group Policy. Using Group Policy simplifies domain administration by configuring security for multiple computers at once. When you modify templates, they do not automatically apply themselves. You must import them using the Security Configuration and Analysis snap-in on a single computer, or by importing a template into a Group Policy object.

Predefined security templates are listed in Table 4.1.

TABLE 4.1

SECURITY TEMPLATES

Template	Filename	Notes
Default workstation	Defltwk.inf	Applied during a clean install of Windows 2000 Professional.
Default server	Defltsv	Applied during a clean install of Windows 2000 Server.
Default domain	Defltdc	Applied during a controller promotion of Windows 2000 Server to a domain controller.
Basic workstation Basic server Basic domain controller	Basicwk.inf Basicsv.inf Basicdc.inf	Basic: Reverts to the default setting applied. Does not modify user rights. Can be used to apply security settings to a computer upgraded to Windows 2000.

Template	Filename	Notes
Compatible workstation or server	Compatws.inf	Compatible: Lowers security settings on common application access files, folders, and registry keys.
Secure workstation or server	Securews.inf	Uses recommended security settings for all security areas except files, folders, and registry keys.
Secure domain controller	Securedc.inf	Settings that impact the operating system are changed. This enables SMB packet signing. It does not change any DACLs. It also warns of the installation of unsigned drivers. Application of this template assumes application of the default (during installation) or basic (after upgrade) templates.
Highly secure workstation or server	Hisecws.inf	Uses settings for network communications. Offers maximum protection for network traffic and protocols
Highly secure domain controller	Hisecdc.inf	used between Windows 2000 computers. No communication takes place with Windows 95 or Windows NT. Packet signing is required, as is signing of drivers. Application of this template assumes that the default (during installation) or basic (after upgrade) template has been applied. Application of this template requires SMB signing; the application of the secure template just enables SMB signing.
Dedicated domain controller	Dedicadc.inf	Can no longer run server-based applications on domain controllers. Default settings for local users are defined like those of workstations and servers.
No terminal services ID	Notssid	Removes the terminal server ID.
Optional components workstation	Ocfilesw.inf	Applies security for optional components, such as DNS and DHCP.
Optional components server	Ocfiless.inf	

Security templates include settings, such as these:

◆ Account Policy settings, such as password, lockout, and Kerberos policies

◆ Local policies, such as user rights and logging

◆ Security for registry keys

◆ Security for the local file system

◆ Security and startup for local services

◆ Group membership (restricted groups)

◆ Event Viewer settings

> **Restricted Groups**   Restricted groups are groups whose member-ship can be tightly controlled. Groups and users not defined in Restricted groups are removed from the group. A typical Restricted group is the Administrators group.

You can modify security templates by copying and pasting, or importing or exporting all or some of the *.inf file attributes. All security attributes can be contained in a security template except IP Security and Public Key Policies. You can create a personal database to store customized templates.

Templates are viewed, defined, or further modified using the Security Template snap-in.

Templates can be applied using the following:

◆ secedit, a command-line tool

◆ The security Configuration and Analysis Tool

◆ Importing to Group Policy objects

Windows 2000 provides the command-line tool secedit.exe to assign security templates to computers.

Templates should not be applied to production systems without test-ing. Areas may change that could affect the operation of applications. To use templates for configuration, follow Step by Step 4.2.

STEP BY STEP

4.2 Implementing Templates Using Security Configuration and Analysis MMC Snap-In

1. Add the Security Configuration and Analysis snap-in to the MMC.

2. Right-click the Security Configuration and Analysis snap-in in the Console window.

3. Click Open Database (see Figure 4.5).

4. If you have not created a database, type the name of the database in the File Name box.

5. If you have created a database, select that database.

6. In the Import Template window, double-click the template to import. By default, the window points to the system-root\security\template folder. The template is imported.

7. Right-click the Security Configuration and Analysis console item.

8. Select Configure Computer Now.

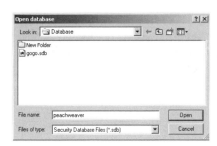

FIGURE 4.5
The Open Database window.

After configuration is complete, to view the information in the database, perform an analysis by following the steps in Step by Step 4.3.

> **NOTE** **What, No "New"?** There is no Create New Database option. You must select Open Database and then enter the name of the new database you wish to create in the File Name text box. When you click the Open button, a database file using that name will be created.

STEP BY STEP

4.3 Analyze Computer Security Settings

1. Right-click Security Configuration and Analysis.

2. Select Analyze Computer Now.

3. The analysis shows the settings in the policy, tells how well the computer matches them, and gives the effective policy. A red X indicates noncompliance. A green check mark indicates compliance.

CREATING OR MODIFYING SECURITY TEMPLATES USING SECURITY CONFIGURATION AND ANALYSIS

If you want to change the security policy on a single machine (one that's not in a domain), open the Local Computer Policy from the Administrative Tools Menu, and make your changes. A Local

NOTE   **Template Location**   Security templates are found in the %system root%\security\templates folder.

Computer Policy cannot override domain-based policy.

To examine or modify a template, use the Microsoft Management Console snap-in Security Template. Instructions are given in Step by Step 4.4.

STEP BY STEP

4.4 Working with Security Templates

1. At the START/Run button, enter MMC.

2. Choose Add/Remove Snap-in from the Console menu.

3. From the Standalone tab, click the Add button.

4. Click Security Templates, and close the Add Snap-in window.

5. Select the template to modify or view.

6. From the Action menu, select Save As.

7. Name the template and click OK.

8. From the console tree, select your new template.

Template Sections

Security settings include these:

- ◆ **Account Policies**—When the Account Policies are set in the Group Policy object for the Domain Controllers, they affect an entire domain. (When set in the Group Policy object for an OU, they affect the local account database of member servers and workstations.)

  - **Password Policy**—Includes password length, history, and complexity requirements.

  - **Account Lockout Policy**—Forces lockout after failed logon attempts, and specifies how long accounts are frozen.

  - **Kerberos Authentication Policy**—Sets maximum lifetime for the ticket.

◆ **Local Computer Policies**—Local Computer Policies set in the Local Security Policy of the computer affect the local computer but may be overridden by policies set at the site, domain, or OU level. If a policy item is not set at any other level, then the local policy remains in effect.

  • **Audit Policy**—Can be set to record successful or unsuccessful attempts at a multitude of tasks. See Chapter 6, "Designing an Audit Policy."

  • **User Rights Assignment**—Controls rights assigned to user accounts and security groups. Determines who can log on locally and who can shut down the system—in other words, who can do what (see Chapter 10 for details).

  • **Security Options**—Windows NT administrators will recognize favorite registry settings, now just a click away. Many of these specific policies are discussed through out the book.

◆ **Event Log Policies**—Controls event log retention, access, and file size.

◆ **Restricted Group Policies**—Manage and enforce membership of built-in or user-defined groups that have special rights. Membership in groups on local computers adheres to the settings here.

◆ **System Services Policies**—Specify startup mode, disable a service, and configure system services to operative with minimum rights and permissions. Also refine auditing to monitor for inappropriate actions by services.

◆ **Registry Policies**—Configure security and auditing for registry keys and subkeys. Information on access permissions is discussed in Chapter 5, "Securing Resources." Information on audit settings is covered in Chapter 6.

◆ **File System Policies**—Configure security for files and folders. Assign a group, such as Administrators, to have full control over folders that are critical (such as system files), and to grant others read-only access. Prevent certain users from viewing files and folders. Also set audit level for files and folders.

Design a security baseline for a Windows 2000 network that includes domain controllers, operations masters, application servers, file and print servers, RAS servers, desktop computers, portable computers, and kiosks.

DOMAIN CONTROLLERS BASELINE

This category considers the basic domain controller definition, describes the available templates, and makes recommendations.

Role Definition

A Windows 2000 Server that has been configured using the Active Directory Installation Wizard is a domain controller. The wizard installs and configures the Active Directory Service. A domain controller manages user logon processing, authentication, and directory searches and also stores directory data.

Domains can have multiple domain controllers. A small organization may need only one domain, while larger organizations with multiple locations may choose to have several domains to ensure high availability and fault tolerance.

Multimaster and single-master directory replication synchronizes directory data on domain controllers. Unlike Windows NT domains, there is no primary or backup domain controller. In Windows NT domains, a single primary domain controller per domain stored the only writeable directory. Multiple backup domain controllers stored read-only copies, which were updated via single-master replication. All Windows 2000 domain controllers store writeable directories.

The default installation for Windows 2000 Server and Advanced Server is the standalone server model. Servers may be promoted to domain controller status or may be demoted (in most cases) by running the dcpromo wizard.

Templates

Three templates are available for domain controllers: basicdc, securedc, and hisecdc. The defltdc template is applied during the domain controller upgrade on a newly installed Windows 2000 Server. An upgraded Windows NT domain controller with the basicsv and basicdc templates applied has security settings equivalent to the freshly installed and promoted domain controller.

Template settings for Account Policies, Local Policies, and Event Log Policies are displayed in tables that follow. None of the templates have default settings for system services set in the templates. System Service settings are discussed, if appropriate under individual roles, or as they apply to other strategies in later chapters. User rights and Restricted groups are also not defined by default in the templates. User rights and Restricted groups are discussed in Chapter 10. Permission settings for registry keys and the file system are analyzed in Chapter 5.

In each template you will find many areas to be "not defined." This simply means that this template will not change any system settings in those areas.

As you examine Tables 4.2 through 4.5, try to notice the difference among the templates. Try to imagine which template would be appropriate for of ITS's domain controllers. Remember that these represent templates; they are meant to be applied against existing systems that have things already set. For example, domain controllers by their nature have Kerberos policy settings. None of these templates will change those settings, if applied.

TABLE 4.2

DOMAIN TEMPLATE ACCOUNT POLICY SETTINGS

Item	basicdc	securedc	hsecdc
Password Policy			
Enforce password history	Not defined	24 passwords remembered	24 passwords remembered
Maximum password age	Not defined	42 days	42 days

continues

| TABLE 4.2 | *continued* |

DOMAIN TEMPLATE ACCOUNT POLICY SETTINGS

Item	*basicdc*	*securedc*	*hsecdc*
Minimum password age	Not defined	2 days	2 days
Minimum password length	Not defined	8 characters	8 characters
Passwords must meet complexity requirements	Not defined	Enabled	Enabled
Store passwords using reversible encryption for all users in the domain	Not defined	Disabled	Disabled
Account Lockout Policy Account lockout duration	Not defined	30 minutes	0
Account lockout threshold	Not defined	5 invalid logon attempts	5 invalid logon attempts
Reset account lockout counter after. . .	Not defined	30 minutes	30 minutes
Kerberos Policy Enforce user logon restrictions	Not defined	Not defined	Not defined
Maximum lifetime for service ticket	Not defined	Not defined	Not defined
Maximum lifetime for user ticket	Not defined	Not defined	Not defined
Maximum lifetime for user ticket renewal	Not defined	Not defined	Not defined
Maximum tolerance for computer clock synchronization	Not defined	Not defined	Not defined

TABLE 4.3

DOMAIN CONTROLLER AUDIT POLICY

Audit Policy	basicdc	securedc	hisecdc
Audit account logon events	Not defined	Failure	Success, Failure
Audit account management	Not defined	Success, failure	Success, Failure
Audit directory service access	Not defined	Failure	Success, Failure
Audit logon events	Not defined	Failure	Success, Failure
Audit object access	Not defined	No auditing	Success, Failure
Audit policy change	Not defined	Success, Failure	Success, Failure
Audit privilege use	Not defined	Failure	Success, Failure
Audit process tracking	Not defined	No auditing	No auditing
Audit system events	Not defined	No auditing	Success, Failure

TABLE 4.4

DOMAIN CONTROLLER SECURITY OPTIONS

Security Option	basicdc	securedc	hisecdc
Additional restrictions for anonymous connections	Not defined	Do not allow enumeration of SAM accounts and shares	No access without explicit anonymous permissions
Allow server operators to schedule tasks	Not defined	Disabled	Disabled

continues

TABLE 4.4 *continued* DOMAIN CONTROLLER SECURITY OPTIONS			
Security Option	*basicdc*	*securedc*	*hisecdc*
Allow system to be shut down without having to log on	Not defined	Disabled	Disabled
Allow ejection of removable NTFS media	Not defined	Administrators	Administrators
Amount of idle time required before discontinuing session	Not defined	15 minutes	15 minutes
Audit the access of global system objects	Not defined	Disabled	Disabled
Audit use of Backup and Restore privilege	Not defined	Disabled	Disabled
Automatically log off users when logon time expires	Not defined	Enabled	Enabled
Automatically log off users when logon time expires (local)	Not defined	Enabled	Enabled
Clear virtual memory page file when system shuts down	Not defined	Disabled	Enabled
Digitally sign client communications (always)	Not defined	Disabled	Enabled
Digitally sign client communications (when possible)	Not defined	Enabled	Enabled
Digitally sign server communications (always)	Not defined	Disabled	Enabled
Digitally sign server communications (when possible)	Enabled	Enabled	Enabled

Security Option	basicdc	securedc	hisecdc
Disable Ctrl + Alt + Del requirement for logon	Not defined	Disabled	Disabled
Do not display last username in logon screen	Not defined	Disabled	Enabled
LAN Manager authentication level	Not defined	Send NTLM response only	Send NTLMv2 response only; refuse LM and NTLM
Message text for users attempting to log on			
Message title for users attempting to log on			
Number of previous logons to cache	Not defined	10 logons	10 logons
Prevent system maintenance of computer account password	Not defined	Disabled	Disabled
Prevent users from installing printer drivers	Not defined	Enabled	Enabled
Prompt user to change password before expiration	Not defined	14 days	14 days
Recovery console: Allow automatic administrative logon	Not defined	Disabled	Disabled
Recovery console: Allow floppy copy and access to all drives and all folders	Not defined	Disabled	Disabled

continues

| TABLE 4.4 | *continued* |

DOMAIN CONTROLLER SECURITY OPTIONS

Security Option	*basicdc*	*securedc*	*hisecdc*
Rename Administrator account	Not defined	Not defined	Not defined
Rename Guest account	Not defined	Not defined	Not defined
Restrict CD-ROM access to locally logged-on user only	Not defined	Enabled	Enabled
Restrict floppy access to locally logged-on user only	Not defined	Enabled	Enabled
Secure channel: digitally encrypt or sign secure channel data (always)	Not defined	Disabled	Enabled
Secure channel: digitally encrypt secure channel data (when possible)	Not defined	Enabled	Enabled
Secure channel: Digitally sign secure channel data (when possible)	Not defined	Enabled	Enabled
Secure channel: Require strong (Windows 2000 or later) session key	Not defined	Disabled	Enabled
Secure system partition (for RISC platforms only)	Not defined	Not defined	Not defined
Send unencrypted password to connect to third-party SMB servers	Not defined	Disabled	Disabled
Shut down system immediately if incapable of logging security audits	Not defined	Disabled	Disabled

Security Option	basicdc	securedc	hisecdc
Smart card removal behavior	Not defined	Force logoff	Force logoff
Strengthen default permissions of global system objects (such as symbolic links)	Not defined	Enabled	Enabled
Unsigned driver installation behavior	Not defined	Do not allow installation	Do not allow installation
Unsigned nondriver installation behavior	Not defined	Warn, but allow installation	Silently succeed

TABLE 4.5

DOMAIN EVENT LOG TEMPLATE SETTINGS

Event Log	basicdc	securedc	hisecdc
Maximum application log size	512KB	Not defined	Not defined
Maximum security log size	512KB	5120KB	10240KB
Maximum system log size	512KB	Not defined	Not defined
Restrict guest access to application log	Enabled	Disabled	Enabled
Restrict guest access to security log	Disabled	Enabled	Enabled
Restrict guest access to system log	Disabled	Enabled	Enabled
Retain application log	7 days	Not defined	Not defined

continues

TABLE 4.5 | *continued*

DOMAIN EVENT LOG TEMPLATE SETTINGS

Event Log	*basicdc*	*securedc*	*hisecdc*
Retain security log	7 days	Not defined	Not defined
Retain system log	7 days	Not defined	Not defined
Retention method for application log	By days	Not defined	Not defined
Retention method for security log	By days	As needed	As needed
Retention method for system log	By days	Not defined	Not defined
Shut down the computer when the security audit log is full	Not defined	Not defined	Not defined

As these tables show, secure and hisecure templates do not define things such as registry and file system settings. This means that the settings made in the default or basic templates continue to be in effect. It also makes quite clear that if a default or basic template has not been applied before the application of the secure or hisecure template, these types of settings (and any others not defined in secure or hisecure) are not applied. To provide the intended security level, make sure that a basic or default template was applied before you apply the add-on templates.

Recommendations for ITS

Domain controllers that do not need to communicate with down-level clients, and that are tuned for security instead of ease of use or performance, should use the hisecdc template. The basicdc template can be used as a starting point. Many good security techniques are contained within it, and it provides excellent security—far more than the default Windows NT setup. The securedc template places the computer somewhere between the hisecure and the default security provided by default setup or basicdc templates.

ITS has stated that it cannot move all its systems to Windows 2000 at first. The company cannot use the hisecdc template as its baseline because it needs to have NTLM and LM backward compatibility. If ITS has one domain, it can start with securedc and modify the template if any connectivity issues arise. The AD Client for Windows 9x enables these platforms to use NTLMv2, which is significantly more secure. NT can also be configured to use NTLMv2. ITS will need to modify settings on clients, domain controllers, and servers to limit connection authentication to this protocol. ITS also will need to develop a migration strategy so that it can move systems that require more security to Windows 2000 first. ITS does need to realize, however, that some version of NTLM will always be present and available for use, even in native mode or a pure Windows 2000 enterprise. The company should make sure that all systems at that point have their settings changed to require NTLMv2.

Operations Master

Directory data in Active Directory is replicated using the multimaster replication model—that is, data can be changed anywhere and will replicate so that all domain controllers hold the same directory. Some changes, however, are more efficiently served when directed by the operations master. Only the operations master accepts requests for such changes.

Five operations master roles exist. They are assigned to one or more domain controllers. These roles are schema master, domain naming master, relative ID master, primary domain controller (PDC) emulator, and infrastructure master.

Forest-Wide Operations Master Roles

Two operations master roles are forest-wide—that is, only one of each is necessary in the forest.

The schema master controls updates and modifications to the schema. To change the forest schema, you must have access to this domain controller and be a member of the Schema Admins group.

Schema Definition   The schema defines the kinds of objects and the type of information about those objects that can be stored in Active Directory.

Two types of definitions are stored: Attributes are defined once and can be used for many classes. Attributes are things such as Description. Classes or object classes describe objects that can be created such as users. Classes are composed of attributes. A user object, for example, has the attributes Home Directory, Name, Network Address, and so on.

Although a set of basic classes and attributes is supplied, the schema can be dynamically extended by defining new classes and attributes. Because schema changes are global and are not reversible, only experienced developers and network administrators should be allowed to extend the schema, and they should do so through the Active Directory Service Interfaces (ADSI).

The infrastructure master should not also be a Global Catalog server. If it is, it will never replicate changes because it believes that everything is up-to-date.

Writes also must be enabled at the schema master.

The domain naming master is in charge of additions and deletions of domains in the forest and of sites. The domain naming master should be located on a system that also contains the Global Catalog.

There can be only one schema master and one domain naming master in the forest at one time.

Domain-Wide Operations Master Roles

Just as some operations master roles are forest-wide, three roles are domain-wide. Although only one schema master and domain naming master will be present in a forest, one of each of the following roles will exist at each domain.

The relative ID master allocates relative ID sequences to each domain controller in its domain. Each new user, group, or computer in a domain gets a unique security ID. This ID is partially composed of a unique domain security ID (one to a domain) and a relative ID (unique to each security ID created in the domain). Objects can be moved within domains using movetree.exe. This cannot be done if the relative ID master operations master is not available.

The infrastructure master updates the group-to-user references when group members are renamed or changed. Updates are made via multimaster replication. The infrastructure master compares its data to the Global Catalog data and requests changes. It then replicates this information to other domain controllers in the domain. During renaming or moving, it may take a while before changes made are reflected in the GUI. This does not mean that group membership or user IDs are temporarily suspended; it is only an artifact of the environment.

The PDC emulator acts as a Windows NT PDC if non-Windows 2000 clients are in the domain, or if Windows NT BDCs are present. It can process password changes and replicate updates to the BDCs. In native mode, the PDC emulator receives preferential replication of password changes, and a failed authentication at another domain controller (due to bad password) will be forwarded to the PDC emulator before the logon is rejected.

There can be only one PDC emulator, one infrastructure master, and one relative ID master in a domain at one time.

Operations Master Locations

The first domain controller created in a new domain becomes the relative ID master, the primary domain controller emulator, and the infrastructure master. These are the three operations master roles in the domain. The first domain created in the forest (the forest root domain) holds the forest-wide operations master roles of schema master and naming master. In a single domain controller domain, that domain controller holds all the roles. A multiple controller domain can have a standby operations master domain controller that can be used in case of failure of the operations master domain controller.

Operation master roles can be moved to other domain controllers. However, the infrastructure master and the Global Catalog host (the domain controller that maintains the Global Catalog) should not be the same domain controller.

NOTE **Global Catalog Composition** The Global Catalog is composed of a replica of every object in Active Directory. This replica contains a limited number of the object's attributes. The global catalog is built automatically by Active Directory replication. Its purpose is to enable network logon by providing universal group membership information to a domain controller, and to enable directory information search regardless of which domain in the forest actually holds the data.

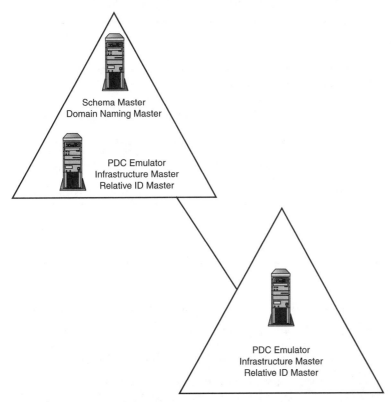

Schema Master
Domain Naming Master

PDC Emulator
Infrastructure Master
Relative ID Master

PDC Emulator
Infrastructure Master
Relative ID Master

FIGURE 4.6
Operations master assignments.

N O T E **Admin Tool Location**   If the Schema Management snap-in is not available, it can be installed by double-clicking on the adminpak.msi file in the installation cd-rom\i386 folder.

Step by Steps 4.5, 4.6, and 4.7 provide information on how you can find the location of the operation masters. You can also use REPLMON (installation CD-ROM, support tools) to see all the operations masters in one tool.

STEP BY STEP

4.5 Identifying Schema Operations Master

1. Open the Active Directory Schema snap-in (schmmgmt).

2. Target the appropriate forest.

3. In the console tree, right-click Active Directory Schema.

4. Click Operations Master.

5. The current schema master appears.

STEP BY STEP

4.6 Identifying Domain Naming Operations Master

1. Open Active Directory Domains and Trusts.

2. Target the appropriate forest.

3. In the console tree, right-click Active Domains and Trusts.

4. Click Operations Master.

5. The current domain naming operations master appears.

STEP BY STEP

4.7 Identifying Domain Operations Masters

1. Open Active Directories Users and Computers.

2. Right-click Active Directory Users and Computers.

3. Click Operations Master.

4. Click the tab of the operations master you wish to identify.

Templates

No special templates are created by default for operations masters.

Recommendations for ITS

No special templates exist for operations masters. The PDC emulator operation master should be configured so that it can communicate with Windows NT BDCs and non-Windows 2000 clients in the domain. This means that when designing templates, you must match the security option LAN Manager Authentication Level with the requirements of these systems. It is always appropriate to save a copy of the original security policy in a database so that it can be reapplied, if necessary.

ITS is probably small enough to have only one domain. Two domain controllers should be sufficient and should provide backup for them.

SERVERS

A server in a Windows 2000 domain can have many roles. A server can be promoted to a domain controller. It can also exist as an application server, a file and print server, a Web server, or a RAS server.

Templates

No secures or hisecss template exists for servers. However, higher-security templates designed for workstations may be used (see Tables 4.6 through 4.9).

TABLE 4.6

SERVER TEMPLATE ACCOUNT POLICY SETTINGS

Item	*basicsv*
Password Policy	
Enforce password history	0 password remembered
Maximum password age	42 days
Minimum password age	0 days
Minimum password length	0 characters
Passwords must meet complexity requirements	Disabled
Store passwords using reversible encryption for all users in the domain	Disabled
Account Lockout Policy	
Account lockout duration	Not defined
Account lockout threshold	0 invalid logon attempts
Reset account lockout counter after. . .	Not defined
Kerberos Policy	
Enforce user logon restrictions	Not defined
Maximum lifetime for service ticket	Not defined
Maximum lifetime for user ticket	Not defined
Maximum lifetime for user ticket renewal	Not defined
Maximum tolerance for computer clock synchronization	Not defined

TABLE 4.7

SERVER AUDIT POLICY

Audit Policy	*Basicsv*
Audit account logon events	No auditing
Audit account management	Not defined
Audit directory service access	Not defined
Audit logon events	No auditing
Audit object access	No auditing
Audit policy change	No auditing

Audit Policy	*Basicsv*
Audit privilege use	No auditing
Audit process tracking	No auditing
Audit system events	No auditing

TABLE 4.8
SERVER SECURITY OPTIONS

Security Option	*basicsv*
Additional restrictions for anonymous connections	None, rely on default permissions
Allow server operators to schedule tasks	Not defined
Allow system to be shut down without having to log on	Disabled
Allow ejection of removable NTFS media	Administrators
Amount of idle time required before discontinuing session	15 minutes
Audit the access of global system objects	Disabled
Audit use of Backup and Restore privilege	Disabled
Automatically log off users when logon time expires	Not defined
Automatically log off users when logon time expires (local)	Enabled
Clear virtual memory page file when system shuts down	Disabled
Digitally sign client communications (always)	Disabled
Digitally sign client communications (when possible)	Enabled
Digitally sign server communications (always)	Disabled
Digitally sign server communications (when possible)	Disabled
Disable Ctrl + Alt + Del requirement for logon	Disabled
Do not display last username in logon screen	Enabled
LAN Manager authentication level	Send LM and NTLM responses

continues

| TABLE 4.8 | *continued* |

SERVER SECURITY OPTIONS

Security Option	*basicsv*
Message text for users attempting to log on	
Message title for users attempting to log on	
Number of previous logons to cache	10 logons
Prevent system maintenance of computer account password	Disabled
Prevent users from installing printer drivers	Enabled
Prompt user to change password before expiration	14 days
Recovery console: Allow automatic administrative logon	Disabled
Recovery console: Allow floppy copy and access to all drives and all folders	Disabled
Rename Administrator account	Not defined
Rename Guest account	Not defined
Restrict CD-ROM access to locally logged on user only	Disabled
Restrict floppy access to locally logged-on user only	Disabled
Secure channel: Digitally encrypt or sign secure channel data (always)	Disabled
Secure channel: Digitally encrypt secure channel data (when possible)	Enabled
Secure channel: Digitally sign secure channel data (when possible)	Enabled
Secure channel: Require strong (Windows 2000 or later) session key	Disabled
Secure system partition (for RISC platforms only)	Not defined
Send unencrypted password to connect to third-party SMB servers	Disabled
Shut down system immediately if incapable of logging security audits	Disabled
Smart card removal behavior	No action
Strengthen default permissions	Enabled
Unsigned driver installation behavior	Not defined
Unsigned non-driver installation behavior	Not defined

TABLE 4.9

SERVER EVENT LOG TEMPLATE SETTINGS

Event Log	securedc
Maximum application log size	512KB
Maximum security log size	512KB
Maximum system log size	512KB
Restrict guest access to application log	Disabled
Restrict guest access to security log	Disabled
Restrict guest access to system log	Disabled
Retain application log	7 days
Retain security log	7 days
Retain system log	7 days
Retention method for application log	By days
Retention method for security log	By days
Retention method for system log	By days
Shut down the computer when the security audit log is full	Disabled

Application Server

Additional security baseline settings for application servers will depend on the server applications that will be running there. If the application meets the specification for the Windows 2000 logo, then all users should be members of the Users group. By default, Windows 2000 gives appropriate nonadministration rights and access to the system. For servers, this includes making the Authenticated Users group a member of the Power Users group. To further secure servers on which only logo applications are run, you can remove this setting. However, if the applications running on the system do not meet the logo requirements, you may need to make all users Power Users to allow them to run the applications. Because Power Users have additional privileges, another way to do this is to use the compatws template. This template will not change policy settings, but it will open up registry and file settings to Windows

NT specifications. This may be adequate for your needs. For more information on Power User access rights, see Chapter 5.

ITS may need to use the compatws template on its SQL Server.

> NOTE
>
> **To Logo or Not to Logo** Any server that is running in compatible mode is considered a security risk. Move toward logoed applications that do not require you to relax security.

File and Print Server

Print servers have special requirements necessary to secure access to printer management. These issues are discussed in Chapter 7, "Designing a Security Group Strategy." Your baseline settings for file and print servers should select the nature of the files stored there and the printers that it controls. Print servers that control check (payroll, accounts payable, and so on) need special attention. One consideration is to set the Unsigned Driver Installation Behavior option to a minimum of Do Not Allow Installation; for maximum security and stability, use the Do Not Allow Installation setting. Similar choices should be made of the Unsigned Non-driver Installation Behavior option. All print servers should enable the security options Prevent Users from Installing Printer Drivers.

RAS Server

Three models for administering remote access permissions and settings exist:

- ◆ **Access by the user**—Determined by remote access permission on the Dial-in tab of each user account.

- ◆ **Access by policy in Windows 2000 native-mode domain**—Remote access permission on every user account is set to Control Access through Remote Access Policy. Users can be permitted explicit allow, explicit deny, and implicit deny. Implicit deny is a situation in which the connection attempt does not match the conditions of any Remote Access Policy. Remote Access Policy is set using the Routing and Remote Access console or the Internet Authentication Service (IAS) console. When multiple RAS servers exist, IAS can provide centralized management of remote users. The RAS servers act as RADIUS clients to the IAS server. Policies set on the IAS server apply to all RAS servers.

◆ **Access by policy in a Windows 2000 mixed-mode domain**—The Control Access Through Remote Access Policy option is not available on the user account. User account settings are set to Allow Access, the default Remote Access Policy is deleted, and new policies are created. Access is based on matching a user account to the conditions of a policy.

RAS servers should be members of the RAS and IAS Servers security group in the Active Directory directory service of their domain. The RAS and IAS Servers groups is used to manage and control these servers.

Permissions for the RAS and IAS security group can be granted using Active Directory Users and Computers.

Because RAS servers allow access to resources on your network from outside your network, they should be high-security machines. RAS servers may also become part of your e-commerce or B2B strategy.

You should export the security settings of the RAS server to a database. (This can be done in Security Configuration and Analysis.) The settings should then be tightened down, and the template should be saved in case it is needed later to serve as the baseline for other RAS servers, or to restore the current server's settings.

As part of your baseline, you may want to specify the authentication service used (Windows, RADIUS, EAP) and the resolution of other security issues (use of reversible encrypted password, smart card remote access, certificate-based EAP). Much of this can be done in the template under Security Options.

More information on the security setting possible for RAS servers and IAS servers is provided in Chapter 13, "Providing Secure Access Between Networks," and Chapter 14, "Designing Security for Access Between Networks."

DESKTOP COMPUTERS

Desktop computers make up the bulk of computers in most companies. It is tempting to classify them as one group and develop a policy for all of them. This is not the way things work, however. Desktop computers are used in different ways, and the abilities and duties of their users vary. Several different polices—and, thus, templates—should be considered. First, determine the roles desktops play, and then develop the policies and templates appropriate for each of them.

Desktop Role

Desktop computers are installations of Windows 2000 Professional. You should set a security baseline for all desktop computers. In many companies, you may have different classes of desktop computers. This includes laptops, whether general, secure, and highly secure. You may even need Windows NT-compatible laptops, in some cases.

Secure desktops are those that may be used by individuals in the more sensitive areas of your company. Financial areas or marketing and engineering areas are good choices. Some of these areas may also need high-security workstations.

Use the representative templates that follow, and adapt them to your information security policy.

You may wish to start with the hisecws.inf template and develop a special template for laptop computers.

The compatws.inf template can be used to assure compatability with applications that do not meet the Windows 2000 logo standard. This template changes settings back to the Windows NT settings for files, registry keys, and permissions and is consistent with most legacy applications. An example is Microsoft Office 97 SR1, which runs well for Power Users or for a user under the compatible configuration, but which does not run well for a normal user after a clean installation of Windows 2000. Office 2000 runs well for users because it meets the Windows 2000 applications standard.

Desktop Templates

The templates for Windows 2000 Professional are similar to those for the server and domain controller. There is one for basic, secure, and high security settings. In addition, one called compatws provides compatibility with legacy applications. Any Desktop configured with the compatws template should not be considered secure (see Tables 4.10 through 4.13).

TABLE 4.10

DESKTOP TEMPLATE ACCOUNT POLICY SETTINGS

Account Policy	basicwk	securews	hisecws	compatws
Password Policy				
Enforce password history	0 passwords remembered	24 passwords remembered	24 passwords remembered	Not defined
Maximum password age	42 days	42 days	42 days	Not defined
Minimum password age	0 days	2 days	2 days	Not defined
Minimum password length	0 characters	8 characters	8 characters	Not defined
Passwords must meet complexity requirements	Disabled	Enabled	Enabled	Not defined
Store passwords using reversible encryption for all users in the domain	Disabled	Disabled	Disabled	Not defined
Account Lockout Policy				
Account lockout duration	Not defined	30 minutes	0	Not defined
Account lockout threshold	0 invalid logon attempts	5 invalid attempts	5 invalid logon attempts	Not defined
Reset account lockout counter after. . .	Not defined	30 minutes	30 minutes	Not defined
Kerberos Policy				
Enforce user logon restrictions	Not defined	Not defined	Not defined	Not defined
Maximum lifetime for service ticket	Not defined	Not defined	Not defined	Not defined
Maximum lifetime for user ticket	Not defined	Not defined	Not defined	Not defined

continues

TABLE 4.10 *continued*

DESKTOP TEMPLATE ACCOUNT POLICY SETTINGS

Account Policy	basicwk	securews	hisecws	compatws
Password Policy				
Maximum lifetime for user ticket renewal	Not defined	Not defined	Not defined	Not defined
Maximum tolerance for computer clock synchronization	Not defined	Not defined	Not defined	Not defined

TABLE 4.11

DESKTOP AUDIT POLICY

Audit Policy	basicwk	securews	hisecws	compatws
Audit account logon events	No auditing	Success, Failure	Success, Failure	Not defined
Audit account management	No auditing	Success, Failure	Success, Failure	Not defined
Audit directory service access	Not defined	Not defined	Not defined	Not defined
Audit logon events	No auditing	Failure	Success, Failure	Not defined
Audit object access	No auditing	No auditing	Success, Failure	Not defined
Audit policy change	No auditing	Success, Failure	Success, Failure	Not defined
Audit privilege use	No auditing	Failure	Success, Failure	Not defined
Audit process tracking	No auditing	No auditing	No auditing	Not defined
Audit system events	No auditing	No auditing	Success, Failure	Not defined

TABLE 4.12

DESKTOP SECURITY OPTIONS

Security Option	basicwk	securews	hisecws	compatwk
Additional restrictions for anonymous connections	None, rely on default permissions	Do not allow enumeration of SAM accounts and shares	No access without explicit anonymous permissions	Not defined
Allow server operators to schedule tasks	Not defined	Not defined	Not defined	Not defined
Allow system to be shut down without having to log on	Enabled	Not defined	Not defined	Not defined
Allow ejection of removable NTFS media	Administrators	Administrators	Administrators	Not defined
Amount of idle time required before discontinuing session	15 minutes	15 minutes	15 minutes	Not defined
Audit the access of global system objects	Disabled	Disabled	Disabled	Not defined
Audit use of Backup and Restore privilege	Disabled	Disabled	Disabled	Not defined
Automatically log off users when logon time expires	Not defined	Not defined	Not defined	Not defined
Automatically log off users when logon time expires (local)	Enabled	Enabled	Enabled	Not defined

continues

TABLE 4.12   *continued*

DESKTOP SECURITY OPTIONS

Security Option	basicwk	securews	hisecws	compatwk
Clear virtual memory page file when system shuts down	Disabled	Disabled	Enabled	Not defined
Digitally sign client communications (always)	Disabled	Disabled	Enabled	Not defined
Digitally sign client communications (when possible)	Enabled	Enabled	Enabled	Not defined
Digitally sign server communications (always)	Disabled	Disabled	Enabled	Not defined
Digitally sign server communications (when possible)	Disabled	Enabled	Enabled	Not defined
Disable Ctrl + Alt + Del requirement for logon	Not defined	Disabled	Disabled	Not defined
Do not display last username in logon screen	Disabled	Disabled	Enabled	Not defined
LAN Manager authentication level	Set LM and NTLM responses	Send NTLM response only	Send NTLMv2 response only; refuse LM and NTLM	Not defined
Message text for users attempting to log on				Not defined
Message title for users attempting to log on				Not defined
Number of previous logons to cache	10 logons	10 logons	10 logons	Not defined

Security Option	basicwk	securews	hisecws	compatwk
Prevent system maintenance of computer account password	Disabled	Disabled	Disabled	Not defined
Prevent users from installing printer drivers	Disabled	Enabled	Enabled	Not defined
Prompt user to change password before expiration	14 days	14 days	14 days	Not defined
Recovery console: Allow automatic administrative logon	Disabled	Disabled	Disabled	Not defined
Recovery console: Allow floppy copy and access to all drives and all folders	Disabled	Disabled	Disabled	Not defined
Rename Administrator account	Not defined	Not defined	Not defined	Not defined
Rename Guest account	Not defined	Not defined	Not defined	Not defined
Restrict CD-ROM access to locally logged-on user only	Disabled	Disabled	Disabled	Not defined
Restrict floppy access to locally logged-on user only	Disabled	Disabled	Disabled	Not defined
Secure channel: digitally encrypt or sign secure channel data (always)	Disabled	Disabled	Enabled	Not defined
Secure channel: digitally encrypt secure channel data (when possible)	Disabled	Enabled	Enabled	Not defined

continues

TABLE 4.12   *continued*

DESKTOP SECURITY OPTIONS

Security Option	*basicwk*	*securews*	*hisecws*	*compatwk*
Secure channel: Digitally sign secure channel data (when possible)	Enabled	Enabled	Enabled	Not defined
Secure channel: Require strong (Windows 2000 or later) session key	Disabled	Disabled	Enabled	Not defined
Secure system partition (for RISC platforms only)	Not defined	Not defined	Not defined	Not defined
Send unencrypted password to connect to third-party SMB servers	Disabled	Disabled	Disabled	Not defined
Shut down system immediately if incapable of logging security audits	Disabled	Disabled	Disabled	Not defined
Smart card removal behavior	No action	Lock workstation	Lock workstation	Not defined
Strengthen default permissions	Enabled	Enabled	Enabled	Not defined
Unsigned driver installation behavior	Not defined	Warn, but allow instal-lation	Do not allow instal-lation	Not defined
Unsigned nondriver installation behavior	Not defined	Silently succeed	Silently succeed	Not defined

TABLE 4.13

DESKTOP EVENT LOG TEMPLATE SETTINGS

Event Log	basicwk	securews	hisecws	compatwk
Maximum application log size	512KB	Not defined	Not defined	Not defined
Maximum security log size	512KB	5120KB	10240KB	Not defined
Maximum system log size	512KB	Not defined	Not defined	Not defined
Restrict guest access to application log	Disabled	Enabled	Enabled	Not defined
Restrict guest access to security log	Disabled	Enabled	Enabled	Not defined
Restrict guest access to system log	Disabled	Enabled	Enabled	Not defined
Retain application log	7 days	Not defined	Not defined	Not defined
Retain security log	7 days	Not defined	Not defined	Not defined
Retain system log	7 days	Not defined	Not defined	Not defined
Retention method for application log	By days	Not defined	Not defined	Not defined
Retention method for security log	By days	As needed	As needed	Not defined
Retention method for system log	By days	Not defined	Not defined	Not defined
Shut down the computer when the security audit log is full	Not defined	Not defined	Not defined	Not defined

Restricted groups are not set in basicwk and hisecws. The Power Users Group is a member of the Restricted groups in the compatwk and securews templates.

Just as fresh server installations use the defltsv template and upgraded systems can have the basicsv template (the equivalent) applied, a fresh installation of Windows 2000 Professional has the defltwk template applied, and an upgraded system may have the basicwk applied. More secure templates assume that the defltwk or basicwk template has been applied and do not apply or reapply those settings.

Recommendations for ITS

ITS will have more than a hundred salespeople in the field with Windows 2000 laptops. The company should attempt to set the highest security baseline it can. There are concerns with the operation of the company's legacy applications. Perhaps the client side of the FullStock application can be the first part prepped to follow logo standards and enable the laptops to be secured. ITS also has a number of desktop computers that will be either Windows 2000, Windows NT, or Windows 98. ITS would do well to start migration of desktop machines to Windows 2000 with machines that operate in more sensitive areas of the company. The company may want to have specific security baselines for different operating systems (yes, Matilda, there are things you can do to secure downlevel clients) as well as different activities or roles.

KIOSKS

Kiosks are special-case machines. Examples include shop floor systems accessed for lookup by many people, or store front or mall machines used to suggest gifts and give directions. Because these machines generally sit in public areas, a good security baseline would be as follows: Remove keyboards and allow only touch screens, mouse devices, or other pointing devices; and remove external access from modems or the network or the Internet unless this is required for the functionality of the machine. If possible, specially constructed hardware should be used to give the machine longevity and prevent abuse. Generally, the machine itself does not hold the only copy of data, so its compromise may be only annoying, not disastrous. In most cases, a logon will not be required. In this case, Windows 2000 can be set to automatically log on in case the machine reboots.

If your organization uses kiosks, you will need to define their purpose and determine what peripherals can be removed and how tightly the system needs to be locked.

SYSTEM SERVICES TEMPLATE SETTINGS

System Services are shown in Table 4.14 for basicsv and basicwk. All other templates do not define them. That is so that when you apply those templates to existing systems, you will not change services relationships that are already set.

TABLE 4.14

SYSTEM SERVICES

Service	basicsv	basicwk
Alerter	Automatic	Not defined
Applications management	Manual	Manual
Clipbook	Manual	Manual
Computer browser	Automatic	Automatic
DHCP Client	Automatic	Automatic
Distributed File System	Automatic	Not defined
Distributed Link Tracking Client	Automatic	Automatic
Distributed Transaction Coordinator	Automatic	Not defined
DNS Client	Automatic	Automatic
Event log	Automatic	Automatic
IPSEC Policy Agent	Automatic	Automatic
License Logging Service	Automatic	Not defined

continues

| TABLE 4.14 | *continued* |

SYSTEM SERVICES

Service	basicsv	basicwk
Logical Disk Manager	Automatic	Automatic
Messenger	Automatic	Automatic
Net Logon	Automatic	Automatic
Network DDE	Manual	Manual
Network DDE DSDM	Manual	Manual
Plug and Play	Automatic	Automatic
Print spooler	Automatic	Automatic
Protected storage	Automatic	Automatic
Remote Procedure Call	Automatic	Automatic
Remote Registry Service	Automatic	Automatic
Removable storage	Automatic	Automatic
RunAs Service	Automatic	Automatic
Security Accounts Manager	Automatic	Automatic
Server	Automatic	Automatic
Simple Mail Transport Protocol	Automatic	Not defined
System Event Notification	Automatic	Automatic
Task Scheduler	Automatic	Automatic
TCP/IP NetBIOS Helper Service	Automatic	Automatic
Windows Time	Automatic	Automatic
Workstation	Automatic	Automatic

REGISTRY AND FILE SYSTEM

The default installation of Windows 2000 Professional sets permission on registry keys and system file folders. These settings are not modified if the secure workstation template is applied, but additional settings are applied if the hisecwk template is applied.

To understand the scope of these settings, view the registry and/or File System portions of the basicwk, securewk, and hisecwk templates.

INSTALLING COMPUTERS WITH ENHANCED AND APPROPRIATE SECURITY

When Windows 2000 is installed, it uses an appropriate default template to set initial settings. If you have many machines to install and have developed security baselines for each type of machine, you can substitute your baseline template to ensure quick compliance with your security policy.

Single-System Installation

The default file used in the configuration of the newly installed machine can be found in I386 on the CD-ROM (deflt##.in_). By storing the installation files on a network installation point and replacing that file with your template, you can start your systems, freshly installed, with the level of security you desire.

Automated Install

To install, many computers develop automated installation. You can find complete instructions for installing Windows 2000 in an automated fashion in the Windows 2000 Resource Kit.

Part of the preparation for automated installs is to create a distribution folder that contains the Windows 2000 installation files as well as any device driver and other files needed. Create a distribution folder for each system platform.

During Windows 2000 installation, the appropriate (*server—defltsv.inf*) file is parsed, and settings are applied. To customize setup to use your security baselines, you could edit the defltsv.inf file and then place your version in the distribution folder that you plan to use for system setup. (On the installation CD-ROM the file is compressed with the .in extension.)

Alternatively, you can create a cmdlines.txt file and place it and your template file in the \OEM subfolder outside the distribution folder. The cmdlines.txt file will have in it the secedit command to apply your template. Then, use the OEMFILESPATH key in the answer file. The answer file is used during an automated installation to replace the information that would need to be typed in during installation.

A third method is to place the secedit command in the GuiRunOnce section of the answer file. This section includes a list of commands that are executed when the first user logs on. GuiRunOnce section of the answer file contains a list of commands to be executed when the user first logs on to the system after the GUI mode portion completes. You will need to make sure that your template file is copied to the newly installed machine.

For more information on automating your installation of Windows 2000, see the "Microsoft Windows 2000 Guide to Unattended Setup" (unattend.doc) on the Windows 2000 CD. It is part of the deploy.cab file in the \Support\Tools folder. You will need to use the Extract command to access the file.

Finally, the best solution is to use Group Policy to ensure that the correct security settings are always enforced for each computer. More information on using Group Policy can be found in Chapter 7.

USING SECEDIT TO APPLY AND ANALYZE SECURITY SETTINGS

Secedit.exe is a command-line tool that can be used to create and apply security templates and analyze system security (see Table 4.15). You can place it in a batch file for automatic analysis, or you can use it at the command line. This tool is extremely useful when configuring or analyzing multiple computers. It also can be used to validate the syntax of a security configuration file.

Take a look at the syntax of this tool:

To validate syntax, enter this:

```
Secedit /validate filename
```

To analyze system security, enter this:

```
Secedit /analyze [/DB filename ]/CFG filename][/log
logpath][/verbose][/quiet]
```

TABLE 4.15

SECEDIT PARAMETERS

Parameter	Explanation
/DB *filename*	This is the path to the security template database.
/CFG *filename*	This is the path of the security template. (Without this, any configuration in the database is used.)
/log *filename*	This is the path to the log.
/verbose	More detailed information is provided during analysis.
/quiet	This suppresses screen and log output. Analysis results still are viewable in Security Configuration and Analysis.
/overwrite	Use this to specify that the new security template should overwrite any template or composite template stored in the database instead of appending it.
/area *area1 area2...*	This indicates security areas to be applied to the system. Default is all. Areas include SECURTYPOLICY, GROUP_MGMT, USER_RIGHTS, REGKEYS, FILE-STORE, and SERVICES.
Machine_policy	Settings for the local computer are identified here. (This is used with the refreshpolicy parameter; it kicks off a refresh of machine policies.)
User_policy	Here you can find settings for the local user account currently logged on. (This is used with the refreshpolicy parameter; it kicks off a resfresh of user policy.)
/enforce	This prompts a refresh, even if no changes have been made to the Group Policy object settings.
/mergedPolicy	This merges and exports domain and local policy settings.

To configure system security, use this syntax:

```
Secedit /configure [/DB filename][/overwrite]
[/areas area1 area2…][/log logpath][/verbose][/quiet]
```

To refresh security settings, enter this line:

```
Secedit /refreshpolicy {machine_policy¦user_policy}
[/enforce]
```

This line is used to export security settings:

```
Secedit /export[mergedPolicy][/DB filename]
[/CFG filename][/areas area1, area2…]
[/log logpath][/verbose][quiet]
```

CHAPTER SUMMARY

KEY TERMS

- Group Policy
- security templates
- Security Configuration and Analysis Template
- security groups
- RAS server
- IAS server
- EAP
- forest
- tree
- Active Directory
- domain
- organizational unit
- operations master
- schema master
- relative ID master
- domain naming master
- primary domain controller emulator
- infrastructure master
- LDAP
- Discretionary Access Control List
- Restricted groups
- secedit
- kiosks

This chapter may have posed more questions than it answered. Just what are all those security options and user rights? What is recommended for an audit and password policy? What security groups exist, and what are their privileges? How are communications secured? Upcoming chapters will define these in detail. Your goal here was to baseline, not to fine-tune the process.

You learned about available security templates that can be selected as baselines for various platforms. You also learned how easy they are to modify and mix and match. In addition, you practiced working with the Security Configuration and Analysis console, and with the command-line tool secedit. The ITS case study defined a situation for you to begin your analysis process.

APPLY YOUR KNOWLEDGE

Exercises

4.1 Configure and Apply a New Security Template

Estimated Time: 30 minutes

1. Open the Security Templates snap-in, and copy the template for a high-security desktop to a file named laptop.inf.

2. Open the laptop.inf template, and configure settings to make a secure laptop configuration.

3. The settings should reflect a good strategy for a traveling salesperson.

4. Save the new template.

5. Apply the template to the current system.

6. Examine the settings.

7. Return your settings to the way they were before by applying the basicwk.inf template.

4.2 Choosing a Security Template

Examine each situation in Table 4.16. Choose the baseline template that the company should start with, and write your answer in the "Baseline Template" column. Templates are basicwk, basicsv, basicdc, compatws, securews, securedc, hisecws, and hisecdc.

Estimated Time: 15 minutes

TABLE 4.16

EXERCISE 4.2: TEMPLATE CHOICES

Situation	*Baseline Template*
ABX Dry-cleaning has a database server that holds customer information. The server does not need to communicate with downlevel machines.	

Situation	*Baseline Template*
Roberta travels with a laptop computer. Her entire business resides on that laptop.	
Ford places kiosks in shopping malls to help customers select new cars.	
The server will be an Internet server.	
RTW Technical College uses a lab file server. Students are constantly curious, so a high audit baseline is needed.	
Kere's Travel, a small home office business, has a single file server.	

Answers are provided in Table 4.17.

TABLE 4.17

EXERCISE 4.2: TEMPLATE ANSWERS

Situation	*Baseline Template*
ABX Dry-cleaning has a database server that holds customer information. The server does not need to communicate with downlevel machines.	hisecdc
Roberta travels with a laptop computer. Her entire business resides on that laptop.	hisecws
Ford places kiosks in shopping malls to help customers select new cars.	hisecws
The server will be an Internet server.	hisecws
RTW Technical College uses a lab file server. Students are constantly curious, so a high audit baseline is needed.	hisecws
Kere's Travel, a small home office business, has a single file server.	basicsv

APPLY YOUR KNOWLEDGE

Review Questions

1. Describe Active Directory and compare it to the Windows NT Directory Services model.

2. If ITS could move all its systems to Windows 2000, what template would you choose for the SQL Server baseline? Why?

3. ITS sales reps will be using laptops running Windows 2000. Which template should they have?

4. ITS has a number of workstations that used in the general operation of business. They are not used for financial processing, nor do they access the FullStock database. Can ITS assign a basicws.inf template as a baseline?

5. List two techniques for using security templates to modify security settings.

6. What is stored in the Active Directory directory store?

7. Which computer operating systems can participate in Active Directory by using the Active Directory client?

8. Compare the location of user IDs and passwords between Windows 2000 and Windows NT.

9. Can users be authenticated (in Windows 2000) by any domain controller in their domain tree? Why?

10. Describe how to edit security templates.

11. How would you apply a security template automatically to many computers?

12. Identify which security template you would use for securing the ITS RAS server and what changes you would make to the template before applying it.

13. Describe the differences between the three domain controller security templates.

Exam Questions

1. What should ITS take into account when creating baselines for its Windows 2000 implementation (pick three)?

   A. Understand the role of each type of computer in the network.

   B. Learn how to change security settings.

   C. Learn how to use security templates to change security settings.

   D. Divide computers into types by domain and organization unit.

   E. Understand Active Directory.

2. ITS has heard that it can structure its Windows 2000 Active Directory to allow the application of different security templates for different types of computers. Help ITS develop a hierarchical structure upon which to base this strategy.

   A. Create an organizational unit composed of several trees. Each tree can represent a different type of computer.

   B. Create a domain for each type of computer ITS has. A template can be applied to the domain that secures the type of computer that is a member of that domain.

   C. Create security groups. Place the users of each type of computer in their own security group. Apply the policy for each computer type to the security group that contains the users who use that type of computer.

APPLY YOUR KNOWLEDGE

D. Create an organizational unit for each type of computer. Place computer accounts for those computers in the appropriate OU. Write and apply the policy to the correct OU.

3. ABC Consulting must upgrade 25 Windows NT Workstations to Windows 2000. The company wants to make sure that high-security templates are applied to all workstations. The procedure that should be followed is which of the following?

A. Do nothing. An upgrade installs the tightest security.

B. Apply the basicwk template and then the hisecwk template.

C. Apply the hiseckwk template.

D. Determine whether the hisecwk template or the securewk template is the template the company wants, and then apply it.

4. Security templates are viewed, edited, and modified in:

A. The Security and Configuration tool set

B. The Security Templates snap-in

C. The Security Configuration and Analysis Snap-In

D. The Active Directory Users and Computers console

E. Security Templates may be edited only using Notepad or some other text file editor.

5. Examine the ITS case study. Which templates would you apply to their computers (pick two)?

A. Laptops for salespeople should probably use the hisecws.inf template.

B. Workstations running legacy applications should use the securews.inf template.

C. Desktops that run Windows 2000-approved applications could have the securews.inf, the basicwk, or the hisecwk templates applied.

D. Desktops in sensitive areas, such as financial services and the warehouse, should use the hisecws.inf template.

E. No additional work needs to be done to the hisecws.inf template to secure the CEO's desktop.

6. John has been asked to develop a security baseline for all domain controllers at Sprint.

Required Result:

The solution needs to be easily implementable, maintainable, and auditable.

Optional Desired Results:

Domain controllers need to be locked down while allowing appropriate access to administrators.

Domain controllers need to be locked down, but accessibility to resources needs to be ensured.

Proposed Solution:

John first organizes his information about the domain controllers into the roles that they will play. He recognizes that some domains may contain resources that are more sensitive than others, and that some domain controllers are performing duties that will require them to be more secure than others. Next he examines the needs of the users in these domains. Then he develops several custom security templates, according to the role of the domain controller groups that he has identified. He tests each template to ensure that it

APPLY YOUR KNOWLEDGE

will be applied appropriately and that the domain controller can function in the manner that it was intended to.

Evaluation of Proposed Solution:

Which result(s) does the proposed solution produce?

A. The proposed solution produces the required result but neither of the optional results.

B. The proposed solution produces the required result and one of the optional results.

C. The proposed solution produces the required result and both of the optional results.

D. The proposed solution does not produce the required result.

7. John has been asked to develop a security baseline for all domain controllers at Sprint.

Required Result:

The solution needs to be easily implementable, maintainable, and auditable.

Optional Desired Results:

Domain controllers need to be locked down while allowing appropriate access to administrators.

Domain controllers need to be locked down, but accessibility to resources needs to be ensured.

Proposed Solution:

John develops a security template based on the hisecdc.inf template. He locks down the system completely and applies the template to a Group Policy object in a test domain. He then tests to ensure that administrators can access the domain controllers.

Evaluation of Proposed Solution:

Which result(s) does the proposed solution produce?

A. The proposed solution produces the required result but neither of the optional results.

B. The proposed solution produces the required result and one of the optional results.

C. The proposed solution produces the required result and both of the optional results.

D. The proposed solution does not produce the required result.

8. Applying a security template to a Windows 2000 system:

A. Overwrites current polices in place.

B. Appends to current policies in place.

C. Defines security settings for all configurable security issues.

D. Does not change file and registry key access permissions.

E. The action of the application is dependent on settings within the policy and how the policy is applied.

9. All directory data replication in Windows 2000 except _____ is accomplished via a multimaster replication model. Name the data and the computer role that performs this replication.

A. Updates and modifications to the schema are carried out by the schema operations master.

B. Additions and deletions of domains in the forest are managed by the DNS server.

C. The forest relative ID master allocates relative ID sequences to each domain controller.

D. All group and user information is replicated by the infrastructure master.

E. The PC emulator is used as an authentication backup system.

F. The backup domain controller replicates SID changes.

10. You could make which three changes to the basicsv template to improve security for a stand-alone server used in the ITS warehouse for product information lookup?

   A. Tighten password policy to enable password complexibilty requirements, enforce history, and set age and password length.

   B. Define lockout policy.

   C. Set strong Kerberos policies.

   D. Turn on auditing and set policies.

   E. Enable the Allow System To Be Shut Down Without Having To Log On option

11. Special consideration for baseline policies for RAS servers are which of the following?

   A. RAS servers cannot be controlled by policy. Access can be set only on the Dial-in tab of the user account.

   B. RAS servers are members of the RAS and IAS Servers security groups.

   C. RAS servers need less secure policies to operate.

   D. RAS servers are managed in the Routing and Remote Access console.

12. The compatws.inf security template:

   A. Is applied to desktops that run legacy applications.

B. Makes the desktop more secure.

C. Overwrites all settings in Account Policy, local computer policy, security options, and so on, when applied.

D. Primarily changes file and registry access settings to allow compatibility with Windows NT-type settings, which these legacy applications need to run.

13. Which of the following is the best way to automate installation of multiple computers with your security baselines?

   A. This cannot be done. You will have to apply security templates manually after systems are installed.

   B. Automatically install all systems and then write a batch file that uses secedit to apply your security baseline.

   C. Create separate distribution folders for each security baseline you have developed. Modify the default security template once for each role, and place in the appropriate distribution folder.

   D. Add a command to the GuiRunOnce section of the answer file to apply the template.

Answers to Review Questions

1. Active Directory is a hierarchical structure composed of forests, which are trees that share a schema; trees, which are composed of domains in the same DNS contiguous name space; and domains, which are composed of computers. Sites are used to map the physical network and to control replication of the directory. The directory

APPLY YOUR KNOWLEDGE

contains objects and attributes. Objects such as users, computers, and printers have physical attributes. Automatic, transitive trusts exist within domains of the forest. Organizational units can be composed of users and computers for granular administration. A user can easily find a printer or a service within the forest by querying the active direction. In the Windows NT domain model, each domain was a separate entity. One-way, nontransitive trusts had to be specifically created and often became unmanageable in large environments. Granular and systems-wide administration was difficult and often was accomplished with third-party products.

2. You should choose hisecws. This presumes that the company's legacy application has been corrected to work with Windows 2000 in this mode. If it has not, the company may need to still relax this baseline. There is no high-security server template because it would be the same as the high-security workstation template. This template would be appropriate because it does not respond to NTLM and LM requests. NTLMv2 or Kerberos must be used for authentication. This template also has strong audit policies and device driver signing policies. Data on this machine is highly critical to the running of the business. It pays to make that machine as secure as possible.

3. Sales reps' laptops are being used in high-risk situations. The reps will be accessing sensitive information and storing it on local hard drives. What happens if one of the machines is lost or stolen? Use the hisecws.inf template. (The defltws.inf template will be applied during installation because the sales reps are getting new laptops.)

4. Workstations used in less sensitive areas do not need the Fort Knox treatment. Generally, you do not spend more money and time on securing something than it will take to replace it if it was lost. However, applying secure templates is painless and quick. A judgement should be made as to whether the company can do so due to legacy applications. The basicwk.inf template can be used as a baseline. However, it will not be necessary to apply it to any systems that are the result of a fresh installation. The defltwk.inf (the basicwk.inf equivalent) template already has applied. The basicwk.inf template can be applied to upgraded workstations.

5. Security templates can be applied directly to the local computer or to a Group Policy object.

6. Servers, printers, files, network users, computer accounts, and groups are stored there.

7. Windows 2000 computers can do so. Windows NT and Windows 98 can do so by adding the respective Directory Services client.

8. Domain user IDs and passwords are stored in the Windows 2000 Active Directory (although local computer user IDs and passwords are still stored in the SAM of the local computer or workstation). Windows NT user IDs and passwords are stored in the SAM.

9. Yes. The AD is replicated to every domain controller in the domain.

10. Edit security templates using the Security Template MMC snap-in, or directly by editing the script file. You may copy and paste parts from one template to another.

11. Use Group Policy (see Chapter 8). In a non-Active Directory environment, secedit can be used.

APPLY YOUR KNOWLEDGE

12. Use the hisecws.inf template. The RAS server will be communicating with the sales reps' laptops in the field, which are Windows 2000 Professional, and the SQL Server, which is also Windows 2000 Professional, so NTLM is not necessary. You will need to configure the RAS server to accept only NTLMv2 and not to respond to a request from a server to which it is attempting to connect. It is also important that this template will not load unsigned drivers. If loaded, unsigned, incorrect drivers could kill the server. That's not a good idea if you depend on it for order entry. You will need to investigate appropriate RAS-related settings and set them (see Chapter 14).

13. The basicdc template does not define account policy settings, audit policy settings, or user rights settings. The only security option set is Digitally Sign Server Communications (When Possible). The event log settings are similar to Windows NT defaults. The securedc template and the hisecdc template have the same password policy settings. The hisecdc template generally has more restrictive settings (but both have more restrictive settings than basicdc), including no authentication by LM or NTLM. (NTLMv2 is allowed.)

Answers to Exam Questions

1. **A, C, E.** Without an understanding of Active Directory, the company will have a hard time with Windows 2000 security. If the company doesn't understand what the computer is being used for and can't interpret that information, it will fail at applying any type of security. Templates for security exist and provide a quick way to set baselines. (See the section "Active Directory Introduction.")

2. **D.** OUs do not contain trees, so answer A is wrong. Although you could create a domain to contain each type of computer, this would be unnecessary, so answer B also is wrong. Answer C is wrong because you cannot apply a template to a security group. Answer D is correct: By placing computers in separate OUs, you can apply different templates to each type of computer. (See the section "Organizational Units.")

3. **B.** Because the computers are upgrades, they will need the basicwk template applied first and then the hisecwk or securewk template. (See the section "Understanding Security Templates and Computer Policy Introduction.")

4. **B.** The Security Configuration tool set is a collection of tools that includes the templates, the Security Configuration and Analysis console, and secedit. (See the section "Creating or Modifying Security Templates Using Security Configuration and Analysis.")

5. **A, C.** The laptops for sales reps need the highest security. Computers that run only approved applications will be capable of applying the templates. Computers that run legacy applications may not even be capable of handling the basicwk or defltwk templates. (See the section "Understanding Security Templates and Computer Policy Introduction.")

6. **C.** John used the correct tools and came up with a modified design of the existing template. The templates can be reapplied as necessary, and systems can be analyzed and audited. This can be done in batch file mode and then can be periodically reviewed. John has tested each template to ensure administrative access and appropriate resource access. (See the section "Understanding Security Templates and Computer Policy Introduction.")

7. **D.** Probably one unrevised template will not be enough for Sprint's large, widely diverse network. Furthermore, John has not does adequate testing to ensure compatibility with needs and requirements of administrators and users. He may have just locked both out of the system and caused other systems to fail. (See the section "Desktop Role.")

8. **E.** Policies can be directed to overwrite or to append to the current policy. (See the sections on "Templates.")

9. **A.** Updates and modifications to the schema are carried out via the schema operations master. Other operations masters exist, but they are not named here. (See the section "Forest-Wide Operations Master Roles.")

10. **A, B, D.** Kerberos cannot be used except in a domain. It is not wise to let systems be shut down by any passing person. It is generally accepted that using a tighter password policy and auditing is a sound security decision. (See the sections "Trusts," "Desktop Templates," and "Domain Controllers Baseline.")

11. **B, D.** RAS servers can be controlled by policies—indeed, the preferred way to control a single RAS server is to develop policies in the Routing and Remote Access console. If multiple RAS servers are used, an IAS server can be used to manage policy centrally. RAS servers are members of the RAS and IAS Servers security group, and you may be able to use this in some security settings to control them or to access them. RAS servers need more security than many systems. (See the sections "Servers" and "RAS Server.")

12. **A, D.** The compatws template was developed to assist administrators in getting legacy applications to work. It does not change security settings except in regard to file and registry key access. This template must be applied to be used. (See the section "Application Server.")

13. **D.** If you apply a baseline after installation, there is always the issue that users will connect to the newly live system before the baseline is applied. If you have only a few different systems, you might want to simply create different distribution folders, but a large number will quickly devour storage space. (See the section "Installing Computers with Enhanced and Appropriate Security.")

APPLY YOUR KNOWLEDGE

Suggested Readings and Resources

1. *Windows 2000 Resource Kit: Windows 2000 Server Deployment Planning Guide.* Microsoft Press:

   • "Developing an Automated Installation"

   • "Developing an Automated Installation of Windows 2000 Professional"

2. Cone, Erick, Boggs, Jon, and Perez, Sergio. 1999. *Planning for Windows 2000.* Indianapolis: New Riders Publishing.

   • Chapter 1, "Windows 2000 Overview"

   • Chapter 3, "Implementing Standards"

3. Sheresh, Beth, and Doug Sheresh. 2000. *Understanding Directory Services.* Indianapolis: New Riders Publishing.

   • Chapter 7, "Lightweight Directory Access Protocol"

   • Chapter 9, "Active Directory"

This chapter covers the following Microsoft-specified objective for the "Analyzing Security Requirements" section of the Designing Security for a Microsoft Windows 2000 Network exam:

Identify the required level of security for each resource. Resources include printers, files, shares, Internet access, and dial-in access.

▶ Access controls are critical in the design of a secure network. They need definition, resource by resource, to ensure this. After all, any object that exists in the Windows 2000 network requires its own Discretionary Access Control List (DACL). It is easiest to examine them by type of object.

CHAPTER 5

Securing Resources

STUDY STRATEGIES

▶ You need to learn the following three things to complete your study of this objective:

- First, learn the type of control available for each type of resource object.

- Next, learn how that control is applied. How are things set by default? Are there multiple ways to apply those controls?

- Finally, make a list of the objects you need to manage in your environment and determine the level of access control to be applied on each.

INTRODUCTION

In planning your security design, you have considered policy settings for different computer roles. You have learned how to create your own templates to assist you in configuring, applying, and maintaining these policies. Now you must consider the establishment of access controls for the resources you have identified. Users must be *authorized* to access objects. Although this may seem like a daunting task, it must be done. It enables you to more easily design other aspects of security and enables a smoother implementation. The information you express is invaluable to the architects of your Windows 2000 infrastructure. Don't forget to examine the default resource protection applied at installation time.

In this chapter you learn the following:

◆ The nature of the resources available for access

◆ The controls available for each resource type

◆ How to apply these controls

◆ Default settings and a special service that helps maintain system files

◆ An introduction to tools that enable you to apply and maintain resource access controls across your enterprise

This chapter considers resources such as file systems (files and folders and shares), printers, registry keys, the Internet, and dial-in access. Chapter 9, "Designing an Encrypting File System Strategy," covers the use and control of the Encrypting Files System (EFS).

You continue to examine the resource security requirements of ITS by looking at their resources and defining the access controls they need. (Chapter 4, "Designing a Security Baseline," introduced the ITS case study.)

APPLYING SECURITY TO FILE SYSTEMS

Identify the required level of security for each resource. Resources include printers, files, shares, Internet access, and dial-in access.

Windows 2000 supports the use of three file systems: NTFS, FAT, and FAT32. NTFS is recommended. FAT32 is similar to FAT except FAT32 supports large disks. These systems are supported primarily for compatibility with Windows 9x and Windows 2000 dual-boot systems. Windows 9x clients can access files over the network on NTFS partitions. FAT and FAT32 can be secured at the share level. They do not provide local file security.

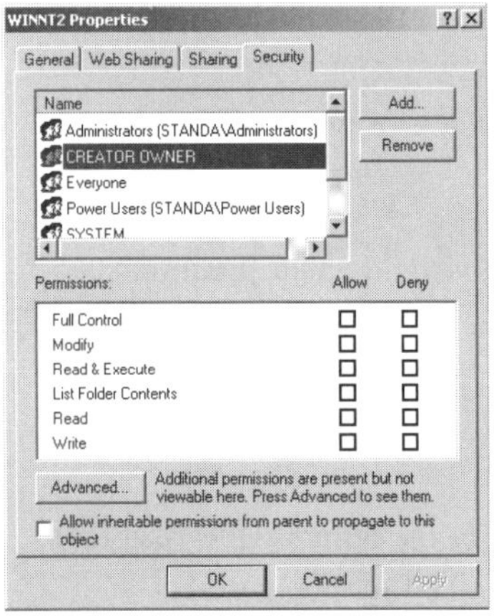

Examining NTFS Features

Windows 2000 offers a new version of NTFS that supports improved file and folder DACLS, Active Directory, domains, sparse files, remote storage, recovery logging of disk activities, disk quotas, better scalability to large drives, and file encryption. You cannot use these features unless you use NTFS as your file system.

Learning File System DACLs

The DACL for each file and folder can be set if you are using NTFS. Windows 2000 offers a refined list of permissions that can be set. The section in this chapter titled "Securing FAT and NTFS Shares" describes share permissions. In addition to allowing different types of access, Windows 2000 also enables you to deny any type of access. Windows NT just enabled you to deny access period.

Folder permissions are actually representative of a logical group of special permissions (see Figure 5.1). The section titled "Special Permissions" discusses folder permissions in detail. The following permissions can be set on each folder:

❖ **Modify.** A combination of List Folder Contents, Write, Delete, and Read Permissions, as follows:

• **List Folder Contents**—See which files and folders are within this folder.

FIGURE 5.1
Folder permissions.

> **NOTE**
>
> **Permission Gotcha #1** Peter has Full Control permission on the folder Stuff. He does not have any permissions on the files and folder within Stuff. Can he delete the file Stuff\johnie? Yes!
>
> This seemingly contradictory situation results from the need to maintain compliance with POSIX.

- **Write**—Add a folder or file to the folder.

- **Delete**—Delete a folder or file from the folder.

- **Read Permissions**—See who has permissions on the folder and what the permissions are.

◆ **Read & Execute**—A combination of Traverse Folder/Execute File, Read Attributes, Read Extended Attributes, and Read Permissions, as follows:

- **Traverse Folder**—If a user does not have permission to view the contents of folder or file, he still can move through this file or folder if the user has the Traverse Folder/Execute File permission. There is also a Bypass Traverse Checking user right. The Traverse Folder permission takes effect if the Bypass Traverse Checking user right is not granted. See Chapter 7, "Designing a Security Group Strategy."

- **Execute File**—Run the program if it is executable.

- **Read Attributes**—Read which attributes are configured and how.

- **Read Extended Attributes**—Read which extended attributes are configured and how.

- **Read Permissions**—Read who has permissions and what they are on this folder.

◆ **List Folder Contents**—A combination of Traverse Folder/Execute File, List Folder/Read Data, Read Attributes, Read Extended Attributes, and Read Permissions, as follows:

- **Traverse Folder**—If a user does not have permission to view the contents of a folder or file, he still can move through this file or folder if the user has the Traverse Folder/Execute File permission. There is also a Bypass Traverse Checking user right. The Traverse Folder permission takes effect if the Bypass Traverse Checking user right is not granted (see Chapter 7).

- **Execute File**—Run the program if it is executable.

- **List Folder**—Lists files and folders in the folder.

- **Read Data**—Read information in folder.

• **Read Attributes**—Read which attributes are configured and how.

• **Read Extended Attributes**—Read which extended attributes are configured and how.

• **Read Permissions**—Read who has permissions and what they are on this folder.

◆ **Read**—A combination of List Folder/Read Data, Read Attributes, Read Extended Attributes, and Read Permissions, as follows:

• **List Folder**—Lists files and folders in the folder.

• **Read Data**—Read information in folder.

• **Read Attributes**—Read which attributes are configured and how.

• **Read Extended Attributes**—Read which extended attributes are configured and how.

• **Read Permissions**—Read who has permissions and what they are on this folder.

◆ **Write**—A combination of Create Files/Write Data, Create Folders/ Append Data, Write Attributes, Write Extended Attributes, and Read Permissions, as follows:

• **Create Files**—Create a file in the folder.

• **Write Data**—Write data in a file.

• **Create Folder**—Create a folder in the folder.

• **Append Data**—Add data to a folder.

• **Write Attributes**—Add or change attributes.

• **Write Extended Attributes**—Add or change extended attributes.

• **Read Permissions**—Read who has permissions and what they are on this folder.

◆ **Full Control**—A combination of all of these listed permissions.

NOTE

Seeing Double? List Folder Contents and Read & Execute seem to have the same group of special permissions. List Folder Contents is only inherited by folder, however, not by files. The choice is not visible when you view file permissions. Read & Execute is inherited by files and folders.

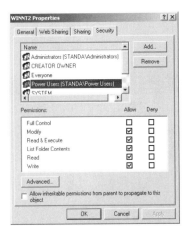

FIGURE 5.2
Discretionary access control settings.

Clicking the Advanced button (see Figure 5.2) enables you to see the list of user and group access levels.

File and Folder Advanced Permissions

The following special or advanced permissions can be set on files/folders. All permissions can be set to "Allow" or "Deny." Special permissions are set by clicking the Advanced button on the Security tab of the file or folder Properties page, selecting a user or group, and clicking the View/Edit button (see Figure 5.3).

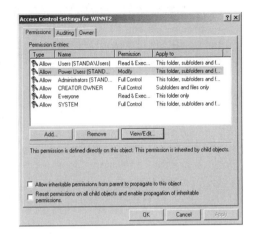

FIGURE 5.3
Special permissions.

◆ **Traverse Folder/Execute File.**

  • **Traverse Folder**—If a user does not have permission to view the contents of folder or file, he still can move through this file or folder if the user has the Traverse Folder/Execute File permission. There is also a Bypass Traverse Checking user right. The Traverse Folder permission takes effect if the Bypass Traverse Checking user right is not granted (see Chapter 7).

  • **Execute File**—Allows or denies running programs.

◆ **List Folder/Read Data.**

  • **List Folder**—Viewing filenames and subfolder names in the folder.

  • **Read Data**—View data in files.

◆ **Read Attributes**—View file or folder attributes. (Attributes are defined by NTFS and include read-only, hidden, and so on.)

◆ **Read Extended Attributes**—View extended attributes. (Extended attributes are defined by programs.)

◆ **Create Files/Write Data.**

  • **Create Files**—Create files in folders.

  • **Write Data**—Change data in file.

◆ **Create Folders/Append Data.**

  • **Create Folders**—Create folders within folders.

  • **Append Data**—Make changes to the end of the file but not change, delete, or overwrite existing data.

NOTE   **Permission Gotcha #2**   If the Managers group has Travers Folder/Execute File permission on the Super Kool Tools folder, do they have the automatic right to execute all program files in that folder? No!

They may not have the right to execute all files because some file permissions may be set on the files.

> **NOTE**
>
> **Permission Gotcha #3** If Tom has the Delete Subfolders and Files permission on the folder Secret, and Tom does not have the Delete permission on the folder Secret\state, can he delete the folder Secret\state? Yes!
>
> Tom can delete the folder because he has the permission on the parent folder and the permissions propagate to the inner folder.

◆ **Write Attributes**—Change attributes of a file or folder.

◆ **Write Extended Attributes**—Change extended attributes of a file or folder.

◆ **Delete Subfolders and Files**—Delete subfolder or file.

◆ **Delete**—Delete the file or folder.

◆ **Read Permissions**—Read file or folder permissions.

◆ **Change Permissions**—Change permissions of file or folder.

◆ **Take Ownership**—Take ownership of the file or folder.

> **NOTE**
>
> **Permission Gotcha #4** Can the owner of a file or folder change permissions on a file or folder? Yes! Can he do so even if he has been specifically denied access to the file/folder? Yes!
>
> Owners of a file or folder can *always* change the permissions.

Understanding Inheritance and Propagation

When a new file is created, it inherits the permissions set on its parent folder. You can block that behavior by selecting This Folder Only in the Apply Onto field when you set up special permissions for the folder (see Figure 5.4). To block inheritance of permission changes to only certain files or folders, clear the Allow Inheritable Permissions from Parent to Propagate to this Object check box on the Security tab of the Properties page for the file or folder.

If the check boxes on permissions are shaded, it means that the permissions have been inherited.

To make changes to inherited permissions, perform one of the following:

◆ Change the parent folder permissions and allow inheritance to change the subfile or subfolder.

◆ Select the opposite permission (Allow or Deny) to override the inherited permissions.

◆ Clear the Allow inheritable permissions from parent to propagate to this object check box.

You can set permissions on a logical drive. These permissions, as well as those set on shares, should be set from the Computer Management console.

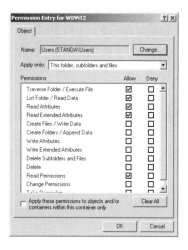

FIGURE 5.4
Preventing permission propagation.

STEP BY STEP

5.1 Setting Logical Drive Permissions

1. Open the Computer Management console.

2. Click Logical Drives in the console tree.

3. Right-click the drive to set permission on.

4. Choose Properties.

5. Choose the Security tab (see Figure 5.5).

6. To add a user or group, click the Add button.

7. Select the user or group and click OK.

8. To change or view permissions, follow these steps:

    1. Select the user or group.

    2. Allow or deny or view permissions in the Permissions window.

    3. Click the Advanced button.

    4. Select the user or group in the Permission Entries window.

    5. Click the View/Edit button.

    6. Allow, deny, or just view permissions.

FIGURE 5.5
Setting permissions on a logical drive.

SECURING OFFICE SERVER EXTENSION

Recently I set up a Web server for a small company. They wanted to use it for internal discussions and collaboration. Our efforts were minimal because they recently purchased licenses for Microsoft Office 2000. I added the Office Server Extensions and *voila!* ... instant collaboration. The system is enjoyed by all.

continues

continued

During and after its installation, I took the following additional steps to secure the server:

- During installation I cleared Allow Basic Authentication Logins for Collaboration. This ensures that access cannot be from some system that might do this.

- Web Subscriptions for Documents was the only option for subscriptions allowed.

- Web discussions were restricted to this server only. If the company gets an external Web server, there would be isolation.

- Anonymous access was restricted.

- Set NTFS DACLs on WINNT\owsconf.log to allow only Administrators and SYSTEM group access.

- Removed the Everyone group the DACL of the Office Server Extension root Help folders.

Examining Shares—FAT and NTFS

Use the Shared Folders console to view and manage connections and resource use for local and remote computers (see Figure 5.6). Only members of the Administrators, Power Users, or Server Operators group can use this console.

Permissions can be set on shared folders for FAT, FAT32, and NTFS partitions. Shared folder permissions on FAT or FAT32 partitions have no effect when the user is logged on locally.

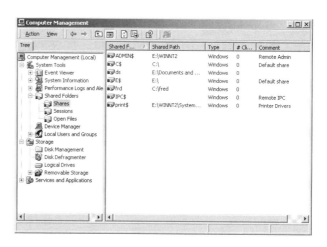

FIGURE 5.6
The Shared Folders console.

In the Shared Folders console, you can do the following:

◆ Create, view, and set permissions

◆ View connected users and disconnect them

◆ View a list of open files

◆ Configure services for Macintosh (only on server)

◆ Limit the number of users of a shared folder

To create a share, follow Step by Step 5.2. To change permissions on a share, follow Step by Step 5.3. To limit the number of users on a share, follow Step by Step 5.4.

STEP BY STEP

5.2 Creating a Share

1. Open the Shared Folders console and select Shares.

2. On the action menu, click New File Share.

3. Enter the folder path or use the Browse button to locate the folder.

4. Enter the share name and the share description in the boxes provided.

5. Select custom permissions such as All Users Have Full Control, Administrators Have Full Control, Other Users Have Read-Only Access, Administrators Have Full Control, Other Users Have No Access, or Customize and Folder Permission.

6. If you selected Customize, you can click the Custom button and add users and use permissions in the Customize Permission dialog box.

7. Click OK.

STEP BY STEP

5.3 Add or Change Permissions on a Shared Folder

1. Open the Shared Folders console.

2. Double-click the shared folder.

3. Select the Security tab.

4. To change permissions, select the user of group to change permissions for.

5. To add a user or group, click the Add button, select the user or group, and click OK.

6. In the Permissions dialog box, click Allow or Deny for each permission.

STEP BY STEP

5.4 Limit the Number of Users of a Shared Folder

1. Open shared folders.

2. Click Shares in the console tree.

3. Double-click the share to limit.

4. Under User Limit, click Maximum Allowed or Allow.

5. If you clicked Allow, enter the number of users.

6. Click OK.

Combining Share Permissions and NTFS Folder Permissions

It is not uncommon to have both share permissions and folder permissions set. The actual permissions that any user can expect depend on how the user is accessing the folder as well as the possible combination of permissions.

If the user is accessing the folder from the local machine, only permissions set on the folder apply. If the user is accessing the folder via the share (access across the network), the combination of permissions must be considered. First each set of permissions should be evaluated separately, and then the two result sets are compared. The most restrictive permissions are those that affect the user's access. The general rule is this: When you use both share permission and NTFS folder permissions, the most restrictive permission is in effect.

To see how this works, consider the share called Payroll on the server called Finance. The share Payroll is in the Data folder on the server.

The data folder has these permissions:

> Administrators: Full Control
>
> Users: Read
>
> FinanceGRP: Modify

The share Payroll has these permissions:

> Users: Modify
>
> FinanceGRP: Read

What access will Users have when accessing the folder across the network? What access will the FinanceGRP have? What access will Administrators have?

To solve the problem, first look at each set of permissions separately. Users have Read access on the folder, and Modify on the share. Which is most restrictive? The Read permission. Therefore, Users have only Read access when accessing the data folder by using the Payroll share.

The FinanceGRP has Modify on the folder data, but Read on the share. Likewise, they also only have Read access on the folder.

Administrators have Full Control on the folder, but no access is listed on the share. Therefore, when accessing the folder across the network, Administrators have no access.

Analyzing Default Settings on System Files

Although Windows NT 4.0 had NTFS and security could be tightened by setting restrictive access permissions, in practice it turned out to be very difficult to do so. In way too many sensitive folders, the default access was Everyone, Full Control. The group Everyone, of course, includes everyone who can gain access to the system. After you realized this, you began the never-ending journey. First you had to determine whom you thought should have access, and then you had to contend with what the system needed access to, and then what various application vendors decided their applications needed to access. There was very little documentation on what the system needed. More than one Microsoft administrator killed his system when he removed the group Everyone, added Administrators, and forgot the SYSTEM account.

This is the problem that the ITS systems administrator was having with his homegrown application. It seems to have been accessing system files or registry keys that it shouldn't have. That is why he may have had to relax security on files and possibly registry keys.

Therefore, he was caught in the worst of circumstances. On the one hand, it was difficult to figure out which system and application files needed to be secured and how; on the other hand, he had to figure out how to relax system security to allow users to do their job.

Windows 2000 makes it easier to secure access to important system files. The system is installed with default system folder permissions that, along with default registry settings, are designed to offer better security right out-of-the-box. If you examine the settings, your will find that member servers and client system computers, system file access is set for the following groups:

◆ Power Users have backward-compatible permissions. Power Users have all access permissions that Users and Power Users had in Windows NT 4.0—that is, Read and Write permission to other parts of the system than their own profile folder.

   Power users can install most applications and have Modify access to %windir% and %windir%\system32.

Power Users have Read-Only access to files that were installed in these directories during setup. So applications that they install can write new files into system directories, but cannot modify Windows 2000 system files. In addition, Power Users cannot install Windows 2000 services.

◆ Administrators, SYSTEM, and CREATOR OWNER have Full Control to file system and registry objects that exist at the beginning of GUI-mode setup. The Administrators group has the same level of rights and permissions as in Windows NT 4.0.

◆ Users have Write access only to the files and registry keys listed in Table 5.1 By default, users may not even be able to read data on the rest of the system.

TABLE 5.1

USER FILE ACCESS

File Path	What Is?	Permission
HKEY_Current_User	User portion of registry	Full Control
%User Profile%	User's profile directory	Full Control
All Users\Documents	Shared Documents Location	Modify
All Users\Application Data	Shared Application Data Location	Modify
%Windir%\Temp	Per-machine temp folder	Traverse, Synchronize, Add File, AddSubdir
\(Root Directory)	Root	Not configured during setup

On servers configured as domain controllers, the following permissions apply:

◆ Everyone reads and writes his or her own profile folders. By default, normal users can only access domain controllers over the network.

◆ Administrators, Account Operators, Server Operators, and Print Operators have the same access permissions as in Windows NT 4.0.

NOTE

Root Rights During installation, Windows 2000 does not attempt to configure permissions on the root directory. This feature is to protect you from destroying permission structures set up on other folders on the install partition. If Windows 2000 were to set permissions on the root folder, it would then try to recursively configure permissions for the entire directory. Applications and data located there might become unusable.

Figure 5.7 shows the logical C: drive, the drive where the system has been installed, and the permissions set at its root.

FIGURE 5.7
Root rights.

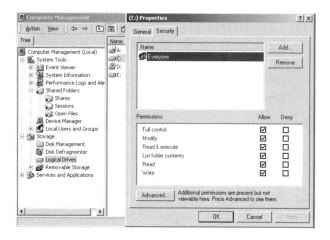

Protecting Windows Files with the Windows File Protection System (WFP)

Let's pretend: You're the *Star Wars* Storm Trooper, and I'm Obi Wan. You click the WINNT folder in Windows Explorer. I say, "This folder contains files that keep your system working properly. There is no need to modify the contents." (see Figure 5.8). Yeah, right. And they'll obey?

ITS's help desk manager complained about users changing things on their systems, loading programs, deleting files, and generally causing unknowing tolls in terms of productivity and his staff's help fixing it. When users select the system folder in Windows 2000, they are warned to leave these files and folders alone. It is just a warning, however; a simple click and they can see the files. Windows 2000

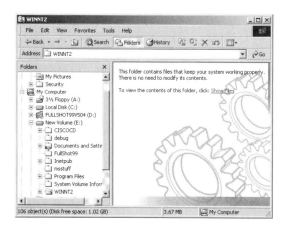

FIGURE 5.8
Soft protection.

does have something better going on behind the scenes. The help desk manager is going to love Windows 2000's Windows File Protection!

Windows File Protection (WFP) keeps systems files, files that were installed by the Windows 2000 setup, from being deleted or over-written. If a program or user attempts to delete, move, or overwrite a protected file, WFP springs into action. Only files digitally signed by Microsoft are allowed to succeed. Other attempts are foiled; WFP grabs a copy of the correct file from the Dllcache folder and places it in its correct system folder. An entry is written to the Event log as well.

Systems administrators and programmers will hate WFP at first, because they cannot manipulate the system's files either. Only Windows 2000 service packs, hot fixes, OS upgrades, and the Windows Update service can replace system files.

Analyzing Default Settings, Other Folders

Folders other than the system folders also have default permission settings. As in all things, you must be the judge of any additional settings needed.

Documents and Settings

Documents and Settings is a folder on the system drive and contains a folder for each user who has logged on to the computer. If user Fred has logged on to the Computer1 Windows 2000 system, for example, a folder called Fred is located underneath the Documents and Settings folder on the computer. Fred's folder holds subfolders for his profile, including the following:

◆ Applications Data

◆ Start Menu

◆ Desktop

◆ Cookies

◆ My Documents

> **NOTE**
>
> **Adding Additional Services**   InetPub is a good example of some choices ITS and anyone who installs an Internet Information Server (IIS) or other additional server services on Windows 2000 is going to have to make. The default setting on this folder is Everyone, Full Control. Its subfolders (AdminScripts, ftproot, iisamples, mailroot) and scripts inherit this setting. Fortunately the root for the World Wide Web root folder has its permissions changed to Administrators, Full Control; and Everyone, Read & Execute, List Folder Contents, and Read. As you know, however, that is not sufficient protection for a Web server's files and data.
>
> If you are going to install IIS or other programs on any of your servers, you need to do some work to ensure the security of server, the program, its data, and your network.

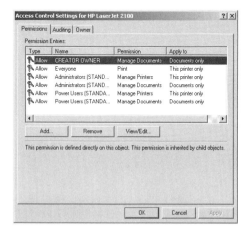

FIGURE 5.9
Printer permissions.

All advanced permissions on the Documents and Settings folder are set for This Folder, Subfolders, and Files. Unless otherwise noted, permissions are set to allow the following:

- ◆ **Administrators**—Full Control.

- ◆ **Everyone, Power Users, Users**—Read & Execute, List Folder Contents, Read. These permissions are also given to them on the All Users and Default Users subfolders.

- ◆ **SYSTEM**—Full Control.

When any user first logs on, a profile folder is created underneath the Documents and Settings folder and the user is given Full Control. Note that the Allow Inheritable Permissions from Parent to Propagate to this Object check box is not selected on the Security tab of the Properties page for profile folders. This means that if you change permission at the parent folder (My Documents and Settings), the changes are not propagated to the profile folders (except Default User and All Users).

ANALYZING PRINTER PERMISSIONS

Printer permissions control who can print, who can manage documents, and who can manage a printer (see Figure 5.9). In making permission-setting decisions, you must determine whether you want to restrict printing access to certain printers. Printers that print sensitive documents such as checks are good candidates for this. Others are printers that are expensive to operate or that need to be reserved for departmental or area use to ensure their availability. By default, the Users group is given Print Permission. This allows the users to print documents, pause, resume, restart, and cancel their own documents and connect to a printer.

After you have determined who should be able to print where, you need to decide whether any of these users should manage documents and choose a group or user to manage the printer. The Manage Documents permission allows Control Job Settings for All Documents and Pause, Restart, and Delete All Documents. In a large organization, you may want to create a group, give it this permission, and then add a reliable individual in remote areas with this permission so that he can manage documents on departmental printers. ITS, for example, gives this permission on the warehouse printers to the warehouse office clerk. She cannot change printer permissions; because she can delete any documents, however, she can delete those that are not printing properly and those that were sent to the printer in error. This practice saves many help desk hours, and limits user frustration with technology.

Manage Printer is a permission that expands these duties to include Share a Printer, Change Printer Properties, Delete Printers, and Change Printer Permissions. The Administrators, Server Operators, and Print Operators groups are given this permission by default. On standalone servers, the Power Users group is given this assignment as well. Printer permissions are set on the Security tab of the Printer property pages.

Although these are the same sets of permission as in Windows NT 4.0, you can explicitly allow or deny *every* Windows 2000 printer permission.

> **N O T E** **Permission Gotcha #5** If a Macintosh computer user can send a document to a printer, he can print it. There is no way to set security settings on a printer for Macintosh users.

ANALYZING REGISTRY KEYS ACCESS

Registry keys have a huge amount of data in them. Much of it is necessary for the very survival of the machine. Herein resides the configuration information for all the system services, for devices, for hardware, and for software. It is only common sense to have granular, discretionary access control.

DACLs

You can set the following registry permissions:

- ◆ **Query Value**—Ask for and get the value of a key.
- ◆ **Set Value**—Change a key value.
- ◆ **Create Subkey**—Create a subkey.
- ◆ **Enumerate subkeys**—List the subkeys.
- ◆ **Notify**—Set auditing.
- ◆ **Create Link**—Link this key to some other key.
- ◆ **Write DAC**—Change permissions.

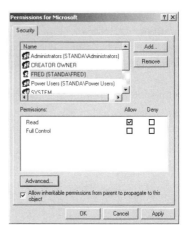

FIGURE 5.10
Does Fred have Read or Special permission, part 1?

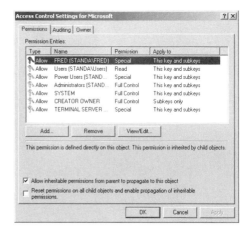

FIGURE 5.11
Does Fred have Read or Special permissions, part 2?

FIGURE 5.12
Fred has Special permission!

◆ **Read Control**—Find the owner of the key.

◆ **Write Owner**—Change ownership of the key.

◆ **Delete**—Delete the key.

Registry permissions, like file permissions, can also be applied by selecting one of two groupings of permissions: Read or Full Control. Full Control, of course, means that the user or group has all the permissions previously listed. Read incorporates the Query Value, Enumerate Subkeys, Read Control, and Notify permissions.

However, you should not be fooled by the indication of Read permission on the Permissions page for a key (see Figures 5.10 and 5.11). It is almost as if Microsoft forgot a check box for Special. If a user or group has Special permission on this key, you will have to look behind this page by clicking the Advanced button (see Figure 5.12). There is no indication on the Permissions page that users have Special permission.

You also need to look at the Access Control Settings for … (Advanced) page to see key ownership, audit settings, and to determine whether the permission applies to This Key and Subkeys, This Key Only, or Subkeys Only.

Examining Default Registry Settings

In a fashion similar to the default protection of important system files, registry key permissions are secured by default. In many cases, the default permission gives only Full Control to Administrators

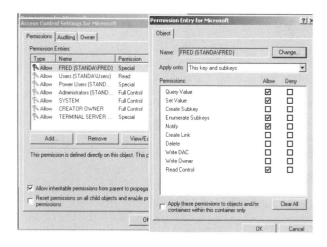

and to the SYSTEM account. The group Everyone may have Read permissions at hive roots, but subkeys are controlled by giving permissions to Power Users and or to Users, Authenticated Users, and CREATOR OWNER as appropriate. Gone are the days of wide-open access by default.

After install, Power Users have backward-compatible permissions for users. Power Users can create subkeys in the HKEY_LOCAL_MACHINE\SOFTWARE\ key. This gives them the ability to install software, which is creating keys and subkeys underneath this root.

Power Users also, like CREATOR OWNER, have Full Control over the subkeys they create, but only the subkeys. This ability to allow the CREATOR OWNER of a key to control it, without inadvertently giving them the ability to control other keys, is an outstanding feature.

Power Users do not have these same rights in other hives. The Hardware hive, for example, does not even list Power Users. Instead, the group Everyone is given Read permission, Administrators and the SYSTEM are given Full Control, and the RESTRICTED group is given Read permissions.

You may want to tighten security more on certain registry keys. You should be aware that, as in Windows NT, any changes to the registry may have unintended and disastrous consequences. Understand thoroughly the nature of the changes you are making, and back up the registry before you make them. Test the results of your changes before putting the system back into production.

Backing Up the Registry

No discussion of security resources would be complete without making sure that a standard is set for registry backup.

You can use the `regedt32 — file\save` key to save the selected key to a file.

You can also use the new Windows 2000 backup tool. Open this tool and select the Backup tab. Then select System State (see Figure 5.13). This backs up the registry, COM+ Class Registration database, and system boot files of the server. It also includes the

Certificate Services database if the system is operated as a certificate server. If it is a domain controller, backup is made of the Active Directory Directory Services database and the sysvol directory.

You can only do this on the local computer.

The registry is saved in the *systemroot*\repair\regback folder and can be used to repair only the registry.

To ensure the best backup practice, Microsoft makes the following recommendations:

◆ Write a backup plan and test it.

◆ Train backup operators. (In minimum- and medium-security networks, grant Backup rights to one user and Restore rights to another; in high-security networks, give Restore rights only to those with Administrator rights.)

◆ Back up complete volumes.

◆ Back up Directory Services database to capture user account and security information.

◆ Backup logs are created by default; print them and keep them.

◆ Maintain at least three copies of your backup. One of them should be kept offsite.

◆ Test your backup (with a restore).

◆ Keep backup device and backup media secured.

NOTE

For More Security The Backup Operators group has privileges to both back up and restore data. You may want to create two groups. Give one the backup right, and the other the restore right. On the other hand, you might want to only give those in the Administrators group the right to restore.

FIGURE 5.13
Backing up the System State.

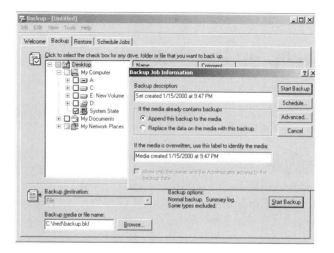

EXAMINING DIAL-IN ACCESS

Dial-in access or the ability to dial-in to the network and use network resources is first controlled by restricting the right to even connect to the network in this manner. (For more information, see Chapter 4 and Chapter 14, "Designing Security for Access Between Networks.")

After users have connected, however, what protects network resources?

In simple environments, and in environments with Windows NT Remote Access Servers that are not using Routing and Remote Access Services, resource access is restricted by setting the ability to access resources on just the RAS server, or throughout the network.

In a Windows 2000 network where the RAS server is a Windows 2000 Server, the preferred way to restrict access to the network is through the Routing and Remote Access console. Policies can be created and maintained through the Remote Access Policies section. Access is controlled based on dial-in properties of user accounts and policies (see Figure 5.14). If multiple RAS servers are necessary, all access can be controlled through central policies on Microsoft Internet Access Server (IAS), an optional Windows 2000 service.

In either case, granular access to resources is controlled by native systems, such as by setting NTFS permissions on files and folders, and registry access permissions by using regedt32.exe.

INTERNET ACCESS

Internet access is an expected component of an enterprise network. The process of securing that access has many parts. Controlling internal access to the Internet is one part of it. Security can be specified by identifying where that access occurs and who will have what access permissions.

First, identify and control the point of access. Do computers have dial-up access via modems? Is there a proxy server on the network? A firewall? A router? Proxy servers serve as an intermediary between users and the Internet. Most enable some form of access control. If you are using Microsoft Proxy Server, you can control access using Windows 2000 users and groups. Although firewalls typically are put into place to block external access to your network, they may also act

FIGURE 5.14
Dial-in access properties.

as guardians of access to the Internet. You must investigate the appropriate means and permission sets available on your proxy servers, firewalls, and routers. Remember that you should have a granular means to do this. You want to do more than allow or deny Internet access; you want to be able to specify the type of Internet resource (WWW server, ftp server, telnet server); and within those broad categories, you want to be able to specify finer ones that address the issue of content and intent.

Finally, address the issue of Internet access to your network. Can external users access your network from the Internet? Can they browse to your external or internal servers? Are additional controls necessary to ensure they have only the access they need? Does your plan include blocking nonauthorized users (employees as well as intruders) from access?

Next, understand that Internet access can mean increased risk of intrusion to your network. Guarding against that possibility, while strengthening internal resources against external attack, is an important part of analyzing security.

ITS does not indicate whether they give their employees Internet access. This would be a point to clarify. They do, however, indicate plans to redesign their main application to offer increased access to their inventory and customer information to their salespeople, access to customer information to the customer, and direct-ordering capabilities. This could be accomplished within the current infrastructure using the same dial-up RAS servers, or they may choose an Internet model. This is one thing you should determine so that you will not be blindsided by this development.

For more information on the tools and the "how to" of securing Internet access, refer to Part V of this book, "Designing a Security Solution for Access Between Networks."

ACTIVE DIRECTORY SCHEMA PERMISSIONS

Permissions within the Active Directory schema are set on each class. Think of an Active Directory schema class as a category, a definition of an object, but not the object itself. If I talk about the schema class Computer, therefore, I am not talking about any particular computer, just a generic description of a computer. Because I have a class Computer in the schema, that means I can store computer objects in Active Directory. The class Computer consists of a list of attributes that describe what a computer is composed of. Some other classes are user, storage, and volume. A class represents the properties or attributes (userSharedFolder, catalogs, userCertificate, logonHours, logonCount, badPwdCount, and so on) used to describe an object. The schema is just a definition for the kinds of objects and the characteristics of those objects that can be stored in Active Directory. Make no mistake, modifying the schema can have earth shattering results. Modifying the schema can mutate Windows 2000 into something wildly different from your out-of-the-box Windows 2000. To modify the schema, you must be a member of the Schema Admins group, and schema updates must be enabled on the Schema Operations Master.

In the schema, you can define and manage the types of classes, the attributes they can have, and who can do what with them. The specific objects stored in Active Directory are managed through the Active Directory MMC snap-ins. To add users or to change their passwords, use the Active Directory Users and Computers console. To specify who can change a user's password, use the Delegation of Authority Wizard.

The following are some basic Active Directory schema permissions:

- Create Child
- Delete Child
- Read Property
- Write Property
- List Contents
- Write Self
- Delete Tree
- List Object
- Control Access

Many other Active Directory permissions exist. The permissions available for any class depend on the class type. For example, the right to Change Password is a permission set on the Computer class. It is granted to the group Everyone by default. This is logical and correct. Everyone ought to be able to change his or her own password. This differs from the Reset Password right. Resetting a password would mean changing someone else's password, definitely a right that should be restricted. Access permissions to Active Directory objects are set through the Active Directory Schema console.

Setting Active Directory schema permissions should be restricted to senior administrators and programmers experienced in Active Directory management. You can find more information on managing the Active Directory schema by accessing Help when the Active Directory schema MMC snap-in is loaded in a console. The Active Directory schema snap-in is not available by default. You must run REGSVR32 to register the console in MMC.

ITS Resource Security Design

It is clear from the default access permissions settings imposed on the file system folders and files, printer objects, and registry keys that Windows 2000 provides fair resource security settings for these objects. Further refinement of these settings will depend on the circumstances that exist in the enterprise. Configuration may need to be tightened or relaxed accordingly. As services beyond those loaded by default are added, more configuration will have to be managed.

What would be appropriate baseline settings for ITS? To answer this, you need to consider three things:

◆ Legacy applications

◆ Down-level clients and servers

◆ Level of risk

Down-level clients and servers have associated authentication issues that were discussed in Chapter 4.

First, will ITS have, or have for some interim time, down-level servers or clients? ITS will have down-level servers and clients into the near future. Because of this, some configuration settings cannot be changed. To maintain communications between servers and clients, for example, NTLM needs to remain as an authentication choice. If the Directory Services Client for Windows NT and/or

Windows 9x is loaded, it will be possible to restrict the authentication to NTLMv2, which is considerably more secure.

Legacy applications can also cause the relaxation of baseline settings. As you know, ITS has its own, homegrown server application. It expressed issues with that application and the need to elevate user privileges to "make it work." A careful investigation of this application and any other legacy applications must be made to determine specific changes that might have to be made. It may be that all that is necessary is to include in the Power Users group any users who need general access to the application. As you have seen, Power Users have extended rights in the system files and registry keys that members of the Users group do not. Windows 2000 Professional includes, by default, the Authenticated Users group as members within the Power Users group. Windows 2000 Server and Advanced Server do not. ITS can add to this group, just those users who need access to legacy applications. (Chapter 7 discusses this topic in more detail.) Over time ITS needs to rewrite its application to adhere to Microsoft logo standards for Windows 2000; then it will be able to tighten security configurations.

If ITS had not had legacy applications, it might have wanted to make adjustments to the baseline for access settings. Doing so requires knowledge of user groups, the registry, and Windows 2000 services and settings. One simple change that could be made is to remove the Authenticated Users group from membership in the Power Users group on Windows 2000 Professional. This limits the access and rights that users logging on to those computers have. Another possibility is to apply secure or high-security templates.

The third area that ITS needs to consider in formulating its security baseline is to gauge its level of risk. By understanding the types of risk its network resources are exposed to, it can more clearly identify needs for special security configuration. Although much activity in risk alleviation is done at the point at which users connect to the network, or connect to a particular machine, other work needs to be done at the network resource level. This work goes far beyond the basic baseline configuration, but may belong to what an individual company considers as its baseline. You can find more information on risk assessment and responding to different kinds of external risks in Chapter 14.

CHAPTER SUMMARY

KEY TERMS

- DACL
- NTFS
- Power User
- CREATOR OWNER
- Everyone
- Users
- WFP
- Manage Printer
- Manage Documents
- Routing and Remote Access
- Routing and Remote Access policy
- class
- object
- attribute
- schema

This chapter has concentrated on the resource access portion of analyzing security requirements. You have looked at the major network resources, files, registry, printers, dial–up access, and Internet access. Windows 2000 has a lot of adjustments that can be made, no?

By now you should have realized that there are many things that need to be done to secure an enterprise. You have begun to see the breadth and depth of the security services available in Windows 2000, and the complexity of the system you are attempting to secure. As you continue your study, nay as you develop your own enterprise security solution, don't forget to revisit these first steps. Good security is multilevel and good security design is too.

APPLY YOUR KNOWLEDGE

Exercise

5.1 Setting Access Permissions

Examine Table 5.2. Read each statement in the Needed column. Decide which tool you would use to set permissions and what permissions you would set. Write in the answers.

Estimated Time: 10 minutes

TABLE 5.2

EXERCISE 5.1: PERMISSION SETTING

Needed	Where to Set	Permission
ITS salespeople need access to customer reports		
Administrators need to keep clerical from running Registry Editor		
Stop Users from accessing check printer		
Manager needs access to Internet		
Deny access to the share Customer folder for Warehouse staff		
Pam needs to be able to read files in the Company folder		
Prevent Sally from deleting files in the Court Documents folder		
Deny Server Operators access to services configuration		
Provide Read access to drive D for all Users		

Review Questions

1. ITS's salespeople are getting new Windows 2000 Professional laptops. What file system should be loaded on the laptops?

2. ITS's help desk manager asks, "Will the new system help me keep Jane from damaging her system by loading games from home?" What is your answer?

3. The systems administrator at ITS is afraid of a long learning curve. He wants to know how difficult it is going to be to secure the file system and registry. What do you tell him?

4. John works in the accounting department. He wants to know how to make the check printer more secure. What would be your plans for securing that printer? How about the other printers?

5. How can external access to the ITS database be controlled? Customers and salespeople will be dialing in. Can settings differ for both?

6. What might ITS have to do to ensure its custom application will run under Windows 2000?

Exam Questions

1. Hillside Nursery ships plants to 1,500 shops around the country. They include growing instructions with each plant on a special label. The labels are printed on three special printers in the warehouse. Three printers are also available for normal printing. The warehouse is some distance away from the rest of the business. What would you suggest for the print permissions on each type of printer?

APPLY YOUR KNOWLEDGE

A. Label printers: Remove Users group; make group that can print; make one person Manage Documents; Administrators, Full control. Regular Printers: Users, Print; Administrators, Full Control.

B. Label printers: Make one person Manage Documents; Administrators, Full Control. Regular printers: Users, Print; Administrators, Full Control.

C. Label printers: Deny Print to Users; make group that can print; Administrators, Full control. Regular printers: Users, Print; Administrators, Full Control.

D. Label printers: Deny Print to Users; make group that can print; make one person Mange Documents; Administrators, Full Control. Regular Printers: Administrators, Full Control.

2. ITS has a legacy application it wants to run on Windows 2000 Professional. (Pick those that apply.)

A. No problem, it will run fine.

B. Because Authenticated Users is a member of Power Users and Power Users can do any-thing, everyone can run the program.

C. Because Authenticated Users is a member of Power Users, and the Power Users group has backward compatibility with the Windows NT 4.0, Users group, if users ran the program before, can run it today.

D. Because the program doesn't directly access the hardware and follows most other Windows NT 4.0 compatibility rules and runs well on NT 4.0, it should run okay.

3. Sally wants to give Frank permission to read a file on the computer that they share. Sally owns the file. What can Sally do?

A. Sally can't give Frank permission because she is not a member of the Administrators group.

B. Sally can't give Frank permission because she does not have the Change Permission permission.

C. Sally can give Frank permission to read her file because she is a member of the Power Users group.

D. Sally can give Frank permission to read her file because she is the file owner, and as CREATOR OWNER she has Full Control on the file.

4. If you change permission on registry keys, what two groups should always be given Full Control?

A. Users and Power Users

B. Administrators and Power Users

C. Administrators and SYSTEM

D. SYSTEM and Power Users

5. Examine Figure 5.15. Who can delete files in msstuff?

A. Fred, John, Nancy, Peter

B. John, Nancy, Peter

C. John, maybe Fred

D. Nancy, John

E. Fred, John, Nancy

F. Fred, Nancy, Peter

G. Fred, Nancy

APPLY YOUR KNOWLEDGE

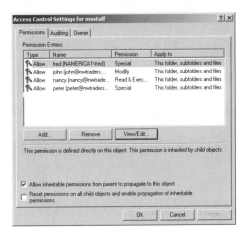

FIGURE 5.15
Who can delete?

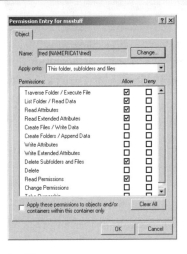

FIGURE 5.16
Can Fred delete?

H. Fred, Peter

I. John

6. Examine Figure 5.16. Fred does not have permission to delete the can.doc file in the msstuff folder. Can Fred delete the can.doc file?

   A. Fred cannot delete; he does not have Delete permission.

   B. Fred can delete because he is a member of the Administrators group.

   C. Fred cannot delete; he needs the Delete, Modify, or Full Control permission on the can.doc file.

   D. Fred can delete. The Delete Subfolders and Files permission implies deletion of all files and subfolders no matter what.

7. The Crown and Sons, Inc. systems administrator needs to design a resource access strategy for his company. He knows that everyone has access to the network and that most storage is for files. A printer in each department will serve most needs. Users are unsophisticated. After they create a file, they should be able to do anything they want with it, but he does not want them assigning permissions at their home-folder level. He should include the following things in his design:

   A. Users will store files on a network file server.

   B. Each will have access to private storage space; he will exclude other users from access to this area.

   C. At their home-folder level, he will give them Read & Execute and Write Permission.

   D. At the home subfolder and file (of their folder), he will give CREATOR OWNER Full Control.

   E. At their folder level, he will give them Full Control.

APPLY YOUR KNOWLEDGE

8. Nancy wants to block permission inheritance from folders to files. She opens the Security page for the file and makes which of the following change(s)?.

   A. Unchecks Reset Permissions on All Child Objects and Enable Propagation of Inheritable Permissions.

   B. Checks the Don't Accept Permissions by Inheritance box on the Security tab.

   C. Unchecks the Allow Inheritable Permissions from Parent to Propagate to this Object box on the Security tab.

   D. Clicks the View/Edit button and selects Don't Accept Permissions by Inheritance from the Apply onto drop-down box.

9. During installation Windows 2000 sets the following permissions on the root folder of the installation volume.

   A. Administrators, Full Control

   B. Everyone, Full Control

   C. Power Users, Full Control

   D. Users, Read & Execute

10. Backing up the registry by using Backup and selecting System State also backs up what?

    A. COM+

    B. System boot files

    C. User profiles

    D. SAM

    E. Network settings

    F. Certificate Services database (if applicable)

G. Active Directory Directory Services database

H. The sysvol directory

Answers to Exercise

The solution to Exercise 5.1 is shown in Table 5.3.

TABLE 5.3

ANSWER TO EXERCISE 5.1: PERMISSION SETTING

Needed	Where to Set	Permission
ITS Salespeople need access to customer reports	Windows Explorer	Allow Read
Administrators need to keep clerical from running Registry Editor	Windows Explorer	Deny Access
Stop Users from accessing check printer	Printer (for check printer)	Deny Print
Manager needs access to Internet	Proxy server, or firewall/router Internet Explorer	Depends on tool
Deny access to the share 'Customer' Folder for Warehouse staff	Computer Management console, or Shared Folders, Share Permissions Tab	Deny Full Control
Pam needs to be able to read files in the Company folder.	Same as above but Security Tab	Allow Read
Prevent Sally from deleting files in the Court Documents folder	Windows Explorer	Deny Delete Subfolders and Files
Deny Server Operators access to services configuration.	Regedt32, HKLM\SYSTEM\ Current ControlSet\ Services	Deny Full Control to Server Operators Group

APPLY YOUR KNOWLEDGE

Needed	Where to Set	Permission
Provide Read access to Drive D for all Users	Computer Management, Logical Drives, D Drive	Allow Read to Authenticated Users

Answers to Review Questions

1. ITS Windows 2000 Professional laptops should have NTFS loaded as their file system. Effective file protection can be implemented. This way data that is on the road can be better secured.

2. Tell the help desk manager that although there is no guarantee that Windows 2000 will totally protect Jane's computer from Jane, Windows File Protection will not allow any program that she loads to overwrite files needed to keep the operating system running.

3. Although it takes time to learn the ins and outs of securing his registry and file system to best suit his systems, both have many default settings that help protect the system right out-of-the-box. You can also tell him about the templates provided for system configuration.

4. John's check printer should have the Print permission assigned to Everyone removed. Instead, Print permissions should be assigned to a smaller subset, perhaps a trusted group within the accounting department. It may also be useful to have an accounting department member assigned the Manage Printers and Manage Documents rights, instead of allowing the Print Operators group this permission. Because CREATOR OWNER also is assigned Manage Documents, he will need to decide whether they should keep this

right. Other printers in the company can start with default rights.

5. External access settings can be controlled through remote access policies, which can differ for customers and salespeople.

6. ITS needs to develop a Windows 2000–compliant version of the product. In the interim, it may have to relax both access privileges and give users elevated rights so that they can run the application.

Answers to Exam Questions

1. **A.** Label printers are for printing labels, not for general use. You might think that people would realize that by themselves, but you'd be surprised how many labels would be wasted. (For more information, see the section "Analyzing Printer Permissions.")

2. **C, D.** Although you cannot be 100% sure, even with all of this going for you, you do stand a reasonable chance. The Power Users group has backward compatibility with user permissions in Windows NT 4.0, and users can run the program in NT 4.0. The program itself isn't causing problems in 4.0. (For more information, see the sections "Analyzing Default Settings on System Files" and "Analyzing Default Registry Settings.")

3. **D.** Sally owns the file. Sally can assign permissions. She does not have to be a member of the Administrators group (A is wrong), nor does she specifically have to have the Change Permission granted (B is wrong). Sally is not a member of the Power Users group (C is wrong). (For more information, see the section "Learning File System DACLS.")

4. **C.** Don't take the chance that you may lock the SYSTEM out of important files, and make sure that someone has rights to set permissions for others. The administrator is the logical person to do this. (For more information, see the section "Examining Default Registry Settings.")

5. **C.** John can delete files because he has the Modify permission. Fred and Peter have special permissions. There is no way to tell from here whether they have Delete permission. (For more information, see the sections "Learning File System DACLS.")

6. **D.** The Delete Subfolders and Files permission on a folder implies that any subfolder or file in that folder can be deleted, even if that file does not have specific Delete permission applied. (For more information, see the section "Learning File System DACLs.")

7. **A, B, C, D.** Users don't need Full Control to create and read their files. To give them permission to assign permissions and to delete these files, CREATOR OWNER needs Full Control but only for subfolders and files. (For more information, see the section "Learning File System DACLs.")

8. **C.** Inheritance can be easily blocked while permissions are changed and reapplied by using this check box. (For more information, see the section "Understanding Inheritance and Propagation.")

9. **B.** Windows 2000 will not tighten security on the root folder because it doesn't know whether other programs and files exist on this volume. If restrictive permission is set on the root folder, it attempts to propagate them through out the structure, and that might destroy carefully designed permission sets or might prevent some application from running. (For more information, see the note "Root Rights.")

10. **A, B, D, F, G, H.** System State's a collection of important files and needs to periodically be backed up. They are collected under this name to ensure they all get backed up. (For more information, see the section "Backing Up the Registry.")

APPLY YOUR KNOWLEDGE

Suggested Readings and Resources

1. Windows 2000 Advanced Server online help system

2. *Microsoft Windows 2000 Resource Kit.* Microsoft Press, 2000

3. Windows 2000 property pages for files, folders, printers, registry, and schema objects

4. Microsoft white papers:

   • A Step By Step Guide to the Microsoft Management Console

• Default Access Control Settings

• Development considerations for File Storage Applications in Windows 2000.

5. Web sites

   • www.microsoft.com/security

   • www.microsoft.com/windows

DESIGNING A WINDOWS 2000 SECURITY SOLUTION

This chapter covers the following Microsoft-specified objective for the "Designing a Windows 2000 Security Solution" section of the Designing Security for a Microsoft Windows 2000 Network exam:

Design an audit policy.

▶ You design security strategies to protect your assets. You determine when special authentication mechanisms are important and where to tighten file access. You delegate management of local and task-oriented resources to the people who best understand them. You reserve global access for the trusted few. Doesn't it make sense to audit the activities of users and the attempts of attackers to see whether your strategies are working? What facilities are available and how are they implemented? You have choices; which should you employ? Where should you employ them? These are the questions you must answer in your quest to design an audit policy.

CHAPTER 6

Designing an Audit Policy

OUTLINE

▶ If you attempted to establish audit policies in Windows NT 4.0 domains, you will appreciate the ease with which you can establish and maintain policies without visiting multiple sites. Pieces of the puzzle are still missing; you still cannot easily manage the thousands of audit messages that a good design generates, and many of the messages are quite cryptic. If you are new to audit policies, you will want to concentrate on understanding why you have the option you do. It is a good practice to read a setting and then question "Why would I want to do this?"

▶ To learn the components of a good audit policy, do the following:

  • Understand the process. Make sure you can explain how auditing information is generated. How does the OS know to report that someone attempted to open a file?

  • Implementing a sample policy is helpful. Use the exercises to learn how. Make sure you understand how auditing is set up.

  • As you examine the possible types of information you can collect, it is helpful to ask "What would getting this information tell me?"

  • Determine your best practices for different classes of systems. Systems that share data with partners, those that allow access into the network from outside, and any servers that handle money or other sensitive data are candidates for special attention.

  • Revisit the security baselines and security template sections in Chapter 5, "Securing Resources," for help in understanding the use of these tools.

INTRODUCTION

It seems rather unfair, doesn't it? You are charged with securing your network. You work hard to learn what to do and to put it into place. Just when you think your job is done, those pesky auditors poke their noses in. This time, head 'em off at the pass and prepare an audit policy that gives them the information they need. You will find it can also become your first line of defense, your first indication that something is wrong, and a good tool to figure out what went wrong. You will find it useful, as well, to help you make legacy applications available to users without giving them broad and elevated privileges.

Remember that this process has two parts. You set up auditing to watch for intruders and to help figure out access problems. Auditors use the results to determine whether systems are configured with proper controls. I recommend that you bring in your information system auditors during your security design process to make sure you are obtaining the information they need as well.

DESIGNING AN AUDIT POLICY

Design an audit policy.

To derive an effective audit policy, you must do the following:

◆ First, learn what can be audited and what useful information it will give you.

◆ Decide which objects you need to audit on a regular basis and what you are looking for.

◆ Derive strategies for gleaning information using periodic or fixed-frame audit techniques.

◆ Learn how to turn auditing on and how to establish each available facet.

◆ Determine how you are going to cope with the multitude of records produced.

WHAT CAN BE AUDITED?

You can configure an audit policy (Security Settings\Local Policy\
Audit Policy) to audit the following events (see Figure 6.1):

- ◆ Account logon events
- ◆ Account management
- ◆ Directory service access
- ◆ Logon events
- ◆ Object access
- ◆ Policy change
- ◆ Privilege use
- ◆ Process tracking
- ◆ System events

In addition, you can configure special security options to allow auditing of the Backup and Restore privilege and the access of global
system objects (refer to Chapter 4, "Designing a Security Baseline").
These audit policies are covered separately because they result in the
generation of massive amounts of data and are not as useful in the
production environment. Auditing global system object access can be
useful in determining the actions of software you are testing and for
determining whether software follows security guidelines before it is
implemented in your environment.

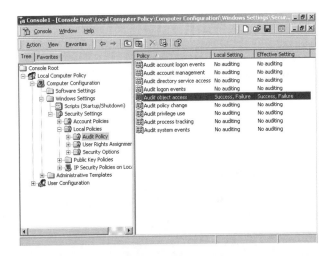

FIGURE 6.1
Configuring audit policy.

Account Logon Events

When a domain controller gets a logon request, this category is activated. This includes the issuing of Kerberos tickets for resource access.

Account Management

Security events are triggered if a user account is created, deleted, or changed.

Directory Service Access

This category is activated when an Active Directory object is accessed. Like file and folder objects, Directory service objects have multiple activities that can be audited. The number and kind of activities depend on the type of object being audited. Setting this category does not automatically generate the thousands of events you might expect. You must visit the property pages of the Active Directory object and set auditing for specific users or groups (see Figure 6.2).

The following list shows some of the activities that can be audited:

- ◆ Full Control
- ◆ List Contents
- ◆ Read All Properties
- ◆ Write All Properties
- ◆ Delete
- ◆ Delete Subtree
- ◆ Read Permissions
- ◆ Modify Permissions
- ◆ Modify Owner
- ◆ All Validated Writes
- ◆ All Extended Writes

- ◆ Create All Child Objects
- ◆ Delete All Child Objects
- ◆ Change Password
- ◆ Receive As
- ◆ Reset Password
- ◆ Send As
- ◆ Validated Write to DNS Host Name
- ◆ Validated Write to Service Principal Name
- ◆ Create IntelliMirror Service Objects
- ◆ Delete IntelliMirror Service Objects
- ◆ Create MSMQ Configuration Objects
- ◆ Delete MSMQ configuration Objects
- ◆ Create Printer Objects
- ◆ Delete Printer Objects

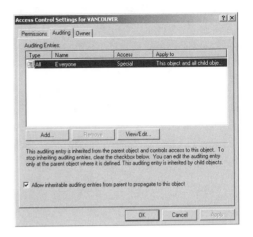

FIGURE 6.2
Setting audit choices on a computer object.

Some of the activities that can be audited for a group are as follows:

- ◆ Full Control
- ◆ List Contents
- ◆ Read All Properties
- ◆ Write all Properties
- ◆ Delete
- ◆ Delete Subtree
- ◆ Read Permissions
- ◆ Modify Permissions
- ◆ Modify Owner
- ◆ All Validated Writes
- ◆ All Extended Writes
- ◆ Create All Child Objects
- ◆ Delete All Child Objects

◆ Add/Remove Self as Member

◆ Send to

Logon Events

Events are recorded when a user logs on or logs off. Audit logon failure to find whether someone is trying a random-password hack. In high-security networks, you may want to audit logon success periodically during heavy vacation times or at any time that you want to find out whether passwords have been compromised.

Object Access

When an object is accessed, this category is activated. As you know, each object has a security descriptor attached to it. The descriptor is composed in part by a Discretionary Access Control List (DACL). The DACL enables fine-grained control of object access. A second part to the security descriptor is the System Access Control List (SACL). The SACL specifies when to record access, or failed access, to the object. You create entries in the SACL when you identify an object for auditing and indicate users and groups to watch for. File and folder access audit is set in Windows Explorer. After you have selected the file or folder to audit, you can audit success or failure of the following activities (see Figure 6.3):

◆ **Traverse Folder/Execute File**—Someone, or an application, opens a folder and passes through it to look below. At the file level, an application is executed.

◆ **List Folder/Read Data**—A folder is opened, or data is viewed.

◆ **Read Attributes**—A file or folder attributes are looked at.

◆ **Read Extended Attributes**—Extended attributes are examined. (Applications create and view extended attributes.)

◆ **Create Files/Write Data**—A file is created or changed.

◆ **Create Folders/Append Data**—A folder is created inside the folder that is audited, or a file within the audited folder is changed.

- ◆ **Write Attributes**—Attributes are set.
- ◆ **Write Extended Attributes**—Extended attributes are set (by an application).
- ◆ **Delete Subfolders and Files**—A file within an audited folder or a folder within an audited folder is deleted.
- ◆ **Delete**—A specific file is deleted.
- ◆ **Read Permissions**—Permissions for a file or folder are read.
- ◆ **Change Permissions**—Permissions for a file or folder are changed.
- ◆ **Take Ownership**—Ownership of a folder is changed.

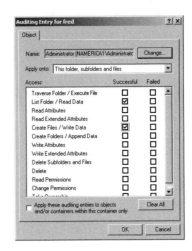

FIGURE 6.3
Setting audit choices on file objects.

Policy Change

When a policy that affects security, user rights, or auditing is changed, an event is generated.

Privilege Use

A user right is used to do something. Every privilege that a user has, even including the right to access a file, is recorded.

Process Tracking

This is used to track what a program is doing while it is executing. It is valuable to the developer during testing. It is also valuable when used to verify that the activities of a supplied program are not doing anything that would compromise security.

System Events

System events, such as shutting down the computer, are recorded.

OBJECTS TO WATCH

Generally accepted best practices, including those recommended by Microsoft for auditing, are as follows:

◆ Audit logon failure to discover random-password hacking.

◆ Audit logon success to discover password compromise (stolen passwords, password break in). If a user is on vacation and an account is being accessed, or if accounts are being accessed at odd hours of the day, you can suspect that someone other than the user is logging on. Remember, however, that auditing passwords for Success or Failure produces records for every active account. You cannot limit your audit to a single user.

◆ Audit user rights, user and group management, policy changes, and system events to learn of misuse of privileges. If a user has been given the rights to manage particular groups and is overstepping his privileges by adding or deleting membership in other groups, a Success audit will catch this. If an Account Operator is attempting to add users to the Administrators group, a Failure audit will catch this.

◆ Set Success or Failure audit for file objects and printers for users and groups that you suspect of improper access or attempted access. Be selective when determining files and folders and users to audit. Each file access generates multiple events, and the audit log can quickly become unmanageable.

◆ Actively monitor when setting Success and Failure on Write access to program files. This may produce a large number of entries. If it does, you may suspect virus or Trojan horse activity.

◆ Be sure to increase the default size of the Security log to handle the larger number of records.

It is much harder to define which file, printer, Active Directory, and registry objects to audit. Only you can determine the sensitive files that need to be audited for attempted access or for a list of who has been in the files. During your planning strategies, you identified files and folders that users would be opening. You should also have identified those objects that are at greatest risk.

To these files, add possible system files that might cause problems. If you will use the repair folder to store a copy of the registry, for example, this is a good choice. Most system files are protected from tampering, but do you need to monitor attempts? See the section "Applying Security to File Systems" in Chapter 5.

There are two approaches to file auditing. One approach finds the more sensitive files and folders and audits their access by everyone, looking for suspicious activity. The other approach attempts to predict suspicious people and audits files specifically for their access attempts. You can use both approaches to your benefit. First, really sensitive files and folders may need to be audited for attempted access by anyone. You can control the audit policy on these files by adding them to the File System folder of the Group Policy for the local computer (see Chapter 8, "Designing Security Policy Inheritance"). Second, it is true that you can sometimes anticipate unauthorized activity by an individual; the problem is the other thousands of individuals for whom you cannot anticipate this activity. So go ahead and audit the activities of folks you find irresistible, but don't forget to set up auditing on sensitive folders and files, registry keys, Active Directory objects, and printers.

USING PERIODIC OR FIXED-FRAME AUDIT TECHNIQUES

All audit purposes are not served by setting an audit policy and dealing with the results. Special techniques are used for special purposes or because of increased suspicious activity.

One such special process is to determine the minimal access requirements to allow legacy applications to run. Legacy applications may not run under Windows 2000 or may not run unless the user is a member of the Administrators group. Rather than needlessly, and dangerously, elevating user privileges, you can audit the activities of the program to determine where the problem lies. Step by Step 6.1 lists the process to follow.

STEP BY STEP

6.1 Auditing for Application Resolution

1. As Administrator, set an audit policy that includes process tracking, registry access, and file access (to do so, enable object access auditing; select specific registry and file objects to audit) from a regular user account.

2. Run the application as the user.

3. Examine audit logs to see what the application is attempting (but failing) to access.

4. Set up a group of application x users. Adjust file, folder, and registry settings to allow access by members of this group.

5. Add a regular user account to the group.

6. Test the application again as this user.

7. Modify where necessary and retest.

8. When everything is working, add users who need access to the group.

NOTE

A Tip Use the Domain Controller Security Policy console (Administrative Tools) to set audit policy for the domain. Settings made here impact all domain controllers in the domain. Use the Domain Security Policy to set audit policy for local databases on servers and professional systems joined in the domain. This is a *very* important distinction. If you set policies in the Domain Security Policy and think they will be in effect for domain controllers, you will be wrong! Any policy set in the Domain Controller Security Policy overrides domain-level settings. The default audit setting for the domain controller is No Auditing; hence, if those settings are still in place, you may wait in vain for a policy to take effect.

CONFIGURING AUDITING

Audit is first turned on and then dignified by detailed inspection and selection. In the Group Policy console (Local Computer Policy in the computer that is not a member of a domain), you create the audit policy by making changes to the Audit Policy folder underneath Local Policies. Although the audit policy is local, settings made at the site, domain, or OU level supercede those made here. Be sure to check the Effective Policy column if you are having trouble setting up auditing. The objects defined here are listed earlier in this chapter. Then, for file, folder, printer, and Active Directory objects, you create the audit policy by selecting the object, assigning users or groups to audit, and determining the items you want to watch for.

To view the results of any audit events, you use Event Viewer to look at them in the Security log (see Figure 6.4). Don't forget to check the Manage Auditing and Security Log user right. If you are not listed there, you cannot view the fruits of your auditing endeavor.

You can audit objects other than files. The following list identifies those objects and explains how to audit them:

◆ **Registry access**—After turning on object auditing, you can audit registry access by setting audit parameters on the Auditing tab of the Advanced Property pages of the registry key. These pages are accessible through the Security menu in the regedt32.exe program. An example of an audit on an object in the registry is shown in Figure 6.5.

◆ **Cluster data**—You set up auditing of cluster data in the same manner that you set up auditing of any file or folder. The difference is that you need to audit on all cluster nodes. Otherwise, you will see only activity when access occurs on the node you have set auditing on. The audit message appears in the Security log of the node that owns the resource.

◆ **Message queues**—You can also audit message queues for access. You set auditing in Active Directory, in the Users group, and in Computers\domain\ou\computer\msmq\queue_folder\queue.

◆ **Routing links for message queues**—You can audit these as well by visiting Active Directory Sites and Services and traversing to the Services folder MsmqSEvices\routing link.

◆ **Printers**—You can set up printer auditing on the Printer properties Security tab.

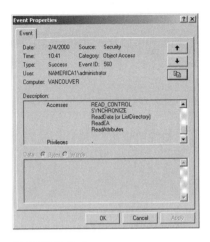

FIGURE 6.4
Making sure you can view the Security log.

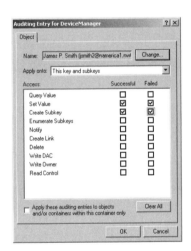

FIGURE 6.5
Setting auditing in the registry.

DETERMINE HOW YOU ARE GOING TO COPE WITH THE MULTITUDE OF RECORDS PRODUCED

The records produced by turning on auditing are recorded in the Security log, which can be displayed by visiting Administrative Tools\Event Viewer. You can view them in that log, export them in comma-delimited or tab-delimited format, and even copy an individual record to a Clipboard.

To manage the logs, you must accomplish two things:

◆ You must manage the log itself.

◆ You must make sense of and manage the data.

Managing the Log

Log settings are specified in the Group Policy Object\Computer Configuration\Windows Settings\Event Log folder. Doing the first part is easy. The log size must be set in anticipation of the amount of data that will be collected. If you will recall, the security templates enlarge the size of the security logs as security auditing increases. If you are unsure of the size of the file needed, remember that you must consider both the number of records and the frequency with which you will be archiving the file and clearing it. In addition to setting Security log size, three log settings are also possible (see Figure 6.6):

◆ Overwrite Events as Needed

◆ Overwrite Events Older than x Days

◆ Do Not Overwrite Events (Clear Log Manually)

If you choose to allow the log events to be overwritten, you may miss important security events. Setting a large file size and monitoring it helps prevent this.

If you specify that events should not be overwritten, you may be surprised to find that the event logs just stop recording events. Once again, you may miss important events. An attacker, realizing this is how you have things set, or assuming a number of administrators will do so, might mount a denial-of-service attack, attempting to fill up the log in hopes of having his real penetration events not recorded.

Alternatively, you could specify that events should not be overwritten and then enable the Shut Down System Immediately if Unable to Log Security Audits security option. An administrator must reset the policy and archive and clear the log file before users can continue using the system.

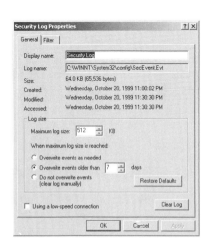

FIGURE 6.6
Changing Security log settings.

Managing Events

Managing events is a lot harder. It is so easy to set auditing and, even when set correctly, be overwhelmed with the multitude of security events appearing in the log. What do they all mean? Who has time to filter them looking for the important ones?

In a smaller environment, the Security log can be filtered manually with meaningful results.

You can filter events by clicking the Filter tab of the Security Log Properties page (see Figure 6.7).

First, you can check or uncheck the type of events for which to filter. The possibilities are as follows:

◆ Information

◆ Warning

◆ Error

◆ Success Audit

◆ Failure Audit

Next, you can select the event source and category:

◆ All

◆ DS (Directory Store)

◆ LSA (Local Security Authority)

◆ NetDDE Object (network dynamic data exchange object)

◆ SC Manager (Secure Channel Manager)

◆ Security

◆ SAM Database (Security Account Manager)

◆ Spooler (Print spooler messages)

Third, you can enter the event ID. You can find a list of event IDs in the w2000event.mdb file, available in the Windows 2000 Resource Kit.

Fourth, you can filter by user or computer name.

Finally, you can filter by first event, last event, or events on date pairs.

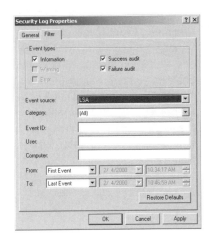

FIGURE 6.7
Setting Security log filters.

N
O
T
E

Recording Event Messages
Viewing the event may not let you see all the information at one time; besides, you may want a printed record. To obtain a full listing of the event message, click the button on the event page to send the information to the Clipboard (refer back to Figure 6.4). Paste the Clipboard contents to a WordPad or NotePad file for printing (see Figure 6.8).

Filtering enables you to narrow the range of data to digest but does nothing to help you identify what that data means. Some of it may be obvious—the indication of a failed file access means that someone is attempting to access a file, for example. Other bits appear meaningless.

Two Windows 2000 Resource Kit utilities, w2000msgs.chm, which contains the most frequent Windows 2000 messages, and w2000events.mdb, an Access database of Windows 2000 events, can help you discover the meaning of these cryptic messages.

Scroll through the w2000msgs.chm tool to find the exact words registered in the event and an explanation of what the record means. There are even useful hints at how to use that information. Consider, for example, the message An Authentication Package Has Been Loaded by the Local Security Policy. This message tells you which authentication package is in use. An authentication package is used by the LSA to authenticate logons. The administrator should periodically verify it. If an incorrect authentication package is substituted for the correct one, the system is under attack—or stupidity.

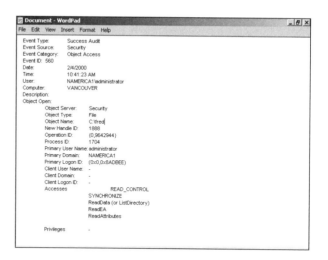

FIGURE 6.8
Recording individual audit events to files.

CASE STUDY: AUDIT POLICY

BACKGROUND

John Smith is the systems administrator with Cote, Inc., a major producer of toothpicks for the specialty food market. He has just been charged with migrating the mixed Windows NT and Novell network to Windows 2000. Cote has had "security events" before; many files on its network file server were deleted when a systems employee left the company, and last week its Web site was defaced.

PROBLEM STATEMENT

A method for auditing activity on all systems must be developed.

Information Systems Manager
We cannot tolerate any illegal, irresponsible activity on our network. I want to know even whether there is a hint of suspicious activity.

Systems Administrator
There are too many systems to watch the logons; besides, if I set up auditing, what's to prevent someone else from changing things? I just don't have the time to set up and maintain auditing.

Information Security
Windows 2000 has audit capabilities? We checked the Security log and didn't find anything there.

Help Desk Staff
Windows 2000, huh? I heard that most of my applications won't run. No one has written the new versions yet. This is certainly going to be fun.

CURRENT SYSTEM

Auditing the system has not been a primary concern.

Systems Administrator
We have no policy in place to tell us what to set up auditing for. That should be written by the auditors, and then they can get the logs and analyze them. I've set the correct access restrictions on the files. That keeps people out. Why, just the other day, I had to make someone a Power User so that he could run a program on his desktop.

Information Security
This has been a big issue with us. Why can't we print out a report on the settings that are made, and why don't we have records to indicate what happened during that Web site break-in?

ENVIRONMENT

The system is composed of a mixture of NT and Novell.

Systems Administrator
There are 2,000 Windows 98 and 30 Windows NT Workstations systems as well as 50 NT Servers and 10 Novell systems at this location. Our 100 branch offices each have an NT Server and 5 to 15 Windows 98 boxes each.

ENVISIONED SYSTEM

A new attention to audit involves a desire for education and a plan to make audit become a regular part of operations, not just something done once in a while (or when there is a problem).

continues

CASE STUDY: AUDIT POLICY

continued

Information Security

I would like to be able to view regular reports on activities. I suspect the systems folks might want to consult with me if they are seeing suspicious activity that needs action. When the auditors come, I would like to be able to have a report that shows them just what we are auditing.

Information Systems Manager

We need to have information at our fingertips. I don't want to find out that our data has been destroyed again.

Systems Administrator

I need to be able to set audit policy once, in one location, and know that it is being followed by all of my systems.

I'd like some lessons in what auditing events mean. I hear there are a whole lot of new events having to do with Active Directory.

I've heard that some legacy applications are not going to run on Windows 2000 due to its more restrictive file and registry settings. From what little I know about the auditing, it might help us determine where things are failing and enable us to modify access rights where necessary.

PERFORMANCE

As always, every new activity can't change the current level of performance.

Systems Administrator

We need to be careful that all this collection of auditing information doesn't slow the system down. What impact will it have on the network? What risks are there to system stability?

Information Technology Manager

We have a commitment to maintain our service level. I will accept no degradation.

MAINTAINABILITY

As manager, I'm not hiring anyone to run around to each system and keep it configured. Find a way to automate it, or do it yourself.

AVAILABILITY

The new activity must not interfere with the operation of the Web site. That must be up all the time.

ANALYSIS

Cote is like many companies. After a "security event" occurs, everyone figures someone should have been watching for things like that. They are in the perfect position to make a difference. They are motivated and have some new capabilities with Windows 2000 to develop an automated audit system that can ensure them of collecting the information they need.

Understanding what to audit and when to audit it will be less of a problem for them than learning how to deal with the plentitude of information auditing provides. As you will learn in later chapters, they can write a policy and then push it out across the enterprise using Group Policy.

CHAPTER SUMMARY

Auditing is not a fun task. Why do you think auditors are such cranky people (sorry Aaron)? Windows 2000 does not make the job of analyzing the auditing results very easy. What it does do is enable the fullest spectrum of audit events for you to pick and choose from. Setting up the policy is a matter for deliberation, consultation with your management, and possibly visiting with your auditors. When you do set up auditing, you need to consider how you are going to deal with the results.

Other uses for the auditing tools are not so hard to see. Programmers and application specialists will no doubt benefit from being able to trace the access path of their programs.

KEY TERMS

- Audit policy
- Domain Controller Security Policy console
- Domain Security console
- SACL

APPLY YOUR KNOWLEDGE

Exercises

6.1   Configure Auditing

Estimated Time: 10 minutes

Configuring auditing properly is important to the overall success of your security design. This exercise takes you through the steps necessary to configure your auditing policies.

1. Create a new text file called secrets.txt.

2. Open the Group Policy object for the domain controller (Domain Controller Security Policy console).

3. Under Local Policies\User Rights Assignment, give yourself the right to Manage Auditing and Security Log.

4. Under Local Policies\Audit Policy, set Success and Failure Auditing for Audit Logon Events and Audit Object Access.

5. Right-click File System and select Add File.

6. Browse to the file secrets.txt you made earlier.

7. On the Auditing tab for this file, add yourself and select Write Data and Read Data access options for successful and failed attempts.

8. Click OK and close all windows.

9. From the command prompt, run
   `secedit/refreshpolicy machine_policy`
   (see Chapter 8 if you're curious).

10. Use Windows Explorer and open the file secrets.txt. Modify the file and save it.

11. Log off the computer. Attempt to log back on with an incorrect password. Do this a couple of times, then use your correct password to log on.

12. Open the Domain Controller Security Policy console. Open the Event Viewer\security log and view the events your activity generated.

Review Questions

1. John Smith of Cote has a number of issues with auditing. List two items that Windows 2000 provides that will assist him in handling his company's audit needs.

2. Jane sets up auditing in Windows 2000. She selects Success and Failure for every category in the Audit Policies section of Local Policies. Does she have an effective audit policy?

3. Pam sets up auditing by enabling Failure for logon events and Success for object access. She also sets up auditing on the secret.txt file by indicating that the Read property should be audited for her account. She attempts to log on repeatedly using the wrong password and opens and changes a file repeatedly, yet she finds no records in the Security log. What could be wrong?

4. You receive a call Monday morning from one of your remote branch offices. There is a domain controller for the London domain present at that location. The systems administrator tells you that at 10:00 a.m., a large number of users cannot log on to the London domain. He found the domain controller had stopped but then come back online. He can log on. What could be the problem?

5. When Fred checks the Security log Monday morning, he finds that Vice President Sam Honglua has logged on over the weekend. "I thought he was on vacation until next month,"

APPLY YOUR KNOWLEDGE

Fred thinks. "I'd better get that report on system security ready for him." Should Fred be so cool and collected?

6. Mary's project development program runs fine on her Windows 2000 Professional computer. When she installs it for other members of her department, they cannot run it. She has John, the network administrator, give these users Administrator accounts on their machines so that they can run the program. Is this the only way to get them access?

7. The auditors think Pete should audit access to the printer used to print checks. Pete finds the property page to do so, but he can't decide which permissions to audit and how. Use the property page in Figure 6.9 to set auditing for the check printer.

8. John has identified 10 files that he needs to make sure access is audited on. Where should he set that access?

FIGURE 6.9
Set printer auditing.

Exam Questions

1. John Smith at Cote sets up a test network to study Windows 2000 auditing. He wants to ensure that events are audited on all domain controllers. Where does he do this? (Choose the best and most complete answer.)

   A. He uses the MMC snap-in Security Configuration Manager to turn on auditing in the Local Policies\ Audit Policy area.

   B. He uses the Domain Controller Security Policy and turns on auditing in the Local Policies\Audit Policy area.

   C. He uses the Domain Security Policy and turns on auditing in the Local Policies\Audit Policy area.

   D. He visits each domain controller and sets Enable Auditing.

2. John has been testing the audit functionality of Windows 2000. He has enabled Failure audit for logon. He has also enabled Success/Failure for object access. He visits several computers and sets up audit on several files. For some files, he denies his account access; for others, he allows it, and then he sets up audit for these files to record success and failure. He logs on to the domain from a Windows 2000 Professional system and then accesses several of the files. When he then begins to look for the audit events, he has trouble finding all those that he expected. Where does he need to look for the events? (Check all that apply.)

   A. In the Security log of the computer on which the event occurred.

   B. In the Security log of each domain controller.

   C. In the Security log of the designated audit repository.

APPLY YOUR KNOWLEDGE

D. In the Security log of the Windows 2000 Professional system he was working from.

3. Peter Furst is a domain administrator for Cote. He has been asked to set up auditing for the check printer, several registry keys, files, and folders. He visits each object and sets the appropriate audit policy. To test his settings, he visits each object. When he examines the Security log, there are no records. He tries accessing them again. Still, there are no records. After lunch, he tries again. Still no records. What has Peter done wrong?

A. Audit policy can only be set by the enterprise administrator.

B. Audit policy for object auditing has to be enabled by setting the policy for Audit Object Access in the Local Policies\Audit Policy section of the Domain Controller Security Policy console.

C. The enterprise administrator has to turn on object access auditing in the Local Policies\Audit Policy section of the Domain Controller Security Policy console.

D. Changes to audit policy are delayed in taking effect. If Peter waits long enough, his changes will take effect, and he will see results in the Security log.

4. Peter, Mary, Fred, Alexandria, and John are arguing about the internal process that generates a security event when an object is accessed. (Auditing has been correctly set up.) Each one has a different opinion, listed here. Which one of them is correct?

A. The DACLs set on the objects tell which user or group will trigger the recording.

B. The SACLs set on the object tell which user or group will trigger the recording.

C. The DACLs set on the object indicate that any access needs to be recorded.

D. The SACLs set on the object indicate that any access needs to be recorded.

E. The ACEs set on the object indicate that any access needs to be recorded.

5. Cote has decided that it will have multiple domains in its Windows 2000 network. Its auditors have written a policy for the items that need to be audited. The policy should be applied uniformly across all domains. How can this be ensured?

A. Audit policy configured for domain controllers in the root domain in the forest will propagate to all domain controllers in the forest.

B. Audit policy configured for the domain controller in the root domain in the forest must be copied to a file and then pasted into the policy console for each domain in the forest.

C. Audit policy can be configured in a template using the Security Configuration and Analysis snap-in. This template can then be imported into the audit policy section for each domain controller.

D. Audit policy can be configured in a template using the Security Configuration and Analysis

APPLY YOUR KNOWLEDGE

snap-in. The template should then be imported into the Security Settings section of the domain controller's Policy console for each domain.

6. Nancy Maggler is in charge of reviewing new applications before they are implemented at Cote. She wants to make sure that each new application is only doing what it has been supposedly designed to do and is not somehow subverting security. She loads the software on a test system and configures auditing to help her determine the activities of the new software. After correctly configuring auditing, she runs the program as a user would and then reviews the Security log. What items in auditing did she turn on? (Choose the best answer.)

A. Logon events, account management, object access.

B. Logon events, system events, privilege use.

C. System events, object access, processing tracking, privilege use, Directory Service access, policy change, account management.

D. Object access, policy change, account management, Directory Service access, privilege use, system events.

7. Windows 2000 Servers (joined in a domain) need an audit policy of their own. You have been given the task of setting this up.

Required Result:

Create an audit policy for Windows 2000 Server. Audit for logon failure and changes to security policies and enable object access auditing.

Optional Desired Results:

1. Ensure that all Windows 2000 Servers in the domain follow the same audit policies.

2. Restrict access to audit logs to a single administrator.

Proposed Solution:

You set up auditing in Windows 2000. In the Domain Controller Security Policy console, you select logon Failure for account logon events and logon events. You select Success and Failure for object access.

Evaluation of Proposed Solution:

Which result(s) does the proposed solution produce?

A. The proposed solution produces the required result and both of the optional results.

B. The proposed solution produces the required result and one of the optional results.

C. The proposed solution produces the required result but neither of the optional results.

D. The proposed solution does not produce the required result.

8. Windows 2000 Servers (joined in a domain) need an audit policy of their own. You have been given the task of setting this up.

Required Result:

Create an audit policy for Windows 2000 Server. Audit for logon failure and changes to security policies and enable object access auditing.

APPLY YOUR KNOWLEDGE

Optional Desired Results:

1. Ensure that all computers in the domain follow the same audit policies.

2. Restrict access to audit logs to a single administrator.

Proposed Solution:

You set up auditing in Windows 2000. In the Domain Controller Security Policy console, you select logon Failure for account logon and logon events. You select Success and Failure for object access. You select Success and Failure for policy change.

Evaluation of Proposed Solution:

Which result(s) does the proposed solution produce?

A. The proposed solution produces the required result and both of the optional results.

B. The proposed solution produces the required result and one of the optional results.

C. The proposed solution produces the required result but neither of the optional results.

D. The proposed solution does not produce the required result.

9. Windows 2000 Servers (joined in a domain) need an audit policy of their own. You have been given the task of setting this up.

Required Result:

Create an audit policy for Windows 2000 Server. Audit for logon failure and changes to security policies and enable object access auditing.

Optional Desired Results:

1. Ensure that all computers in the domain follow the same audit policies.

2. Restrict access to audit logs to a single administrator.

Proposed Solution:

You set up auditing in Windows 2000. In the Domain Controller Security Policy console, you select logon failure for account logon and logon events. You select Success and Failure for object access and Success and Failure for policy change. In User Rights Assignment, you give yourself the Manage Auditing and Security Log privilege.

Evaluation of Proposed Solution:

Which result(s) does the proposed solution produce?

A. The proposed solution produces the required result and both of the optional results.

B. The proposed solution produces the required result and one of the optional results.

C. The proposed solution produces the required result but neither of the optional results.

D. The proposed solution does not produce the required result.

10. John has to review audit events in the Security logs for Cote. He wants to make sure that he can effectively manage the Security logs. What things should he do? (Check all that apply.)

A. Set the log properties. John can determine the log size and needs to establish a policy for log retention.

APPLY YOUR KNOWLEDGE

B. Use event log filtering.

C. Audit selectively.

D. Use the wide variety of built-in reports provided with Windows 2000.

Answers to Review Questions

1. Audit policy can be controlled globally. Event logs can be restricted to management by one person. There is a comprehensive set of auditing tools and opportunity to get the information needed.

2. No. Jane will get lots of data, but will have a hard time using it. She will get logon records for everyone who logs on. That's hardly worth it. She won't get any auditing of specific file, registry, or printer objects because that has to be enabled on each of the objects she wants to audit.

3. Two possibilities: The policy doesn't take effect immediately, and she may just need to wait; and, Pam may be setting the policy in the Local Security Policy console, and it is being overridden by the domain policy.

4. Check to see whether the security option Shut Down System Immediately if Unable to Log Security Audits is set. This option shuts down the computer when the audit log is full. When the system reboots, only an administrator can log on. To correct the situation, the audit log needs to be archived and then cleared. The security option needs to be reset.

5. Fred might want to suspect that the vice president's account has been compromised. He should check to see whether the vice president is still on vacation and then take appropriate steps. This presumes the vice president does not have RAS or VPN access to the network while he is on vacation.

6. Mary should ask that the program access be audited to see whether an alternative solution exists. It is possible that just granting access to certain files and maybe registry entries will be enough to allow users to run the program without giving them elevated privileges. Other choices might be to make them members of the Power Users group or that the application of the compatibility security template may be enough.

7. See Figure 6.10.

8. That depends on whether the files are located only on the local machine, on every computer, or on all domain controllers. There are three possibilities, The Domain Controller Security Policy, the Domain Security Policy, and the local file system. Assuming that the files are located only on the local computer, John should use the file system to set up auditing.

FIGURE 6.10
Auditing printer use.

APPLY YOUR KNOWLEDGE

Answers to Exam Questions

1. **B.** Choice A would be correct if he then imported the template into the Domain Controller Security Policy. Choice C sets auditing for local server and professional systems, but not for domain controllers. Choice D is preposterous (and would be overwritten by Domain Controller Policy anyway). (See the section "Configuring Auditing.")

2. **A.** Audit events are always recorded on the computer on which they occurred. (See the section "Determine How You Are Going to Cope with the Multitude of Records Produced.")

3. **B.** Before these objects can be audited, you must enable object auditing for object access in the policy console. Domain administrators can set audit policy, so choices A and C are incorrect. Choice D is also incorrect. Although changes in policy are delayed in taking effect, if object access auditing has not been enabled, waiting alone will not bring any results. (See the section "Configuring Auditing.")

4. **B.** SACLs, or system access control lists, include the name of the individual or group to watch for access from as well as the type of access to audit. Choice D is incorrect because SACLs do not turn on auditing for every access, just those users you specify. DACLs are access control lists and are not used in auditing; therefore, choices A and C are incorrect. Choice E is incorrect because ACEs are the access control entries that make up DACLs and SACLs. They specify the user or group to audit or allow access and the type of access or audit event. They do not require that all access be recorded. (See the section "Object Access.")

5. **D.** A policy can be configured in a template, and the template can then be imported in each domain's Domain policy. Choice A is incorrect because domains are security boundaries. Each domain needs configuration. Choice B is incorrect because you cannot copy policy. Choice C is incorrect. It is not necessary to import the policy to each domain controller, only to each domain. (See the section "Configuring Auditing.")

6. **C.** Although an argument could be made to audit all areas, choice C is the most complete because it includes process tracking. This audit policy is rarely used for anything but tracking the processes of programs. It can be used to assist programmers in their efforts as well as be used as an aide for security professionals who are determining what an application actually does. (See the section "Process Tracking")

7. **D.** Because you set the policy in the Domain Controller Security console, it impacts only domain controllers in the domain. You also have not set the management of the logs to one person or turned on policy change. (See the section "Configuring Auditing.")

8. **D.** You still have not set the policy for policy change or management by one administrator. (See the section "Objects to Watch.")

9. **B.** Because Peter sets the policy in the Domain Controller Security console, it impacts only domain controllers. (See the section "Configuring Auditing.")

10. **A, B, C.** There are no standard reports. (See the section "Managing the Log.")

Suggested Readings and Resources

Microsoft Windows 2000 Resource Kit Utilities:

elogdmp.exe—Dump information from event logs

showpriv.exe—Show users and groups granted a privilege

svcacls.exe—Set access control lists on service objects

svcmon.exe—Service monitoring tool

w2000msgs.chm—Windows 2000 error and event messages help

Crystal Reports 6.0—Event log viewer

Auditpol.exe—Modify audit policy from command line

CyberSafe Log Analyst—Security event log analysis tool

Dumpel.exe—Dump event log into tab-separated text file

Enumprop.exe—Enumerate properties of directory service object

Findgrp.exe—Find group membership for a specified user

Gpresult.exe—Find result Group Policy has had on currently logged on user on current computer

Showacls.exe—Enumerate access rights on files , folders

Showmbrs.exe—Show user names of members of given group

Showgrps.exe—Show groups user is member of

Subinacl.exe—Obtain security information on files, registry keys, and services

This chapter covers the following Microsoft-specified objectives for the "Designing a Windows 2000 Security Solution" section of the Designing Security for a Microsoft Windows 2000 Network exam:

Design a security group strategy.

▶ A security group strategy should identify the additional security groups you will create, establish their scope, and identify membership requirements. Not everyone is created equal. No one assignment of rights strategy is possible for the diverse users and information resources in your enterprise. You've spent considerable time determining who needs access to what; now you must determine how to make sure that everyone has only the access they need. Let the operating system help you do that. You must understand the security principal, security group, and privilege assignment model of Windows 2000. Then you can match your users to these groups and privileges and, where necessary, extend the model to meet your needs.

Design a delegation of authority strategy.

▶ The concept of delegation of authority is not a new one to managers. What is new in Windows 2000 is the capability to make the delegation of administrative tasks very granular. To take advantage of this opportunity, you must consider during your design stages when decisions about the creation of domains and OUs are being made. You will need to determine the need for specific administrative tasks, who should be given the responsibility, and where the resources they need to manage should be located.

CHAPTER 7

Designing a Security Group Strategy

▶ If you are familiar with Windows NT, you will be tempted to skip the first part of this section and rely on your existing knowledge. Don't. While many things are the same, there are some new wrinkles to groups. There's a new type, the Universal group, that you will want to know about. Also new are Domain Local groups, which can be shared among all Windows 2000 members of the domain, not just domain controllers. There are new arrangements of rights and privileges to understand, new group nesting rules, a new interface to get used to. You'll also find new ways that all these can be used.

▶ So, rearrange your understanding of Windows NT users and groups to accommodate the differences in Windows 2000.

▶ Next, take a look at the possibilities extended by delegation of authority. Do you need to allow the management of groups of users? What about specific resources? In Windows NT 4.0, you created separate resource domains or used default management groups such as Server Operators or Account Operators. In a smaller organization, this may have been adequate to meet your needs. Larger organizations, and organizations with reasons to granularize management tasks, found this limiting—or, worse, created many otherwise needless domains. Is this your situation?

INTRODUCTION

What are your security group needs? Do you have resources that require restricted access? Does your distributed management structure demand partitioning of administrative tasks? Who needs the ability to access what when? Previously you developed lists of resources and users. You documented how the resources are used, who should have access, what type of access they needed, and who should manage them. Now you will design the groups, define memberships, and arrange privileges to fulfill those needs.

Before you can implement an effective security group strategy, your must learn the built-in users, groups, and permissions that are available. The first thing this chapter does is define these for you.

Next, you will learn the Window 2000 basic user management philosophy. Yes, it follows and extends the Windows NT 4.0 approach. There are new security structures and Active Directory to contend with, however, so you cannot rely on your Windows NT knowledge to take you all the way.

As you begin to formulate your security group strategy, keep in mind the changes to the Windows 2000 domain structure. Most likely you will have fewer domains than before. You will want to review the concept of the organizational unit (OU). The OU becomes your secret weapon in the fight to minimize the extent of any elevated privileges that you grant nonadministrative users. It is at this level, not the domain level, that you partition resources and management of groups. Delegation of authority within Windows 2000 is ubiquitous. If you do not understand this principle, you are missing one of the most useful changes to the Windows administrative model.

Finally, some example strategies for security group design will be presented and discussed.

BUILT-IN USERS

Design a security group strategy.

Security groups are composed of users and other security groups. I know that should be obvious, but it's amazing how often otherwise intelligent, well-meaning individuals design security infrastructure

---

NOTE

Distribution Groups? Security Groups?   These are two group types in Windows 2000. Security groups are similar to Windows NT 4.0 groups. Distribution groups are lists; they can be used for email.

and fail to keep that in mind. Only a couple default users exist in Windows 2000, but you should know something about them. Similarly, there are several built-in security groups that each has its own unique rights and access privileges. Finally, multiple property settings can be established to assist in the management of users.

The Administrator account is the default administrative account created during installation. The individual installing the system can select an initial password. The Administrator account is all-powerful on the system. It is automatically a member of the Administrators group on a workstation or member server, and it cannot be deleted, disabled or removed. You wouldn't want to lock yourself out of your computer, would you?

If the server is promoted to a domain controller, the Administrator account becomes a member in the following groups:

- ◆ Domain Admins
- ◆ Domain Users
- ◆ Enterprise Admins
- ◆ Group Policy Creator Owners
- ◆ Schema Admins

The Guest account is also created during installation. It is a member of the Guests group on the local system. Its purpose is to provide an account that can be used by the user who may need occasional access to the computer or to some resource on the computer. Because this account does not require a password, it can make access convenient and dangerous. The Guest account is dangerous because administrators forget about its existence; they forget that this account can be used by anyone. If the Guest account is enabled, users whose accounts have been disabled can use it. If your strategy is to disable accounts when users leave the company, or if you have set account policy to disable accounts after unsuccessful logins, you may still be vulnerable to abuse by foe and former employee alike. This account is disabled by default.

One of the most often-requested security strategies is how to further secure the Guest account. In addition to making sure that this account is disabled by default, you can explicitly grant it no access to especially sensitive files, set its logon hours to be nonexistent, and

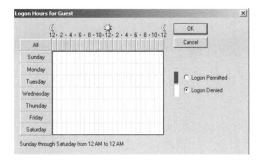

FIGURE 7.1
Restricting the Guest account.

restrict its capability to log on by allowing the Guest account to log on only from a nonexistent system. That is, the administrator will use the property pages of the Guest account and, on the Account tab, Log On To button, check the This User Can Log On To: The Following Computers radio button. Then the administrator can enter the name of a workstation that does not exist. If the workstation does not exist, even if the guest account becomes enabled, no one will be able to use it because it is impossible to log on from a computer that does not exist; furthermore, there are no legal logon times for this account (see Figure 7.1). Another step could be adding the Guest account to the user right Deny Access To This Computer From The Network. For more information on account settings, visit the "User Rights and Privileges" section, later in this chapter.

TYPES OF GROUPS AND GROUP SCOPE

Groups in Windows NT were either global with domain level scope, or local with local scope. Four types of security groups exist in Windows 2000: Computer Local, Domain Local, Global, and Universal. Each group has its own scope, or range of impact.

Computer Local

A Computer Local group exists only on a single computer. No other computer in any workgroup or domain recognizes these groups. They can be used to define access to this computer's resources and privileges. Local groups are the Administrators group, the Guests group, the Users group, and the Power Users group. By default, the local Administrator account belongs to the Administrator's group. You can use this account, or additional accounts that you add to this local group, to administer this computer. No Computer Local groups exist on domain controllers.

Domain Local

Domain Local groups can be used to give broad access to resources on any computer in the domain. Members of these groups can be from the local domain as well as from other domains. In a mixed-mode domain, Domain Local groups can be used only on Windows 2000 domain controllers. By definition, mixed-mode domains can contain Windows NT 4.0 domain controllers. Windows NT 4.0 did not have Domain Local groups. Because these domain controllers do not know what a Domain Local group is, they would not be capable of accepting them for any purpose.

Global

Global groups are good choices for establishing a one-to-one relationship between groups of people and job functions. For example, if all accountants need access to various files and folders on several servers in the domain, it makes sense to create a group that can be used for access control assignment. Because global groups can be used throughout the domain, after the resource access is established, it is easy to add or remove users and give them immediate and efficient access to files and folders they need. (It is also easy to remove users who leave the department.)

Global groups can have only members who come from the local domain.

In native mode, global groups can be nested. This enables you to model the elaborate overlapping access needs of your organization or to scale large group structures.

Universal

Large, multidomain organizations need the capability to assign access to multiple, similar groups that exist in many domains. Universal groups, then, can be used for this purpose. Global groups can be members of Universal groups. Use this strategy to reduce replication traffic. Global groups may be volatile, and at any rate represent the possibility for many members and changes. Changes to Universal groups are replicated as their membership is stored in the Global Catalog. Changes to the Global Catalog take time to replicate; therefore, by adding Global groups to Universal groups, you will see replication only once, for the addition or deletion of the Global group. Changes to the Global group membership are replicated within the domain, but not within the forest. Universal groups are granted access to local resources by giving them membership in Domain Local groups. This is pictured in Figure 7.2. The Domain Local group is given access to resources on the disk pictured on the right side of the figure.

Where does the Universal group fit in? You cannot create a Universal group unless a domain is in native mode. In a forest with a single domain in native mode, you can create Universal groups. However, their true advantage is found in multiple domain forests. In either case, a domain's Universal group membership is stored in the domain and in the Global Catalog. Because the Global Catalog is forest-wide, membership can be determined from any domain. In a single-domain forest, Universal group membership can be determined from the Active Directory database of the domain.

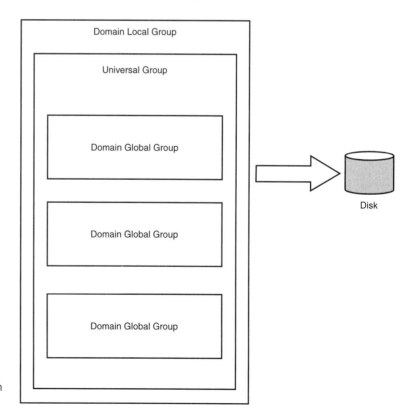

FIGURE 7.2
Universal groups given membership in Domain Local groups.

By definition, then, a single domain in mixed mode will not benefit from Universal groups, nor can it have these groups. Still, you may want to create the Universal groups in anticipation of growth to a multidomain forest.

Group Strategies

If you are familiar with Windows NT group strategies, you probably learned about AGLP, which reminded you to add users to Global groups, add Global groups to Local groups, and assign permissions to Local groups. This strategy is still useful in Windows 2000. In fact, in mixed-mode domains, this is the strategy to follow. You may want to modify it slightly to use Domain Local groups where possible because they can be granted access to all computers in the domain; this may simplify administration. (By definition, Local groups exist on only a single computer.)

In a native-mode domain, where you can create Universal groups that can contain members from multiple domains, and where you can nest Global groups, you can expand this strategy to UGUDLP. Place users in Global groups, and place Global groups in Universal groups. Place Universal groups in Domain Local groups, and give permissions to local objects to Domain Local groups. This strategy is pictured in Figure 7.3.

Put Global Groups in
Universal Groups

Put Universal Groups in Domain Local Groups.
Grant Domain Local Groups Resource Access

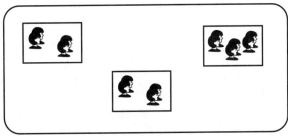

FIGURE 7.3
Who manages what?

You decide which OU to create a group in based on how the group will be administered. If groups will be managed at the OU level and contain only domain members, the groups can be created as global groups. Global groups can have access throughout the domain but cannot contain members from outside the domain. If you need to give these groups access outside the OU, and if the domain is in native mode, it is a simple matter of nesting them into Universal groups or other Global groups.

You also can manage Domain Local groups or Universal groups at the OU level. To manage membership in any group, position the group in the OU hierarchy where management can be assigned via delegation to the appointed manager.

You decide who to add to what group based on the access needed and the group scope.

The administrator who has been delegated administration over the OU will maintain management of the members within the group. In a hierarchical situation—say, one with OUs within OUs—the child OUs can have their own groups and cannot administer groups created in the parent OU.

Remember that domains are security boundaries. Be careful to design the group strategy to fit your organization. Although changes can be made later (by moving groups), it may be impractical.

> **NOTE**
>
> **Group Movement** Investigate the utilities movetree and ADMT. Beware of moving groups; you may affect security assignments. However, you can change the group scope to Universal before moving Global groups, and then move the groups between domains while maintaining current security assignments.

Groups with Domain Local scope are used to manage access to resources in a single domain. You create the Domain Local scope group and give it resource access privileges; then you add to it groups with Universal scope, Global scope, Accounts, or Domain Local scope.

DEFAULT GROUPS

Two main types of groups exist within Windows 2000: distribution groups and security groups. Security groups are used to allow access to systems and recourses. Distribution groups are used as mailing lists. Security groups can also be used as mailing lists. You cannot assign rights or resource access permissions to distribution groups. Therefore, when authorization information is compiled for a user, their membership in distribution groups is left out of the picture.

Use distribution groups for mailing lists. This can have considerable effects in reducing the amount of information that must be conveyed across the network, in reducing the size of the access token generated, and in reducing the amount of time necessary to determine access rights and thus logon. The access token is composed of the SID of the user and the SIDs of the groups of which a user is member. For more information on access tokens, see the later section "Using Security Groups to Provide Resource Access."

You can create distribution groups and security groups. There are no default distribution groups, but there are default security groups. Understand these first, before you create your own. Two types of default, or built-in, security groups exist: explicit, those we can change the membership of, and implicit, those which obtain their membership due to an activity they are engaged in. Explicit groups can be further segregated into built-in (local) and global (domain) groups.

Explicit Default Groups

Domain controllers, servers, and Windows 2000 Professional computers all have local groups. The types of groups that exist vary. Standalone servers and Windows 2000 Professional have Computer Local groups:

- ◆ Administrators
- ◆ Power Users
- ◆ Users
- ◆ Guests
- ◆ Backup Operators
- ◆ Replicator

Domain controllers have a slightly different set of user groups. These groups are Domain Local groups. A list of these groups can be found in the Active Directory Users and Computers console in the Builtin folder (see Figure 7.4).

- ◆ Account Operators
- ◆ Administrators

◆ Backup Operators

◆ Guests

◆ Print Operators

◆ Replicator

◆ Server Operators

◆ Users

Keep in mind the scope of the group when you examine default logon rights and permissions. Default rights and permissions indicate what a member can do; scope indicates where a member can do it. To properly design your group strategy, you need to match scope and rights to users' needs.

Account Operators

Account operators can create, delete, and modify user accounts and groups within the domain. They cannot place themselves or anyone else in the Administrators group or any of the other operator groups. Add users here who are to be trusted with managing groups of regular users.

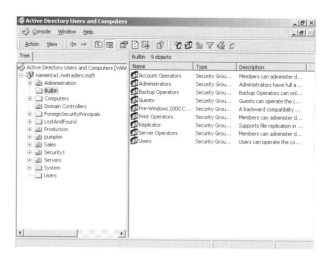

FIGURE 7.4
Domain Local groups.

Administrators

Administrators can do anything. The scope of the group may be Local Computer or Local Domain, depending on where it exists. Thus, a member of the Administrators group on a Windows Professional computer has only broad-ranging powers on that system. When that computer joins a domain, that user has no rights or privileges in the domain until he or she is assigned some.

In a domain, a local Administrators group exists on each computer. The Domain Admins global group from the domain that the computer is a member of is automatically a member of the Administrators group. To give individual administrative control throughout the domain, place users in the Domain Admins global group. Many administrative duties can also be done by members of Operator groups, but specific rights retained for Administrators only are as follows:

- ◆ Install the OS
- ◆ Install components such as drivers and services
- ◆ Install service packs and hotfixes
- ◆ Install windows updates
- ◆ Repair the operating system
- ◆ Configure machine-wide parameters, including access controls and audit functions, password policy, and kernel mode driver configurations, among others
- ◆ Add, delete, and modify members of Administrator groups and Operator groups

Backup Operators

Members of the Backup Operators group can back up and restore all domain controllers using Windows Backup. To improve security, many companies split the duties of backup and restore. They do not use the Backup Operators group, but they create two new groups—one for each operation.

Power Users

The Power Users group combines many of the functions of the Account Operators and Server Operators groups. The group exists only on servers and Windows 2000 Professional systems. For all practical purposes, members in Power Users have many of the privileges that those in the Users group had in Windows NT. Power Users can install software that does not install system services and can do the following:

◆ Install software (unless it installs system services)

◆ Create local users and groups

◆ Modify users and groups that they have created

◆ Create and delete non-administrative file shares

◆ Change System Time

◆ Change the Display settings

◆ Configure shares

◆ Configure Power settings

◆ Create, manage, delete, and share local printers

Power Users cannot take ownership of files and folders unless explicitly assigned this right. Power Users also cannot access other user data on NTFS volumes.

Guests

The Guests group gives no default permissions or rights. The things that its members can do are restricted to the privileges and permissions that you grant that group, with one exception. A guest user is a member of the implicit group Everyone. This means that any access rights the group Everyone has are also available to the Guest group. To avoid problems, it is a good idea to severely restrict the access rights of the Everyone group to limit the damage that can be done.

Print Operators

The Print Operators group manages printers. In Chapter 5, "Securing Resources," you learned the access rights involved in managing and using printers. Members of the Print Operators group have all those rights and privileges.

Pre-Windows 2000 Compatibility Access

This group was created for use by administrators who must support applications that are compatible with Windows NT 4.0, but not the stricter security requirements of Windows 2000. The group has read access on all groups and users in the domain. Instead of completely removing the default stricter access settings of Windows 2000, this group can be used to assign access to registry keys, files, and folders that default security settings would deny. Later, when legacy applications are replaced with Windows 2000-compliant applications, access using this group can be removed. The default, stricter access controls that were left in place will manage access.

Replicator

The Replicator group is created to hold a user that will be used to log on to the file replication service. It should never be used to log on.

Server Operators

Members of the Server Operators group can perform regular administrative tasks. They can share disk resources, back up and restore files on a domain controller, and shut down or restart the server.

Users

Those in the Users group do not have broad powers. However, these users can do anything that the administrator has given them privileges to do. Like Power Users, these users can also install programs that do not install system services, but the programs they install cannot be used by anyone else but them.

Predefined Groups: Domain Global and Domain Local Groups

Domain Global groups and other predefined groups are found in the Active Directory Users and Computers console in the Users folder (see Figure 7.5.) Predefined groups include groups for users and computers. Domain Global group membership may or may not convey explicit privileges. For example, the Domain Users group is used to contain users, and then they themselves can be made members of Computer Local groups. Other groups, such as Enterprise Administrators, have specific preassigned privileges. Some global groups are automatically made members of corresponding Computer Local groups.

Domain Global and Domain Local groups and Universal (in native mode) groups for users are listed in Table 7.1:

TABLE 7.1

DOMAIN GLOBAL, DOMAIN LOCAL, AND UNIVERSAL GROUPS

Group (Obtain Privileges from This Group)	Mixed Mode	Native Mode	Member of
Domain Users	Global		Users
Domain Admins	Global		Administrators
Domain Guests	Global		Guests
DNS Administrators	Global	Domain Local	
Cert Publishers	Global		
Enterprise Admins	Global	Universal	Administrators
Group Policy Creator Owners	Global		
Schema Admins	Global	Universal	

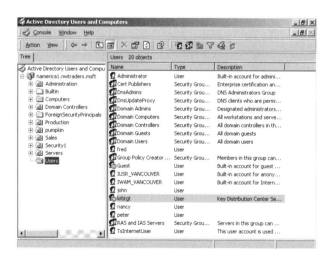

FIGURE 7.5
Domain Global and Domain Local groups.

New Windows 2000 user groups with specific privileges are further described here:

◆ Like the Domain Admins and Enterprise Admins groups, the DNS Administrators group has full control over DNS servers in the domain. Use this group to give DNS administrative privilege without making a user Domain or Enterprise Administrator.

◆ Cert Publishers manage Certificate Services.

◆ Users in the Enterprise Admins group are given broad rights in the forest. Specific privileges are reserved for Enterprise Admins. By default, Enterprise Admins have full control over all objects in a forest. This account has administrative rights in all domains in the forest as well. By default, the root domain in the forest includes this group and places its Administrator account as a member of this group. Membership in this group (or in the Administrators group of the root domain) is required to promote a Windows 2000 Server to be a child domain in the forest.

◆ Group Policy Creator Owners create and manage group policies.

◆ Schema Admins manage the schema.

Computer groups is a new feature of Windows 2000. Although computers in Windows NT 4.0 were classified as domain controllers, member servers, and workstations, there was no opportunity to assign these computers policies or privileges as a group. You installed a computer into a computer role (domain controller, server, or workstation), and that was pretty much it. Membership in Computer groups extends the concept of role to one of control. You cannot create new Computer groups, but you can organize computers within domains and organizational units.

Computer groups are these:

◆ RAS and IAS Servers, which can access remote access properties of users. (Domain Local scope grants no default membership.)

◆ Domain Controllers, which manage Active Directory and other computers. (Global scope applies to all domain controllers in the domain.)

◆ Domain Computers. (Global Scope allows all member servers and workstations to be joined in the domain.)

◆ DNS Update Proxy. (DNS clients are allowed to update DNS updates for other clients without taking ownership of the DNS resource records.)

The computer groups RAS and IAS Servers and DNS Update Proxy are two new groups that you can find more information on in Chapter 13, "Providing Secure Access Between Networks," and Chapter 12, "Designing Windows 2000 Network Services Security," respectively.

Implicit Groups

In addition to groups and users that can be created and/or managed by the Administrators group, several implicit groups exist as well. These groups have membership based on the activity of the user, not by administrator selection:

◆ **Everyone**—All security principals plus anonymous users

◆ **Interactive**—Users logged on locally

◆ **Authenticated Users**—Have been authenticated

◆ **Creator Owner**—The user who either created the object or is currently the owner of the object

◆ **Network**—The user currently accessing resources across the network.

◆ **Dialup**—Users using RAS

◆ **Anonymous Users**—The user who is touching resources but is not logged on as a user with a Windows 2000 account

USING SECURITY GROUPS TO PROVIDE RESOURCE ACCESS

What's the point here? To create a complicated security structure, or to get the job done? Security groups exist to make administration easier and to mitigate risk from attack. Carefully planning their location, scope, and membership saves time.

The basic process is simple.

1. Determine where groups will be administrated; this tells you where to create them.

2. Determine membership for groups.

3. Determine scope based on required membership and your policy for access flexibility. Scope is also based on the mode of the domain, native or mixed. Mixed-mode domains create more restrictions for group assignments.

Native mode and mixed can be defined as follows:

Native mode—Typically you will create Domain Global groups at the domain or OU level. Users from the domain are added to these Domain Global groups. Domain Local groups are given access to resources. Domain Global groups are added to Domain Local groups. They can also be added to other Domain Global groups in the same domain, or to Universal and Domain Local groups in any domain.

Mixed mode—Group membership is the same as it would be in a Windows NT 4.0 domain. How could it be any different? Some variations are not possible. For example, Domain Global groups are treated as if they are Global groups in Windows NT 4.0; Domain Local groups are different than Windows NT 4.0 local groups. Windows 2000 Domain Local groups can be used throughout the domain. Windows NT 4.0 Local groups are available only on the local computer on which they are created. Windows 2000 does have Machine Local groups as well, which exist on standalone servers, member servers, and Professional systems. These groups are equivalent to Windows NT 4.0 Local groups.

Group membership is outlined in Figure 7.6 and detailed here:

In native mode, groups can contain the following:

◆ Domain Local groups can contain user accounts, Global groups, Universal groups from any domain in the forest, and Domain Local groups from the same domain.

◆ Domain Global groups can contain user accounts and Global groups from same domain only.

◆ Universal groups can contain user accounts, Global groups, and other Universal groups from any domain in the forest.

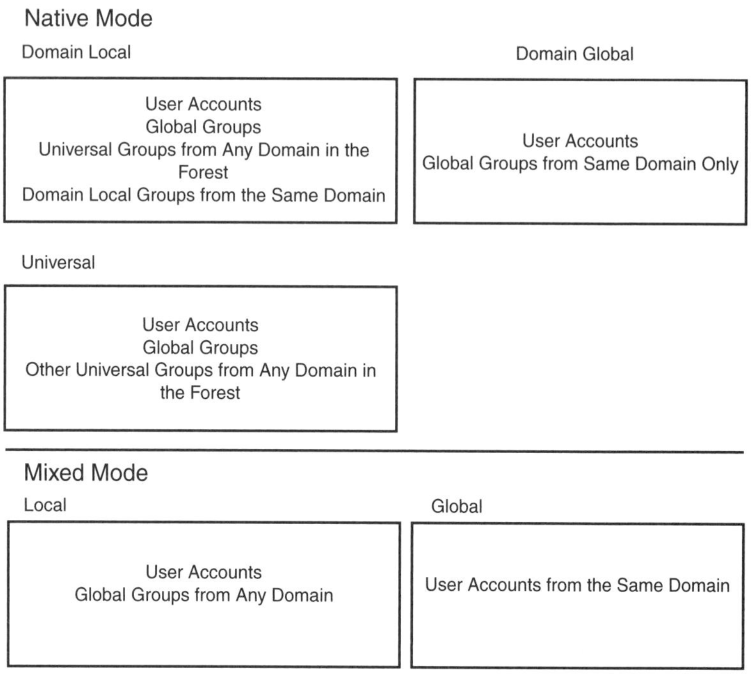

FIGURE 7.6
What groups can include is based on domain mode: mixed mode or native mode.

Native Mode

Domain Local

Domain Global

User Accounts Global Groups Universal Groups from Any Domain in the Forest Domain Local Groups from the Same Domain

User Accounts Global Groups from Same Domain Only

Universal

User Accounts Global Groups Other Universal Groups from Any Domain in the Forest

Mixed Mode

Local

Global

User Accounts Global Groups from Any Domain

User Accounts from the Same Domain

In mixed mode, groups can contain the following:

◆ Domain Local groups can contain user accounts and Global groups from any domain.

◆ Domain Global groups can contain user accounts from the same domain.

◆ There are no Universal groups in a mixed-mode domain.

When designing your group strategy, keep in mind your Active Directory; likewise, when designing your Active Directory, keep your group strategy in mind. Unless you are able to immediately upgrade all Windows NT domain controllers to Windows 2000, or unless you start clean with a pure Windows 2000 enterprise, you will have to wait for many of the new advantages. The exception is that you now can create OUs and base your security group design on multiple OUs instead of multiple domains.

The best plan to follow is to design for the pure Windows 2000 enterprise, and then work back to a design that is restricted by your realities.

Using Nested Groups

You've seen how, by definition, groups can contain other groups. A good strategy is to use this concept, known as nested groups. Use parallel groups to contain users from special areas of administrative control. The parent group will not contain any users of its own, but it will either be given access to resources or be placed in a group that has access to resources. By placing your user member groups in the parent group, you give them access to the resource while allowing local administrative control.

To see what this entails, imagine a database server that contains product information. Sales personnel from every division of the company need read access to the database. The corporate headquarters administrator creates a Universal group called ProductInfo (see Figure 7.7). Domain Global groups are created in each division's domain to hold local salespeople. These groups are named DpInfoNY, DpInfoCA, and DpInfoNJ. These three groups are placed in the Universal group ProductInfo. A Domain Local group, ProdInfoAccess, is given read access to the product database. When the ProductInfo group is placed in the local group ProdInfoAccess, all salespeople have read access to the database.

An even more distributed approach can be used, creating groups at the OU level. In either case, local administrators determine membership in the local groups and manage the user accounts. If a new database server is brought online, access can be given to a Domain Local group, ProductInfo can be placed in that group, and all sales personnel have access. If a salesperson in New York leaves, all that need be done is to remove him from the Domain Global group DpInfoNY. If a new salesperson joins the company in California, place him in the DpInfoCA Global group.

This strategy also can help you avoid replication conflicts. A replication conflict can occur when two different administrators from different domain controllers in two different sites make changes to the same group simultaneously. (The changes are made to different users.) If the changes are made faster than replication can occur, one of the changes will be lost.

This is because when changes are made to group membership (add or remove) the entire group membership attribute is replicated, not just the changes in membership. If each administrator was making a change to different groups, two groups would replicate, so there

FIGURE 7.7
Using a Universal group.

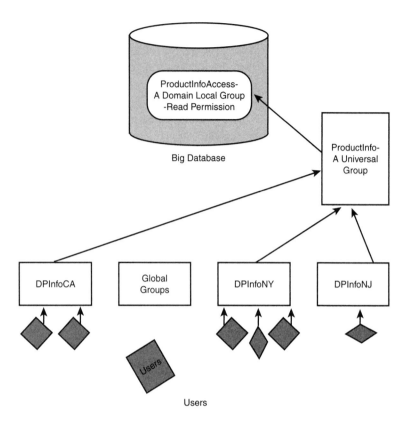

would be no chance of replication conflict. Furthermore, if the group existed only on a single domain controller, there would be no need for replication to occur at all. This is a win-win situation because you have sidestepped the issue.

Access to Files, Folders, and Registry Keys

As you learned in Chapter 5, file and folder access is controlled by permissions set on folders and files. Each built-in group, and some Domain Global groups, are controlled in Windows 2000 with a default settings on files, folders, and registry keys. The settings make sense according to the defined needs of the groups. Thus, those in the Administrators group have broad access, whereas those in the Users group have minimal access.

EXAM TIP

Keep User Management Local
Create Domain Global groups and place users only in the domain controller groups that exist on that domain controller. To allow access to resources within that domain, create Universal groups or Domain Local groups. Access is granted to Universal groups or Domain Local groups, and then Domain Global groups from any domain can be included in the Universal group or Domain Local group.

This can cause some problems with legacy applications. You must understand the needs and requirements of any legacy application and thoroughly test access before deploying it in the Windows 2000 domain. If you cannot provide the level of access for users that you want, you may want to consider placing those users who need access to this application in the Power Users group. Power Users members have essentially the same rights and access privileges that the Users members did under Windows NT. If your application could be run by mere users under Windows NT, Power Users members should be able to run it now. (As you learned earlier, use of the Compatibility security template, which lessens security to match Windows NT 4.0 security, may also be an answer.)

If you want to be assured that applications are built to run well in a Windows 2000 computer, look for the Windows 2000 logo. Window 2000 application specifications can be found at `http://msdn.microsoft.com/winlogo/win2000.asp`.

Default security group permissions are described in Table 7.2.

TABLE 7.2

DEFAULT SECURITY GROUP FILE PERMISSIONS

Group	Member Servers/ Professional	Domain Controllers
Everyone	Read-only permissions many places, and undefined in others. Watch out for volume root permissions—see the note that follows	Same access.
Users	Read-only permission in most places. Read/write permission in their own profile folders. Cannot install applications that install system services.	Same access, but only over the network. Users cannot log on interactively to domain controllers. This is a big change from Windows NT.

continues

Volume Permissions Gotcha! During installation, Windows 2000 has no way to determine what other applications and preset access permission exist on the volume you have selected for installation. Therefore, it provides the group Everyone full control at the root. If it applied more restrictive permissions at this time, it would then propagate these restrictions throughout the volume. This might rearrange the application or your desired permission arrangement. To ensure security on the root, apply permissions that are more restrictive after installation. (One way to do that, of course, is to apply the BASIC template using the Security Configuration and Analysis snap-in.

TABLE 7.2	*continued*	
DEFAULT SECURITY GROUP FILE PERMISSIONS		
Group	*Member Servers/ Professional*	*Domain Controllers*
Power Users	Permissions are aligned with those of Power Users and Users in Windows NT 4.0. Read/write permission is granted to Power Users on folders other than their own profiles.	Not applicable.
Administrators	Same level as for Windows NT 4.0. Access everywhere. Total control over the system.	Same. An administrator who is a local administrator is not automatically given privileges on a domain controller when his server joins the domain.
Account Operators, Server Operators, Print Operators	Not applicable.	Same rights as in Windows NT. Access to particular files and folders is explicitly given, however.

SIDS, ACLS, and RIDS

Security primitives are unique identifiers used by the operating system to determine access rights and privileges. Each security principal is assigned a security identification (SID). This SID is composed of parts such as the revision number, the name of the authority that assigned the SID, the domain, and a variable number of relative identifiers (RIDs). The RID is what uniquely identifies the security principal.

Resources such as files, folders, and printers have security descriptors (see Figure 7.8). Their security descriptor includes a Discretionary Access Control List (DACL). DACLs are composed of Access Control Entries (ACEs), which are SIDs plus the access privileges allowed to that SID.

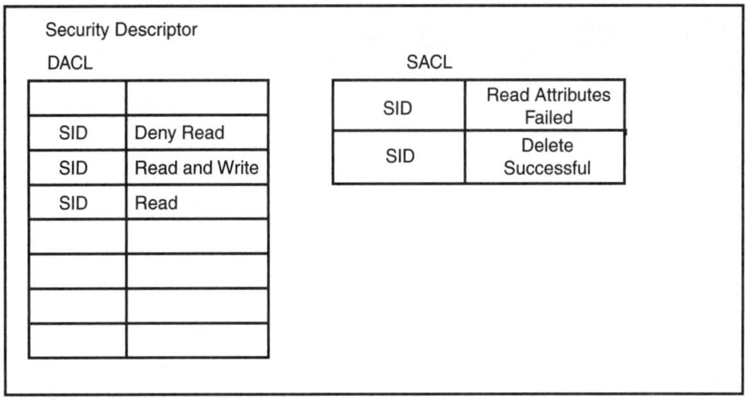

FIGURE 7.8
Security descriptor.

At logon, a user's identifying SIDs (his SID plus the SIDs of his group memberships, plus the SIDs of his privileges, and any SIDs in the SIDHistory attribute) are gathered. This information is used to create an access token for the user. When the user attempts to access a resource, the SIDs in his access token are compared to the SIDs in the file ACL. (See Chapter 10, "Designing an Authentication Strategy," for more information on access tokens and the logon process).

NOTE **SID History** In Windows NT 4.0, a SID was assigned when a user account was created and then remained that user's SID forever. In Windows 2000, when a user is moved from one domain to another, his SID changes. His old SID becomes a part of his SID history so that his defined privileges and access can be determined.

Additional Group Strategies

Additional good group strategies are these:

◆ Follow the pattern of default groups, and create groups composed of users with similar roles. Name the group according to the role the users play. A group composed of project or team members is a good way to begin.

◆ At logon, your system determines the groups you are a member of; if you are a member of multiple groups, this will take longer. Follow the nesting group strategy outlined previously to reduce the number of groups your users are members of. (The upper limit of group memberships is 1,000 groups, but this is theoretical and varies.)

◆ Determining membership in a Universal group (in a native-mode domain) requires the Global Catalog to be available when multiple domains exist in the forest. Cached credentials can be used if the Global Catalog is not available.

RESTRICTED GROUPS

Restricted group Group Policies can be defined to enforce the membership of groups. The Group Policy contains the list of members in the indicated group. By defining the policy centrally, you prevent administrators from changing group membership at the local computer level. A user who has been given administrator privileges at the local level cannot add or remove users to the Restricted membership group.

Let's say that you have given Fred Pumpkin membership in the Administrators group on the server CompanyMail. Fred Pumpkin wants to include his friends in this group as well. If you make this local Administrators group a Restricted group, you can control its membership. Fred cannot add or remove users from the local Administrators group, even though by definition he would normally have the right to do so. Membership in Restricted groups should be made at the OU level where the group is located.

For more information policies and how to manage them, see Chapter 8, "Designing Security Policy Inheritance."

TERMINAL SERVICES

If Terminal Services are installed on a Windows 2000 system, user rights are predefined but can be modified. The first restriction is that any user who wants to use Terminal Services to access the computer must be granted logon locally rights. These rights are granted depending on the terminal server mode. There are two modes for terminal server. In the remote administration mode, only members of Administrators can log on locally. In the application sharing mode, all domain Users group members can log on. On a member server, the Domain Global users group is automatically a member of the Local users group.

While a user is remotely logged on to the terminal server, that user is automatically a member of the Terminal Services Users local group.

Terminal Services should not be installed in application sharing mode on a domain controller. If you do so, any privileges you define for these users is available to them on all domain controllers in the domain. For example, because the users now have logon local rights (to access the applications on the domain controller), they will be able to sit down at any domain controller and log on interactively.

TOOLS FOR MANAGING USERS

In a domain, users are managed from the Active Directory Users and Computers console. Users can be added to the Users container, or to OU containers for which Administrators members or other have rights assigned. Property pages make configuring users easy and complete.

A standalone Professional or member server has local groups and users. These can be managed in the Local Users and Groups console.

USER RIGHTS AND PRIVILEGES

User rights include logon rights and privileges. Logon rights consist of a list of rights associated with the ability to attempt authentication to a type of computer, through a particular process or as a particular type of user. Privileges include the possible things a user can do after logging on. In both cases, rights and privileges may be assigned or denied.

Logon rights and privileges usually are assigned to groups of users. However, there is nothing preventing the assignment of these rights and privileges to individual users, except that it is not good, efficient practice.

The groups in Tables 7.3 and 7.4 have default logon rights and privileges.

TABLE 7.3

ADMINISTRATORS ONLY

	Logon Right	Privilege	Information
Log on as a batch job	X		Log on using a batch facility.
Create page file		X	Create a page file.
Debug programs		X	Debug low-level objects such as threads.
Force shutdown from remote systems		X	Shut down a computer remotely.
Load and unload device drivers		X	Install and uninstall device drivers.
Manage auditing and security log		X	Specify resources to audit access to. View and clear security logs. This privilege does not include the privilege to set system audit policy.
Modify firmware environmental variables		X	Change system environmental variables stored in nonvolatile RAM.
Take ownership of files or other objects		X	Even if permission does not include access for this user, ownership can be taken.

TABLE 7.4

ADMINISTRATORS AND OTHER GROUPS

	Right or Privilege	*Admins Plus?*	*Information*
Access this computer from a network	Right	Everyone, Power User	Connect to computer across a network.
Log on locally	Right	Backup Operator, Power User, Everyone (client or standalone server)	Sit at console and log on interactively.
Back up files and file folders	Privilege	Backup Operator	File and folder permission cannot keep them from copying files to backup tapes using a backup program.
Bypass traverse checking	Privilege	Everyone	Even if no access to a folder is granted, a user can access files within the folder when given appropriate privileges.
Change System Time	Privilege	Power Users	Set computer time clock.
Increase scheduling priority	Privilege	Power Users	Boost the priority of a process.
Profile a single process	Privilege	Power Users	Sample a process, a useful tool for developers.
Restore files and file folders	Privilege	Backup Operators	Restore backed-up files and folders, even without specific permissions set.
Shut down the system	Privilege	Backup Operators, Everyone, Power Users, Users	Shut down the system interactively.

Several deny access rights exist, which means that you can selectively and explicitly deny access to a particular computer, resource, or logon right. This helps to granularize these rights. For example, all Domain Admins members would normally have the right to log on

FIGURE 7.9
Denying network logon.

to any computer in the domain (see Figure 7.9). You may wish to keep Joshua Celery from accessing the SQL database server. Simply give his account the Deny Access To This Computer From The Network and Deny Local Logon logon rights. This will not affect his ability to access other computers in the domain.

In addition, the Logon As A Service logon right is granted only by default to the Local Systems account.

DELEGATION OF AUTHORITY

Design a delegation of authority strategy.

Delegation of authority mitigates the risk of granting users sweeping control over entire domains. You can give users administrative rights for a single organizational unit or OU hierarchy within a domain. Those rights may or may not include rights within OUs that are nested within them. You will still have Domain Admins with broad access permissions and domain-wide privileges, but you can reserve membership and grant it to only highly trusted administrators.

To delegate authority effectively, you must participate in the design of OU hierarchy within Active Directory. OUs may be created for several reasons. Often they are created in alignment with business structure, such as divisions or departments. If this is not carefully considered, it may create extra work when users change departments without any benefits. Structure without purpose is rarely adequate and can be destructive. However, OUs created to delegate administrative tasks can often improve efficiency and security. It may be desirable to delegate control by physical location, by business unit, or by role or task.

A business department such as Human Resources often needs to modify characteristics of users. Within a domain, an OU created for this department can contain users (see Figure 7.10). A Human Resources administrator can be granted privileges to manage these accounts without giving them privileges to, say, install services on domain computers. Within that OU, other OUs can be nested to further delineate privileges, or other OUs can be created within the domain to allow control of resources such as printers or files by other administrators.

Each division within a company may desire to control access to its own files and folders. Divisional OUs may also represent separate physical locations. It only makes sense to let local administrators

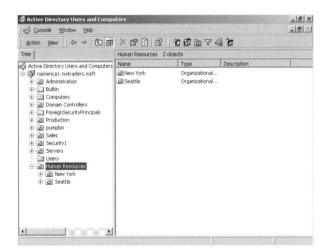

FIGURE 7.10
The Human Resources OU.

control their own resources. Imagine controlling folder access on a server in Berlin by administrators located in New York. This situation was often the reason for creating separate domains in Windows NT 4.0. With Windows 2000, unique OUs can be created to allow control of division-owned or physically located objects.

To allow this type of delegation, create the appropriate OU hierarchy. Your knowledge of company hierarchy, physical locations, task orientation, security risks, and politics will guide these decisions.

To delegate administrative authority, you can directly modify the DACLs of the OUs, or you can use the Delegation of Control Wizard from the Active Directory Users and Computers console (see Figure 7.11). Two types of control are available. You can delegate object creation and deletion permission on particular classes of objects within an OU. Object classes include users, computers, and so on. You can also delegate permissions such as updating specific attributes on all objects within an OU. For example, help desk personnel could be given permission to reset passwords on user accounts within particular OUs. (Policy would dictate how they would prove the identity of the user asking for the password reset.)

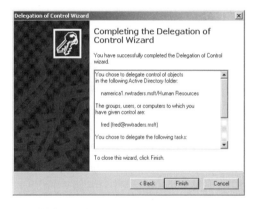

FIGURE 7.11
Delegation of Control Wizard.

Further delegation of control can be accomplished at both lower and higher levels:

◆ By directly delegating permission to change attributes at the container level. The container may be a file folder or a printer.

◆ By delegating administration for a domain within a forest.

According to Microsoft, delegation of authority carried out effectively within a domain or forest reserves only the following rights for Domain Administrators:

◆ Installation of new domain controllers.

◆ Creating initial OU structure. (Within an OU, additional OUs can be created by local administrators.)

◆ Fixing mistakes.

All other privileges and rights should be delegated to local administrators or those given OU-level responsibilities.

Let's look at an example of a division OU. If AB Chalmers, Inc., were to purchase Peterson's SoftAce, the AB Chalmers domain could create an autonomous OU and give Peterson's SoftAce local administrators the ability to manage it. Here are the steps they would follow.

1. Create an OU called SoftAce within the Chalmers domain.

2. Create a Domain Local group called SoftAce Admins.

3. Give the SoftAce Admins group the Full Control Of Object and All Other Objects permission on the SoftAce OU.

Members of the SoftAce Admins group can not only manage the SoftAce OU, but they also can create OUs within that OU. They will have Full Control permission on those OU objects as well.

Control of objects within an OU can also be delegated on an object-by-object basis. Consider the object types within the OU before making design decisions. Object types are as follows:

◆ User accounts

◆ Computer accounts

◆ Groups

◆ Other OUs

Control consists of the ability to completely control the objects within the type, to create objects of that type, or to modify objects of that type.

Ask yourself the same questions about OU objects that you did for files and folders. In a company of any size, large or small, some objects require closer scrutiny and demand tighter access control and policy management than others. Your previous investigations should have located those objects; now you have a strategy for protecting them that also allows you to narrow their control to specific users or groups. In a small company, the domain administrator may be a trusted member of corporate management, and there is little need to restrict his privileges or go to extreme measures to delegate authority to individuals. The domain administrator can be responsible for all objects and administrative tasks within the domain, and users can be granted access as necessary to files, folders, printers, and other resources. In a large, complex organization, or one with out-of-the ordinary security needs, however, more comprehensive granular methods are needed.

Group Policies can be associated with OUs as well. For more information see Chapter 8.

Finally, you can hide the existence of objects by creating an OU and restrict the List Contents right for that OU. If you create an Accounting OU, you can place Accounting group databases and check printers within that OU and give List content rights only to appropriate accounting personnel.

To see how to use the Delegation of Control Wizard, see Step by Step 7.1.

STEP BY STEP

7.1 Using the Delegation of Control Wizard

1. Open Active Directory Users and Computers.

2. Right-click the object that you wish to delegate control of.

3. Select Delegation Control.

4. Click Next.

5. Use the Add button to add groups or users to delegate control to.

6. Click OK.

7. Check the box for the task you wish to assign, or create a custom task to delegate.

8. Click the Finish button.

CASE STUDY: DAVISON AUTOMOTIVE—SECURITY GROUPS

BACKGROUND

Davison Automotive has experienced rapid growth and is showing the effects. The company serves the automotive aftermarket and provides parts and supplies to retailers, garages, and consumers. After many years of operating as a traditional wholesaler/mail-order business, Davison Automotive brought up an e-commerce site to move its mail-order business into the future. The company was so successful that it has just completed a business-to-business rollout of a new site just for retailers and repair shops. Unlike many companies that move to the Internet, Davison Automotive is keeping its staff of salespeople to provide the personal touch to larger dealers and to provide in-house phone and email support.

PROBLEM STATEMENT

Like many companies, Davison Automotive needs to get it done now! This is superceded only by the need to do it the right way.

Information Systems Manager

We have really outgrown our way of thinking. We realize that we need to be a little more careful in how much responsibility we give to everyone. We just grew fast, and it was easier to simply add someone to a group with more privileges or to assign access by individuals than it was to carefully think it through. My background is with the AS/400, and I just left the PCs up to my PC guy.

Systems Administrator

You simply won't believe it. I didn't when I came to work here. Almost 50% of the company had some Administrative rights, and some folks were also in multiple administrative groups unneces-

sarily. There is still a lot of duplication. There just hasn't been the time to figure out what would happen if I removed these folks from the groups they were in.

Cleaning up the file server has been a pain. Some files have hundreds of users allowed access—that's right, by their user ID, not because of their membership in some group.

We recently moved the inventory and accounting databases off the AS/400 to SQL Server 7.0. Everything is working well, but we've still go some legacy user issues due to the short amount of time we took in transferring the system.

There's simply no way I'll ever be able to get it worked out. I'm really looking forward to the new system. I'm going to finally get a chance to align things properly.

Sales Manager

My sales folk need information fast. I want to make sure that they can get to the databases and get customer information on-the-fly. In the past, I could just added their names to the list when I hired someone new. Who's going to do that for me now?

Help Desk Staff

We need to be able to reset passwords when people call.

CURRENT SYSTEM

The current system reflects the management philosophy of management by current need and belief. Each administrator made changes, and the next one changed them again. No clear plan or policy really exists.

CASE STUDY: DAVISON AUTOMOTIVE—SECURITY GROUPS

Human Resources Director

When a new employee is hired, I turn over his or her information to Information Systems. There's a form I fill out. I know there are lots of complaints about how long it takes to get people on the system, but there's so much to do to get them oriented and on their way. Honestly, we don't want to send any information along to other departments before the people are actually here.

I would like the ability to add each new employee to the data system when that person arrives. I used to be able to do that, and I don't know why I can't anymore.

And when someone leaves, oh, such a problem. I do all the paperwork, and there's so much to do. I hadn't thought about what happens to their records in the system. I know I let payroll know when that person's last day is.

Accounting Manager

I agree with Information Systems—there's far too much freedom around here. Just anyone can access my server. The database is secure—at least, I'm told it is. But it scares me that someone might have the ability to get into the payroll data or something.

Warehouse Manager

Some of these guys out here can't remember to come to work in the morning, and you want them to remember their password? Really, all most of them need is to be able to look up locations of parts and inventory.

Now, the shipping department needs to scan in the shipment contents and be able to enter num-

bers and print shipping information. But they can't ship anything unless an order is entered elsewhere and is in the system.

ENVIRONMENT

A large investment in PC technology exists.

Information Technology Manager

We used to have an AS/400 for our accounting and inventory databases. We are looking to move them from Windows NT to Windows 2000 DataCenter Server next year, if that works out. We have a large number of networked PCs and NT Servers. Our Web site is run on Windows NT.

System Admin

Currently there are 300 PCs here at headquarters. We will be upgrading them to run Windows 2000 Professional. Our outside sales staff (200) have laptops. We have regional warehouses in 16 states. Each one has from 5 to 50 office folks and many warehouse staff. The Web server is currently on 10 NT servers.

ENVISIONED SYSTEM

Windows 2000 has been chosen for the new system, and this presents an opportunity to revise the user, group, and privilege system.

Information Systems Manager

Each user should have only the privileges and access rights needed to do his or her job. We will manage user accounts but may delegate authority to some key areas to ease administrative burden.

continues

CASE STUDY: DAVISON AUTOMOTIVE—SECURITY GROUPS

continued

Systems Admin

The following Administrative roles will be created:

- **Domain Admins**—This will be a very small group that will perform only high-level duties and fix problems.

- **Account Operators**—A little bit larger number of people will have authority to work with accounts at the domain level.

- **Server Operators**—Only personnel who are full-time network or systems admin types will belong to this group.

- **Print Operators**—This group will consist of only personnel who are full-time network or systems admin types.

Other administrative responsibilities will be delegated. To accomplish this, OUs will be created. Some of the OUs and their rationale are listed here:

- In anticipation of moving the inventory database to Windows 2000 DataCenter Server, an OU will be created to hold network servers. Two OUs will be nested underneath: one for the test server and one for our production SQL 7.0 servers. Other databases and resources that have to do with products can also be in this OU. Authority for management of the computers here will be delegated to various personnel, including the database administrator.

- OUs will be created under the DataCenter Server OU, to hold additional servers that may be used for accounting, sales information, and other functions as necessary.

- Help Desk personnel can be given delegated authority in each user OU to reset passwords.

The following groups and structures will be created:

Domain Global:

- SalesMidWest

- WarehouseGeneral

- Office

Domain Local:

- InventoryAccess

- InventorySales

- InventoryLimited

Resource Access Will be Accomplished by doing the following:

Read and write access to the inventory database will be given to the InvenetoryAccess Domain Local group. Read-only access will be given to InventoryLimited.

InventoryLimited will have as member groups the Office and WarehouseLimited groups. All office and warehouse personnel who need to just read data can be placed in these member groups. There will also be a Wfloor user account created, which will be a shared account to be used at kiosks on the warehouse floor. By making this group a member of the WarehouseLimited group, workers can access limited inventory information without logging on.

CASE STUDY: DAVISON AUTOMOTIVE—SECURITY GROUPS

The InventorySales group will be given broader access to the inventory database and to customer information. The various Sales user groups will belong to this group.

SECURITY

The new ability to delegate administrative tasks will help Davison Automotive secure their systems.

Systems Admin

By carefully selecting whom to delegate authority to, and by limiting those persons' roles to just the part of the company and the privileges needed, we will be able to control and secure access to our systems.

Accounting Manager

Finally, accounting for the accountants.

PERFORMANCE

This arrangement should make log on faster because the token size will be reduced. There will also be more time to devote to improving performance because less time will be spent fighting fires.

MAINTAINABILITY

Delegation of authority is an opportunity but can be a liability as well. People will have to be trained, and someone will have to review their work.

AVAILABILITY

The sales manager insists: "Just make sure my guys can get on the system when they need to, and that means from day one."

ANALYSIS

Davison Automotive has a lot of work to do. New systems do present opportunities to correct problems created in previous ones. However, without a lot of work, the problems with the old system still will be present in the new one. Fortunately, the company look as if it is committed to properly planning and implementing the system.

As indicated, delegation could be the company's saving grace, but it could also be its downfall. The ability to give people the authority they need, such as resetting passwords to help desk individuals, is golden. Sorting out how to group users and computers so that authority may be delegated, and so that only the necessary authority is given to the right people, will take some planning. A methodology also has to be devised to review these activities, both to make sure that they are being done properly, and also to determine whether any adjustments need to be made.

The company will need to make a careful evaluation of its current business operation, plan the new implementation, and test it extensively before deployment.

CHAPTER SUMMARY

KEY TERMS

- delegation of authority
- security group
- security principal
- distribution group
- built-in groups
- group scope
- Computer Local group
- Domain Local group
- Domain Global group
- Universal group
- Computer groups
- implicit groups
- native mode
- mixed mode
- nested groups
- security descriptor
- RID
- SACL
- DACL
- Restricted groups
- Enterprise Admins
- Delegation of Control Wizard

This chapter provided an introduction to the new security group structure in Windows 2000 and gave you a peek at the ability to delegate authority. Now that you have learned the concepts and rationale behind the new group structure in Windows 2000, you are ready to move on with your design. Don't forget to revisit your structure as you expand your knowledge. You may find a number of uses for the new Universal groups—and certainly for delegating authority.

APPLY YOUR KNOWLEDGE

Exercises

7.1 Creating an OU and Group Structure

Estimated Time: 30 minutes

1. The OU structure in the case study is incomplete. What additional OUs would you create?

2. The list of groups is incomplete. What additional groups would you add?

3. On your Windows 2000 domain controller, add this OU structure. You can use the diagram in Figure 7.12 to plan your structure before entering it. (To create an OU, right-click the domain or OU in which to create the OU, select New and then OU, and then name the OU.) You can create groups as well. (To create a group, right-click the OU or domain the group should be in, select New, and then select Group. Finally, name the group.)

4. Create computer accounts in the resource OUs to represent database servers. Computer accounts are created by right-clicking the OU, selecting New and then Computer, and then entering the name of the computer.

5. Create one Administrator account and at least two accounts for every group. Define a manager for Sales, Accounting, and Warehouse. Define an operations manager and a database administrator as well.

6. Who should be a member of the Domain Admins group?

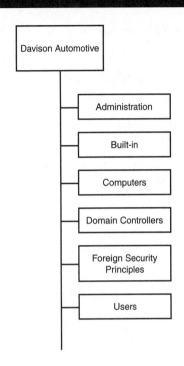

FIGURE 7.12
Planning an OU structure.

7.2 Delegating Authority

Estimated Time: 30 minutes

Use the Delegation of Authority Wizard to assign user responsibility to managers for Warehouse, Sales, and Human Resources. To do this, the previous exercise needs to be completed.

Use the Delegation of Authority Wizard to assign computer resource responsibility to the operations manager (see the following steps).

Delegation of Control

1. Right-click the database computer.

2. Select Delegate Control, and click Next.

APPLY YOUR KNOWLEDGE

3. Use the Add button to add Operations Manager.

4. Click Next.

5. Select the radio button for Create A Custom Task To Delegate, and click Next.

6. Select the radio button for Only the Following Objects in the Folder.

7. Check the boxes for Computer Objects, Shared Folder Objects, and click Next.

8. Check the box for General.

9. Check Permission boxes for Read and Write.

10. Click Next, and then click Finish.

Log on as each of the managers, and add users to their OUs.

Creating Users in OUs

1. Right-click the OU.

2. Select New, and then select User.

3. Enter a minimum of the username and user logon name.

4. Click Next.

5. Click Finish.

Review Questions

1. John is the newly appointed administrator in the EastCoast.SmithBrothers.com domain. He is asked to help Human Resources by creating lists of users that can be used for email distribution. There are 100 different lists. John creates 100 security groups and adds the appropriate users to these groups. Soon after this, users and their managers are complaining that logon time in the domain has increased significantly. Why might this be? What should John do about it?

2. Nancy is busy adding restrictions to the Guest account. She limits its logon hours to 0 and adds a nonexistent computer account as the only workstation that the Guest can logon from. Her boss, Peter, finds her doing this and tells her it's a waste of time—after all, he says, the Guest account is disabled by default. Which one of them is right?

3. John is a member of the Server Operators group. He wants to shut down the database server from the domain controller. He finds that he does not have the right to do that. The database server is at another location. Short of going there, who can he ask locally to do this for him?

4. Mary is a member of the Administrators group. Several users in her domain need to run legacy applications. As an Administrator, Mary can run the application. As members of the Users group, her users cannot. Mary does not want to make these users members of the Administrators group on their Windows 2000 Professional computers. Can she give them membership in any group that might work? Is there any reason not to give them membership in that group?

5. The DNSAdmins group is a Domain Local group in a native-mode domain. Sally is a member of this group. This group is given full control of the DNS server on the domain controller by default when it is installed. Another DNS server service is installed on a member server. Will Sally have administrative responsibility on that DNS server?

APPLY YOUR KNOWLEDGE

6. Peter has to assign users to groups and give groups access to resources. He creates the following groups: LocalBackup, GlobalBackup, LocalRestore, and GlobalRestore. (Groups with a preface of Local are Local groups; groups with a preface of Global are Global groups.) He wants to use these groups to assign responsibility for backup and restore in his 10-computer, native-mode Windows 2000 domain. Detail the process he uses.

7. Why would you use a Universal group instead of a Domain Global group? When would you use a Domain Global group instead of a Universal group?

8. Describe how to use the built-in groups, your own groups, and delegation of authority to granularize responsibilities and access permissions within a domain.

9. What is an Enterprise Admin group, and where would this be used?

10. What does membership in the Interactive group versus the Network group mean?

11. On a newly installed Windows 2000 Server, who will be able to access files in the root?

Exam Questions

1. You give Nancy Smith membership in the local Administrators group on domain controller ServerA. How do you make sure that she does not extend membership in the Administrators group, or any other group, administrative privileges? Select the best answer.

   A. Use Active Directory property pages for Nancy Smith, and set her privileges to Self Only.

   B. Add Nancy Smith to the Account Operators Group instead.

   C. Define a Restricted group policy that includes the Administrators group and the Power Users group for ServerA.

   D. Monitor the Administrators group.

   E. Define a Restricted group Group Policy that includes the Administrator group, the Account Operators group, the Print Operators group, and the Server Operators group.

2. You want to have remote administrative privileges on your domain controller. What is the most secure way to do that?

   A. Install terminal services in the remote administration mode.

   B. Install terminal services in the application sharing mode.

   C. Create a strong password for the administrative account you will use for this.

   D. Create a Restricted group policy and include the Administrators group on the server.

3. You do not want to create needless Administrators, but you need to have a user who can change the system time on some servers. The servers are member servers or standalone servers. You want to give the user as few additional administrative privileges as possible. What group do you make the user a member of?

   A. Power Users

   B. Server Operators

   C. Account Operators

   D. DNSAdmins

APPLY YOUR KNOWLEDGE

4. When you change domain mode to native, you can change group scope from Global to Universal. Why would you elect to do this?

   A. Because Global groups can contain only Local groups, and Universal groups can contain Global groups, this gives you better access to forest-wide resources.

   B. Global groups can be given access to any resource throughout the forest, but Universal groups can be given access to other forests.

   C. Global groups can be given access to any resource in the forest; so can Universal groups. However, Global groups can be nested in Universal groups. This simplifies the implementation of groups strategy. You can place one Universal group in any Domain Local group and obtain access to the resources that the Domain Local group has been given. All members in all Global groups will have that access.

   D. Universal groups can contain users from throughout the forest. You place users in the Universal groups and place the Universal groups in Global groups. You can then place the Global group in the Domain Local resource and simplify your group strategy.

5. Jesus Smith is the administrator for the Relzo domain. He must decide upon a group membership strategy to help him administer the domain.

Required Result:

Management of all user accounts and groups except Administrative groups should be done by the Human Resources Department. Management of desktop PCs should be given to help desk personnel. They should be able to load software, configure and reload systems, if necessary, and reset passwords.

Optional Desired Results:

Users managing users or computers should be limited to the areas defined. Only the privileges they need should be given to them. There should be no possibility that they have privileges in other areas of the infrastructure.

The structure should be extensible as the company grows.

Proposed Solution:

OUs are created for Human Resources (user management) and help desk personnel. Users in Human Resources are selected for membership in the Account Operators group. Help desk personnel are placed in the Server Operators group.

Evaluation of Proposed Solution:

Which result(s) does the proposed solution produce?

   A. The proposed solution produces the required result and both of the optional results.

   B. The proposed solution produces the required result and one of the optional results.

   C. The proposed solution produces the required result but neither of the optional results.

   D. The proposed solution does not produce the required result.

6. Jesus Smith is the administrator for the Relzo domain. He must decide upon a group membership strategy to help him administer the domain.

Required Result:

Management of all user accounts and groups except Administrative groups should be done by the Human Resources department. Management

APPLY YOUR KNOWLEDGE

of desktop PCs should be given to help desk personnel. They should be able to load software, configure and reload systems, if necessary, and reset passwords.

Optional Desired Results:

Users managing users or computers should be limited to the areas defined. Only the privileges they need should be given to them. There should be no possibility that they have privileges in other areas of the infrastructure.

The structure should be extensible as the company grows.

Proposed Solution:

Two new groups are created. The Domain Local group HumanR is placed in the Account Operators group and is given additional rights to fit the job requirements. The Domain Local HelpDesk group is given membership in the Power Users group on the desktop PCs. The group is given additional rights as necessary so that members can do their job.

Evaluation of Proposed Solution:

Which result(s) does the proposed solution produce?

A. The proposed solution produces the required result and both of the optional results.

B. The proposed solution produces the required result and one of the optional results.

C. The proposed solution produces the required result but neither of the optional results.

D. The proposed solution does not produce the required result.

7. Jesus Smith is the administrator for the Relzo domain. He must decide upon a group membership strategy to help him administer the domain.

Required Result:

Management of all user accounts and groups except Administrative groups should be done by the Human Resources department. Management of desktop PCs should be given to help desk personnel. They should be able to load software, configure and reload systems, if necessary, and reset passwords.

Optional Desired Results:

Users managing users or computers should be limited to the areas defined. Only the privileges they need should be given to them. There should be no possibility that they have privileges in other areas of the infrastructure.

The structure should be extensible as the company grows.

Proposed Solution:

OUs are created for Human Resources (user management) and help desk staff. Domain Global groups are created, one for Human Resources called HumanRDG, and one for the help desk called HelpDeskDG. Two Domain Local groups, HumanR and HelpDesk, are also created. The HumanR group is delegated authority in the HumanReources OU to manage users. Appropriate privileges are given. The HelpDesk group is delegated authority in the HelPDesk OU and is given every possible privilege in the OU. The HelpDeskDG group is made a member of the HelpDesk group. The HumanRDG group is made a member of the HumanR group.

APPLY YOUR KNOWLEDGE

Evaluation of Proposed Solution:

Which result(s) does the proposed solution produce?

A. The proposed solution produces the required result and both of the optional results.

B. The proposed solution produces the required result and one of the optional results.

C. The proposed solution produces the required result but neither of the optional results.

D. The proposed solution does not produce the required result.

8. Jesus Smith is the administrator for the Relzo domain. He must decide upon a group membership strategy to help him administer the domain.

Required Result:

Management of all user accounts and groups except Administrative groups should be done by the Human Resources department. Management of desktop PCs should be given to help desk personnel. They should be able to load software, configure and reload systems, if necessary, and reset passwords.

Optional Desired Results:

Users managing users or computers should be limited to the areas defined. Only the privileges they need should be given to them. There should be no possibility that they have privileges in other areas of the infrastructure.

The structure should be extensible as the company grows.

Proposed Solution:

OUs are created for Human Resources (user management) and help desk staff. Domain Global groups are created, one for Human Resources called HumanRDG, and one for the help desk called HelpDeskDG. Two Domain Local groups, HumanR and HelpDesk, are also created. The HumanR group is delegated authority in the HumanReources OU to manage users. Appropriate privileges are given. The HelpDesk group is delegated authority in the HelPDesk OU and is given rights to deal with the computers. The HelpDesk group is also given the permission to reset passwords in the HumanResources OU. The HelpDeskDG group is made a member of the HelpDesk group. The HumanRDG group is made a member of the HumanR group.

Evaluation of Proposed Solution:

Which result(s) does the proposed solution produce?

A. The proposed solution produces the required result and both of the optional results.

B. The proposed solution produces the required result and one of the optional results.

C. The proposed solution produces the required result but neither of the optional results.

D. The proposed solution does not produce the required result.

APPLY YOUR KNOWLEDGE

9. Cher is a member of the Accountants group, the Managers group, and the Sales group. The Sales group is given read permission on the Whatisthis folder. The Managers group is given read, write, and delete privileges on the Whatisthis folder. The Accountants group is given Modify permission on the Whatisthis folder. You do not want Cher to be able to delete files in the Whatthis folder. What do you do (pick two)?

   A. Remove Cher from the Managers group and the Accountants group.

   B. Remove Cher from the Managers group.

   C. Remove Cher from the Managers group and the Accountants group, and create a new group that has the same privileges they do, except Delete permission in the Whatisthis folder. You place Cher in the group.

   D. Leave Cher's group membership alone. Give Cher the Deny Delete permission in the Whatisthis folder.

Answers to Exercises

Exercise 7.1

1. These OUs should be created:

   • A Human Resources OU will be created, and all employees will be created under this OU or an OU nested underneath. Routine account administration will be delegated to management in Human Resources.

   • A sales OU will be created under the Human Resources OU and will contain sales personnel. Authority to do routine account administration will be delegated to management in sales.

   • An information systems OU will be created under the Human Resources OU and will contain information systems personnel. Authority for management will be delegated to Information Systems.

   • In anticipation of moving the inventory database to Windows 2000 DataCenter Server, an OU will be created to hold network servers. Two OUs will be nested underneath, one for the test server and one for the production SQL 7.0 servers. Other databases and resources that have to do with product can also be in this OU. Authority for management of the computers here will be delegated to various personnel, including the database administrator.

   • OUs will be created under the DataCenter Server OU to hold additional servers that may be used for accounting, sales information, and so on.

   • Help desk personnel can be given delegated authority in each user OU to reset passwords.

2. These additional groups should be added:

   • SalesMidWest
   • SalesEastCoast
   • SalesWestCoast
   • GAccounting
   • WarehouseGeneral
   • WarehouseLimited
   • Office

APPLY YOUR KNOWLEDGE

These Domain Local groups should be added as well:

- InventoryAccess
- InventorySales
- InventoryLimited
- Accounting

3. See Figure 7.13 for solution to item 3.

4. See Figure 7.13 for solution to item 4.

5. This is a simple process of adding users on the domain controller.

6. Only the Administrator should be member of the Domain Admins group.

Answers to Review Questions

1. The SID of each security group a user is a member of will be accumulated and added to the access token each time that user logs on. This can slow logon and negatively affect performance. Distribution group SIDS are not evaluated at logon. John should create distribution groups for each mail list and place users in them. Then he should remove the security groups he created.

2. Nancy is correct. Although the Guest account is disabled by default, it can be enabled. Additional action is necessary to ensure that if it becomes enabled, it is not abused. The Guest

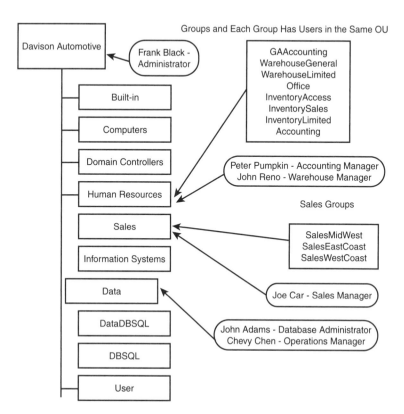

FIGURE 7.13
OUs, groups, and users.

account is a member of the Everyone group, so everywhere the Everyone group can go, so can the Guest account.

3. John needs to ask the administrator. The administrator can log on as a batch job, create a page file, debug programs, force shutdown remotely, load and unload device drivers, manage the auditing and security log, modify firmware environmental variables, and take ownership of objects. He can also change a security configuration even if permissions are set to deny him access. He merely takes ownership and then assigns himself, or anyone else, the access he wants.

4. Many applications that users could run under Windows NT 4.0 do not run under Windows 2000. Because the Power Users group is given registry and file access similar to that of the Users group in Windows NT 4.0, it may be that she can place her users in the Power Users group on their system and solve the problem. Mary may want to investigate other possibilities because she is giving the users additional privileges as well. The Power Users Group can log on locally to a server (if members are running applications on their Professional systems, this is not a problem; they would have to be members of the Power Users group on the server to log on locally to the server using that privilege), change the system time, increase scheduling priority, and profile a single process.

5. Computer Local groups can exist only on member servers and Windows 2000 Professional. They can be used to define security for locally stored resources. Alternatively, Domain Local groups can be used in a Windows 2000 native-mode environment to define security on any computer joined in the domain. The Domain Local group DNSAdmins is given Full Control, by default, to any new DNS server. Because Sally is a member of this group, she will have administrative control of the new DNS server.

6. Peter makes sure that the LocalBackup and LocalRestore groups are Domain Local groups. At the domain controller, he places the GlobalBackup group in the LocalBackup group, and the GlobalRestore group in the LocalRestore group. Then, on each server, he gives the appropriate Domain Local group the appropriate privilege to back up or restore. He places appropriate users in the GlobalBackup and GlobalRestore groups.

7. Use a Universal group when you have multiple similar groups that exist in many domains. They can be collected into single Universal group, which then can be given membership in Resource Local groups. Universal groups exist only in native-mode domains. In a large enterprise consisting of many native-mode domains, it will be easier to use Universal groups to collect Domain Global groups. In smaller organizations, and in mixed-mode domains, you will use Domain Global groups. Universal groups cannot be used in mixed-mode domains.

APPLY YOUR KNOWLEDGE

8. Determine where built-in groups will serve, while realizing that they cannot be restricted as groups you create. Create global groups that match job functions. Create OUs to contain users and computers for roles or other reasons. Delegate authority within OUs to created groups.

9. Enterprise Admins is a group with default privileges in every domain in the forest. These members also can be granted other privileges and permission in every domain in the forest.

10. Membership in the Interactive group means that you have logged on locally. Membership in the Network group means that you have accessed the computer over the network.

11. A newly installed Windows 2000 Server gives the group Everyone access to the root. Therefore, any files not otherwise protected may be vulnerable.

Answers to Exam Questions

1. **E.** Ordinarily, this is just what Nancy could do. If you create a restricted group policy and place the Administrators group from that server in it, you would be able to manage membership in this group using that policy. Nancy will not be able to place anyone in any group for which you create a restricted policy. Answer C would work if ServerA was a standalone server. Answer D might work if you had the time, but then Nancy could still add users to the Account Operators, Server Operators, and Print Operators groups. Answer B would keep Nancy from adding administrators, but would it give her the privileges you want? (See the section "Restricted Groups.")

2. **A, C, D.** Installing Terminal Services in application sharing mode would give every user the rights to log on locally. This is not a good idea. Install Terminal Services in remote administration mode. While you are at it, make sure that the Administrator account password on this system is strong. Finally, if you have a large system and want to control membership in administrative groups, you may want to consider creating restricted group policies. (See the section "Terminal Services.")

3. **A.** Power Users have some administrative privileges. They can change the system time and increase scheduling priority. This group has the least additional privileges of the groups mentioned. Therefore, Power Users is the correct answer. (See Table 7.4 and "Power Users.")

4. **C.** You use Universal groups to contain multiple Global groups from many domains in the forest. Then a single Universal group can be used to grant access or privilege in any domain by placing it in the appropriate Domain Local group. (See the section "Universal.")

5. **D.** Although placing users in the Account Operators group will allow them to manage users, and although they will not be able to add users to Administrative groups, the Server Operator group will not give help-desk personnel enough privileges to do the job they need to do because they will not be able to reset passwords. In addition this group would give them rights they do not need, and which could be abused. (See the sections "Explicit Default Groups" and "Using Security Groups to Provide Resource Access.")

APPLY YOUR KNOWLEDGE

6. **C.** Now Human Resources and help desk personnel can do their jobs. This will not turn out to be an extensible structure if the company grows much. The Power Users group is a Computer Local group, and visiting each PC to make sure that it has the new group HelpDesk in it will be labor-intensive. Because the group is local to the domain, it cannot be extended to other domains. Both groups are Domain Global groups, so it will not be possible to restrict their privileges to some part of the domain, nor can these groups be fine-tuned by granting only some privileges to some resources to some people. (See the sections "Explicit Default Groups" and "Using Security Groups to Provide Resource Access.")

7. **B.** The use of OUs and Domain Global and Domain Local groups makes this a very extensible structure. Help desk and Human Resources people can do their jobs. Help desk people have too many privileges, however, so the results in answer A are not produced. (See the sections "Explicit Default Groups" and "Using Security Groups to Provide Resource Access.")

8. **A.** Finally, groups and OUs are appropriately assigned. Privileges are granted, but not too many. (See the section "Explicit Default Groups" and "Using Security Groups to Provide Resource Access.")

9. **D.** Use the new granular Deny permission to fine-tune accounts with multiple group assignments. This will keep the proliferation of groups to a minimum and enable you to precisely control access to important files and folders. (See the section "User Rights and Privileges," and Chapter 5.)

Suggested Readings and Resources

1. *Microsoft Windows 2000 Resource Kit.* Microsoft Press, 2000.

2. *Microsoft Windows 2000 Resource Kit: Deployment Planning Guide.* Microsoft Press, 2000.

   • Chapter 10, "Determining Domain Migration Strategies"

   • Chapter 11, "Planning Distributed Security"

3. Boswell, William. *Inside Windows 2000 Server.* New Riders, 2000. (Chapter 10, "Managing Active Directory Security.")

This chapter covers the following Microsoft-specified objective for the "Designing a Windows 2000 Security Solution" section of the Designing Security for a Microsoft Windows 2000 Network exam:

Design the placement and inheritance of security policies for sites, domains, and organizational units.

▶ You can implement security polices in Windows 2000 by creating appropriate Group Policies and linking them to Group Policy containers. Group Policy containers (GPCs) hold collections of computers or users. Sites, domains, and organizational units (OUs) are GPCs. Planning what to apply where is the major design issue. A sound understanding of the process is necessary because improperly created or applied policy can have major impacts on system operation, performance, and security.

CHAPTER 8

Designing Security Policy Inheritance

▶ The first step here is to get comfortable with the tools used to apply Group Policy, and then examine the why of using Group Policy to applying security policy.

▶ Read, understand, and practice using the Security Configuration Editor to create, modify, and use security templates to fashion security on the local machine. Chapter 4, "Designing a Security Baseline," can help you with this area.

▶ Read the section in this chapter on creating Group Policy objects (GPOs) using the Group Policy console.

▶ Read the section in this chapter on creating Group Policy using templates.

▶ Practice creating a simple Group Policy and applying it to the local computer.

▶ Practice creating a simple Group Policy and applying it to an OU so that it affects other computers in the domain.

▶ Study the scenario in the case study.

▶ Learn about the impact of multiple policies at various levels and the tools available to change default behavior.

▶ Use the case-study information to design Group Policies for the Tremain Polson domain, and then compare your results with the case study's proposed plan. Did you agree with the proposed solution? Why or why not?

▶ Consider your own company and its needs, and practice by designing a Group Policy plan for it.

INTRODUCTION

Although most of the hoopla about Windows 2000 Group Policy centers around the reduced Total Cost of Ownership that can be brought about by managing computer and user configurations, another major advantage of this tool is its capability to assist in the implementation and maintenance of security policy. Just as administrators can control the proper settings on display drivers and avoid help desk calls, security professionals can set policy for authentication, user rights, registry and file access, and much, much more. They can do this for an entire enterprise, and yet, if required, make the implementation granular so that it impacts only a single user or a single machine.

The process for doing this is through the implementation of Group Policies. To effectively implement Group Policy, you should first understand what they are. Then you need some time to learn how to choose and use the tools available. You should also learn the Group Policy Inheritance Model as well. After you are comfortable with these operations, you can predict whether a particular setting will be applied to a computer or user group. You will understand what policy should be entered at which level (site, domain, or OU) to have the desired effect.

Finally, you can design a Group Policy model that effectively distributes the desired security policies throughout your organization.

Understanding, modeling, testing, and designing Group Policy for security purposes is a challenging and time-consuming task. Remember, however, when tested and ready, you can push policy across the enterprise to all Windows 2000 computers and maintain these security settings from a central place.

CASE STUDY: TREMAIN POLSON SECURITY POLICY DESIGN

BACKGROUND

Tremain Polson is a $1.8 billion manufacturer and marketer of personal care and household products. Its hair-care products and skin-care creams are leaders in their class. In addition, the company also owns Siddhartha Herbal Beauty Supply. Products are marketed both in the United States and internationally.

Tremain Polson, a family-founded and still family-run company, prides itself on a corporate culture built on honesty, respect, and ownership. This has long meant very open communications and open information systems. Folks are just used to being able to go anywhere, see and do anything. Recently their Web site was hacked, and a database containing accounting information was breached.

PROBLEM STATEMENT

Internet presence was established a tad too hastily.

Information Systems Manager

Putting the company on the Internet created a security hotspot. We're so naive here. I guess we left ourselves open. We've slapped together protection for that server and removed any connection with our internal network. Meanwhile we are evaluating security needs internally. We don't think it was just chance that the accounting database was attacked. As much as we just can't imagine the possibility, we believe some insider information was used. We've got to be careful, however; most folks here are honest, good people, and we don't want to offend them. We just need more control over our systems. We need a

way to quickly put new security decisions into place and make sure they stay there without being obtrusive.

We had made the decision to move to Windows 2000 with all new applications and hardware and had begun a test lab a month ago. I believe it has the tools we need to manage our servers and our people. In light of our recent security issues, we're going to migrate all servers to Windows 2000 as fast as we can develop a reasonable plan.

Systems Administrator

In the past, we've had rather loose security to be sure. Tightening controls has been suggested but always turned down as offensive and not necessary. This company is proud of its corporate citizens. It has been pretty shocking to discover that everyone is not as straightforward and respectful of property. Now, at least we have the opportunity to put together a plan that will protect our systems.

Accounting Manager

Really, it's quite simple. Only my group should have any access to the accounting database. I don't know what the fuss is. I trust my children, too, but I don't give them credit cards. They just are not mature enough to handle the responsibility. Folks here have got to get over that one big family thing.

Furthermore, not everyone in my group should be able to get everywhere. I have folks who shouldn't be allowed to see anything except what they are currently entering. We should separate the accounts payable folks from the billing folks and

continues

CASE STUDY: TREMAIN POLSON SECURITY POLICY DESIGN

continued

the payroll folks and establish a few controls here. Our internal auditors should be able to see everything, change nothing. What's so difficult about that?

Human Resources VP

I'm afraid of the consequences of all the increased security. Many of our associates have been with the company for their entire careers. They are used to being treated as people, not "accounts" or "users." Whatever we do needs to work behind the scenes. If it changes the way they are used to working, I need to know about it. We can turn this into another family activity, a way to protect our jobs and our families by protecting our company's assets.

CURRENT SYSTEM

An open, non-restrictive, company policy prevails.

Human Resources Manager

When new associates join us, they are welcomed with our open-arms policy. No one is restricted from going anywhere. Everyone is asked to share in the work, and no idea is ever ignored. Each associate shares in the profits of the company. Computer access is open and very available, from terminals on the shop floor, to desktops, laptops for traveling folks, and Palm organizers for anyone who wants them. We want our people to be informed and have the tools they need to do their job.

People are given a logon account and password that they are asked to change when they first log on. Plant workers have an account, but usually use the kiosks and terminals in the plant area that are always on and connected to the resources they need.

Accounting Manager

Anyone can sit down at a computer anywhere and all the tools that person needs to do his job (and anyone else's) are available. All desktop computers look and act alike. In my department, we are very cognizant of the confidentiality of the information that we are working with and the need to work only in our areas.

I'm not too sure how well things are protected, however. I thought there was some security in place, but it really wasn't of any concern. Computer systems are not my job; accounting is.

Asiago Plant Manager

I've got a lot of computer equipment out here. I can't be watching what folks are doing every second. Everything we do now is computerized from the mixing and bottling to the packing and shipping. The systems work great. We haven't had a computer-related work stoppage or slowdown in years. It's pretty much the same at all our plants.

We have some terminals used only for specific jobs, such as scanning barcodes on product into inventory systems, or in the packing and shipping areas. We also have a lot of desktop boxes

CASE STUDY: TREMAIN POLSON SECURITY POLICY DESIGN

always up and running. We use them for any-thing—for checking order and production status, inventory information, product location, you name it. There's a lot of data out there, and we need to get to it. I can do so from any one of a hundred stations.

ENVIRONMENT

A mixed platform environment exists.

Information Technology Manager

Here at headquarters we have almost a hundred Windows NT Servers. We have a few UNIX systems that mainly run legacy applications. We have a commitment to moving these legacy systems to Windows 2000 Data Center Server when it's available. Each plant and warehouse location has its own complement of servers and workstations. Database information is replicated between the plants and warehouses, so everyone knows what's going on at each plant. I believe we have about 20,000 desktop machines.

Systems Admin

My group is responsible for all these systems. Our security is password based. Although we use NTFS, we haven't really developed the permission system because it's too hard to keep the information current on who needs access to what. We are aware of a number of security patches, registry hacks, and other things that can make our

systems more secure, but we are fighting a losing battle. It's just too difficult to keep up with it. We tried scripting the changes and applying them across the board, but only the most basic of things can be done that way. Then, when it gets changed for some reason, we have no really good way of determining whether it has been changed, changed back, or whatever. There are just too many things to work with, and we are learning more every day.

Systems fall into about 20 different groups, from databases, to plant information systems, to intranet servers. Desktop systems are generally configured exactly the same way because it's easier.

ENVISIONED SYSTEM

Control needs to be established where it is necessary. It can be left alone in other places. A hierarchy of Windows 2000 OUs and a well-thought-out Group Policy design is the goal.

Accounting Manager

My people, and my people only, can access any accounting information. Others may have forms they fill out that may feed information into our system, but they can't touch it, or see it after it is there.

My people will do their jobs like they always have. They won't know that there may be some areas of the database that they can't get to.

continues

continued

Information Systems Manager
We believe we need to make many changes, but one of the first ones is to design our systems so that we have as few domains as possible and within them a number of appropriate organizational units. By separating computers and users into rational groups, we can delegate their management, and we can apply security selectively.

Systems Admin
The first part of the design places similar systems into OUs within the Corporate domain. I see an OU for each of the following:

- **High-security servers**—These servers will be servers, like Accounting and Human Resources databases, that require extra security precautions. We plan to implement IPSec for all communications with these servers, as well as other security options and policies.

- **Intranet servers**—These servers require a different security model. Although they can be more open than the high-security servers—they won't require an IPSec connection, for example—they require considerations different from normal file and print servers.

- **File and print servers**—Common security issues should be manageable for all these systems.

- **Kiosks**—The plant has far too much openness on the plant floor. Most stations are used only to check information, because special barcode and laser systems are used for recording. Yet the stations are complete desktops and allow access to all areas of the company. We'll lock these systems down so that they are like virtual libraries with access only to plant-related information to help folks on the plant floor. We're considering other kiosks in other areas of the company, and it may be they will be in this OU, the restrictions will be the same, and the data may differ, but that can be handled.

- **Desktop**—I believe there will be a hierarchy here. We'll start with a top layer of security settings that should be common to all, and nest within this OU a couple of different OUs. At the first level beneath Desktop will be at least two OUs (each has as a parent, the Desktop OU). One will be for very locked-down systems, such as those in the customer service call center. For the other, less-intensively controlled systems, we may need a third layer to allow the use of Group Policy to control software settings and machine configuration settings. The Desktop OU structure could also include user accounts. The accounts would be placed in the appropriate OUs—for example, customer service accounts in the very locked-down OU.

I'll need to share this system with our applications people and the hardware guys and further extend the design to include software installation, logon scripts, hardware management, and so forth. It'll be awhile before we roll out the desktops, so we've got some time.

CASE STUDY: TREMAIN POLSON SECURITY POLICY DESIGN

Meanwhile we can institute the policies for our servers and tighten security. We'll be able to use Security Configuration and Analysis to develop templates for each of the OUs, to test them, and to periodically make sure they are still configured correctly. We can use Group Policy and import the templates to Security Settings.

SECURITY

Security needs to be established. Plans include creating a design for each type of computer and user.

Information System Security

I'm new here, but come from a company where security was paramount. I'm amazed at the lack of security concern evident in the current systems. I'm impressed by the willingness to move into the real world and institute a few controls. As I see it, here are a few of the controls to establish for each OU identified.

We've decided that user accounts won't exist in these first OUs, so we will not be setting more restrictive user rights assignments at this time within these server OUs. Desktop OUs will have user and computer settings. We'll have a high-security Desktop OU that we can put users, such as auditors, in and give their desktop machines an IPSec Policy, for example. Here's an example description of OU Security Settings.

High-Security Servers:

- Security options
  - **Additional restrictions for anonymous connections**—No access permitted without explicit anonymous permissions.

- **Amount of idle time required before disconnecting**—15 minutes.

- **Clear virtual memory pagefile when system shuts down**—Enabled.

- **Do not display last username in logon screen**—Enabled.

- **Message text for users logging on**—Defined.

- **Message title for users logging on**—Defined.

- **Recovery Console: Allow automatic administrative logon**—Disabled.

- **Recovery Console: Allow floppy copy and access to all drives and all folders**—Disabled.

- **Rename administrator account**—Yes.

- **Rename guest account**—Yes.

- **Restrict CD-ROM access to locally logged on user only**—Enabled.

- **Restrict floppy access to locally logged on user only**—Enabled.

- **Shutdown system immediately if unable to log security audits**—Enabled

- **Unsigned driver installation behavior**—Do not allow installation.

- **Unsigned non-driver installation behavior**—Do not allow installation.

- Event logs
  - **Retention method for security log**—Do not overwrite events.

continues

CASE STUDY: TREMAIN POLSON SECURITY POLICY DESIGN

continued

- · **Restrict Guest access to application log**—Enabled.

- · **Restrict Guest access to security log**—Enabled.

- · **Restrict Guest access to systems log**—Enabled.

- · **Restricted Groups**—All administrative groups will be defined at the domain level and entered as restricted groups.

- · **System Services**—A number of system services will be disabled to prevent their use on these systems, including DNS server, Fax service, FTP Publishing, IIS Admin, Internet connection sharing, Telnet, Trivial FTP Daemon, World Wide Web Publishing.

- · **Registry and File System**—Follow registry permission as outlined in high-security template, and adjust for software as applicable

- · **IPSec policy**—Required for all communications with these machines.

Information Auditor

I like the way Group Policies work. You've just made my job easier. I can use security templates in MMC to make sure the policies decided on are being used.

PERFORMANCE

Attention to the impact of new security policies will prevent policies from negatively impacting performance.

Systems Admin

The specs we've seen show that using IPSec alone will decrease performance by more than 20%. We'll need to provide hardware acceleration to assist us in handling that extra load. There are some new network interface cards to which the Windows 2000 TCP/IP stack can offload the encryption part of the IPSec.

Using Group Policies can make logon and startup times longer. I'm going to test our design. It's relatively flat, so it shouldn't present much of a problem; but then everyone hasn't really had time to consider how he or she wants to use it. The high-security server groups won't have user accounts, so we can disable that functionality. The policy will take less time to process.

Information Technology Manager

I've been given a solid budget for hardware improvements that will enable us to counter any performance hits due to security. We've got to make sure that at each step we design an efficient system, however, so we place the hardware only where we need it. Adding more hardware doesn't solve a design error.

We must not allow our desire for security to get in the way of production. Response time should be the same as it is now, if not better. There are also people to consider here. We want the new security to be as unobtrusive as possible. If it takes me a long time to log on, I'm going to know something is happening.

CASE STUDY: TREMAIN POLSON SECURITY POLICY DESIGN

MAINTAINABILITY

After being implemented, the system must have minimal maintenance expenditure.

Accounting Manager

Are all these gewgaws and policies going to continue to work? You're talking about a lot of new technology here. Can you keep it up? I've heard there are 63,000 known bugs in Windows 2000. That's a lot.

Information Technology Manager

That bug statement was taken out of context. There may be issues; there always are. But I rely on sound data from people I know and trust, not the media. I've seen the stats from several test sites and places already in full production. Basically, keeping the system up and running is not a problem. Keeping our policies in place won't be either. We can constantly monitor the policy state, and it is reapplied automatically. We control it centrally.

AVAILABILITY

The system must be up 24 × 7. I don't want another outage like the Web site going down.

ANALYSIS

Tremain Polson has a rich, complex system with a large requirement for flexible security policies. This is the perfect environment for Windows 2000. They do not have to implement a strict, "one-fits-all" policy to obtain security. Each resource and situation can be evaluated, grouped for efficiency, and have an appropriate policy applied. Policies can be centrally maintained.

There is a lot of work to do here, and the company must be careful to fully test each policy with the types of users that will have to interface with it. Because the system has been so open in the past, they would do well to engage their employees in the design effort. That is, they could be informative as to the need for security to be tightened in some circumstances. After all, no one seriously considers leaving all of his money hidden out in the cookie jar. Most people have bank accounts and insist on them being kept secure. Now, the extra penny jar? Everyone is welcome to it. Employees also want to feel safe themselves. How can they feel safe if they come to believe that outsiders can enter their work world and destroy data. Data that they, the employees, have worked hard to gather.

Security is important, and most people believe in it. With group policies, Tremain Polson has the opportunity to put the pieces together in a manner that will suit all.

WHAT IS GROUP POLICY?

Design the placement and inheritance of security policies for sites, domains, and organizational units.

Group Policy is an expression of the desired computer and user configuration settings for an organization. All Windows 2000 computers—Professional, Server, Advanced Server, domain controllers, and standalone systems—can be controlled using Group Policy. If these computers are joined in a Windows 2000 domain, their configuration settings and those for users that use them to log on to the domain can be established and maintained from a central location. If the computers are not part of a Windows 2000 domain, a Group Policy (called in this instance, the Local Computer Policy) can be designed to control computer configuration and to selectively apply user settings on that machine.

Group Policy is part of IntelliMirror. (Other parts are Active Directory, Synchronization Manager, Offline Files, and Remote Installation Services.) IntelliMirror is designed to assist in desktop configuration management. The discussion here centers on the use of Group Policy to implement and maintain security policy. Chapter 12, "Designing Windows 2000 Network Services Security," addresses the security aspects of Remote Installation Services. For information on how to use Group Policy and other aspects of computer management, see the Suggested Readings and Resources at the end of this chapter.

You can use Group Policy to set computer configuration options such as the following (see Figure 8.1):

◆ **Security Settings**—You can use Group Policy to set many security settings for implementation across sites, domains, and OUs. A number of security templates can assist you in this development, including the following:

  • Account Policies (These settings are only changeable at the domain level. No changes to domain-level settings can be made at the OU level. Setting changes made there will affect local SAM settings for member servers and Professional.)

  • User Rights Assignment, Audit Policy and Security Options

  • Settings for Event Logs

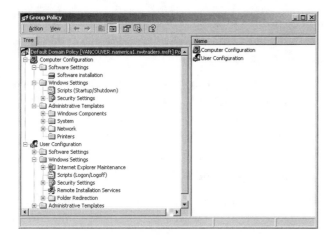

FIGURE 8.1
Default domain GPO.

- Restricted Groups

- System Services

- Registry and File System (access to particular paths can be specified by entering them and then setting permissions)

- Public Key Policies

- IP Security Policy

◆ **Administrative Templates**—ADM files are Unicode text files that list categories that can be set in the Group Policy snap-in. It also lists registry locations where settings are made. System.adm, Inetres.adm and conf.adm are installed. You can create custom ADM files to extend this section of Group Policy. Settings made here are added to the Policy portion of the appropriate HKEY_CCURRENT_USER or HKEY_LOCAL_MACHINE part of the registry.

  - Desktop appearance such as existence of a Run option on the Start menu, the icons that exist on the desktop, the screen saver, and the color of the screen

  - System service settings such as Automatic and Manual

  - Internet Explorer settings

  - System settings such as logon, disk quotas, DNS, client, Group Policy, and Windows File Protection

   - Network settings such as whether a user can configure his
     offline file settings, and whether network connection shar-
     ing is enabled

   - Printer settings such as whether printers are automatically
     published in Active Directory

◆ **Scripts**—Logon, logoff, boot, and shutdown scripts.

◆ **Software Installation**—Installation, updates, and uninstalls
can be arranged according to GPC.

◆ **Folder Redirection**—Users' folders can be stored on the network, but appear to the users to be located on the current
computer.

The items and their settings are contained in a Group Policy
template. The template is divided into two sections: Computer
Configuration and User Configuration.

You can learn more about most Group Policy setting by opening the
GPO, double-clicking on a policy, and examining the Explain tab.
(GPOs are stored in Active Directory. Their templates, gptemplates,
are stored in the domain sysvol folder.) Each item, with the exception of Security Settings, has an Explain tab. There is also a
Windows 2000 Resource Kit reference file, GP.chm, which lists
these details.

The name Group Policy comes from the fact that it represents a collection, or group, of policies. It has nothing to do with Windows
2000 security groups. Group Policies cannot be applied to Windows
2000 security groups; as previously stated, they are applied to a GPC.

GPCs are Active Directory objects that have been given GPO attributes (sites, domains, and OUs). Each GPC can have multiple policies
applied; these subcontainers contain Group Policy information of a
particular type. A Group Policy may contain all configuration information necessary for a GPC, but this is not always the case. Although
one Group Policy might be sufficient for a particular GPC, other
GPCs may need several. One policy might contain only information
about the IPSec policy, whereas another might contain the Public
Key policy. By creating separate subcontainers for these policies, we
can more minutely manage policies on different issues and control to
whom the policies apply. It is always wisest to stick to as few policies

per GPC as possible. Group Policies applied to sites affect all domains at the site. Group Policies applied to a domain affect all users and computers in the domain. Policies applied to OUs affect users and computers in that OU as well as, by inheritance, the users and computers in any OUs nested underneath it (see Figure 8.2).

Where Does Group Policy Live?

Group Policy is actually expressed in two parts: Group Policy templates that define the Group Policy settings, and registry settings and other components of Group Policy that must be applied at the client level to put Group Policy into action.

Group Policy templates store Group Policy settings. They are stored as INF files in the domain controller, sysvol folder. You modify their settings by using the Group Policy console and exporting the changed template back to the sysvol folder. GPO components are stored in the GPC and in the Group Policy template. When you create a new GPO, its template is stored in the sysvol folder with a folder name of the GUID of the GPO created. Each template is placed in its own <systemroot>\SYSVOL\sysvol\<domain name>\Policies \<GUID\ folder (see Figure 8.3). Within this folder are folders for ADM, machine and user components, as well as a GPT.INI file. The machine folder includes registry.pol, which contains registry settings applied to computers. This file is downloaded when a computer starts, and is applied to the HKEY_LOCAL_MACHINE key of the registry. The User folder contains a registry.pol file that holds the user settings of the policy. This folder is downloaded when a user logs on and is applied to the HKEY_CURRENT_USER registry key. The Adm folder contains the ADM files for the object. The GPT.INI file stores information including whether client-side extensions contain user or computer data, whether the Computer or User portion is disabled, and the version number of the Group Policy snap-in that was used to create the object.

The local Systems Policy is stored in the <systemroot>\system32\ GroupPolicy folder on the local machine.

FIGURE 8.2
Multiple policy OU.

NOTE

Granularizing GPOs To granularize the application of a particular Group Policy, you use the Security page of the GPO. Both the Read permission and the Apply Group Policy permission are necessary before a Group Policy can be applied. By default, Authenticated Users is given these permissions on each new Group Policy. However, you may remove the Apply Group Policy permission and Add security groups to whom you want to give the Apply Policy permission. Therefore, you control which groups of users have which policies applied, by placing appropriate users in the GPCs, writing appropriate policies, and by assigning security groups the Read and the Apply Policy permissions within that container for each Group Policy.

FIGURE 8.3
GPO template storage is in the sysvol folder.

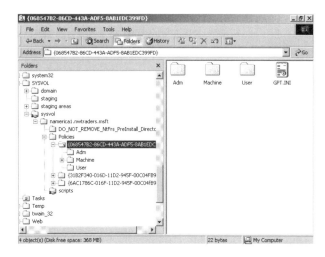

To distinguish which Group Policy is applicable to which GPC, GPOs are linked to GPCs. Polices are linked to a specific GPC. A policy may be linked to more than one GPC. Options such as No Override and Block Inheritance are applied to the links. Group Policies are linked to GPCs through the Group Policy page of the object's Properties page.

When settings are applied to the client registry, they are applied to the Policy section of the appropriate registry key.

GROUP POLICY APPLICATION

Group Policies are applied at three distinct times and in a well-defined order: at computer boot, at user logon, and periodically throughout the day.

1. At boot, Group Policy settings under the Computer Configuration part of all applicable GPOs are processed. At the Gastro company on the Accounting Manager's computer (which is part of the Accounting OU), Local Computer Policy settings are applied, then domain settings, then Managers OU policies, and then Accounting OU policies.

2. Next, any startup scripts are run. Each script must run and complete before the next script can begin. Therefore, if there is a script in the Managers OU and the Accounting OU, the Managers OU script will run and finish. Then the Accounting OU GPO script will run.

3. At user logon, all settings under the User Configuration part of all applicable (associated with that user account) GPOs are processed.

4. Next, logon scripts associated with Group Policy are run.

5. Finally, logon scripts associated with a user account are run.

Group Policy settings, with the exception of software installation and folder redirection, are refreshed throughout the day, throughout the network. When changes are made to policy, a policy refresh occurs at client computers every 90 minutes. Domain controllers refresh their policy every 5 minutes. These times can be adjusted in the Administrative Templates part of the GPO.

If you are changing policies and need them to take effect in a more timely fashion, you can kick-start Group Policy application by using the secedit command reviewed in Chapter 4. As you recall, you must enter the following command from a command window:

```
Secedit /refreshpolicy Machine_policy
```

Creating, Editing, and Applying Group Policies

The following list shows you how to create, edit, and apply Group Policy settings:

◆ To edit a GPO, open the Group Policy console and its extensions, and select a GPO.

◆ Use the Security Templates snap-in to create templates that can be imported to the Group Policy Security Settings section. You can store your new templates in %systemroot%\security\ templates until you need them. Templates are not applied automatically; you must import them into a GPO or apply them using the Security Configuration and Analysis snap-in (see Figure 8.4).

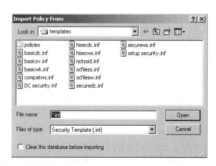

FIGURE 8.4

Importing a template into Group Policy.

NOTE

Can Multiple Admins Modify a GPO at the Same Time? Group Policy is focused on the domain controller that is the PDC operations master (known as the PDC Emulator). This prevents multiple administrators from editing a GPO at the same time. If the PDC Emulator is not available and an attempt is made to edit Group Policy, however, you will be allowed to override this option and modify Group Policy from a different domain controller. In this case, it is possible for multiple administrators to have the opportunity to change Group Policy at the same time. If conflicts appear, the final change wins. To avoid problems and conflicts, never override unless you are sure that others are not editing policy and the last changes have already been applied everywhere.

◆ To edit or create a new GPO, open the Properties pages of sites, domains, and OUs and select the Group Policy tab.

To build a GPO, you must create a new Group Policy template or edit one that already exits. In addition, security templates (default or developed) can be applied to the Security Settings part of the GPO. You have already examined the Security Configuration and Analysis and Security Template snap-ins, and used the Security Templates snap-in to edit and create security templates, so next I explain creating and editing GPOs.

GPOs can be edited in two places: the Group Policy console, and by opening the GPO from the Group Policy Properties page of the GPC. To create new policies, you use the GPC Group Policy Properties page.

Editing a GPO in the Group Policy Console

To examine or edit a GPO, you load it in the Group Policy console (see Step by Step 8.1). Changes made in the console are changed in the GPO immediately. They are applied to computer and users as per normal conditions (boot, logon, refresh times). Therefore, take care to test the results of Group Policy changes before applying them to a production system. The Group Policy console has no Read-Only mode.

STEP BY STEP

8.1 Exploring the Group Policy Console and Editing the Local Computer Policy to Change the Device Driver Code Signing Policy

1. Type `mmc` in the Start, Run dialog box.

2. Select Add, Remove Snap-in from the Console menu.

3. Click Add and select Group Policy; then click Add.

4. Use the Browse button to note the different Group Policies. (It is here that you select the policy you want to edit.) Then return to the Local Computer Policy.

5. Click OK, Finish, Close, and then click OK.

6. The Group Policy is added to the console.

7. Expand the Policy tree, and select System under User Configuration\Administrative Templates.

8. In the Policy window, double-click Code Signing for Device Drivers.

9. Click the Explain tab and read about the policy.

10. Click the Enabled radio button.

11. Select Warn from the drop-down window.

12. Close the Group Policy console.

Create a New Group Policy Object

New GPOs are created by opening the GPC at the site, domain, or OU level (see Step by Step 8.2). The New button exists on the Group Policy page of the OU Properties pages (see Figure 8.5).

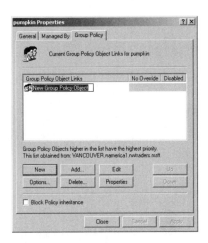

FIGURE 8.5
Creating a new GPO.

STEP BY STEP

8.2 Creating a New Group Policy Object

1. Right-click the site, domain, or OU object in Active Directory Users and Computers, and select Properties.

2. Click the Group Policy tab.

3. Click the New button.

4. Name the new policy.

5. Click the Edit button and set configurations.

6. Close the console when finished.

Importing a Security Policy

Working with Group Policies in either of the previous scenarios can be frustrating and dangerous, because policies are live while they are being created. When working with security policies, an easier tack to take is to create the security template using Security Templates in MMC (see Chapter 4). Then import the security policy into the GPO. The policy changes should, of course, be thoroughly tested before you import them.

To import the security policies, use the steps outlined in Step by Step 8.3.

STEP BY STEP

8.3 Import Security Policy

1. Open a Group Policy for editing.

2. Expand the Windows Settings folder.

3. Right-click the Security Settings folder and select Import Policy.

4. Select the Security template.

Group Policy Filtering and Delegation

The management of GPOs can be delegated along with the management of objects with an OU or other containers. You can delegate responsibility for managing links, creating GPOs, and editing GPOs.

To administer Group Policy, users need permission to log on to a domain controller. A good practice is to create a security group of those users who are going to be given GPO permissions and give them the Log On Locally right.

To narrow the application of a Group Policy, you can filter by security group. You do so by using the Security tab of the GPO Properties pages. Any filtering done here affects the entire GPO. You cannot pick and choose the parts of the object by which to filter. Users who have the Apply Group Policy and Read access to the object receive the settings in it. By default users cannot modify information in the GPO, but will have the GPO applied to them if they are subject to its policy according to their location in Active Directory. Remove Group Policy Read and Apply Group Policy permissions for any users who do not need them. Removing Read permission is not necessary to keep the users from getting the policy. Removing Read, however, prevents these users from reading the policy and improves their logon times.

GROUP POLICY INHERITANCE

A user or computer object may inherit multiple policy settings from multiple policies depending on its container's position in the Active Directory hierarchy and the application of Group Policy linking options. Settings from one policy may be applied in addition to the settings from the previous policy, or may override settings if there is a conflict.

The behavior of Group Policy inheritance is controlled by four configurations:

◆ Default Behavior

◆ Override

◆ Block Inheritance

◆ Loopback

Override and Block Inheritance are two options that are not applied unless specifically chosen by the user with the authority to create and implement Group Policies. A third Group Policy option, Loopback, is primarily used in kiosk operations and is explained later.

Default Behavior consists of the following:

◆ Computer Group Policies are applied when the computer is booted.

◆ User Group Policy is applied when a user logs on.

◆ Policies are reapplied throughout the day.

◆ Local Computer Policy is applied.

◆ Any site policies are applied.

◆ Any domain policies are applied.

◆ OU policies are applied.

◆ If OUs are nested, each inner nested OU Group Policy is applied.

◆ At each level, all applicable Group Policies are applied in the order specified by the administrator.

◆ Finally (excluding the Local Computer Policy), the policy closest to the user or group is also applied.

At each policy level, settings that are not in conflict are applied. Therefore, Group Policy can be thought of as the cumulative effect of all the policies in the hierarchy. If conflicts occur, they are resolved by allowing each successive policy to overwrite settings made by the earlier policy. Settings at any level that are "not configured" do not overwrite earlier settings.

Look at Figure 8.6 for a simple example of what default behavior means. Fred works on the help desk in the Johnco.com domain. His account is in the NewYork\IT\Help Desk OU. Any site and domain policies are applied to Fred, as well as any policies in the New York, IT, and Help Desk OUs. Mary also works for Johnco, and her account is in the Human Resources\Sales OU site, and domain policies apply to Mary, but also policies in the Human Resources and Sales OUs. John's account is also under the Human Resources OU but in the Accounting OU, so site and domain policies apply; because his account is in the Human Resources\Accounting OU, however, policies from the Human Resources and Accounting OUs apply. Only the policies in their specific OU hierarchy apply.

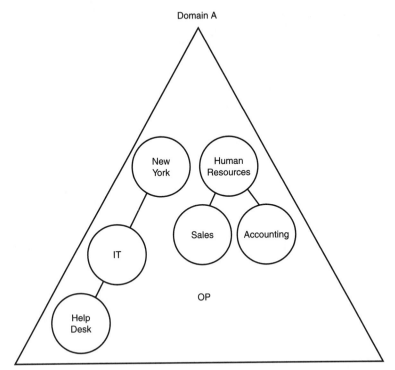

Domain A

New York

Human Resources

IT

Sales

Accounting

OP

Help Desk

FIGURE 8.6
Which policies apply?

Therefore, although Mary, John, and Fred receive the Johnco.com site and domain policies, only Mary and John receive the Human Resources policies, and only Fred receives the New York, IT, and Help Desk policies. (Of course, any other users and computers in any of these OUs receive the policies.)

You can see another example by looking at the structure and policies of Gastro Enterprises.

Gastro Enterprise is a large, international conglomerate with offices on three continents. They have three domains: the North American domain, the Australian domain, and the Asian domain. The Asian domain of Gastro Enterprises has configured Group Policy security settings to allow LM, NTLM, or NTLMv2 authentication (see Figure 8.7). At the Managers OU level, a policy has been written

FIGURE 8.7
Gastro Group Policy inheritance.

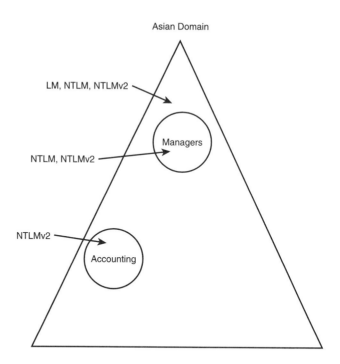

and applied that allows NTLM or NTLMv2 authentication. Nested within the Managers OU is the Accounting OU, which has a Group Policy set to allow only NTLMv2 authentication. Which policy applies to computers within the Accounting OU? Which policy applies to computers within the Managers OU? Which policy applies to all other computers in the Asian domain? Why did Gastro write the policy this way?

If you followed the rules previously given, you no doubt know now that the Accounting OU computers can use NTLMv2 for authentication, whereas the Managers OU computers can use NTLMv2 or NTLM. All other computers can use NTLM, NTLMv2, or LM for network authentication. Of course, all Windows 2000 computer use Kerberos for network authentication by default.

Joe Smith is an auditor hired by Gastro. He is given an account in the domain and placed in the Accounting OU. He brings in his brand new laptop that is running Windows 98 and soon finds that he cannot access network computers in the Accounting OU. His Windows 98 computer does not have the Directory Services client and so can only do LM authentication. (For information on the Directory Services client, and the different authentication protocols, see Chapter 10, "Designing an Authentication Strategy.") Nancy Peters, who is manning the help desk that day, gets his call. After she verifies that Joe is supposed to have access to the Accounting computers, she contacts Peter Johnson, who has the authority to manage the Group Policy settings on the Accounting OU. Mary tells him that the auditor needs access. Because he sees Joe as a temporary worker and he has no policy to refer to, Peter takes the easy way out. He changes the authentication policy for the Accounting OU to allow LM authentication. Because the Accounting OU is the OU closest to Joe's account, the LM setting overrides the earlier NTLMv2-only setting. Joe can log on and do his job.

What has happened here? Has a lower-level administrator changed corporate policy concerning authentication? Sure, all users in the Accounting OU have computers that allow them NTLMv2 authentication. Because policies are applied periodically, and because their computers can now use LM, however, eventually all computers in this OU may be using LM authentication. (You would need to examine the Domain Controller Group Policy settings to completely understand whether this would happen.) This change in policy has made their accounts more vulnerable to network attack.

This situation should not have happened. Obviously, Peter should have consulted with someone else before making such a change. Other solutions could have been found—for example, obtaining a license of the Directory Service client for Joe's computer, or providing a computer for Joe to use. Ideally, policy should have covered what to do when outside contractors wanted to use their computers on the Gastro network. The problem becomes, is there a way within Group Policy to prevent such a change? There is, but let's first explore a little more of what a wayward or unsophisticated lower-level administrator can do to subvert authority.

Blocking Inheritance

The second mode of inheritance is the Block Inheritance option. Set this option to block any policy from above from being inherited. In the earlier example, the setting of one item that conflicted with an inherited policy caused a conflict resolved by the "closer-wins" rule. If other settings had conflicted, they also would have won. To avoid having to set hundreds of items to counteract inherited policy, the

Block Inheritance option can be set. This allows and makes easier the configuration of a unique policy for a single GPO. Of course, it also enables a rogue administrator to ignore corporate policy and establish local policy the way he sees fit.

What if, regardless of the rightness or wrongness of the use of this option at a low level, policies must be implemented across the domain?

Preventing Override

The third mode of inheritance is the No Override option. This option allows a GPO to be set so that it cannot be blocked by a lower-level object. Use this policy to prevent the blocking of company-wide business rules or security policy. Once set, lower-level GPOs will merge with higher-level objects as before, but the higher-level GPO will now win any conflict. In addition, any low-level object with Block Inheritance set cannot block the inheritance of the higher GPO. No Override can be applied to any GPO at any level. If there are multiple NO Override settings within a hierarchy, the highest-level No Override wins.

Gastro could have avoided the example problem by setting No Override at the Domain Level OU. Even if Peter set his GPO in the Accountants OU to allow LM authentication, the No Override policy would have prevented it from having any effect (see Figure 8.8).

You should use No Override and Block Inheritance with care, and sparingly. Each can contribute to confusion in troubleshooting Group Policy problems, in lengthy logon times, and network performance issues.

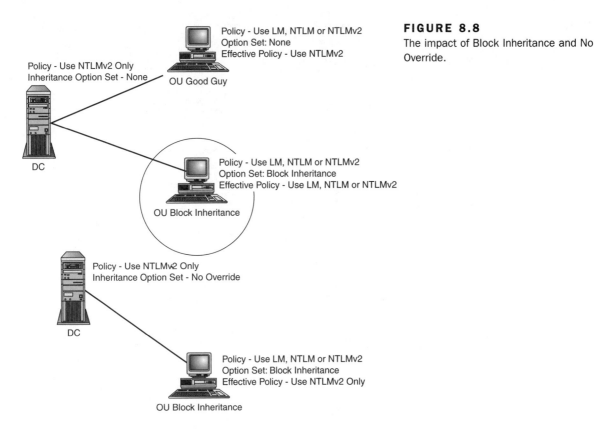

FIGURE 8.8
The impact of Block Inheritance and No Override.

CONTROLLING GROUP POLICY WITH GROUP POLICY

It should come as no surprise that configurable items dealing with Group Policy are set within Group Policy itself (see Figure 8.9). Traverse the Administrative Templates folder in the Computer Configuration part of the GPO until you come to the Group Policy folder (Computer Configuration\Administrative Templates\System\ Group Policy).

Here you find settings for Group Policy processing as a whole, and for the processing of select folders within the Group Policy. Table 8.1 lists Group Policy processing as a whole.

FIGURE 8.9
Controlling Group Policy with Group Policy.

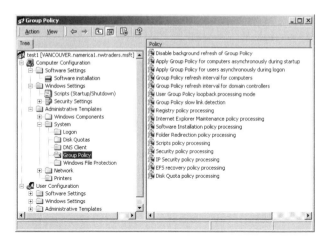

TABLE 8.1

GROUP POLICY POLICY SETTINGS

Policy	*Explanation*
Disable background refresh of Group Policy.	Group Policy is not updated so long as a computer is in use (a user is logged on). When the user logs off, Group Policy is updated.
Apply Group Policy for computers asynchronously during startup.	The system can display the logon prompt before all policies have been applied. This makes it appear to the user as if logon time is reduced; however, the users interface may not be really ready for use.
Apply Group Policy for users asynchronously during logon.	The system can display the desktop before updating Group Policy. If Group Policy affects the appearance of the desktop, its appearance may change as policy finishes applying.
Group Policy refresh interval for computers.	The frequency for background updating (updating while the computer is being used) is specified here. By default the set ting is every 90 minutes with an offset of 0 to 30 minutes so that not all policies on all computers attempt to update at the same time. The frequency can be set from 0 to 64,800 min utes (45 days). A setting of 0 attempts to start the updating every 7 seconds. Short update times are not very useful because they may interfere with network usage and user work.
Group Policy refresh interval for domain controllers.	Here you specify the background update policy for domain controllers. Group Policy is updated by default on domain controllers every five minutes. Any setting on this policy at the Local Computer Policy setting level is ignored. Frequency and recommendations are the same as the settings above.

Policy	*Explanation*
User Group Policy Loopback processing mode	Alternate user policies are applied on this computer when a user logs on. A computer with this setting determines the application of policies. Although usually a user's Group Policy settings are applied no matter which computer he logs on to, if this policy is set, the computer Policy Settings determine the settings a user receives. Quite often this setting is used for kiosk computers in malls and airports, classroom or library computers, and any computer that needs to stabilize to one consistent configuration. There are two modes to select here: Replace, which indicates that user settings defined in the computers Group Policy settings replace the user policies normally set by the user; and Merge, which means the computer-defined user settings merge with the user-defined user settings. If conflicts occur, the computer's Group Policy user settings win.
Group Policy slow link detection.	A rate of data transmission assigned here is compared with the actual rate of data transmission from the domain controller to the computer. If the domain transfer rate is slower than the policy rate, the link is considered slow and an action can be specified by the program implementing the policy. The rate set is in kilobits per second.

Policy settings for some folders contain options that determine whether they are updated depending on slow links, whether someone is logged on, and whether the policy has changed.

By default, when a slow link is detected, the following processing occurs:

◆ Security settings and Administrative Templates update, even over a slow link.

◆ Software installation, scripts, folder redirection, and Internet Explorer maintenance does not occur.

All settings in the Administrative Templates make changes to the registry. Policy determines whether those settings are updated during background processing, or whether they are processed even if GPOs have changed. The reasons to apply this policy are twofold. First, if settings are changed to program registry settings while they are in use, they may become unstable and cause the program to crash. Second, if users change settings during the operation of a program, it may not be a good idea to refresh the policy setting while they are working and thus change the setting back the way it was.

Table 8.2 lists the folders with these types of policy settings and the ones that they can set.

TABLE 8.2

GROUP POLICY SETTINGS FOR SUBSECTIONS OF GROUP POLICY

Policy Folder	Slow Link Processing	Refresh While Computer Is Being Used	Refresh Even if Policy Has Not Changed
Registry (Administrative Templates)		X	X
Internet Explorer	X	X	X
Software Installation	X		X
Folder Redirection	X		X
Scripts	X	X	X
Security	X	X	X
IP Security	X	X	X
EFS Recovery	X	X	X
Disk Quota	X	X	X

CLIENT-SIDE PROCESSING

The client participates in the processing of the policy. Client-side DLLs are used if a policy is implemented which requires them. The DLLs are as follows:

- USERENV.DLL (Registry)
- DSKQUOTA.DLL (Disk Quota)
- FEDPLOY.DLL (Folder Redirection)
- GPTEXT.DLL (Scripts)
- APMGMTS.DLL (Software Installation)
- SCECLI.DLL (Security)

◆ GPTEXT.DLL (IP Security)

◆ SCECLI.DLL (EFS)

◆ IEDKCS32.DLL (Internet Explorer maintenance)

If the GPO does not have any settings in the corresponding Group Policy template, the DLL is not used.

Client-side settings that use client-side extensions are considered preferences, not Group Policy settings. Client extensions are MMC snap-ins and therefore are registered in the following:

```
HKEY_LOCAL_MACHINE\SOFTWARE\Microsoft\MMC\SnapIns \<guid>
```

and in

```
HKEY_LOCAL_MACHINE\SOFTWARE\Microsoft\Windows NT\
Current Version\Winlogon\GPExtensions\GUID
```

Client extensions are limited to a total of 60 minutes for all of their processing. If any process is not finished after that time limit, it stops and policy settings do not process. You cannot change this time limit by using Group Policy.

POLICIES FOR WINDOWS NT AND WINDOWS 9X COMPUTERS IN A WINDOWS 2000 DOMAIN

Not all computers will be immediately migrated to Windows 2000. In fact, many enterprise systems will continue to have Windows NT Server and Workstation computers and Windows 9x computers for some time to come. How do Group Policy settings impact these computers? Are utilities available to assist in the management of these clients?

Windows NT and Windows 9x do not have Group Policies; instead, they have a tool called the Systems Policy Editor. This tool enables administrators to load configuration files and selectively apply configuration settings to computers, users, and/or groups. A systems policy file (ntconfig.pol for Windows NT, config.pol for Windows 9x), after created using the tool, is stored at the Windows NT 4.0 logon share (%system root%\system32\repl\import\scripts). At logon the registry settings contained in the policy are applied to the local registry. If you want to apply Window NT 4.0 and/or Windows 9x policies to these computers when using a Windows 2000 domain controller, you must put the policy files in the NETLOGON share, which is in %systemroot%\SYSVOL\sysvol*domainname*\SCRIPTS. (Where *domainname* is the fully qualified domain name of the domain.)

The Systems Policy changes are written directly to the registry of the local machine. This practice, called *registry tatooing*, means that changes made this way can be reversed only by implementing a different policy, or by direct editing of the affected computer registry. Removing the policy from the logon share does not remove the settings from the local computer. More than one careless Windows NT administrator has locked herself out of a computer by applying improper policy settings. Untested policies can mean a lot more work, not less work.

Group Policy does not tattoo the registry. Changes made are stored in a separate registry key. When policies are evaluated (at boot, logon, and periodically), registry settings are examined and applied, policy objects in the organization are downloaded to the specified registry location, and then this policy root is examined and applied. If a policy has been removed, it cannot be applied, and pre-policy settings remain in the registry.

Group Policy is a better system, isn't it? So should you abandon Systems Policy?

Unfortunately, the only computers that can use Group Policy are Windows 2000–based computers. Group Policy has no effect on Windows NT or Windows 9x computers. These computers must be managed by creating POL files with Poledit, the Systems Policy Editor. You use Poledit on Windows 9x to create a config.pol file, and on Windows NT to create a ntconfig.pol file.

In a mixed Windows NT and Windows 2000 domain, the following should take place on Windows 2000 computers (see Figure 8.10):

1. When the Windows 2000 computer has a Windows NT domain computer and user account (neither the computer nor the user exists in Active Directory), the Local Group Policy for the computer is applied at startup. When the user logs on, the Systems Policy for the user is applied.

2. If the computer and user accounts are both on Windows 2000 domain controllers (both in Active Directory), the Windows 2000 computer Group Policy is applied at startup. When the user logs on, the Windows 2000 User Group Policy is applied.

3. If the computer is managed in a Windows NT 4.0 account and the user is managed in a Windows 2000 account (a Windows NT domain account computer, but the user is in Active Directory), when the user logs on, the computer gets Systems Policy, and the user receives the Group Policy to which he is set. No Systems Policy for the user is applied.

4. If the user is managed in a Windows NT 4.0 account domain and the computer is managed in a Windows 2000 domain, at system startup Group policy for the computer is applied. When the user logs on, Systems Policy is applied. No Computer System Policies are applied.

When a computer is upgraded to Windows 2000, its registry settings from the Windows NT 4.0 Systems Policy settings are not changed. These settings are persistent. You may need to plan for removal of old Systems Policy settings, or to provide a clean install of the Windows 2000 operating system.

When the user account is moved from Windows NT 4.0 to the Active Directory, any settings applied through Systems Policy are not removed from the registry. Planning for removal of these settings should be a part of the migration strategy.

DESIGN

The successful design of the placement and security policies depends on your understanding of the following:

◆ The organization's business needs

◆ How to apply Group Policy in Active Directory

◆ How to plan for Group Policy to follow administrative needs

◆ Recognition that the security policy requirements are only one part of Group Policy

FIGURE 8.10a
Mixed-client policy application.

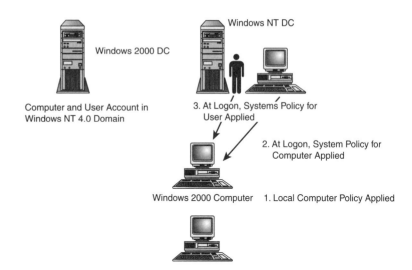

FIGURE 8.10b
Computer and User Account in Windows 2000
Domain.

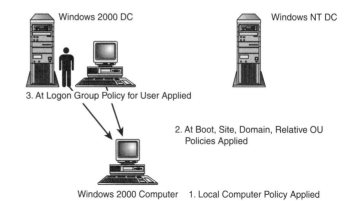

You may be tempted to begin planning the design of Group Policy
Security Settings without checking with your Computer
Configuration counterparts. Because Group Policies impact users
and computers at all levels of the organization, and because the existence of multiple polices impacts performance both at the network

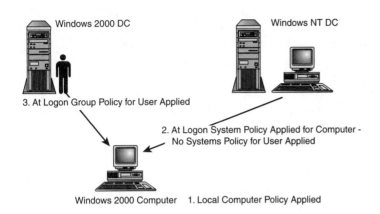

FIGURE 8.10c
Computer Account in Windows NT, User Account in Windows 2000 Domain.

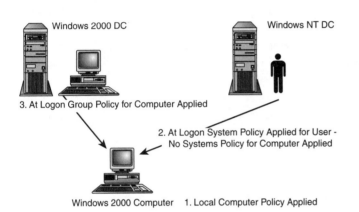

FIGURE 8.10d
Computer Account in Windows 2000, User Account in Windows NT Domains.

traffic level and at the user logon level, neither one of you should be designing Group Policies in a vacuum. Just as you worked with IT management to develop the game plan for delegating authority over groups of computers and users, you must continue joining forces to determine the placement and extent of Group Policy.

As you know each step in the design process may send you back to other areas to compare notes and make sure the design still works. Your original concepts of OU creation for the delegation of authority may not fully meet the needs of IT management for Computer Configuration management. It may not meet the needs of security configuration and management. It might be mostly okay, but you may need to make changes as you begin to work with the security components of Group Policy. That is why you plan and design *before* implementation.

You have completed the first step in your design plans if you have developed an understanding of what Group Policy is and how it works. Step two is to merge your security requirements with Computer Configuration models and apply the structure over the site, domain, and OU hierarchy.

To do this, obtain a copy of the required configuration model from that planning team. Make sure it identifies which site, domain, or OU at which the planned configurations are directed. Discuss with them the business needs behind the plan. You must keep the business needs of an organization in mind when planning security.

Business Needs

To plan for Group Policy implementation, you must know the business needs of the company. Group Policy settings enable very comprehensive management of clients. Business needs generally dictate the level of control incorporated. In a highly structured environment, users are restrained from making configuration changes to desktop systems. In public environments (kiosks, libraries, public schools, for example), configuration settings are made to minimize the damage often done by overzealous configuration of user settings by people with little knowledge and then left to be used by users with less knowledge.

Where security is concerned, strict implementation of security policy is the rule. Either a policy should be followed, or it is not a policy. However, each business must decide for itself the policies that should be followed.

Designers, developers, and implementers of security policy should, however, keep in mind the business needs of the organization. A strict security policy may hinder employee operations and guest activities. A decision must be made on which wins, user convenience or security. Good security can be nonobtrusive and noninvasive. Much of what is chosen may depend on the perceived risk, as well as the special demands of particular business operations.

When designing the security side of a Group Policy hierarchy, close attention to business needs results in a coordinated effort. Business needs and security needs should be complementary, not counterproductive.

The level of configuration management depends on the level of service expected by the company from IT. The level of security management depends on the security policy ascribed to by management. Here's where the conflicts may arise and security must win. Where management may specify that users have configuration control over desktop PCs, security policy may dictate, and enforce the items users may configure. Consider, for example, password complexity rules. Users may want to keep things simple when logging on to their local machine; security policy, however, dictates and enforces a more complex arrangement.

Security Needs

Computer security in an organization needs to follow prescribed rules and be implemented across the entire organization. In addition, security needs may vary at many levels. Certain areas of the company and the uses of certain machines may dictate a varied security policy.

The first step in determining the security components of the organization's Group Policy design is to determine the level at which different security policies should be applied. Look for the following separation points:

◆ Are there security policy aspects that should be implemented consistently across the organization at every site and location?

◆ Are there site-dependent security policy aspects?

◆ Are there security policy aspects that vary by domain?

◆ Are there security policies that may vary within the domain depending on the computer or users involved?

As you perhaps are anticipating, your job is going to be one of laying out the security requirements at each level and then determining where best the policy should be implemented. Take, for example, organization-wide security policy. This might be something like smart cards required for logon or an audit policy. There is no "super-site" that contains all other sites and presents an object in the Active Directory. Therefore, you cannot create a policy and place it in one place and expect policy to propagate throughout the organization. You could, however, insist on the linking of a particular "organization-wide" policy template to each and every site in your organization. This policy could be prepared centrally, and the permission to edit it denied. Enterprise administrators could retain the right to link the policy to their site, but not to change the policy. The CREATOR OWNER of the policy could retain that right. On the other hand, you may determine that network and system performance may dictate that no Group Policy be implemented at the site level unless it is specifically aimed at managing traffic over slow network links.

If your organization has a single site, applying Group Policy at the site level does dictate a security policy for the entire organization, and the decision becomes one of determining whether this makes sense (performance and policy wise).

An organization with one site and one domain needs only to apply the policy at the domain level. This is the same as applying it at the site level and simplifies many things. Keep life simple; apply the policy at the domain level.

If you want the simplest model for Group Policy management, create all GPOs at the domain level, including the Domain Controller Policy and Domain Computer Policy OUs. Do not create any additional OUs. No conflicts, such as those possible with an extensive domain-OU hierarchical approach, will occur. You cannot, however, delegate administration of the Group Policies. All administration must take place at the domain level.

Keep separate in your mind the Group Policy hierarchy from the Active Directory domain hierarchy. Whereas domain hierarchies show domains as child domains of other domains, this has no affect on the inheritance of GPOs. Domains are security boundaries, and Group Policies implemented at the domain level extend only to that domain. A Group Policy may be linked to multiple domains, but a

Group Policy linked to a parent domain has no impact on that domain's child domain. Keep in mind that a domain that links Group Policies from another domain creates an increase in network traffic. You might be better off if you create a new Group Policy in the second domain, with the same settings. Group Policy cannot be copied. However, the templates that you create to manage security settings within Group Policy can be changed.

Some settings must be set only at the domain level. Other settings can be set at any level. Common settings applied at the domain level include the following:

◆ Password

◆ Account

◆ Kerberos Policy

◆ Public Key Trust List

◆ User Rights

◆ File/Registry DACLs

◆ Audit/Event Logs

◆ Local Policies

Of course, most of these settings can also be set at the OU level and therefore may be overridden.

Of these password settings, account lock-out policies, and Kerberos, policy must be set at the domain level only.

If you need to control the application of Group Policy by collections of users or computer, you want to apply the policy at the OU level. You can also delegate control of Group Policy at this lower level. If you need to control administration of the OU GPOs, do not delegate administration of these OUs or restrict the authority to other privileges within the OU.

Typical OU-level security settings include the following:

◆ User Rights

◆ File/Registry DACLs

◆ Audit/Event Logs

◆ Local Policy

◆ EFS Policy

Remember that policies are inherited and policies at a lower level merge with those from an upper layer. If there is a need for different policies at a lower level, only organization-wide policies should be placed in a site-level policy.

In your early work on your security design, you identified computers and applications and their security needs. You also identified users and the level of access that they required. Now is the time to map this information to GPOs. In Chapter 7, "Designing a Security Group Strategy," you considered the creation of OUs to establish a delegation-of-authority framework. One of the issues you considered was the uniqueness of security policy for particular users and computers.

With your increased knowledge of the application of Group Policy, review that plan for its security policy fit. Ask the following questions:

◆ Do proposed OUs allow security policy to be applied uniquely where necessary?

◆ Does the level of OU nesting require unique Group Policy at each level?

◆ Does the OU structure suggest additional nested OUs will be required to implement distinct Group Policies?

◆ Does the OU structure suggest additional OUs will be required to implement distinct Group Policies?

◆ Does your design minimize the number of GPOs?

Designing Group Policy Application

As you know, Group Policy application depends on its location in the Group Policy hierarchy, options, and, within a GPC, the order set by the GPO administrator. For GPCs with multiple GPOs, the order of processing depends on the order listed within the container. The last GPO processed wins in the case of conflict.

By default, GPOs affect all computers and users that are part of the GPC. The primary filter for GPO in domain- and site-level GPO is to place the GPO lower in the hierarchy. Therefore, to apply a GPO to users in Domain A, but not in Domain B of Site 1, a GPO is created for each domain. To apply policy to a distinct set of users within Domain A, an OU is created, and these users are moved to the OU. Within OUs, by default, authenticated users receive GPOs, because this security group is given the Apply Group Policy and Read permissions. To further filter GPO and apply policies to specific groups, apply security permissions from the Security tab of the GPO. Add the security group that should have the policy applied and give them Read and Apply Group Policy permission. Remove the Authenticated Users Group. Only the group that has been given Read and Apply Group Policy permission will process the policy. In Figure 8.11, John Doe has only the Read permission. The Front Office group has the Read and the Apply Group Policy permission. The policy changes the screen color to red. John's computer screen will not change to red because he does not have the Apply Group Policy permission. The computer screens of Users in the Front Office group will be red. You may want to create a new GPO that can be applied to other security groups within the same OU.

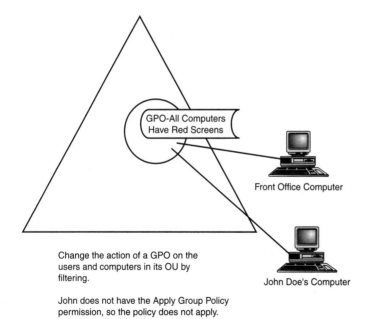

Change the action of a GPO on the users and computers in its OU by filtering.

John does not have the Apply Group Policy permission, so the policy does not apply.

FIGURE 8.11a
Filtering GPO.

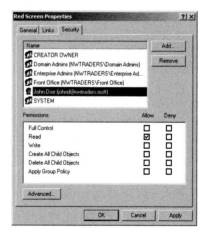

FIGURE 8.11b

Planning for Administrative Needs

Administration of GPOs is available at the following three levels:

◆ **GPO Creation**—CREATOR OWNER. Whoever creates it, owns it.

◆ **Modify**—Users in the GPO ACLs with permissions to Write, Modify Permissions, Create, and Delete.

◆ **Link**—Users in Active Directory given the permission to link GPO to GPCs. Linkers do not have to have Modify or Create permissions.

The rights to create, modify, and link GPOs throughout Active Directory can be delegated to appropriate personnel. A standard practice is to create standard GPOs that lower-level (probably OU) administrators can link to their GPC for which they have been delegated control.

TESTING AND DOCUMENTING GROUP POLICY

During the design process, you specify which security policies should be implemented in which GPOs and where GPOs should be linked. During your test, you continue to modify these notes as you learn the effectiveness of your design. These design notes are used in a formal implementation plan and should become an integral part of your system documentation.

Before implementing Group Policy, you need to test the final design. You should ensure that the test models and the production system are as close as possible. You want to test GPOs from the perspective of users and administrators. Are conflicts resolved in the manner you desire? Do security policies restrict appropriately? To think like users who have no clue about your security policy structure is difficult. Don't! Use two types of people in your test scenarios.

First, use typical users who just want to get their work done. Make sure they attempt all job duties and listen to their comments on timing issues, their complaints about things they think they ought to be able to do, and their worries about the safety of objects for which they are responsible.

Second, if security policy is to be thoroughly tested, you should have it tested by people who want to bypass it. Find users, or even outside contractors, and charge them with "getting in" to secure areas of your test network. In reality, they will not be breaking into company resources, but into servers, files, folders, and other objects that represent those resources. These break-ins provide a source of knowledge that you can use to refine your security policy so that it does work as intended. Test it again to make sure.

Test possible scenarios. Log on as representative users. Follow software-testing routines, such as the following:

- ◆ Compose a list of "types" of users. If it is not possible to log on as one of each type of user, pick representative users—for example, one from each domain, site, OU, and filtered group within OUs.

- ◆ Log on from portable computers in each location the portable computer user might use.

- ◆ Test mobile users by dialing in, connecting directly at the user's organization, office, and at other company locations if appropriate.

If you are having problems, you can use the GPResult.exe command-line utility from the Windows 2000 Server Resource Kit to check Group Policy setting in effect on a particular computer and the user currently logged on. This gives you good feedback. You can determine whether the policies you expected to be in use have been applied.

BEST PRACTICES

According to Microsoft, you should do the following:

- ◆ Limit use of Block Inheritance and No Override options.

- ◆ Limit use of GPOs linked across domains.

- ◆ Limit the number of GPOs that affect a particular user or computer. Logon and startup time increase in direct proportion to the number of GPOs that must be processed.

◆ Use security groups to filter GPOs, thus reducing the number of GPOs any user logon must process.

◆ Disable the User or Computer Configuration parts of a GPO if the GPO is assigned to a GPC that does not contain that object. By disabling the Computer Configuration part of a GPO that sits on an OU that contains only users, you have reduced the number of objects the computer startup process has to process.

◆ Wherever possible, group related settings on a single GPO.

In addition, consider doing the following:

◆ Design your computer/user security policies from the top down, but implement them from the bottom up.

◆ Develop security policies in the Security Templates console and save as a template. Test thoroughly, and then roll out by importing policies to the Security Settings portion of the appropriate GPO.

◆ Try to implement security settings on an existing GPO. Group Policy design should include the design of security policy settings for Group Policy. This minimizes the impact of security settings on performance by limiting the number of objects and conflicts.

◆ Fewer GPOs = Best Design. This reduces the amount of network traffic and reduces the amount of time necessary to log on.

◆ GPO needs should dictate the need for a new OU, not the other way around.

◆ Each GPO should map to one site only, or one domain, or one OU container. This minimizes confusion, conflicts, and network traffic. By not linking GPOs across domains, you reduce logon time.

◆ Fewer GPOs Per User = Best Design. A GPO with dozens of settings processes quickly compared to dozens of GPOs with one setting per GPO.

CHAPTER SUMMARY

You can effectively implement security options throughout your enterprise by taking full advantage of Group Policy. You create GPOs within GPCs (sites, domains, OUs). Group Policies are inherited by objects lower in the hierarchy. (Site policies are inherited by domains, domain policies take effect in OUs, OU policies affect OUs nested underneath them.) Each Group Policy has multiple areas for configuration of computer and user items. Some of these items are security options.

Designing the implementation of security policies by using Group Policy consists of matching security requirements to applicable containers within Active Directory. Existing site and domain objects can be utilized, as well as OUs. OUs should be created to allow the correct administration of computers and users. If their design has considered security policy as well as computer configuration and user desktop appearance, the job becomes one of selecting the correct Windows 2000 security policy to match your organization's policy, at each level.

You can design security templates in the Security Templates snap-in. You can test them by first using the Security Configuration and Analysis snap-in to apply the policy to a single test machine, and then by importing them into a GPO on a test domain. Finally, they are imported to GPOs in the production domain.

GPOs are stored in Active Directory. Their templates, gptemplates, are stored in the domain sysvol folder.

KEY TERMS

- Group Policy
- Group Policy object (GPO)
- Group Policy container (GPC)
- linking
- Apply Group Policy
- Group Policy filtering
- Group Policy template

APPLY YOUR KNOWLEDGE

Exercises

8.1 Creating an OU Hierarchy

Estimated Time: 25 minutes

1. On your test system, create the OU structure indicated in the earlier "Tremain Polson Security Policy Design" case study.

2. Create the security template for the High-Security group by following the next set of steps. You may leave out IPSec Policy for now (use Step by Step 8.4).

   a. At Start, Run, type **mmc**.

   b. Open the Security Template snap-in by selecting the Add/Remove Snap-in from the Console menu.

   c. Right-click the hisecws template, and click Save As.

   d. Name the template hiserver.inf, and click Save.

   e. In the tree, double-click the hiserver.inf template.

   f. Change any settings necessary to match the policy defined in the case study.

   g. Save the template and exit the console.

3. Import the template to the Security Settings portion of the GPO for the OU you created for the high-security servers.

8.2 Modifying the hiserver.inf template

Estimated Time: 20 minutes

1. Open the hiserver.inf template you created for the High-Security group.

2. Are there settings you would change for the Web Server group? What are they? Remember that these computers are in a different domain. Does that change your entries?

3. Make a list of these setting changes.

4. Implement them by creating a new template and applying it to the OU you created for these servers.

Review Questions

1. Explain the relationship between Group Policy, GPOs, and GPCs.

2. Circle the items in the following table that cannot be controlled using Group Policy.

APPLY YOUR KNOWLEDGE

Software Installation	Distribution Group Membership
Logon scripts	User rights
Required password length	Internet security zones
Registry key permissions	Allowing users to browse printers
Security group membership	Removing the Run button from the Start menu
Domain membership	Redirect the location of all users' My Documents folders to a file server
Who can be in a security group	Redirect a specific security group's My Documents folder to a file server
Group Policy	Disable Add/Remove Programs in Control Panel

Group Policy Information

Local Computer Policy

Templates

Settings applied to HKEY_LOCAL_MACHINE

Settings applied to HKEY_CURRENT_USER

Information on whether the computer portion is disabled

ADM files for the object

Settings applied to HKEY_USERS

5. Describe the process by which Group Policy is applied to Sally and her Windows 2000–based computer. Assume Sally has just arrived and turned on her Windows 2000–based computer.

6. How will you manage policies for Windows NT and/or Windows 98 computers?

7. The case study mentioned that servers would be immediately upgraded to Windows 2000 and Group Policy designed to control security settings. Because some of those security settings will apply to users who will be connecting to these servers, what will have to happen to user computers that are still Windows 9x or Windows NT?

8. What happens if Tremain Polson computers used to connect to high-security servers are moved to areas that will be used by people who do not have the authority to use these systems? Might settings remain in the registry that would allow someone to more easily attack the high-security systems? Might settings unduly restrict the new user's activity?

9. Can multiple administrators change Group Policy at the same time? If they can, what will happen if they do?

3. Tremain Polson has listed several types of OUs for which they want to create GPOs. To what other types of containers can they apply Group Policy?

4. Match the following Files with the relevant Group Policy–related information.

Files

registry.pol in the machine folder

registry.pol in the user folder

GPT.INI

INF files

policy files stored at <system root>system32\GroupPolicy

files stored in the sysvol folder on the domain controller

APPLY YOUR KNOWLEDGE

10. Tremain Polson has indicated a need for kiosk computers on the plant floor. What feature of Group Policy ensures that no matter who logs on to this computer, very specific user policies are applied? How will this help Tremain Polson?

Exam Questions

1. Tremain Polson wants to effectively use Group Policy. They want to organize their computers and users so they can write policies to administer them. What type of object should they organize their users and computers into so they can do this?

   A. Security Groups

   B. Groups of Users

   C. Groups of Computers

   D. The Computers Object in Active Directory Users and Computers

   E. Organizational Units

2. Joe Smith manages Group Policy for the Tremain Polson Desktop OU. He writes a policy for the Desktop\Call Center OU. Call Center Computers and users are part of this OU. All employees who work in the Call Center have their account in this OU and are members of the Customer Service Group. Many contractors also work in the call center. They are given user accounts in the Call Center OU and in the Contract security group. Joe wants to clean up his Group Policy so he opens the Properties\Security page for the only policy written for the OU. He adds the Customer Service Group and grants them the Read and Apply Group Policy permissions. He then removes the Authenticated Users Group. The Call Center Manger calls to say that suddenly, tempo-

rary workers are not getting the more restrictive Call Center policy applied when they log on. What does Joe need to do to fix the situation?

   A. He needs to remove the Apply Group Policy permission from the Customer Service Group.

   B. He needs to add the Manage Group Policy permission to the Customer Service Group.

   C. He needs to add the Contract group and give them Read and Apply Group Policy permission.

   D. He doesn't need to do anything, contract workers don't need to have the more restrictive settings applied.

3. Tremain Polson does not want to take a chance that any policy in any OU will be applied to Domain Admins. For each new GPO they need to do the following:

   A. Remove the Domain Admins Read permission

   B. Give the Domain Admins the Full Control permission then they can change the policy the way they want it.

   C. Add appropriate groups to each policy. Give them the Apply Group Policy permission. Remove the Domain Admins Group.

   D. Add appropriate groups to each policy. Give them the Apply Group Policy permission. Remove the Authenticated Users Group.

   E. Add appropriate groups to each policy. Give them the Read and Apply Group Policy permissions. Remove the Authenticated Users group.

4. I have three OUs nested in this order: Human Resources, Management, and Executives. Authority is delegated to manage each of the

APPLY YOUR KNOWLEDGE

OUs. If the person in charge of the Executives OU wants only his policy to apply he can:

A. Do nothing, his policy will automatically win in the case of any conflict.

B. Since many of his settings are 'not defined' he must choose the Block Inheritance option for his Group Policy.

C. Since many of his settings are 'not defined' he must choose the No Override option for his policy.

D. He must choose the Only This Policy Applies option for his policy.

5. I have three OUs nested in this order: Operations, Warehouse, Arcadia Warehouse. Authority is delegated to manage each of the OUs. The person in charge of the Arcadia Warehouse OU does not want his policy to be modified and has applied the correct option to prevent this. As Domain Administrator, I must enforce certain security policies on all computers at all warehouses. I determine that Arcadia is blocking the application of this policy. I can add the following option to my domain level policy, and Arcadia will not be able to block the policy from being applied.

A. No Override.

B. Block Inheritance

C. Only This Policy Applies

D. No Blocking

6. Sally has been working at her desk all day long. She has not logged off and then on, nor has the computer been rebooted. The Group Policy Settings have been changed. When will they be applied to Sally and/or her computer?

A. When she reboots.

B. When she next logs on.

C. In 5 minutes

D. In 90 minutes

E. In 120 minutes.

7. The Group Policy for all Domain Controllers has changed. When is the new policy applied?

A. AT reboot.

B. When someone logs on.

C. In 5 minutes

D. In 90 minutes

E. In 120 minutes.

F. When the Group Policy Service is stopped and then restarted.

Use the following information to help answer the next several questions: Some domain controllers at Tremain Polson are upgraded to Windows 2000. Some desktop computers are upgraded to Windows 2000 Professional, some of the Windows 2000 Professional systems have computer accounts in the Windows NT 4.0 domains, and some have accounts in the Windows 2000 domains. Some users accounts are migrated to the Windows 2000 domains, and some are left in the Windows NT 4.0 domains.

APPLY YOUR KNOWLEDGE

8. Peter's computer is running Windows NT. His computer is a member of a Windows NT domain. He logs on to a Windows 2000 domain. Policy settings are applied in the following manner:

    A. The computer gets Systems Policy, the user gets Group Policy.

    B. Group Policy is applied to both the computer and the user.

    C. The computer and user get Systems Policy.

    D. The computer gets Group Policy, the user gets Systems Policy.

    E. The computer gets Systems Policy. The user does not get Group Policy or Systems Policy.

9. Fred's computer is running Windows 2000. His computer is a member of a Windows NT domain. He logs on to a Windows 2000 domain. Policy settings are applied in the following manner:

    A. The computer gets Systems Policy, the user gets Group Policy.

    B. Group Policy is applied to both the computer and the user.

    C. The computer and user get Systems Policy.

    D. The computer gets group policy, the user gets Systems Policy.

    E. The computer gets local policy, the user gets Group Policy.

10. Peter's computer is upgraded to Windows 2000 and joined to the Windows 2000 domain. What happens to the Systems Policy applied when his computer ran Windows NT?

    A. Nothing, no Systems Policy was ever applied to his computer.

    B. The settings are removed since he no longer has any contact with a Windows NT domain controller.

    C. The settings remain. Group Policy will not apply until you remove them.

    D. The settings remain. Group Policy will apply.

Answers to Exercises

Answer to Exercise 8.1

1. It is always a good idea to sketch out what your OU structure might be before implementing it. There will be one OU for each of the items in the following list:

    • High-security servers

    • Intranet servers

    • File and print servers

    • Kiosks

    • Desktops (within this OU are nested other OUs)

    • Call center

    • Others

Then add the OUs to the Active Directory Users and Computers console (see Figure 8.12).

APPLY YOUR KNOWLEDGE

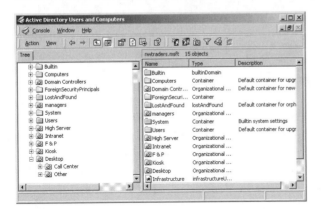

FIGURE 8.12
The OU structure.

Answer to Exercise 8.2

You should change the following settings:

Although the case study does not list extensive requirements for configuring its Web servers, it does mention that no IPSec will be required. You could choose to implement IPSec to block unnecessary protocols. These are public Internet sites. More information about IPSec is contained in Chapter 15, "Designing Security for Communication Channels." Revisit early chapter sections on risk and use your own experience to choose settings that you believe should be different for Tremain Polson's Web servers.

The enhanced security settings are all applicable except the Services settings. The World Wide Web service needs to be set to Automatic. We can, however, disable the server and workstation services, because all external access will be via the Web.

Because these systems are part of a separate domain, and are member servers, only the Local Administrator and Guest accounts will remain. These local accounts, as well as domain-level

accounts, will have a strict password and account policy set.

- Enforce password history, 24.
- Maximum password age, 42 days.
- Minimum password age, 2 days.
- Minimum password length, 8 characters.
- Passwords must meet complexity requirements, Enabled.
- Account is locked out until administrator unlocks it.
- Account will lock out after 2 invalid logon attempts.
- Reset lockout count after 30 minutes.

Audit policy is set to audit for success and failure of the following:

- Logon events
- Account management
- Directory services access
- Logon events
- Object access
- Policy change
- System events.

User rights are set to allow a typical user-level account no access. Because public access is through the IUSR_*server* account, this account can be severely restricted through the Registry and File System objects. Local policy for each Web server will further restrict these settings to keep public access to only Web-site files. All groups will be placed in the restricted groups and their membership controlled centrally.

APPLY YOUR KNOWLEDGE

(Your answer may differ somewhat.) The idea here is to lock down the system as much as possible using Group Policy, because it can be centrally controlled and managed and is reapplied periodically. In production systems, security settings should follow your organization's policy, which should incorporate the latest lessons learned.

Answers to Review Questions

1. Group Policy is the utility that allows centralized control of desktop appearance and security settings, and software installation GPOs are the collection of policies that will be applied to users and computers within the GPC. Group Policy containers are Active Directory objects that can hold users and/or computers and accept Group Policy application.

2. Distribution group membership is the only thing that is listed here that cannot be controlled through Group Policy.

3. Group Policy can only be applied to GPC. Current GPCs in Active Directory are sites, domains and OUs.

4. Files are matched here with the relevant Group Policy–related information:

FILES	*Group-Policy Information*
Registry.pol in the machine folder	Settings applied to HKEY_LOCAL_MACHINE
Registry.pol in the user folder	Settings applied to HKEY_CURRENT_USER
GPT.INI	Information on whether the computer portion is disabled
*.inf files	templates
policy files stored at <system root> system32\GroupPolicy	Local computer policy
files stored in the sysvol folder on the domain controller	Adm files for the object

5. During system start up the computer policy is applied. First the local computer policy, then the site, then domain, then OU and any nested OUs. When Sally logs on, the user policies are applied. First local, then site, domain, OU and nested OU. If multiple policies apply from the same OU level, they are applied in administrator specified order.

6. Since only Windows 2000 computers are affected by Group Policy, you should uses Systems Policy to manage these other computers.

APPLY YOUR KNOWLEDGE

7. To obtain full benefits and maintain the level of security required on some servers, some user computers may need to be upgraded. If any servers have IPSec implemented, all their clients must be upgraded to Windows 2000. If servers require NTLMv2, either the Active Directory services client will have to be loaded on the client, or the client system will have to be upgraded to Windows 2000. Inspection of who has authority to access these servers will indicate the possible group of users affected. Inspection of the policies written for these computers will determine how many of these user computers need to be upgraded and how quickly.

8. Group Policy does not tattoo the registry. Therefore, settings made on desktop computers that connected to high security servers are not persistent. Likewise restrictive settings will not be in place either. However, cached logons and pagefile data could be a source of concern. The computers should be shut down, moved, and rebooted.

9. Group Policy is focused on the Operations Master. This prevents multiple administrators from changing Group Policy at the same time. If this domain controller is not available, you can override the default setting and allow Group Policy changes to be written to other Domain Controllers. This opens up the possibility that multiple administrators could make changes simultaneously. If there is a conflict, the last in wins.

10. Group Policy has a Loopback feature that allows specification of user policy that must be reinforced on a computer. If someone logs on, his or her settings are applied, but then the original settings are reapplied. This setting can be for override or to merge with the user settings. This will help Tremain Polson because it will force the application of security settings and desktop settings applicable for these exposed machines on the warehouse and plant floor. Even if the computers are rebooted and someone logs in with more authority, the default settings will be applied.

Answers to Exam Questions

1. **E.** Group Policy is applied to groups of users and groups of computers, but those groups are organized into sites, domains and OUs. (See section "What is Group Policy.")

2. **C.** By default Authenticated User has these settings. That is why the original policy worked for both Customer Service and Contract groups. To filter Group Policy by security group, you add groups to have policy applied and remove Authenticated Users. Authenticated Users was removed and Customer Service added. So only Customer Service would have the policy applied. To fix this, add the Contract group and give them Read and Apply Policy permissions. (See section "Group Policy Filtering and Delegation.")

3. **E.** Domain Administrators need Read and Write and Create and Delete to write or edit policies. They have those permissions by default. They do not have the Apply Group Policy Permission, which is necessary for policy to be applied. However, they are members of the Authenticated Users group, which does have this permission. To make sure they don't have policy applied, you must remove this group and add in the groups that should have group policy applied, then give them the Read and Apply Group Policy permissions. (See section "Group Policy Filtering and Delegation.")

APPLY YOUR KNOWLEDGE

4. **B.** Only the Block Inheritance Option will assure that none of his settings are changed. It is common practice to leave alone many settings—not set them. Although it is true that his settings will win in the case of a conflict, the Non Define setting allows policy inheritance from GPCs above the current container. (See section "Group Policy Inheritance.")

5. **A.** When No Override is added as an option to a policy, its settings can not be blocked by lower level Block Inheritance settings. (See section "Group Policy Inheritance.")

6. **D.** Group Policy settings are refreshed throughout the day. A user does not have to log off or reboot to get them. By default Group Policy is refreshed every 90 minutes. Actual times could vary, depending on network and local activity. (See section "Controlling Group Policy with Group Policy.")

7. **C.** Unlike normal computers, the group of computers—Domain Controllers—will refresh their Group Policy every 5 minutes. (See section "Controlling Group Policy with Group Policy.")

8. **E.** Only Windows 2000 computers are subject to Group Policy. This eliminates answers A, B, and D. Because Peter logs on to a Windows 2000 domain, no Group Policy is applied. Windows NT Systems Policy for the computer is applied. (See section "Policies for Windows NT and Windows 9x Computers in a Windows 2000 Domain.")

9. **E.** Fred's computer is subject to Group Policy. However, since it's a member of an NT domain, it does not receive Group Policy from the Windows 2000 domain. It does, however, have a local Group Policy that will be applied. (See section "Policies for Windows NT and Windows 9x Computers in a Windows 2000 Domain.")

10. **D.** Systems Policy settings are persistent. They will remain in the registry. Any Group Policy settings will be applied, however, they are not persistent. (See section "Policies for Windows NT and Windows 9x Computers in a Windows 2000 Domain.")

Suggested Readings and Resources

1. *Microsoft Windows 2000 Server Resource Kit, Distributed Systems Guide.* Microsoft Press, 2000.

   - Chapter 21, "Introduction to Desktop Management"

   - Chapter 22, "Group Policy"

   - Chapter 25, "Troubleshooting Change and Configuration Management"

2. Charlie Russell and Sharon Crawford, *Windows 2000 Server Administrators Companion*, Microsoft Press, 2000.

   - Chapter 9, "Managing Users and Group"

This chapter covers the following Microsoft-specified objective for the "Designing a Windows 2000 Security Solution" section of the Designing Security for a Microsoft Windows 2000 Network exam:

Design an Encrypting File System strategy.

▶ The Encrypting File System (EFS) is a new feature in Windows 2000. It enables users to encrypt files and folders. Administrators need do nothing to enable this capability. If folders are encrypted, users need do nothing to encrypt and decrypt any file they place in the folder. What you must do is determine whether you want to disable this capability anywhere, who should be in charge of recovery keys, and where the files should be stored.

CHAPTER 9

Designing an Encrypting File System Strategy

▶ The best way to understand EFS is to get some practice with it. Use the exercises at the end of the chapter to encrypt files and then move them around. Create files as one user and attempt to read and then recover flies as another. What happens when you place an encrypted file on a remote drive? What happens when encrypted files are copied to floppy disks? After you have answered these questions by working with the file system you will be better prepared to design a strategy for its use in your organization.

INTRODUCTION

The ability to encrypt files and folders is a powerful feature of Windows 2000. Traveling users can protect their files and folders in case they are lost, and all users can ensure that the data they create remains confidential. Proper use of this feature means understanding its ins and outs. Make sure you design-in user training, or its value will soon be useless. You can head off troubles for your help desk and avoid security breaches by clearly identifying its principles to all. Reliance on this feature, like reliance on seat belts not properly anchored to the car chassis, can cause you headaches.

REVISITING ITS

In Chapter 4, "Designing a Security Baseline," you learned about the ITS company, which sells products to truck stops. Its salespeople enter, store, and retrieve data to their laptop computers. If you will remember, there were a number of concerns about the possible exposure of confidential information.

◆ Our customer inventory information is confidential. Imagine what would happen if our competitors could get at our information. It hasn't happened yet, but I hear a lot about disgruntled employees destroying information, or spying on their own company and selling information to its competitors. I need to know that can't happen here.

◆ Our sales reps use a handheld barcode scanner to scan shelf labels at the stores. They enter inventory counts at that time. Each rep is expected to visit each of his customers to take monthly inventory. When the count is complete, the information is transmitted via phone lines back to Akron and the inventory database gets updated.

◆ Our sales reps can dial in to our system in the morning and see the same reports. He then calls the customer to get order approval.

Sales Manager

◆ Our reps are getting new laptops, and they will be able
to download customer inventory information to them. They
can show the reports to their customers and enter orders,
check payment history, and display new product catalog
information. If Internet connectivity is possible, they will
be able to get current information and even place the order
before leaving the store.

◆ The sales reps are now going to have lots of confidential
customer and company information on their laptops. What
happens if the laptop is lost or stolen?

◆ The reps are good salespeople, not computer nerds. We don't
want the new laptops and system to put any new pressure on
them to learn new computer skills.

ITS could use EFS to alleviate many of these concerns. As you learn
about EFS, therefore, keep ITS in mind.

ENCRYPTING FILES—USER PROCESSES

To the user, encrypting files merely means setting an attribute on
a file or folder (see Figure 9.1). One just needs to follow the
procedure in Step by Step 9.1.

STEP BY STEP

9.1 Encrypting Files or Folders

1. Right-click the file or folder in Windows Explorer on an
NTFS5 partition.

2. Select Properties.

3. Click the Advanced button.

continues

FIGURE 9.1

Setting the encryption attribute.

continued

4. Click and select the Encrypt contents to secure data option.

5. Click OK twice.

If you select a file, the file is encrypted. If you select a folder, all files in the folder (and all that are added) are encrypted.

Users continue to use files in a normal manner, but it is impossible for another user to read the encrypted files. Ah, you have just stumbled on a truth: EFS is *not* a way to protect files that must be shared among users. You cannot give multiple users access to encrypted files. Other pertinent facts include the following:

NOTE   **Making It Easy**   If a folder has been encrypted for users, they do not have to set the attribute.

◆ Encrypted files that are moved remain encrypted even if the destination folder is not encrypted.

◆ Encrypted files copied to an unencrypted folder on the same volume remain encrypted.

◆ Encrypted files or folders moved to a volume that is not NTFS (such as one formatted with FAT or FAT32, or a floppy disk formatted with FAT) can become decrypted.

◆ You cannot encrypt system files.

◆ Any user who has Deletion permission in that folder can delete encrypted files.

◆ Encrypted files remain encrypted if backed up using Microsoft Backup.

◆ Encrypted file information might appear as clear text in the paging file during reading and use by an application. To secure this information, set the policy to clear the paging file at user logoff.

◆ You cannot compress an encrypted file or encrypt a compressed file.

Remote Encryption

Encryption can be accomplished across the network, but it is not recommended. The rational behind this is that the data traveling across the network is not protected. So, when I access my network file server files from my workstation, while I am reading them, anyone who can sniff the network can read them as well (see Figure 9.2).

If additional protection is put in place—for example, the use of IPSec to encrypt data traveling across the network—the use of encrypted files on a remote folder can be practical and safe.

To enable remote encryption, you must designate the file server as "trusted for delegation." You can do so on the server's Properties pages in the Active Directory Users and Computers console (see Figure 9.3). The computer must have this property set because it will be acting as the user (the user's "delegate") when it encrypts or decrypts the file.

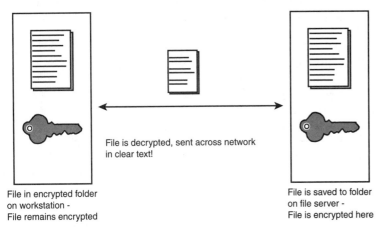

File is decrypted, sent across network in clear text!

File in encrypted folder on workstation - File remains encrypted

File is saved to folder on file server - File is encrypted here

FIGURE 9.2
File data is not encrypted as it travels on the network.

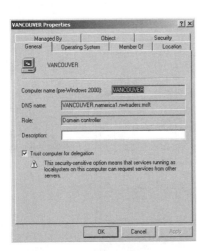

FIGURE 9.3
Trusted for delegation.

ENCRYPTING FILE SYSTEM INTERNALS

Windows 2000 EFS uses the Expanded Data Encryption Standard (DESX) 56-bit encryption algorithm. When encrypted, each file receives a unique encryption key. Think of this like you do a session key in a Kerberos client/server authentication session. The file encryption key is used to encrypt the file. This key is then encrypted with the user's public key. To decrypt the file, the user's private key is first used to decrypt the encryption key, which is then used to decrypt the file. Thus, this system uses both public/private key pairs and session key algorithms (see Figure 9.4).

The File Encryption Key (FEK) is also encrypted with the recovery agent's private key. The recovery agent can use the new key to recover encrypted files in the owner's absence. Using a public/private key system ensures that only the user and the recovery agent can decrypt the file (see Figure 9.5).

Private keys are kept in the key store. The encrypted session key (the FEK) is stored in a Data Decryption field attached to the EFS file. The copy of the FEK encrypted with the recovery agent's key is stored in the attached Data Recovery field. Even though the location of this key is well known, an attacker would need to have a copy of the user's private key to decrypt it because the FEK is encrypted with the user's public key (or the recovery agent's key).

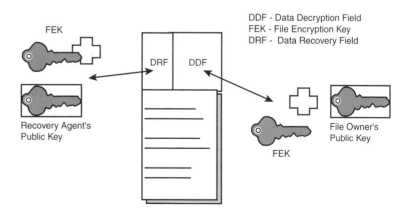

FIGURE 9.4
Encrypted file structure.

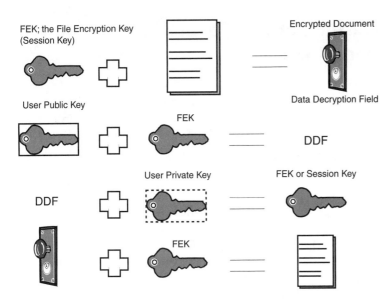

FIGURE 9.5
EFS keys and the encryption-decryption process.

The session key is also encrypted with the recovery agent's public key and stored in a special field, the Data Recovery Field (DRF). The DRF can contain information for multiple recovery agents.

The Security subsystem manages encryption of files and folders. You do not have to be online to use file encryption.

Levels of Encryption

Five levels of encryption protect encrypted files, as follows:

1. EFS provides a key (the FEK), and the file is encrypted.

2. The user's public key and the recovery agent's public key are used to encrypt the FEK. These keys are stored in the user's certificate store.

3. The Protected Storage service generates a user master key. This key is used to encrypt the user's private key.

4. The Protected Storage service encrypts the master key twice— one time for user storage, and one time to provide a backup (or recovery) key.

5. If you want to, you can use a system key to protect all master keys.

Certificate and Private Key Generation and Storage

Users' keys are stored in their personal certificate store. The keys are in Documents and Settings*username*\\ApplicationData\\Microsoft\\SystemCertificates\\My\\Certificates (see Figure 9.6). The certificates are written to the user's store in the system registry when the user logs on. Users with roaming profiles can have certificates follow them wherever they log on.

Certificates can be found using the Certificates console under Certificates - Current User\\Personal\\Certificates (see Figure 9.7). The recovery agent's certificate is in the personal certificate store that belongs to the recovery agent account. You can tell that it is the recovery agent because it lists File Recovery under the Intended Purpose column (versus the Encrypting File System entry of the user's personal certificate).

Recovery agent certificates can also be viewed in the Encrypted Data Recovery Agents folder of the Group Policy console.

Certificates hold public keys. Public keys are meant to be, well, public.

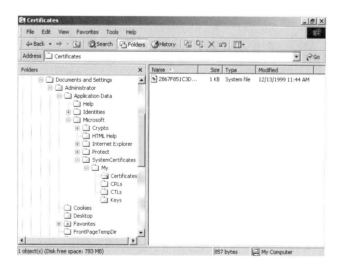

FIGURE 9.6
Certificate location.

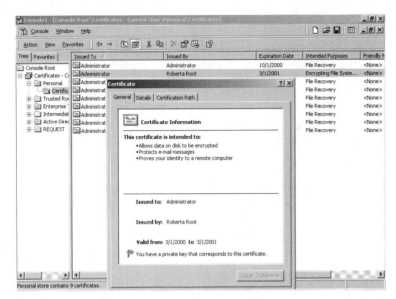

FIGURE 9.7
Viewing a certificate.

Private keys, however, need extra protection. Files in the RSA folder (the private key folder) are themselves encrypted with the user's master key (using RC4). You can tell this folder should not be removed, renamed, or relocated; the file system would not know where to find your keys! You can export EFS private keys for protection. Remember, however, that you should export certificates and the private keys to a securable medium. If you were to export them to a floppy disk, and then delete them from the folder, the user would have to use the private key floppy disk to read the file. The user would then also have to protect the floppy disk; that said, you might find this preferable to worrying about data on the hard drive.

Private keys are found in the user profile. They are under *root*\Documents and Settings*username*\Application Data\ Microsoft\Crypto\RSA (see Figure 9.8).

The master key is encrypted twice (by the Protected Storage service) and then stored in the user profile under *root*\Documents and Settings*username*\Application Data\Microsoft\Protect.

Hash-Based Message Authentication Code (HMAC) and the SHA1 message digest function is used to create a hash of the encryption of the user's master key (160-bit RC4), the user's SID, and the user's logon password.

FIGURE 9.8
Locating private keys.

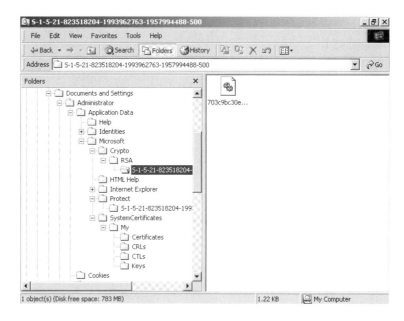

The domain controller, using HMAC and SHA1 on the master key and the domain controller's own master key, makes a backup/restore form and returns it to the user's Protect folder.

The domain controller's master key is stored as a global LSA secret in the HKEY_LOCAL_MACHINE/SAM key in the registry.

The three folders involved—the Certificates folder, the Protect folder, and the RSA folder—are kept unencrypted by leaving their system attribute set.

If the user changes her password, it will be detected and the user's master key will be re-encrypted with the new password used in the algorithm.

RECOVERY POLICY

A recovery policy is automatically put into place when Windows 2000 is installed. The default recovery agent is the Administrator account. If you have a Certificate Authority (CA), you can generate a certificate for the recovery agent. If this is available, the EFS uses the CA to request certificates instead of using its own. Using a CA rather than the native EFS certificate process can ensure greater security because the CA can generate certificate revocation lists and can provide a centralized place to control and manage recovery agents. If your organization needs this kind of sophisticated management of documents, using a CA is the way to go. For more information on Certificate services, including their hierarchy design, see Chapter 14, "Designing Security for Access Between Networks."

You can change recovery policy through the Group Policy console. It is maintained in the Local Computer Policy\Public Key Policies\Encrypted Data Recovery Agents. You can add additional recovery agents, create a new file recovery certificate, and delete the recovery policy (see Figure 9.9).

Do *not* delete the recovery policy unless you want to remove the user's capability to encrypt files. Do not delete the recover agent's certificate; otherwise, you create an empty policy. This has the same effect: If the user has created encrypted files prior to this process, those files are nonrecoverable.

Instead, to remove the possibility that a theft of a computer can mean decryption of encrypted files by someone who cracks the Administrator (recovery agent's) password, you can export and back up the certificate to a safe location. Don't forget to remove the certificate from the Administrator account. You can then import it if necessary to do file recovery. Microsoft recommends that recovery certificates should always be locked in a safe for use only when required. To recover files, follow the procedure in Step by Step 9.2. Remember that the encrypted files are still only as protected as the user password is able to resist guessing or cracking.

EFS policy is configured locally on standalone computers that are not members of a domain. Domain members can have their policy controlled at the domain or organizational unit (OU) level.

To set a policy for only some computers that are members of a domain, you must set a policy at a higher level than the local computer. If you set no policy or an empty policy on the local computer, site, domain, or OU policy will override it. Setting no policy at a domain or OU level disables EFS there. The local computer can

> **NOTE**
>
> **No CA Necessary**   The EFS does not need a CA to operate and make available encryption and a recovery policy. It just may work better with one.

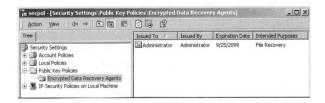

FIGURE 9.9
Recovery policy.

have its own policy. You must apply an empty policy at the domain or OU level to remove EFS at that level and all the levels below. For more information on Group Policy settings, see Chapter 8, "Designing Security Policy Inheritance."

To perform file recovery, follow the procedure in Step by Step 9.2.

STEP BY STEP

9.2 File Recovery

1. If the recovery agent certificate and private key have been exported, import the certificate and private key to the recovery computer. To import the certificate, follow steps 2 through 11.

2. Log on as the designated recovery agent. For extra security you can create a new account for this purpose. You will be importing the private key.

3. Open the Certificates snap-in (choose My User Account) in an MMC console.

4. Right-click the Personal\Certificates folder, and click Import.

5. In the Certificate Import Wizard, click the Next button.

6. Browse for the file (on the floppy disk you stored the certificate and private key on).

7. Select the file and click Next, and then click Finish.

8. Obtain the file to be recovered. It can be emailed using secure email, or backed up to a removable medium and restored to the recovery computer. (Backed-up encrypted files remain encrypted.)

9. Use the cipher /d command to decrypt the file. If only the files to be decrypted are in the D:\Etemp folder, run the following command from that folder (for more information on the cipher command, see below):

   ```
   cipher /d D:\Etemp\*.*
   ```

   Alternatively, you could use the interface and remove the check from the Encrypt option on the Properties page of each encrypted file.

10. Transport the decrypted files over a secure medium to the proper computer.

11. Delete the recovery certificate and private key from the recovery user account. (It should still be on the removable medium for safekeeping.) You could also delete the user account, if your policy is to create a new recovery account each time recovery is necessary.

THE CIPHER COMMAND

For those who prefer it, and/or for ease of administration, all encryption management can be done at the command line, or in batch files by using the cipher command. The user must be using the command on files that belong to him, or he must be the recovery agent.

The cipher command consists of a number of switches followed by the path of the file to be affected.

Table 9.1 lists the parameters that you can use with this command.

TABLE 9.1

CIPHER SWITCHES

Switch	Application	Example
/e	Encrypt	cipher /e C:\payroll\june5.xls
/d	Decrypt	cipher /d C:\payroll\june5.xls
/s:dir	Apply action to all folders and all subfolders	cipher /d /e /s:payroll
/a	Apply action to files with specified names	cipher /d /e /a june*
/I	Continue even after error messages (by default cipher stops)	cipher /e /I /a june*
/f	Force encryption or decryption even if files are marked as encrypted or decrypted	cipher /e /f c:\payroll\june.xls c:\payroll\may.xls
/q	Report only essential info	cipher /d /q C:\payroll\june.xls
/h	Display files with hidden or system attributes	cipher /d /s:payroll /h

DESIGNING A STRATEGY FOR EFS

Design an Encrypting File System strategy.

You must make several decisions about an Encrypting File System strategy.

- ◆ Should users have this capability?

- ◆ Should the EFS use its own certificates, or should a CA be used?

- ◆ What should be involved in user training for use of the system?

- ◆ Who should be able to recover files?

- ◆ Should strict policies about the necessity of encrypting files be in place?

- ◆ Should additional security be put into place to allow remote encryption and decryption of files?

Should Encryption Be Allowed?

Do nothing, and users can use EFS. Few users probably will, however, because no data will be encrypted if the attribute is not set on files and folders. With luck, users who discover this capability will use it appropriately. Again with luck, no data will be lost because of missing recovery agent certificates or empty recovery policies.

You should probably determine your strategy. Because recovery policy can be controlled at the domain level for all domain member computers, you can effectively remove this capability. You can, however, also remove it for some computers, while allowing its use by others. You have already seen in Chapter 7, "Designing a Security Group Strategy," how delegation of authority can be managed at the OU level; high-risk computers can be given EFS capabilities at this level. Question whether laptops and high-risk systems need a different policy than the majority of your systems.

Do You Need a Certificate Authority?

What is your expertise in the management of a CA? Do you have any other reason for developing a public key infrastructure (PKI)? What are the risks that someone will have access to sensitive files? Just how sensitive are these files anyway?

Research and development information is critical to the survival of many companies. Long before the current crop of hackers, crackers, and malfeasants could say "corporate espionage," individuals were running around attempting to steal these types of secrets. To protect this information by encryption is paramount to its security. A CA offers flexibility and increased control over the process.

When I travel, I like to maintain the privacy of projects and processes I am working on, as well as personal notes and information. In that, I'm much like many of you. It is not likely that a stolen laptop would bring anyone data of any value, but I still don't like the thought of someone pouring through my personal data. It's unlikely that a CA needs implemented here, at least not to manage these systems and their file encryption.

In between, somewhere, is the harder decision to make. You must weigh the additional overhead of establishing and maintain a CA against the increase security control obtained.

What Should Be Involved in User Training for Use of the System?

Now that you realize that a misunderstanding of EFS can result in exposing private information by copying encrypted files across the network (or to non-NTFS volumes), you should consider designing-in user training. This training can be packaged in with other training on the use of the new operation system and/or as part of your security-awareness training.

Training should include exercises that demonstrate the strength of the encryption process, its ease of use, how it may be compromised, and its recovery capabilities.

Who Should Be Able to Recover Files?

After users know that encrypted files can be recovered, they are going to ask who is this person who can read their private file. You had better have an answer! In many instances, the access to recovery agent capabilities can be controlled and secured by creating special recovery agent accounts strictly controlled and used only for this purpose.

You might want to create an account especially for areas of control. Departments, such as Research and Development, might want the recovery agent account to be managed by an individual within their own department, for example, perhaps by the department head.

Remember, however, that recovery is just that. It is meant to be used in an emergency to decrypt files that would be lost because the individual who encrypted them has left the company. If the user forgets his password, the administrator can reset the account password.

Finally, the recovery key should never be left on the system; instead, keep it in a safe place and attach it only for the purpose of recovery. For extra security, the user account used for recovery can be newly created at the time of recovery and/or protected by allowing only smart card logon for this account. You can also lock away the necessary smart card.

Should Strict Policies About the Necessity of Encrypting Files Be in Place?

This is a policy decision that needs to be made at the corporate or division or departmental level, not by designers of EFS strategies. If this is policy, however, you can enforce to some degree by setting up systems and maintaining them with strict policies on where data is saved and by setting the encryption attribute on these folders. You can prevent users from changing attributes on files and folders. Remember that after a folder has been marked "encrypt," the process of encryption and decryption is transparent to the user.

You can prevent users from copying files to floppy disks by removing floppy drives from computers. You can prevent users from copying files across the network by not giving them privileges to save files on any network computer. If desirable, you can implement additional security to allow network copying of encrypted files.

Should Additional Security Be Put into Place to Allow Remote Encryption and Decryption of Files?

You must weigh the impact of such a procedure against the benefit it allows. You can also isolate this practice to selected computers and file servers and protect them by encrypting all communication with them. To find out more, take a look at Chapter 15, "Designing Security for Communication Channels."

Without a CA, Can Files Be Recovered if User Keys Are Lost?

If there is no CA, can data be lost? If your system lacks centralized control and the user's computer crashes, taking the user's private key with it, how can you recover encrypted files stored on backup media? If you have exported the local administrator's certificate and private key, you can use them for data recovery. Alternatively, if you have implemented roaming profiles, the user may be able to log on from another computer and recover files from backup.

BEST PRACTICES

To use EFS to the best advantage, you need to consider what is best for your organization. Some guidelines follow.

◆ Train users in the nature of encrypted files.

◆ Encrypt folders, not files.

◆ Encrypt the My Documents folder and the Temp folders.

◆ Do not allow users to access encrypted folders across the network unless additional processes are in place that provide for security of data as it travels across the network.

◆ Export and then remove recovery agents from traveling machines and store in a secure place. Stolen, lost, or compromised machines will not have a security policy and therefore cannot be used to "recover" encrypted files.

◆ Keep a recovery agent archive. If recovery agents are changed, older files may remain that have been encrypted with their keys. Lose the key, and there will be no way to decrypt the file.

◆ Use Active Directory and use Group Policy to implement a central recovery agent, or implement Certificate Services and do the same.

CHAPTER SUMMARY

KEY TERMS

• Data Decryption Field (DDF)

• Data Recovery Field (DRF)

• File Encryption Key (FEK)

• Recovery agent

• cipher

You have just learned about a very important new feature in Windows 2000. The Encrypting File System gives your users a way to protect their local data. You must understand its proper use, what it is and is not, and how to set up a proper recovery policy. As you continue to study Windows 2000, think about how you could use this feature in conjunction with other features to fully protect what needs to be protected.

APPLY YOUR KNOWLEDGE

Exercises

9.1 Exploring the Encrypted File System

Estimated Time: 30 minutes

1. Create three users: UserA, UserB, UserC.

2. Log on as UserA.

3. Create a folder, Secret, and encrypt it.

4. Create a new file, secrets.txt, and store it in the Secret file folder.

5. Close the file.

6. Open the file. Can you read it?

7. Share the folder and make it Full Control to Everyone.

8. Log off and log on as UserB.

9. Attempt to open the file secrets.txt. Can you open it?

10. Create your own file and save it in the Secret folder. Were you able to do so?

11. Log off and log on as UserC.

12. Access the folder.

13. Attempt to open the file(s). Were you successful?

14. Log off and log on as Administrator.

15. Attempt to open the file secrets.txt. Can you open it?

9.2 Recovering an Encrypted File

Estimated Time: 15 minutes

1. Log on as UserA.

2. Back up the secrets.txt file.

3. Open UserA's Certificate snap-in in MMC.

4. Open the Personal\Certificates folder.

5. Right-click the File Recovery certificate and click on All Tasks\Export.

6. In the Certificate Export Wizard, click Next.

7. Select Yes, export the private key; then click Next.

8. Select Personal Information Exchange, Enable Strong Protection, and Delete the Private Key if the Export Is Successful; then click Next.

9. Type the word **password** in the Password and Confirm Password boxes, and then click Next.

10. Use the Browse button to browse to the floppy drive, and then name the file.

11. Click Save. Then click Next.

12. Click Finish.

13. Log off and log on as UserC.

14. Restore the encrypted file to its own folder. (Name the folder Etemp).

15. Attempt to read the file. Can you?

16. Open your personal Certificates snap-in in MMC.

APPLY YOUR KNOWLEDGE

17. Right-click the Personal\Certificates folder.

18. Select Import.

19. Use the wizard to import the certificate and key you stored earlier.

20. Open a command prompt.

21. Use the following cipher command to decrypt the file and read it:

    ```
    cipher /d D:\Etemp\*.*
    ```

22. Can you read the file?

Review Questions

1. John encrypts his Documents folder and uses it to save all his files in. Are John's files always secure?

2. Peter and John want to share files by attaching them to email. Is using EFS a viable approach?

3. Systems administrator Charlie sets up a folder for Mary to use on the network file server. Mary wants to be sure that the files are not readable by anyone else. "No problem," Charlie tells her, "I'll set up the folder so whatever you save there will be encrypted. Only you will be able to decrypt the file." Is there anything wrong with this strategy?

4. EFS can be used to keep files safe from snooping by others who gain access to the user's hard disk. What protection mechanisms keep others from decrypting the files?

5. Why must there be a recovery agent?

6. Why does the Protected Storage service encrypt the master key twice?

7. Why is the FEK encrypted in the users public key? Why not just use another session key?

8. Why give the recovery agent his own key pair. Couldn't he just be given access to the user's private key?

9. Can batch processing be used to encrypt and decrypt files?

10. What are the recommended best practices?

11. Is it necessary to install a CA to use EFS?

Exam Questions

1. ITS wants to allow its salespeople to store files on a server for retrieval when they are on the road. The company wants to maintain tight security and ensure that no salesperson can accidentally read another salesperson's files.

   Required Result:

   All files stored on the file server should be encrypted.

   Optional Desired Results:

   There should be no chance that anyone who can sniff the network could capture file data as files are being read or written to the file server.

   Each user's files should not be readable by other individuals.

   Proposed Solution:

   EFS is used to encrypt a folder on the file server for each user.

APPLY YOUR KNOWLEDGE

Evaluation of Proposed Solution:

Which result(s) does the proposed solution produce?

A. The proposed solution produces the required result and both of the optional results.

B. The proposed solution produces the required result and one of the optional results.

C. The proposed solution produces the required result but neither of the optional results.

D. The proposed solution does not produce the required result.

2. ITS wants to allow its salespeople to store files on a server for retrieval when they are on the road. The company wants to maintain tight security and ensure that no salesperson can accidentally read another salesperson's files.

Required Result:

All files stored on the file server should be encrypted.

Optional Desired Results:

There should be no chance that anyone who can sniff the network could capture file data as files are being read or written to the file server.

Each user's files should not be readable by other individuals.

Proposed Solution:

EFS is used to encrypt a folder for each user on the network file server. IPSec is used to set up a secure pathway between the user and the file server.

Evaluation of Proposed Solution:

Which result(s) does the proposed solution produce?

A. The proposed solution produces the required result and both of the optional results.

B. The proposed solution produces the required result and one of the optional results.

C. The proposed solution produces the required result but neither of the optional results.

D. The proposed solution does not produce the required result.

3. John needs to recover files encrypted by Mary, who left the company. To do so, he does what? (Select two)

A. Backs up the files to be recovered, restores them to a server, and imports the recovery agent certificate and private key to his certificate store on the server. Uses the cipher command to decrypt the files.

B. Backs up the files to be recovered using the Windows 2000 Backup program, restores them to a server, imports the recovery agent certificate and public key to his certificate store on the server. Uses the cipher command to decrypt the files.

C. Backs up the files to be recovered. Copies them to a floppy disk. Uses the cipher command to decrypt the files.

D. Backs up the files to be recovered, restores them to a server, imports the recovery agent certificate and private key to his certificate store on the server. Opens Windows Explorer. Opens the advanced Properties page for each file and clears the encrypted box.

APPLY YOUR KNOWLEDGE

4. Peter is giving a demonstration for the sales manager to prove the security of the file system and to show him why they must train the salespeople not to move or copy the files. Which of the following processes will result in the file still being encrypted?

   A. Moving an encrypted file to a folder that is not encrypted, but is NTFS.

   B. Copying an encrypted file to a folder that is not encrypted, but is NTFS.

   C. Copying an encrypted file to a FAT32 volume.

   D. Copying an encrypted file to a floppy disk.

   E. Backing up an encrypted file to a floppy disk using the Windows 2000 Backup program.

5. The ITS sales manager wants to know about the file encryption key. Because a new key is generated for every encrypted file, the key has to be available somewhere to decrypt the file. Peter tells him the key is placed in a field attached to the file. Anticipating the sales manager's question about the security of the key, he gives the following process explanation regarding the use of public and private keys in EFS.

   A. The encrypted file is encrypted using the user's public key; the user's private key is used to decrypt the file.

   B. The encrypted file is encrypted using a session key, the session key is encrypted using the user's public key, the user's private key is used to decrypt the session key, and the session key is used to decrypt the file.

   C. The encrypted file is encrypted using a session key, the session key is encrypted using the user's public key, the recovery agent's private key is used to decrypt the session key, the session key is used to decrypt the file.

   D. The encrypted file is encrypted using a session key, the session key is encrypted using the user's private key, the user's public key is used to decrypt the session key, the session key is used to decrypt the file.

6. John is in charge of preparing the laptops of the salespeople for a test of the system. He needs to get two laptops ready. He has been told to make sure that the recovery agent key does not remain on the laptops. To ensure this for each laptop, he does what?

   A. Imports the recovery agent certificate and private key to a floppy disk and locks the floppy disk in a storage cabinet.

   B. Exports the recovery agent certificate and private key to a floppy disk and locks the floppy disk in a storage cabinet.

   C. Exports the recovery agent certificate and private key to a floppy disk. He checks the Delete Private Key option. He stores the floppy disk in a storage cabinet.

   D. Exports the recovery agent certificate and private key to a floppy disk. He checks the Delete private key option. He places the floppy disk in the laptop bag with the laptop because the salespeople will need it to decrypt files.

APPLY YOUR KNOWLEDGE

7. Charlene changes her password. What happens to the user's master key?

    A. Nothing. The master key has nothing to do with the user's password.

    B. The master key has to be regenerated by the Protected Storage service (using the backup of the user's private key it made), because the user's encrypted master key is hashed using HMAC and SHA1 over the user's master key, the user's SID, and the user's logon password.

    C. The password change is detected and the Protected Storage service automatically rehashes the user's master key using HMAC and SHA1 over the user's master key, the user's SID, and the user's logon password.

    D. The master key doesn't change. Charlene won't be able to decrypt her files. The recovery agent can be used.

8. You are asked to develop the recovery policy for ITS. You recommend the company changes the policy to use a central recovery agent. Now they want you to implement this strategy. After opening the policy, the first step you take is what?

    A. Add new recovery agents.

    B. Remove the original recovery agent.

    C. Delete the recovery policy.

    D. Allow more than one user to share certificates and keys.

9. To keep hackers who steal laptops from cracking the Administrator (recovery agents) password and decrypting encrypted files, you should do what?

    A. Remove the Administrator account.

    B. Nothing. Files can be encrypted only while the computer is offline. They cannot be decrypted.

    C. Export the recovery agent private key and certificate and delete the recovery agent private key.

    D. Export the user's private key and certificate.

    E. Make sure that the Local Administrator account has as uncrackable password.

10. ITS does not want its office workers to encrypt files. To prevent them, you can do what?

    A. Disable encryption policy.

    B. Remove the recovery agent.

    C. Remove the user's certificate.

    D. Uninstall EFS.

    E. Tell them that their files will be lost if they encrypt them. EFS encrypts only and doesn't decrypt.

Answers to Exercises

9.1   Exploring the Encrypted File System

1. Create three users: UserA, UserB, UserC.

2. Log on as UserA.

3. Create a folder, Secret, and encrypt it.

4. Create a new file, secrets.txt, and store it in the Secret file folder.

5. Close the file.

6. Open the file. Can you read it? *Yes*!

7. Share the folder and make it Full Control to Everyone.

8. Log off and log on as UserB.

APPLY YOUR KNOWLEDGE

9. Attempt to open the file secrets.txt. Can you open it? *No!*

10. Create your own file and save it in the Secret folder. Were you able to do so? *Yes!*

11. Log off and log on as UserC.

12. Access the folder.

13. Attempt to open the file(s). Were you successful? *No!*

14. Log off and log on as Administrator.

15. Attempt to open the file secrets.txt. Can you open it? *Yes!*

9.2   Recovering an Encrypted File

1. Log on as UserA.

2. Back up the secrets.txt file.

3. Open UserA's Certificate snap-in in MMC.

4. Open the Personal\Certificates folder.

5. Right-click the File Recovery certificate and click on All Tasks\Export.

6. In the Certificate Export Wizard, click Next.

7. Select Yes, export the private key; then click Next

8. Select Personal Information Exchange, Enable Strong protection, and Delete the private key if the export is successful; then click Next.

9. Type the word **password** in the Password and Confirm Password boxes, and click Next

10. Use the Browse button to browse to the floppy drive, and then name the file.

11. Click Save. Then click Next.

12. Click Finish.

13. Log off and log on as UserC.

14. Restore the encrypted file to its own folder. (Call the folder Etemp.)

15. Attempt to read the file. Can you? *No!*

16. Open your personal Certificates snap-in in MMC.

17. Right-click the Personal\Certificates folder.

18. Select Import

19. Use the wizard to import the certificate and key you stored earlier.

20. Open a command prompt.

21. Use the following cipher command to decrypt the file and read it:

```
cipher /d D:\Etemp\*.*
```

22. Can you read the file? *Yes!*

Answers to Review Questions

1. If John doesn't copy his data to a floppy disk, or to a FAT or FAT32 volume, the answer is a big "well maybe." He might be using an application that saves files to a Temp folder. Although the files are there, they are not encrypted. John can fix this; he just needs to encrypt the Temp folders too.

2. No. EFS is a personal encryption system. Encrypted files cannot be shared.

3. The files will not be encrypted as they move across the network.

APPLY YOUR KNOWLEDGE

4. The user's private key is encrypted in the user's master key. This is then hashed before storage.

5. A recovery agent is necessary in case a user leaves the company. Without his password, no one can log on as that user and recover the files. A recovery agent solves this problem.

6. The Protected Storage service is making a backup key, one that it can access (because no user password is included in the hash).

7. The session key is more vulnerable to attack. A public/key private key pair is, in this case, considered to be more secure.

8. Keeping the user's private key private ensures that no one else can obtain it. (Private keys are for use by individuals, not a group of individuals.)

9. Batch processing can be used to encrypt or decrypt files. Use the cipher command.

10. It is recommend that you encrypt folders, not files. Encrypt Temp folders as well as the My Documents folder. Do not set up remote encryption without managing the encryption of data as it crosses the network, export and then remove recovery agents from traveling machines, and keep a recovery agent archive.

11. You do not need to install a CA to use EFS. It generates its own public and private key pairs. Using a CA may provide significant benefits, however, so you should investigate this possibility if you already have reasons for establishing a PKI, or if you want to provide a better system of file recovery.

Answers to Exam Questions

1. **B.** Although this is not a good result, the required result did not specify the issue about network transport. Perhaps it is a very small and contained network and the risk is considered slight. (For more information, see the section "Encrypting File System Internals.")

2. **A.** Now the system is secure end to end, except for Temp folders; but once again, that was not a requirement. (For more information, see the section "Encrypting File System Internals.")

3. **A, D.** John must have all three: the encrypted file (not the backup of it), the recovery agent's certificate and private key, and must use either the cipher command (A) or the interface. Choice B is wrong because it stipulates the public key; the private key must be used. Choice C is wrong because when an encrypted file is backed up by the Windows 2000 Backup program, you can copy it to a FAT folder and then restore it, and it will remain encrypted. (For more information, see the section "Encrypting File System Internals.")

4. **A, B, E.** Encrypted files do not remain encrypted if copied to a FAT or FAT32 volume. A floppy disk cannot be formatted with NTFS, so copying encrypted files to them removes the encryption. (For more information, see the section "Encrypting Files—User Processes.")

5. **B.** The user's public and private key pair must be used. To ensure no one can decrypt the file except the user, the private key must be used for that process. The public key would be available to others. (For more information, see the section "Encrypting File System Internals.")

APPLY YOUR KNOWLEDGE

6. **C.** The certificate and key are "exported." The private key should be deleted and the floppy disk safely stored. Choice A is incorrect because the key must be exported, not imported. Choice B is very close, but would leave the private key on the system. Choice D is wrong because the recovery agent key is not necessary. The salesman's public and private keys are used by the salesman. (For more information, see the section "Encrypting File System Internals.")

7. **C.** The Protected Storage service detects the password change and goes to work. (For more information, see the section "Certificate and Private Key Generation and Storage.")

8. **A.** You add a new recovery agent, or agents. Choice B is wrong; you should never remove the original agent without first providing another agent. Removing an agent is not the same as exporting the agent certificate and private key. Choice D would delete the ability to use EFS. Choice D is incorrect because you cannot share encrypted files by sharing certificate and keys. You cannot share these keys. (For more information, see the section "Recovery Policy.")

9. **C.** Export the certificate and private key and delete the key. Choice A is incorrect; the Administrator account cannot be removed. Choice B is wrong because files can be decrypted offline. Choice D stores only a copy of the user's certificate and key. Choice E is wrong because no password is uncrackable given enough time. (For more information, see the sections "Recovery Policy" and "Encrypting File System Internals.")

10. **A.** Choice B is wrong because you may not be able to remove the recovery agent (by default, the local administrator). Choice C is incorrect; removing or exporting the user's certificate and private key is a little impractical, and policy might be set elsewhere to allow the user to request a new certificate. Choice D is incorrect because EFS cannot be removed; you can only disable it. Choice E is incorrect: When did your users last listen to you? (For more information, see the sections "Encrypting File System Internals" and "Recovery Policy.")

Suggested Readings and Resources

1. *Windows 2000 Server Resource Kit: Distributed Systems Guide.* Microsoft Press, 2000.

   • Chapter 15: The Encrypted File System

2. Microsoft White Paper: "The Encrypting File System" from www.microsoft.com/windows2000.

This chapter covers the following Microsoft-specified objectives for the "Designing a Windows 2000 Security Solution" section of the Designing Security for a Microsoft Windows 2000 Network exam:

Select authentication methods. Methods include certificate-based authentication, Kerberos authentication, clear-text passwords, digest authentication, smart cards, NTLM, RADIUS, and SSL.

▶ Authentication is the process of proving that you are who you say you are. Many methods of authentication are used by systems in the enterprise. A typical IT person will have used as many as 10 or more during his or her career. From experience, you know that no authentication system is secure against every attack. You want the best security, but you realize that this may come at too high a price for every access to every system. You know that some systems cannot participate in some authentication schemes. So, what should you choose for your Windows 2000 network? What's native, and what must be added on? Do special circumstances require special products and standards? How will your authentication scheme work with other operating systems? Rather than putting off authentication issues until a groundswell of complaints about multiple passwords brings you screaming to the books, or until an intruder discovers an unprotected back door, use this opportunity to design authentication into your system. Explore your cornucopia of options, and select the methods for each authentication challenge in your enterprise.

CHAPTER 10

Designing an Authentication Strategy

Design an authentication strategy for integration with other systems.

▶ The first step in designing an authentication strategy is to determine what's going on in your Windows 2000 network. Next, you must find and, if necessary, implement strategies that will bring alternative OSs into your fold. Most of the authentication systems that you have studied are standards that are implemented throughout the world. Does the Windows 2000 implementation play well with these others? Which authentication methods can be used as interfaces with them? Of these, which will you use and where?

▶ This is not a subject that is usually presented so as to make it more easily understood. It's also not a subject that a lot of us know that much about. Personally, I groan when someone pulls out the flow charts and starts explaining Kerberos, or RADIUS, or public key infrastructure (PKI). Somehow, it seems like the discussion of these subjects brings out the worst in the best of us. For a moment, I'm transported back to grad school and Calculus III, with thoughts of how I'm ever going to pass the exam. Then I'm spaced out, off in another world, not listening. To implement any of these authentication strategies—indeed, to decide whether I want to implement them—I need to know all I can about them. I just find it hard to sit through long, dry explanations of them.

▶ I'll try to do my part to make the information easier to understand: I'll try to present lots of details without being boring. Experience is the best teacher, but much of this detail is not something that you can write up in an exercise. In later chapters, you will learn more about some of the features, such as RADIUS and PKI. You should learn about them by setting them up in your test lab. Should you memorize what works with Kerberos and what works with NTLM? When should you use a RADIUS server and when should you use SSL? I don't know that you can do all that by memory alone.

Instead, you should follow this credo: If you work with it, you'll know it because you've done it. For your part, you're still going to have to spend the time. Here's how to attack this part of your struggle:

- Read the case study to get the big picture.
- Read and study a particular authentication algorithm and description.
- Review related questions.
- Review the written descriptions, flow charts, and other materials.
- Return to the "Review Questions" and "Exam Questions," and answer the questions. Pay particular attention to how you think that this particular mechanism fits into your enterprise.
- Start on a different authentication mechanism and follow the same path.
- Compare the two methods. Are they complementary? Could one be used in place of the other? Would you have a choice? Would they be more likely used internally, or would they be used to authenticate entry from outside your network?
- Continue on, after each method, and consider it against what you have learned before. Classify each in your own mind.
- When you have examined them all, do so again.

INTRODUCTION

If I have a key to your house or the pass code to your alarm, then I can do great damage. To secure your home against intruders, you may have invested time and money in a security system. You at least gave it some thought. ("Hey," you asked the rental agent, real estate agent, or new roommate, "How do I get the key to get in?")

Keeping your network safe from intruders also starts at the front door. You need a way of determining who should be let in. Taking the time to examine the available Windows 2000 methods for authentication and determining how they fit your enterprise will go a long way toward providing you with a solid security design. You've looked at business, technical, and security requirements; now it's time to start on the design.

This chapter provides you with knowledge of the authentication methods possible with Windows 2000 and helps you select those to meet the needs you have already defined.

WINDOWS 2000 SECURITY MODEL

Select authentication methods. Methods include certificate-based authentication, Kerberos authentication, clear-text passwords, digest authentication, smart cards, NTLM, RADIUS, and SSL.

To make choices regarding authentication, you must first learn a little bit about the Windows 2000 architecture. Consider the authentication model, the Security Support Provider Interface (SSPI). Review the security subsystem. What are the parts? How do they work together? These are two models you must consider when examining Microsoft security.

SSPI is the glue that allows Windows 2000 to offer a varied authentication, message integrity, and message privacy for any distributed application protocol. It frees application developers from struggling with the appropriate way and how to implement security. Programmers write to the SSPI interface and do not worry whether the underlying authentication process used is Kerberos, NTLM, Schannel SSL/TLS, or Distributed Password Authentication (DPA).

Think about it. If I have a DCOM application, a mail client, or a Web server, or if I just want to access a file, the only concern I have is whether it can talk SSPI. SSPI is supported by Windows 2000, Windows NT, Windows 98, RPC run-time for Windows 95, MS-DOS, Windows 3.11, and Macintosh. Figure 10.1 displays the interface.

Windows 2000 Architecture

The Windows 2000 security architecture consists of components in Active Directory and in the operating system. Active Directory stores security policy and account information. The operating system implements the security model while trusting information stored in the directory.

Components of the Security Subsystem

Local accounts are stored in the Windows 2000 registry, and local logon is similar to that of the Windows NT 4.0 model. Local logon uses components that you may be familiar with.

The standalone, workgroup-oriented Windows 2000 Server or Professional keeps its accounts in the Security Accounts Manager (SAM) and follows the same process as it did for Windows NT 4.0.

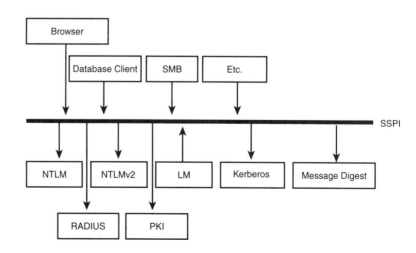

FIGURE 10.1
SSPI interface to multiple authentication services.

The user's account is passed to the local security authority (LSA), which hands off authentication to NTLM. When a user attempts to access a resource, the Security Reference Monitor (SRM) validates his permissions. These components make up parts of the security subsystem and are further defined here.

◆ **Security Reference Monitor (SRM)**—The SRM checks user permissions to access objects. It enforces access validation and audit policy. SRM is used by both kernel and user modes, and it generates the audit messages.

◆ **SAM**—In Windows NT 4.0, the SAM was the repository for all account information. It is still used to store local user accounts. Every Windows 2000 Server, Advanced Server, and Professional system has a SAM when installed. This is used to store the original installation Administrator account. When a server is promoted to domain controller, SAM accounts are no longer accessible.

◆ **Local Security Authority (LSA)**—The LSA generates the access tokens, manages local security policy, provides interactive user authentication, and hands off authentication to the Kerberos client or NTLM protocols for network-based authentication.

KERBEROS—NATIVE WINDOWS 2000 AUTHENTICATION

To understand Windows 2000 implementation of Kerberos, you must understand Active Directory. Active Directory is the framework upon which everything in Windows 2000 revolves. Ignore it, and you are forced to memorize millions of details or forever be confused by the actions of the servers in your network. Kerberos defines the rationale behind the framework on which Active Directory lies.

You don't have to do anything to implement Kerberos in Windows 2000—it will be used by default to authenticate network users using Windows 2000 clients who are logging into a Windows 2000 domain. The Windows 2000 domain controller will negotiate authentication protocols with other clients unless you configure it to prevent this.

Kerberos is an IETF standard for authentication. Developed by the Massachusetts Institute of Technology in the 1980s, Kerberos is considered a secure authentication protocol. Many operating systems other than Windows 2000 have used Kerberos for a long time, and this offers some interoperability opportunities as well.

> **NOTE**
>
> **Request For Comment**   RFCs are standardized algorithms developed by volunteer committees. Although anyone can submit an RFC draft to the Internet Engineering Task Force (IETF), a long, laborious process is involved in obtaining consensus and actually moving the draft to proposed standard and finally Standard. RFCs are meant to be algorithms, so implementation is left up to the implementer. To learn more about RFCs, visit the IEFT Web site at www.IETF.org. To find a copy of the Kerberos (or any other) RFC, visit www.rfc-editor-org/rfcsearch.html.

IETF Standard and Microsoft's Implementation

To fully appreciate Kerberos, you should obtain a copy of the IETF RFC 1510 and study it. In the minutia of its design, you will find many sound security principles. In the details, you will find the answers to questions that may arise long after you have passed the exams. You also will find answers to questions from any peers who certainly will condemn Microsoft for not following the standard even if though they have not read it. You can then join them with real facts, or refute their claims as you see fit.

Meanwhile, to understand how authentication works in Windows 2000, you must not worry about whether each detail of the specification followed or "improved." Instead, concentrate on what does happen. What follows is a presentation of Kerberos, paralleled with specific Windows 2000 details.

First, some basics:

The basic process that Kerberos uses for authentication is this: The username and password that an individual enters at logon is used to determine whether that person is who he says he is. That's it. To do this, several things take place. A ticket (a Ticket-Granting Ticket, or TGT) is generated that can be used later to request a session ticket, or a ticket to access a particular server. This server may be a file server, print server, or application server. The original ticket is locally cached in protected storage by the client system. The user is not asked to re-enter a username and password. The process for the first authentication on the system, the request for a session ticket, and the request for access to the resource server are described in three Kerberos subprotocols or message exchanges, the Authentication Service Exchange, the Client/Server Authentication Exchange, and the Ticket-Granting Service Exchange, respectively.

Kerberos Components

A Kerberos system is made up of several elements:

◆ **Authentication Server**—This server performs authentication of the client against the Kerberos Distribution Center (KDC). In Windows 2000, this is implemented as a service: the Authentication Service (AS).

◆ **Ticket-Granting Server**—This server grants tickets for resource servers to authenticated clients. In Windows 2000, this is implemented as the Ticket-Granting Service.

◆ **Kerberos Distribution Center (KDC)**—In Windows 2000, the KDC is a service that is itself composed of two services, the Authentication Service and the Ticket-Granting Service.

◆ **Key storage**—In Kerberos classic, a database called the Kerberos Database (KDB) stores keys. Windows 2000 uses Active Directory for key storage.

◆ **Kerberos Administration Server (KADM)**—All modification of the KDC is done from the KADM. Windows 2000 domain controllers are responsible here.

◆ **Kerberos realm**—A logical organization of Kerberos servers and clients, Windows 2000 uses the word *domain* instead of *realm*.

Active Directory contains information about users. In a traditional Kerberos KDB, it contains user IDs and passwords. Its record structure is defined by the following fields:

◆ Principal identifier

◆ Principal secret key

◆ Principal key version

◆ Maximum lifetime for tickets

◆ Maximum total lifetime for renewable tickets

This information and more is kept in Active Directory under Windows 2000.

Kerberos Message Exchanges

Kerberos consists of three message exchanges that define communications between the Kerberos client and the Kerberos Server: the Authentication Service Exchange (AS), the Ticket-Granting Service Exchange (TGS) and the Client/Server Service Exchange (CS). Each exchange has two primary messages, a client request and a server response (see Table 10.1).

TABLE 10.1

KERBEROS MESSAGES

Exchange	Request	Response
Authentication Service Exchange	KRB_AS_REQ	KRB_AS_REP
Ticket-Granting Service Exchange	KRB_TGS_REQ	KRB_TGS_REP
Client/Server Service Exchange	KRB_AP_REQ	KRB_AP_REP

The Authentication Service Exchange

The Authentication Service Exchange (AS) is used for initial authentication, for changing passwords, and to request access to an application server or service.

In traditional Kerberos preauthentication, the presentation of credentials to the Authentication Server (AS) before asking for access to some application, is not required. The process is described. Instead, the client asks for a ticket; it does not send a password. The client does not use its password as the key to encrypt a random string. The client's request merely provides its identification (client name and realm) and tells where it wants to go (server, service, or application name).

In Windows 2000, preauthentication is required, but it can be disabled for interoperability purposes. The client uses the password entered by the user at logon to encrypt a timestamp of its current time. This is used as a key to encrypt data sent to the server. This key then is included in the client's request to the server. The standard indicates that for preauthentication, the password must be used to encrypt a random string. It also provides for the use of the client's timestamp instead. The client clock must be synchronized to the KDC clock. By default, if these clocks vary by more than 5 minutes, authentication will fail.

The traditional Kerberos Authentication Server responds by returning a ticket for the requested server, or by returning a TGT that must be presented to a Ticket-Granting Server to obtain a ticket for the requested server. If preauthentication is not requested, the AS does not validate the client because it has no credentials to validate the client with. If the client ID exists in the database, a ticket is returned in the response. The ticket may be for the Ticket-Granting Server or for the requested server.

The Windows 2000 AS validates the client's credentials. It always returns a ticket for the Ticket-Granting Server.

The Windows 2000 Authentication Exchange algorithm consists of three parts: client preparation and request (KRB_AS_REQ), server evaluation and response (KRB_AS_REP), and client reaction. The client begins the process:

1. The user enters a user ID (principal identity) and password.

2. Windows 2000 uses a one-way hashing function (DES-CBC-MD5) to convert the password to a cryptographic key (the principal long-term key) and stores it in its credentials cache.

3. The nearest available domain controller is located using DNS lookup. All Windows 2000 domain controllers run the Kerberos AS and TGS services.

4. The KRB_AS_REQ is prepared and sent to the Authentication Server.

The KRB_AS_REQ message includes the following components:

◆ Preauthentication data (the client time encrypted with the principal's long-term key)

◆ Principal name (user ID)

◆ Server name

◆ Client time (must be the same time used to create the preauthentication data)

◆ Address (IP address) or addresses that are assigned to the client

Next, the server processes the request (see Figure 10.2):

If the server is a Windows 2000 Server, or preauthentication is requested, the following occurs:

1. The server looks up the principal in the KDC (Active Directory).

2. The server retrieves its copy of the user's long-term key.

3. The server encrypts the client-provided client time with the retrieved long-term key.

4. The server compares its result to the provided preauthentication data from the client.

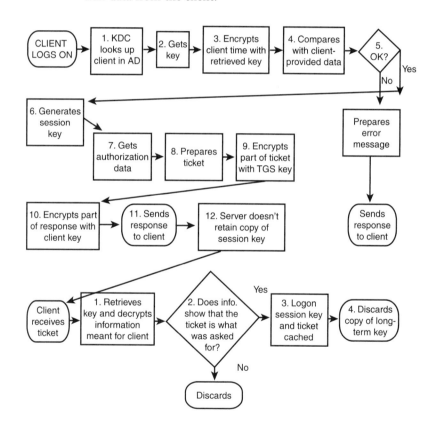

FIGURE 10.2
The AS message exchange.

5. If there is a match, the server continues on; otherwise, an error message is sent to the client.

6. The server randomly generates a session key to be used by the client in future conversations with the Ticket-Granting Server (Windows 2000 always) or the desired application server.

7. Microsoft only: The server looks up the principal's group membership information and the privileges the user or these groups have in this domain.

8. The server prepares the ticket.

9. The encrypted part of the ticket (which includes the session key) is encrypted with the key of the destination server.

10. The server encrypts a portion of the response (including the client's copy of the session key) with the client's key.

11. The server sends the response (KRB_AS_REP), which includes the ticket, to the client.

12. The server does not retain a copy of the session key.

The KRB_AS_REP includes the following fields:

◆ Message type

◆ Data encrypted in the client key:

  • Session key

  • Key expiration date

  • Time of authorization

  • Start time (when the ticket will be good from)

  • End time (when the ticket expires)

  • Server domain—The domain of the server the ticket is meant for (in Windows 2000, the domain of the TGS)

  • Server name

◆ The ticket (see Table 10.2)

TABLE 10.2

THE TICKET

Field	Information	Matches Encrypted Client Data in Response?
Session key	Key provided by AS Server.	Yes
Client domain	Identification of client because client may be accessing resources in another domain.	No
Client name	Name of the client that submitted the request.	No
Transmittal list	Names of servers that touched this ticket.	No
Authorization time	Time that the ticket was generated. You'll see that this is used in later algorithms to evaluate whether the ticket is valid.	Yes
Start time	Time that the ticket will become usable. The Kerberos standard allows for "postdated tickets."	Yes
End time	Ticket expiration time.	Yes
Authorization data	The standard allows for the use of this field for authorization data, but does not specify its contents. In the Microsoft implementation, this field contains: User SID, SIDs of groups user is a member of, SIDS of the user's rights.	No

When the client receives the ticket, the following should occur:

1. The client uses its cached, long-term key to decrypt its portion of the ticket. It retrieves its copy of the session key (in Windows 2000, now known as the logon session key).

2. The other information is used to verify that the client did receive what it asked for and to identify the ticket for use later.

3. The logon session key and the ticket are cached in the Kerberos credentials cache in volatile memory (never on disk).

4. The Windows 2000 client discards its copy of its long-term key. Any future exchanges with the KDC will use the logon session key.

Several points are of note here:

First, the password is not sent across the network at all. The AS has a copy of the password in its database and does not need to see a copy. The AS uses exactly the same algorithm to encrypt the timestamp provided by the client as the client does, so it can then compare the two to authenticate the client. A secondary authentication occurs as well. Because the information returned to the client is encrypted using the client's key, only the client (or someone possessing the client's key) can decrypt it and retrieve the session key and other information needed to use the ticket. This is why the Kerberos standard does not require preauthentication. If the response is hijacked from the network data stream, it will be useful only to someone who also possesses the client key.

Second, the majority of the ticket is encrypted in the key of the destination server (an application server, or the TGS in Microsoft). The KDC does not need to remember the session key because the two parties that need it can obtain it. The ticket is encrypted in the server key, so the client cannot access its data, nor can anyone except the holder of the server key. When the client establishes a conversation with the server (the TGS or other server), that server will use its key to decrypt the ticket and obtain the session key, which will be used for future communication. A rogue client could not simply create a ticket, even though it knows its format, because it would not know the server key. To attack an application server, the hacker would have to possess the keys for both a valid client and the server, as well as the exact specifications of the message format.

Third, the use of authentication start and end times not only establishes when the ticket is valid and when it expires, but it also gives the client and the destination server further information to prevent replay attacks. Because the authentication time is included in the ticket, the destination server can compare this with the current time. Policy within the Kerberos domain (realm) dictates a maximum life-time for any ticket. The server can reject any ticket whose authoriza-tion time goes against policy when compared with the current time.

Finally, a ticket that has been captured by an attacker will therefore expire. The attacker cannot spend time at his leisure working on the encryption before mounting a replay attack.

More information on the uses of the fields provided in the ticket is included in discussions on the other exchanges.

The Ticket-Granting Service Exchange

To copy a file, use a service, or print a report, the client must have a ticket for the server that has that resource. In the Kerberos standard, that type of ticket may be obtained from the AS or by using a TGT and obtaining a session ticket from the Ticket-Granting Server. In the standard, the TGT is often used as a way to obtain tickets for application servers that are not in the client's realm. Windows 2000 clients receive TGTs when they preauthenticate (log on), and they use the TGT to obtain destination session tickets as they request use of network resources.

The process of using a TGT, similar to that of obtaining a TGT, involves four parts: preparing and sending the request (KRB_TGS_ REQ), validating the request, responding to the request with a reply (KRB_TGS_REP), and acting on the reply (see Figure 10.3).

To prepare and send the request, do the following:

1. The user attempts to access or use some resource.

2. The client checks for a valid session ticket. If one is found, it is used; if not, the process continues.

3. The client checks the Kerberos cache for a valid TGT. (It knows this from the information in the reply that stored in cache with the ticket.)

4. The client prepares an authenticator. The authenticator includes the client's current time. The authenticator is encrypted in the session key (the Windows 2000 logon session key).

5. The client sends the authenticator and the TGT to the TGS in the KRB_TGS_REQ.

FIGURE 10.3
The TGT exchange.

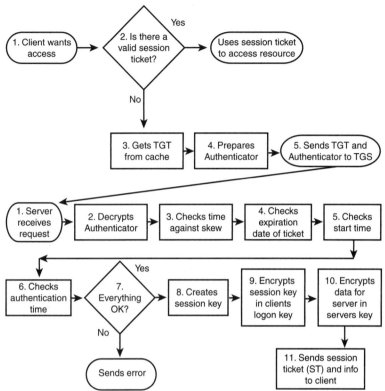

The KRB_TGS_REQ is mostly made up of the same fields as the KRB_AS_REQ. This makes sense because the standard allows the KRB_AS_REQ to get a direct response in the form of a ticket to the requested server. The two messages would have to have most fields in common. The KRB_TGS_REQ also incorporates additional information:

◆ **The authenticator**—Because the ticket has a range of valid usage time, the authenticator marks the request as current. This information can be used to detect replays.

◆ **Authorization data**—Windows 2000 uses this field to include the authorization data included in the KRB_AS_REP. It's not used by the TGS, but it will be needed in the new ticket. (The standard does not require this.)

◆ **Additional items**—In the standard, there is allowance for additional tickets to accompany this request.

NOTE

TGT to the TGS in the KRB_TGS_REQ
That's Geek Speak—K-Geek Speak, to be specific. Don't worry, though, you'll soon catch on. Like the Hooked On Phonics man says, just sound it out. The Ticket-Granting Ticket is sent to the Ticket-Granting Server using the Kerberos Ticket-Granting Service Request. That's what you'd want the client to do right? I know I don't want it sent to me.

The Ticket-Granting Server receives the request and does the following:

1. The TGS receives the request and decrypts the TGT.

2. The TGS uses the session key found in the TGT to decrypt the authenticator.

3. The time in the authenticator is compared to the current (server) time. If the times vary by more than a policy skew time, the request is rejected. This is done to prevent replay attacks. By default, the skew time is 5 minutes.

4. The expiration date on the ticket (the end time) is checked against the current time to determine whether the ticket is valid.

5. The start time on the ticket is compared with the current time to determine whether the ticket is valid.

6. The authorization time on the ticket is compared with the current time to compare with policy to see whether the ticket is valid. The authorization time may also be compared to a "hot list" of times that match the time at which invalid tickets may have been issued.

7. If everything is okay, the process continues; otherwise, an error message is sent to the client.

8. The TGS creates a random session key to be used by the client and the server to which the client is requesting access.

9. A copy of the session key and other data for the client is encrypted with the client's logon key.

10. A copy of the session key and other ticket data is encrypted with the requested server long-term key. This, plus some additional clear-text information, becomes the ticket.

11. The encrypted session key, the encrypted server long-term key, plus other identifying clear-text parts (see the previous ticket description) are returned to the client in the KRB_TGS_REP.

The client receives the request and does the following:

1. The client uses its long-term session key to decrypt the session key.

2. The session key, identifying information, and the ticket are added to the credentials cache.

You should take note of a few points:

The Ticket-Granting Ticket may be reused. In Windows 2000, it is used throughout the logon session to obtain credentials for use in accessing resources. This reduces the network traffic that would be incurred if the client could or did access the AS each time it wanted a ticket for a new resource. Because the ticket can be reused, additional checks are needed to reduce the possibility of its capture and use by rogue clients. The solution: the authenticator. By requiring that a new authenticator accompany any ticket (not just the TGT), the server on the other end has one more tool to help it verify that this is a legitimate request.

The ticket can use this tool in the following way. Because the authenticator is encrypted in the session key, the possibility that it is compromised is also reduced. If the ticket is stolen from the network, an authenticator is necessary to make the ticket valid. To create a valid authenticator, the attacker needs the session key that matches the one in the encrypted portion of the ticket, as well as the key for the client that is recorded in the encrypted portion of the ticket. To obtain the session key and knowledge of who the client is, the attacker needs the server's long-term key.

Finally, did you notice that the time in the authenticator is compared to the current time? The authenticator can't be stolen off the network and then used at a later time.

The Client/Server Exchange

Here's where the real authentication takes place. It's like you get a ticket on the Train Bound for Glory and then at the gate they ask you again for your ID. Did you expect that just because you had a ticket you could get on board?

Kerberos is doing its job to protect your network assets. Before it turns the discussion over to a decision on what you can do after you get there, it calls a halt at the door to let the application server check your credentials.

This exchange, known as the Client/Server Service Exchange, is much different than the two others. After all, you are not merely requesting a ticket or logging on, but you finally are asking for the goods. The process is similar, but different as well. There is preparation and a request message. There is validation and response, both to

> **EXAM TIP**
>
> **TRAC** Tickets can be reused. Authenticators cannot.

the validity of the ticket and to the request for information or service. A reply message is specified, but it may not be returned (see Figure 10.4).

Once again, the client begins the process:

1. Client retrieves session ticket for the server to which it wants access.

2. The client prepares an authenticator by encrypting its current time with its logon session key.

3. The authenticator and the session ticket (ST) for the required service (server) are sent to the server in the KRB_AP_REQ.

The server receives the request and does the following:

1. The server decrypts the session ticket using its long-term key.

2. The server uses the session key to decrypt the authenticator.

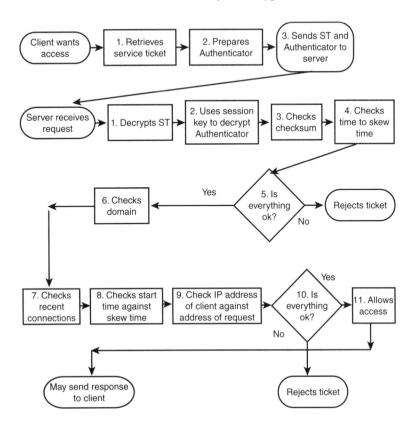

FIGURE 10.4
The CS exchange.

3. The checksum in the authenticator is checked against a checksum that the server makes over the authenticator. If these are not the same, the authenticator has been tampered with and the ticket is rejected.

4. The server compares the client time from the authenticator to its time. The two times cannot differ by more than the policy skew time.

5. If the time difference is okay, the process continues.

6. The realm (domain) of the client and the client name are compared between the ticket and the KRB_AP_REQ information. These must match, or the ticket is rejected.

7. The server maintains a list of recent connections. It checks this list looking for one that matches the client time, server time, and client name. If it finds one, this request must be a replay and is rejected.

8. The server checks the start time of the ticket against its time. The start time cannot be earlier than the server time minus the skew time.

9. The server checks the IP address of the client in the ticket against the IP address of the request. The two must match.

10. If all tests are passed, the server may send a reply, KRB_AP_REP. According to the standard, however, this is not necessary.

11. The server then uses whatever authorization scheme is required by the application the user is accessing (Discretionary Access Control Lists [DACLS] to security IDs [SIDS], among others). This step is not part of Kerberos.

Error Messages

Each of the exchanges may return error messages to the Kerberos client. These are discussed in the next sections.

> **EXAM TIP**
>
> **Authentication Is *not* Authorization**
> Authentication is the process of proving that you are who you claim to be. Authorization is the process of determining whether you can access the data or printer, or use the service that you have requested. While Kerberos does allow for the *transport* of authorization data in the tickets, it does not specify anything about that data or how it will be used.

Inter-Realm/Interdomain Access

A session ticket for a server may be granted only by the Ticket-Granting Server (service) in the same realm (domain) as the server (only the domain controller in that domain will know the server's password). How then can the client access resources in another realm?

The client must obtain a Ticket-Granting Ticket to the Ticket-Granting Service in the resource's domain. How can this be accomplished?

This is where the concept of trust is used. Two realms, or two Windows 2000 domains, that have established a trust relationship have a shared password or interdomain password. (In the words of the Kerberos RFC, they have an "inter-realm secret key".)

This interdomain password can be used to encrypt communications between them and, you guessed it, to allow the creation of TGTs.

The process (see Figure 10.5) goes like this:

1. A user in domain A wants to access a server in domain B.

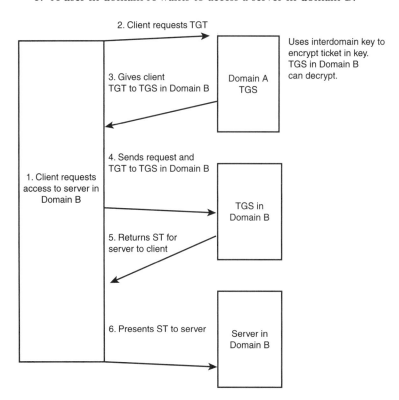

FIGURE 10.5
Interdomain access.

2. The user's TGT is sent to the KDC in domain A, the user's domain.

3. The domain A KDC returns a TGT encrypted with the inter-domain password (instead of the local TGS password). This TGT will be used to contact a KDC in domain B.

4. The user sends this TGT to the KDC in domain B to request a session ticket for the target server.

5. The KDC in domain B validates the TGT and returns a session ticket to the user.

6. The session ticket is used to access the server in domain B.

Unlike a Windows NT 4.0 domain, in Kerberos realms and Windows 2000 domains, trust is transitive and goes both ways. This means that the domain controller need store only the interdomain password for the domains it directly has a trust relationship with. Users in domains with trust relationship to other domains can access resource in domains directly trusted and in those trusted by these other domain.

If domain A trusts domain B, and domain B trusts domain C, then domain A trusts domain C (see Figure 10.6). Security principals in domain A can obtain TGTs for domains B and C. In fact, all security principals in domains A, B, and C can obtain TGTs for domains A,

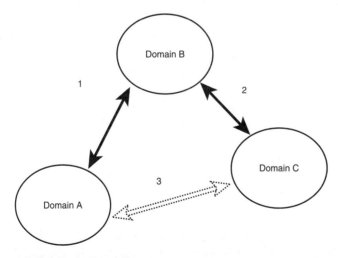

1. Domain A trusts Domain B
2. Domain B trusts Domain C
3. Then Domain C trusts A (this trust is not explicit)

FIGURE 10.6
Transitive trust.

B, and C. Whether they can do anything useful in those domains with that TGT depends on the rights and privileges given to them by administrators in those domains. The administrators can grant access without creating additional accounts for them. And that's another story (see Chapter 7, "Designing a Security Group Strategy").

Additional Notes on the Microsoft Implementation

The Kerberos credentials cache is protected by the Local Security Authority (LSA) and is managed by the Kerberos Security Support Provider (SSP). This SSP runs in the context of the LSA. The LSA calls the SSP to cache and obtain or remove tickets, session keys, and other information from the cache. When a security principal logs off or the system is shut down, any objects stored in the cache are destroyed.

The security principal's long-term password (the hashed logon password) is kept by the LSA. If the TGT expires while the user is still logged on, the LSA can use this to obtain a new one without requiring the user to re-enter a password.

What if the application that the client is using requires additional services on a server different from the server for which the client's session ticket is written? For example, Joe User is looking up data in a database on server A. The database application on A needs to check data that exists on server B. The application is running under the context of the user—how can access to server B be secured? Windows 2000 provides access to this server through the concept of delegation. The client can forward its TGT to server A. Here it uses a flag. The standard provides for the use of several flags that can modify the standard algorithm. The FORWARDABLE flag is one of them. This is required because the IP address in the TGT won't match that of the requesting computer, server A. Server A sends a KRB_AP_REQ to the KDC with a request for a session ticket for server B.

Server A can be used in this way only by the client, if server A is marked as "trusted for delegation." Generally, you want to limit the servers in a domain that clients can trust for delegation so that the

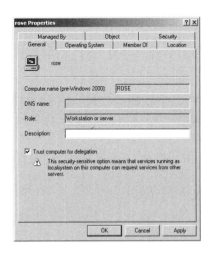

FIGURE 10.7
This computer is "trusted for delegation."

privilege has less chance of being abused. In addition, you can configure this privilege so that not all users in a domain have it. The feature can be disabled at the computer account level, and, of course, a policy can be created and applied at the OU level.

A server is marked as "trusted for delegation" on its general property page in Active Directory Users and Computers.

Flags

Flags are used to request and respond to special options about tickets such as the FORWARDABLE flag mentioned previously. Some flags are used by the client as requests, and some are used by the server to respond. The flags are listed in Table 10.3.

TABLE 10.3

FLAGS

Client Flag	Server Flag	Information
FORWARDABLE	FORWARDED	The FORWARDABLE flag tells the TGS that it can issue a TGT to a client with a different IP address than on the included TGT. When a session ticket is issued, it includes the FORWARDED flag. The FORWARDED flag tells the server that the session ticket was forwarded.
PROXIABLE	PROXY	The PROXIABLE flag (which can be used only by the TGS) tells another TGS that it can issue a TGT to a client with a different address than in the TGT. The PROXY flag tells the server that the ticket was issued by proxy. This flag could be used by the client to obtain tickets to be used by other servers for it.
RENEWABLE	RENEWABLE	Tickets may be renewed. The RENEWABLE flag allows the KDC to renew the ticket unless the renew-till time has been passed.

continues

TABLE 10.3	*continued*

FLAGS

Client Flag	Server Flag	Information
INITIAL	INITIAL	According to the Kerberos standard, the INITIAL flag on a ticket indicates that the session ticket was created by the Authentication Service, not the Ticket-Granting Service. Because Windows 2000 Authentication Service does not issue session tickets, but just TGTs, the INITIAL flag on a ticket means that it is a TGT.

Kerberos Policies

Kerberos is the default network authentication protocol for Windows 2000. Windows 2000 computers will use this protocol by default without any intervention by users or administrators. Configuration policies are set by default, and adjustments can be made to them.

To determine the policies in place in a domain, open the Domain Policy console and expand the Kerberos Policy entry.

Domain Kerberos policies can be analyzed and configured using the Security Configuration tool set. Default settings are illustrated in Table 10.4.

You can define security configuration in the Group Policy snap-in. Kerberos Policy is set at the domain level; you cannot have a different one for OUs within the domain.

TABLE 10.4

DEFAULT POLICY SETTINGS IN WINDOWS 2000

Policy	Windows 2000 Default	Kerberos RFC Recommendation
Are tickets renewable?	Yes	Yes
Are tickets proxiable?	Yes	Yes

Policy	Windows 2000 Default	Kerberos RFC Recommendation
Are tickets forwardable?	Yes	Yes
Maximum ticket lifetime (MaxTicketAge)	10 hours	1 day
Maximum renewable ticket age (MaxRenewAge)	7 days	1 week
Maximum session ticket lifetime (MaxServceAge)	10 hours	No recommendation in RFC 1510
Maximum skew time (difference in computer clocks, MaxClockSkew)	5 minutes	No recommendation in RFC 1510
Enforce user logon restrictions (look at user rights policy on target computer first) (TicketValidateClient)	Enabled (1 means enabled)	No recommendation in RFC 1510

You can adjust policy to increase security precautions. Remember that you also may be affecting the performance and efficiency of your servers.

These two suggestions will make your policy more efficient:

◆ Decrease the maximum ticket life to force frequent changes of session keys. This reduces your exposure to attacks on session keys.

◆ Allow renewable tickets. When tickets are renewed, new session keys are created. This is more efficient then creating an entirely new ticket. Renewing a ticket also requires a new authenticator.

TCP or UDP?

Windows 2000 Kerberos uses TCP for transmission. The Kerberos RFC specifies UDP, but Windows 2000 messages may easily exceed the size limitations of a UDP packet (1500 octets using Ethernet). The larger size of Windows 2000 messages is due to the use of authorization information included in the message. Remember, according to RFC 1510, authorization information can be included. If interoperability with non-Microsoft realms is required, the messages will not include Microsoft authorization data and may use UDP.

Distributed Services Use Kerberos Authentication

Kerberos is used for authentication on all distributed services in Windows 2000, including these:

◆ Print spooler service

◆ Local access to Internet Information Server

◆ CIFS/SMB remote file access

◆ LDAP queries to Active Directory

◆ Certificate requests from domain users and computers to Microsoft Certificate Server

◆ DFS management

◆ IPSec host-to-host authentication

◆ Quality of service reservation requests

◆ Remote computer management via RFC

NATIVE MODE VERSUS MIXED MODE

When you install a Windows 2000 domain, it is in mixed mode. Mixed mode means that you can have Windows 2000 domain controllers and Windows NT 4.0 backup domain controllers in the domain. This is to allow interoperability until the Windows NT backup domain controllers are migrated to Windows 2000. When all domain controllers in the domain are Windows 2000, you must change the domain structure to native mode. Windows NT stand-alone servers, Windows NT Workstations, and Windows 9x clients still can participate in and access data in the domain. However, if you have a Windows NT BDC operating in the domain, and you change your domain to native mode, you will lose the capability to synchronize the domain accounts with that BDC. More information can be found in Chapter 7. This issue is mentioned here because putting a domain in native mode is often confused with eliminating the use of NTLM, LM, and NTLMv2, and, therefore, the total reliance for authentication on Kerberos. This does not happen when a domain moves from mixed mode to native mode, but the availability of different types of security groups does change.

NTLM, LM, AND NTLMv2

The use of NTLM, LM, and NTLMv2 for network authentication is considered much more of a security risk than the use of Kerberos. Unfortunately, you will always have the possibility of authentication using NTLM, LM, and/or NTLMv2. However, you do have options that will enable you to reduce your risk by limiting the use of these protocols to certain servers, by insisting that clients use the strongest protocol available to them, by using NTLMv2 with Windows NT 40, and by enabling the use of NTLMv2 on Windows 9x by using Directory Services Client for Windows 9x.

To restrict the use of these protocols, you will make policy settings in Windows 2000, and registry settings in Windows 9x and Windows NT 4.0. More information is found in the later section "Using NTLM for Downlevel Clients."

When is Kerberos used? It is always attempted first by Windows 2000 clients. However, you cannot enforce its usage.

> **EXAM TIP**
>
> **What Gives with Local Logon?** All this conversation about Kerberos and network authentication obscures the situation where you are logging on interactively. What happens here? Kerberos, NTLM, LM, NTLMv2 are all *network* authentication protocols. Local logon is handled by the LSA, but the entered password is hashed and compared to the password in the local registry. If users have local accounts on member servers or Windows 2000 Professional, the information is kept in a protected section of the local registry.

USING NTLM FOR DOWNLEVEL CLIENTS

Windows NT 4.0 uses NTLM, NTLMv2, or LM, depending on which client or server it is talking to and how it has been configured. Windows 9x uses LM. By default, Windows 2000 has enabled LM, NTLM, and NTLMv2. As noted previously, you can eliminate the use of these protocols within your domain, if your domain is a pure Windows 2000 domain.

If your domain is not purely Windows 2000, then you must retain Windows 2000's capability to use these protocols, while mitigating the threat to your systems. Several Windows 2000 policy settings and Windows NT/Windows 9x registry settings can be used to do so.

The first question about NTLM and LM then, is whether you need it as part of your authentication policy. If you do not, then your policy is easy, but you must remember to have your policy propagate to all systems.

The second question to ask where access is necessary to Windows 2000 computers by users with non-Windows 2000 computers. You may find that you need to reallocate computers and upgrade computers for the best possible situation. If you have data and services that need especially secure policy settings, you can disable NTLM and LM on those servers. The servers will send only NTLMv2 and will refuse LM and NTLM responses. You then must provide users who need to access those computers with Windows 2000 upgrades. If desired, you may create some settings in between—for example, you may require the use of NTLMv2 to access certain or all servers. You then create make the required policy or registry settings on the computers that will access these servers. You can enable the use of NTLMv2 by Windows 9x computers by installing the Directory Services Client.

The Oswanee Credit Bureau, described in the case study at the end of this chapter, will still have downlevel clients in its domain and won't be capable of shifting those clients to less secure areas of the company, for two reasons. First, there are no plans to rapidly replace the desktop systems at all. Second, just about everything in the company is dealing with data that must be secured at the highest level.

What's the Fuss?

The LAN Manager (LM) authentication protocol was developed for use by the old LAN Manager network server. It was integrated into the Windows 95 and Windows 98 operating systems. To support connectivity to these systems, Windows NT supports LM as well as its own NTLM protocol. The LM protocol is not as strong, however, because although the passwords can be longer than seven characters, they can be attacked in seven-character chunks. In addition, the LM protocol does not differentiate between uppercase and lowercase letters. NTLM takes advantage of all 14 characters and allows lowercase letters. Strong passwords in which the NTLM protocol is used take a very long time to be broken. (Weak passwords can be broken in seconds, though.)

For information on the estimated time for breaking passwords, see www.rsa.com/des/.

The issue is that Windows NT 4.0 accepts LM by default and also stores a copy of the LM password in the registry. Both LM and NTLM passwords are used during authentication, so attackers can more easily crack passwords for NT. (The weak LM password is cracked and then is used to crack the NT password—they'll be the same, with the possibility of some difference in letter case.)

What's a Strong Password?

One Microsoft recommendation (from a white paper on securing Windows, which is available at www.Microsoft.com/security) is to have 11 characters, of which 4 are uppercase, numbers, or punctuation, to create a minimum of a DES key space of $7.2 *10 **16$ possible combinations.

The hisecure template suggests either characters and the complexity set of using a combination of three of four choices from among uppercase, lowercase, numeric, and punctuation characters.

Even the 11-character password can be cracked in three to six days with equipment (including hardware accelerators, at an estimated cost of $250,000).

See http://www.eff.org/descracker.html for more information.

What's NTLMv2?

NTLMv2 has a key space of 128 bits. Generally speaking, a larger key space means a more secure key. Windows NT 4.0 client and server must use SP4 or above. The HMAC-MD5 algorithm (RFC 2104) for message integrity checking is used as well.

NTLMv2 has a datagram variant that supports session security and 128-bit encryption for message confidentiality, but this must be configured.

To insist on the use of NTLMv2 by Windows 2000 clients and/or servers, you use Group Policy. First consider the implications for downlevel clients. Implementing NTLMv2 for downlevel clients requires registry edits. You must modify the following registry key (see Figure 10.8).

Registry key: HKLM\System\CurrentControlSet\control\LSA

Value: LMCompatibilityLevel

Value TYPE: REG_DWORD – number

Range: 0–5 (the choices are outlined in Table 10.5)

Default: 0

<table>
<tr><td colspan="3">**TABLE 10.5**</td></tr>
<tr><td colspan="3">**MAXIMIZING AUTHENTICATION USING LMCOMPATIBILITYLEVEL**</td></tr>
<tr><td></td><td>*Definition*</td><td>*Notes*</td></tr>
<tr><td>Level 0</td><td>Use LM response and NTLM response; never use NTLMv2 session security.</td><td>Default.
Windows NT 4 (SP4 or higher) clients can connect to Windows NT SP3 servers, but will use LM and NTLM.</td></tr>
<tr><td>Level 1</td><td>Use NTLMv2 session security, if negotiated.</td><td>See Chapter 12, "Designing Windows 2000 Network Services Security."

SP4 clients connecting to SP3 servers will use LM and NTLM.</td></tr>
<tr><td>Level 2</td><td>Send NTLM authentication only.</td><td>A client configured this way will not be capable of connecting to Window9x and below.</td></tr>
<tr><td>Level 3</td><td>Send NTLMv2 authentication only.</td><td>This level should be set on servers, to allow Windows 9x clients to connect.</td></tr>
<tr><td>Level 4</td><td>DC refuses LM authentication.</td><td>Windows 9x clients can't connect.</td></tr>
<tr><td>Level 5</td><td>DC refuses LM and NTLM authentication (accepts only NTLMv2).</td><td>Windows 9x clients can't connect. Windows NT clients without service pack 4 or higher cannot connect.</td></tr>
</table>

EXAM TIP

Timing Is Everything Watch out for time difference between clients and servers. If the time is more than 30 minutes apart, authentication can fail. The server may think that the client challenge expired.

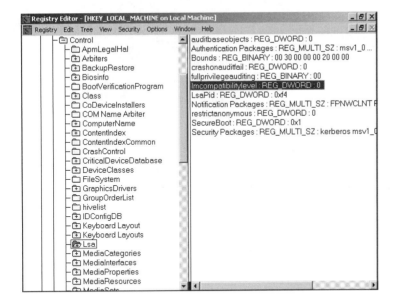

FIGURE 10.8
Setting LMCompatibility level.

Session security is used for communications between client and server after a connection is established. Authentication must occur first; it's the client proving to the server that it is indeed a valid client.

Setting LMCompatabilityLevel in Windows 2000 is easy: You use Group Policy. The option is set in the Computer Configuration\ Windows Settings\Security Settings\Local Policies\ Security Options section of the Group Policy Object for the OU that contains the computers that need to have this level of NTLMv2 authentication applied. The Security Option is LAN Manager Authentication Level (see Figure 10.9). You define the policy setting by checking the appropriate box. You have five choices that correspond to Table 10.5:

◆ Send LM and NTLM responses

◆ Send LM and NTLM (Use NTLMv2 session security, if negotiated)

◆ Send NTLM responses only

◆ Send NTLMv2 response only

◆ Send NTLMv2 response, but refuse LM

Be sure to make settings on the client side as well.

FIGURE 10.9
Setting LMCompatibilityLevel using Group Policy.

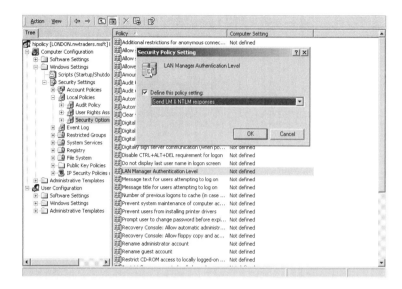

DIGEST AUTHENTICATION

Digest authentication is an alternative to using Windows Integrated Authentication with an Internet server.

Windows NT IIS implementation has been capable of using the Windows NT authentication process to authenticate users without passing passwords in clear text.

Windows-integrated authentication is limited for these reasons:

◆ Clients must have a Windows NT account on the IIS Server or in its domain or one it trusts.

◆ This method of authentication is not supported by non-Microsoft servers.

◆ Windows-integrated authentication cannot pass through a firewall via a proxy unless tunneled.

◆ Delegation to other servers, for example SQL server, will not work with NTLM.

◆ This method is supported only by IE 2.0 and above; other browsers cannot be used.

Digest authentication does not solve all these issues, but it is a viable alternative:

◆ Digest authentication does not send the password in the clear text across the network.

◆ This method uses a challenge/response mechanism.

◆ Although it is not yet a standard, there is an IETF RFC draft (2069). Thus, if this RFC is agreed upon, a chance exists that all browsers will support it.

You can implement digest authentication as an option when configuring IIS 5.0 on Windows 2000 (see Figure 10.10). The IIS 5.0 implementation follows the RFC draft.

To configure digest authentication in IIS 5.0, follow this process:

1. Windows 2000 must be in a domain.

2. Verify the existence of the IISUBA.DLL on the domain controller (copied during server setup).

3. Configure accounts in the domain to have the Save Password as Encrypted Clear Text option enabled (from the Account tab of the User Properties page).

4. Select the User Must Change Password at Next Logon option. (Passwords must be reset for digest authentication to work.)

5. Configure IIS 5.0 to use digest authentication. This can be done from the Computer Management console or from the Internet Information Services console.

   • In the Computer Management Console, expand Services and Applications, and right-click Internet Information Services to set properties for the entire Web server. Or, expand the object to select a Web site, and right-click to set properties for just that site.

   • Click Properties.

   • On the server page, click the Edit button to edit master properties.

   • Click the Directory Security tab.

   • Click the Edit button in the Anonymous Access and Authentication Control frame.

   • Select Digest Authentication for Windows Domain Servers.

FIGURE 10.10
Selecting digest authentication in IIS 5.0.

With digest authentication configured, the browser request to a Web page on an IIS 5.0 server is challenged. The browser must be capable of responding with the digest, or nonce, to be allowed access. Because this is a new standard, only browsers that support HTTP 1.1 will be capable of using this authentication method.

Digest authentication is a step above basic authentication because passwords are not sent in clear text. However, you must change settings to allow unencryptable passwords to be stored, so many consider this method to add undue security risks to the environment. Passwords are not usually stored in an unencryptable form. By not storing a decryptable password, another layer of security is added.

Using Certificate-Based Authentication

Certificate-based authentication in Windows 2000 is primarily accomplished by setting up a public key infrastructure (PKI). This may be done by installing Certificate Services, or by using third-party Certificate Authority Services. The process and issues of setting up a public key infrastructure in Windows 2000 is covered in Chapter 11, "Designing a Public Key Infrastructure." Before determining whether certificate-based authentication should be implemented in your organization, you should read this chapter and investigate other resources.

By directive, your authentication strategy might include a PKI, or you might want to determine whether you want to allow for its implementation at a future date. This chapter begins your studies by introducing some definitions and common practices.

Applications for Digital Certificates

Some of the ways to use PKI in your enterprise are listed here:

◆ To secure Web communications and Web sites

◆ To secure email

◆ To digitally sign files to provide proof of origin (device drivers, for example)

◆ To implement smart card authentication

◆ To secure the EFS recovery agent

◆ To provide IPSec authentication

Definitions

The definitions provided here are generic and condensed. See the details provided in Chapter 11.

Certificate

A certificate binds a user and a public key. The standard certificate definition used by the Internet community and many others is the X.509 Public-Key Certificate (RFC 2459). Pretty Good Privacy (PGP) is another type. As you learned in Chapter 9, "Designing an Encrypting File System Strategy," Windows 2000 uses certificates to control recovery. (EFS provides its own certificates without network administrator interference, but to provide a centralized recovery policy, Certificate Services is required.)

A certificate includes a serial number, the name of the issuer, an expiration date, the certificate owner, the public key, and owner attributes.

The secret key of the matched public key/private key that complements this public key is stored elsewhere. (It is not part of the certificate.)

Certificate Authority (CA)

The Certificate Authority (or Certification Authority, as the RFC specifies) issues the certificates. The CA digitally signs the certificate. If we agree to trust the CA, then we will accept the certificate as proof of user identity. Therein lies the rub. Who should our CA be? Although a lot of controversy surrounded the initial implementation of Web-based certificate authorities (the U.S. Post Office even thought that it should be the public Certificate Authority—can you imagine?), Verisign, Thawte, and a few others have become de facto public Certificate Authorities.

Of course, you can set up your own Certificate Authority by installing Certificate Server on Windows NT 4.0 from the Windows NT 4.0 Option pack, or Certificate Services on Windows 2000. However, you then will have to establish trust relationships with anyone outside your company to which you want to present your certificates. (This type of trust is a certificate trust relationship, not a Windows 2000 direct trust.)

The responsibilities of the Certification Authority are as follows:

◆ Confirm identity of applicants for certificates

◆ Create and issue public/private key pairs and certificates

◆ Maintain and issue the certificate lists and revocation lists (certificates that are invalidated before their expiration date)

◆ Perform key recovery

Certificate Repository

The certificate repository is a centralized place that can be accessed to find the certificate for all participants. If I want to verify that I have received a message from you, and if you have signed it with your private key, I need to locate your public key. Because that is contained in your certificate, I need to find it. It would become impractical very shortly to keep a copy of all the certificates in my system. Windows 2000 certificates are kept in Active Directory and are mapped to security principals.

Public Internet Server certificates are provided to us by the server when we connect to it. We can verify the certificate because it is signed by the CA, and we have a copy of the CA's root certificate in our browser.

Public Key/Private Key

In a public key infrastructure, authentication is accomplished by asymmetric cryptography. Unlike Kerberos, which uses a shared-key, symmetric cryptographic approach, PKI uses a key pair. It is as if you and I each have a key to a box. Our keys are different, but each can unlock the box. To exchange messages, you can lock the message in the box using your key. You send the box to me. I use my key to open it. The two keys we have are a set.

The system works because the public key of the pair is offered to anyone. The private key is kept private and is available only to the owner. Let's assume that I want to send a message to you. I have two choices. I can encrypt the message using my private key or your public key. First, if I encrypt it using my private key, you can read the message using my public key, but then, so can anyone else. This will not make our conversation private, but because only I could have my private key, it does assure you that it came from me. This is known as digital signing (see Figure 10.11).

If I want the message to just be between you and me, I use your public key to encrypt it. Then only you can read the message. This is called sealing the message (see Figure 10.12).

Incidentally, I could have done both sign and seal. Then the message would be private, and you would know that it came from me.

A PKI can be used for client and server authentication.

A PKI can be used for client and server authentication.

PKI for Server and Client Authentication

SSL is the de facto standard used for secure connections between browsers and servers on the Internet. SSL was developed by Netscape and is primarily used to authenticate the server to the browser using public key technology. (SSL also can be used to authenticate clients, but it is rarely used in this manner.)

SSL3, better known as Transport Layer Security Protocol, or TLS, is a standard proposed by the IETF. While the Windows NT 4.0 option pack Certificate Server used public key technology to implement SSL/PCT protocols, Windows 2000 provides more advanced Certificate Services.

PKI Standards

No one standard exists for public key infrastructure. To understand it fully, you should investigate the current drafts available from the IETF Web site. Drafts for you to review are listed here:

FIGURE 10.11
Signing.

Signing

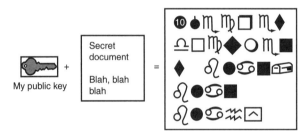

FIGURE 10.12
Sealing.

Sealing

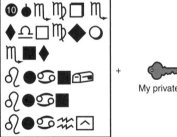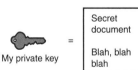

- ◆ RFC 2459, "Public Key Infrastructure Certificate and CRL Profile"

- ◆ RFC 2585, "Internet X.509 Public Key Infrastructure Operational Protocols: FTP and HTTP"

- ◆ RFC 2246, "The TLS Protocol Version 1.0"

- ◆ Public Cryptography Standard (PKCS), at `www.rsa.com/ rsalabs/pubs/PKCS`

◆ U.S. government site, at `http://csrc.nist.gov/pki`

◆ Canadian government site, at `www.cio-dpi.gc.ca/pki/`
   `splash_e.html`

PKI is a choice mentioned by Oswanee in the case study accompanying this chapter. There seemed to be some interest in implementing it among credit bureaus. Credit bureaus share information for credit reporting purposes. You contact a credit bureau to do research on someone's credit before granting that person a loan. It makes sense that the data needs to be protected and yet should clearly be available to the right people. A PKI might be a viable solution, especially because there seems to be an indication that other credit bureaus are implementing such a structure.

Windows 2000 Implementation

Windows 2000 integrates public key cryptography into the familiar security token structure. Certificates are mapped to existing security principal accounts in Active Directory. In this way, the authorization structures for users and groups that are already defined can be used to support access control. No separate database of privileges is necessary.

External users—that is, users who do not have a Windows 2000 domain account—can be granted access to Windows 2000 resources. This is done by associating an external user or users to an existing Windows 2000 account that then is used for access control. The user must be authenticated based on a public key certificate issued by a trusted Certificate Authority.

In this manner, businesses can grant access to users from their business partners. The mapping of users can be a one-to-one scenario (one account exists for each certificate issued) or a many-to-one scenario (many users can use the same certificate). The Certificate Authority must be configured for the external user's certificate as a trusted CA.

SMART CARDS

The need for tighter security has never been greater, and yet the basis for all our security efforts is based on an extremely weak and frail component: the human being who has to select, enter, and maintain a password. The algorithms for encrypting these passwords can be made stronger, as you have seen. The definition of what constitutes a password that is hard to crack can be explained, required by written policy, and partially enforced through digital policy. But nothing can protect us from users who write down passwords and tape them underneath their keyboards or in other more conspicuous places, who share them with friends, and who ignore written policies.

Nothing except the implementation of some other form of secret key, that is. A strong authentication process can be implemented by requiring a two-factor authentication. Two-factor authentication consists of requiring the user to present an identity-encoded physical object and a password. You probably have used this already. If you have accessed your bank account using an ATM card and a personal identification number (PIN), you have used two-factor authentication.

The science of biometrics has produced a number of devices that seek to use something physical about the user to identify him to the computer. Some use fingerprint analysis, some retinal scans, and others hand geometry or facial contour. Many of these devices are available in the marketplace today. If they don't have a driver for Windows 2000, they probably will in the very near future.

Another physical device that can be implemented without requiring body part identification is a smart card. You must have a smart card reader attached to the computer, insert a valid smart card, and enter your password or PIN. The private key is in a chip on the smart card. I suppose that a smart card could be stolen, but it would be useless without the PIN. Your security is still reliant on a piece of information that probably will be written down, but you have made it much harder to use the password because it is useless without the card.

Smart cards can also be used for SSL authentication and to secure email.

Windows 2000 supports smart cards and readers that are compliant with Personal Computer/Smart Card (PC/CS). Drivers are provided for plug-and-play smart card readers.

WHAT DOES A SMART CARD DO?

The smart card contains your private key, other logon information, and your public key certificate. To use it, you insert it into the card reader attached to the computer system and type in your PIN.

Okay, so you're sold on smart cards. What's it going to cost? Before deciding on using smart cards for authentication with Windows 2000, you must consider the additional cost of such an operation. Items to consider are the following:

◆ The need to install Microsoft Certificate Services.

◆ The number of users that you will be including in this strategy.

◆ How you will verify users (initial identification) for smart card issuance. Will you need to do background investigations?

◆ What will you do when users lose or forget their cards? Will you authorize temporary alternative? Send them home? Issue new cards?

The following standards apply:

◆ ISO 7816, International Standards Organization standard, covering interoperability at the physical, electrical, and data-link protocol levels

◆ 1196 (EMV), adopted by Visa, Europay, MasterCard, Visa, and others

◆ European telecommunication industry Global System for Mobile Communications (GSM)

◆ Personal Computer/Smart Card workgroup specifications, available at www.smartcardsys.com (HP, Microsoft, Schlumberger, and Siemens Nixdorf, based on 7816)

Microsoft's implementation involves a standard model for interface readers, a device-independent API for enabling smart card applications. See www.microsoft.com/smartcard for details.

The following APIs can be used:

◆ CryptoAPI is a cryptographic API for writing a Cryptographic service provider (CSP).

◆ Scard COM is a noncryptographic interface implementation for accessing generic smart card-based service from a different language. A set of COM interfaces. Use to build interfaces.

◆ The Win32 API, base-level API on which others are built.

◆ Readers for Windows 2000 must conform to PC97 or PC98 hardware design and to Microsoft implementation of the PC/SC Workgroup 1.0 specifications.

INTEGRATION WITH WINDOWS 2000 KERBEROS

Windows 2000 Kerberos has been extended to allow smart card authentication. This extension (PKINIT) is not part of the current Kerberos standard, but it has been proposed.

The smart card can be used to authenticate to Windows 2000 using this extension to the Kerberos standard.

1. The user inserts the smart card and is prompted to enter a PIN.

2. The built-in smart card driver interface validates the entered PIN with that stored on the card and then provides the certificate stored on the card to the Local Security Authority (LSA).

3. The LSA passes the request to the Kerberos authentication package on the client.

4. Kerberos send an AS request to KDC on DC for authentication. It includes the x.509 certificate (from the smart card) in the preauthentication data field of the AS request.

5. The KDC builds a certification path from the certificate to a root CA in the system root store.

6. In Windows 2000, the CA must be an enterprise CA published in Active Directory (preventing a rogue CA certified in another CA hierarchy from issuing a certificate in the domain).

7. KDC uses the public key from the certificate to verify the signature.

8. KDC verifies that the timestamp is within the skew time to detect a replay attack.

9. KDC looks in Active Directory for account information.

10. TGT is encrypted using random key (the session key).

11. The client verifies the KDC signature by building a certificate path from the certificate to the trusted root CA, using the KDC public key to verify the reply signature.

12. From here on out, it's the standard Kerberos activities to obtain required TGTs and session tickets.

For offline logon, the users private key must be available. The private key is needed to decrypt credentials on certificate. It is encrypted using the user's public key,

Smart card support is integrated with Crypto API, Secure Sockets Layer, and TLS. You don't need to know about smart cards to use them for authentication.

INTEGRATION WITH WINDOWS 2000 PKI

Smart cards require the configuration of Certificate Services, smart card readers, and preparation of the smart cards. More information related to the use of smart cards with your PKI is included in Chapter 11.

The usual implementation requires at least one smart card enrollment station with a smart card reader and an authorized user. This is where smart cards will be created. The user must be issued an Enrollment Agent Certificate.

> **EXAM TIP**
>
> **Smart Cards in Windows 2000**   To support smart card logon to Windows 2000 domains, you must have Windows 2000 Certificate Services installed. You cannot use third-party or standalone CAs.

Integration with SSL

Using IE, the server could be IIS or some other Web server supporting SSL or TLS.

A secure session is established during public key authentication with a key exchange to derive a unique session key. The user certificate can be mapped to a user or group account that has access control privileges.

> **EXAM TIP**
>
> **Forcing Smart Card Logon**   To force smart card logon, enable the policy Disable Ctrl + Alt + Del, and configure each account to require smart card logon.

A test certificate server is available at `http://sectest.microstof.com` for developer use and testing and demonstration purposes.

Should smart cards be used by everyone?

For the security policy with the most punch, most workers should be issued smart cards. Users with administrative privileges in the network may want to use alternative methods. Smart cards can be issued to normal users, contractors, suppliers, and anyone else who needs access to network resources.

Because smart cards also can be used for SSL and remote access authentication, their use for your extended population is also recommended.

If users are required to implement operations that require secondary authentication, which requires entering a username, domain name, and password, the use of smart cards may not be feasible for them. If users are required to join computers to domains, to promote servers to domain controllers, or to configure remote network connections, they will need traditional logon capabilities.

Interactive policies that influence the use of smart cards are discussed here.

The option Smart Card Required for Interactive Logon is configured per user. When this is enabled, the user will not be able to log on from a password prompt or from the command line. This policy applies to interactive and network logons; it does not apply to remote logon.

The On Smart Card Removal option is configured per computer. If a user has logged on using a smart card and the smart card is removed, the computer is locked. Another user will not be able to access the computer.

Separate policies must be established for using smart cards remotely; these are covered in Chapter 13, "Providing Secure Access Between Networks."

Setting Up Smart Card Logon

A number of processes must be accomplished to establish the use of smart cards in Windows 2000. Be sure to include the following steps in your planning process:

1. Establish a smart card policy.

2. Set up a Certification Authority.

3. Set up an enterprise CA to issue smart card certificates, including Enrollment Agent Certificates.

4. Set security permissions in each domain. Three templates are involved: Smart Card User, Smart Card Logon, and Enrollment Agent Certificate.

5. Set up an enrollment station.

6. Set up smart cards for each user.

7. Install smart card readers on user computers.

8. Train users in logging on with smart cards (see Step by Step 10.2 in the following section).

Supported Smart Cards

Support for the GemSAFE and Cryptoflex smart cards is included in the default installation of Windows 2000. This means that your system is configured for their use. To use other RSA-based cryptographic smart cards, the vendor must supply a cryptographic service provider (CSP) for the card that is written to the CryptoAPI using the Smart Card Software Developers Kit available through MSDN.

The private key/public key management works via Windows 2000 Certificate Services. PIN management is via the smart card itself, not Windows 2000.

STEP BY STEP

10.1 Log On with a Smart Card

1. At the Windows 2000 logon screen, insert the smart card into the smart card reader.

2. The smart card prompts you for your PIN.

3. Enter your PIN.

SSL

Netscape designed the Secure Sockets Layer Protocol 3.0 (SSL) to provide message integrity, data encryption, server authentication, and optional client authentication. An SSL server and an SSL browser are necessary for operation.

SSL is used to encrypt credit card transaction on the Internet. You can set up an SSL-enabled IIS 5.0 server.

IIS can also be used to mix basic authentication with SSL.

RADIUS: INTERNET AUTHENTICATION SERVICE

Remote Authentication Dial-In User Service (RADIUS) is an authentication protocol used to authorize dial-up and tunneled users. It is used quite prevalently by Internet service providers to verify user access to their service. You can find the IETF proposed standard in RFC 2058 and RFC 2059. Windows 2000 includes an implementation of RADIUS called the Internet Authentication Service (see Figure 10.13).

The IETF Standard

NOTE

RADIUS Client   A RADIUS client is any server that can connect to the RADIUS server. A NAS server is a RADIUS client when it asks the RADIUS server for authentication and authorization information. A RADIUS server can be a RADIUS client when it forwards this request to another RADIUS server.

The first point of contact for a user attempting to connect to your network through RADIUS is the Network Access Server (NAS). A NAS can be the endpoint to a tunnel, or simply an endpoint that in at the entry/exit point of the larger world (the Internet, for example). The NAS becomes the client in a client/server relationship with your RADIUS server.

The RADIUS client passes user information to RADIUS servers and acts on their response. The RADIUS official port for authentication is UDP 1812. Older RADIUS servers may still support port 1645.

The RADIUS server does the authentication part and returns configuration information so that the user can access services on your network.

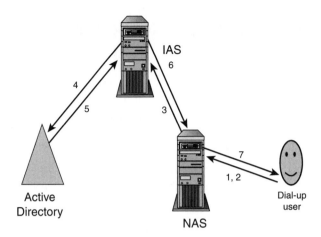

FIGURE 10.13
RADIUS authentication.

User passwords are sent encrypted (RSA message digest algorithm MD5) between the NAS and the RADIUS server. All communications are based on a shared secret that is never transmitted across the network.

Authentication is actually performed by various protocols, including Point-to-Point Protocol (PPP), Password Authentication Protocol (PAP), Challenge, Handshake Authentication Protocol (CHAP), rlogin, and others.

RADIUS authentication works as follows, per RFC 2138:

1. The client system creates an Access Request message, which includes the username, password (as a message digest using [RSA MD5]), client ID, and port ID.

2. The Access Request message is submitted to the RADIUS server via the network.

3. The RADIUS server receives and validates the shared secret.

4. If an Access-Accept message is returned, it will have the configuration data needed by the client to access services on the network (for example, IP address, subnet mask, and so on).

N O T E **Vulnerability** Even though the RADIUS server has authenticated the client, the authenticated session is not protected from hijacking, and there are no controls in place to prevent this. When the RADIUS server manages the authentication, the RADIUS server steps out of the picture.

RADIUS Challenge Response Authentication

Typically a challenge response authentication provides the user with a number that needs to be encrypted in some manner and given back to the server. Authorized users may have special equipment (a smart card or accelerator board), or at least knowledge of the algorithm and perhaps a shared secret that allows them to easily return the correct results. Because the number is unpredictable and unlikely to be repeated, there is a good chance that the response is from an authorized client.

In a large system that deals with multiple types of clients, another server external to the RADIUS server may come into play here. No longer is this a system that merely has a database of users; the RADIUS server has a database of the types of devices and systems that may need to respond to the challenge, and it can provide a challenge appropriate for that type of client. Thus, if one client uses smart cards and another uses merely an algorithm that is understood and performed by the OS, they both receive a challenge that they can respond to.

The challenge may even be entered by the user into some external device that supplies an answer that the user must enter into the client software on his system.

RADIUS Accounting and Authorization

A RADIUS server also can be configured to collect information about logon requests, denials, account lockout, and other usage information (logon and logoff records).

Authorization for remote access can be controlled via policy and can include the time of the day or month, the type of medium (ISDN, modem, VPN tunnel), the phone number called, the phone number called from, the RADIUS client, and so on.

Microsoft's Internet Authentication Service (IAS)

Internet Authentication Service is Microsoft's implementation of RADIUS. IAS uses the Windows 2000 Active Directory for authentication.

Basically, this process occurs:

1. A remote user dials into a network access server (NAS). This can be a Windows 2000 RAS server configured to use RADIUS for authentication.

2. The NAS negotiates a connection with the client by starting with the most secure protocol first (EAP, MS-CHAP, CHAP).

3. The NAS acts as the RADIUS client and sends a RADIUS Access Request packet to the IAS server.

4. IAS forwards a request for authentication to the Windows 2000 Active Directory.

5. If the logon is valid, a success response is returned to the IAS.

6. If authenticated, the IAS checks its remote access policies and the user's dial-in properties to decide what to do. If there is an access policy that matches the user's request, then IAS sends an ACCESS-ACCEPT packet back to the NAS.

7. If not authenticated, or if there is no matching policy, IAS returns an ACCESS-REJECT packet to the NAS, which then disconnects the user.

8. If the IAS does not respond, the NAS will attempt to use the backup server.

9. The NAS uses authorization information included in the ACCESS-ACCEPT packet to determine the user's network access privileges and establishes the user's connection.

10. The NAS sends an ACCOUNTING-START request to the IAS server.

11. The IAS responds affirmatively.

12. If the IAS does not respond affirmatively, the NAS resends its ACCOUNTING-START. If it still doesn't get a response, the NAS contacts the backup server.

13. The user finishes his work and disconnects.

14. The NAS sends an ACCOUTING-STOP request to the IAS server.

15. The IAS responds affirmatively.

IAS Authentication Protocols

IAS can be used to authenticate a variety of users using a variety of authentication protocols, including these:

◆ PAP

◆ CHAP

◆ MSCHAP

◆ Extensible Authentication Protocol (EAP), which allows the addition of other authentication protocols and methods. EAP is often used to support smart cards, certificates, on-time passwords, and token cards.

◆ Dialed Number Identification Service (DNIS), based on the number called by the user

◆ Automatic Number Identification Service (ANI), based on the number called from (with caller ID)

◆ Guest Authentication

Centralizing User Authentication with Remote Access Policies

RAS servers can implement Remote Access Policy. If you have very many RAS servers, the management of these policies becomes a challenge. Unlike many other policies, Remote Access Policy is configured on the RAS server, not in the Group Policy console.

The answer is IAS because it can be used to centralize control over remote user authentication. You establish remote access policies on the IAS server and configure all your RAS servers to be RADIUS clients. Any policies on the RAS servers will be ignored, and policies established on the IAS server will control the RAS servers.

Remote access can be based on the following:

◆ User membership in a Windows 2000 security group

◆ Time of day or day of week that the request is made

◆ Type of medium (ISDN, modem, VPN tunnel) used

◆ DNIS (phone number called)

◆ Phone number called from

◆ Whether the user is connecting from a partner's network or the local corporate network

◆ Where the RADIUS client request came from

Uses of RADIUS

RADIUS is used to authenticate users for two purposes:

◆ Access to the Internet

◆ Remote access to internal networks

RADIUS is often used to provide users access to the Internet. It is often outsourced to the Internet service provider. We will take a closer look at the use of IAS in Chapter 13.

RADIUS is also used to provide authenticated access from outside the network. It works with an NAS. IAS supports many different types of NAS, including Routing and Remote Access.

Routing and Remote Access also can authenticate users by using the Windows NT 4.0 or Windows 2000 domain controller database. It can be programmed with policies and can record information to the IAS log files. IAS also can manage Routing and Remote Access. To give IAS control over remote access servers, configure Routing and Remote Access to use RADIUS Authentication and RADIUS Accounting. So, why would you do this? IAS can manage more than one Routing and Remote Access Service. You manage multiple RAS servers from one place, and all the accounting and auditing information is in one place as well. IAS can even do authentication, authorization, and logging for outsourced remote access connections.

If you are an ISP, you can use IAS to manage subscribers. Using Remote Access Policies, you can set up multiple service plans, restricting premium access to users who pay more money.

When to Use RADIUS and When to Use RAS

RADIUS is an authentication service that can be used to handle a large volume. Although RAS is extensible by using numerous RAS servers, there is no built-in way to manage multiple RAS servers easily, and no way to have central reporting. This is where RAS shines. RAS servers can communicate with each other, passing off searches for clients. If so developed, clients can use multiple RADIUS servers. Central management and central reporting are supported. The NAS becomes the point of entry, redirecting its inputs to multiple RADIUS servers.

RADIUS Review

Clearly, RADIUS is a special system of authentication designed to provide controlled access between two networks. It does not replace the need for a centralized database of user identification and information. The following characteristics might be indications that a RADIUS solution will work for your company:

◆ You need to provide remote access to a large number of your users.

◆ You need to tightly control user access to the Internet.

◆ You want to set up a way to authenticate and authorize partner access to your network.

◆ You are an ISP looking for a robust solution that offers a way to connect multiple types of clients with varied access rights.

WINDOWS 2000 KERBEROS INTEROPERABILITY

Windows 2000 follows the RFC 1510 Kerberos standard for MIT version 5. So, it should be capable of interoperating with other MIT Version 5 implementations, right? Well, the Microsoft Windows 2000 Kerberos implementation can interoperate with other Kerberos implementations, but it's not perfect. Microsoft has done a few things differently (see the earlier section, "Kerberos—Native Windows 2000 Authentication"), and some things may be done differently in those other installations. So the answer is, maybe. The next section uses information available from Microsoft to discuss the ways that Windows 2000 Kerberos can interoperate with other implementations.

> **NOTE**
>
> **For More Information** Basic information is included here, along with information on the configuration items needed to integrate common features. Before attempting a UNIX/Windows 2000 interoperation, you should visit www.microsoft.com/WINDOWS2000/ library/planning/security/ kerbsteps.asp and download a recent copy of the white paper "Step-by-Step Guide to Kerberos 5 (krb5 1.0) Interoperability." This document appears to be a living document, and new information may be added at any time.

MIT v5 Kerberos: Kerberos Classic

As you recall, Kerberos Classic uses the word *realm* instead of *domain*, uses UDP instead of TCP, and allows the direct issue of session tickets in the Authentication Protocol. A few more flags also are available, including POSTDATED, INVALID, and VALIDATE. POSTDATED is used to issue a ticket for use later. The ticket is not valid until that date and is marked with an INVALID flag. To use the ticket, it would need to be sent to the TGT with the VALIDATE flag set. Microsoft always insists on preauthentication, although the standard seems to indicate that it is rarely used. Microsoft also extends its implementation of the standard with capabilities for smart card logon and uses the Authorization field of the ticket to include Windows 2000 user and group SIDS. Windows 2000 uses Active Directory to store security principal IDs and secret keys, while Kerberos Classic maintains a database on the Kerberos server.

Classic Kerberos operates with the concept of the Kerberized application. Kerberized applications include any application that uses Kerberos for network authentication. Windows 2000 is considered a Kerberized application. Kerberos classic also has Kerberos utilities that are used to manage credentials. One way to understand classic implementation of Kerberos and how they might interoperate with Windows 2000 is to understand these utilities (see Table 10.6).

TABLE 10.6

KERBEROS UTILITIES

Utility	Information	Standard	Implementation Specific
Kinit	Log in to the realm using a key derived from the password.	Yes	
Klist	View the cached credentials (tickets).	Yes	
Kdestroy	Destroy the credentials cache (use at logout to keep from use by others).	Yes	
Kpasswd	Change passwords.	No	Yes
Kpropd	Use a daemon that accepts changes to the UNIX Kerberos database from the master Windows 200 Key Distribution Center for the slave.	No	Yes
Kadmin	Used by Kerberos administrators to update accounts.	Yes	

The Kerberos Distribution Center is a network service that accepts requests for tickets, validates identity, and grants tickets. A common implementation might include a master Kerberos Distribution Center and several slaves. The slaves keep a recent copy of the key database (KDB) and are updated by the Kpropd daemon. Kpropd accepts changes from the master Kerberos Distribution Center. This replication process is not defined in the standard.

Windows 2000 Clients in a Classic Realm

Can Windows 2000 clients participate in a classic Kerberos realm? Yes, if they are configured to do so. Let's say that you are a university or some other long-time UNIX-based shop. You would like to provide access for students and professors to your UNIX servers, but you do not want to install another network OS server just for that purpose.

On the UNIX side, accounts will have to be implemented for each Windows 2000 user, or a decision will have to be made to use a one-to-many mapping strategy, such as using a guest account on the UNIX server and allowing all Windows 2000 clients to use it.

Configuration of the Windows 2000 Professional computers is done by using the KSETUP utility to configure the alternative KDC. (By default, the Windows 2000 Professional computer will look for a Windows 2000 KDC.) In short, the following must be done:

◆ Create a host principal for the computer using KADMIN.

◆ The Windows 2000 Professional system should be set as a member of a workgroup, not a domain.

◆ The KSETUP utility is used to set the UNIX realm, to set a local password, and to map local machine accounts to Kerberos principals.

UNIX Clients in a Windows 2000 Domain

If you are primarily a UNIX shop, if you have mixed UNIX and Windows clients, and if you need access for both services and applications running on Windows 2000 domain controllers, you can accomplish this by configuring the UNIX clients to use the Windows 2000 KDC.

Security principals (user accounts) need to be set up for the UNIX clients in Active Directory. UNIX clients will use kinit to log on to Windows 2000 using Kerberos and request certificates. The accounts are represented in Active Directory in the same way as accounts in Kerberos realms. After logon, a TGT is returned and stored by the UNIX client in its credentials cache. This TGT can be presented by the client to the Windows 2000 AS when access to files or applications is needed. Only tickets issued from a Windows 2000 KDC will contain authorization information that will allow the UNIX clients to access network resources. The UNIX Kerberos utilities Kdestroy and Klist will work as well.

Two configuration steps must be taken:

◆ MIT Kerberos clients must configure the Krb5.conf files to use Windows 2000 Kerberos as their KDC server, and the Windows 2000 domain as their Kerberos realm.

◆ Windows 2000 Server is configured to support MIT-format passwords.

- On the DC hosting the KDC, the KDCSVC notification package must be present.

- The password for the krbtgt user account must be changed. This will change the KDC's password format.

- Set up user accounts for the MIT clients.

- Create computer accounts for host (UNIX) security principals.

- Use KTPASS to configure the account for the host.

The Multiclient, Multi-KDC Mix

What if there are Kerberos classic realms and Windows 2000 domains, and Windows clients and UNIX clients? Interoperability can be accomplished here as well.

Scenarios are explored in Table 10.7:

TABLE 10.7

KERBEROS MIXED SCENARIOS

Clients	KDC	Resources	K Logon	Notes
Windows 2000 Professional	Windows 2000 MIT realm	Windows 2000 and UNIX	Windows 2000 KDC	Establish one-way trust between Windows 2000 and UNIX realm.
				Windows 2000 clients can access UNIX resources.
Windows 2000 Professional and UNIX	MIT realm Windows 2000	Windows 2000 and UNIX	MIT KDC	Establish a two-way trust between Windows 2000 and MIT.

Can UNIX clients access Windows 2000 services? Can Windows 2000 systems access UNIX services? In mixed scenarios, if trusts have been appropriately set up, access can be provided. It is even possible, by creating a two-way trust and providing other configuration, to give Windows 2000 and MIT Kerberos clients appropriate access. Clients have access to Windows 2000 resources through the Windows domains and access to Kerberized applications on the UNIX servers through the MIT realm logon. Account mapping is used. Accounts must be synchronized between the domain/realm.

To give Windows clients access to UNIX services, the services must support GSS-API, and some configuration is necessary. On the Windows 2000 domain controller, a service instance must be created in Active Directory. This is done with the KTPASS utility.

WINDOWS 2000 PKI
INTEROPERABILITY

In this suspicious world, trust in oneself is important, but in the business world there must be trust between organizations. PKI is about trust, but to use a PKI between partners, there must be some way for each to trust the other. Trust can be established between two PKIs, or both may trust some external PKI. How does Microsoft's PKI implementation stack up? According to the Microsoft white paper "Public Key Interoperability," the following is true about third-party PKI integration with Windows 2000.

Third-Party PKI and Windows 2000 PKI

Perhaps you want to share information with another business that is using another PKI, or perhaps you already have a third party PKI in house. How well can you integrate the two? Like most interoperability questions, the answer is a resounding, "It depends."

You will be looking for particular characteristics of the third-party PKI that will enable its use and will match them to your needs. Examining the following items can help you determine whether a PKI can interoperate with Windows 2000.

◆ To be used with EFS, a third-party PKI certificate needs to contain the enhanced key usage extension for EFS and use the Microsoft RSA Base cryptographic service provider to manage the private key.

◆ Third-party certificates can be mapped to user accounts in Active Directory. Thus, they can be used for authorization purposes.

◆ Third-party root certificates can be used to establish trust with a third-party Certificate Authority.

Third-Party PKI Without Windows 2000 PKI

The exclusive use of a third-party PKI with Windows 2000 is possible. Each third-party PKI will have its own set of successes and limitations. Some of the areas that may cause problems are listed here:

◆ Windows 2000 computers can self-enroll only with a Windows 2000 PKI. Self-enrollment can mean that less administrative time is spent on the PKI.

◆ Windows 2000 MMC snap-ins cannot be used to manage third-party PKI.

◆ Third-party applications that use CryptoAPI to manage their certificates can use roaming profiles.

◆ The issuing CA for smart card logon must be a Windows 2000 Enterprise Certificate Server.

WINDOWS 2000 AND MACINTOSH INTEROPERABILITY

Interoperability between Windows 2000 and Macintosh clients consists of these elements:

◆ File sharing via File Services for Macintosh

◆ Printer sharing via Print Server for Macintosh

◆ Windows 2000 AppleTalk Routing (support for AppleTalk Phase 2)

◆ Dial-up access to AppleTalk network via Windows 2000 RAS server

◆ Secure logon using the Microsoft-User Authentication Module (MS-UAM), or clear-text logon using the Apple Standard UAM

File Services for Macintosh

Although it is not necessary to run the AppleTalk protocol to provide File Services for Macintosh on Windows 2000, you may do so for other reasons. Macintosh systems (with the AppleShare client version 3.7 or later) can run the AppleTalk Filing Protocol (AFP) over TCP/IP. The AppleTalk Filing Protocol is used by Macintosh systems for file sharing over a network.

Macintosh file systems are different from those used on Windows 2000. However, the Windows 2000 NTFS file system can provide the necessary facilities and permission translations so that Macintosh clients can read, edit, and write files to an NTFS volume on the Windows 2000 Server.

File Services for Macintosh must be added to the Windows 2000 Server, and specific volumes must be identified for use by Macintosh clients. Windows clients that are authorized to do so can also read, edit, and write files on this volume.

Print Server for Macintosh

Services for Macintosh can be configured to permit the following:

◆ Allow non-Macintosh clients to access PostScript printers that are part of the AppleTalk network.

◆ Allow Macintosh clients to print to any Windows 2000 network-connected printers.

◆ Provide spooling for Macintosh clients. Macintosh clients can go on with other work while preparation of the print job and its printing continue in the background.

◆ Solving the "LaserPrep Wars" condition. This condition exists in some AppleTalk networks when Macintosh clients have different versions of PostScript printing information. Each print job from a different client can result in extra work by the Laser Printer because it must load a different version of a Laser Prep file.

Typical problems encountered include these:

◆ Quality of output, which can be improved with third-party image processor packages.

◆ Authentication. Macintosh clients can access any network printer, regardless of Windows 2000 printer authentication settings. For a workaround, see the Server Resource Kit.

Support for AppleTalk Phase 2

It is not necessary to configure the AppleTalk protocol stack in a Windows 2000 network to provide file and print services. Support for this protocol exists so that Windows 2000 can provide AppleTalk routing for an AppleTalk network.

File Services can run over a TCP/IP network.

AppleTalk networks may be composed of small physical networks connected by routers. A Windows 2000 Server can be configured as an AppleTalk router and can contain an unlimited number of network interface cards to provide services to multiple AppleTalk networks.

Before configuring support for AppleTalk routing, consult the Windows 2000 Server Resource Kit.

Dial-Up Access for Macintosh Clients

To use dial-up access to an AppleTalk network via a Windows 2000 RAS server, the Macintosh client must use a PPP client that supports the AppleTalk Control Protocol (ATCP).

On the Windows 2000 RAS server, the AppleTalk Protocol is installed during installation of the File and Print Services for Macintosh or separately. The ATCP protocol is installed automatically if the Remote Access Service has already been installed.

MS-UAM versus UAM

Several possibilities are available for authentication by Macintosh clients on the Windows 2000 network. Clients can access resources as a guest, if the guest account is activated. They also can use the AppleShare client software, the Macintosh User Authentication Module (UAM), or the Microsoft User Authentication Module (MS-UAM).

The AppleShare client provides for the use of a clear-text password. If you want to require encrypted password use by Macintosh clients, you must implement either the UAM or the MS-UAM.

The Macintosh standard UAM encrypts the password, but passwords are limited to eight characters. The MS-UAM can use passwords of up to 14 characters. In both cases, the actual password is not sent over the network. Rather, the client participates in a challenge/response system similar to the Windows authentication process. The server sends the client a string that the client encrypts using the user-entered password. This is returned to the server. The server compares this with the result it has obtained by performing a similar process.

The down side of integration with a Macintosh client and requiring an encrypted password is that the server must store the passwords in reversibly encrypted form. This means that the storage of passwords is not as secure as the usual process is to store passwords in nonreversible encrypted form.

Services for Macintosh does not provide Kerberos authentication.

WINDOWS 2000 NOVELL INTEROPERABILITY

Windows 2000 has a new set of Novell interoperability services. Microsoft Services for NetWare v.5 (SFNWS) contains the following tools:

◆ Microsoft Directory Synchronization Services (MSDSS)

◆ File Migration

◆ File and Print Services for NetWare v.5

◆ File and Print Services for NetWare v.4

◆ Directory Service Manager for NetWare (DSMN) for managing NetWare 2.x and 3.x binderies

The last two tools are the same as those available with Windows NT 4.0.

MSDSS is a tool that allows the bidirectional synchronization of data between the Novell directory services (NDS) and Active Directory. Synchronization of data between Active Directory and NetWare 3.x bindery services is one-way.

MSDSS functions like a connector between the two directories. Sessions are started manually or automatically, collect the configuration changes, and then publish to the other directory.

Passwords that are administered in Active Directory can be synchronized with accounts in NDS and maintain the one user ID, one password objective of single sign-on. Password synchronization is one-way. You change the passwords in AD, and they are passed to NDS. NDS is responsible for encrypting the password and placing it in the directory. This synchronization can be disabled.

WINDOWS 2000 UNIX INTEROPERABILITY

In addition to configuring Kerberos realms and domains for authentication communication, Microsoft Services for UNIX can be used for one-way password synchronization between Windows 2000 and UNIX systems. This also can be configured to interoperate with UNIX NIS domains. Network Information Services is a namespace administration system for UNIX systems used to organize UNIX hosts into an administrative group. A number of other UNIX utilities are available for interoperation.

Password synchronization is accomplished by setting up pods, or logical collections of UNIX hosts. Nonsecure and secure password synchronization can be configured. Nonsecure password synchronization passes the password over the network in clear-text and is not recommended, but it does not require that any changes be made to the UNIX host. Password update is done using the native rlogin daemon. Secure password synchronization is configured by installing the Single Sign On Daemon (SSOD) on the UNIX host. One is available at this time for HP-UX, SunOS, and Digital UNIX. Sample source code is provided by Microsoft if you want to write your own password synchronization daemon.

Here's how it works. The password synchronization daemon detects password changes and sends them to the password synchronization daemon on each UNIX host. If the UNIX hosts are part of an NIS domain, the changes are made on the NIS domain master. The NIS domain master then propagates the changes to the other hosts in its domain.

SNA SERVER AND AUTHENTICATION IN THE IBM MAINFRAME AND AS/400 WORLD

Microsoft SNA Server provides a gateway between a Windows network and an IBM mainframe and AS/400. SNA Server 4.0 can provide single sign-on. Windows 2000 user accounts can be mapped to multiple hosts. Manual password synchronization can be done by administrators. Mapping can be one-to-one or one-to-many. Users are autologged on to the host application.

SNA Server can provide secure transmission of passwords if a channel attachment or dedicated Token Ring LAN connection is used between the host and the SNA Server. The user logs on to the Windows 2000 domain, and the password is never transmitted in the clear. (Many emulator desktop products transmit the user password in the clear; they can be configured to use SNA Server, and this problem is resolved.)

Third-party products can bring two-way password synchronization and integration with host security products such as RACF and Top Secret.

WHAT WORKS FOR YOU?

Design an authentication strategy for integration with other systems.

Now that you've seen the panoply of authentication products available in a Windows 2000 enterprise, what works for you? There are almost too many choices, but it really boils down to using the information that you have collected previously to map the best strategy for your current and projected needs. The first step, mapping your information system, you have already completed.

If you have digested all the information up to this point, then you have completed the second step of investigating the possibilities. Now it's a matter of putting the two together. The following charts (Tables 10.8 and 10.9) should help you. As you fill them out, remember to think into the future, and don't forget that you need to answer the questions at least twice: once for your situation today, and the second for some time in the future.

Finally, compare your two sets of answers. Weak security authentication areas may resolve themselves based on your scheduled system upgrades. New opportunities may be right ahead.

TABLE 10.8

AUTHENTICATION GIVENS/BEST PRACTICES

	Default	*Current Configuration*	*Best Practice*	*Long Term*
Will you be retaining Windows NT?	NTLM, LM		NTLMv2	
Will you be retaining Windows 9x?	LM		NTLMv2	
Will you be retaining Macintosh?	UAM or AppleShare		UAM	

	Default	Current Configuration	Best Practice	Long Term
Will you be retaining Novell?	None		MSDSS	
Will you be retaining UNIX?	None		Kerberos	
Will you be retaining IBM mainframe or AS/400?	None		SNA Server	

TABLE 10.9

SUPER SECURITY CONSIDERATIONS

	Yes/No	
Do you have interbusiness data-sharing needs?		Consider RADIUS, PKI
Do you have problem securing passwords?		Consider smart cards
Do you need to secure sections of your network?		Consider RADIUS, VPNs, PKI
Do you need to protect or restrict Internet or intranet Web access		Consider digest authentication IIS 5.0
Do you need to set up or maintain an e-commerce site?		Consider SSL/TLS, other Certificate Services

CASE STUDY: OSWANEE CREDIT BUREAU

BACKGROUND

Oswanee Credit Bureau maintains credit histories in the southern United States. It shares its information and receives reciprocal information from other credit systems. Like most credit bureaus, Oswanee does collections.

Oswanee has been in business since—well, since people decided that they didn't have to pay bills. It has grown from a completely pen-and-pencil shop to a hodgepodge of applications, hardware, and software.

Problem Statement

A collection of different, incompatible systems has caused problems for everyone. Data is difficult to access, and use of the system requires the use of multiple passwords.

Information Systems Manager

We've had problems for years with all these disparate systems. Each new system is supposed to solve our problems, but it introduces new issues instead. One system can't talk to the other, and those that can—well, our folks have multiple passwords, with all that entails. We have security issues as well, so we can't easily move to a new, less expensive system.

Systems Administrator

It's a full-time job just keeping everyone straight. Our credit bureau side of the fence, the reporting and maintaining of credit history, uses one system; our collections operations use another. Our management uses a third. A lot of our people need access to all the systems. This requires them to have separate passwords. We maintain pretty strong security here, so everyone has to change their passwords frequently.

The information we deal with has to be kept strictly confidential; we have applications that encrypt sensitive data. That means using another password—sometimes many, depending on how we're using the password(s). When data is exchanged with other credit bureaus, the exchange takes place across a dedicated line.

Office Manager

I don't understand why I have to have all these passwords and accounts. They get in the way of doing my job. Truthfully, I used to keep a list in the upper-right drawer of my desk until I was told not to. I find it difficult to remember them all. Just when I think I've got it, I'm told to change them. Why can't I just have one?

CURRENT SYSTEM

An unwieldy system exists in which no one seems to know exactly what access a particular account may give, or whether any inactive accounts are really inactive, or held as backup by a senior individual.

Information Systems Manager

There is no central clearing house for user accounts and password. When someone new comes on board, we see what that person needs and get it to him.

CASE STUDY: OSWANEE CREDIT BUREAU

Systems Administrator

People don't always get the logins they need. In some systems, I could just give them access, but here I have to be extremely careful. That logon and password may allow entry into systems that certain people shouldn't see. The managers sometimes give me conflicting information. To make it worse, many "old–timers" have multiple accounts. It's difficult to determine whether those accounts are still required. I can't just delete inactive accounts, though—these folks may decide they need to use them.

Collections Manager

It works.

Credit Manager

In the last place I worked, we ran a much tighter ship. We have little control here. People write down their passwords. We get new ones and new accounts each time someone gets scared that too many people know how to get to too much information. That seems to be the solution. Change the account names and passwords.

ENVIRONMENT

The system consists of AS/400, Windows 98, and Windows NT.

Information Technology Manager

We have our credit reporting system on the AS/400, collections on UNIX and our general office on Windows NT.

Systems Administrator

There are multiple desktop Windows 98 systems. A few of the collection agents are still using terminals. They'll get new machines next month. We are using Kerberos for authentication. That's one of the reasons we are going with Windows 2000. That data is not going to be moved. The AS/400 lease is up in two years, and we will be looking a alternatives. Meanwhile, we need to keep things running.

ENVISIONED SYSTEM

The goal is single sign-on. This is something that everyone agrees on. Suggestions of PKI and smart cards have been made.

Information Systems Manager

We want to move to a system that will allow our folks to log on once and forget about it. If our different systems need different accounts and passwords, we need to automate the synchronization of this information.

Systems Administrator

I've been reading up on SSO. Single sign-on, that's what we need. This will allow us to take a major consumer of our time, resetting passwords and trying to make sense out of a morass of accounts, and allow us to concentrate on *who* should have an account and where. The credit bureau manager went to a conference last month and came back all hot to implement a PKI. He says that the other credit bureaus are moving

continues

continued

forward and that we can integrate with them. Then our access to their information will be easier, and we can be assured that any access we allow to our information is controlled.

Office Manager

Let's make life easy. One password. And it never changes.

Collections Manager

Here we go again, another new system that's supposed to bring us to nirvana. We'll cope somehow, I suppose. Are we going to be able to keep our files private? I had to fight really hard to get the money to purchase software to do that. I hope it still works on the new systems. Will it mean another password? Here we go again.

Credit Manager

I want to see my people using smart cards. That way no one can break in and change someone's credit history. They would have to have a card!

SECURITY

Any changes cannot weaken the security; they should strengthen it.

Information Systems Manager

We cannot afford to allow improper access of this information.

Systems Administrator

This is our first assignment. Keep the information private, and keep access restricted. We'll continue to search for the best ways to do this.

PERFORMANCE

When the daily activity is examined, all agree that in many activities, a little longer time spent in processing is really not a concern. The major issue will be response time for queries.

Information Systems Manager

Security can come at a cost in more than money. Many of the techniques we have tried in the past decreased performance. Because things do need to have a high degree of security, we can afford a little latency and a little degradation of service, but our agents cannot be left waiting for information.

Systems Administrator

A lot of our batch system updates with other credit bureaus can be done at night and early in the morning, when waiting doesn't matter that much. If we can log on once, then when folks do that in the morning, they are getting coffee. The Kerberos system on our UNIX box is quite efficient and doesn't cause any delays during the day.

Office Manager

Our system seems to be pretty quick.

Collections Manager

My people spend a lot of time on the phone. The information about their clients is usually pretty static. After all, we're dealing with people who have a hard time making a payment once a month. It's hardly relevant what happened 5 minutes ago. However, when they do make a payment, the system needs to update.

CASE STUDY: OSWANEE CREDIT BUREAU

MAINTAINABILITY

Having one account should make the system easier to maintain.

AVAILABILITY

The system needs to be available 24×7. Credit checks are being done by dial-up. We want to move that to an online system, so it's critical that any system we use works automatically and can be kept up all the time.

ANALYSIS

Oswanee Credit Bureau has an enormous opportunity here to take advantage of the opportunities for integration and single sign-on that Windows 2000 brings. It can immediately reap this benefit while evaluating the implementation of a public key infrastructure and possibly smart cards. Careful testing will show whether this is feasible in the credit bureau's environment. Because much of the company's work involves sharing of information with other credit bureaus, Oswanee Credit Bureau will have to be careful to test with them as well.

CHAPTER SUMMARY

KEY TERMS

- digest authentication
- Authentication Server
- Ticket-Granting Service Exchange
- Client/Server Service Exchange
- KDC
- TGT
- session ticket
- SSP
- HMAC-MD5
- 509.v3 certificate
- CryptoAPI
- cryptographic service provider (CSP)
- Kpropd daemon

This has been an arduous journey into the specialized part of security called authentication. You have learned about the new Windows 2000 de facto standard for authentication, Kerberos. You've seen how it will replace NTLM, but only in a Windows 2000 to Windows 2000 communication. NTLM and LM will be around, as long as you have Windows 98 and Windows NT in your network. As you have seen, a lot can be done to improve the security for those systems as well. In addition to looking at the basics, you've spent time looking at other authentication technologies, including RADIUS, smart card integration, and PKI. These technologies will be revisited in the chapters ahead.

APPLY YOUR KNOWLEDGE

Exercises

10.1 Install and Configure the AD Client for Windows NT and Windows 98

Estimated Time: 20 minutes

1. Log on to the Windows 2000 domain from two different Windows 98 machines and a Windows NT system to verify that you can do so. What authentication process is being used?

2. Inspect the Windows NT registry to determine whether any settings for increased strength of NTLM authentication have been set.

3. Install the Directory Services Client on one of the Windows 98 systems and on the Windows NT system. The Directory Services Client for Windows 98 can be found in the i386\clients folder on your installation CD-ROM. To install it, run the executable from your Windows 98 system. Accept all defaults when prompted. The client for Windows NT should be available with service pack 7 for Windows NT 4.0.

4. Log on from each upgraded system to the Windows 2000 domain. Which authentication system is being used?

5. Adjust the Windows 2000 domain policy to restrict logon to accept only NTLMv2.

6. Log off and then log on again. Were you able to do so?

7. Use the Windows 98 system that was not upgraded to log on to the domain. Were you able to do so? Why or why not?

10.2 Choose Authentication Approach

Estimated Time: 15 minutes

Match the request, or the existence of software and/or hardware, with the potential authentication strategy. You may reuse strategies. All of them may not be used.

| TABLE 10.10 |

EXERCISE 10.2: AUTHENTICATION STRATEGY

This Exists or Has Been Requested	You Possibly Need	Choices
Windows 2000		Digest authentication
Large number of users, a need to control access to the Internet, and a centralized policy		Kerberos
UNIX		Directory Services Client for Windows NT
AS/400		Directory Services Client for Windows 9x
Windows 98		Smart card
Windows NT		RADIUS
A need to authenticate visitors to a Web site		SNA Server
Increased security needs, strong authentication		PKI
A need to share data by allowing business partners access to internal servers		

APPLY YOUR KNOWLEDGE

Review Questions

1. The Security Support Provider Interface makes a programmer's job easier and ensures that authentication is handled appropriately for every application. Why is that?

2. Where is user account information stored in Windows 2000?

3. Why does Kerberos issue the security principal a ticket to get a ticket?

4. What are the three Kerberos message exchanges, and how are they used?

5. What is preauthentication? Is it required in Kerberos? In Windows 2000 Kerberos?

6. Of what use is the client timestamp in the authentication process?

7. The Kerberos standard specifies the use of UDP for transmission. Why does Microsoft use TCP?

8. Can you get rid of NTLM, LM, and NTLMv2 on your network? Explain.

9. A public key infrastructure uses what kind of cryptographic process?

10. Explain two-factor authentication.

11. IAS can be used to authenticate users who request access to the Internet and what else?

Exam Questions

1. Information in the Kerberos TGT is kept confidential by encrypting parts of using cryptographic keys. The following is true:

   A. Part of the ticket is encrypted with the key of the client, and part of the ticket is encrypted with the key of the Ticket-Granting Ticket Server.

   B. Part of the ticket is encrypted with the key of the Ticket-Granting Ticket, and part of the ticket is encrypted with the key of the client.

   C. Part of the ticket is encrypted with the key of the domain controller, and part of the ticket is encrypted with the key of the client.

   D. Part of the ticket is encrypted with the key of the TGS, and some information for the client is encrypted with the key of the client.

2. Kerberos is all about authentication. Authorization data:

   A. Is never part of a Kerberos ticket.

   B. Is carried in the Authorization data field of the Kerberos ticket.

   C. Is carried in the client as part of the KRB_AS_REP.

   D. Is used to authorize activity on the destination server.

   E. Is used to authenticate the client on the destination server.

APPLY YOUR KNOWLEDGE

3. The authentication time is listed in the ticket so that:

    A. It can be compared with the current time and current policy for ticket life to tell whether the ticket is possibly part of a replay attack.

    B. It tells the server whether the ticket is valid.

    C. It can be used by the both the client and the server to make correct entries in their audit logs.

    D. It can be compared to the skew time to see whether it's a valid ticket.

4. The authenticator accompanies the session ticket.

    A. The authenticator holds a copy of the current client time.

    B. The time in the authenticator can be used to detect replays.

    C. A new authenticator must be used each time.

    D. The authenticator contains a copy of the client password.

5. Trust in Windows 2000 is transitive. Domains A, B, and C are part of the same AD tree. Jane needs to access resources in domain C. Her account is in domain A. The administrator of domain C wants to give her access to the resources in his domain. Can he do this? What about the administrator in domain B? Can he give Jane access to resources?

    A. The administrators in domains B and C can give Jane access to resources in their domains without creating a user account for her.

    B. The administrator in domain B can give Jane access to resources without creating a user account for her, but the administrator in domain C must create an account for her before he can grant her access to resources.

    C. The administrator in domain C can give Jane access to resources without creating a user account for her, but the administrator in domain B must create an account for her before he can grant her access to resources.

    D. Before either administrator can give Jane access to resources in his domain, he must create an account for her.

6. Joe is querying database server X. Server X needs to access a database on server Y. Can this be done?

    A. Yes, If Joe's ticket is marked FORWARDABLE.

    B. Yes, if server X is marked as trusted for delegation.

    C. Yes, if the application requested and got a ticket for both server X and server Y, and then passed them both when it authenticated with server X.

    D. A and B must be true.

    E. A and C must be true.

    F. It is not possible for server X to access data on server Y.

APPLY YOUR KNOWLEDGE

7. The Oswanee Credit Bureau is implementing Windows 2000. Because of the long time some transactions can take, the company feels that it needs to make an adjustment to the Kerberos policy. Which part of the policy should be changed?

   A. Tickets are RENEWABLE.

   B. Tickets are PROXIABLE.

   C. Tickets are FORWARDABLE.

   D. The maximum ticket lifetime is one day.

   E. The maximum renewable ticket age is one week.

   F. The maximum session ticket lifetime is seven days.

   G. The maximum skew time is 5 minutes.

   H. Logon user restrictions is enabled.

8. A native mode Windows 2000 domain:

   A. Consists of Windows 2000 domain controllers and Windows NT domain controllers.

   B. Consists of Windows 2000 domain controllers and Windows NT backup domain controllers.

   C. Cannot contain any Windows NT computers.

   D. Cannot contain any Windows 98 or Windows 95 computers.

   E. Cannot contain any Windows NT domain controllers.

9. The Directory Services Client for Windows NT and Windows 9x:

   A. Allows these clients to use the Kerberos protocol.

   B. Allows these clients to use the NTLMv2 protocol.

   C. Allows these clients to access and interact with Active Directory.

   D. Allows a Windows NT domain controller to store a copy of the AD.

10. Oswanee Credit Bureau wants to move credit check queries online. The company wants authorized business and other credit bureaus to make inquiries via a private Web site that the company will build. Oswanee Credit Bureau cannot control which browsers or even which operating systems their customers may use, but the company needs to make sure that these users have an account in the Oswanee system. Which authentication method should be used?

    A. Windows integrated authentication plus SSL

    B. Digest authentication plus SSL

    C. Basic authentication plus SSL

    D. IPSec plus SSL

APPLY YOUR KNOWLEDGE

11. A meeting of an the Association of Credit Bureau Managers is discussing the use of digital certificates. The members of this association do not have a background in information systems and shortly discover that they are hopelessly confused about what digital certificates can be used for. They call you and ask you to give them some examples. You respond with the following. (Check all that apply.)

    A. Implement smart card authentication

    B. Secure email

    C. Authenticate your client to any Web server that requires you to have a certificate

    D. Record your ownership of stock

12. Oswanee has decided to implement smart cards. The company is investigating the steps needed. You have been called in for advice and say that, for the basic service of user authentication, the company should do this: (Check all that apply.)

    A. Use Scard COM to develop a cryptographic services provider for the smart card

    B. Use CryptoAPI to build a cryptographic service provider for the smart card

    C. Configure Certificate Services

    D. Purchase smart card readers and cards from GemPlus or Schlaumberger

13. Oswanee Credit Bureau states that it has a UNIX-based Kerberos on one system. The company does not want to get rid of this system; instead, it wants to integrate the UNIX system with Windows 2000. What are some of the issues that might prevent this from being a possibility?

    A. MIT Kerberos does not insist on preauthentication, but Windows 2000 does.

    B. The UNIX system might be MIT version 4.0.

    C. MIT Kerberos uses UDP, and Windows 2000 uses TCP.

    D. Several complicated steps must be done to fully integrate the systems.

Answers to Exercises

Answers to Exercise 10.1:

1. NTLM is being used.

4. NTLMv2 is being used.

6. Yes, this was possible.

7. No, this was not possible. Windows 98 uses LM. Windows 98 with the Directory Services Client installed uses NTLMv2.

Answer to Exercise 10.2:

Match the request, or the existence of software and/or hardware, with the potential authentication strategy.

TABLE 10.11

SOLUTION TO TABLE 10.10 IN EXERCISE 10.2: AUTHENTICATION STRATEGY

This Exists or Has Been Requested	*You Possibly Need*
Windows 2000	Kerberos
Large number (several thousand) of users and a need to control access to Internet, and a centralized policy	RADIUS
UNIX	Kerberos
AS/400	SNA Server
Windows 98 for Windows 9x	Directory Services Client

APPLY YOUR KNOWLEDGE

This Exists or Has Been Requested	*You Possibly Need*
Windows NT for Windows NT	Directory Services Client
A need to authenticate visitors to a Web site	Digest authentication
Increased security needs, strong authentication	Smart card
A need to share data by allowing business partners access to internalservers	PKI

Answers to Review Questions

1. The Security Support Provider Interface represents one interface to the programmer. No matter what actual authentication protocol is used, the programmer can write to one API. The programmer does not have to know which authentication protocol will be used.

2. Domain user account information is stored in Active Directory. Local account information is stored in SAM.

3. A ticket to get a ticket is one way to ensure that a user does not have to present credentials again during the session. The users have no way of knowing which servers they will need tickets for, so getting a general ticket that also will allow them to request and get tickets for another server is a good thing.

4. The Authentication Exchange serves the first purpose of client authentication on the network. The TGT Exchange gets the user a ticket that can be reused throughout the daily session, and the Client/Server Exchange gets the user to the server that is required for whatever he wants to do.

5. Preauthentication is the process of authenticating a Kerberos client with the first AS message. It is not required by the standard.

6. The client timestamp is used to protect against replay attacks. The timestamp is encrypted with the session key. The server uses its key to decrypt the session key and then uses it to decrypt the timestamp.

7. Microsoft uses TCP because, by adding authorization data, the possible size of the message can be increased above the maximum size that UDP can handle.

8. You can get rid of LM. You can get rid of Windows NT and Windows 98/95 and configure Windows 2000 LM compatibility level to use only NTLMv2. You also can banish LM if you use the Directory Services Client for Windows NT and for Windows 9x, and configure all systems to use only NTLMv2. However, even in a pure Windows 2000 world, you cannot eliminate the possible use of NTLMv2.

9. A pubic key infrastructure uses an asymmetric cryptographic function.

10. Two-factor authentication is the use of two factors, using something that is unique, such as a password embedded in a smart card, and something that only the user could know, such as a PIN number.

11. IAS also can be used to control access from outside your enterprise.

APPLY YOUR KNOWLEDGE

Answers to Exam Questions

1. **D.** Part of the ticket is in clear text, and part is encrypted in the key of the destination server (the Ticket-Granting Server). Information for the client is encrypted, but it is not part of the ticket. (See the section "Kerberos Message Exchanges.")

2. **B.** It is part of the standard that authorization data can be carried in this field. For Windows 2000, this data consists of a list of SIDs: the SID of the user, SIDs of any groups the user is a member of, and SID history. (See the section "The Authentication Service Exchange.")

3. **A, B.** The authentication time gives the server a time to compare with its own time, so it knows how old the ticket is. Compared to its policy for age of the ticket, this may possibly help detect a replay attack. (See the section "The Authentication Service Exchange.")

4. **A, B, C.** The authenticator is used to help prove that the ticket is a valid ticket. To look inside the authenticator, the server must decrypt the ticket and get the session key, and then use this to decrypt the authenticator. The server then can check the time against its own time. If the difference is more than the policy skew time, this determines that the ticket is invalid. (See the section "The Client/Server Exchange.")

5. **A.** Trust in Windows 2000 is automatically transitive if domain controllers are members of the same forest. If an administrator in any domain in the forests needs to provide access to users from other domains, he or she can do so without creating additional accounts. Therefore B, C, and D are incorrect. (See the section "Inter-Realm/Interdomain Access.")

6. **D.** Answers A and B must be true. If the server is not marked for delegation, server X cannot act in the client's behalf. The alternative would be to have the client get tickets for both servers X and Y. (See the section "Additional Notes on the Microsoft Implementation.")

7. **G.** The skew time is the time between the time in the authenticator and the server time. By default, if this is more than 5 minutes, the request is dropped. If Oswanee feel that this is not a long enough time, it can change it in the Kerberos policy. The ticket flags are not relevant here (answers A, B, and C are wrong), nor are the ticket lifetimes (answers D, E, F are wrong). (See the sections "The Ticket-Granting Service Exchange" and "The Client/Server Exchange.")

8. **E.** Native mode means no Windows domain controllers. Windows NT, Windows 98, and Windows 95 clients can still participate in a native-mode domain. (See the section "Native Mode versus Mixed Mode.")

9. **B, C.** A computer must be a Windows 2000 computer to use the Windows 2000 version of Kerberos for authentication. (See the sections "NTLM, LM, and NTLMv2" and "Using NTLM for Downlevel Clients.")

10. **C.** While basic authentication would provide a clear-text password, by combining it with SSL, the application can be written to request the password after the SSL connection is established. Thus, the password will be part of the encrypted communication, and any browser that understands SSL can be used. Answer A is wrong because most browsers do not understand Windows integrated authentication. Answer B, digest authentication, seems okay, but browsers

APPLY YOUR KNOWLEDGE

would have to be HTTP 1.1-complaint. For answer D, while IPSec could secure communications, many systems do not have this built in. (See the section "Digest Authentication.")

11. **A, B.** A PKI can provide digital certificates, for use by smart card authentication and secure email. These certificates also can be used for authenticating users to the system and for authentication with Web servers. However, answer C is too broad. A server may require a certificate, but just having a certificate does not allow you access to any Web server. You must have one that that the Web server recognizes as trusted. Answer D is incorrect because, while conceivably a program could be written to do something with stock ownership and digital certificate, stock ownership certificates are not the same as digital certificates. (See section "Applications for Digital Certificates.")

12. **C, D.** The company will have to implement Certificate Services. Oswanee can use the provided drivers if it elects to, and no extra programming is needed—just the purchasing of the cards

and readers. Answers A and B, therefore, are incorrect. (See the section "Smart Cards.")

13. **B, D.** Integration of Windows 2000 Kerberos with versions of Kerberos other than MIT version 5.0 may be impossible. All instructions state that Kerberos version 5.0 is necessary. A number of steps must be done, and the complexity of the task requires decisions on what parts need to be integrated and where to perform the steps. Answer A is incorrect because this possibility is not a problem. The MIT Kerberos standard allows preauthentication but does not insist on it. Windows 2000, on the other hand, always preauthenticates. When Windows 2000 is working with an implementation that does not require preauthentication, it will not perform it. Answer C is incorrect because the reason that Windows 2000 uses TCP is because the size of its Authentication field may mean that the packet exceeds the maximum size for a UDP packet. When communicating with the UNIX system, this authorization data is not necessary, and UPD can be used. (See the section "Windows 2000 Kerberos Interoperability.")

Suggested Readings and Resources

1. Microsoft Windows 2000 Resource Kit: *Windows 2000 Distributed Systems Guide*. Microsoft Press, 2000.

   - Chapter 11, "Authentication"

   - Chapter 13, "Choosing Security Solutions That Use Public Key Technology"

   - Chapter 16, "Windows 2000 Certificate Services and Public Key Infrastructure"

2. Microsoft white paper: "Smart Card Logon"

3. Microsoft white paper: "Public Key Interoperability"

4. "To disable LM authentication on Windows NT" (Tech Net, PSS ID Q147706)

Suggested Readings and Resources

5. URLs

- Microsoft test certificate server
  www.wectest.microsoft.com

- Smart card manufacturers:

  - www.bull.com

  - www.gemplus.com

  - www.chipcard.ibm.com

  - www.slb.com (Schlumberger)

- Internet drafts for the IETF Public Key
  Working Group (PKIX): www.ietf.org/html.
  charters/pkix-charter.html

- ITU x.509 specification describing certificate
  format: www.itu.int/

- Public Key Cryptography Standards (PKCS):
  www.rsa.com/rsalabs/pub/PKCS

- PC/SC Personal Computer/Smart Card
  specifications: www.smartcardsys.com/

- Descracker: www.eff.org/descracker.html

This chapter covers the following Microsoft-specified objective for the "Designing a Windows 2000 Security Solution" section of the Designing Security for a Microsoft Windows 2000 Network exam:

Design a Public Key Infrastructure.

- Design Certificate Authority (CA) hierarchies.
- Identify certificate server roles.
- Manage certificates.
- Integrate with third-party CAs.
- Map certificates.

▶ Today's organizations require security above and beyond the traditional user ID/password approach that has proved so vulnerable. Web-based applications, e-commerce, mobile users, and companies whose public role exposes them to every form of digital criminality are seeking guaranteed security. Although no one has found such a perfect solution, many think that the extra trouble and time spent implementing a public key infrastructure (PKI) gives them an edge in the impending apocalypse. It is a PKI's duality that gives credence to its promise.

▶ A PKI establishes a system of asymmetric key pairs for use in authentication. Users from within and outside of an organization can be vetted and assigned keys. These keys can be linked to access rights, enable closer control over recovery agents in the Encrypting File System (EFS), coupled with smart cards, serve as server authenticators for Web sites, and secure servers of any type. A PKI can go a long way toward implementing tighter security.

CHAPTER 11

Designing a Public Key Infrastructure

OBJECTIVES

▶ Implementing a PKI is not as simple as assigning user ID and password pairs, or even as simple as handing out plastic smart cards and readers to be used in their stead. Implementing a PKI demands a degree of sophistication and knowledge and a willingness to learn yet another new technology.

▶ You must configure Certificate Authorities (CAs) and choose or create trusted roots. For safety's sake, hierarchies are planned and the root CA is taken offline and often placed in a vault. The public key in the public/private pair is issued with a certificate, and certificates require management. This is not some drawing on a chalkboard to be implemented by paper-credentialed bozos yearning for excitement, entertainment, and ersatz. This stuff *demands* your thoughtful attention.

OUTLINE

STUDY STRATEGIES

▶ Remember, a PKI is basically another scheme for controlling access to your systems. If you analyze it, it consists of credentials (a whole database of credentials in fact), a scheme for getting those credentials to users, another scheme for determining who can have the credentials, another for removing credentials from the system, and another to confirm the veracity of the presented credentials. Unlike many authentication systems, however, PKI provides a little twist. One half of the key pair assigned to every user is available for anyone to see.

▶ Interested? What you need to know about PKI is this:

    • What is the CA and why should you trust it?

    • Why is there a certificate hierarchy and how do you create one?

    • Where does trust begin? How can you change that?

    • What are the roles of different CAs?

    • What is a certificate revocation list (CRL) and why do you need one?

    • How do you manage CAs, certificates, and CRLs?

    • What are CAs used for?

    • What is a public and private key?

▶ If you can thoroughly explain these things and how to put them into operation, you have got the essence of PKI. Then you need to understand the business reason for the PKI to determine how to design a PKI for a given situation. The case studies section and the questions at the end of this chapter give you some practice in doing that.

INTRODUCTION

Not that long ago, I attended a conference in which one of the speakers made this statement (somewhat paraphrased here): "There are going to be two types of IT folks in the near future. Those who understand and use PKI, and those who are saying, 'Would you like some french fries with your hamburger?'" Well, that hasn't happened yet, but there is considerable more interest in PKI today. At the time this statement was made, PKI was the provision of security and IT professionals at large companies who had extreme security needs, some Exchange Server trainers who implemented the Key Management Server, and the folks at Netscape who were plugging this new technology called Secure Sockets Layer (SSL) that they said would revolutionize the way people purchased their Christmas presents.

Today, all you have to do is write PKI on a bar napkin, and you can assemble a paying crowd of people who want to talk about it.

What is it, then, and how does it work? What does Windows 2000 offer to assist you? How can you best integrate it into your enterprise?

A PKI is the technology, hardware, and software that supports the use of public/private key pairs for authentication between servers and clients.

Public/private key pairs are asymmetric keys used in the process of authentication. In typical key, shared key, or secret key technology, you and I share a secret. This secret, or key, is used to obscure or scramble or encrypt any messages that we send between us (see Figure 11.1). It can also be used to prove identity, as described in previous chapters.

In public key technology, a key pair is used. A message, or bit of data, is encrypted with one key and can only be decrypted by using the other key. One key, called the public key, is stored where anyone who knows its location can get it. The other, the private key, is kept secret by its owner.

Symmetric Encryption

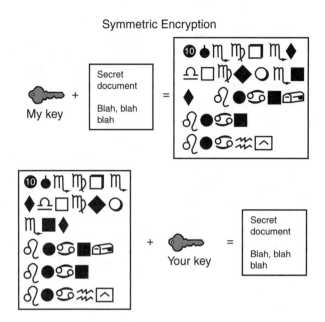

FIGURE 11.1
Shared key encryption.

Let's pretend that I want to invite you to lunch on Thursday but I don't want anyone else to know. I obtain your public key from a public directory of keys. I encrypt the message using your public key and send it to you. Because you are the only holder of your private key, you can decrypt the message. To agree to come to lunch (after all, I'm buying), you locate my public key, encrypt the answer, and send it to me (see Figure 11.2). When I receive it, I use my private key to decrypt it and know that my wallet is going to be a little lighter on Thursday.

Sound good? It gets better.

In our little scenario, how do you know the message hasn't been tampered with? How do you know the message really came from me? You don't. Although only you could read the message (only you have your private key), anyone might have intercepted the message and replaced it with one of his own. Others wouldn't be able to read the original message, but they might delight in confusing you. You would receive a message, decrypt it, and if it said it was from me, you would have no way of knowing whether it was.

FIGURE 11.2
Public key/private key encryption.

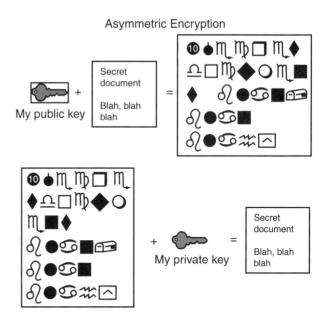

Asymmetric Encryption

You and I could do something else. This time, before I send my message to you, I use a one-way algorithm to create a digest of the message. I encrypt this digest with my private key. I send the encrypted digest, and the message that has been encrypted with your public key, to you. When you receive the message, you use my public key to decrypt the digest. You then use the same one-way algorithm I used to encrypt the message. You can compare the digest you create with the now decrypted digest I sent. If they compare exactly, no one has tampered with the message, and you know I sent the message. (The digest was encrypted with the private key that only I hold. You decrypted it with my public key and the digests matched). You now know the message is from me, and you decrypt the message with your private key and happily repeat the process in reverse to accept my invitation.

This process of encrypting something with a private key, for decryption by the public key, is called digital signing. It can be used for nonrepudiation or truly proving that the message came from the individual who claims to have sent it. It can be used without the encryption of the main message body. (Often, we don't care who might know the contents of a message; we just need to know, without a shadow of a doubt, who it came from.)

In addition to just proving that a message came from the person who signed it, signing has implications for e-commerce and other transactions in our digital world. After all, signing could prove that you used your credit card to buy that Porsche online.

In summary, for purposes of authentication, public/private key scenarios provide a more secure way for us to answer the immortal question "Am I who I say I am?"

Windows 2000 comes with optional installed Certificate Services. With it, you can set up your own PKI to manage file encryption keys; create a digital marketplaces on the Web; support smart card authentication systems; and manage the authentication of employees, contractors, and business partners within your network.

Before you do this, you should spend some time understanding and then designing your Certificate Services. Start with the following basic information:

◆ Basic definitions

◆ Certificate server roles

◆ Certificate Authority hierarchies

◆ Certificate lifecycle

◆ How certificates are mapped to Active Directory objects

After you have learned the basics, you should design and test a PKI. If you will need to interoperate with a third-party PKI, you need to spend time studying the issues that such a scenario may bring to your design. A section on how Certificate Services can integrate with third-party CAs finishes this chapter.

BASIC DEFINITIONS

You have already learned that key pairs are fundamental to the definition of a PKI. Each participant in the system owns a public and a private key. Where do these keys come from and where do they reside?

To join the system, each applicant goes through an enrollment process. This process produces the public/private key pair and returns a certificate and a private key. The certificate contains the public key, identifying information, and is signed by the CA that issued it. Certificates issued by different PKI systems or for different purposes may have different information on the certificate. Microsoft Certificate Services certificates follow the v.509 standard. The structure of the certificate used is described in the later section "Certificate Lifecycle—Managing Certificates."

The one-way encryption algorithm mentioned previously may be one of several hash algorithms (see Figure 11.3). Special hash algorithms are designed for this purpose. These hash algorithms, if used on the same block of data, always arrive at exactly the same result. We can compare it byte for byte. Conversely, no other block of data produces exactly the same result; that is, two different messages, if hashed with the same algorithm, will never produce exactly the same result. No collisions will ever occur.

If users of our Certificate Services are going to enroll and obtain a certificate, from whom do they receive it? In the parlance of PKI, an issuing server is called a Certificate Authority. The CA can belong to some external entity, such as VeriSign or Thawte. Our complete PKI can consist of obtaining keys from these organizations and insisting that they be used in our enterprise. We could also hire some other company to set up and maintain our PKI for us. Or, using Microsoft Certificate Services, we could do that for ourselves.

NOTE

Hash: It Is Not Your Mothers Roast Beef When you install Certificate Services, you can choose the hash algorithm to be used. The selection of available algorithms varies depending on the cryptographic service provider (CSP) that you select. Although all the hash algorithms are considered safe and appropriate, you may need to match the hash algorithm with the one used by some third-party CA with which you want to interoperate.

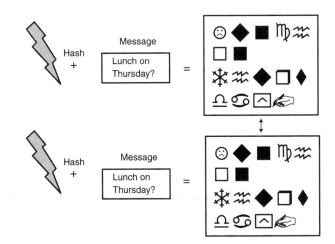

FIGURE 11.3
One-way hash algorithm.

The CA will issue our users certificates and private keys. The CA also has a certificate, a server certificate, which can be used to authenticate the server. Now you can establish that the server you are talking to is the server you think it is.

In deciding which way to go, you should be aware that the owner of the CA controls the polices used by the CA. No one standard is used. Public CAs, of course, rely on your trust for their existence, and so follow a set, published standard for the issuance of certificates, as well as their expiration or revocation. If you install Certificate Services, you need to implement a policy to be used internally. If you want to create a structure to be used by partners, or trusted by others, you may need to modify that policy accordingly. If you are setting up an e-commerce Web site, you might want to invest in a server certificate from one of the trusted CAs on the Internet.

Just as certificates are issued according to some policy, certificates are given a lifetime. Usually there is provision for renewal, but also for expiration. To assist users of certificates in identifying valid certificates, the CA publishes a CRL. You can search this list to determine whether a certificate has been revoked.

A CSP is the actual code used to encrypt, decrypt, encode, and perform authentication. A CA requires a CSP to function. Although Microsoft Windows 2000 provides a default, the Microsoft Base Cryptographic Provider v 1.0, you may require or desire a third-party CSP to allow Microsoft Certificate Services to function with third-party PKI-enabled applications or hardware. You must select the CSP provided by Gemplus or Schlumberger, for example, if you want to enable smart card services using their smart cards and readers.

The CSP creates and destroys keys, and uses the keys to perform operations (encrypt, decrypt). Third-party CSPs may implement the CryptoAPI in different ways. They may use different strength encryption algorithms or provide interfaces for hardware such as smart cards.

Other available CSPs include the following:

◆ Gemplus GemSAFE Card CSP v1.0

◆ Microsoft Base DSS Cryptographic Provider

◆ Schlumberger Cryptographic Service Provider

CryptoAPI is Microsoft's application programming interface that provides functions for encryption, descriptions, and digital signing. A programmer can use these functions to implement a specific CSP that has been written to the CryptoAPI. The CSP does the actual encryption. Another name for CryptoAPI is CAPI.

Certificate trust lists (CTLs) are used to establish trust between your organization and another. If a CA that you trust trusts their root, this may not be necessary. If their root is a self-signed root (as is your enterprise root CA), however, you can use a trust list to identify for which purposes you will trust certificates signed by this foreign CA.

A certificate is just a data structure that contains information necessary for the operation for which it is a certificate. A user certificate has a copy of the user's public key, for example, a certificate serial number, the user's name, a list of uses for which the certificate is intended, and other identifying information. A server certificate includes a list of uses for which the certificate is intended, the name of the CA to whom the certificate was issued, by whom the certificate was issued, valid dates, certificate version, serial number, signature algorithm, issuer, valid from, valid to, the public key, CA version, CRL distribution point, and other information (see Figure 11.4).

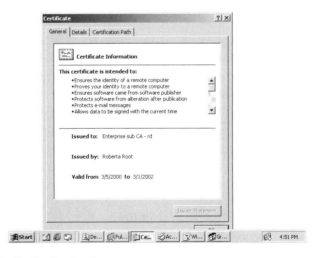

FIGURE 11.4
Viewing a certificate.

Windows 2000 PKI

The Windows 2000 PKI is composed of the following:

- ◆ Active Directory
- ◆ Certificate Services
- ◆ PKI-enabled applications

Active Directory is used to publish certificates and CRLs. Certificates and CRLs can also be published on Web pages, smart cards, disks, and compact discs.

Certificate Services provides the tools that enable your organization to create, manage, and use their own CAs, as well as to issue digital certificates.

PKI-enabled applications use your PKI for encryption and authentication. Windows 2000 provides the following PKI-enabled applications:

- ◆ Encrypting Files System
- ◆ Smart Card Services
- ◆ Internet Explorer
- ◆ IPSec
- ◆ Internet Information Server

Other PKI-enabled Microsoft applications include the following:

- ◆ Microsoft Money
- ◆ Microsoft Outlook
- ◆ Microsoft Outlook Express

Of course, many third-party applications are PKI enabled. You should check for their compatibility with Microsoft PKI, however, before making them part of your security design.

Protocols

Microsoft PKI components were developed to use industry-standard encryption technologies and can utilize SSL for secure Internet communications. SSL can be used to authenticate clients and servers; it is used most currently to authenticate the Internet Information Server as part of secure e-commerce transactions. Windows 2000 PKI can also implement IPSec for secure data communications at the IP layer; this can be used by applications that do not utilize SSL.

Current Uses for Windows 2000 PKI

Certificates are used in Windows 2000 for the following purposes:

◆ Server authentication (e-commerce)

◆ Client authentication (remote access, smart card)

◆ Encrypting File System

◆ IPSec (network traffic encryption)

◆ Code signing (active content)

◆ Secure email

CERTIFICATE SERVER ROLES

Identify certificate server roles.

When you install Certificate Services on a Windows 2000 computer, you create a certificate server. During the installation process, you are asked to choose a role for this CA (see Figure 11.5):

◆ **Enterprise root CA**—Most trusted CA in enterprise; requires Active Directory.

◆ **Enterprise subordinate CA**—Issues certificates and obtains certificate from another enterprise CA.

◆ **Standalone root CA**—Most trusted CA in hierarchy; doesn't require Active Directory.

◆ **Standalone subordinate CA**—Issues certificates and obtains certificate from another CA.

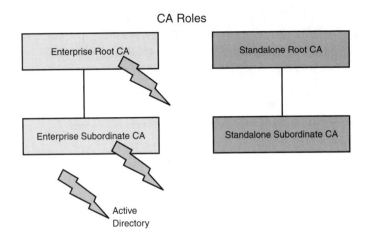

CA Roles

FIGURE 11.5
Certificate Authority roles.

All CAs have CA certificates. The difference is this: The root CA does not require a certificate issued by some other CA. Its certificate is self-signed. As you can see, the enterprise CA roles are linked to Active Directory.

Root CA

Any root is the most trusted CA in an organization's PKI. You want to plan and provide extra security for this server. This CA issues server certificates for all other CAs in your enterprise. Typically, the root CA is often kept offline where it cannot be easily compromised. The enterprise root CA at Microsoft, for example, is kept offline and in a biometrically protected vault.

The root CA issues a certificate for subordinate CAs. These subordinate CAs may be permitted to issue certificates that create other CAs, and/or they may be used to issue certificates to users of your organization's information systems. A root CA and its subordinate CAs create the organizations certification hierarchy.

If a root CA were to be compromised, certificates could be issued and used to establish subordinate CAs that could then issue certificates that would be entirely useful in your organization. All your certificate-based authentication would be suspect.

In the Microsoft Certificate Services world, there are two types of root CAs; the enterprise root CA and the standalone root CA. The major difference is that the enterprise root CA requires Active Directory, and the standalone root CA does not. Unless the right to install an enterprise CA has been delegated, only an enterprise administrator can install enterprise CAs. Another difference is that the maximum length of the CA certificate lifetime is longer for a standalone root CA.

The enterprise root CA uses Active Directory to validate requestor's permission to obtain the type of certificate requested. Large number of users can be granted certificates without administrative intervention.

A standalone root CA does not require Active Directory and may or may not be a member of a domain. Administrators must validate certificate requests. For extra security, disconnect it from the network and place it in a secure area.

Subordinate CA

A subordinate CA is one that has obtained a certificate signed by the root CA in your organization. This CA is used to directly issue certificates to users of the system, or to additional subordinate CAs. It may be a general purpose CA that issues several types of certificates, or it may be dedicated to a particular type. Separate CAs for issuing smart card certificates, or for issuing certificates for business-partner employees, are often established. These CAs can also issue server certificates to other subordinate CAs, thus further extending the certification hierarchy (see Figure 11.6).

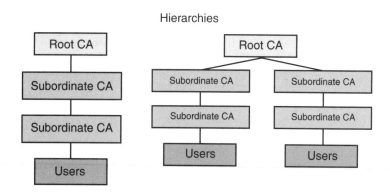

FIGURE 11.6
CA hierarchy.

Microsoft Certificate Services allows two types of subordinate CAs: enterprise CAs, which require Active Directory, and subordinate CAs, which do not.

A standalone subordinate CA can operate within a CA trust hierarchy or as a solitary certificate server. Standalone subordinate CAs are used to issue certificates to users outside your organization.

Installation Requirements

To install an enterprise root CA or an enterprise subordinate CA, the following conditions must be met:

- ◆ You must be a member of Enterprise Admins.

- ◆ Windows 2000 DNS must be available.

- ◆ Active Directory must be available.

- ◆ You must have privileges on DNS, Active Directory, and CA servers.

- ◆ To publish certificates in AD for other domains, the server you install the CA on must be a member of the Cert Publishers group.

To install a standalone root or a standalone subordinate server, you must be an administrator on the server to which you want to install the CA.

INSTALLING CERTIFICATE SERVICES

Certificate Services comes with Windows 2000 Server and Advanced Server. It is not installed by default. You may select it as an option during installation, or you may install it afterward.

To install Certificate Services and begin implementation of your PKI, complete the following steps to install an enterprise root CA (Step by Step 11.1) and an enterprise subordinate CA (Step by Step 11.2). Tables following these procedures provide more information about some of the choices that you have.

NOTE

What's in a Name?   Many reasons exist for changing a server name, but just as many reasons exist not to. Early installers of Exchange Server found out that although you could physically change the name of the computer, you could not do so and hope to retain the Exchange Server. Windows 2000 prevents you from changing the name of the server, and from adding to or removing from a domain, after the installation of Certificate Services.

Name your computer and establish its domain status *before* you install Certificate Services.

STEP BY STEP

11.1 Installing the Root CA

1. Log on as an enterprise administrator.

2. Open Control Panel, Add/Remove Programs.

3. Click Add/Remove Windows Components.

4. Click the Components button.

5. Click the box next to Certificate Services.

6. Click Yes when reminded that you cannot change the computer name after the installation of Certificate Services.

7. Click Next.

8. Select Enterprise Root CA.

9. Click Advanced Options to note the cryptographic service providers and the settings to be used in generating key pairs (see Tables 11.1 and 11.2). Accept the defaults and click Next.

10. Enter Identifying Information. CA name, Country/Region, and Valid for are required (see Table 11.2).

11. Click Next.

12. In the Data Storage Location dialog box, you can specify the location for databases and logs or accept the default. In this case, accept the default.

13. Click Next.

14. If asked whether it is okay to stop IIS services, click OK.

15. Insert the Windows 2000 Server (or Advanced Server) CD-ROM when asked or point to another location for the installation files.

16. Click Finish.

DEFAULT AVAILABLE CRYPTOGRAPHIC SERVICE PROVIDERS

Cryptographic Service Providers	Hash Algorithms Available
Microsoft Base Cryptographic Provider	MD4, MD5, SHA-1
Microsoft Base DSS Cryptographic Provider	SHA-1
Gemplus GemSAFE Card CSP v 1.0	All the above as well as the following
Schlumberger Cryptographic Service Provider	All the above as well as SSL3 SHAMD5

Table 11.2 shows your installation choices.

CERTIFICATE SERVER INSTALLATION OPTIONS

Option	Description	Notes
CA Type	Enterprise root CA, enterprise subordinate CA, standalone root CA, standalone subordinate root CA.	See the previous section "CA Roles."
Advanced Options	Cryptographic Service Provider.	Microsoft provides a default, the Microsoft Base Cryptographic Provider; this is the code that performs the authentication and encryption. See the previous section "Basic Definitions."

continues

TABLE 11.2 *continued*

CERTIFICATE SERVER INSTALLATION OPTIONS

Option	Description	Notes
	Hash Algorithm. (Default is SHA-1, others are MD4 and MD5, and SSL3 SHAMD5.)	The availability of hash algorithms depends on the CSP selected.
	Key Length (Default is 512 bit for Microsoft Base Cryptographic Providers. 1024 is available and recommended for a root CA; also available are 2048 and 4096.)	You cannot change the key size if you check Use Existing Keys.
	Use Existing Keys (You select this option if you are relocating, restoring a previous CA.)	Check Use the Associated Certificate to ensure a certificate identical to the preceding one.
Name	Up to 64 characters to identify the CA in Active Directory.	
Organization	Enter the name of the organization that owns the CA.	
Organizational Unit	Indicate the name of the organizational unit within which the CA resides.	
City, State, Province	Enter the name of the city, state, or province.	
Country/region code	Required by X.500	Use the drop-down box to select the code. United States is US; Canada is CA.
E-mail	Enter the email address of the CA administrator or an individual designated to handle email about the CA.	

Option	Description	Notes
Valid for	The time this CA is valid.	Settable only in root CA.
Data Storage Location	Local storage area must be specified.	Default location is \<systemroot\>\ system32\CertLog for both the configuration data and the log.
		You may specify a shared folder; by default, this is \<systemroot\> \CAConfig.

After installation, you can manage the CA from the Certificate Authority console.

An additional component, the Certificate Services Web Enrollment Support, is added. These are Web pages that can be used to request certificates. Locate them at `http://name of CA server/certsrv`.

A Certification hierarchy is created by installing subordinate CAs. During installation, you must obtain a certificate for this CA. (The root CA creates its own certificate; it is, in essence, self-signed.) The parent CA can be either online (Step by Step 11.2) or offline (Step by Step 11.3). The process varies a little and so is described here in two separate step by steps.

STEP BY STEP

11.2 Installing a Subordinate CA (Enterprise Root CA Online)

1. Log on as an enterprise administrator.

2. Open Control Panel, Add/Remove Programs.

3. Click Add/Remove Windows Components.

4. Click the Components button.

5. Click the box next to Certificate Services.

continues

continued

6. Click Yes when reminded that you cannot change the computer name after the installation of Certificate Services.

7. Click Next.

8. Select Enterprise Subordinate CA.

9. Enter Identifying Information. Note that "Valid for" says "Determined by Parent CA." The life of a subordinate CA cannot be longer than the life of its parent.

10. Click Next.

11. In the Data Storage Location dialog box, specify a location for database and logs or accept the default. Accept the default.

12. Click Next.

13. On the Certificate Request page, click the Browse button and select the previously installed enterprise root CA (see Figure 11.7).

14. Click OK, and then click Next.

15. If asked whether it is okay to stop IIS services, click OK.

16. Insert the Windows 2000 Server (or Advanced Server) CD-ROM when asked, or point to another location for the installation files.

17. Click Finish.

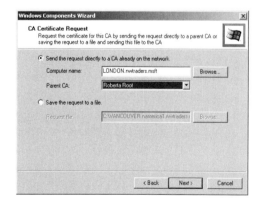

FIGURE 11.7
You must identify where to get the subordinate CA certificate.

STEP BY STEP

11.3 Install a Subordinate CA (Enterprise Root CA Offline)

1. Log on as an enterprise administrator.

2. Open Control Panel, Add/Remove Programs.

3. Click Add/Remove Windows Components.

4. Click the Components button.

5. Click the box next to Certificate Services.

6. Click Yes when reminded that you cannot change the computer name after the installation of Certificate Services.

7. Click Next.

8. Select Enterprise Subordinate CA.

9. Enter Identifying Information. Note that "Valid for" says "Determined by Parent CA." The life of a subordinate CA cannot be longer than the life of its parent.

10. Click Next.

11. In the Data Storage Location dialog box, specify location for database and logs or accept the default. Accept the default.

12. Click Next.

13. Select Save the request to a file. (The file is saved with an .req extension.)

14. If asked whether it is okay to stop IIS services, click OK.

15. Insert the Windows 2000 Server (or Advanced Server) CD-ROM when asked, or point to another location for the installation files.

16. Click Finish.

17. Use the saved request file to request a subordinate CA certificate from the enterprise root CA (see Step by Step 11.4).

18. Install the provided certificate on the subordinate CA (see Step-by step 11.5).

STEP BY STEP

11.4 Request a Subordinate CA Certificate

1. Open Internet Explorer.

2. Enter the address `http://name of server/certsrv`.

continues

continued

3. Enter the account name and password if requested.

4. Select Request a Certificate and click Next.

5. Select Advanced Request and click Next.

6. Select Submit a certificate request using a Base64 encoded PKCS#10 file or renewal request using a Base64 encoded PCCS#7 file. Then click Next.

7. Open the file created previously (titled *fully qualified domain name of server_name of CA*.req) in Notepad, and select the content and copy to the Clipboard.

8. Paste the contents into the window provided by the wizard (see Figure 11.8).

9. Use the drop-down box under Certificate Template to select Subordinate Certificate Authority.

10. Click Submit.

11. On the Certificate Issued page, click Download CA Certificate.

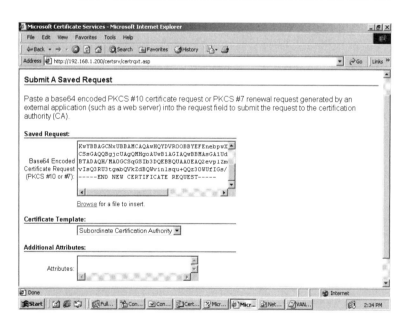

FIGURE 11.8
Paste the certificate file contents into the window.

12. Choose Save This File to Disk. The file is called certnew.cer by default.

13. Save the file to a floppy disk.

14. Close Internet Explorer.

STEP BY STEP

11.5 Install a Subordinate CA Certificate

1. Open the Certificate Authority console on the subordinate CA server. Note that the CA icon has a red mark on it to show that it is not valid.

2. Right-click the CA icon in the tree and select All Tasks\Install CA Certificate.

3. Load the floppy disk with the required certificate file and navigate to this file. Double-click the file.

4. The system loads the file, starts Certificate Services, and places a green check mark on the CA icon.

CONFIGURING A CA

After the CA has been installed, what are your options? There are settable properties, policies, and other items with which you can work. You may want to do the following:

◆ CA backup and restore.

◆ Specify location where a CRL and a certificate for this CA can be located (see Figure 11.9).

◆ Add and remove exit module.

◆ Determine where certificates are published (Active Directory or file system).

FIGURE 11.9
Specify CRL and certificate location.

◆ Set permissions (Enroll, Manage, Read).

◆ Configure Policy Settings.

To configure the CA, open the Certificate Authority console and right-click on the CA. Choose Properties.

You can configure the location of the CRL if you need additional locations. By default there is a file at `http://name of server/name of ca.crl`. You can add other locations.

Policy Settings specify existing certificate types that can be issued and for what they can be used. An existing policy can be deleted, and new policies can be added. You might not want a particular CA to be allowed to issue subordinate certification authority, for example, so you could remove this policy. Or you might want to implement IPSec, Smart Card Services, create enrollment agents, Exchange Users, and so on. To add these policies, you must expand the CA tree and select New after right-clicking on the Policy Setting folder. Then select them from the Select Certificate Template dialog box. Table 11.3 outlines policies and their certificates.

TABLE 11.3

**DEFAULT CA POLICIES DESCRIBE AVAILABLE
CERTIFICATE TEMPLATES USES**

Policy	*Certificate Purpose(s)*
EFS recovery agent	File recovery
Basic EFS	Encrypting File System
Domain controller	Client and server authentication
Web server	Server Authentication
Computer	Client and server authentication
User	EFS, secure email, client authentication
Subordinate certification authority	All
Administrator	Code signing, Microsoft trust list signing, EFS, secure email, client authentication

Backing Up and Restoring the CA

Microsoft recommends using Microsoft Backup to back up the entire server on which the CA resides. The CA is backed up as part of the System State option. You can, of course, only back up the CA from within the Certification Authority console, but you must remember to also back up the IIS metabase.

CERTIFICATE AUTHORITY HIERARCHIES

Design Certificate Authority (CA) hierarchies.

Certificate Authority hierarchies consist of a self-signed root CA and multiple subordinate CAs. The subordinate CAs have a certificate issued by the root, and trust is then inherited from the root.

EXAM TIP

Just How Important Is IIS?   If you restore the CA to a server whose IIS metabase has been damaged or lost, the IIS will fail to start and therefore Certificate Services will fail to start! Always make sure you are backing up the IIS metabase. This is another reason why Microsoft recommends backing up the entire server, not just the CA.

Hierarchies are thought to provide better security and improved scalability. They certainly provide a flexible administration support model. Commercial CAs Thawte, GTE, VeriSign, and others support this model. The following PKI-enabled applications support this model:

◆ Internet Information Server

◆ Netscape

◆ IE

◆ Apache

CA security is important; in the hierarchical model, however, the security of some roles is more important than others. The root CA needs to be highly secure, and access to it can be limited to provide this most trusted element the most security. Intermediate CAs, those directly below the root CA in the hierarchy and used to issue server certificates to those below, can be kept more secure, less available; whereas with each successive distance from the root, subordinate CAs can be more accessible. Indeed, it is these CAs that issue end-entity or user and non-CA server certificates.

Designing a hierarchy consists of determining the best depth and breadth that will maintain security and yet not interfere with productivity and performance. Depth involves distance from the root CA, whereas breadth allows different CAs to be used for different purposes—issuing smart card certificates rather than certificates for email, for example.

According to Microsoft, a depth of 3–4 CAs allows the best operations and security compromise (see Figure 11.10). With this level of CAs, you can place the first and second tiers offline for security purposes. A shorter hierarchy decreases security and can provide operational problems because the secured, offline root must frequently be accessed. A deeper hierarchy produces little benefit.

Hierarchy breadth can allow the implementation of technology domains (application-specific CAs, as previously mentioned) or increase your CA capacity (see Figure 11.11). It can also model your organizational structure, by providing separate CAs for geographical or other divisional lines. Organizational model, geography, and enrollment policies, and enrollment availability may also influence this part of the hierarchy.

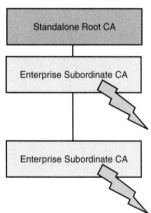

3-Tier CA Hierarchy

Standalone Root CA

Enterprise Subordinate CA

Enterprise Subordinate CA

FIGURE 11.10
A three-tier CA hierarchy.

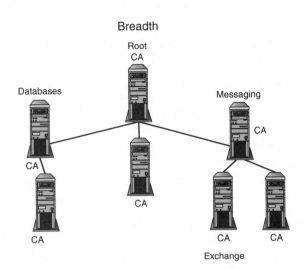

Breadth

FIGURE 11.11
Hierarchy breadth allows implementation of technology domains or follows organization structure.

Enrollment availability may not be an issue because enrollment/renewal is infrequent, often every 6 to 12 months. Multiple CAs can increase the availability if necessary. CAs do not share keys. They obtain their trust from the root CA. Multiple CAs can also protect distant locations from network outages.

Updating the CRL may cause a problem, as if there were no valid CRL. Any revocation check will fail. You may want to publish the CRL frequently, to allow more downtime if problems occur. CRL distribution can fail for two reasons: If the network link is down, it cannot be distributed; if the CA goes down, the CRL is not updated. No certificate can be used if the CRL in unavailable because its validity cannot be checked.

Policy and Performance—Getting the Right Information Down

When designing your CA hierarchy, you should also design a certificate policy. This policy would include the specifications that tell you what the finished design is expected to handle.

You should understand, for example, the number and type of users that will be using Certificate Services. Are they all just requiring certificates for smart cards? Are certificates for EFS centrally managed? Are special applications required? Which ones? Are you expected to integrate with third-party CAs? Which CAs? For what? Will partners require access to your organization's resources? Does it make sense to issue them certificates from your CA, or to import their PKI certificates and map them to user IDs in Active Directory?

What risks are involved in these operations?

What is the required certificate lifetime? What is the revocation latency—how long before a certificate is revoked, is it in the CRL available to all clients and applications in the enterprise? Revocation latency is based on the interaction between the time required for forest replication and the time set for CRL publication. Changing the CRL publication period can impact revocation latency.

How will users register? Usually this is the domain administrator's responsibility because then one authority manages domain and PKI naming. Will users visit an enrollment agent, or request certificates through the wizard or through Web pages? What sort of a demand will either option place on resources? What extra security may be required on Web site locations where users may request certificates and CRLs?

Which users can register? For what type of certificate?

How long is the certificate lifetime? Default CA policy prescribes the CA certificate issuance to be for one year. This is adjustable via the registry. Default CA policy prescribes a certificate template setting of one year. This is not configurable.

Testing

All the previous factors can influence the demand placed on the CAs and prove the hierarchy lacking or sufficient to handle the load. You will want to test your model to prove both functionality (does it work under a load) and usability (does the model work for security and convenience as well as performance).

Your design should be created early enough to allow time to plan for the necessary resources and for testing. The design should be lab tested and in a pilot program before being deployed in production.

You should test the following:

◆ CA backup and restore.

◆ Renewal of the CA (down to a hardware rebuild).

◆ Enrollment and revocation procedures.

◆ Applications.

◆ Interoperability with third-party PKIs.

◆ Set short certificate lifetimes in the pilot so that you can test what happens when certificates need to be renewed.

◆ Pad the CRL to expected size (10% of population; Microsoft suggests 90% of certificates will not be revoked).

◆ Test across a forest.

◆ Check distant network locations for loss of service.

CERTIFICATE LIFECYCLE—MANAGING CERTIFICATES

Certificates do not last forever. Each issued certificate has a lifetime. Although most certificates are renewable, nonrenewed certificates expire. The certificate lifecycle identifies what happens to a certificate from creation to expiration and the modules of the CA involved at each point (see Figure 11.12).

A certificate's lifecycle has the following stages:

◆ CA is installed and CA certificates issued.

◆ CA issues server, user, and other certificates.

◆ If necessary, certificates are revoked.

◆ Certificates are renewed or expire.

◆ A CRL is published.

◆ CA's certificate is renewed before it expires.

◆ CA is revoked or is retired.

From the client perspective, enrollment (or the process of obtaining a certificate) begins when a user requests a certificate using the Certificate Request Wizard (if requesting a certificate from an enterprise CA) or the certificate server Web pages (if requesting a certificate from an enterprise CA or a standalone CA). The type of

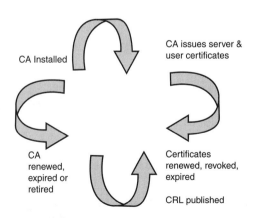

FIGURE 11.12
The certificate lifecycle.

certificate requested determines the template used. Templates available are listed in the CA Policy Settings folder. Certificates available from an enterprise CA include the following:

- **Administrator**—Used to authenticate clients and EFS, secure mail, CTL signing, and code signing.

- **Authenticated Session**—Used to authenticate clients (users or computers).

- **Basic EFS**—Used for EFS operations.

- **CEP Encryption (offline)**—Used to Enroll Cisco Systems routers for IPSec. If a certificate is not issued for the router, and they are not enrolled, any IPSec transaction that includes the router's interaction cannot proceed.

- **Code Signing**—Used for code-signing operations. Code signing is the process in which a private key is used to "sign" the code. A public key can be used to verify.

- **Computer**—Used to Authenticate client computers and servers.

- **Domain Controller**—Used to Authenticate domain controller.

- **EFS Recovery Agent**—Used in EFS recovery operations.

- **Enrollment Agent**—Used to authenticate administrators who request certificates on behalf of other computers.

- **Exchange eEnrollment Agent (offline)**—Used to Authenticate Microsoft Exchange administrators.

- **Exchange Signature Only (offline)**—Used by Exchange Server for client authentication and secure mail signing.

- **Exchange user (offline)**— Used to authenticate clients and secure mail.

- **IPSec**—Used for IPSec authentication.

- **IPSec (offline)**—Used for IPSec authentication.

- **Root Certification Authority**—Used in Root CA installation operations (cannot be issued from a CA).

- **Router (offline)**—Used to Authenticate a router. (If the router doesn't have a certificate, and it is required that it be authenticated, it will not be able to.)

◆ **Smart Card Logon**—Used to authenticate clients, secure mail, logging on.

◆ **Subordinate CA (offline)**—Used to issue certificates for subordinate CAs.

◆ **Trust List Signing**—Used to sign CTLs.

◆ **User**—Used to authenticate clients, EFS, secure mail.

◆ **User Signature Only**—Used to authenticate client and secure mail signing only.

◆ **Web Server (offline)**—Used to authenticate Web server.

The types of certificates actually issued by the enterprise CA are specified in the enterprise CA's certificate-issuing policy. Standalone CAs do not use certificate templates.

You start the Certificate Request Wizard from the Certificates snap-in module by right-clicking the store name—Personal, for example, to request a personal user certificate (see Figure 11.13).

Web-based enrollment pages are located at http://<server name>/certsrv.

Enterprise CAs use information in Active Directory to authenticate the requestor and determine other certificate information.

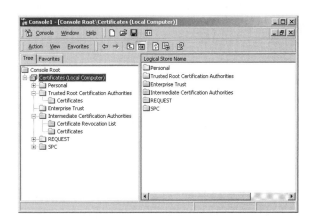

FIGURE 11.13
Logical certificate stores.

Manage certificates.

Much of the certificate lifecycle is self-managed. Enterprise CAs issue certificates automatically, expired certificates pass out of existence, revoked certificates are placed on a CRL, and the CRL is periodically published. Other processes can be completed manually. Some of these processes include the Web interfaces for requests, accepting requests (requests made to standalone CAs must be approved by an administrator), revoking certificates, manually issuing a CRL, and so on.

The administrator must automate some enrollment processes in Public Key Policies. Computers associated with a Group Policy automatically receive computer-related certificates when they next log on.

To automate the issuance of computer certificates (to be used to authenticate the computer), complete Step by Step 11.6.

STEP BY STEP

11.6 Create Public Key Group Policy

1. Open Active Directory, Users and Computers.

2. Right-click on the OU in which to create the policy.

3. Click Properties.

4. Click Group Policy.

5. Click New (or open an existing policy).

6. Navigate to Windows Settings\Security Settings\Public Key Policies.

7. Right-click on Automatic Certificate Request Settings and select New\Automatic Certificate Request.

8. Click Next.

9. Select Computer from the list of templates provided.

10. Select the CA that should issue the certificate.

11. Click Finish.

Requests for certificates that are not automatically issued can be found in the Pending Requests Folder of the Certification Authority console. Certificate requests can be removed, issued, or denied through the Web interface or through the Certification Authority console.

To check on a pending certificate, complete the procedure in Step by Step 11.7.

STEP BY STEP

11.7 Look for Pending Requests

1. Open the Certification Authority console.

2. Expand the tree.

3. Open the Pending Requests folder and look for the certificate. (You can filter the list by any valid certificate field or type.)

4. If the certificate request is not in this folder, check the Issued Certificate folder and the Revoked Certificates folder.

Issued certificates are stored in certificate stores. Stores are of two types: physical and logical. Physical stores represent the actual physical location (either in the system registry of the computer or in Active Directory). (For increased security, the certificates may be stored on a smart card.) Logical stores are used to group certificates in functional categories and contain pointers to the physical stores.

You can use the Certificates console to manage the certificates in the certificate stores. Open the Certificates console to view the certificate stores.

When viewing the certificate store, you will find certificates of many kinds in addition to those requested from the Microsoft Certificate Services CA (see Table 11.4). Double-clicking any certificate exposes its properties.

TABLE 11.4		
LOGICAL CERTIFICATE STORES		
Logical Store	*Purpose*	*Notes*
Active Directory User Object	Certificates published in Active Directory for this user	Only shown in console for user.
Enterprise Trust	Certificate Trust Lists	If a certificate has a path to a CTL. it is trusted by the computer as specified in the CTL.
Intermediate Certification Authorities	Certificates for CAs that are not trusted roots	Subordinate CAs.
Personal	Individual certificates	Your user certificate.
Request	Pending or rejected requests	
SPC	Certificates of software publishers trusted by this computer	Software is downloaded without prompting. By default empty.
Trusted Root Certification Authorities	Certificates for root CAs	If a certificate has a certification path to a root CA here, it is trusted.

Administrators can use the Certificates console to issue, revoke, publish a CRL, and export and import certificates. They can manage their own certificates or those for other users.

Revoked certificates are published on a CRL. This list is published automatically, but may be manually published as well (see Step by Step 11.8).

STEP BY STEP

11.8 Manually Publishing a CRL

1. Open the Certification Authority from Administrative Tools.

2. Click Revoked Certificates in the console tree.

3. Right-click and then click All Tasks, Publish.

4. Click Yes when asked whether you want to overwrite previous CRL.

5. The CRL is published to Active Directory and/or <system root>\system32\CertSrv\CertEnroll\.

Normally certificates expire at a predetermined date, if they are not renewed. However, there may be a reason for revoking a certificate. Someone leaves the company, for example, or is transferred to another section for which the certificate is no longer any good. Certificates should also be revoked if there is reason to believe that the key has been compromised, or some other security issue has occurred which makes it suspect.

> **EXAM TIP**
>
> **Is My CRL Out-Of-Date?** Yes! If the client has a cached copy of the CRL that hasn't expired, and a new CRL has been issued, the client CRL is out-of-date.

Certificates are revoked from the CA. When you right-click on the certificate and select All Tasks, Revoke Certificate, you have the opportunity to enter a reason code:

◆ Unspecified

◆ Key Compromise

◆ CA Compromise

◆ Change of Affiliation

◆ Suspended

◆ Cease of Operation

◆ Certificate Hold

Certificates identified as Certificate Hold can be unrevoked, left until they expire, or have their reason code changed. Revoked certificates appear on the next CRL.

Certificates can be imported and exported in a number of formats (see Table 11.5). You may want to do so to move certificates to smart cards, other computers, or obtain a copy of the CA certificate so that you can install a subordinate certificate. When you export a certificate using PKCS #12, the private key associated with the certificate is only exportable under the following conditions:

◆ The certificate is for EFS or EFS recovery.

◆ The certificate was requested using the Advanced Certificate Request Web page and Mark keys as exportable was selected.

TABLE 11.5

CERTIFICATE EXPORT AND IMPORT FORMATS

Format	Description
Personal Information Exchange (PKCS#12)	Transfer of keys from one computer to another, or from a computer to removable media
Cryptographic Message Syntax Standard (PKCS#7)	Transfer of certificate and all certificates in its path: computer to computer, or computer to removable media.
DER-Encoded Binary X.509	Interoperability with non-Windows 2000 CAs (uses the .cer extension)
Base64-Encoded X.509	Interoperability with non-Windows 2000 CAs (uses the .cer extension)

Adding a Certificate Template

To add functionality to the Windows 2000 PKI, you may need to add a new certificate template as part the process. To add IPSec functionality to your Windows 2000 computer, for example, you must enable CAs to issue IPSec certificates (see Step by Step 11.9).

STEP BY STEP

11.9 Adding IPSec Certificate Templates and Enabling CAs for IPSec

1. Expand the server CA in the Certificate Authority console.

2. Right-click Policy Settings and point to New.

3. Click Certificates to Issue.

4. Click IPSec in the Select Certificates Template dialog box.

5. Open an MMC console and add the Certificates snap-in.

6. When asked which type to manage, select Computer Account and click Next.

7. Select Local Computer in the Select Computer dialog box, and then click Finish.

8. Verify that the root certificate is present in the Local Computer/Trusted Root Certificate Authorities folder.

9. Verify that the root certificate is present in the Local Computer/Personal folder.

10. Right-click on this folder and select All Tasks, Request New Certificate.

11. Click Next in the wizard.

12. On the Certificate Template page, select IPSec, select Advanced Options, and then click Next.

13. On the Cryptographic Service Provider page, click Next.

14. On the Certification Authority page, browse and click the server CA for your server. Click Next.

15. In the Friendly name box of the Certificate Friendly Name and Description page, type **IPSec Certificate**. In the Description field, type **Domain controller certificate for IPSec**, and then click Next.

16. Click Finish, and then click OK.

Command-Line Functions

Three command-line functions exist to assist you in administering Certificate Services. These tools extend the functions and enable closer control of a CA than the graphical interface does. These command-line functions are as follows:

- ◆ CertUtil
- ◆ CertReq
- ◆ CertSrv

CertUtil

CertUtil offers a number of functions useful in managing, upgrading, and diagnosing a CA. Caution needs to be used with these commands. Only experienced programmers or administrators should have access. The primary syntax is as follows:

```
Certutil [options] [switch]
```

Table 11.6 shows a partial list of other syntax.

TABLE 11.6

CERTUTIL SYNTAX

Syntax	Action
Certutil -?	Display command options.
Certutil –decode infile outfile	Decodes Base64-encoded file and writes result to outfile.
Certutil –decodehex infile outfile	Decodes hexadecimal-encoded file specified by infile and dumps to outfile.
Certutil –dump	Dumps the CA's configuration information.
Certutil –encode infile outfile	Encodes the infile to Base64 and writes result to outfile.
Certutil –error errorcode	Displays error message text for the error code.
Certutil –getconfig	Gets default configuration string and displays it.
Certutil –store certificate storename	Displays certificates in the Local Machine certificate store. If the store isn't named, the CA store is used.
Certutil –verify certificate [cacertfile]	Verifies the certificate was issued using the CA certificate specified by CAcertfile. If CAcertfile is not specified, the certification path is constructed using certificates installed on the computer, and all of them are verified to see whether they have been revoked.
Certutil –verifykeys keycontainername CACertfile	Verifies public/private key set in the key container.
Certutil –verifystore Certificatestorename [certindex]	Like –store, but verifies associated private keys if they exist, and builds a chain from the installed CA and root certificates and verifies all certificates in the chain.
Certutil – ConvertMDB	Used on a Certificate Server 1.0 as well as on Windows NT Server 4.0 that has been upgraded to Windows 2000 with Windows 2000 Certificate Services. This command converts the old database records to the current database.

CertReq

You can use CertReq to request certificates from the command prompt (see Table 11.7). The syntax is as follows:

```
CertReq [-rpc][-binary][-config] configstring][-attrib
attributestring] [requestfile[certfile[certcahifile]]]
Certreq -retrieve [-rpc][-binary][-config
configstring][requested][certfile[certchainfile]]]
Certreq -?
```

TABLE 11.7

CERTREQ COMMAND OPTIONS

Option	Description
-attrib	Attribute name, value string pairs.
-binary	Output files in binary format rather than Base64 encoded.
-config configstring	Server\CA configuration string. To obtain the default, use a single dash (-) as the configstring.
-rpc	Use RPC server connection rather than DCOM.
-retrieve	If the certificate is not issued automatically, a requestedid is returned to the requestor. Use certreq -retrieve to obtain the certificate after it has been issued.
-?	Show help
RequestFile	Base64 encoded or binary input filename. Can be PKCS #10, PKCS #7, or KeyGen tag format.
Certfile	Base64-encoded, X-509 output filename
CertCahinFile	Base64-encoded, PKCS #7 output filename
ConfigString	Server name and CA name separated by a backslash.
AttributeString	Name and value string pairs separated by a colon. Separate pairs by a \n.
	Example: Name1: Value\n Name2: Value\n

CertServ

CertServ.exe starts Certificate Services as a standalone application rather than a Windows 2000 service. You must stop the Certificate Services before you run CertServ. This is diagnostics mode and should only be used as such.

Diagnostic Aids for Troubleshooting Certificate Services

Several tools may assist you in diagnosing Certificate Services issues. Table 11.8 lists them.

TABLE 11.8

TROUBLESHOOTING TIPS

Tip	Description
Diagnostics mode	To run in diagnostics mode, first stop Certificate Services. Then type `Certsrv -z` at the command line. This starts the CA as a standalone application rather than a Windows 2000 service. A log of actions displays in the console window.
Help	Look for troubleshooting tips by going to Troubleshooting after searching on Certificate Services in Help.
Check authentication methods	If you are using Web pages to request certificates, and the Web server is not located on the same computer as the CA, you need to select Basic Authentication and protect these pages using SSL.
Confirm the validity of the certificate	Open the Certificates snap-in and double-click on the certificate. Check to see whether the certificate has expired, was issued by a non-trusted CA, or has been revoked.

MAPPING CERTIFICATES

Map certificates.

To allow users who are not members of your company access to your resources, you may have decided on a PKI. To allow users who do not have an account in Active Directory to authenticate, the following must be true:

- ◆ The user needs a certificate.
- ◆ You have created a user account for use by this user or many external users.

◆ The certificate must be issued by a CA listed in the CTL for the site, domain, or OU in which the user account is created.

◆ You must map the external user certificate to the Active Directory account (see Step by Step 11.10).

A Certificate Authority Trust can be established by your internal Windows 2000 enterprise root CA. Windows 2000 will then distribute the root certificates. Other root certificates can be distributed using Group Policy (see Figure 11.14).

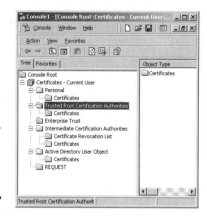

FIGURE 11.14
Group Policy can distribute a trusted root certificate.

STEP BY STEP

11.10 Mapping Certificates

1. Open Active Directory, Users and Computers.

2. Select Advanced Features from the View menu.

3. Expand Domain in the console tree.

4. Click the user container (Users or the OU).

5. Click the user account in the Details pane.

6. From the Action menu, click Name Mappings.

7. Click Add on the X.509 Certificates tab (see Figure 11.15).

8. Enter the name and path of the CER file that contains the certificate to map to this user account.

9. Click Open.

10. Choose one: one-to-one mapping, or many-to-one mapping (see Table 11.9).

FIGURE 11.15
Adding certificate mappings.

You determine the type of mapping you want based on your desired use of the certificate. If you want to be able to restrict an individual, or to audit access at the individual level, for example, select one-to-one. A certificate is mapped to one user account. If you need to provide access to a group of individuals but do not require the ability to provide access or audit activity on the individual level, choose many-to-one. In this case, you can create a rule that indicates all certificates issued by a particular CA will be mapped to this one account. In this way, for example, you could provide access to multiple employees of a firm that has installed its own CA, without creating multiple user accounts (one for each user). You then have only to provide access rights for this one user.

Two types of many-to-one mappings exist. In the Issuer many-to-many type, any certificate issued by the selected CA will be mapped to the account; whereas in the Subject many-to-many type, the subject must be matched. Subject identifies the particular type of certificate, such as user, file encryption, or IPSec.

You should choose Use Subject of Alternate Security Identity if multiple types of certificate exist and you want to be specific about which ones are mapped to the user account you have selected.

TABLE 11.9

DETERMINING MAPPING TYPE

Mapping Type	Use Issuer for Alternate Security Identity	Use Subject of Alternate Security Identity	Definition
One-to-one	Selected	Clear	Map certificate to one account.
Many-to-one	Clear	Selected	Any certificate with the same subject is mapped to the user account regardless of issuer.
Many-to-one	Select	Clear	Any certificate that has the same issuer to the user account, regardless of the subject of the certificate.

THIRD-PARTY INTEGRATION

Integrate with third-party CAs.

Windows 2000 PKI is based on standards and is interoperable with other PKI products. Interoperability with specific products varies because these products may have chosen to follow proprietary methods or may have implemented the standard in a slightly different way. Many of the issues of interoperability are detailed here. For more information, see the Microsoft White Paper "Public Key Interoperability" available from the www.microsoft.com/windows Web site.

Two different tracks for interoperability need to be examined. In one track, you must interoperate Microsoft PKI with a third-party PKI. They both exist in your environment. In the second track, only the third-party PKI is used.

Common operations such as CA trust, certificate enrollment, certificate path validation, revocation status checking, and use of public key–enabled applications may be fully supported, supported with workarounds, or not supported in an integrated PKI. You can often anticipate whether Windows 2000 PKI will interoperate with another PKI by examining the goals of each PKI implementation and the standards that they adhere to.

Microsoft's stated goal for PKI in Windows 2000 was to enable the platform for e-business opportunities. Internet standard protocols such as Kerberos 5.0, SSL, TLS, and IPSec are used. The PKI is also integrated with Microsoft's Active Directory Service and the operating system Security Services.

If Microsoft's PKI is going to interoperate with other PKIs, those other PKIs must be using the same standards.

Microsoft standards include the support of ITU X.509 version 3 and version 1 certificate formats, and a number of standard cryptographic algorithms.

Cryptographic algorithms (key minimum/maximum length may vary depending on export restrictions) include the following:

◆ **RSA**—Rivest-Shamir-Adleman developed various cryptographic algorithms that now contain the leading title RSA. These algorithms are the most widely used public key cryptographic algorithms. The Microsoft Base Cryptographic Provider and the Microsoft Enhanced Cryptographic Provider use RSA technology to provide digital signing as well as other cryptographic functions.

◆ **DSA**—Data signing and signature verification is provided in the Microsoft Digital Signature Standard (DSS) Cryptographic Provider using the Digital Signature algorithm (DSA).

◆ **DH**—Diffie-Hellman key exchange (an algorithm for using public/private keys to exchange session keys) is provided by the Microsoft Base DSS and Diffie-Hellman Cryptographic Provider.

◆ **RC2, RC4, and RC5**—RSA algorithms used in symmetric encryption algorithms.

◆ **DES40, DES56, and 3DES**—Versions of the Data Encryption Standard, a U.S. government standard for symmetric encryption. DES40 uses a 40-bit key, whereas DES56 uses a 56-bit key. 3DES uses three keys.

The following public key standards are supported:

◆ **PKIX**—Internet drafts, including RFC 2459 from the PKI working group

◆ **X.509**—ITU specification that describes certificate format

◆ **PKCS**—Public Key Cryptography Standards specifications

◆ **TLS**—Drafts from the IETF Transport Layer Security working group.

◆ **S/MIME**—Drafts from the IETF S/MIME Mail Security working group

◆ **Kerberos**—RFC 1510 and PKINIT from IETF Common Authentication Technology (CAT) working group

◆ **PC/SC**—Personal Computer/Smart Card specifications

How can you evaluate third-party PKIs for possible interoperability? If you examine the uses of PKI in the Microsoft enterprise, it shakes out like this:

◆ Third-party PKIs that want to issue certificates for use by the EFS must issue certificates that contain the enhanced key usage extension for EFS and the CA must use the Microsoft RSA Base CSP to manage the private keys associated with these certificates. The Microsoft RSA Base CSP can issue certificates, or they may be imported using the PKCS #12 file format.

◆ Group Policy can be used to establish trust of a third-party CA. CTLs can be used to certify other PKIs. A trusted administrator signs CTLs. The time period and uses of CAs identified with the CTL can be controlled. Therefore, you might identify a third-party CA as trusted to issue certificates for users, which then can be mapped to Active Directory and issued for remote authentication, but not to issue certificates that can be used locally or for EFS recovery agent.

◆ Third-party PKIs that will exist alone in the Windows environment can be tested, and there is a logo standard that is evidence of how well they interoperate with Windows 2000 features, including Active Directory. Applications that worked in the Windows NT environment should work in Windows 2000. New features available in Windows 2000 will not be available if the Windows 2000 PKI is not used.

Features that do not work with third-party PKIs include the following:

◆ Auto enrollment and renewal of machine certificates.

◆ Windows 2000 PKI management tools.

◆ Applications that do not use CryptoAPI cannot use roaming profiles to store user certificates.

◆ If the third-party PKI replaces the Windows 2000 Graphical Identification and Authentication (GINA), component of the logon process that collects data from the user, support for smart card logon is removed.

◆ The smart card logon certificate must be issued by a Windows 2000 enterprise CA published in Active Directory for the domain. (Therefore, a foreign CA can't name-spoof attack and gain entry into your network.)

◆ The issuing CA for smart card logon must be Windows 2000, but the parent or root CA can be a third-party CA.

◆ EFS automatic enrollment.

Limitations and Annoyances

Windows 2000 PKI may differ in some aspects that may prevent or limit interoperability with third–party PKIs. These differences include the following:

◆ **Key import and export**—Interoperability can be expanded if the capability for key export and import is there.

◆ **Algorithms and key length**—Key length can be a problem if one PKI supports large public key lengths and the other does not. The exchange of symmetric keys will not be possible. Key exchange and digital signature between PKIs do not have to use the same key lengths. Symmetric key algorithms do require the same size keys. Symmetric key algorithms are used in PKI to bulk encrypt and to establish secure communication channels.

◆ **Trust model**—Windows 2000 uses a rooted Hierarchical Trust Model. This has been described previously in the section "Designing CA Hierarchies." Other trust models include the Network Trust Model described later.

◆ **Trust path**—Also called trust chains. The way a trust path is created may vary, and this may cause compatibility issues. For example, if they vary, the ability to compose a trust path back to the root may be impossible and the certificate may be rejected.

◆ **Directory requirements**—Windows 2000 PKI takes advantage of Active Directory, but can be established and run without Active Directory.

◆ **Online/offline requirements**—Windows 2000 CA can be taken offline to protect private keys. Some third-party CAs require their CAs to remain online.

◆ **Dual key-pair requirements**—Windows 2000 supports both single and dual key pairs. This allows more opportunities for interoperability. Some PKIs require one or the other. In the dual key-pair scenario, a separate pair is used for signing than for sealing.

◆ **Partitioned CRLs**—Partitioned CRLs is an optional feature in the IETF RFC 2459 standard. It is designed to limit CRL maximum size. Windows 2000 does not support this standard.

◆ **Optional extensions**—Each PKI may choose to use optional extension. The options they choose to support may be different. A PKI may reject a certificate from another PKI that uses an optional extension that it does not, and vice versa.

◆ **Application support**—Many PKI-enabled applications may have trouble interoperating with certificates issued by different PKIs. Email is one of those applications. Even if you have only one PKI in your organization, if you are exchanging email with someone whose organization uses a different PKI, you may have trouble using secure email. Outlook Express, for example, may be able to process the third-party email, but the reverse may not be true if the third-party email requires the CA's presence in its directory.

◆ **Hardware support**—User and computer keys should be stored in hardware devices for better security. The Microsoft PKI operates with many different hardware vendors. A hardware abstraction layer is provided to allow applications to ignore hardware information involved in key storage. Crypto API is used by Windows API to provide this support. It uses the PC/SC standard not PKCS #11 to communicate with smart cards and readers. Other vendors use PKCS #11 or other standards. Microsoft requires hardware devices to support Plug and Play and Power Management features.

◆ **Certificate information**—Certificates bind a name to a public key value. How certificate information is represented can determine the level of interoperability between two PKIs.

◆ **Encoding formats**—Windows 2000 supports encoding formats specified by RFC 2459 as well as Unicode. Name information can cause interoperability problems if the encoding formats are not supported.

◆ **Authority Information Access (AIA)**—The AIA field is used dynamically in chain building. Windows 2000 supports and uses this field if it is present and necessary. Some PKIs do not and require a global directory or pushing of all certificates to the client. This may not be practical in an environment where PKIs need to operate across company boundaries and/or over the Internet.

◆ **CRL Distribution Point (CDP)**—The CDP tells the PKI where to look for a CRL. Because CRLs may have short lifetimes, a client must periodically look for new CRLs. Having the CDP allows it to do this.

◆ **Basic Constraints**—This extension identifies which certificates are CA certificates and which are end-entity certificates. Windows 2000 rejects certificates that do not have this extension.

◆ **Subject alternate name**—S/MIME and IPSec use Subject alternate name to obtain more information about the name. Windows 2000 enters email name, user principal name, and DNS name.

◆ **Extended Key Usage (EKU)**—This extension allows certificates to be identified as to what they can be used for. Therefore, a certificate issued for EFS cannot be used for smart card authentication and vice versa.

Windows 2000 Certificate Services conquers some of these restrictions. Windows 2000 CAs can import and export certificates and keys and support a number of algorithms and key lengths. A more insurmountable problem may be the trust model and/or the way certificate trust chains are built.

Trust Models

As you know, the Windows 2000 has a Hierarchical Trust Model.

Some say that hierarchical models are more scalable and easier to administer. In the hierarchical model, each CA plays a role and does not depend on the others for operation. CAs are either a root or a subordinate. Each CA uses its own key to sign certificates.

Management of each CA can be by different peoples. Therefore, the New York division can manage its own CA and control who gets issued a certificate. Because the corporation root CA signs its CA certificate, it trusts certificates from other CAs with the same root. This separation of powers allows the root CA to be stored offline and secured in a vault or even an offsite location. It never has to be exposed to the network. Deciding whom to trust is straightforward, with many applications delivering a chain of certificates that terminates in a trusted root CA. Either the root is trusted or it is not.

The Network Trust Model allows each CA to be self-signed (see Figure 11.16). Trust is based on cross-certificates. For trust to exist between two CAs, they each must be cross-certified with each other. You can think of each CA as being both a root (with other CAs subordinate) and a subordinate at the same time. In a Network Trust Model, a global directory is necessary to allow discovery of cross-certificates. (Otherwise each CA would need to be cross-certified with all other CAs.)

Network Trust Model

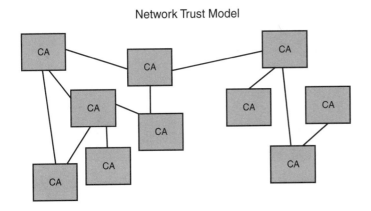

FIGURE 11.16
Network Trust Model.

Certificate Chain Building

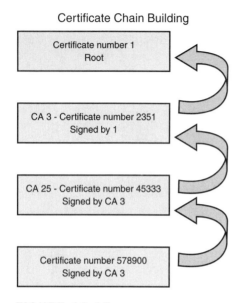

FIGURE 11.17
Certificate chain building.

Chain Building

If a client does not recognize a certificate, how does it determine trust? The client tries to verify the certificate by building a chain (see Figure 11.17). Each link in the chain is from a CA certificate to its parent in an attempt to go from an unknown CA to one that the client does trust (bottom-up), or the other way around (bottom-down). It is as if in trying to determine whether you can trust a fellow traveler, you attempt to find some common friend or business relationship in common. It is the old "do you know, I know" dance.

Windows 2000 chain building is bottom-up. Chain building follows this process:

1. The trusted certificate chain delivered with the certificate is examined for possible links to the trusted CA.

2. If the path is not complete, the Authority Key Identifier (AKI) field on the certificate is used to find the parent certificate(s) on the local computer.

3. If the path is not complete, the AIA field in the certificate is checked for location information to obtain parent certificates from the location specified.

4. If the path is not complete, the issuer name information in a certificate is used to find a parent certificate.

Optional Extensions

Issuer Distribution Point is an extension. Per the standard, when a PKI marks an extension as critical, it cannot interoperate with a PKI that does not support that extension. Certificates or CRLs issued by the PKI without the extension are rejected by the PKI that supports it. Internet Explorer and Internet Information Server fail this type of revocation check by a third-party CA.

Microsoft PKI clients do not process CRLs containing critical extensions. CRLs with critical extensions are rejected. To check revocation information, the CRL for each CA in the certificate chain must be local to the client or a URL must be provided in the CDP.

CASE STUDY: TREMAIN POLSON PKI

BACKGROUND

Tremain Polson is the company you previously examined in Chapter 8, "Designing Security Policy Inheritance." The company began its Group Policy design and decided to implement complex passwords as part of its high-security domain policy.

PROBLEM STATEMENT

Like most companies, change is hard. Proposals for stricter security are often met with resistance.

Information Systems Manager

It has become evident that attempting to institute complex passwords is going to be a struggle. We know we need to have better security, yet I'm meeting quite a lot of resistance to our proposed policy.

Systems Administrator

If we tighten the password policy too much, I believe folks will find a way around it. Right now we ask people to change their password every 60 days, and we have our settings so they must not repeat their password. We ask, but don't monitor, that passwords be composed of upper- and lowercase letters and numbers. Most people try to follow this policy, but quite frankly, many don't. Those that do, often write down their passwords in their daytimers, or personal phonebooks. It's all too easy to find out someone's password. Then there's the issue of leaving the computer logged on and of using the password at multiple computers. Too often people forget, or allow someone else to use their password.

Human Resources Manager

What happened to one big family? I can't believe how hung-up these guys are getting on security. I've got people who are excellent workers but forget their password because we ask them to change it too often. Now you're going to make the policy more restrictive?

Help Desk Staff

I spend a good part of my day resetting passwords for people who can't remember them. I wonder how many of them leave the password the same as I set it? Oh I set User Must Change Password, but everyone knows you can just type in the same password.

CURRENT SYSTEM

The current password policy does not insist on complex passwords.

Systems Administrator

The current password policy is this: It must be changed every 60 days, history is 12, no lockout policy, minimum length 8 characters.

Accounting Manager

I make sure my people follow the policy.

Warehouse Manager

In the plant and out here, most people don't log on. The shift supervisor may have to log on if a computer gets rebooted or something, but mostly we leave the system up all the time and logged on; that way folks can step over to a system and find the information they want. Data gets entered mostly by scanners and little handheld units.

continues

CASE STUDY: TREMAIN POLSON PKI

continued

ENVIRONMENT

Desktops are primarily Windows NT and Windows 98.

System Administrator

Our desktop systems are scheduled for replacement with Windows 2000. We are designing our migration strategy now.

ENVISIONED SYSTEM

Smart cards can be used to make logon more secure while making it easier for all individuals A CA hierarchy must be designed.

Information Systems Manager

We see smart cards as an answer. Each person who needs to logon will have a smart card. That way we can use extremely complex passwords, but no one has to remember them. To use smart cards, we will have to implement a PKI. We already had this in the plans because certain computers are required to use IPSec for all communications. Having a PKI also enables us to implement more control over the recovery agent keys for EFS.

Information Security Officer

We have decided on a multilevel CA hierarchy. The root, of course, will issue certificates to the second-level CA.

Our pilot project here at headquarters will utilize one CA to issue smart card certificates and one CA to issue certificates for the Encrypting File System and the IPSec computers. These CAs will be enterprise CAs because they will need to be integrated with Active Directory to issue smart cards for authentication, and to automatically issue certificates for IPSec and EFS.

I'm really excited about the possibilities of this approach. We'll use a smart card enrollment station in Human Resources and designate someone to issue the smart cards. We feel that the Web enrollment pages are nice, but offer possibilities for abuse, and may be very confusing to our people. People will feel more comfortable with the cards that way too. It'll be like getting a key to your office; no big deal.

SECURITY

Smart cards will provide excellent security. The company is going to have to develop policies for protecting its CA and for all of the routine activities and for disaster planning.

Accounting

Smart cards will work very well thank you.

Human Resources

We'll have the enrollment station. We've asked around and found that most people don't have any problem using a smart card. They are used to ATM machines and the cards look the same. They even have to have a pin number to use them. The biggest problem seems to come from the issue of getting one. People don't seem to

CASE STUDY: TREMAIN POLSON PKI

understand the process. They get confused. So we'll do it for them. Right along with getting them their standard first-day paperwork out of the way, They'll get a smart card.

We're also the logical place for folks to come if they leave their card at home or lose it. Our plans are to make temporary ones for them

Systems Administrator

We've got work to do on the policy. At the domain level, we'll set Public Key, which is a subset of Group Policy, to allow smart cards to be issued. We'll also need to cover automatic enrollment for most servers. This is also where we will specify the EFS data recovery agents. The secure server OU, of course, gets the IPSec policy, and server and desktop enrollment can be automatic for computers in that OU.

Accounts Receivable Clerk

Phew. I don't have to type in my ID and a password that I never can seem to remember? I'm usually pretty good at keeping control of my ATM card. I'll like using a smart card.

PERFORMANCE

Careful testing will help determine the impact, if any, of Certificate Services and smart card logon.

Systems Admin

It's going to take time to work out how it all fits together, but I think it is going to save us time and be more secure. With Windows NT, the setup was easy; it was the long-term maintenance that

became labor intensive. With Windows 2000, smart cards, and PKI all this, it seems like it's a lot more in the setup and understanding, but lots of tools will help make the day-to-day much easier.

Information Technology Manager

They say that we're going to experience some degradation because we are giving the system one more thing to do when users log on.

MAINTAINABILITY

Equipment, planning, and proper installation will all contribute to the long-term effectiveness as well as the long-term maintainability of the system.

Human Resources

We must make sure the equipment we purchase for the desktops will stand up to the daily use it is going to get.

Information Technology Manager

We will have to make sure we have spare readers. The cost seems quite low according to their expected lifetime.

The CAs shouldn't experience too much activity because users get a card good for an entire year.

AVAILABILITY

By leaving the third-level CAs online, the CRL is always available. Other CAs can be brought online for some of the other locations. If the CRL is not available, no authentication occurs.

continues

CASE STUDY: TREMAIN POLSON PKI

continued

ANALYSIS

A carefully planned and implemented PKI can have a number of benefits for Tremain Polson, including smart card logon, control over EFS recovery agents, and the availability of certificates for IPSec. One of their first steps is to plan the CA hierarchy.

Using several layers is good. A good place to start is to plan for a subordinate CA that issues server certificates to an intermediate layer of CAs only. The root CA need never be online and can be locked away and physically protected as well. The intermediate CA(s) can be restricted to the issuing of server certificates for the third layer. This third layer of CAs can be used to issue user certificates. The user certificate CAs can be restricted to just issuing user certificates and not be authorized to issue server certificates. Because these CAs get their authority via their own certificate signed by the level above, they operate independently of each other once established.

The root standalone CA can always be offline and kept in a vault. It will only be accessed if another level-two standalone subordinate CA is needed, or when renewing the level-two CA certificate, or when replacing the level-two CA. The level-two CA can also be kept offline. The level-three enterprise subordinate CAs will be kept online to issue user-level certificates and CRLs. User-level CAs can be segregated by purpose to spread the load and to delegate responsibility. Human Resources can be in charge of smart card certificates, but not IPSec or EFS recovery agent certificates.

Table 11.10 sums it up.

TABLE 11.10

TREMAIN POLSON CA HIERARCHY

Role	On or Off	Level	Certificates Issued	Certificate Lifetime
Standalone root	Offline	1	Server	10 years
Standalone subordinate	Offline	2	Server	5 years
Enterprise subordinate	Online	3	EFS and IPSec	1 year
Enterprise subordinate	Online	3	Smart card	1 year

The control over EFS will also be good. Although some companies are uncomfortable with users being able to encrypt files on the desktop, they recognize the value of keeping information confidential for folks on the road. Recovery, however, always remains a concern. Making it available at the cost of allowing the administrator to be one who holds the recovery agent keys and of having those keys available online is not an option. You can use Certificate Services to appoint a different recovery agent.

CHAPTER SUMMARY

Designing a PKI causes you to detail many things. The procedures are not complicated, but the continued operation and maintenance of a PKI can be awkward, at best, if careful design, planning, and implementation is not done. You must make several important decisions. You must decide where the root CA should be kept, how long CA certificates should be, what depth the CA hierarchy should be, and for which purposes the PKI should be used.

To get the most out of a PKI, you need to determine whether you need to interoperate with another PKI now or in the future. You need to develop a clear policy of operations and choose who will manage the PKI. You should look ahead to many other uses for the PKI and use sound testing practices to determine whether you have a valid design.

KEY TERMS

- Public key infrastructure (PKI)
- Certificate Authority (CA)
- digest
- Certificate Services
- hash algorithm
- certificate revocation list (CRL)
- cryptographic service provider (CSP)
- CryptoAPI
- enterprise CA
- standalone CA
- subordinate CA
- root CA
- IIS metabase
- CertUtil
- CertReq
- CertSrv
- certificate mapping
- MSGINA
- GINA
- Network Trust Model
- Hierarchical Trust Model

APPLY YOUR KNOWLEDGE

Exercises

11.1 Establish Certificate Services

Estimated Time: 15 minutes

Use detailed steps from Step by Step 11.1 and 11.2 to assist you with this exercise.

1. Use Add, Remove Programs, Windows Components, and select Certificate Services.

2. Select Enterprise Root CA.

3. Select a key length of 2048 bits.

4. Name the CA and fill out other Identifying Information.

5. Use the Validity Duration box to specify a lifetime of five years.

11.2 Configure Certificate Services

Estimated Time: 15 minutes

1. Open the Certification Authority console (Start, Programs, Administrative Tools).

2. Right-click the CA node and click Properties.

3. Click Policy Module.

4. Click Add to add another distribution point for the CRL. Why might this be important?

5. Click Exit Module and examine the exit module listed. What does the exit module do?

6. Close the Properties page.

7. Right-click the Revoked Certificates node and change the CRL publish interval to six months. Why might you do this? When would you Disable Scheduled Publishing?

8. Right-click the Policy Settings node of the CA.

9. Click New and click Certificate to Issue. Add a certificate from the list.

11.3 Configure Public Key Policy

Estimated Time: 15 minutes

1. Open the Group Policy snap-in focused on the default domain policy.

2. Open the Computer Configuration, Security Settings, Public Key Policies node.

3. Right-click the Automatic Certificate Request Settings node.

4. Click New.

5. Select a computer certificate template and click Next. Computers within this scope are issued a certificate the next time the computer restarts and logs on.

6. Select your CA and click Next. (Multiple selections can be made, but only one CA will process.) What's good about multiple selections?

Review Questions

1. In a public/private key encryption system, the public key is available to anyone. How are messages kept secret if the key is known by all?

2. Explain how public/private key can be used for nonrepudiation.

3. What will happen if the CRL is not available?

4. If the root CA is placed offline, how can the PKI function?

APPLY YOUR KNOWLEDGE

5. To set up the use of smart cards for authentication, or to use third-party PKI-enabled applications, you need to make some changes to Certificate Services. What are the items you may need to change?

6. You have partners you would like to grant access to certain resources on your network. Your business partner has his own PKI. Can this be done? How?

7. How could you control what the employees of your business partner could do within your network?

8. The Windows 2000 system your root CA is installed on crashes. You bring it back up and Certificate Services fails to start. All attempts to start the service fail. Thinking the system might be corrupt, you restore the CA from a backup of the CA (not a complete system backup). Certificate Services still won't start. A closer inspection reveals that IIS isn't starting either. What could the problem be? Can you recover? If so, how? If not, what should you have done to avoid this scenario?

9. Tremain Polson establishes a PKI (see case study). They have three layers, and the third layer has two CAs. They use this for their test at headquarters. The test is successful and now they must go into production. They have locations in six other countries and two other locations in the United States. Assume that they test collected all the correction information. The test showed that a single CA was adequate for issuing the certificates needed for EFS, smart cards, and IPSec. Is there any reason they shouldn't reduce the number of level-three CAs to one? Would any CAs be necessary offsite?

10. Can the Web server you are using to place enrollment pages and CRLs on the Web be on a separate machine from the CA? If so, is there anything that needs to be done to ensure secure authentication?

Exam Questions

1. Tremain Polson is wondering whether any other applications that it uses or wants to use are PKI enabled. The company is using the following applications. Which ones are PKI enabled?

   A. SMS

   B. Microsoft Money

   C. Microsoft Outlook

   D. Microsoft Word

   E. Internet Information Server

2. Certificates can be used for the following purposes:

   A. EFS

   B. SMS

   C. IPSec

   D. Code-signing active content

   E. Smart cards

3. Agatha Jones of Tremain Polson is setting up the first enterprise subordinate CA. The process fails. What are two possible reasons for this?

   A. Agatha is not an enterprise administrator.

   B. Active Directory is not available.

APPLY YOUR KNOWLEDGE

C. An enterprise subordinate CA cannot be set up without a certificate from Verisign. Agatha does have one.

D. Agatha is trying to set up a subordinate CA on a member server. It must be set up on a domain controller.

4. Stuart Edwardson installs the standalone root CA. It is not placed online. He then visits the Web site `http://Caservername/certsrv` and requests a certificate for an enterprise CA. The default location for certificates is the root of the installation volume. When Stuart looks there, he does not find a certificate. What could have happened?

A. He hasn't installed Active Directory yet.

B. No standalone certificate is automatically issued. An administrator has to visit the CA and approve the issue or rejection of the certificate request.

C. The subordinate CA must be online when it issues server certificates.

D. A standalone CA cannot issue a certificate for an enterprise CA.

5. The standalone subordinate CA

A. Is the most trusted CA.

B. Requires Active Directory.

C. Does not require Active Directory.

D. Cannot be taken offline.

6. Tremain Polson has decided that it can improve business by allowing major suppliers access to specific resources on their network. To do so the company wants to allow these suppliers authentication via its PKI. One of its suppliers has a PKI and Tremain Polson would like to import its

certificates. What are the steps that must be taken? (Check all that apply.)

A. Use a third party such as VeriSign or Thawte to establish trust; because they both have trust in the third-party CA, they trust each other's certificates.

B. Create an account in Active Directory.

C. Add the external CA to the CTL for the domain.

D. Import the certificates.

E. Issue certificates for each new user and send them to the individuals at the suppliers who need access.

F. Map the external user certificate to the Active Directory account.

7. Interoperability between Windows 2000 Certificate Services and third-party PKIs may be limited by any of the following:

A. Use of a different trust model.

B. Difference in cryptographic algorithms.

C. Replacement of MSGINA by the third-party PKI.

D. Failure of the third-party PKI to submit to the Microsoft PKI interoperability testing process.

E. Failure of the third-party PKI to use CryptoAPI.

F. Failure of the third-party PKI to support Kerberos.

G. The third-party PKI cannot import or export certificates.

APPLY YOUR KNOWLEDGE

8. Tremain Polson wants to also utilize a third-party PKI with Windows 2000. Which of the following interoperability issues between Windows 2000 Certificate Services and a third-party PKI prevent Tremain Polson from adopting the third-party PKI?.

   A. Difference in key length.

   B. Differences in trust model.

   C. Differences in cryptographic algorithms.

   D. Replacement of MSGINA by the third-party PKI.

   E. Failure of the third-party PKI to use CryptoAPI.

   F. Failure of the third-party PKI to use Kerberos.

   G. The third-party PKI cannot integrate with Active Directory.

   H. The third-party PKI cannot import or export certificates.

   I. The third-party PKI insists on using dual-key pairs.

9. Tremain Polson will leverage their installation of Certificate Services to manage certificates for EFS.

   Required Result:

   Certificates for EFS will be managed by Certificate Services.

   Optional Desired Results:

   A recovery procedure is established and removes the administrator as the recovery agent for encrypted files. Another individual will be assigned that role.

Laptops will receive a revised, high-security template. Employees who travel with these laptops receive instructions on how to use the security features.

Proposed Solution:

The complete proposed CA hierarchy is installed and tested. A new recovery agent certificate is created for the designated individual.

Evaluation of Proposed Solution:

Which result(s) does the proposed solution produce?

   A. The proposed solution produces the required result and both of the optional results.

   B. The proposed solution produces the required result and one of the optional results.

   C. The proposed solution produces the required result but neither of the optional results.

   D. The proposed solution does not produce the required result.

10. Tremain Polson will leverage their installation of Certificate Services to manage certificates for EFS.

    Required Result:

    Certificates for EFS will me managed by Certificate Services.

    Optional Desired Results:

    A recovery procedure is established and removes the administrator as the recovery agent for encrypted files. Another individual will be assigned that role.

    Laptops will receive a revised, high-security

APPLY YOUR KNOWLEDGE

template. Employees who travel with these laptops receive instructions on how to use the security features.

Proposed Solution:

The complete proposed CA hierarchy is installed and tested. A new recovery agent certificate is created for the designated individual. The recovery agent certificate and associated private key are exported from each laptop. The user's EFS certificate and associated private key are exported to a floppy disk. The floppy disk is provided to the user of the laptop with instructions for keeping it secured and separated from the laptop during travel.

Evaluation of Proposed Solution:

Which result(s) does the proposed solution produce?

A. The proposed solution produces the required result but neither of the optional results.

B. The proposed solution produces the required result and one of the optional results.

C. The proposed solution produces the required result and both of the optional results.

D. The proposed solution does not produce the required result.

Answers to Exercises

Exercise 11.2, Item 4. Adding another distribution point, say a Web page location, can make it easier for clients to find the CRL.

Exercise 11.2, Item 5. The exit module specifies a loca-

tion where the certificate should be published. A certificate request specifies a publication location; an exit module enables this. By default, an enterprise CA publishes certificates to Active Directory.

Exercise 11.2, Item 7. You make the CRL longer if you don't think you will have many certificate revocations. You might disable CRL publication because the CA is offline. You can create a CRL manually when necessary.

Exercise 11.3, Item 6. Having multiple selections available means any CA selected can process the request. You've just built in some redundancy.

Answers to Review Questions

1. The public key must be public so that it can be easily found. Anyone may use it to encrypt a message to its owner. However, only the holder of the private key can decrypt the message. It is this reliance on a key pair that keeps the message safe. If the algorithm that produces such a key pair is sufficiently complex, it is impossible, given the public key, to calculate the private key.

2. If the private key in a public/private key pair is used to encrypt some data, only the public key can decrypt it. If the ciphertext can be decrypted with the public key, only the holder of the private key could have encrypted it. This proves that the message, was, without a doubt, encrypted by the holder of the private key. Most people are willing to accept that this will establish nonrepudiation. (The holder of the private key might argue that his key was stolen.)

3. If the system has been configured to check the

CRL to determine the validity of the certificate and a valid CRL is not available, the certificate is rejected as invalid.

4. The root CA is used only to establish the hierarchy and provide server certificates for CAs in the intermediary layers below it. After these CAs have been established, they do not need to be able to connect to the root CA. A CRL can be issued manually periodically and posted where it can be accessed. So the root CA can be taken offline and protected.

5. To enable the use of smart cards or to use third-party PKI-enabled applications, you probably need to load the appropriate cryptographic service provider. You may also need to add certificate templates, and establish a process for certificate enrollment.

6. Partner access to your resources when the partner has an established PKI can be done by establishing the partner's CA as a trusted entity. You use a CTL to establish what the partner's certificates can be used for in your environment. A user account(s) will need to be established for use by the partner's employees. The partner's certificates need to be imported into Active Directory and then mapped to this user account(s).

7. You control your partner's activities using a CTL and through ACLs. Restrictions can be defined when you configure the CTL.

8. The IIS metabase may be corrupted. To restore the CA you need to restore the metabase. If this is the problem and you do not have a backup of the IIS metabase, you cannot restore your CA. The IIS metabase is necessary or the IIS services will not start. If IIS doesn't start, your CA will not start. To prevent catch-22s like this, make

sure that you are backing up the IIS metabase, or preferably, you are doing a system backup that would have done this for you. Don't forget to include a backup of the System State.

9. Tremain Polson may reduce the number of level-three CAs to one at corporate headquarters unless they determine that they would like to separate the administration and processing of the different types of certificates. The original rationale was to separate the functions that were put into place to provide tighter security for critical servers. (IPSec), so they may decide to remain with this separation of duties and keep two level-three CAs at headquarters. The larger issue here is the possible need for CA at the other company locations. They need to examine the speed of links between the locations and the frequency with which certificates and the CRLs will be renewed. It is possible that not every location will need a CA because certificate renewal is infrequent. If the CRL is not available, however, problems will arise.

10. The Web server for enrollment pages does not have to be physically on the CA computer. If it is on a different computer, however, you must change the authentication to Basic, and protect this Web server with SSL.

Answers to Exam Questions

1. **B, C, E.** SMS and Microsoft Word are not PKI enabled at this point. (For more information, see section "Basic Definitions.")

2. **A, D, E.** Certificates could be used to authenticate to an SMS server, but there is no integration with the product. (For more information, see section "Current Uses for Windows 2000 PKI.")

3. **A, B.** Two important requirements for setting up any Enterprise CA are that Active Directory be available and that the individual doing the setup either be an enterprise administrator or have been delegated the right to set up the enterprise CA. Choice C is incorrect; it is not necessary to obtain a certificate from VeriSign to set up any CA. Choice D is also incorrect; a CA may be set up to a member server, or even a standalone server. (For more information, see section "Root CA.")

4. **B.** A standalone CA requires an administrator to issue or reject certificate requests. Choice A is incorrect; the standalone CA does not require Active Directory. Choice C is incorrect because the subordinate CA does not have to be online; in fact, the root subordinate CA should not be online, ever. Choice D is incorrect; a subordinate root CA can issue certificates for an enterprise CA. (For more information, see section "Installing Certificate Services.")

5. **C.** The standalone subordinate CA requires a certificate issued from either the root CA or another subordinate CA. (For more information, see section "Certificate Server Roles.")

6. **B, C, D, F.** Answer A or Cross-certification of their CAs, or some custom development of trust in a shared root—both parties use the third-party as their root—is one way to go, However, the most secure, least-intrusive, easiest way is to establish Active Directory user accounts and map imported certificates to these accounts. Choice E is wrong because no new Windows 2000 certificates are necessary if the supplier has already established its own CA and it can issue certificates usable by Windows 2000. (For more information, see section "Mapping Certificates.")

7. **A, B.** If the two PKIs use different trust models, this usually prevents interoperability except on the most basic levels. Common applications such as email are probably broken. If the two PKIs do not share at least one cryptographic algorithm in common, they cannot communicate. If the third-party PKI replaces MSGINA, it cannot be used for producing smart card certificates; however, other functions may work just fine. The lack of existence of Microsoft interoperability testing results, or a logo proving interoperability, only shows the PKI has not been tested by Microsoft; it does not mean the PKI won't interoperate with Microsoft's PKI. If the third-party PKI does not use CryptoAPI, it cannot take advantage of roaming profiles; however, other functionality is not hampered. The use or not of Kerberos by a third-party PKI does not prevent the third-party PKI from interoperating with Microsoft's PKI. The capability to import and export certificates reduces interoperability, but may not prevent it. (For more information, see section "Third-Party Integration.")

8. **A, B, C, D.** The first thing that should come to mind is Tremain Colson's reliance on smart cards. If the third-party PKI needs to provide this service, it cannot. If the third-party PKI cannot match Microsoft key lengths, trust model, and cryptographic algorithms, problems will also arise. Microsoft Certificate Services can use either single- or dual-key pairs, so Choice I is not an issue. For information on other items, see the answer to Question 7. (For more information, see section "Third-Party Integration.")

9. **C.** If Certificate Services is present, EFS leverages its use. If it is not, EFS issues its own certificate for the currently logged-on user. This meets the

APPLY YOUR KNOWLEDGE

requirement. Although the administrator is removed as the recovery agent in this scenario, no other individual is given this role. There is also no process put into place for securing EFS on laptops. (For more information, see section "Policy and Performance—Getting the Right Information Down.")

10. **C.** As in Question 9, EFS uses Certificate Services. Although a new recovery agent certificate is produced, there is no indication that the administrator's certificate is removed. Therefore the administrator could also read the encrypted files. Certificates and private keys are exported from laptops; however, there is no mention of "removing" the private keys. The export process merely places a copy of the certificate and key where requested; it does not delete the private key unless it is required to do so. (For more information, see section "Policy and Performance—Getting the Right Information Down.")

Suggested Readings and Resources

1. Microsoft Official Curriculum course 2151: Microsoft Windows 2000 Network and Operating System Essentials, Module 5.

2. Online Help article: Certificate Checklists—Deploying Certification Authoritative and PKI for an Intranet (search under "certificates/checklist" in Windows 2000 Help).

3. *Microsoft Windows 2000 Resource Kit: Distributed Systems Guide.* Microsoft Press, 2000.

- Chapter 16: Windows 2000 Certificate Services and Public Key Infrastructure

- Chapter 13: Choosing Security Solutions That Use Public Key Technology

- Chapter 14: Cryptography for Network and Information Security

- Chapter 15: Encrypting File System

Suggested Readings and Resources

4. Windows 2000 Resource Kit: *Deployment Planning Guide.* Microsoft Press, 2000.

    - Chapter 12: Planning Your Public Key Infrastructure

5. Web Sites

    - PKIX working group: www.ietf/org/html.charters/pkix-charter.html

    - X.509: www.itu.int/

    - PKCS working group: www.rsa.com/rsalabs/pubs/PKCS

    - TLS: www.ietf.org/html.charters/tls-charter.html

    - S/MIME working group: www.ietf.org/html.charters/smime-charter.html

    - Kerberos: www.ietf.org/html.charters/cat-charter.html

    - PC/SC: www.smartcardsys.com

    - Federal PKI efforts: http://csrc.nist.gov/pki/

    - Canadian government: www.cio-dpi.gc.ca/

This chapter covers the following Microsoft-specified objectives for the "Designing a Windows 2000 Security Solution" section of the Designing Security for a Microsoft Windows 2000 Network exam:

Design Windows 2000 network services security.

- Design Windows 2000 DNS security.

- Design Windows 2000 Remote Installation Services (RIS) security.

- Design Windows 2000 SNMP security.

▶ Every network service that you implement opens new holes that intruders can use to attack your network. To understand this, you only need open up any IT publication, Webzine or print, and read of the latest attack scenarios. Security lists and bug lists are full of the implications of insecure network services.

▶ The best recommendation that anyone can make seems to be to remove unnecessary services. If you don't need a basement door, why provide a hole through which vermin of all kinds can creep in?

▶ The next best recommendation is to identify all network services and provide the best defense possible. Identify known holes or good practices. Follow the recommendations for configuration, and fix holes as they are discovered. It's horrible enough to be robbed; it's worse when it's the result of having left the doors or windows unlocked.

CHAPTER 12

Designing Windows 2000 Network Services Security

▶ The best practice here is to become thoroughly comfortable with the services selected for design. When you know how normal operation is configured, you will be able to identify potential security flaws. Familiarity with the service brings the ability to block problems before they become problems and to be able to secure the service.

▶ Don't become a victim of the Chicken Little syndrome. These little guys run around yelling about perceived weaknesses in networks. The weaknesses may or may not be there—how do you tell, and how do you protect against them? That's the level of knowledge required here. No one can possibly know all the present, past, and future integrity scams on every service. If you know the service, you may be able to predict whether it is vulnerable, determine whether it is properly configured, or at least know where to look and how to test for the new piece of sky that someone sees falling.

INTRODUCTION

On a standalone system, limited attacks can result in damage to the system or in loss of confidential information. While some people argue these systems are the least protected and therefore the most vulnerable, fewer opportunities exist for attack. A simple house has but a single door and a limited number of windows. There are few points of entry and, therefore, limited access to protect. If the house is in the country, fewer folks want to get in, and physical access to the access points is limited by distance.

Now put that house in the city. It instantly becomes vulnerable to attack from at least a dozen directions, including access from the air, buildings that surround it, underground tunnels, and a range of scams for gaining entrance through the door and windows. In the same way, when you put a computer on a network, you've magnified its vulnerability. For the house, we prescribe additional locks, bars, and training for its owners. For computers on a network, similar efforts need to be made.

Later chapters deal with securing the communication pathways. Previous ones have concerned themselves with authentication and authorization. Here you will investigate several network services and learn how they may be best secured. While you will limit your attention to Domain Name Service (DNS), Remote Installation Service (RIS), and Simple Network Management Protocol (SNMP), the principles you learn can be applied to any network service.

DNS SECURITY

Design Windows 2000 DNS security.

DNS security in Windows 2000 is intertwined with the new features of Dynamic DNS and Dynamic Host Control Protocol (DHCP). You cannot consider one without the other. This section will accomplish the following:

◆ Describe the changes to DNS that allow dynamic update of IP addresses.

◆ Explain how the tradition brought to you by DHCP's dynamic assignment of IP addresses has morphed into features that extend to the dynamic updating of IP addresses.

◆ Discuss possible problems and security issues that result from this process.

◆ Define and explain *secure dynamic update,* the features that, if properly applied, allow you to keep these exciting features from becoming new holes in the fabric of your network.

Windows 2000 Dynamic DNS

As you know, Domain Name Service provides name resolution services. It maintains a list of computer names and IP addresses in a hierarchical searchable database. Its records typically are kept in zone files and are manually updated. At a minimum, an address record or resource record contains the fully qualified domain name (FQDN) of the computer and its IP address.

DNS in Windows 2000 supports dynamic DNS updates. DNS resource records can be automatically updated by computers and by the Windows 2000 DHCP server. Also new to Microsoft DNS in Windows 2000 is the capability to secure DNS using Active Directory-integrated zone files and the capability to register and use service (SRV) records.

SRV records are registered by services with DNS so that clients can locate services by using DNS. An example of an SRV record is the Kerberos resource record, which allows a Kerberos client to find a domain controller. When this record is placed in DNS, clients can use it to locate domain controllers nearby. Every domain controller registers services by creating SRV records in DNS. The records are created automatically and are added to DNS database using the dynamic update protocol.

All DNS records are kept in zone files or, if the zone is an Active Directory-integrated zone, in Active Directory. Each zone file represents computers in a contiguous address space.

DNS Server Zone Types and Zone Replication in Windows 2000

Zone files represent contiguous address spaces or DNS domains. Traditional DNS consists of two zone types: primary and secondary. These are called *standard primary* and *standard secondary* in Windows 2000. New in Windows 2000 is the Active Directory-integrated zone. Windows 2000 zone files are defined as follows:

◆ **Standard primary**—This is a read/write zone file. Changes to records are recorded in this standard text file.

◆ **Standard secondary**—This is a read-only zone file. Changes recorded to the primary file are replicated to a secondary file. Secondary zone files are used to distribute the workload across computers and to provide backup.

◆ **Active Directory-integrated**—New in Windows 2000, this zone file exists only in Active Directory, not in a text file. Updates occur during Active Directory replication, which can simplify planning and configuration of the DNS namespaces because you don't need to tell DNS servers to specify how and when updates occur. Instead, Active Directory maintains the zone information. No primary and secondary zones exist in an Active Directory-integrated DNS zone. (However, you can create a standard secondary zone and point it to an Active Directory-integrated zone.)

If your Active Directory consists of a single domain, there is no need for a secondary or backup file to spread the workload or to be available in case of disaster if you have configured DNS on multiple domain controllers. The workload is spread over multiple computers by virtue of AD replication, and multiple copies of the zone file are always available.

In a multiple-domain Active Directory, you may need to create standard secondary zones that replicate data held in Active Directory-integrated zones. This is because the replication of Active Directory-integrated zone information is limited to the domain in which the zone is created. The standard secondary zone can assure the availability of another domain's zone information. This is especially useful in providing backup and availability of reverse lookup zones and in providing local zone information in remote sites where you do not want to have a domain controller.

In traditional DNS and in standard and primary zone files, data is replicated from the primary to the secondary zone. In Windows 2000, it is updated by incremental zone transfer (IXFR), which replicates changes only to the zone file, not the whole file.

Secondary zones are created to provide additional copies of zone file information. When the secondary zone file is created, it receives a copy of the current primary zone file. When new hosts and other records are added to the primary zone file, they are not automatically added to every secondary zone file. Replication must be configured between the primary and secondary zone files.

Active Directory-integrated zone files automatically replicate zone information as part of Active Directory replication. Every domain controller for the domain that is configured to be a DNS server will receive all changes to zone information (see Figure 12.1). There is no need to set up zone replication separately. Each of these domain controllers can be used to make changes to the zone information. Because replication is managed by the Active Directory replication process, it is multimaster.

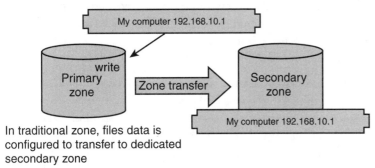

In traditional zone, files data is configured to transfer to dedicated secondary zone

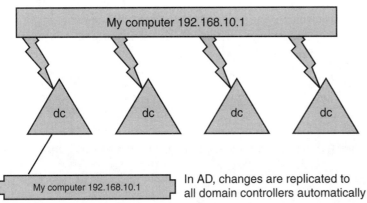

In AD, changes are replicated to all domain controllers automatically

FIGURE 12.1

Updating zone file records in Active Directory.

As in traditional DNS, you can configure subdomains. In Windows 2000, you can then delegate authority to manage the DNS subdomain on a departmental or other basis within the organization.

You can do this by opening the DNS console from Administrative Tools, right-clicking on the name of domain to delegate, and then clicking New Delegation to start the Delegation of Authority Wizard.

Resource Records

DNS is used for the resolution of computer names to IP addresses, but it also is used for the resolution of IP address to computer names. How is this accomplished? There are two resource records for every computer—a forward lookup and a reverse lookup record. The forward lookup is the A record, and the reverse lookup is the PTR record.

New Security Challenges with DNS

In the pre-dynamic DNS world, you controlled the DNS server by controlling access to the server. You controlled access to the records of computers and IP addresses in the server by controlling access to the software used to modify the files. Whether files were modified by text editors or GUI interfaces, the process was essentially the same: You controlled who could modify the DNS files.

With Windows 2000, you still control local access to the DNS server. If the DNS server is traditional—that is, its records are located on a server—you control who can use the Administrative console and who can locally access the files in the same manner as you control access to any other service and its files. If the DNS server is integrated into Active Directory, you have additional controls available to control access to all records. More information can be found in the section "Configure the Zone for Secure Dynamic Update," later in this chapter.

In either case, dynamic DNS changes your approach to security. In traditional DNS, administrators manually enter computer names and addresses. In dynamic DNS, client systems and DHCP servers may be capable of registering computer names and IP addresses with the DNS server. This is a good thing. This is also a bad thing.

NOTE

Why Would I Need to Look Up a Computer Name by Address?   If I attempt to download an application that includes encryption technology stronger than what is allowed for export, the downloading application will attempt to determine whether the IP address that I am downloading to belongs to a computer in the United States. This is done by looking up the resource record for the IP address in DNS. Because the address resides in a DNS server, it can be traced to ownership and location. If the program can find that out, I get my download; if it cannot, I don't.

It is good because you can use DHCP to dynamically manage network IP addressing. When IP address assignments are made or changed, they automatically are entered in the proper DNS zone. This reduces the administrative overload of managing the address assignments.

This is also a bad thing because IP address assignments are automatically entered. Think about it. If the computer name and IP address are dynamically being entered and/or modified in the zone, how are you controlling these entries? By default, you are not. Any Windows 2000 computer that is configured will update its resource record with the Windows 2000 DNS server whether or not that address is assigned by the Windows 2000 DHCP server. Furthermore, every computer that uses the Windows 2000 DHCP server can have its resource record updated by the DHCP server.

To discover the issues and how to secure DNS while allowing dynamic update, you must first examine the default behavior of DHCP. Next, determine the recommended ways to secure dynamic update. Finally, think about its operation from two views. First, think about this from the view of just simple confusion that might exist on your network with and without the added security. Second, consider this from the view of someone who wants to create havoc on your network.

Default Behavior: DHCP Updating of DNS

Whether or not you utilize DHCP in your network, Windows 2000 computers can update DNS with their domain name and IP address. When a Windows 2000 DHCP server assigns addresses to them, Windows 2000 clients register or modify their host address (the A record) dynamically to the DNS server database. The DHCP server registers the PTR or reverse lookup record to the DNS server. If DHCP is not used, the Windows 2000 client can update both the A and the PTR records. Windows NT and Windows 9x computers cannot dynamically update DNS, but if they are using DHCP, the DHCP server can be configured to update both records for them.

> **NOTE**
>
> **Standards, Anyone?** To consult the standards for dynamic DNS, you may want to examine three IETF RFCs: RFC 2136, "Dynamic Updates in the Domain Name Systems" (DNS UPDATE); RFC 2137, "Secure Domain Name System Dynamic Update"; and RFC 2078, "Generic Security Service Application Program Interface (GSS-API)."
>
> Windows 2000 dynamic update follows the specification in RFC 2136. Windows 2000 secure dynamic update follows the GSS algorithm for TSIG (GSS-TSIG) IETF draft.

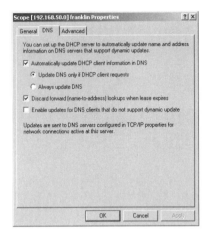

FIGURE 12.2
Update options.

Here's how it works in Windows 2000.

By default, the DHCP server registers and updates Windows 2000 clients with DNS based on the request made by the DHCP client (see Figure 12.2). The Windows DHCP client can request a specific way in which DHCP updates the client's A and PTR records. By default, clients request and get to update their own host or A record, and the DHCP server is allowed to update the PTR record. Make sure that you are using this method if you have multihomed computers that are using DHCP. If you do not, the A and PTR records will be replaced for all records for this client whenever they are updated. In the DNS server, then, the computer will appear to have one address.

Other options for DHCP are listed here:

◆ **ALWAYS**—DHCP always registers and updates the client information, both the A and the PTR resource records. DHCP examines the FQDN option of the DHCPREQUEST message to get the client name and IP address and uses this information to update the DNS server. This reduces network traffic between clients and the DNS server. You also can use this for security reasons, as you can then centrally control DNS updates. (Only the DHCP server is allowed to update DHCP assigned records.).

◆ **NEVER**—DHCP will never update the record. The client computer must register the resource records, or they must be updated by an administrator.

◆ Windows NT and Windows 9*x* computers cannot request DHCP registration or dynamically update DNS on their own. DHCP can be configured to update both records. Because older clients do not have the FQDN option in the DHCPRE-QUEST message, the DHCP server generates an FQDN by adding the domain name defined for the scope of addresses that the client is using to the client name in the DHCPRE-QUEST message. The DHCP server then sends the A and PTR records to the DNS server.

To make any of these changes to the DHCP server, perform the steps listed in Step by Step 12.1.

STEP BY STEP

12.1 Configure Dynamic Update for DHCP Server

1. Open DHCP console.

2. Right-click scope to configure.

3. Click **DNS** tab.

4. Select from the following:

a. Automatically update DHCP client information in DNS. Whenever information changes, (such as failure to renew lease), DNS is updated.

b. Update DNS only if the client requests it. The Windows 2000 client may be doing the updating of both the host and PTR record. If this is the case, the DNCP server should update only if some Windows 2000 client is configured to request updating by DHCP.

c. Always update DNS. Even if a Windows 2000 client does not request updating by DHCP, the DHCP server should do the update.

d. Enable updates for DNS clients that do not support dynamic update. Select this if you want DHCP to update records for clients such as Windows 98 and Windows NT that cannot update records for themselves.

The actual dynamic update process depends on the operating system of the client computer, the configuration changes to the DHCP server and the DNS server, and whether or not the address is assigned by DHCP or statically. By default, a Windows 2000 computer with a statically assigned address updates DNS like this:

1. The client queries the name server for the primary name server and the authoritative zone for the name it is updating.

2. Client sends a dynamic update (A and PTR records) to this server.

3. The authoritative server checks to see whether there is any reason to reject the update.

4. If there is no reason to reject the update, the changes are made.

5. The server replies to client and reports success or failure.

The Dynamic Update Process for DHCP Clients

From the client perspective, the dynamic update process consists of several possible actions. These options (see Figure 12.3) depend on any negotiation between the client and the server as to who should update DNS. These options are listed here:

1. The Windows 2000 DHCP client negotiates with the DHCP server during lease or renewal to determine which computer updates A and PTR records. The FQDN option (option 81) of the DHCPREQUEST packet is used to provide the DHCP server with the fully qualified domain name of the client.

2. The non-Windows 2000 DHCP client does not negotiate. The DHCP server will update both records if it is configured to do so.

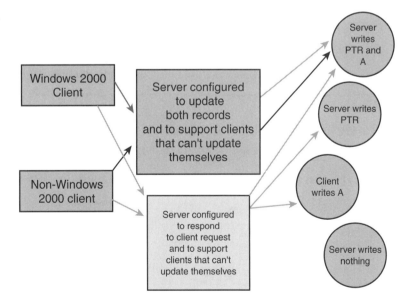

FIGURE 12.3
Windows 2000 DHCP client update.

3. Depending on negotiation, the client, the server, or both send a dynamic update request to the primary DNS server that is authoritative for the name to be updated. The server uses the FQDN option to return information to the client in the DHCPACK message about its registration on the client's behalf.

Dynamic Update Process for Non-Windows 2000 Clients

Non-Windows 2000 clients who can use the Windows 2000 DHCP server to obtain an IP address cannot register their IP address with the Windows 2000 DNS server. The DHCP server, however, can be configured to update the records for these clients. It can register both the A and the PTR record for these clients. If the DHCP server is enabled to update these clients, the process is as follows:

1 The DHCP server obtains the name of the client from the DHCP REQUEST packet.

2. The server appends the domain name for that scope.

3. The server registers the A and PTR resource records.

Preventing Dynamic DNS Registration

A Windows 2000 computer can be configured to not dynamically register its address. You might want to do this if you want all dynamic updates to be done by the DHCP server. To do so, follow the steps in Step by Step 12.2.

NOTE **Updates for What and When?** Windows 2000 clients can send updates for DHCP adapters, static adapters, and remote access adapters. Information is sent to the DNS server by the DHCP client that is active on all clients, even if they do not get an IP address from DHCP.

Updates occur as follows:

- Every 24 hours
- If TCP/IP addressing is changed
- If the DHCP address is renewed or a new lease is obtained
- If a plug-and-play event occurs
- If an IP address is added or removed from the computer for static adapter, with no restart needed
- If the user issues IPCONFIG/registerdns

STEP BY STEP

12.2 Preventing a Windows 2000 Computer from Dynamically Registering Its Address

1. Right-click My Network Places, and click Properties.

2. Right-click Connection to Configure and click Properties.

continues

continued

3. Select TCP/IP.

4. Click Properties.

5. Select the Advanced button.

6. Select the DNS tab.

7. Clear the Register This Connection's Address in DNS check box.

Dynamic Confusion

Can things get out of hand by themselves? Yes. Can they be purposefully screwed up? Yes.

To discover how, think about this: What happens when a client logs on and attempts to register its IP address in a DNS zone, but finds that another computer has already registered that address? What happens if someone installs an unauthorized DHCP server? What happens when a client lease is not renewed?

Name Spoofing

When a client attempts to register its name and IP address but finds it already there, by default it changes the registration to show its current IP address. This means that any client machine on the network can change the IP address of any other machine. Phooey. That would sure put a cork in your bottle. The next request for name resolution would erroneously send communications to the new address. This interruption in communications would be mild to severe, depending on the computers involved. Any accidental or purposeful misnaming of a computer can cause a problem. What if the computer name chosen was the name of your domain controller?

You can prevent this behavior by configuring the DNS zone for secure update (see the later section "Configure the Zone for Secure Dynamic Update"). If this is not possible, you can make the registry change on the Windows 2000 client computers listed in Step by Step 12.3.

STEP BY STEP

12.3 Preventing Name Resolution Security Issue

1. Open regedt32 and navigate to
HKEY_LOCAL_MACHINE\SYSTEM\
CurrentControlSet\Services\Tcpip\Parameters

2. Add the DisableReplaceAddressesInConflicts entry.

3. Enter a DWORD value of 1.

The value of 1 will prevent the client from overwriting a name that is the same as the one it is trying to create. A value of 0 replaces the default action.

Rogue DHCP Servers

If a rogue DHCP server (one that is not part of the formal network architecture) is installed, problems can result. This rogue server either might refuse to renew leases or might hand out inappropriate addresses to client computers on the network. These addresses might duplicate legal addresses or give client computers addresses that prevent them from communicating on the network. By dynamically registering these incorrect addresses, more confusion is created.

Any company or training center that has run a Windows NT administration course without protecting its internal network from the classroom has seen this issue.

Just as there are two servers involved in the dynamic registration process, there are two servers to secure. To provide secure dynamic address updating, you must secure the DHCP server as well as the DNS server.

One step in this process is to prevent unauthorized DHCP servers from operating. To do this, register the server as authorized in Active Directory. This will prevent rogue Windows 2000 DHCP servers from operating in your network.

When a DHCP server starts, it discovers the directory service enterprise root by talking to other DHCP servers. It then does a self-check with Active Directory to see if it is authorized. If it is not, the

DHCP service does not start, and the server will not make lease assignments. (Oh, whoops, I don't have a driver's license, so I won't drive that car). Although this may not be adequate to prevent non-Windows 2000 DHCP servers from operating, it does prevent the accidental or purposeful operation of the readily available Windows 2000 DHCP server.

Here's how the authorization process works:

1. During service start, the DHCP server sends out a DHCPINFORM broadcast using the limited broadcast address 255.255.255.255.

2. Operating, authorized DHCP servers on the network respond with a DHCPACK reporting the root domain of which that server is aware.

3. The starting DHCP server queries Active Directory for a list of authorized DHCP servers for its network.

4. If it finds itself in the list, it starts.

5. If it doesn't find itself in the list, it logs an error in the event log and does not respond to client requests.

6. Every 5 minutes, every DHCP server rebroadcasts the DHCPINFORM message to detect other DHCP servers to determine whether there is any change in their authorization status. (They can thus be started or stopped by the change in their status.)

The list of authorized servers is contained in the DhcpServer object in Active Directory. For authorization to work properly, the first DHCP server must participate in Active Directory and must be in the domain as a domain controller or a member server, not in a workgroup (see Figure 12.4). To authorize a DHCP server, you must be a member of the EnterpriseAdmins security group. (This right can be delegated).

To authorize a DHCP server in your enterprise, follow the steps in Step by Step 12.4.

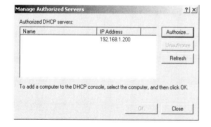

FIGURE 12.4
Authorized DHCP start process.

STEP BY STEP

12.4 Authorizing DHCP Servers

1. Open the DHCP console.

2. Right-click DHCP.

3. Click Manage Authorized Servers.

4. Click Authorize.

5. Type the name or IP address of the server to authorize, and click OK.

Scavenging Records

If a client lease is not renewed, the actions of the DHCP server vary depending on how it is configured. If it has been configured to add A and PTR addresses, then it will remove them from DNS. If it is configured to add only the PTR record (as is the default for Windows 2000 clients), then it removes only the PTR address. You can imagine the confusion of extinct IP addresses cluttering up the DNS server. Although a client may obtain a new lease and thus modify its DNS record to show the correct address, there exists a possibility for confusion if the client machine is not being used or has been moved to another location, and thus another zone. The DHCP server can be configured to remove the A address when the lease expires.

When a lease expires, the DHCP server will delete the records it created. In many cases, this will be only the PTR record because the client created the A record. You can configure the DHCP server to delete the A record as well. Use Step by Step 12.5.

STEP BY STEP

12.5 Configure DHCP Server to remove A resource records when lease expires.

1. Open the DHCP console and select the DHCP server.

2. Right-click the scope and click Properties.

3. Select the DNS tab.

4. Select Discard Forward (Name-to-Address) Lookups When Leases Expire.

Resource Record Ownership Issue

If a DHCP server registers a record, it becomes the owner. Only it can remove or update the record. This means that the client cannot update its own record! What if the DHCP server is decommissioned? Outdated records may remain until an administrator removes them.

However, there is a built-in security group DnsUpdateProxy. Objects created by this group have no security, and the first user (not a member of this group) to modify a record associated with the client becomes its owner. If you put all DHCP servers in this group, any DHCP server is authorized to update or remove records in DNS.

By default, this group has no members. Add your DHCP servers to this global security group, but be aware that the records created by members of this group are not secure and may be changed by any authenticated user or computer.

Securing Dynamic Updates

How can you eliminate the confusion and possible attacks that can result due to dynamic updates? Some of the issues have been detailed previously, but the major concern remains: How do I assure that only authorized and valid records are placed in the zone files, and that they are never modified by unauthorized agents? One possibility is to disable dynamic updates (see Step by Step 12.6). This is not recommended, however. If you do so, remember that using DHCP will dynamically assign addresses to clients, but those addresses will not be in DNS. You will need to make static entries in DNS, including recording all the SRV resource records (that's a lot of manual management), and then risk that they will be out-of-date. Or, you may need to use WINS for name resolution.

STEP BY STEP

12.6 Preventing DNS Dynamic Update

1. Open the DNS console.

2. Right-click on the zone to configure.

3. Open the property pages.

4. On the General page, change Allow Dynamic Updates? to No (see Figure 12.5).

A second possibility is to use Active Directory-integrated zones instead of the more traditional zones, and configure the zones to accept only secure updates. When Active Directory-integrated zones are used, you can protect the DNS server from unauthorized updating by configuring secure dynamic updates. There are other advantages as well:

◆ No single point of failure.

◆ Fault tolerance. All zones are primary zones. Each server that hosts a zone maintains it, but all records are replicated in Active Directory.

◆ Single replication topology is used. No separate zone transfer takes place. Replication is done in Active Directory replication; you don't configure replication for DNS separately.

◆ Secure dynamic updates are possible. You can set permissions on zones and records within those zones. Updates that use dynamic update protocol can be updated only by the computer that owns the record.

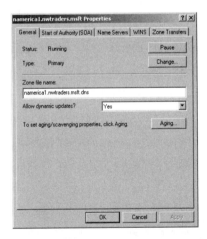

FIGURE 12.5
Determining whether to allow dynamic updates.

Active Directory-integrated zones can be created only on servers that are configured as domain controllers and configured to run the DNS service.

Zones can be created as Active Directory-integrated zones when installing the DNS server, or they can be converted (see Step by Step 12.7). To convert a zone, the server must be a domain controller, and Active Directory must be present. During conversion, the zone file is copied into the Active Directory and is deleted on the server.

STEP BY STEP

12.7 Converting to Active Directory-integrated DNS Zones

1. Open the DNS console.

2. Right-click on the zone folder you want to convert.

3. On the General page, click the Change button next to the zone type.

4. Select Active Directory-integrated (see Figure 12.6).

5. Click OK three times.

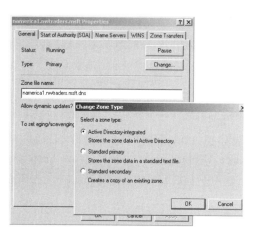

FIGURE 12.6
Changing the zone type.

When you have established the Active Directory-integrated zone, how do you protect it?

In a perfect world, you want to control who can make changes to the DNS zone files. You want only computers with existing domain accounts to be capable of updating DNS records.

Active Directory-integrated DNS zones can be configured for secure dynamic update. Secure dynamic update protects zones and resource records from being modified by users without authorization. You specify which users and groups can modify zones and resource records using DACLs. Inactive directory DNS zones cannot be configured for secure dynamic update.

Secured Active Directory-integrated zone files can protect themselves in three ways:

◆ Only computers that own the DNS record can update the record. The computer that creates the record owns it.

◆ Only computers with domain accounts can create DNS records.

◆ The authoritative server accepts updates only from client computers and servers that are authorized to send dynamic updates. You can protect zones and resource records against modification by unauthorized users because you can specify computers users and groups that are authorized to modify zones and resource records.

How is this done, and what happens when it is?

First, the zone must be configured for secure dynamic update, and then DACLs must be set. To understand the process, you will need to learn more about GSS-API.

Configure the Zone for Secure Dynamic Update

Any primary zone can be configured for dynamic update. Only Active Directory-integrated zones can be configured for secure dynamic update.

To configure Active Directory-integrated DNS zones for secure update, change the Allow Dynamic Updates? box in the zone property pages to Only Secure Updates.

You then must specify which computers and users can create or modify dnsNode objects in the zone. Because the Authenticated Users group receives Create permission by default, any authenticated computer or user can create new objects in the zone. Object creators have full control over the object. Use the Security tab of the object to further control who can make changes.

To control who can make updates to a specific FQDN, enter or select the FQDN in the DNS console and modify its DACL to allow only a particular computer, user, or group of users to change any records associated with this FQDN. Although it would be extremely time-consuming to attempt to modify all DNS records, you will want to secure servers and their resource records to keep them safe from unauthorized modification.

Next, consider changes at the client level.

Changes at the Client Level

If a zone is configured for secure dynamic update, the client tries a dynamic update. If it fails, the client negotiates secure dynamic update. You can configure the client to always try insecure or secure updates. The registry entry is UpdateSecurityLevel.

The registry entry can be set to 256, 16, or 0:

256: secure update only

16: use insecure update only

0: secure if dynamic is refused (this is default)

Add the entry to:

HKLM\system\CurrentControlSet\services\Tcpip\Parameters

GSS-API: The Generic Security Service Application Program Interface

The IETF RFC 2078 (GSS-API) draft is supported by Windows 2000. Other relevant RFCs that are not supported are RFC 2535, "Domain Name System Security Extensions," and RFC 2137, "Secure Domain Name System Dynamic Update." GSS-API is security services–independent; that is, it does not consider which security mechanism is being used.

GSS-API uses tokens to pass security contexts. The client creates a token and sends it to the server; the server may return a token to assist in the negotiation of the security context. The security context has a limited lifetime.

The algorithm used by Windows 2000 is defined in the Internet draft "GSS Algorithm for TSIG (GSS-TSIG)," which uses Kerberos version 5 as the underlying security. Resource records used are listed here:

◆ **TKEY**—Transfers security tokens client to server and server to client, and establishes secret keys

◆ **TSIG**—Sends and verifies digitally signed messages

The secure update process involves a number of steps (see Figure 12.7):

1. The client queries the local name server to find an authoritative server for the name to update.

2. The client attempts an insecure update.

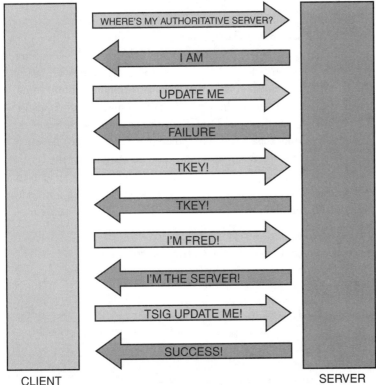

CLIENT   SERVER

FIGURE 12.7
Secure update flow chart.

3. The server refuses the insecure update.

4. The client and server begin the TKEY negotiation. What security do client and server both use?

5. TKEY tells the client to use Kerberos.

6. The client and the server perform mutual authentication.

7. A security context is established including the TSIG key.

8. The client attempts update with TSIG.

9. The server uses security context and TSIG to verify the client.

10. The server attempts to add, delete, or modify a resource record in Active Directory that is requested. The change is made if the client has proper permissions.

11. The server replies to the client indicating success or failure.

Security for Non-Windows 2000 Clients

These clients do not support the FQDN option. You can configure the DHCP server to make updates for them. The DHCP server is a member of the DNSUPdateproxy group. Ordinarily, the computer that places the record in DNS becomes the owner and, with secure updates, must manage it after that. You can see how without some special process, allowing the DHCP server to make secure updates on behalf of the client, the DHCP server becomes the owner of the record, and only that server can update that name. Other servers (backup servers, for example) cannot update the name if the IP address of the client changes. If the client computer is upgraded to Windows 2000, the Windows 2000 computer also could not update the IP information. Therefore, do not allow the DHCP server to make secure updates for these clients.

Instead, make these DHCP servers members of the DNSUPdateproxy group. This group has no security, and any computer can take over objects.

If the DHCP server also serves Windows 2000 computers, putting it into the DNSUpdateProxy group does not affect their ownership of the A record if they register it (as they do, by default).

> **WARNING**
>
> **Warning! Do Not Make a DHCP Server a Member of DNSUPDAT if the DHCP Server Is Installed on a Domain Controller** If you do this, then any user or computer will have full control of DNS records on all the domain controllers unless you modify the corresponding DACLs. This is because a DHCP server runs under the computer account; if installed on DC, it has full control over the DNS objects stored in Active Directory. If it has been configured to perform updates on behalf of clients, it can take ownership of any record, even in zones configured for secure dynamic update.

Other DNS Tips, Tricks, and Helpful Commands

If you have configured all clients to use a proxy server, and if you are using the proxy server to control access to and from the Internet, you will often find that users look for and find ways around the proxy server. To prevent them from going around the server, reconfigure the root domain of your internal DNS servers. This is also useful in preventing users from accessing the Internet in an environment where Internet access is not allowed.

The DNS root domain contains information on top-level DNS servers, such as servers in the .com domain. Top-level servers contain information on second-level servers. Resolving host-names begins with your local DNS server looking in its own database and then starting at the root and searching. If users can't find the top-level Internet root, then name resolution on the Internet will fail and users will not be able to surf Internet sites using conventional names. To create a new root zone for use in this scenario, use the new zone wizard and create a root zone that is represented by a period (.).

RIS SECURITY

Design Windows 2000 Remote Installation Services (RIS) security.

Remote Operating System Installation is a feature of Windows 2000 that is designed to automate installation of Windows 2000 Professional.

Remote Installation Services (RIS) is a service that allows installation of Windows 2000 Professional from a RIS server. The RIS server can deliver unattended system setup, fast recovery, and a network client computer configuration enabled for the remote-boot Preboot Execution Environment (PXE).

RIS can support Windows 2000 clients whose operating system needs to be restored, or new clients that have never had an operating system installed. It cannot be used to upgrade existing operating systems to Windows 2000 from downlevel Windows clients.

WARNING

WARNING! DACL Security If you put the DHCP server in this group, modify the DACL of the DNS of the DHCP server so that it has security.

NOTE

Helpful Commands Flushing DNS cache on computer: `ipconfig/flushdns`

If you are using dynamic update protocol to register names with DNS, and the IP address appears to be missing, you can force renewal of the registration:

Windows 2000: `ipconfig/registerdns`

Windows NT: `Ipconfig/release`, followed by `Ipconfig/renew`

Windows 9x: `Winipcfg/renew`

NOTE

Refusing Helpful Responses By default, the TCP/IP client or resolver accepts responses from servers that it did not query. This speeds performance but can be a security risk. You can configure the client not to accept these "helpful" responses:

Add the registry entry `QueryIPMatching` with a value of 1 (REG_DWORD) to HKEY_Local_Machine\SYSTEM\CurrentConrolSet\Services\DnsCAche\Parameters.

RIS allows the creation of a computer account in Active Directory, if configured to respond to any request for service from an authenticated user. In addition, you can define computer naming policy and the container within which the computer account is created.

You do this by setting a policy that defines naming, as in Step by Step 12.8.

STEP BY STEP

12.8 Define Computer Naming Policy

1. Open the Active Directory Computers and Users console.

2. Right-click the RIS server and select Properties.

3. Click Remote Install/Advanced Settings.

4. Click New Clients.

5. Define computer naming. (See instructions in Help and in the resource kit.)

6. Determine the location for the computer in Active Directory by selecting from the following:

   - **Default Directory Service Location**—(Set to Computers). The client becomes the computer in the same domain as the RIS server.

   - **Same Location as the User Setting Up the Computer**—This specifies the same container where the user's user object is located.

   - **A Specific Directory Service Location**—Specify which container you want. This allows you to specify a specific OU to contain all computers that have been installed by a particular RIS server.

To utilize the services of RIS, specific hardware and software requirements must be met. In addition, security considerations should be a part of the design and implementation of this service.

Requirements for RIS

To utilize RIS, you must have the following:

◆ RIS installed on a Windows 2000 Server.

◆ A DNS server must be present on the network (any DNS server that supports service records [SRV RR] [RFC 2782] and the dynamic update protocol [RFC 2136]).

◆ A DHCP server must be present on the network. Remote boot clients will obtain an IP address from the DHCP server.

◆ Access to Active Directory (membership in an Active Directory domain). RIS uses Active Directory to locate clients and other RIS servers.

◆ Client machines that meet certain hardware requirements.

These are the RIS clients hardware requirements:

◆ P-166 or better Net PC PXE-based, with remote boot enabled

◆ 32MB RAM

◆ 800MB or larger disk drive

◆ DHCP PXE-based boot ROM version l99c or later, or network adapter supported by RIS boot floppy disk

These requirements are not very stringent, and a large number of PCs will meet or exceed the requirements. PC98 or NetPC standards require PXE-based boot-enabled hardware.

If you choose to allow authorized users to create their own computer accounts and install the OS, you must do the following:

◆ Set the RIS server to Respond to Client Computers Requesting Service.

◆ Give the user a domain user account and password.

◆ Give the user read permission, and create computer object permission on the organizational unit that you have specified to hold the new computer account.

Security Issues

RIS is a powerful service that allows the administrator to provide operating system remote, automated installation, and repair. How could this be abused?

◆ Unauthorized users might install rogue computers by contacting RIS servers and installing Windows 2000 Professional.

◆ Rogue computers might join an Active Directory domain and thereby gain access to information resources within that domain.

◆ Rogue RIS servers might be installed.

◆ The ROM sequence is not secure, no packet encryption is used, client or server spoofing may be possible, and wire-sniffing-based mechanisms can see the activity.

◆ When a RIS boot disk is used, the login information is stored in clear text.

◆ RIS can be used to prepare an image not just of the OS, but of a preconfigured desktop, so the possibility exists of using it to prepare an image of a computer with data on it and then placing that image on another rogue computer.

Designing Security for RIS

Securing RIS requires knowledge of its operation and the requirements of your organization. Several features of RIS can be configured to make it more secure.

To restrict which computers can update or install the OS, you configure the RIS administrative option Do Not Respond to Unknown Client Computers (see Figure 12.8). When this option is checked, only computers that exist in or that have been prestaged (that is, those that have a computer account created in Active Directory) can access the RIS server. The RIS server checks Active Directory to verify that a computer account exists.

You can assign computer accounts to specific RIS servers.

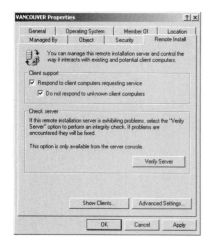

FIGURE 12.8
Restricting RIS.

To prestage computer accounts, you create them in Active Directory in the normal manner, or you create the computer account using the computer GUID. The GUID is in the system BIOS of the computer; you may find it also listed on the outside of the computer case.

Users then can install an OS on the prestaged client if they have the right to read and write all properties on the specific computer object (not the container) that was created. The user also needs the right to reset and change his password.

Clients can also be restricted by using Group Policy, as in Step by Step 12.9.

STEP BY STEP

12.9 Restricting RIS Client Options with Group Policy

1. RIS policy settings are applied by default in the Default Domain Policy Object item. Open Active Directory Users and Computers from the Administrative Tools menu.

2. Select the domain (or select an OU that contains the users you want to control).

3. Right-click the object, Click Properties, and then click the Group Policy tab.

4. Select the Group Policy object to modify or create a new one.

5. Click Edit.

6. Click User Configuration\Windows Settings\Remote Installation Services.

7. In the Details pane, double-click Choice Options.

8. Set desired settings for the users this policy affects: Automatic Setup, Custom Setup, Restart Setup, and Tools. For information on each of these settings, see Table 12.1. Each policy can be configured as follows:

   - **Allow**—Users are allowed to access that option in the Client Installation Wizard.

   - **Don't Care**—Users receive policy from parent container.

   - **Deny**—Users are not allowed to access that installation option.

9. Click OK.

TABLE 12.1

CHOICE OPTIONS FOR RIS POLICY

Policy Option	Notes
Automatic Setup	Automatic Setup does not provide the user client choices during setup. The administrator is responsible for most configuration.
Custom Setup	Using this option provides a choice of computer name and location within Active Directory.
Restart Setup	If a setup fails before completion, turning on this option allows the setup to attempt a continuation instead of starting again at the beginning.
Tools	Remote installation tools are provided by independent software vendors (ISVs) or original equipment software vendors (OEMs). They may be things such as flash bios or other maintenance and troubleshooting tools. The tools can be used by administrators to help troubleshoot problems because, before installation of the operating system, the hard disk might be empty. These tools also provide an easy way to update client computer systems.

To prevent rogue RIS servers, make sure that you control who can authorize RIS servers on the network. RIS servers must be authorized to run before they can accept requests. See Step by Step 12.10 for instructions on performing this procedure.

STEP BY STEP

12.10 Authorizing a RIS Server

1. Log onto the domain where the RIS server resides (you must be a member of the Enterprise Admins group).

2. Open the DHCP Management snap-in.

3. Right-click the DHCP root note in the Scope pane.

4. Click Manage Authorized Servers.

5. Click Authorize, and enter the IP address or name of the RIS server. Then click OK and click Yes.

Designing RIS Services for Large Organizations

In large organizations, you may want to set RIS servers for specific purposes. Some could be designated to install only new OSs; others could be used only for service repair requests.

In any organization, you will want to control the number of administrators that are allowed to install or configure RIS servers. In larger organizations, this becomes a greater issue because it can easily get out of control.

As an added precaution, configure the Boot Information Negotiation Layer (BINL) to use Active Directory to check credentials. The BINL listens for and answers DHCP (PXE) requests and service client installation requests. By configuring it to check credentials, you are adding another layer of security.

SNMP

Design Windows 2000 SNMP security.

SNMP is a network management protocol used with TCP/IP networks. The standard includes:

◆ **RFC 1213 MIB**—This is a set of objects that can be managed. This includes items such as network interfaces, a routing table, an ARP table, open TCP connections.

◆ **RFC 1902**—This details Structure for Management Information (SMI), which describes the syntax for referencing and storing MIB data.

◆ **RFC 1157**—This defines Simple Network Management Protocol and communication between devices.

A central host can use SNMP to manage many devices, including servers, routers, and hubs. Agents are loaded on devices, and management software runs at the central location.

Windows 2000 implements versions 1 and 2C. The agent is optional on Professional. Windows 2000 provides only the agent, not the management software application. APIs (WinSNMP API and the Management API) can be used to develop management applications. SNMPUtil.exe is a tool on the Windows 2000 installation CD that is a simple example of how a management tool might be developed.

A management system can request information and make configuration requests information for the following:

◆ Protocol ID and stats

◆ Hardware/software configuration

◆ Device performance stats

◆ Device errors

◆ Other statistics

Because most configuration information is read-only, SNMP configuration requests may not always be granted.

Agents respond to management system requests, but they can be configured to generate activity in response to event triggered alarms or traps. An example of this might be reboot. These traps can notify the management station that a security event has occurred.

SNMP uses UDP port 161 to listen for messages and UDP port 162 for SNMP traps.

SNMP messages are as follows:

◆ **GET**—Obtain report information.

◆ **GET-NEXT**—Browse the hierarchy of objects.

◆ **SET**—Configure.

◆ **GET-Bulk**—Get as much information as possible so that I don't have to keep asking.

◆ **NOTIFY**—Trap message.

SNMP Security Settings

SNMP agents respond to requests for information, so this information should be restricted. Only rudimentary security configuration is available. SNMP is configured from the Computer Management Console/services/SNMP object. Configuring security for SNMP may include any of the following:

◆ Configure traps to do security checking.

◆ Join hosts and agents to SNMP communities, and use these to authenticate SNMP messages.

◆ Secure SNMP messages with IP security.

Configure Traps

Traps are configured to generate a message when an event occurs. Such events might be requests for information from an unknown management system or for password violation.

A trap is configured with the hostname and IP addresses of the management system. Traps are configured in Windows 2000 from the SNMP Properties dialog box.

Configure Communities

An SNMP community is a collection of hosts identified by a name you assign. Community names are just made-up names and have no connection with domain or workgroup names. You use community names to authenticate SNMP messages. Hosts can belong to several communities at the same time. Agents do not accept requests from management systems that are not in one of its communities.

In addition, you can configure permission for the communities on the Security tab of the SNMP Properties dialog box. Permissions available are listed here:

◆ None or Notify causes the agent to discard requests and send an authentication trap.

◆ Read Only does not allow the processing of SET requests. The requests are discarded, and a trap is entreated.

◆ Read Create and Read Write allow processing of all requests, including SET.

Other options include setting which hosts packets will be accepted from. They include:

◆ **Accept SNMP packets from any host**—Default.

◆ **Accept SNMP packets from these hosts**—A list of acceptable hosts represents acceptable management systems.

Secure SNMP Messages with IP Security

You can implement IP security to secure SNMP messages. This is an all-or-nothing venture, though. If you do so, you must configure all SNMP-enabled systems to use IPSec.

By default, IPSec will not encrypt the SNMP protocol messages. You will need to create a filter for traffic between management systems and agents. To learn more about IPSec, see Chapter 15, "Designing Security for Communication Channels."

CASE STUDY: LUCKY TOWN SCHOOL DISTRICT

BACKGROUND

The Lucky Town school district is comprised of 3 high schools, 21 elementary schools, and 9 middle schools. A district office is located next door to the original high school campus. The school system has always prided itself on being technologically advanced. It has had computer labs for many years and now features multiple computers in every classroom. Students, teachers, and staff receive computer training as part of multiple grants and program initiatives.

PROBLEM STATEMENT

Windows 2000 has been installed throughout the school district. All computers run Windows, with the exception of two labs at the one elementary school. The district superintendent has read about teenagers hacking into computer systems and wonders if the district system is secure. All aspects of information systems security will be reviewed. The first topic to come under scrutiny

was passwords, and that has been delegated to a committee for research. Luckily, the subject of network services sounded a little incomprehensible to the district supervisor, so he has delegated that to the systems administrator and his staff of three.

The IT staff feels that a pretty secure system has been set up.

The school staff and teachers complain a lot about inconsistencies in the system and how difficult it is to use. They point to having to type in IP addresses, whatever those are, to receive their email and to access some programs at district offices. Some office computers can be used to enter information at district headquarters, and some cannot. When the help desk is asked why, staffers cannot figure out why. The business teachers at the high school are particularly vocal. They feel that they are responsible, computer-literate adults who should have more control over their own systems.

CASE STUDY: LUCKY TOWN SCHOOL DISTRICT

When new lab computers arrive, it takes several weeks before district personnel arrive to set up the systems and install Windows 2000.

When a machine crashes and needs to be rebuilt, a similar wait is experienced.

CURRENT SYSTEM

Two Windows 2000 domains exist in a single forest. The root domain, district.huzzah, contains district records. Only staff, teachers, and information systems staff have user accounts in this domain. Computer accounts consist of Windows 2000 domain controllers, standalone servers, and Windows 2000 Professional systems that are used at district headquarters. No student lab computers, local school computers, or student accounts exist in this domain. The second domain, SchooLabs, has a domain controller at every school and one at district headquarters. An OU for each school has been created, and underneath each OU is an OU for each lab located at the school and an OU to contain student accounts. Each lab OU has the computer accounts for computers within each lab. Teachers have user accounts at the school OU level. Students have accounts at the school.student OU.

The DNS servers are two domain controllers in the district.huzzah domain. They are located at district headquarters. One hosts a standard primary zone, district.huzzah, and the other hosts the standard secondary zone and the district DHCP server. The district.huzzah zone contains the subdomain SchooLabs.district.huzzah. Zones are configured to accept dynamic updates.

No school has a primary or secondary DNS zone server. Schools are linked to the district office primarily via direct dial-up.

Each school has at least one file server that is used by teachers and staff for storage and that stores copies of district-wide information.

There is no district Web server. Internet access is accomplished via dial-up modems in some labs and a proxy server at larger schools.

PROPOSED SYSTEM

The standard primary zone will be changed to an Active Directory-integrated zone. This zone will be configured for secure updates only. A RIS server will be installed at district headquarters and used to build or repair computer systems at district headquarters and at the schools. Only the systems administrator will be allowed to configure and manage the RIS server and kick off the process of building or repairing systems.

PERFORMANCE

The addition of the RIS server should help get new equipment configured faster.

MAINTAINABILITY

Because computers are already configured into OUs, the capability to set up and control new systems will be easy to continue.

continues

CASE STUDY: LUCKY TOWN SCHOOL DISTRICT

continued

ANALYSIS

Setting up Active Directory-integrated zones is a good idea. The school district can control dynamic updates and be assured that only authorized computers are doing the updating. The DHCP server, however, should not be on a domain controller. This might allow unauthorized users or computers full control of DNS records corresponding to the domain controllers.

Because the child domain, SchooLabs.district.huzzah DNS, will be managed as a subdomain in the district.huzzah zone, there is no need to set up a separate DNS zone for it. However, because the school computers must access a DNS server across dial-up lines, name resolution outside of their subnet will still be a problem. (Note the complaints in the earlier section "Problem Statement.") It is not a wise idea for users to have to enter IP addresses. That not only confuses the user, but it allows IP addresses of possibly sensitive servers to be available publicly. The district could implement a DNS server on the file server and create a secondary zone. Replication could then be established between the secondary zone server and the Active Directory-integrated zone. In this manner, local name resolution can be accomplished. This also provides off-site backup of zone file information, if that ever is needed by the district in an emergency. By definition, a secondary zone is a read-only copy, so local personnel would not be able to make changes to records in the zone file.

Adding a RIS server is a good idea as well because it will help the district set up new systems in an efficient manner. However, doing a RIS install across a dial-up line is impractical, if not impossible. The district will either end up setting up systems at district offices and physically moving them to the schools (another time delay) or abandoning the project. A RIS server could be established at each school and provide for OS installation locally. Security settings can ensure that only authorized systems are capable of using the service. Management of the service can be retained by district personnel.

CHAPTER SUMMARY

Three Windows 2000 services were analyzed to determine special security considerations that they present. You will use this information in your planning and design efforts. If these services are used in your design, be sure to include decisions on the implementation of appropriate security guidelines. Although every network is not the same, the same considerations need to be weighed.

Does the service present new risks to the organization by its implementation? Does some feature of the service expose some new security risk or allow you to control or ameliorate some risk? What can be done to counter this issue, or how can the feature be used to its advantage?

Finally, how should you attack the design and use of other services in Windows 2000? Have you noticed a strategy?

◆ Determine what the service does and how it does it.

◆ If it is applicable and necessary in your organization, look for security vulnerabilities.

◆ Plan your design to include steps that will use security features to your advantage, or that will mitigate the impact of using this service.

KEY TERMS

- trap
- community
- SNMP agent
- SNMP management system
- RIS
- remote OS
- PXE
- secure dynamic update
- standard primary zone
- standard secondary zone

APPLY YOUR KNOWLEDGE

Review Questions

1. How does the DHCP server know the FQDN of the client so that it can properly register the PTR record?

2. How can you use client side configuration changes to prevent the default DHCP server behavior toward registering IP addresses?

3. What is the advantage of making the DNS zone files Active Directory-integrated?

4. What is the default action if a Windows 2000 computer attempts to register its name and IP address with DNS, and finds that another computer has already registered that name and address? Is this a problem? Can this action be changed?

5. How can you prevent administrators from installing DHCP servers on your network?

6. Can Windows 2000 securely interoperate with third-party dynamic DNS servers that have implemented RFC 2137, "Secure Domain Name System Dynamic Update"? Why or why not?

7. RIS can be used to install Windows 2000 Professional on a computer that does not have an operating system. An account for the computer in Active Directory can be created during this process. Is this operation secure? If you don't think that it is, is there a way to make it more secure?

8. If you remove all community names from the SNMP agent interface, which management system will be capable of obtaining information from the SNMP agent?

9. Explain how SNMP agents can be used to alert administrators of unauthorized attempts to log on to secured servers.

Exam Questions

1. The Lucky Town school district wants to control all computers in the district. The district wants to ensure that its DHCP servers do all dynamic updates. All computers are Windows 20000. The file server and the principal's computer at each school are assigned a static IP address. All other Windows 2000 Professional computers are assigned addresses by DHCP. Assuming that no changes are made to either the client configuration or that of the Windows 2000 DNS server, what needs to be done to ensure that no computer dynamically updates its own IP address?

   A. Nothing needs to be done. The DHCP server will automatically dynamically update all records.

   B. Any Windows 2000 computers with static addresses must have dynamic addressing turned off. The DHCP server will automatically update all records.

   C. All Windows 2000 computers must be configured to not dynamically update their own address. The DHCP server needs to be configured to update both the A and the PTR records.

   D. All Windows 2000 computers must be configured to not dynamically update their own address. The DHCP server needs to be configured to update both the A and the PTR records. Computers with static IP addresses will have to be manually updated in the DNS zone file.

2. The Lucky Town school district wants to make sure that DNS records can be updated even if the original DHCP server is replaced or additional

DHCP servers are built. The district has configured secure updating and placed the DHCP
server in the DnsUpdateProxy group. Does the
district need to do anything to secure the DHCP
server or other computers because of this?

A. No. This group is designed to participate in
the secure update zone.

B. If the DHCP server is not located on a
domain controller, the DHCP server is running under the context of the domain controller system and has full control of the DNS
objects stored in Active Directory.

C. The DHCP server host (A) record is not
secure. Because the computer is in the
DnsUpdateProxy group, it does not own any
record that it updates, including its own.
Change ownership on this record to prevent
unauthorized computers or users from
changing it.

D. Every computer DNS host record will have to
be configured to make sure that only it can
update its DNS record.

3. Paint Productions, Inc., is setting up DNS. The
company would like to use any new features that
Windows 2000 has to offer. Staffers notice the
DnsUpdateProxy group and wonder how it can
be used. They have asked you to participate in
their efforts. You tell them that DnsUpdateProxy
is used for which purpose?

A. To contain all computers that have the privilege of updating their records in an Active
Directory-integrated zone that has been configured for secure update

B. To contain all the users who have the privilege of updating a computer's DNS records in

Active Directory-integrated zone that has
been configure for secure update

C. To contain all the computers that have the
privilege of updating their records in an
Active Directory-integrated zone that has
been configured for dynamic update

D. To contain the DHCP servers that will be
updating DNS records for computers in an
Active Directory-integrated zone

4. You are setting up RIS. You want users to have
some choices when installing the operating
system, such as naming their computers, but do
not want them to be able to use diagnostics tools
or upgrade the bios, even if you have such tools
available on the system for your use in troubleshooting. In the Group Policy object for the
domain, you select Remote Installations Services.
Then you open Choice Options in the Details
pane. You make the following settings:

A. Automatic Setup: Allow; Custom Setup:
Allow; Restart Setup: Allow; Tools: Allow

B. Automatic Setup: Don't Care; Custom Setup:
Allow; Restart Setup: Allow; Tools: Deny

C. Automatic Setup: Don't Care; Custom Setup:
Deny; Restart Setup: Allow; Tools: Deny

D. Automatic Setup: Don't Care; Custom Setup:
Allow; Restart Setup: Allow; Tools: Allow

5. To establish secure dynamic DNS updating with
Windows 2000, you must:

A. Make sure that your DNS zones are Active
Directory-integrated zones.

B. Not run the DHCP service on the domain
controller if you are using the DNSUpdate
proxy group.

C. Configure the zone to accept only secure updates.

D. Specify users and computers that are authorized to modify zones and resource records.

E. Configure clients to use secure update only.

6. Windows 2000 can update DNS with records of its IP addresses for:

A. DHCP adapters

B. Static adapters

C. Remote access adapters

D. Multihomed adapters

E. Multiple adapters in the same computers

7. Windows 2000 computers send updates on their IP address(es) when?

A. Every 48 hours

B. When TCP/IP configuration changes

C. When an IP address is added or removed and the computer is not restarted

D. When the user runs the Update IP Address Wizard

8. To lock down the RIS service, what do you do?

A. Set the RIS server to Respond to Client Computers Requesting Service.

B. Prestage computer accounts in Active Directory.

C. Give the user read permission and create computer object permission on the organizational unit that you have specified to hold the new computer account.

D. Create computer accounts in Active Directory using the computer GUID found in the BIOS of the computer.

E. Define the computer naming policy.

F. Restrict RIS client options with Group Policy.

9. Steps that can be taken to secure SNMP on your network include which of the following?

A. Configure traps to do security checking.

B. Set permissions for SNMP agents in Active Directory.

C. Make sure that all hosts and agents are part of appropriate SNMP communities.

D. Make sure that the community Public is listed in the list of approved communities.

E. Limit the installation of the SNMP agent to necessary devices.

F. Secure SNMP messages with IPSec.

10. The Altair community is established to provide SNMP agents to share information with management applications. The administrator suspects that a rogue management application is working the network and obtaining information via this community. To stop a possible attacker from obtaining device information while he investigates, the administrator reconfigures the community permissions on agents. Which of the following does he do?

A. Sets the permission for the Altair community to None

B. Sets the permission for the Altair community to Read Only

C. Sets the permission for the Altair community to Read Create

APPLY YOUR KNOWLEDGE

    D. Sets the permission for the Public community to None

    E. Sets the permission for the Public community to Read Only

    F. Sets the permission for the Public community to Read Create

Answers to Review Questions

1. If the client is a Windows 2000 client, the DHCP server gets the FQDN from option 81, an optional parameter in the DHCPREQUEST packet. If the client is not a Windows 2000 client, then the DHCP server creates a FQDN from the client name in the DHCPREQUEST packet and the domain name that is authoritative in the scope from which it is assigning an IP address.

2. By default, the DHCP server may register a client's A or PTR record, or both. The DHCP server is following the REQUEST of the Windows 2000 client. You can configure the client to request ALWAYS (DHCP always does the registration of A and PTR records) or NEVER (DHCP will never update the record; the client must do so).

3. Active Directory-integrated zone files have multiple advantages. Dynamic updating of IP addressing can be made more secure. The zones benefit from Active Directory replication: There is no single point of failure, and you do not have to set up or separately manage another replication structure in your network. The zones are fault-tolerant as well, so changes can be made on any copy of the zone and be replicated to all copies.

4. By default, a Windows 2000 computer that attempts to register its computer name and IP address in DNS and that finds that another computer has registered it will overwrite the existing record. This is not good because the address it is overwriting may actually be the legal one. This default would allow a rogue computer to overwrite important records, including those of servers on your network. To prevent Windows 2000 clients under your control from doing this, you can make a registry change. To prevent a rogue computer from doing this, you should use Active Directory-integrated zones and secure the update process. Properly setting up secure dynamic update prevents the overwriting of DNS resource records.

5. You cannot prevent administrators from installing the DHCP service on your network. However, you can prevent unauthorized Windows 2000 DHCP servers from operating on your network. Each Windows 2000 server checks itself at startup and then periodically to see whether it is among the listed authorized DHCP servers on the network. If it is not listed, the service will not start and the DHCP server will not respond to clients.

6. Windows 2000 uses the IETF RFC 2078 draft "Generic Security Service Application Program Interface." It does not support RFC 2137, so it cannot securely interoperate with third-party DNS servers that only use this approach.

7. To securely operate RIS, you must configure RIS to Do Not Respond to Unknown Client Computers. This will prevent any non-prestaged computer from installing the Windows 2000 operating system via this RIS server. Prestaging a computer means to create a computer account for that computer in Active Directory.

APPLY YOUR KNOWLEDGE

8. If there are no community names in the SNMP agent, the agent will not communicate with any management system.

9. SNMP agents can be configured to send a trap message to the management system when unsuccessful attempts are made to log on to the device.

Answers to Exam Questions

1. **D.** By default, Windows 2000 computers attempt to update their own DNS record. If they receive their address via DHCP, they share this responsibility with the DHCP server. To make the DHCP server responsible for all updates, you must configure the clients not to update and then configure the DHCP server to update for all clients. The statically addressed computers' records cannot be updated dynamically because you have turned off that feature. Answer C is wrong because it doesn't plan for this. (See the section "Default Behavior: DHCP Updating of DNS.")

2. **C.** The DHCP server host or A record could be updated by any computer because placing the DHCP server in the group allows this. Answer B is wrong. If the DHCP server *is* located on a domain controller, then this is a problem. (See the sections "Resource Record Ownership Issue" and "Securing Dynamic Updates.")

3. **D.** DnsUpdateProxy group is used for DHCP servers. (See the section "Securing Dynamic Updates" and "Resource Record Ownership Issue.")

4. **B.** Tools must be set to Deny, and Custom Setup must be set to Allow. Restart wasn't mentioned, so it could be Allow or Deny. Automated should be Don't Care. Answer A is wrong because Tools is set to Allow. Answer C is wrong because Custom Setup is set to Deny. Answer D is incorrect because Tools is set to Allow. (See the section "Designing Security for RIS.")

5. **A, B, C, D.** Simply making the DNS Zone Active Directory integrated will not secure dynamic DNS updates. You must configure the zone to allow only secure updates and configure it to allow updates by users and computers. Setting the clients to Secure Only is a good extra precaution, but the clients by default will attempt an insecure update first and then a secure update when that fails. Proper configuration of the server will insist on the secure update process. (See section the "Securing Dynamic Updates.")

6. **A, B, C, E.** Windows 2000 will update only the first address on its adapter if the adapter holds multiple addresses. The DHCP server must be set to Update DNS Only if DNS Client Requests (this is the default); otherwise, when one adapter update is made, DHCP will update all known records for this computer to the same IP address. (See the section "The Dynamic Update Process for DHCP clients.")

7. **B, C.** Windows 2000 also updates its IP address every 24 hours. There is no wizard that will update the IP address. (See the section "The Dynamic Update Process for DHCP Clients.")

APPLY YOUR KNOWLEDGE

8. **B, F.** If you set the RIS server to Respond to Client Computers Requesting Service, you are allowing any computer to load the OS and add its computer account to Active Directory (if the user account has the appropriate permissions). If you give the user read permission and create computer permission, you have given that user the right to add a computer account to Active Directory. If the RIS server allows the user to load the OS, that user will be able to add the computer account. Although you can create the computer account in Active Directory by using the GUID of the computer, this is no guarantee that if the computer account doesn't have the GUID, it won't install and create a computer account. (See the section "Designing Security for RIS.")

9. **A, C, E, F.** There is no way to set permissions for SNMP agents in Active Directory. Leaving the community Public in the list of communities opens up the agent for attack because this is a well-known community name. (See the section "Configure Communities.")

10. **A.** Setting the permissions on the Public community will not keep attackers from using the Altair community. None or Notify are the only permissions that will totally keep the agent from responding. (See the section "Configure Traps.")

Suggested Readings and Resources

1. *Microsoft Windows 2000 Resource Kit: TCP/IP Core Networking Guide.* Microsoft Press, 2000.

   - Chapter 4: "Dynamic Host Configuration Protocol"
   - Chapter 5: "Introduction to DNS"
   - Chapter 6: "Windows 2000 DNS"
   - Chapter 10: "Simple Network Management Protocol"
   - Appendix E: "DHCP Options"

2. Iseminger, David. *Active Directory Services for Windows 2000 Technical Reference.* Microsoft Press, 2000.

   - Chapter 14: "Administratively Leveraging Active Directory Services"

3. RFCs, drafts, and working papers available from ietf.org

   - "Secret Key Establishment for DNS (TKEY RR)"
   - "Secret Key Transaction Signatures for DNS (TSIG)"

4. URLs

   - http://windows.microsoft.com/windows2000/ reskit/webresources (search for IETF Internet draft "Interaction Between DHCP and DNS")
   - www.ins.com/knowledge/whitepapers/ win_2k_dns_integration.asp ("Windows 2000 DNS Integration," by Morgan Stern)
   - www.isc.org (Internet software consortium [ISC])

DESIGNING A SECURITY SOLUTION FOR ACCESS BETWEEN NETWORKS

This chapter does not cover specific exam objectives but provides detailed information on the tools needed to design secure communications and connections between networks, which are covered in Chapter 14, "Designing Security for Access Between Networks" and Chapter 15, "Designing Security for Communication Channels."

CHAPTER 13

Providing Secure Access Between Networks

INTRODUCTION

To design secure communications and connections to, from, and between networks, you need to examine the tools available to do so. Some of these tools, such as those that make up a public key infra-structure, you have already examined. Others are described in this chapter and the next. Each tool, process, or protocol described here can be put to practical use in your designs. Not detailed here, but used in the design examples, is the IP Security protocol IPSec, which is covered in Chapter 15, "Designing Security for Communication Channels."

Your knowledge of these tools will enable you to make better design choices. Although no exam objectives explicitly mention these services, you could hardly design secure access to and between private networks without detailed knowledge of them.

The following services and processes contribute to secure network communications:

◆ NAT and Internet Connection Sharing

◆ Proxy server

◆ Routing and Remote Access Services

◆ Internet Authentication Services

◆ Virtual private networking

◆ Terminal Services

In Chapter 14, you will see that some of the solutions may use one of these services. Others may use several.

NAT AND INTERNET CONNECTION SHARING

Network Address Translation (NAT) is an IP router defined in RFC 1631. NAT is used to hide internal IP addresses by inserting new IP addresses and possibly new TCP/UDP port numbers of packets from one network before they are forwarded to another. NAT is also used to connect many computers to the Internet without having a corresponding number of valid Internet addresses. Private network addresses can be mapped to one or to multiple Internet addresses. Mapping can be dynamic or static. Private IP addressing (defined in RFC 1918) can be used for the internal, private network.

The private IP addressing scheme includes several ranges of IP addresses that are not usable on the Internet. Companies can use these for computers that do not directly connect to the Internet. When these computers need Internet access, they must use a proxy or other address translation scheme. NAT can do this. The computer address (and maybe the port of the source computer) is replaced by the NAT server with a legal Internet address. When the response is returned to the NAT server, NAT replaces the translated address with the private address.

The private address ranges are listed here:

◆ 10.0.0.0–10.255.255.255 (10/8 prefix)

◆ 172.16.0.0–172.31.255.255 (172.16./12 prefix)

◆ 192.168.0.0–192.168.255.255 (192.168./16 prefix)

NOTE **IPSec and NAT—No Way** IPSec encapsulates and encrypts the entire payload. The only part of the packet that is not encrypted is the source and destination IP address. Because the port number cannot be determined, you cannot use NAT to forward IPSec packets.

NAT editors can be used to configure the NAT component to translate the payload beyond the IP, TCP, and UDP headers that are handled by default. File Translation Protocol (FTP), Internet Control Message Protocol (ICMP), Point-to-Point Tunneling Protocol (PPTP), and NetBIOS over TCP/IP are examples of protocols that require this action. Windows 2000 includes built-in NAT editors for these protocols and proxy software for H.323, Direct Play, Lightweight Directory Access Protocol (LDAP) Internet Locator Service (ILS) registration and Remote Procedure Call (RPC).

NAT is part of the Windows 2000 Routing and Remote Access Protocol. It is also available as part of the Internet Connection Sharing feature of the Dial-up connections folder. Internet Connection Sharing uses a scaled-down version of NAT. Its version of NAT is less configurable than that in the Routing and Remote Access Protocol.

NAT adds no additional authentication or other security configuration or processes.

Internet Connection Sharing (see Figure 13.1) should be used only by a home office or small office. It can be used to share a dial-up or VPN connection back to the main office among other computers connected on the LAN.

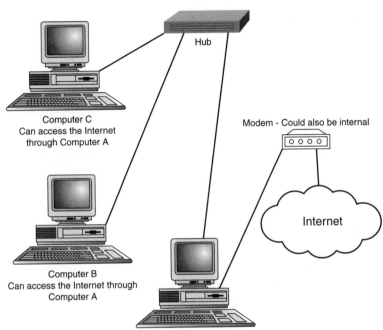

FIGURE 13.1
Internet Connection Sharing.

Hub

Computer C
Can access the Internet
through Computer A

Modem - Could also be internal

Internet

Computer B
Can access the Internet through
Computer A

Windows 2000 Professional computer with
Internet connection sharing configured
and a single connection to the Internet through an ISP

ROUTING AND REMOTE ACCESS SERVICES

Windows 2000 Routing and Remote Access Services is composed of the following:

◆ Routing Information Protocol (RIP) version 2, the routing protocol for IP and IPX

◆ Open Shortest Path First (OSPF) routing protocol for IP

◆ Demand-dial routing

◆ ICMP router discovery

◆ Internet Group Management Protocol (IGMP) and multicast boundary support

◆ Remote Authentication Dial-In Service (RADIUS) client

◆ IP and IPX packet filtering

◆ Point-to-Point Tunneling Protocol (PPTP) support for router-to-router VPN connections

◆ Routing and Remote Access Console and Netsh (command line) for administration

◆ Network Address Translation (NAT)

◆ Integrated AppleTalk routing

◆ Layer 2 Tunneling Protocol (L2TP) over IP Security (IPSec) support for router-to-router VPN connections

◆ Support for client-to-router VPN connections

Using these technologies, a Windows 2000 Server can become a multiprotocol router, a demand-dial router, and a remote access server. To enable secure network connections and communications, you may use Routing and Remote Access Services to establish a remote access server or a demand-dial router.

Remote Access Server

The remote access server accepts Point-to-Point Protocol (PPP) connections. PPP can be configured to require authentication. The Windows 2000 PPP infrastructure provides support for the following:

◆ Dial-up remote access

◆ VPN remote access using either PPTP or L2TP over IPSec

◆ On-demand or persistent dial-up demand routing

◆ On-demand or persistent VPN demand-dial routing

A connection is truly a connection when the user is authenticated by the network, and when verification is done on the security principal and the user is authorized for dial-in access to the network. Authentication may be via Windows authentication (your user ID and password are correct). Authorization is via Remote Access Policies, which verify that the connection is allowed.

The Routing and Remote Access Server (RRAS) may also be configured to accept only Remote Authentication Dial-In User Service (RADIUS), in which case the dial-up credentials are passed to the RADIUS server for authentication and authorization. Remote Access Policy is then centralized at the Internet Access Server (IAS, Microsoft's implementation of the RADIUS service), not at the RRAS server.

Figure 13.2 shows the authentication and authorization process when the Routing and Remote Access Server uses Windows authentication.

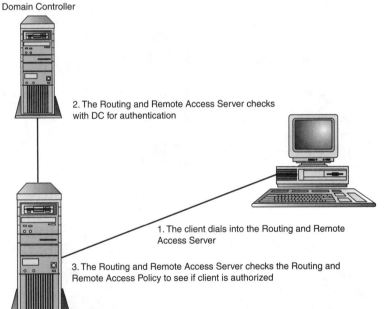

Domain Controller

2. The Routing and Remote Access Server checks with DC for authentication

1. The client dials into the Routing and Remote Access Server

3. The Routing and Remote Access Server checks the Routing and Remote Access Policy to see if client is authorized

Routing and Remote Access Server

FIGURE 13.2
Authentication and authorization.

NOTE

IAS—The Windows 2000 RADIUS
Windows 2000 includes a RADIUS
server that is known as the Internet
Authentication Service. If this RADIUS
server is used, Windows 2000
authentication is used (between the
IAS server and the DC), and authorization is accomplished by using the dial-
up properties of the user account and
the Remote Access Policies set on
the IAS server. The RRAS server acts
as a RADIUS client and authenticates
to the IAS server. More information on
IAS is provided later.

Figure 13.3 shows the authentication and authorization process when the Routing and Remote Access Server uses RADIUS.

Secure remote access may be accomplished by requiring the following:

◆ Authentication

◆ Mutual authentication

◆ Data encryption

◆ Remote access lockout

Authentication

Authentication is configured by using the Security tab of the Routing and Remote Access Server (RRAS) properties pages. RRAS servers are managed from the Routing and Remote Access console. Alternatively, the `netsh ras aaaa set authentication` and `netsh ras aaaa set authserver` commands can be used.

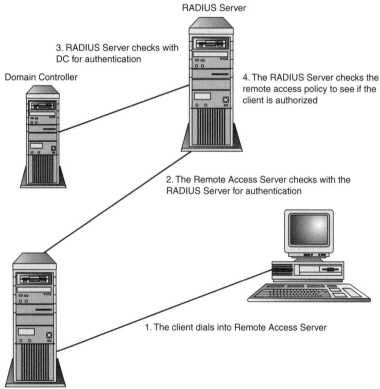

FIGURE 13.3
Authentication and authorization with RADIUS.

Routing and Remote Access is always installed when Windows 2000 is installed, but it is left in an unconfigured state. To enable Routing and Remote Access, perform the steps in Step by Step 13.1.

STEP BY STEP

13.1 Enable Remote Access Services

1. Open the Routing and Remote Access console.

2. Right-click the Local Server icon.

3. Select Configure and Enable Routing and Remote Access.

4. Select Remote Access Server from the Common Configurations page of the Routing and Remote Access Server Setup Wizard.

5. Accept defaults for remaining pages of the wizard (or select RADIUS for authentication, if desired and available).

6. Right-click the Local Server icon and choose Properties.

7. Select the Security tab.

8. Select Windows Authentication or RADIUS Authentication for the Authentication Provider drop-down box.

9. If RADIUS is selected, you must use the Configure button to identify the RADIUS server.

10. Click the Authentication Methods button and select the method desired (see Figure 13.4).

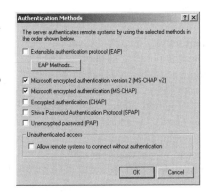

FIGURE 13.4
Authentication methods.

If the Windows Authentication method is chosen, a member server must become a member of the RAS and IAS Servers security group. This will be done automatically if the domain administrator enables the server. If the server is enabled by another user, then the domain administrator must place the server in this group before it can respond to calls. You can further define authentication by choosing a method. Methods available are defined in Table 13.1.

TABLE 13.1	
REMOTE ACCESS AUTHENTICATION METHODS	
Protocol	*Notes*
Extensible Authentication (EAP)	Further configured through Remote Access Policies. Choice is dependent on EAP methods installed. May include smart card, MD5-Challenge, TLS, and RADIUS.
Microsoft-encrypted authentication version 2 (MS-CHAP v2)	LAN Manager encoding is not supported. Mutual authentication is required. Separate keys are used for transmitting and receiving data. Keys are based on user's password and an arbitrary challenge string. A different key is used for every string.
Microsoft encrypted authentication (MS-CHAP)	Routing and Remote Access Server requires only an MD4 hash of the password to validate because the user's password is stored as an MD4 hash.
Encrypted authentication (CHAP)	Password is never sent over the link. MD5 used for challenge hash. Protects against replay attacks (uses arbitrary challenge string) and does not require server authentication.
Shiva Password Authentication Protocol (SPAP)	Used by remote access client to authenticate itself to a Shiva remote access server. Win32 clients can to authenticate to the remote access server. More secure than PAP, but less than CHAP or MS-CHAP.
Unencrypted password (PAP)	Plain-text authentication. Can be used by Win-32 clients to access older remote access servers, and for non-Windows clients to connect.
Unauthenticated access	No authentication required.

NOTE

Client Impact on Authentication
While it is possible to configure a remote access server to not require authentication, a client configured to require authentication using MS-CHAP v2 or EAP-TLS will force authentication negotiation or disconnect. This is because these protocols require server authentication.

Data Encryption

Data encryption will encrypt communications between the remote access client and the Routing and Remote Access Server (see Figure 13.5). If encryption is required from the client to the destination server, you will need to use other techniques such as IPSec to create an encrypted end-to-end connection (see Figure 13.6). An end-to-end connection is established after the remote access connection has been made.

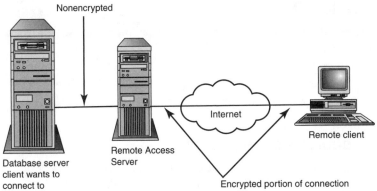

FIGURE 13.5
Data encryption: remote access server – client.

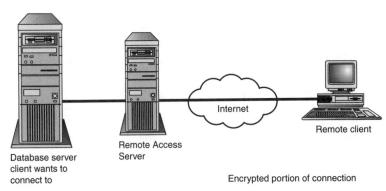

FIGURE 13.6
IPSec end-to-end encryption.

The encryption secret key is negotiated during the authentication process. Data encryption is possible only when using EAP-TLS or MS-CHAP. All Windows clients and remote access servers support Microsoft Point-to-Point Encryption Protocol (MPPE). This protocol uses the Rivest-Shamir-Adleman (RSA) RC4 stream cipher and 40-bit, 56-bit, or 128 bit keys.

Callback

Callback can be configured to call back the user after the connection has been authenticated and authorized. A traveling user can give the server a number to call back, thus saving phone charges. However, for secure callback, callback is configured to always call back a single number.

Caller ID

Caller ID is used to verify that a call is coming from a specified number. This is configured on the user properties sheet of dial-up connections. It will work only if the caller's phone line, the phone system, the remote access server's phone line, and the Windows 2000 driver for the dial-up equipment all support caller ID.

Remote Access Lockout

Remote access lockout can be configured to limit the number of authentication fails allowed before remote access is denied. This may foil a dictionary attack. A dictionary attack can consist of an automated attempt using thousands of words against the password. If lockout has not been configured, the dictionary attack may succeed.

Lockout parameters are set in the registry using two entries: MaxDenials, the maximum number of failed attempts (0 is disabled), and ResetTime, the number of minutes before the failed attempts counter is reset (0xb40, or 2,880, is the default).

The location of these values is at HKEY_LOCAL_MACHINE\ SYSTEM\CurrentControlSet\Services\RemoteAccess\Parameters\ AccountLockout.

If an account is locked, a registry subkey, domain name:*username*, will appear at the same location. To reset the account, delete this subkey.

Authorization

Authorization is based on the dial-in properties of a user account and Remote Access Policies. Dial-in properties are configured in the user properties pages on the Dial-In tab (see Figure 13.7). Access is allowed, denied, or controlled through Remote Access Policy.

When set, Remote Access Policies can impact remote access, service, and the Windows 2000 Internet Authentication Server. If the IAS server is used, all remote access policies are centrally configured and are controlled from the IAS server. Policies set on any Routing and Remote Access Servers that use the IAS server for authentication are ignored. To manage users on a per-user basis, you can set remote access permission on the user accounts and modify the properties of the default policy *Allow access if dial-in permission is enabled*. This policy is located below the server in the Routing and Remote Access

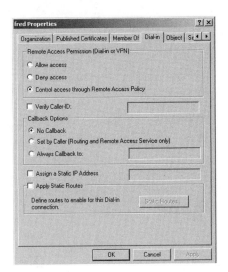

FIGURE 13.7
Dial-in access properties.

Console/Policies container (see Figure 13.8). If the RRAS server is configured to use the IAS server, policy must be set on the IAS server.

The default Remote Access Policy will deny connections unless access is specified on a user basis. The policy is set by default to cover all hours and all days. This can be modified using the Edit button. Additional policies can be configured to cover different time spans or different configurations, according to the policy profile. To set the profile, click the Edit Profile button.

The profile can be configured to restrict or allow access according to a number of authentication, encryption, dial-in, and other constraints. This is where you also limit access by group instead of individual user. Policies, then, can be used to configure different sets of conditions for different groups of individuals. To standardize multiple policies across multiple Routing and Remote Access Servers, you must install, configure, and run Windows 2000 IAS and configure each Routing and Remote Access or VPN server as a RADIUS client. As RADIUS clients, the RRAS servers will receive their Remote Access Policy from the IAS server.

FIGURE 13.8
Default Remote Access Policy.

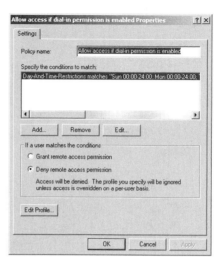

Authentication settings parallel those set for the Routing and Remote Access server. If multiple authentication choices are set on the server, you can configure different polices to use one, several, or none. Thus, a profile could be configured for clients that cannot perform one of the more secure authentication methods. Clients that can perform more secure authentication will use a different profile. When the less secure group of clients is upgraded, the profile can be easily removed.

Encryption choices are these:

◆ No encryption

◆ Basic

◆ Strong

The type of encryption used depends on the type of connection made. Table 13.2 outlines the choices.

TABLE 13.2

REMOTE ACCESS PROFILE ENCRYPTION CHOICES

Connection	Basic	Strong	Strongest
Dial-up and PPTP	MPPE/40-bit	MPPE/56-bit	MPPE/128-bit
L2TP over IPSec	56-bit DES	56-bit DES	3DES

Advanced settings are used only if RADIUS authentication is used; they are ignored by the Routing and Remote Access Server using Windows authentication.

IP properties allow control over IP assignment, including whether the client is allowed to request an address or whether the server must supply it. In addition, you can apply packet filters during the connection for either direction. You add filters that specify source and destination address, source and destination mask, protocol, source port or type, and destination port or code. Filters may be either exclusionary or inclusionary. Thus, you may select Permit All Traffic Except Those Listed Below, or Deny All Traffic Except Those Listed Below.

Dial-in constraints allow the following:

- ◆ Setting idle disconnect time
- ◆ Restricting session time
- ◆ Restricting access days and times
- ◆ Restricting dial-in to one number only
- ◆ Restricting dial-in media

If you have many dial-up numbers configured for your Routing and Remote Access server, it is useful to be able to restrict a security group to using a particular number.

NOTE **Achieving Strongest Encryption** To achieve this setting, you must load the Strong Encryption Pack. You should check Export/Import rules before doing so.

Demand-Dial Routing

Local area network connections and permanent wide area network connections are always available. Any packets that need to travel from one point to another can do so without waiting for a connection. A demand-dial interface can be either connected or disconnected. If a packet needs to travel across the demand-dial interface, the connection must be established before it can do so.

Establishing this connection may take some time—in fact, the connection establishment delay, as it is known, can take from 3 to 5 seconds for ISDN lines, and from 10 to 20 seconds for analog phone lines. This delay can have serious consequences if an application is attempting to run over the connection. If the delay is longer than the application timeout, the application will fail. This is why browser attempts may fail on the first attempt, but if retried, connect. The first attempt established the connection, but the browser timed out. The second attempt, or refresh, simply used the already established connection.

Demand-dial routing is a feature of Windows 2000 Remote Access Services. It is the forwarding of packets across a PPP link. This is not the same as remote access, which allows a client to dial into a remote server. Demand-dial routing connects networks, and multiple sessions can occur over this connection. Connections are configured router to router. You can configure idle disconnect behavior (the idle disconnect time) timeout or establish a persistent connection if this is required to support applications that may otherwise time out before a connection is made.

Router connections are authenticated by adding a user account to the server and configuring the router to use this account.

Demand-dial routing can be used to establish connection to the Internet, between branch offices, and for router-to-router virtual private network (VPN) connections. (While typical VPN connections are established across persistent WAN links such as T1, demand-dial connections can be used for this purpose if such connections are not available, or if less expensive, time-sensitive connections are desired.)

Establishing and Securing Demand-Dial Interfaces

To allow a router to be an answering router, an account must be created in the Users group of the domain or the server that will receive the call. This account is added during the installation of the Demand-Dial router using the Demand Dial Interface Wizard if you select Add A User Account So A Remote Router Can Dial In from the Protocols and Security page of the Demand Dial Interface Wizard (see Figure 13.9)

If you want only one-way connections (only one router will be capable of initiating the connection), do not select this option on the router that will be initiating the call. See Table 13.3 for an example of one-way connections. Here, The New York Branch office will be dialing in to HeadQTRS. The interface at HeadQTRS is called NewYork, and a dial-in user account of that name is created. The NewYork branch will use that account. The two user accounts must also have the same password.

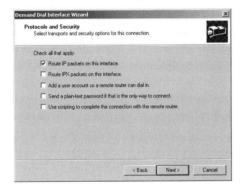

FIGURE 13.9
Creating a user account for the dial-up.

TABLE 13.3

ONE-WAY INITIATED CONNECTION CONFIGURATION

Router	Name of Local Interface	Dial-In User Account	Name of Remote Router Interface	Dial-Out User Account
Headquarters	NewYork	NewYork		
New York Branch Office	HeadQTRS		NewYork	NewYork

Table 13.4 shows an example of two-way user account configuration. The Dial In user account will be given the name that you establish as the name for the demand-dial interface, and you will be able to select a password for use during connections. The account is created for you and is added to the Domain Users group of the domain of which the demand-dial server is a member. The password is set to never expire. Dial-in credentials are used by the dialing router, so the credentials you establish here must be configured as the dial-out credentials on the other demand-dial router. The dial-out credentials are configured with the user account name, domain, and password of the account used by the other router (see Figure 13.10.)

TABLE 13.4

TWO-WAY INITIATED CONNECTION CONFIGURATION

Router	Interface	Dial-In User Account	Remote Router Interface	Dial-Out User Account
Headquarters	NewYork	NewYork	HeadQTRS	HeadQTRS
New York Branch Office	HeadQTRS	HeadQTRS	NewYork	NewYork

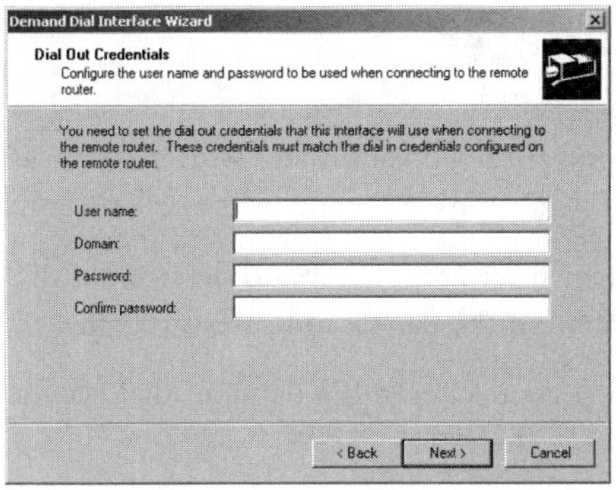

FIGURE 13.10
Determining two-way or one-way connections.

After installing a demand-dial interface, you configure it using property pages. Possible changes to security setting on the connection include these:

◆ Set a callback number. The number should be the number of the other demand-dial router. This ensures that only a connection with this router can be made.

◆ Require data encryption. (None is the default.)

◆ Change password settings from the default Require Secured Password to the option Allow Unsecured Password.

◆ Use Advanced settings to do the following:

 • Allow optional encryption, require encryption, or disallow encryption

 • Select authentication protocol

The security feature set for demand-dial routing is the same as it is for remote access connections. When encryption is required, the type of encryption used is configured in the Remote Access Policy.

After an interface is configured, you cannot change the user account used by the dial-in interface. To change the account, you create a new demand-dial interface. You change the password of the account in the normal manner. You can change the user account information for the dial-out interface.

Routing Process

When demand-dial interfaces have been established at complementary routers (one at each location you will be connecting to), demand-dial connections are made in the following manner:

1. The router receives a packet and determines the best route to use to forward the packet to its destination.

2. If the best route chosen is a demand-dial interface, the connection state is checked.

3. If the connection state is Connected, the packet is forwarded. If the connection state is Disconnected, the Dynamic Interface Manager is called and asked to start the demand-dial interface.

4. The Dynamic Interface Manager checks the policy settings (hours, filters)

5. If the connection is allowed, the Dynamic Interface Manager gets the `<system root>\System32\ras\router.pbk` (the configuration of the interface).

6. If the connection is dial-up, numbers are called and a physical connection is made.

7. If the connection is a VPN connection, tunnels or IPSec security association is established.

8. If the physical connection is made, a PPP connection is negotiated with the endpoint.

9. Authentication is accomplished via Windows authentication or RADIUS authentication, as specified in the configuration.

10. Any static routes configured for the user account of the calling router are configured as static routes for the answering router.

11. The router.pbk of the answering router is checked for the name of the demand-dial interface that matches the user credentials of the calling router. If this is found, the connection setting is changed to a connected state.

12. The calling router can now forward packets across the connection. Packets will be subject to the packet filters configured on the demand-dial interface.

Remote access services on a server can be enabled for either demand-dial routing, remote access, or both.

Demand-dial routing is established separately from remote access, but shares many of the same features and configuration, including policies, authentication protocols, encryption, and troubleshooting facilities.

INTERNET AUTHENTICATION SERVICES

Internet Authentication Services (IAS) is a Microsoft Windows 2000 implementation of Remote Authentication Dial-In User Service (RADIUS). The RADIUS protocol can be examined in RFCs 2138 and 2139. IAS can be used to perform centralized authentication, authorization, and accounting of dial-up and virtual private network remote access and demand-dial connections. It should be used in connection with Windows 2000 Routing and Remote Access Services.

IAS can be used to authenticate remote access requests against Windows 2000 native-mode or mixed-mode domains, Windows NT 4.0 domains, or a Windows 2000 local account database if the IAS server is installed on a standalone server that is not a member of a Windows 2000 domain.

Table 13.5 delineates the authentication features that are present in each situation.

TABLE 13.5

IAS AUTHENTICATION SERVICES

	2000 Native	2000 Mixed or NT 4.0	Standalone
Manage access permission through groups	X		
Connect remote network to office network	X		
Support for User Principal Names (UPN)	X		
Users can retain the same UPN, regardless of domain	X		

continues

TABLE 13.5 | *continued*

IAS AUTHENTICATION SERVICES

	2000 Native	*2000 Mixed or NT 4.0*	*Standalone*
Allow access	X	X	X
Deny access	X	X	X
Control access through Remote Access Policy	X		X
Caller ID	X		
Callback options	X	X	
Static IP address	X		
Static routes	X		
EAP-TLS	X		

You use Routing and Remote Access Services to manage remote access connections if your remote access requirements allow you to focus on one server in one location, and if the configurations and policy settings meet your needs. You use IAS when your requirements exceed those available with Routing and Remote Access Services, and when you need centralized authentication, accounting, and authorization data maintenance.

IAS is often used in the following ways:

◆ For dial-up access to your network

◆ To enable outsourcing of remote access through service providers

◆ For Internet access

◆ To establish limited extranet access for business partners

◆ To manage VPNs

Users do not dial directly into or connect to IAS servers. Instead, they dial remote access servers, which act as IAS clients that connect to IAS. The remote access server can be a Windows 2000 remote access server, another remote access server, or even a simple hardware-based port server (although, in this case, a remote access proxy is required). These remote access servers are often collectively referred to as the Network Access Server (NAS). A simple description of IAS connections and authentication would be the following (see Figure 13.11 for a picture of just such a connection):

1. The client computer dials the NAS server.

2. The NAS acts as the RADIUS (IAS) client and connects to the IAS server.

3. The IAS server connects to a Windows 2000 domain controller for authentication of the client connection.

4. The domain controller responds to the IAS server.

5. Presuming authentication, the results are returned to the NAS, which then allows the connection of the client to the network.

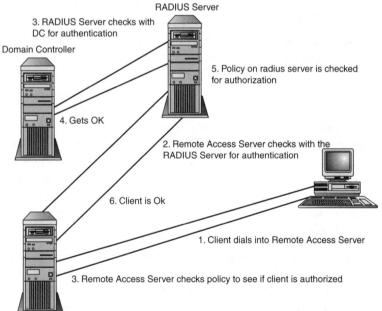

FIGURE 13.11
Remote access with Internet Authentication Services.

IAS Security Feature Set

A number of features make IAS well suited for these roles. Many of these features extend the feature set of remote access.

Centralized User Authentication

IAS supports a number of authentication methods, including these:

◆ All password methods supported within PPP.

◆ Extensible Authentication Protocol for using smart cards, certificates, one-time passwords, and token cards.

◆ Guest authentication, with no name or password during the authentication process. The Guest account is used for identity of the caller.

◆ Automatic number identification/calling line identification (ANI/CLI), based the on number from which the user calls (ANI is caller ID).

◆ Dialed Number Identification Service (DNIS) (based on number called by the user).

In addition to these methods, management of authentication can include the capability to outsource dialing to an ISP. Users connect to the ISP before establishing the VPN tunnel. This is extremely useful because it can enable access worldwide if the ISP supports it. Thus, when traveling, I would have a list of phone numbers in the cities I might be staying in. To connect back to headquarters, I would dial the local number and make the dial-up connection, and then the VPN could be established between my client and the corporate endpoint.

The ISP forwards authentication and usage records to the company's IAS Routing and Remote Access Server. The company controls user authentication and can track usage. The ISP is responsible for providing adequate hardware and dial-up connections. Infrastructure costs and phone charges are reduced, while authentication-based security is maintained.

User authentication is via Windows 2000 or Windows NT domain user accounts.

Policies

Appropriate access to the network can be configured via Remote Access Policies. This allows greater control and flexibility while simplifying basic access. Instead of configuring access via individual user account, access can be configured via security group. IAS and Routing and Remote Access share Remote Access Policies. If Routing and Remote Access is configured for RADIUS, the policies and logging of the IAS server are used. Policies can be configured to control access via conditions such as these:

◆ Membership in Windows 2000 security groups

◆ Time of day, or day of week of the connection

◆ Phone number user calls from

◆ Phone number the user calls

◆ Type of media (ISDN, mode, VPN)

◆ Type of VPN (PPTP or L2TP)

Each policy contains a profile that further controls connection parameters, such as these:

◆ User requests for specific IP address

◆ Permit or deny authentication method

◆ Connection idle time

◆ Maximum session time

◆ Encryption settings

◆ Packet filters

◆ Force creation of mandatory tunnel

Centralized Administration

IAS can centrally administer multiple Routing and Remote Access Servers, auditing, and usage information.

IAS can control connection configurations for multiple remote access servers. If a remote access server follows the RADIUS standard, IAS can manage it.

IAS collects usage information from every NAS. Audit information such as authentication accepts and rejects, and usage information such as logon and logoff records is written to log files. These logs can be imported into a database that then can be analyzed by third-party software.

RADIUS Protocol

RADIUS is an industry standard that provides authorization, authentication, identification, and accounting services. User information is sent to a RADIUS server from a dial-up server. RADIUS servers have been typically located at Internet service providers. The ISPs then established dial-up servers and leased accounts on these servers to the public. The dial-up server is known as the RADIUS client. When a user dials the dial-up server, the process continues like this:

1. The dial-up server (the RADIUS client) creates a RADIUS access-request packet that contains the user's name, password, client ID (the ID of the dial-up server), and port ID (the port on the dial-up server) the user is accessing.

2. If a password is present and encryption of the password is part of the authentication protocol used, the password is encrypted according to that standard.

3. The packet is sent to the RADIUS server. The packet can be resent, if no reply is returned. The client also can forward requests to alternative servers or servers.

4. The RADIUS server receives the request packet and validates the RADIUS client. Digital signatures are checked. (A shared secret is established when clients are authorized in the RADIUS configuration and in the client configuration.)

5. If the connection is not valid, the packet is discarded. If the connection is valid, a database of users is examined to find the user that matches the name in the packet. The database includes a list of requirements for each user, such as password verification.

6. If the username is present but cannot be validated, an Access-Reject packet is returned to the RADIUS client.

7. If the name and conditions are met, a list of configuration parameters is returned in a Access-Accept packet to the RADIUS client. (This could include IP address, subnet mast, packet filters, and so on.)

IAS Authentication Process

In the Microsoft world, the Microsoft Routing and Remote Access server may use any RADIUS server that meets the IETF standards. However, using the IAS server offers many advantages, including full integration. In a pure Microsoft solution, the Routing and Remote Access Server is the RADIUS client or NAS. Figure 13.12 provides

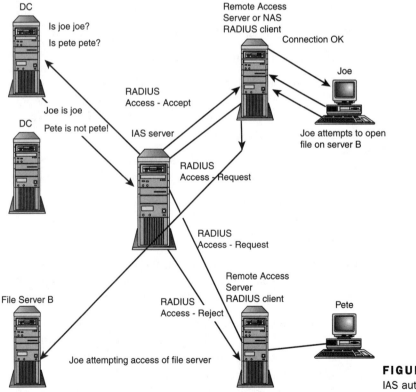

FIGURE 13.12
IAS authentication process.

an illustration. Here's how a client connection using these services will happen.

1. A user attempts a dial-up connection to the NAS.

2. The NAS negotiates a connection (or tries to) using the most secure protocol first, followed by the next-secure protocol until a connection is made.

3. The NAS passes the authentication request to the IAS server in a RADIUS Access-Request packet.

4. The IAS server verifies that the RADIUS client sending the packet is valid. This is done via IP address checking, password checking, and other attributes. The use of digital signatures can also be configured. Passwords used are the shared secret configured between the server and the client when the connection interface was configured. The shared secret can use alphanumeric and special characters, and is case sensitive.

5. Auto Reject is checked (see the next section, "Auto Reject").

6. If validation fails, the packet is discarded.

7. Realm-striping and name-cracking are performed, if necessary. Checking is done for authentication plug-ins and remote access account lockout (see the later sections "Name-Cracking" and "Remote Access Account Lockout").

8. If validation is successful, the IAS server forwards the user credentials to a Windows 2000 domain controller for validation.

9. MS-CAHP, CHAP, and PAP submodules are used for authentication (see later section "MS-CHAP, CHAP, and PAP Submodules").

10. The user account is checked for Account Lockout, Account Disabled, or Password Expired. If the account is not valid, an Access-Reject packet is returned to the NAS.

11. If user credentials are approved, Remote Access Policies and dial-in properties (on the user account) are checked before authorizing the request (see later sections "Authentication and Authorization Plug-Ins" and "Remote Access Account Lockout").

12. If EAP authentication is the protocol used for the connection, EAP authentication takes place here. EAP authentication is checked first for a matching EAP type; if one is found, then EAP authentication continues. If no matching type is found, an Access-Reject packet is sent.

13. If the user connection is denied, the IAS server sends a RADIUS Access-Reject message to the NAS.

14. A check is made for authorization plugs-ins.

15. If the user connection is allowed by policy and/or user dial-in properties, the IAS sends a RADIUS Access-Accept to the NAS that sent the Access-Request packet. The Access-Accept message contains connection information based on policy and user-account configuration.

Auto Reject

Auto Reject is a feature of IAS that allows immediate rejection of Access-Requests when the username in the packet matches a value specified in a registry entry. No authentication processing is required, nor is an authentication log entry made. This feature prevents denial-of-service attacks by known user accounts that are not authorized for remote access.

To configure the registry entry, enter the username in the Ping User-Name setting under HKEY_LOCAL_MACHINE_SYSTEM\ CurrentControlSet\Services\IAS\Parameters.

Guest Access and Other Realm-Stripping Rules

User identity is determined if the username is not in the Auto Reject name. User identity is used by IAS to identify the user for authentication and authorization. In most cases, it will be the username attribute of the Access-Request packet. If there is no username attribute, identity is set to the Guest account or an account listed in the `default user Identity` registry value at HKEY_LOCAL_MACHINE\ SYSTEM\CurrentControlSet\Services\RemoteAccess\Policy.

IAS also can be configured to use another Access-Request attribute for the user identity by setting User Identity Attribute in the registry at HKEY_LOCAL_MACHINE\SYSTEM\CurrentControlSet\ Services\RemoteAccess\Policy.

By default, that setting is 1 for the username. It can be changed to other values and is useful in unauthenticated access authentication mode connections. For example, to configure ANI authorization (authorization based on the number the user calls from), set this value to 31 and establish a user account for each user who will be calling. For their account names, use the phone number they will call from. (If I will use the phone number 559-4609 to dial in, then my username for my Windows 2000 account will be 5594609.)

In the non-Microsoft world, a RADIUS server contains a database of users. In a large network of dial-up servers, the realm name would be used to determine which RADIUS server to forward authentication requests to. Usernames would also include a realm name. Realm names can be prefixes (tagteam/peterb) or suffixes (peterb@tagteam) Realm-stripping describes the process of stripping the realm name from the username before the user database is checked for the existence of the username. In the IAS world, realm names are not used, but requests from dial-up servers that do use a realm name could provide a problem. IAS can be configured to strip the realm name from the username before attempting authentication via the domain controller.

Name-Cracking

Name-cracking is the process used to resolve the username attribute in the Access-Request packet to a user account name. If a user principal name, Lightweight Directory Access Protocol (LDAP), distinguished name (DNA), canonical name, or some form of name other than a user account name is received by IAS, IAS will query the Active Directory Global Catalog to resolve the name. If the username doesn't include a domain name, IAS supplies the domain name by using the domain name for the domain of which it is a member, or the domain name supplied in the registry setting: HKEY_LOCAL_MACHINE\SYSTEM\CurrentControlSet\Service\ RasMan\PPP\ControlProtocols\BuiltIn.

Authentication and Authorization Plug-Ins

Optional plug-ins can be created using the IAS SDK. Authentication and authorization plug-ins can either accept, reject, or continue the processing of the Accept-Reject packet. If an authentication plug-in specifies that the process is to continue, either another plug-in will be checked or the normal authentication process will continue.

Remote Access Account Lockout

Remote access lockout is configured through the registry of the IAS server. It is not account lockout that is configured on the user account configured through Group Policy. Remote access account lockout is configured to prevent dictionary attacks. For configuration instructions, see the section "Routing and Remote Access Service."

MS-CHAP, CHAP, and PAP Submodules

Submodules are used to authenticate the remote access client. The username and password are checked against those in the accounts database of the server or the domain. Group membership information is returned to the IAS server so that it can be used to determine which Remote Access Policy is valid.

Policy Evaluation

A Remote Access Policy must be found that matches the connection. (A default policy exists for simply validating connections for which the user account is configured to accept dial-up connections.) If no policy is found that matches, an Accept-Reject packet is sent and an event is logged.

Tunneling and IAS

Tunnels can be configured between the IAS server and different parts of the network. More information about tunneling is included in the later section "Virtual Private Networking."

Tunneling can be either voluntary or compulsory. In voluntary tunneling, the client issues a VPN request. The tunnel negotiation takes place after the initial connection request is granted. First the client requests a network connection that is negotiated by the NAS with the IAS server. Then the client requests a tunnel connection with the network tunnel server. Because the tunnel server is on the network, the NAS and the IAS are in the picture again. Upon completion of the tunnel authentication request, the IAS is dropped from the picture just as it is after the approval of any other connection. IAS is used to authenticate a connection, not to maintain it. Figure 13.13 shows a picture of a voluntary tunnel between a client and the network tunnel server.

A compulsory tunnel is one that is made on behalf of a client computer. It ensures that a tunnel is used. The user is not aware of the tunnel, nor does his computer become a tunnel endpoint (one side of a tunnel connection). Some other device becomes the endpoint of the tunnel that connects to the ultimate destination endpoint. In IAS, that tunnel will be created between the dial-up server or NAS and the IAS server. This would be extremely useful if the dial-up server was located at your ISP and needed to connect to your IAS server at your location. You could even use tunnels nationwide to connect across the Internet to your centrally located IAS server, thus avoiding large phone bills.

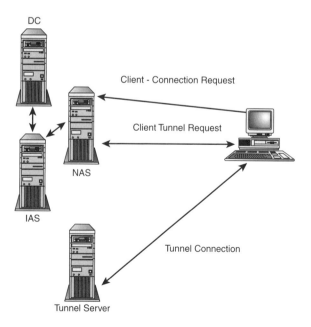

FIGURE 13.13
Voluntary tunnel.

Dial-up servers are available that can act as a tunnel endpoint. The server is known as a Front End Processor (FEP) if it uses PPTP, as an L2TP Access Concentrator (LAC) if L2TP is used, and as an IP Security Gateway if IPSec is used. Generically, the initials FEP are used in Figure 13.14 to represent any one of these.

This scenario may include an ISP IAS server to authorize the tunnel connection. The client dials into the ISP NAS. The NAS connects to the ISP IAS that authorizes the tunnel and returns an IAS Access-Accept message that includes tunnel parameters. If the ISP IAS is required, it can establish the tunnel connection.

The NAS or the IAS at the ISP makes the tunnel connection to the organization's IAS. A PPP message is sent to the dial-up client to restart authentication. The ISP tunnel endpoint encapsulates it and sends it through the tunnel. The organization tunnel server accepts the packet and forwards it to the organization IAS server. If the IAS server authenticates and authorizes the client connection, the tunnel server completes the tunnel connection for that client. All data that the client sends uses the tunnel. The tunnel connection can be used by multiple clients, if they are authenticated and authorized by the IAS server.

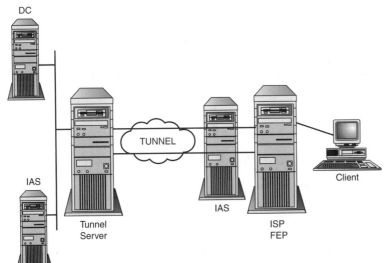

FIGURE 13.14
IAS compulsory tunneling.

The tunnel is called as a compulsory tunnel because the tunnel is created without the client's participation, and all network traffic must travel between the tunnel endpoints. Remember though, that data from the client to the ISP is not passing through a tunnel, so any security benefits such as encryption of data do not occur.

IAS Authorization and Remote Access Policies

IAS authentication attempts to verify that a requesting client is who he says he is. IAS authorization determines whether that user has remote access privileges. Authorization is configured via Remote Access Policies. IAS shares the Remote Access Policies with the Routing and Remote Access Services—that is, no separate configuration is done. If the Remote Access Services are configured to use Windows authentication, the Remote Access Policies of the Routing and Remote Access Server (configured in the Routing and Remote Access console) will be used. If the Remote Access Services are configured to use RADIUS, then the Remote Access Polices of the centralized IAS server are used. Policies are configured in the IAS console.

To ensure centralized management of a single set of Remote Access Policies (policies will be applied across a set of Routing and Remote Access Servers or VPN servers), use the steps outlined in Step by Step 13.2.

STEP BY STEP

13.2 Configure Centralized Remote Access Policies

1. Install IAS.

2. Configure IAS with RADIUS clients, one for each remote access or VPN server.

3. Create the policies on the IAS server.

4. Configure the remote access servers as RADIUS clients to the IAS server. (Any locally configured policies will be ignored.)

Vendor Profiles

IAS can support vendor-specific attributes (VSAs). These attributes include items such as these:

◆ Vendor ID

◆ Vendor type

◆ Data type

◆ Format

To enable vendor specific attributes in IAS, you add the attribute to a dial-in profile by using the Advanced property page.

Policy Administrative Models

Three models of administration exist:

◆ Access by user

◆ Access by policy in a Windows 2000 native-mode domain

◆ Access by policy in a Windows 2000 mixed mode domain

Access by user is the default policy and allows the configuration of remote access permissions by using the Dial-In tab of the user account. Remote access permission is enabled or disabled on a user-by-user basis. Policies can be written to enforce connection settings such as encryption, but not to deny or accept access.

To establish Access By Policy In A Windows 2000 Native-Mode Domain, remote access permission on every user account is set to Control Access Through Remote Access Policy. Policy then can be used to control which groups of users have remote access. Access is granted or denied by policy. The default policy is to deny access. If it is put into place and is not modified, no user has access. If it is changed to allow access, all users have access. Windows NT RAS or IAS servers cannot be used in this situation.

Access By Policy In A Windows 2000 Mixed-Mode Domain is set by changing the Remote Access Policy on every user account to Allow Access. (In a mixed-mode domain, the user setting Control Access Through Remote Access Policy is not available.) You delete the default policy Allow Access If Dial-In Permission Is Enabled. Then policy is used to define allowed connection types.

VIRTUAL PRIVATE NETWORKING

Virtual private networking is the act of setting up a connection between two parts of a private network across a shared network such as the Internet so that it emulates a private link. Data is encapsulated or given a header that includes routing information. Data may be encrypted for confidentiality. The link is set up between two endpoints, either a client and a router, or two routers. This connection is called a virtual private network (VPN).

The logical path from endpoint to endpoint is often called a tunnel (see Figure 13.15).

One way to think about a VPN is to consider air travel. While I cannot fly, by "encapsulating" myself aboard an airplane, I can travel through the sky from city to city. All I need to know about the path the airplane takes is which airplane to board. My ticket gives me that information (think of the ticket as the header with the routing information). I don't care how the plane gets me there, as long as it does so. (I may care how quickly I get there and whether I have to make stops and board different planes along the way, but that's another story.) As far as the air or the airplane is concerned, it doesn't care if I speak English, French, or German—if I have a ticket, I'm transported. If you bend reality for a moment, think of the airplane as a sort of tunnel through the sky, with one endpoint being the starting city and the other being the destination.

Like the airlines, the tunnels created by a VPN connection can use elaborate authentication procedures to determine which packets can travel them.

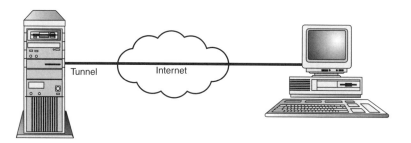

FIGURE 13.15
VPN connection.

Like the airplane, users use a VPN to transport something from one endpoint to the other. Telecommuters, or road warriors, can use the connection to tunnel through the Internet. To users, it's no different than a normal dial-up connection, except they may be communicating at less cost, if their call would have been long distance. The company realizes two benefits: security and reduced communication costs.

In addition, companies can set up routed VPN connections between offices and can create logical dedicated WAN links over the public Internet. Local ISP dial-up lines are used instead of long-distance dial-up or leased lines.

Microsoft Windows 2000 VPNs consist of VPN servers, VPN clients, and VPN connections. The portion of the connection over which your encapsulated data passes is called a tunnel. To create the connection, you must use a tunneling protocol such as PPTP or L2TP. The tunnel crosses a network that is known as the transit internetwork.

VPN Connections

Two types of connections are possible: the remote access connection and the router-to-router connection. The remote access connection is made between a Windows client and the Routing and Remote Access Server. The router-to-router connection is established between two Routing and Remote Access Servers. In the router-to-router VPN connection, the calling router becomes the VPN client. VPN connections can be established across any IP network. Many VPN connections are designed to be established across the Internet (see Figure 13.16), but there is no reason that a VPN tunnel cannot be created across a private network to establish secure communications.

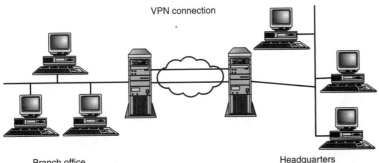

VPN connection

Branch office

Headquarters

FIGURE 13.16
Connecting two sites across the Internet.

Connections include the following properties:

◆ Encapsulation

◆ Data encryption from one tunnel endpoint to the other. The process used depends on the tunneling protocol used and how it is configured.

◆ Authentication. Both user information and data can be authenticated. Authentication can be configured to authenticate the client only, or both the server and the client. Data can contain a cryptographic checksum based on a shared secret key. This allows either endpoint to ensure that data received originated from the other end.

◆ Address and name server assignment. The VPN server establishes a virtual interface that consists of an IP address for the client and for itself, and the IP address of the DNS and/or WINS servers in the server environment. This information is delivered to the VPN client if the connection is approved.

Managing User Access and Authentication via Remote Access Policies

You can manage user access by setting remote access permission on user accounts to Allow Access. Then you can manage the type of connection by policy. If only VPN access is allowed, delete the default policy Allow Access If Dial-In Permission Is Enabled, and then create a new policy for VPN access. If both remote access and VPN connections are allowed, keep the old policy, but place the new VPN connection policy above it so that it is processed first.

Authentication can be configured to allow either Windows or RADIUS authentication. This works like that for remote access authentication; if Windows authentication is selected, authentication is via Windows mechanisms. If RADIUS is selected, user connections are authenticated using RADIUS, with the VPN server acting as the RADIUS client.

Tunneling Protocols

Two options exist for tunneling protocols for Windows 2000 VPN connections:

◆ PPTP

◆ L2TP over IPSec

PPTP is described in RFC 2637. PPTP requires an IP connection between the client and the server. The connection can be made via dial-up. Authentication is via the same mechanisms as PPP. Encryption can be accomplished with Microsoft Point-to-Point Encryption (MPPE) if EAP-TLS or MS-CHAP is used. Encryption is link to link—that is, from the client to the server. Data that travels from the server endpoint across its network to other computers is not encrypted. End-to-end encryption can be accomplished if IPSec is used after the tunnel is established.

Four encapsulation processes complete the PPTP encapsulation (see Figure 13.17):

1. The data payload is encrypted and encapsulated with a PPP header.

2. The PPP frame is encapsulated with a modified GRE header.

3. The GRE–PPP encapsulated payload is encapsulated with an IP header that includes source and destination addresses of the PPTP client and the PPTP server.

4. The IP datagram is encapsulated with a header and a trailer for the data-link layer technology of the physical interface.

Generic Routing Encapsulation (GRE) is documented in RFC 1701 and 1702. GRE's protocol number is 47; it is modified for use by PPTP.

MPPE encryption uses the Rivest-Shamir-Adleman (RSA) RC4 stream cipher. A stream cipher can change the encryption key for every packet. The changing keys can be duplicated at the receiving

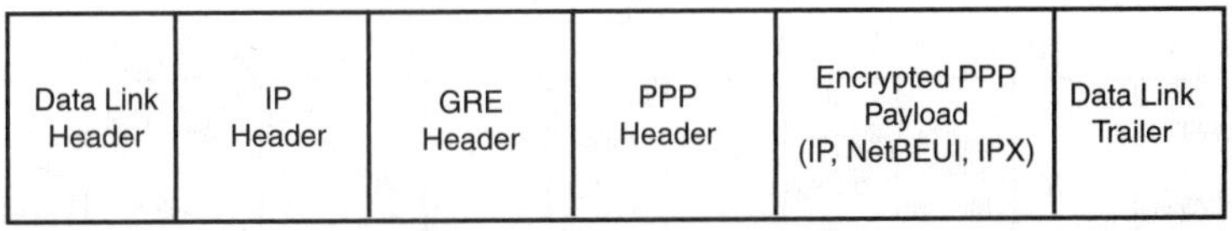

Data Link Header	IP Header	GRE Header	PPP Header	Encrypted PPP Payload (IP, NetBEUI, IPX)	Data Link Trailer

FIGURE 13.17
PPTP tunneled data structure.

end if the receiving end and the sending end begin with the same key, and if both understand the key generation process. The key generation process is significantly mathematically complicated, so it cannot be anticipated and thus broken by would-be hackers. MPPE for VPN includes a sequence number in the packet so that the receiving end can calculate encryption keys for packets that arrive out of order. MPPE can use 40-bit, 56-bit, or 128-bit encryption keys. Use the 40-bit key for compatibility with non-Windows 2000 clients. The highest strength available (and allowed) on both clients is negotiated during connection. If the VPN server requires higher encryption strength than the client supports, connection is rejected.

Layer 2 Tunneling Protocol (L2TP) is the IETF-recommended combination of Cisco Systems, Inc., L2F and PPTP, as described in RFC 2661. L2TP data encapsulation is five-part. L2TP alone does not provide encryption; you must configure encryption using IPSec (see Figure 13.18.)

1. The PPP payload is encapsulated with the PPP header and L2TP header.

2. The L2TP-encapsulated packet is encapsulated with a UDP header with source and destination ports set to 1701.

3. Depending on policy, the UDP message is encrypted and encapsulated with an IPSec Encapsulation Security Payload (ESP) header and trailer, and an IPSec Authentication (AH) trailer (see Chapter 15, "Designing Security for Communication Channels").

4. The IPSec-encapsulated packet is encapsulated with an IP header containing the source and destination IP address of the VPN client and VPN server.

5. The IP datagram is encapsulated with a header and trailer for the data-link physical interface.

In either case, the data-link physical interface specifies the final encapsulation. For example, an Ethernet interface requires an Ethernet header and trailer, while a dial-up, analog phone line requires a PPP header and trailer.

FIGURE 13.18
L2TP Encapsulation.

Data Link Layer	IP Header	IPSec ESP Header	UDP Header	L2TP Header	PPP Header	PPP Payload	IPSec ESP Trainer	IPSec ESP Auth Trainer	Data Link Trailer

Authentication with IPSec over L2TP is two part—both computer
and user authentication is performed. This mutual computer
authentication between the VPN client and the VPN server is
accomplished using IPSec certificates. IPSec certificates must be
installed on both computers. User authentication is the same as it is
for PPTP. L2TP tunnel authentication can be authenticated during
the tunnel establishment. By default, this is not done.

Encryption is provided by IPSec. Both DES with a 56-bit key and
Triple DES (3DES) are available. New DES encryption keys are
generated after every 5 minutes or 250MB of data transferred. New
3DES keys are generated after every hour or every 2GB of data
transferred. AH connections use new hash keys after every hour or
2GB of data transferred. For more information on IPSec, see
Chapter 15.

Data authentication and integrity uses either Hash Message
Authentication Code (HMAC) Message Digest 5 (MD5), which
produces a 128-bit hash of the payload, or by the HMAC Secure
Hash Algorithm (SHA), which produces a 160-bit hash. Using a
hashing algorithm for integrity and authentication works because
the two different hashes of the same message (data payload), which
use the same algorithm and the same key, will produce the same
message digest (result). The hash, or message digest of the payload,
can be sent with the payload (both the data and the message digest
are encrypted before being sent). At the receiving end, the encrypted
payload (digest and data) is decrypted, leaving the data and the
digest. A separate hash of the unencrypted data produces a new message digest, which should match the one that arrived with the data.
If it does, the data has not been tampered with during transport.

Packet filtering can be configured to make sure that the VPN server
performs only routing between the VPN clients and the intranet,
not between other others.

IPSec policy can also be set to determine information about
shared keys.

Demand-Dial VPN

As mentioned in the earlier section, "Demand-Dial Routing,"
demand-dial routing can be used to configure a VPN connection.
Demand-dial VPN connections require two demand-dial interfaces

on the VPN client (the calling router). The answering router needs only one demand-dial interface, unless it also is allowed to establish a connection using the demand-dial router.

The first demand-dial connection is used to establish the dial-up connection to the ISP, and the second connection is used to establish the router-to-router VPN connection. Of course, this is possible only if the ISP allows demand-dial connections for its customers. Figure 13.19 diagrams this type of connection.

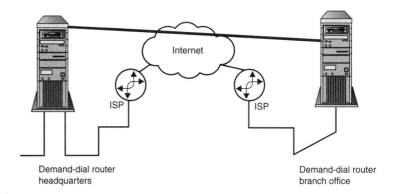

FIGURE 13.19
Demand-dial router-to-router VPN connection.

TERMINAL SERVICES

Terminal Services provides access via a Terminal Services client to a Windows 2000 Server. Clients send only keystrokes and mouse clicks. All processing occurs on the server.

General Information

Terminal Services is available over any TCP/IP connection, including the following:

◆ Remote access

◆ Ethernet

◆ Internet

◆ Wireless

◆ WAN

◆ VPN

Terminal Services clients are available for Windows clients (provided by Microsoft) and for other clients (via third-party products).

◆ Windows for Workgroups 3.11 and up

◆ Windows CE devices

◆ MS-DOS

◆ UNIX terminals

◆ Macintosh clients

Terminal Services provides Windows 32-bit application emulation. Because only keystrokes and mouse-clicks cross the network from the client and displays from the server, network bandwidth usage is minimized. Centralized security is provided by the data center deployment.

Terminal Server Modes

Two modes are available: remote administration, which allows two connections, and application. If the server will be accessed across routers and through firewalls, you must be sure to allow access for the Remote Desktop Protocol (RDP) at port 3389. Conversely, if you do not wish client access across routers and firewalls, make sure that this port is blocked.

Windows 2000 Terminal Services runs on standalone member servers or domain controllers. Do *not* install Terminals Services in application sharing mode on a domain controller. If you do you, will give the Domain Users group logon local permission on the domain controller. This, of course, is not a good thing.

Security Structure

Security structures are these:

◆ User profiles

◆ Group Policy

◆ NTFS

◆ User rights

◆ Single-application access

◆ Guest access

◆ Data encryption

User profiles can be established for Terminal Services users. If users already have a Windows 2000 profile, the Terminal Services profile can be set up separately. Administrators control access to applications by using mandatory profiles.

Group Policy can be used to centrally manage registry settings (including security settings) specific for Terminal Servers. Different sets of policies for application usage can be applied to Terminal Services users by placing the Terminal Servers in a separate OU. Other policy settings (except application usage) will be the same on Windows 2000 as in Windows 2000 Terminal Services.

NTFS should be the only file system used, and care should be taken to assign appropriate permissions to folders and files. You may need or want to set up specific user areas where user–specific application settings can be stored. User areas can be protected from usage by other users. Application files and folders also can be protected against misuse.

User rights are set by default for Terminal Services. A Terminal Server used in application sharing mode gives all members of the Users group logon local rights. You can change this default. (The right to log on locally is necessary for gaining access to a Terminal Server.) A Terminal Server in administrative mode gives rights to only an administrator on the computer. Users logged on to Terminal Server using the RDP client are automatically members of the Terminal Services Users local group. You control Terminal Services users by controlling this group.

Terminal Services users cannot invoke the Windows Installer. This means these users cannot install missing parts of applications. It also means that users are prevented from installing any kind of an application on the Terminal Server.

You use the Terminal Services configuration tool to give users permissions and to disconnect sessions.

You can configure a user for single-application access. To do so, you configure the client through the Client Connection Manager to start a specific application for the user. You then can distribute the client to all users that will use only that application.

You can configure guest access so that users can connect without entering a username and password. This is done through the Client Connection Manager.

Data transfer can be encrypted. Three levels are available:

◆ **Low**—RC4 with a 56-bit key, 40-bit key for RDP 4.0 clients. Client-to-server (server-to-client unencrypted) password entry and data is protected.

◆ **Medium**—Traffic in both directions is encrypted.

◆ **High**—RC4 with a 128-bit key.

> **WARNING**
>
> **Are You Sure You Want Uninvited Guests?**   If you use this feature, anyone can access the Terminal Server without a user ID and password if they have a Terminal Services client.

> **NOTE**
>
> **Terminal Server Tips**
>
> • Smart cards cannot be used for Windows 2000 Terminal Services authentication.
>
> • Disable FTP service to prevent access to the file system.
>
> • Terminal Services can be accessed using L2TP or PPTP over the Internet.
>
> • Remove OS/2 and POSIX subsystems.

CHAPTER SUMMARY

This chapter has examined major Windows 2000 services that can be used to assist you in protecting your network. You have learned how Routing and Remote Services can be used to secure your network in the following ways:

◆ Protecting internal addresses via NAT

◆ Authenticating all remote access users via a wide range of methods

◆ Authorizing users and groups by Remote Access Policies

◆ Providing and protecting a demand-dial router

KEY TERMS

• Network Address Translation

• Internet Connection Sharing

• virtual private network

• Terminal Services

• IPSec

• Point-to-Point Tunneling Protocol (PPTP)

CHAPTER SUMMARY

- Layer 2 Tunneling Protocol (L2TP)

- demand-dial routing

- RADIUS

- Internet Authentication Service (IAS)

- realm-stripping

- name-cracking

- tunneling

- compulsory tunneling

- GRE

◆ Providing connectivity to RADIUS servers for authentication

◆ Providing data encryption for remote access sessions

◆ Providing easily configurable VPN connections using L2TPover IPSec or PPTP

APPLY YOUR KNOWLEDGE

Review Questions

1. How is NAT different from Internet Connection Sharing?

2. Explain the difference between the two Routing and Remote Access Services authentication providers?

3. What must be done to allow the remote access user to use a smart card for authentication?

4. What is the difference between demand-dial routing and a dial-up connection?

5. How can a demand-dial connection be secured?

6. Who or what is the RADIUS client? On what system is it configured?

7. Describe the process by which a call to an ISP can be authenticated through a company's Active Directory.

8. How can policies be used to control access via IAS? Where are these policies configured?

9. Can users be specifically blocked? Can you prevent denial-of-service attacks by known user accounts?

10. VPNs can be established using Routing and Remote Access Services. They can be router to _____ and _____ to router.

11. Connections have what possible security properties?

12. Two separate VPN protocols exist. What are they, and what is one reason for using one over the other?

Answers to Review Questions

1. Internet Connection Sharing is a scaled-down version of NAT. It is less configurable.

2. The two authentication methods are Windows authentication and RADIUS. Windows authentication uses the normal authentication practices of the domain or standalone server (if the server is not joined in the domain). RADIUS authentication is managed by the Internet Access Server. This server centralizes Remote Access Policies, can be configured to collect audit information, and uses Windows authentication. If the Windows authentication method is chosen, Remote Access Policies configured on the Routing and Remote Access Server are used.

3. When an authentication provider (Windows or RADIUS) is selected, an authentication method needs to be selected. To provide support for smart card authentication, you must choose the Extensible Authentication (EAP) option. Of course, other configuration of the Certificate Authority and the smart card client is necessary.

4. A dial-up connection is established between a client and a remote access server. It must be dialed and then wait for a connection to be established. A demand-dial router makes a connection router to router and can be configured to time out and disconnect, or to keep a persistent connection open.

5. A demand-dial connection can be secured by setting a call-back number, requiring data encryption, and requiring a secured password.

APPLY YOUR KNOWLEDGE

6. The RADIUS client is the remote access server. When the Routing and Remote Access server is configured to use RADIUS as an authentication provider, then it becomes the RADIUS client.

7. A user connects to the ISP. The ISP and the company have a compulsory tunnel configured between them. The connection is made through this tunnel to the company's IAS server, which contacts Active Directory for authentication.

8. Policies are configured on the IAS server. They can be configured to control access via membership in security groups, time of day, phone number of user, phone number called, type of media, and type of VPN.

9. A registry entry can be made that allows the IAS server to automatically reject an access request made by a user whose name matches the entry. The rejection occurs prior to authentication attempts and can aid in blocking denial-of-service attacks.

10. VPNs can be established using Routing and Remote Access Services. They can be router to router and client to router.

11. Connections have authentication, encapsulation, and data encryption security properties.

12. You can use either PPTP or L2TP over IPSec. PPTP can use NAT, and L2TP over IPSec cannot. L2TP over IPSec is considered the more secure. PPTP is considered to be less processor-intensive.

Suggested Readings and Resources

1. Atkins, Derek (ed.). *Internet Security, Professional Reference, Second Edition.* New Riders, 1997.

   • Part II: Gaining Access and Securing the Gateway

2. Chapman, D. Brent and Elizabeth D. Zwicky. *Building Internet Firewalls.* O'Reilly, (1995).

3. Kaeo, Merike. *Designing Network Security.* Cisco Press (1999).

   • Part III: Practical Implementation

This chapter covers the following Microsoft-specified objectives for the "Designing a Security Solution for Access Between Networks" section of the Designing Security for a Microsoft Windows 2000 Network exam:

Provide secure access to public networks from a private network.

▶ It is not enough to offer access to the Internet. You must ensure that this access does not allow intrusion from the Internet back to your network. You also need to give consideration to employee activity on the Internet. Are they being good virtual net-citizens? Are they using the privilege to assist them in their work, or has it become a replacement for work?

Provide external users with secure access to private network resources.

▶ Do you join forces with your business partners across the ether? Are your Web sites resources for potential and current customers? Do you support an e-commerce site? You must be aware of the potential risks for each participant in these endeavors. Not only should you ensure that this access is controlled and limited to the resources designated, you must ensure that these external users suffer no ill actions by virtue of connection with your network.

Provide secure access between private networks.

- **Provide secure access within a LAN.**
- **Provide secure access within a WAN.**
- **Provide secure access across a public network.**

CHAPTER 14

Designing Security for Access Between Networks

▶ Outside influences are not the only issues. Many statistics point to major problems with internal workers being major causes of data theft, corruption, and systems abuse. Can you protect sensitive systems on your LAN? How about those across the city or across the world? Just because you have dedicated lines between company locations does not mean you can rest. Each connection point can be a source of risk.

▶ Finally, have you moved from dedicated lines to virtual private networks (VPNs) that connect branches or divisions across the Internet? What additional risks will you encounter here? I am reminded of the first pioneers as they wandered their way across the Great Divide. They took what they thought was adequate protection. For some it was, for others it wasn't. Those who remained vigilant had the better chance of reaching their destination.

Design Windows 2000 security for remote access users.

▶ Gone are the days when every worker worked at the office. There are distinct advantages to providing telecommuters and road warriors direct access to your network—business advantages, that is. For the information systems professional, this access from without can become quite a challenge. How do you ensure that all users of this resource are authorized? How do you protect not only the company assets on the inside, but those that reside on users' systems outside your embrace?

▶ As you study, keep in mind common risks and protective measures. Each company must weigh risk versus cost to determine the strategy that should be followed. What you should know is the respective merits, properties, and implementation strategies of each tool or method. It is only by knowing what you have to work with, and what you need to protect, that you will be able to best devise a plan to follow.

INTRODUCTION

Access to company information needs to be controlled from all perspectives. It is not enough to control access generically via resource permissions or user logon. Although these are important foundations, you must take a look at all the possible ways that resources might be accessed and design a strategy to protect your resources from each.

1. You want to determine whether local area network protection is sufficient. Do you have other operating systems in your network? Have appropriate security measures been taken?

2. Examine the risks brought by allowing your users access to the Internet. Are you sure that no intruder can obtain access this way?

3. Are you allowing access through the Internet or other public networks to your network? Do you have Web servers or dial-up connections? Can remote users (at branch offices or on the road) obtain entry?

4. Are trusted partners allowed access of any sort? Are domain trusts set up between your private networks? Are special Web servers, file servers, databases, dial-up lines, or other entry points available to them?

Investigate each potential risk, and then design and implement a security plan for each possible point of access.

Are you getting the picture that security needs to be considered everywhere? It can easily become your entire orientation to infrastructure design.

Now that you have studied the major security practices and tools that Windows 2000 has to offer and how to implement them, it is time to take a look at the big picture and investigate how to use them to protect your networks from penetration by malicious individuals, while still ensuring secure connectivity for those authorized. This chapter paints security with broad strokes. Each potential area for protection is examined and possible designs developed.

Additional products, such as firewalls, proxy servers, and messaging servers, are incorporated into the designs. For more information on these products, see the section "Suggested Readings and Resources" at the end of this chapter.

SECURE ACCESS TO PUBLIC NETWORKS

Provide secure access to public networks from a private network.

Many companies do not have an Internet or public network access policy. That is, they may or may not have direct lines, firewalls, and support staff to help when there is a problem; but they do not have an official, printed, in-your-face directive dealing with the following:

◆ How public networks including the Internet can be accessed

◆ When they can be accessed

◆ Who can access it

◆ The purposes Internet access can be used for

◆ What can be downloaded, opened, and stored on company networks

Irrespective of company property use, legal issues, and work-avoidance issues, public network access (and the lack of a policy on its access) raises many security issues that should be addressed.

Johnson Automotive, this chapter's case study, did not have a policy and found that every major location had arranged for its own Internet access. Some had no protection on the connection. Others had multiple modems installed. Because no policy or attempt at coordination and instruction was made, many employees had desktop modems as well. Long after formal ISP contracts were signed and firewalls in place, two locations still had users who bypassed this security and used dial-up modems to access private services.

Unsupervised, unprotected, and uncontrolled public network access risks the following:

◆ The introduction of viruses—Trojan horses, malicious scripts, and so on—from Web sites, chat rooms, or private email.

◆ Attacks on internal computers by malicious outsiders who use the connection as a point of ingress to network resources.

◆ The use of compromised company computers in coordinated attacks on Web sites and other companies (such as the distributed denial-of-service attacks in February 2000, which crashed major Web sites).

◆ Use of company computers for cyber-fraud, pornography, or other illegal activity.

◆ Work stoppage or slowdown due to misuse of privilege, or flooding of corporate networks with data from external networks.

◆ Exposure of company network information, such as internal addressing schemes, which can be used for attacks.

Although it is impossible to eliminate every risk entirely, you can reduce their probability. To do so, you must focus on the following six areas:

◆ Protect internal networking address schemes from exposure on the public network.

◆ Set up server-side configuration to control content access (and level of such access) in the event of a security breach.

◆ Set up client-side configuration to mitigate the risk.

◆ Allow only specific protocols to exit and return the organization's boundaries.

◆ Limit exit and entry points to the network.

◆ Consider policy, procedure, and politics.

Protect Internal Network Address Schemes

Knowledge of internal network address schemes might enable an attacker to obtain additional information that could be used in a targeted attack (the address of a database server, for example). You can hide internal addresses in two ways: Network Address Translation (NAT) and the use of a proxy server.

NAT maps internal addresses and ports to external addresses and ports. Many routers and firewalls can be configured to perform this function. Windows 2000 provides NAT capabilities as a part of the Routing and Remote Access service. Figure 14.1 shows how NAT can protect internal addressing schemes.

Microsoft Proxy Server substitutes its address for the source address of every packet that it passes to the external network. A common way to configure Proxy Server is to use two network cards: one on the internal network so that it can be contacted by internal computers, and one on the external network. Routing between the network cards does not occur. For a packet to be forwarded to a computer on the Internet, the server must process it. Because the Proxy Server keeps a cache of recently visited Web sites, the packet may not even be delivered to the external network. If it is, the internal address

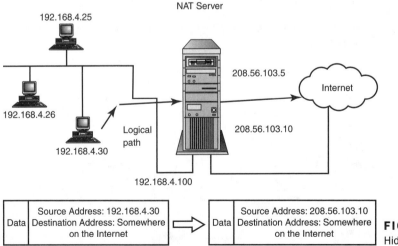

FIGURE 14.1
Hiding internal addresses with NAT.

never accompanies it. Proxy Server 2.0 can also be used to filter exiting and returning packets by protocol and by port. Those that you have filtered out do not pass.

Figure 14.2 shows the placement of a proxy server to protect internal address schemes. Both processes, use of a proxy server or NAT, protect internal addressing schemes.

If you use NAT or a proxy server to hide internal addressing, you may benefit by configuring your internal DNS server to hold only internal addresses. Complete the job by removing the default root, which contains addresses for root Internet servers. Without this information, systems that attempt to "go around" the proxy server will be limited in their capability to access Internet resources. Because the proxy server sits with one interface on the external network, it can access an external DNS for name resolution. The proxy server is configured with an external DNS server as its primary DNS server.

Server-Side Configuration

To protect servers, first determine their level of exposure. In a simple network scheme, all internal servers sit behind a firewall. If the firewall is breached, all servers are at equal risk. In a larger, more complex network, some servers may be more exposed than others. If this is so, they may need additional security arrangements.

For all servers, you should take appropriate precautions, including the following:

◆ Limit and protect administrator accounts.

◆ Assign user accounts with care, with user rights and resource access restricted as appropriate.

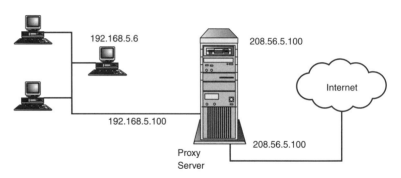

FIGURE 14.2
A proxy server protecting internal address schemes.

◆ Protect data via DACLS.

◆ Fix and/or block known security holes by using the requisite service packs and hot fixes.

◆ Audit sensitive files, registry keys, and objects; and review Security logs for suspicious activity.

If servers are used for a particular purpose (such as database, messaging, connectivity, authentication, and so on), you should establish and maintain appropriate security measures.

Client-Side Configuration

You can set up client computer configuration similarly to servers with regard to access, user rights, and resource protection. In addition, because most client systems will use Web browsers to access the Internet, strict limitations on their configuration can further protect the client system and your internal network. The amount of predetermined configuration you do depends on your organization's policy, but you can effectively maintain this level of protection by using Group Policy.

Other client applications used to access the Internet may need security configuration as well. You may be able to use Group Policy for these, too. You must also decide which applications may be used.

Restricting Protocols That Cross Boundaries

Whatever the reason for accessing the Internet is no reason to allow unrestricted access from the Internet to your network. If your only use for the connection is to access Web sites, you may want to allow only HTTP traffic. Many routers, Proxy Server 2.0, and dedicated firewall systems can minutely control which protocols and ports allow traffic to pass in either direction. You must consider the following three things:

◆ What will you allow to pass and in which direction?

◆ How will you control it?

◆ Where will the control or "firewall" be placed?

Determining which protocols to pass is usually fairly straightforward: Determine the use of the connection; determine the protocols required for this use; and block all other protocols. Think of the blocking process as an encompassing wall, with a guardian at the gate. If a traveler (packet) arrives, the door is opened only if his family name is on the guard's list. Smith, Jones, HTTP, come on in. Peters, White, NetBIOS, nope, sorry, not today. Remember that inbound and outbound activity must be accounted for.

A point to remember is that there must be a way for the response to any internal-to-external communication to be returned. A request from my computer to www.microsoft.com travels from my computer, through my firewall, across the Internet, and arrives at the www.microsoft.com Web server. The server's response (a Web page and all its accoutrements) must return through the Internet to the firewall and to my computer. I need to give the guard two rules: one to let HTTP out, the other to let HTTP in.

So, if the firewall is allowed to pass HTTP back into the network, does that expose the network to attack? Maybe. And maybe you have the type of guard who watches "conversations," not single packets. This type of protection matches incoming and outgoing packets. If I send a request to www.microsoft.com, it seems reasonably safe to return a packet to me from them. This is known as *stateful inspection*.

At any rate, the desire here is to limit exposure. There is no perfect protection from public networks, unless you just do not connect to them.

How you control the information flow? This depends on the size of the company, the perceived risk, and the strategies already in place.

For a smaller company there are many routers that include firewalls. These routers are often called packet-filtering routers and may be limited in their capability to protect your network. Then again, they may provide all the functionality that you need. If a company has purchased a router for ISDN, or T1 connectivity, they possibly already have a firewall and don't know it. To find out, inspect the router's documentation, visit the router company's Web site, or visit the company. Don't stop there. Determine the appropriate configuration, set it up, and test it. Figure 14.3 presents an arrangement for a small company.

If the company has chosen Proxy Server, they may choose to use it for its packet-filtering as well as for its proxy-serving capabilities.

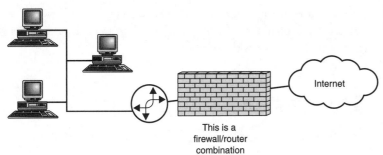

FIGURE 14.3
Small network protection.

This is a
firewall/router
combination

Larger companies may want to invest in a full-blown, dedicated fire-wall. You can find numerous products that allow tight protection of boundaries. These products tend to be much more expensive than packet-filtering routers and may require more extensive training and knowledge for configuration and management.

Whatever your choice, make sure that the firewall is correctly config-ured and that it is not the entire security defense for your network.

Limiting Portals

One of the easiest mistakes to make when providing secure access to public networks is to forget that securing one access point is not enough. If dial-up lines remain after the main Internet access is secured, you have no security. A decision must be made, policy written, and enforced. If you control the number of gateways to the universe, you stand a better chance of keeping space aliens from getting through.

Policy, Procedure, and Politics

You cannot ignore office politics when designing security solutions. Understanding the unwritten rules and the personalities that follow them will help you to more easily obtain the information you need to create your design and enable you to more easily obtain approval for implementation. Remember the business reason for security: to protect the company's property. Remember that its implementation often appears to stand in the way of getting the job done.

Find the business need behind the activity. Determine how security can help meet that need.

Does a written policy or unwritten procedure conflict with your proposed security plan? The key here is to work with people and not let it become a "you versus them" issue.

SECURE ACCESS TO PRIVATE NETWORK RESOURCES

Provide external users with secure access to private network resources.

To provide secure access from public networks to your private resources, you may want to determine the purpose of the access. Is it to allow the public access to your organization's public Web site? Do you want to exchange email with other companies via the Internet? Do you have databases to share with trusted partners? Are you engaging in business-to-business e-commerce?

To secure resources, use DACLs and auditing. Reduce user accounts on the exposed machines to the defaults. Protect these accounts with complex passwords. Use the "no access/no time/no where" practice on the Guest account. This practice makes sure that the Guest account is disabled but doesn't rely on it. It does not let one little option stand between a secure network and one that can easily be penetrated. To lock down the Guest account, just follow these few extra steps:

1. Change the permitted logon hours to none by selecting all hours in the GUI and marking them not allowed. Now the Guest account has no hours during which it can log on.

2. Change the permission to log on from the following workstation to limit allowable workstation to the name of some workstation that does not exist. Because the workstation does not exist, there is no workstation the Guest account can use to log on.

3. Choose an extremely complex password. The default is that the Guest account has no password whatsoever.

4. Rename the Guest account.

Set security templates accordingly and apply them using Group Policy.

Demilitarized Zones

Your strategy for protection may depend on the type of access you will allow and to whom you are allowing it. You may find that the best course of action is to isolate the exposed server and allow no connecting point between that server and your internal network (see Figure 14.4).

You may determine that you need to set up a demilitarized zone (DMZ) that partitions your network and leaves vulnerable machines grouped in a relatively isolated area. To reach your internal network, attackers would need to breach two loggerheads, not just one. Figure 14.5 shows one solution to this problem, the screened subnet where email servers and Web servers are behind the firewall but placed on a separate subnet from the rest of the network. Traffic is filtered at the firewall and only appropriate packets are allowed across and then specifically directed to the appropriate server. A packet directed to an internal Web server, for example, would not even breach the firewall.

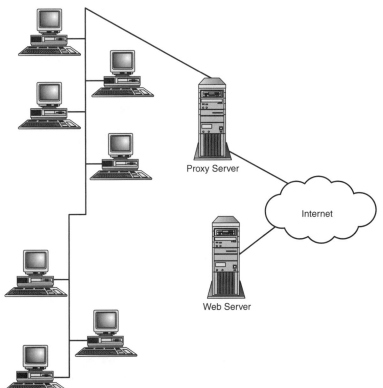

FIGURE 14.4
Isolating the server.

FIGURE 14.5
The DMZ.

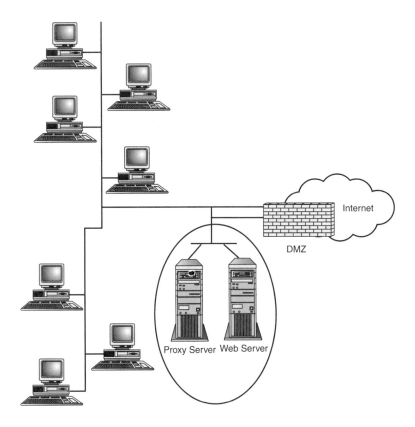

If you think you need more protection, the layout in Figure 14.6 may meet your needs. As the figure shows, two firewalls protect the network. The DMZ sits between them. If a server in the DMZ is compromised and used to attack internal machines, the second firewall would have to be breached.

E-Commerce Solutions

E-commerce presents special issues. Not only do you need to secure the e-commerce server from attack and keep your network safe from people attracted by the server, you also have a duty and obligation to keep the customers safe while they visit your cyber-store. You need

FIGURE 14.6
Using two firewalls.

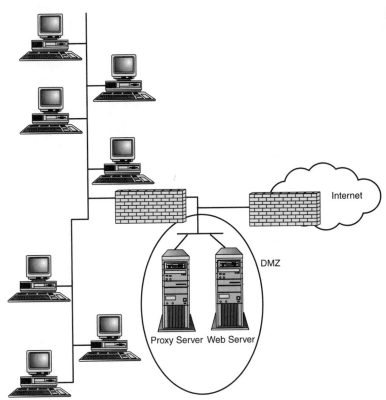

to keep their data private while they are there and after they leave. You want to protect your data as well.

Currently, that means using SSL for all transactions. As you have learned, this requires obtaining a server certificate from one of the public Certificate Authorities (CAs), installing the certificate, and keeping it current. You may also choose to store purchase, pricing, and inventory information in databases external to the Web server and DMZ. Communication between your Web server and its external databases can be via IPSec. In this configuration, the internal firewall does not perform NAT. Figure 14.7 illustrates this process.

FIGURE 14.7
Secure Internet e-commerce transaction.

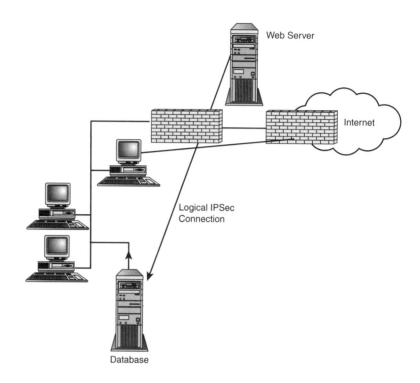

In the future, you might decide to secure transactions by offering customer public key/private key certificates to be used for all transactions. This would have the added advantage of authenticating the client to the server and thereby reduce credit card fraud. Figure 14.8 is the design proposed by Johnson Automotive's retail management for a PKI Customer Promise Plan (PCPP). PCPP uses customer certificates, server certificates, and IPSec to deliver a more secure consumer Web-retail experience.

Secure Access Between Private Networks

Provide secure access between private networks.

Any company that has multiple locations has faced the task of providing connectivity between those locations. This has taken many forms, from private leased lines, to shared Frame Relay, to VPNs constructed across the Internet. Today's enterprise organizations also

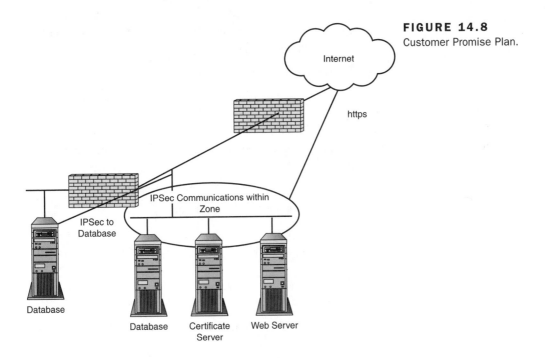

FIGURE 14.8
Customer Promise Plan.

demand connectivity with their business partners. Suppliers, business customers, and trusted partners in joint projects all want to be able to communicate instantly to trade goods and ideas. Security has never been more paramount.

The security of their connections needs to be designed into the connectivity type chosen. Part of ensuring secure access is to begin with security right within the smallest component of the network, the LAN. Your design should begin there and then expand to cover the following:

◆ Secure access within a WAN

◆ Secure access across a public network

Security and the LAN

Provide secure access within a LAN.

Secure access within a LAN requires the following:

◆ Securing administrative access and assigning administrative roles

◆ Understanding and dealing with IP risks and using IPSec for data encryption and/or signing

◆ Controlling access to shared resources

◆ Securing non-Microsoft client access to shared resources

As usual, securing administrative access follows the rules expressed in earlier chapters on groups (Chapter 7, "Designing a Security Group Strategy"), audit (Chapter 6, "Designing an Audit Policy"), and policy (Chapter 8, "Designing Security Policy Inheritance"):

◆ Limit the number of administrators.

◆ Delegate authority to nonadministrative users for specific administrative tasks.

◆ Audit administrative duties.

◆ Use Restricted groups to contain administrative roles.

◆ Ensure that administrators limit their logons and use runas to fulfill that part of their role.

One of the major issues concerning IP is that it was developed during much friendlier times. A number of IP utilities and protocols allow unrestricted access to systems. Telnet, for example, allows administrative access to systems. A password is requested, but passed in clear text across the network. To counter this affect, you can prohibit Telnet servers on your systems, prevent the Telnet protocol from passing through routers and firewalls, or secure any Telnet communications with IPSec.

If you were to use a network monitor to "see" your network communications as an intruder would, you would notice that much information that could assist an intruder to attack your network is available. Although it may not be practical to hide every communication, you may determine that it is necessary to use IPSec for data encryption to protect sensitive communications.

Sound security includes addressing the issues of data resources, whether they are within databases or just stored on file servers. In the Microsoft world, access to local file systems can be protected by setting DACLs on the folders and on the files themselves. Local access can also be controlled in Windows 2000 by using the

Encrypting File system (EFS). Remember that EFS protects files for *individuals*; it is not a way to share encrypted files between users.

Shared resource access should also be designed with security in mind. You must consider the following points:

◆ The DACLs of files and folders manage access to data.

◆ DACLs set on the share control access to the file system.

◆ Although permissions set on shared folders and permissions set on the share combine to determine whether access is permitted, care should be taken to set appropriate access first on the folder.

◆ Access to the file system is controlled by many shares. Any share point allows access to files and subfolders. If share points above a subfolder (which is also shared) are weaker, access to the folder may be gained when a direct connection may have been prevented. Strict settings on the subfolder prevent this oversight from allowing access.

◆ The result of the combination of share permissions and folder permissions always results in the most restrictive action winning. Therefore if Mary has Read permission on the share, but Read and Write permission on the folder, when she connects across the network, her access is limited to Read.

◆ Access from a local logon is not affected by share permissions. If Mary could log on locally, the share permission would have no affect and she would have Read and Write permission. Figure 14.9 illustrates the point.

The first step in securing access by non-Microsoft clients to shared resources is to secure shared access for Microsoft Clients. Next, determine which non-Microsoft clients will be allowed to access each share. There is no point in providing access for Macintosh clients if you have no Macintosh systems. When you add any service that you don't need, you needlessly expose your network to attack. It is not that these particular services are especially vulnerable, it just that every service can be used as a point of attack. The less points of access you provide, the easier it is to secure your network. Every excess service provides possible points of attack. Don't create security holes; don't install unnecessary services. Finally, you must determine how non-Microsoft

FIGURE 14.9
Share and folder permission combos.

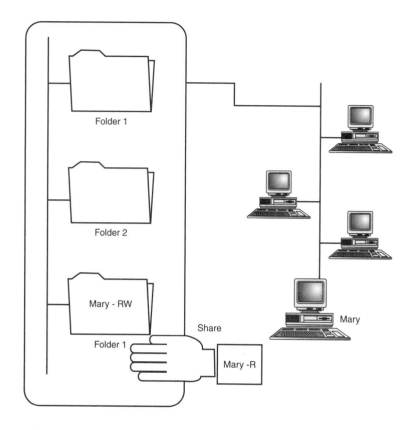

clients will access the shares, and apply appropriate security responses. You must investigate, design, and secure the following areas:

◆ Providing secure access for UNIX clients

◆ Providing secure access for Novell clients

◆ Providing secure access for Macintosh clients

Providing Secure Access for UNIX Clients

Services for UNIX (SFU) is a separate product available to provide integration between Windows and UNIX. Windows 2000 provides printing services for UNIX. Three areas of access for UNIX clients need to be secured:

◆ Shared files and printers

◆ Password synchronization

◆ Telnet

Sharing Files with NFS

Microsoft Server for NFS (Network File System) allows UNIX clients to access shared files on a Windows 2000 Server. In the Network File System (used in the UNIX world), the server file system is logically "mounted" on the client, and to the client, the file system appears to be local. This logical representation is similar to the share mapping expressed in Windows clients, although the actual process is much different. As far as the users are concerned, the idea is the same; they can read and write to files without worrying about where the file actually is.

Administering Server for NFS is done via a Windows 2000 configuration utility.

Two issues concern security: The UNIX client must have an account in the Windows 2000 system, and share and file access must be permitted for this account.

UNIX identifies users by user ID (UID) and group ID (GID). Windows identifies users by user id (SID) and group id (SID). To provide access for UNIX users, each UNIX user and group must be mapped to Windows 2000 users and groups. In Figure 14.10, an account is created on Windows for user NancyS. She is automatically

NOTE
More Detail on NFS NFS, based on RFCs 1094 and 1813, is a standard for file access across a network. The sharing of files is based on the Open Network Computing Remote Procedure Call (ONC-RPC). Remote Procedure Calls (RPC) are described in RFC 1831, 1050, and 1057. Open Network Computing External Data Representation (XDR), described in RFCs 1832 and 1014, is used for data transmission.

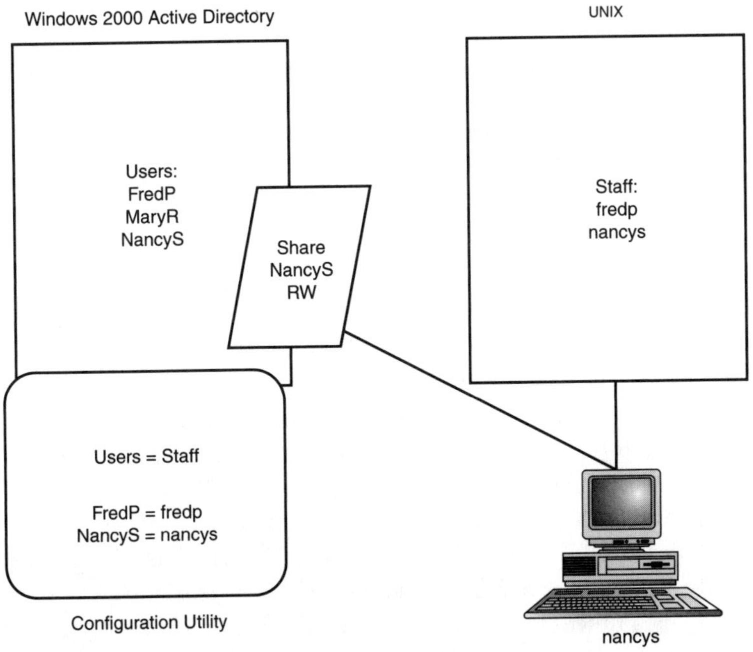

FIGURE 14.10
Mapping UNIX users and groups.

made a member of the Windows 2000 Users group. She already has an account, nancys, on the UNIX system where she is a member of the staff group. On the Window 2000 system in the Server for NFS Administration utility, the Windows user NancyS is mapped to the UNIX user nancys. The Windows group Users is mapped to the UNIX group staff.

The secrets.doc file is created on a Windows 2000 Server volume called stuff in the G:\Stuff\ folder. The Users group is given Full Control. NancyS takes ownership of the file and grants Full Control for herself and the staff group and gives List Permissions for Everyone. When she mounts the volume and lists the directory from her UNIX client, the file appears listed as follows:

```
Rwxrwxr_x 1 nancys staff          2118  Feb 3 12:56
secrets.doc
```

The first nine characters represent permission available (in groups of three) to the group, owner, and other.

UNIX users who have permission can use the UNIX chgmod or chgrp commands to change file permissions. The impact on the existing permission in Windows 2000 is determined by the settings in the Server for NFS. Administrators can force these files to continue to maintain the inherited permissions of the parent directory on the Windows 2000 system.

To provide secure access for UNIX clients to NTFS partitions, you must ensure that original permissions set on the mountable volumes are correct (as well as the permissions on folders and files within the volume). UNIX users must be placed in appropriate UNIX groups, and finally, UNIX users and groups must be mapped to appropriate Windows 2000 user ids and groups. Secure access can be controlled only if UNIX administrators and Windows 2000 administrators cooperate to carry out the design.

Print Services for UNIX

Print Services for UNIX is provided with Windows 2000. After it is installed, it provides printing from a UNIX client that has an RFC-compliant version of Line Printer Remote (LPR). Print privileges do not give UNIX clients printer management access to the Windows 2000–controlled printers. The Windows 2000 Server merely runs the lpdsvc service that responds to an lpr command. The lpdsvc service is the Line Printer Daemon that receives print jobs from an LPR utility.

Password Synchronization

Services for UNIX can be used to synchronize passwords between UNIX computers and Windows 2000 computers. An administrator can configure the system so that changes to Windows 2000 user passwords for accounts mapped to UNIX accounts in Services for UNIX are propagated to UNIX systems. The data can be sent as encrypted text (using Triple DES, or as clear text using the UNIX rlogin command). The UNIX system places the password in its files in the format it requires.

Password synchronization can only occur where the Single Sign-On Daemon (SSOD) is installed on all UNIX systems that want to synchronize passwords. (Unless, of course, you are using the network management system NIS. If you are using it, you can install the SSOD only on the NIS server, and it will propagate the changes out to the servers that it controls.) The SSOD daemon comes with Services for UNIX but is not available for all varieties of UNIX. This password synchronization is one-way. If passwords are changed on the UNIX side, they are not propagated to the Windows 2000 Server. Figure 14.11 illustrates the password-synchronization process.

> **N O T E**   **3DES**   3DES, or triple DES, is a version of the Data Encryption Standard that encrypts the data three times. DES is a symmetric key algorithm. This means that the keys, or shared secret(s), must be known to both sides of the communication. You will want to coordinate password synchronization with your UNIX counterpart.

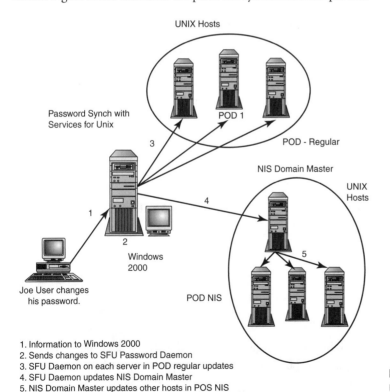

1. Information to Windows 2000
2. Sends changes to SFU Password Daemon
3. SFU Daemon on each server in POD regular updates
4. SFU Daemon updates NIS Domain Master
5. NIS Domain Master updates other hosts in POS NIS

FIGURE 14.11
UNIX/Windows 2000 password synchronization.

Telnet

Windows 2000 provides a Telnet server that allows 2 concurrent connections. The Telnet server included with Services for UNIX supports a maximum of 63. Telnet allows a connection to a remote server. It is often used to remotely administer a UNIX server.

If you use a Windows NT 4.0 or a Windows 2000 client that has a Windows 2000 user account, you can configure your systems so that the client will be authenticated by the Windows 2000 Server using the NTLM network-authentication protocol and passwords will be encrypted. You must provide the client with a copy of the Telnet utility from Services from UNIX, and you must configure the Telnet server to require NTLM authentication.

If your client is a UNIX client, which does not support NTLM, the password traverses the network in clear text. NTLM settings can be adjusted in the registry or, preferably, by using the Telnet Server Administration tool.

To manage Telnet security, there are four possibilities:

◆ Allow any access.

◆ Allow only NTLM access.

◆ Attempt NTLM authentication first, and then use clear text.

◆ Restrict Telnet access to sessions using IPSec.

Changes to NTLM settings are made in the registry by using the Telnet Server Administrator and selecting Option 3. Table 14.1 explains the possible settings.

TABLE 14.1

SETTING NTLM PARAMETERS FOR TELNET

Setting	Option
0	Default: Don't use NTLM.
1	Try NTLM; if fails, use clear-text username and password.
2	User NTLM only.

The Telnet Server Administrator utility also enables you to obtain information about users and to disconnect any user session.

To ensure optimum security over a Telnet session, you want to implement the IPSec requirement. Because Telnet provides administrators very powerful options in managing a server, you want to restrict Telnet access. For more information on Telnet, see RFC 854. At least make the NTLM registry settings so that non-Windows NT or Windows 2000 clients have no access. (Remember, Windows NT 4.0 clients need the SFU client.) Then control administrative privileges thoroughly as well as permissions on folders and files.

Providing Secure Access for Novell Clients

Novell clients may use TCP/IP or IPX/SPX to communicate with the Novell server. For them to access Microsoft shared resources, two things must be true: The Windows 2000 Server must be running NWLink, Microsoft's implementation of IPX/SPX; or the Novell client must be running TCP/IP, and the user of the Novell client must have an account and password on the Windows 2000 system.

If you have chosen to use Client or Gateway Services for NetWare, you want to coordinate activities with your NetWare administrator. The NetWare administrator will want to consider resource access on the NetWare servers and will only grant user access and accounts appropriately. Gateway Services allows access through a single point for multiple users from your side of the network. On the NetWare side, it is represented by a single point. All access to NetWare resources through this portal are the same for every Windows user to whom you grant permission. Remember this, and restrict the membership in this group accordingly.

Providing Secure Access of Macintosh Clients

Windows 2000 provides access to shared resources for Macintosh clients through AppleTalk network integration. This is an outgrowth of the Windows NT 4.0 Services for Macintosh. Both shared file resources and printers controlled by Windows 2000 can be made available to Macintosh users by setting up the following functions:

◆ Installing (and enabling) the AppleTalk protocol or TCP/IP protocol on the Windows 2000 Server. (AppleTalk is installed but not enabled automatically when you install other Macintosh services; see Figure 14.12.)

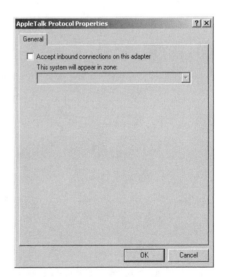

FIGURE 14.12
Enabling AppleTalk.

◆ Installing File Services for Macintosh, including making sure that an NTFS partition is available with a size restriction matching the capabilities of Macintosh clients. (Different versions of the Macintosh file access protocol have different restrictions—from 2GB on OS 7.5 and earlier, 4GB on later versions, and no restrictions on clients that use AppleTalk File Protocol 2.2.)

◆ Installing Print Services for Macintosh.

◆ Establishing network connectivity.

◆ Establish network security including volume permission.

◆ Establish file security.

◆ Establish printer authentication.

Establishing network connectivity should be your first step. You have several choices:

◆ If the Macintosh clients use Ethernet, you make no changes.

◆ If the Macintosh clients use LocalTalk, you should either install a LocalTalk card on the server or install Ethernet cards on all the Macintosh computers that need to access the shared resources. Alternatively, you can install an Ethernet/LocalTalk router.

◆ If there is some combination of LocalTalk, Token Ring, and/or Ethernet, you may need to install a Token Ring and a LocalTalk card on the server, or make a decision on changing all the clients to one standard that can be met by the server(s).

Obviously, the least confusing of all these is to standardize on Ethernet or Token Ring, if that is your current networking standard, and to outfit the Macintosh clients accordingly. This may not be possible, and you may not want to do this for other reasons. You may choose to ignore LocalTalk at the server level and only provide Ethernet cards for those Macintosh machines whose users have a need and permissions to access server resources. This can assist you in limiting access to network resources that need to be secured more closely.

File Services for Macintosh requires you to identify the partitions that will be made available to Macintosh clients. Although this is a restriction resulting from the file-handling changes that must be made to support Macintosh users, it can also assist you in securing network resources. Macintosh users will be unable to access resources on servers unless the server has File Services for Macintosh installed, and on those servers, only volumes that have be established as available to Macintosh users can be accessed. Windows users can also access these volumes, so Macintosh and Windows users can share files and folders. Macintosh-available volumes can also be protected with a volume password. You add the password when you configure the volume. This is like adding a password to shares in Windows 9x. The Macintosh user is required to enter a volume password in addition to a user id and password to access the volume. Complete network security by securing files and folders in the normal manner.

When configuring network security, you must ensure that Macintosh users have Windows 2000 user ids and passwords and you must select the most secure Macintosh authentication method. Methods include the following:

◆ Allowing guest access

◆ Allowing clear-text passwords

◆ Using Apple standard encryption (up to 8-character passwords)

◆ MS- User Authentication Method (UAM) (up to 14-character passwords)

Encrypted options use the password to encrypt a server- provided random number that is then sent over the network. The password is never sent. The server must store the user's password in reversibly encrypted form, encrypt the same number, and compare the two to complete authentication.

> **NOTE**
>
> **Finally, a Use for User Primary Group**
> This option, available in the Windows 2000 user properties, applies to Macintosh users. This group should be the one that the Macintosh user uses most frequently. When the user creates a folder on the server, the primary group becomes the owner of the folder.

File security for Macintosh-accessible volumes is secured in the normal manner from the Windows 2000 perspective. From the Macintosh perspective, files and folders reflect Macintosh permissions and appropriate changes can be made using Macintosh permission settings.

The file permissions recognized and used by Macintosh on Windows 2000 volumes depends on the Macintosh version.

Macintosh systems prior to OS 8.5 use the following:

◆ See Files (see and read files in a folder)

◆ See Folders (see folders within a folder)

◆ Make Changes (modify file content, rename, move, create, and delete files)

Macintosh systems OS 8.5 and later support Windows 2000 privileges:

◆ Read-Only

◆ Write-Only (add files or folders)

◆ Read and Write (add, delete, change)

◆ None (prevents access)

Macintosh users recognize three types of users and groups:

◆ Owners

◆ User/Group

◆ Everyone

This reflects the philosophy that a file or folder is either private (one owner needs to see, use it), group available, or public property. Macintosh users support only folder-level permissions—that is, files within a folder cannot have different sets of permissions. If more granular file permissions are set in Windows 2000, the more restrictive permission wins and you may lock your Macintosh users out of them.

Windows 2000 Read Permissions translates to Macintosh See Files, Folders Permission. Windows 2000 Write, Delete Permissions translates to Make Changes.

Printer Authentication is not natively provided by Macintosh networking. If a Macintosh user can access a printer across the network, he can print to it.

However, you can restrict Macintosh users as a group. To do so, you create an account and use this account as the account that authenticates the MacPrint service (see Figure 14.13). Set user DACLs on the printers using this account. (see Figure 14.14). All Macintosh users have the privileges that are assigned to this user. Therefore, you may keep Macintosh users from using a printer by not giving this account printer privileges on the printers.

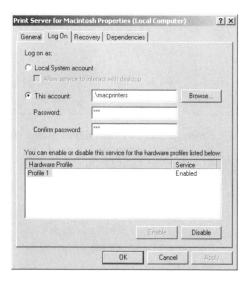

FIGURE 14.13
Setting the MacPrint user account.

Securing WAN Access

Provide secure access within a WAN.

Secure access across a WAN includes access across dedicated links, Frame Relay, and ATM.

Although dedicated connections would seem to provide the ultimate in security, you should still maintain your server, file system and user policies. You might consider smart card or certificate deployment to aid in security efforts.

Tunneling across WAN links can also be a good policy. By providing a VPN connection, you are layering security.

You can use Internet Authentication Server to authenticate access from branch offices via WAN links as well as dial-up lines.

Nothing precludes establishing a firewall or limiting protocol access.

Finally, you can use IPSec to secure data transfer as necessary.

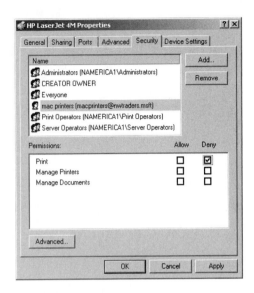

FIGURE 14.14
Setting Macintosh printer privileges.

Secure Access Across a Public Network

Provide secure access across a public network.

Providing access across a public network includes the following:

◆ Providing access between trusted partners

◆ Providing access between organization locations

◆ Providing telecommuters and road warriors access to company facilities across Internet links

The third access scenario, providing telecommuters and road warriors access, is fully described in the following section on providing secure access for remote access users.

Providing access between organizational locations and between trusted partners follows similar patterns, with the degree of security being placed on the other side of the endpoints accounting for the major difference. On either side of the connection, architecturally they may differ, because organizational members may belong to the same tree, forest, or domain as those with whom they are communicating. Trusted partners do not have this advantage, but access may be provided by establishing a trust between domains, establishing a domain for use by trusted partners, or providing access by mapping trusted partner user certificates to Windows 2000 domain accounts.

These scenarios require strict attention to detail, as well as increased vigilance (because the medium of transport is public). Both participants, be they members of the same organization or trading partners, need to be aware of the additional risks. Public networks, such as the Internet, can provide the advantages of reduced cost and ready availability, but also the problems inherent when dealing with the unknown. There will always be a "new" attack mechanism to protect against. There will always be the chance that reduction in reliability or bandwidth availability may be encountered.

Security cannot be gradually "built" in as the need or requirement is established. The best, most secure, afforded solution should be chosen the first time. Here are major opportunities for PKI initiatives and VPNs. PKI will be used for authentication, and VPNs to restrict connectivity and to ensure the confidentiality and integrity of data that crosses the public network. As you can see, the following two areas need design:

◆ Securing resources at either end of the connection

◆ Securing data communications over the public network

Securing Resources

Possible solutions for securing resources include using PKI for authentication, and controlling access by limiting access to special applications such as messaging servers, terminal services, or Web services.

PKI can be used for authentication and to map business partners to internal user accounts. These accounts, and the Certificate Trust Lists (CTL) that enable the use of foreign certificates, can be used to control access and restrict privileges within the network. You want to limit trusted partner access to internal resources. There is also no reason to assume that because users are from the same organization that security should be more lax. Limiting access can be done by assigning resource permissions and restricting rights and by placing shared resources in screened subnets or DMZs. Figure 14.15 shows this approach to communication across the public network.

Providing terminal services consists of establishing a terminal server, possibly in a separate domain. The Windows 2000 Server with terminal services implemented in Application Sharing mode would host the application(s) that organization locations or trusted partners would share. All foreign accounts could be restricted to this server(s), and internal accounts could be maintained via trust. All access to private resources would be through application(s) on the terminal server and through terminal server clients provided to all valid users of the servers.

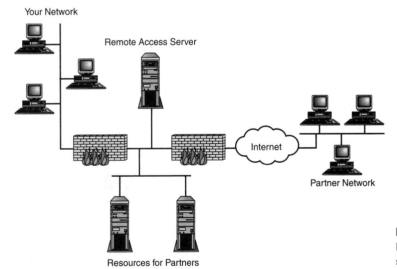

Your Network

Remote Access Server

Internet

Partner Network

Resources for Partners

FIGURE 14.15
Limiting Access for partners using screened subnets.

Securing Data Communications

Data communications needs to be secured. You must assume that someone other than the two parties is interested in the conversation and act accordingly. Simple solutions such as S/MAIL and SSL can provide some access to resources across the Internet. SSL, although primarily used for server authentication, can be used for mutual authentication. If required resources are placed on Web servers or in protected databases accessible to these servers, access can be secured by restricting access to private users.

Communication between terminal services clients and terminal servers located across the public network can be secured by using data encryption provided within the client/server relationship. Set the encryption level to high to provide encryption in both directions as well as 128-bit encryption (see Figure 14.16). Be sure to investigate export and import rules if your connections cross national boundaries.

A VPN can be established between trusted partners or between organizational locations. The type of VPN (server to server, or client to server) and the protocol chosen (PPTP or IPSec over L2TP) depend on the requirements of the connection, as well as the resources available at both ends. IPSec is wonderfully flexible and a number of essentially tunnels within tunnels can be planned that allow flexibility and security for communication. You should examine the following chapter for more information on this solution. Some examples of VPN tunnels follow.

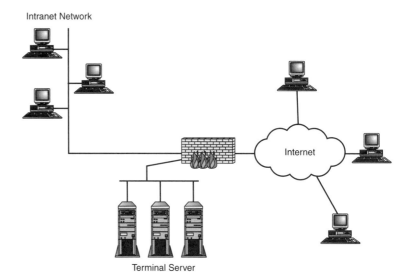

FIGURE 14.16
Securing communications with terminal services.

One approach is to create a tunnel between locations with a Windows 2000 Server at either end. All communications are secured between the endpoints (see Figure 14.17).

This design does not account for the security of data after it leaves the tunnel endpoint, or from the initiating computer to the beginning tunnel. It may be necessary to require client-to-server tunneling, either through the endpoint established or as separate tunnels (see Figures 14.18 and 14.19). IPSec is sufficiently flexible to accomplish this.

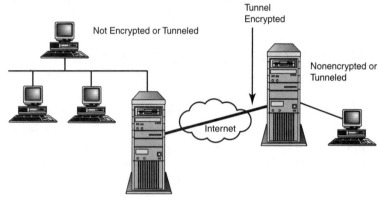

FIGURE 14.17
Endpoint to endpoint security.

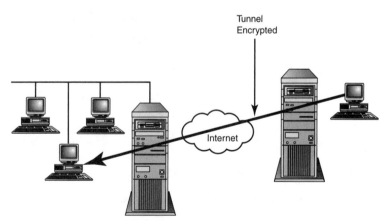

FIGURE 14.18
Client-to-endpoint tunnel.

FIGURE 14.19
Client-to-destination tunnel.

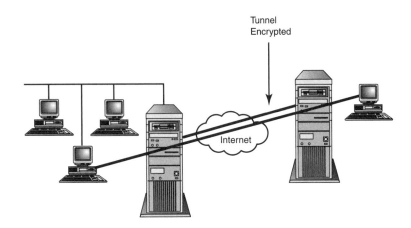

Sharing Databases with Trusted Partners

Many good examples of business-to-business (B2B) sites can be found, and many more are proposed and implemented every day. In the past, inter-business electronic purchasing was established by leased lines or Frame Relay. Now it is accomplished via the Internet. To protect both purchasers and sellers, a good start is to establish a PKI. Because the system is selling to business customers, you may choose to establish your CA as the trusted root and grant user certificates to trading partners. Secure communication can be established by setting up a VPN. Access to your VPN endpoint may be from client systems at the customer or through gateways established by ISPs.

If your purpose is to share information with trusted partners while working on a joint project, a different arrangement may be made. A PKI may already exist at the other company. To control their access to your information, you can do the following:

◆ Create user accounts in Active Directory.

◆ Modify DACLs on resources you want partners to access.

◆ Establish a CTL indicating the uses to which certificates from that source can be used.

◆ Import your business partner's certificates and map certificates to the user accounts.

Johnson Automotive (this chapter's case study) has begun working with ITS (previous case study) in an effort to crack the truck-stop market. As you will recall, ITS markets everything from potato chips to luggage, soft drinks to toys, tools to coffee pots at truck stops across the country. Johnson Automotive will open databases of product information and in-stock information so that ITS can more readily promote Johnson's products. In exchange, ITS will allow Johnson access to customer data by geographical region, which will enable Johnson to better plan inventory and warehousing strategies. To secure access to this information, a trust relationship between company domains has been established. On Johnson's side, an IAS server will serve as a central authentication and accounting database for access to the database. ITS will use a single remote access server. A VPN tunnel will connect the two companies and establish compulsory tunneling for all access between the two (see Figure 14.20).

This form of inter-business communication is becoming more prevalent as companies attempt to find new ways to benefit business partnerships and to find new ways to partner. The challenge then becomes to provide a secure way to allow only the access desired. Thoroughly protecting each partner's network requires cooperation and vigilance. Almost every aspect of security design for Windows 2000 networks will be called into play.

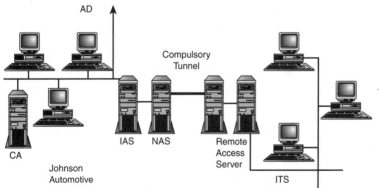

FIGURE 14.20
ITS and Johnson Automotive B2B.

Secure Access Through Messaging

Two ways to provide secure access through messaging are email and public folders. You can use Microsoft Exchange Server for both.

First, users of the messaging system should understand its unique position in today's communication systems. Email is everywhere, yet email is vulnerable to attack, denial of service, spam relay, and just plain old-fashioned interception.

To provide secure access via email, it is important to judge the degree of security required. The prospects can be broken into four classes:

◆ Mail needs to make it to the mail server and arrive intact.

◆ No one but the intended recipient should be able to read secure messages.

◆ The physical mail server requires securing.

◆ Public folder access should be restricted.

The first case is a question of securing the mail server and securing the transport. If the transport is via the Internet, usually the arrival of mail is not in question. If this becomes a concern, especially for partner mail or inter-organizational mail, alternative links might be in order, such as direct lease line, direct dial, or some other connectivity method. Alternatively you could establish and use a VPN between the endpoints for this type of mail.

If messages themselves need to be secure, there is only one solution: message encryption. You can accomplished this in a number of ways including S/MIME, Exchange Server Keys, and third-party products.

Securing the mail server demands strict security of the system itself first. Start with basic security of the OS, and then apply recommended service packs, fixes, configuration, and registry tweaks. Placement of the server is also important. Because mail servers stand between external and internal systems, they are often placed in a DMZ or screened subnets. Depending on the number of mail servers involved, you may want to consider placing a single mail server in the DMZ and other mail servers safely within the organization. All mail is received by the DMZ mail server and forwarded to internal servers. The DMZ mail server holds no mailboxes; it just serves as a forwarding point, and of course is aware of the address of internal servers. By exposing only this server externally, only this server faces the direct brunt of an external attack. This server can also serve as the public folder server, and thus expose only those folders that you want to.

Alternatively, you could use an Exchange Server exclusively for communications with trusted partners. Public folders, restricted to their eyes only, can be protected. Direct lines or VPNs can be established to protect communications between companies.

WINDOWS 2000 SECURITY FOR REMOTE ACCESS USERS

Design Windows 2000 security for remote access users.

Remote access users can consist of users from other company locations, telecommuters and employees on the road, and business partners.

You have already spent time considering data communications security and various scenarios for providing security of resources at the endpoints. This section discusses remote authentication, the security of data in mobile environments, and how to put this together with the other technologies to present full solutions.

Remote authentication has been discussed in earlier sections. You have also read about such methods as using SSL with Web services, adding domain trusts, and PKI solutions. If more comprehensive authentication and accounting is required, consider a solution that uses Windows 2000 Routing and Remote Access, and/or Internet Authentication Services (IAS). You have already studied the way that these services work. How can they be integrated into your security solution? When are they most appropriate?

If you have large numbers of dial-up users, you may already be using some form of a remote access server. If you are accessing the Internet through an ISP, you most assuredly are. When considering remote access solutions, you may want to consider outsourcing all but authentication to reduce your infrastructure requirements, as well as technology expertise. In this scenario, you can still maintain control of authentication by using IAS. As described in the preceding chapter, you place a remote access server at the ISP that acts as the RADIUS client to your IAS server (see Figure 14.21). A tunnel is provided to ensure the security of communications between the servers. You and your ISP may also want to consider placing an IAS server at their location to authenticate access to the tunnel.

This is also a good solution when you need to provide remote access for users in other locations. By selecting an ISP with locations that match your needs, you can provide secure remote access. If you have traveling users, choose an ISP with nationwide (or if necessary, worldwide) access points. Some ISPs may also be able to provide you

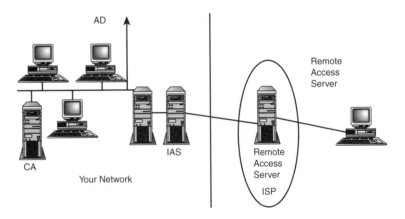

FIGURE 14.21

Sharing remote access responsibilities with the ISP.

with better quality of service, and possibly more secure arrangements, because they can route your communications across their backbone network (see Figure 14.22) instead of relying strictly on links shared with other ISPs.

You may also choose to locate all hardware and software on your network (see Figure 14.23). In either case, be sure to provide adequate backup for the IAS server.

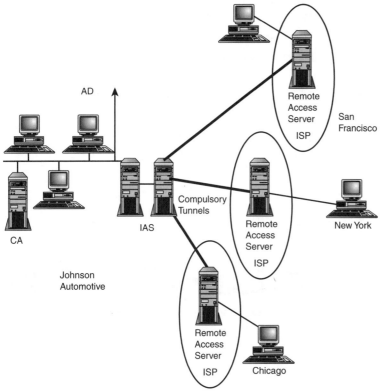

FIGURE 14.22
In-house remote access solution.

FIGURE 14.23
Johnson Automotive remote access.

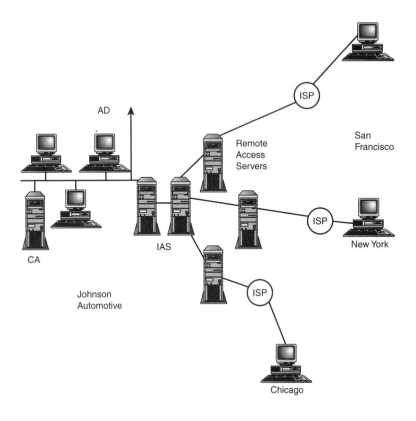

CASE STUDY: JOHNSON AUTOMOTIVE

BACKGROUND

Johnson Automotive manufactures and markets products for the automotive aftermarket. It provides franchise services for more than 1,000 independent store owners and manages 629 company-owned stores. Stores are primarily in the Northeastern and Midwestern states, with a growing number of locations in the Western part of the country. Founded in 1921, the company has a long history of providing quality products and service. They have been innovative in marketing and sell directly to consumers through their Foxboro, Massachusetts Web site. A private consumer and business credit card system ensures a steady trade from automotive hobbyists and car repair businesses as well as from private fleets. Stores stock parts, accessories, tires, and batteries. Company-owned stores also provide dealer-quality automotive repair and maintenance services.

Franchise systems are run from Charlotte, West Virginia. Other locations in Milwaukee and Phoenix act as distribution centers. Grain Valley, Missouri provides packaging and repackaging of private-label Johnson Automotive parts and accessories as well as the acquisition of "produced-for" Johnson Automotive products. Grain Valley also manages the sales force.

CASE STUDY: JOHNSON AUTOMOTIVE

PROBLEM STATEMENT

Access to internal systems has been provided on a piecemeal basis. There has been no thought or overall plan to the process. New technologies have fostered discussions on the need to coordinate activities.

Information Systems Manager

I would have to admit that the communications between divisions and to and from our stores has grown up as a hodgepodge of links. Each one was put in when a need was perceived, with no overall planning or discussion on cost or the overall impact to our data systems. As a result I think we have suffered every calamity that came along. We have been big victims to the Melissa virus and other email-born problems. Costs are skyrocketing. Management is complaining that people spend too much time on the Internet. Our business partners are clamoring for a better way to work together. Just last week, purchasing discovered a place where a large number of our accessory lines can be purchased online. It requires connectivity between us and the company that handles the sales. I'm sure there are other business-to-business scenarios like that, and wonder why our marketing people are not proposing such a venture for us as well.

We think we have got a handle on the Internet connections, but we may be living in a dream world. It is not so much corporate I worry about, it is all our other offices that don't have a clue. They are repeating the mistakes we have made.

We have a unique opportunity here. Everyone is interested in the new technologies and ready to change. We have been able to get IT people from the different locations together to plan the corporate infrastructure.

Headquarters Systems Administrator

It used to be that I could just manage headquarters. We had a couple of connections to other locations, but they were Frame Relay and not a problem. Basically we were just collecting sales information and sending email. Now I have requests from everyone—business partners, branch offices, stores. They all want to link up to get information from us. We have dealt with this request in a rather piecemeal fashion.

Infrastructure Team Leader

For the first time, we can look at the big picture and design a strategy for now and the future.

Charlotte

Our connection has worked fine in the past, but it is terribly expensive. I have heard of companies using the Internet for communications to reduce costs, and I would like to do that.

Milwaukee

We do not provide Internet access for all our users. We have decided that too many risks are involved.

continues

CASE STUDY: JOHNSON AUTOMOTIVE

continued

Phoenix

The data center here has to deal with mainframe, UNIX, Novell, and Microsoft. I want to be sure any internal connectivity we have doesn't allow breaches in security. All our planning can be wiped out if some Joe can directly get into files from his UNIX client.

Grain Valley

I currently have 1,000 plus salesmen on the road all the time. I need to make sure that they have secure access to everything from sales literature to inventory and calendars. They enter orders, check on deliveries, and learn about new products from their laptops and a connection in their hotel or at a customer site.

EveryWhere, Inc.

We have been your ISP in Charlotte and Milwaukee and have been asked to propose a plan for worldwide Internet services for your company. I believe we have some ideas that will help you maintain costs.

CURRENT SYSTEM

A variety of connections exists. Access to external networks, internal networks, and the Internet is not consistent across branches.

Headquarters Systems Administrator

We use Frame Relay connections between Charlotte and headquarters and Phoenix. A T1 line connects us to Milwaukee. Branch offices use dial-up to connect with us to upload sales information.

Infrastructure Team Leader

Each location has pretty much had to fend for itself. Each location has an Internet connection.

EveryWhere, Inc.

Charlotte has a persistent ISDN connection to us. They are using NAT to connect to the Internet with a packet-filtering firewall on the router.

Milwaukee has a T1 connection, their own domain name, and a Class C address pool.

Charlotte

All stores have access to a private Web site where they can query for inventory information.

Grain Valley

We maintain our own remote access servers to provide access to sales staff. Currently we maintain several toll-free number lines.

SECURITY

Consistency can be established by setting baselines and requiring a level of security be established for communications between plants.

Headquarters Systems Administrator

Security baselines for systems including Web servers, database servers, domain controllers, workstations, and servers will be developed. They can be maintained through Group Policy.

CASE STUDY: JOHNSON AUTOMOTIVE

Infrastructure Team Leader

IPSec over L2TP or PPTP (where necessary due to NAT) tunnels will be provided for secure communications between distribution centers and headquarters. Tunnels will link trusted partners to DMZs where B2B Web sites and other information sharing can occur. Client-to-server tunnels with the modus operandi for salesmen. These VPNs will be established over the Internet where possible. A Public Key Infrastructure will be established to provide security between partners and to allow the requirement of smart cards for logon access to any headquarters system. Smart cards and PKI will also allow the central management of encryption keys and certificates for EFS on traveling computers.

EveryWhere, Inc.

You have charged us with hosting your remote access capabilities. We will coordinate efforts with each distribution center and headquarters to provide connectivity with tunnel endpoints, and to ensure communications between remote access servers and your centralized IAS servers. We will provide a list of local phone numbers for all cities where we have locations or form cooperating ventures with other ISPs. You will use these numbers to produce a phonebook for salesmen and other traveling and remote users. We will continually update you as numbers are added or changes are made.

PERFORMANCE

Performance goals are important here. Access needs to be immediate at any time.

Systems Admin

Store accesses to inventory information must be accomplished within three to five seconds. These folks are conditioned to instant availability of product. Because not all stores are company owned, we must always provide a quick response or they will look elsewhere.

Information Technology Manager

Databases, Web servers, mail servers. Any information services must be available 24 × 7!

MAINTAINABILITY

Maintenance of the new requirement will be provided by use of Group Policy, education of all information systems personnel, and adequate staffing.

Headquarters Systems Administrator

Group Policy will be used extensively to maintain our security policy and to ensure availability of resources.

Infrastructure Team Leader

Our team will be increased to numbers needed to support these new technologies. Members will receive ongoing training of the highest quality. Members will be centrally trained but will be located at distribution centers. "At-large" members will circulate to maintain communications and services for company stores, and liaison with franchise members and business-to-business projects.

continues

CASE STUDY: JOHNSON AUTOMOTIVE

continued

AVAILABILITY

24×7, Web sites, databases, tunnels, all components used between and for stores, the distribution center, trading partners.

ANALYSIS

Huge issues of access control face Johnson Automotive. The dual problems of new technology and lack of consistency in the current system might be overwhelming. However, the desire to implement the new technologies may prove to be one of those rare opportunities that allows all parties to cooperate. No one has to lose face because everyone is changing his system. If handled properly, everyone comes out a winner. Corporate information systems leaders will have to make sure to continue to include other locations in the ongoing discussion, design, implementation, and maintenance.

CHAPTER SUMMARY

The potential for disaster is high, the simple solution is nonexistent, and expertise is in short supply. You must craft your design for access between networks with care and maintain it with vigilance. By the time you have completed your design, the possibility of new security developments being available to plague your solution is high.

What's the answer?

You can never design the perfect security solution, because security needs and risks are ever changing. What you can do is design flexible solutions that operate at the highest security level that is affordable and reasonable for the situation. Carefully lay out the requirements, risks, and possibilities. In this chapter, you have examined the possible solutions for different requirements. To provide the best solution for the proposed use, you must continue to study the technology as well as the way it is used.

KEY TERMS

- Remote Procedure Call (RPC)
- External Data Representation (XDR)
- Line Print Remote command (LPR)
- Line Printer Daemon (LPD)
- Triple DES (3DES)
- SSOD
- Telnet
- Services for UNIX (SFU)
- NWLink
- AppleTalk
- LocalTalk
- Service for Macintosh (SFM)
- Universal Authentication Module (UAM)
- S/MAIL secure email

APPLY YOUR KNOWLEDGE

Exercises

14.1 12-Pack Pick

Estimated Time: 15 minutes

Match the need for network communications with the security solutions. (Multiple answers may exist for some statements).

TABLE 14.2

EXERCISE 14.1: 12-PACK PICK

	Situation Requires	Solution
1	Centralized authentication and accounting	
2	Secure access across the Internet	
3	Access to resources by Macintosh clients	
4	Sharing information with business partners	
5	e-commerce – B2B	
6	Securest logon on	
7	Mobile workers	
8	Secure access to the Internet	
9	Limit exposure of shared resources to untrusted network	
10	Remote usage of single application	
11	Control of EFS recovery agent key	
12	Database replication across WAN links	

The following list gives possible answers for Table 14.2:

Solution	
RADIUS	Proxy server
IAS	SSL
Routing and Remote Access	PKI
Terminal services	EFS
S/MAIL	Firewall
DMZ	Database replication
Screened subnet	SFU
Secured Exchange Server public folders	SFM
VPN	NWLink
IPSec	Telnet
PPTP	Smart card
NAT	

14.2 Johnson Automotive Remote Access Design

Estimated Time: 30 minutes

1. Make a list of locations that require remote access.

2. Make an architectural drawing that indicates the locations of remote access servers, IAS servers, and logical tunnels.

APPLY YOUR KNOWLEDGE

Review Questions

1. You have installed a firewall between the Internet and the rest of your network. Should you assume all access to your network from the outside is now appropriately controlled? Why or why not?

2. How does NAT or a proxy server protect internal addressing schemes?

3. What is meant by "limiting and protecting administrator accounts?"

4. How can this be accomplished with Windows 2000?

5. Why are office politics important in security design and how should you deal with them?

6. Explain how a screened subnet can protect an Internet-connected network.

7. You want to give access to resources to individuals from a trusted partner. You have established a PKI and so have they. How can you provide that access using certificates?

8. ABC, Inc. has 3,000 insurance agents. These agents need to communicate on a regular basis with their main office. Explain how to accomplish this without providing phone lines at the office for direct-dial remote access.

9. You have UNIX, Macintosh, and Novell users in your enterprise. You would like all of these users to be able to access files stored on Windows 2000 Server. Describe how you would do that.

10. Why is Telnet considered a security risk? Can you do anything about that?

Exam Questions

1. Securing file resources to be used by Macintosh and Windows users.

Required Result:

Three volumes should be set so that Windows and Macintosh users can access them. Two of the volumes should be available to all users. One should be restricted to the ArtDept group. All users have Windows accounts and passwords. The ArtDept group has been created. A second, 12GB drive has been added to the server.

Optional Desired Results:

Fourteen-character passwords should be allowed.

Access to network printers should be restricted. Macintosh users should be kept from printing to the FP13 printer.

Proposed Solution:

File Services for Macintosh is installed. Three partitions are created on the drive, each 4GB in size. MS – UAM is loaded on all Macintosh systems.

Evaluation of Proposed Solution:

Which result(s) does the proposed solution produce?

A. The proposed solution produces the required result and both of the optional results.

B. The proposed solution produces the required result and one of the optional results.

C. The proposed solution produces the required result but neither of the optional results.

D. The proposed solution does not produce the required result.

APPLY YOUR KNOWLEDGE

2. Securing file resources to be used by Macintosh and Windows users.

   Required Result:

   Three volumes should be set so that Windows and Macintosh users can access them. Two of the volumes should be available to all users. One should be restricted to the ArtDept group. All users have Windows accounts and passwords. The ArtDept group has been created. A second, 12GB drive has been added to the server.

   Optional Desired Results:

   Fourteen-character passwords should be allowed.

   Access to network printers should be restricted. Macintosh users should be kept from printing to the FP13 printer.

   Proposed Solution:

   File Services for Macintosh is installed. Three partitions are created on the drive, each 4GB in size. MS – UAM is loaded on all Macintosh systems. A password is placed on one of the volumes and given to the ArtDept group.

   Evaluation of Proposed Solution:

   Which result(s) does the proposed solution produce?

   A. The proposed solution produces the required result and both of the optional results.

   B. The proposed solution produces the required result and one of the optional results.

   C. The proposed solution produces the required result but neither of the optional results.

   D. The proposed solution does not produce the required result.

3. Smith-Hyatt, Inc. has a large number of remote access users who dial in to numerous locations. They would like to have centralized administration and accounting of these users. What is the best solution?

   A. Routing and Remote Access Service

   B. Internet Authentication Services

   C. Public Key Infrastructure

   D. Proxy Server

4. Johnson Automotive has asked you to design their new B2B Web site. Security structures you will want to incorporate into this Web site might be what?

   A. Certificates

   B. VPN

   C. Routing and remote access

   D. NAT

5. Routing and Remote Access is installed. You now need to configure authentication. You can choose either of which two?

   A. Kerberos

   B. Basic

   C. Windows Authentication

   D. RADIUS

   E. IAS

APPLY YOUR KNOWLEDGE

6. Johnson Automotive has multiple sites that require remote access. They have chosen to use IAS for authentication. Next they need to choose the authentication method. What are the possible secure choices?

   A. EAP

   B. IPSec

   C. PAP

   D. MS-CHAP

7. Johnson Automotive developed a test system with one Routing and Remote Access server in place. They wrote Remote Access Polices to control access. The test was successful. They added more Routing and Remote Access servers and made all RRAS servers (including the test server which they moved into a production role) RADIUS clients. They configured their IAS server to have the policies that proved so successful on the test system. A user dials in. Which policies affect this user?

   A. The policies on the remote access server to which the user connects are followed.

   B. The policies on the IAS server are used.

   C. The policies on the remote access server are parsed first, and then the policies on the IAS server are evaluated.

   D. The policies on the IAS server are parsed first and then the policies on the remote access server are evaluated.

8. Johnson Automotive wants to provide secure remote access to an application for their salespeople on the road.

Required Result:

Secure access for remote clients via the Internet as well as dial-up must be provided to a time-reporting application.

Optional Desired Results:

The clients should have only to provide a username and password. They should not have to hunt for an application and start it.

The clients should be able only to use the connection to run this application.

Proposed Solution:

Terminal services is set up in Application Sharing mode on a standalone Windows 2000 Server. The Client Connection Manager is used to configure the clients so that an authenticated connection starts the time-reporting application. Group Policy is established to secure the terminal server. All users who will use the application are placed in a separate OU. NTFS is the only file system used on the server and permissions are set properly. Data encryption is set to high.

Evaluation of Proposed Solution:

Which result(s) does the proposed solution produce?

   A. The proposed solution produces the required result and both of the optional results.

   B. The proposed solution produces the required result and one of the optional results.

   C. The proposed solution produces the required result but neither of the optional results.

   D. The proposed solution does not produce the required result.

APPLY YOUR KNOWLEDGE

9. Johnson Automotive wants to provide secure remote access to an application for their salespeople on the road.

   Required Result:

   Secure access for remote clients via the Internet as well as dial-up must be provided to a time-reporting application.

   Optional Desired Results:

   The clients should have only to provide a username and password. They should not have to hunt for an application and start it.

   The clients should only be able to use the connection to run this application.

   Proposed Solution:

   The application is installed on a standalone server in the DMZ. A VPN tunnel endpoint is created using Routing and Remote Services. A group is created and contains all the clients allowed to access the application. A Remote Access Policy is created to allow only access by this group. NTFS permissions are used to restrict users to the folders and files necessary to run the application.

   Evaluation of Proposed Solution:

   Which result(s) does the proposed solution produce?

   A. The proposed solution produces the required result and both of the optional results.

   B. The proposed solution produces the required result and one of the optional results.

   C. The proposed solution produces the required result but neither of the optional results.

   D. The proposed solution does not produce the required result.

10. To ensure secure access to resources in a LAN, you should do the following:

    A. Control membership in administrative groups.

    B. Devise restrictive rules and policies for Internet access.

    C. Install Routing and Remote Access Services.

    D. Apply file and registry permissions

    E. Delegate administrative tasks and use Group Policy to maintain security settings.

Answers to Exercises

14.2 The solution to Exercise 14.1 is presented in Table 14.3.

TABLE 14.3
EXERCISE 14.1 ANSWER: 12-PACK PICK

	Situation Requires	Solution
1	Centralized authentication and accounting	RADIUS (IAS)
2	Secure access across the Internet	VPN, SSL
3	Access to resources by Macintosh clients	SFM
4	Sharing information with business partners	VPN, PKI, IAS, IPSec, terminal services, SSL
5	e-commerce – B2B	VPN, PKI, IAS, IPSec, terminal services, SSL
6	Securest logon on	Smart card
7	Mobile workers	EFS, VPN, IAS
8	Secure access to the Internet	Proxy server, fire wall

APPLY YOUR KNOWLEDGE

	Situation Requires	*Solution*
9	Limit exposure of shared resources to untrusted network	DMZ or screened subnet
10	Remote usage of single application	Terminal services
11	Control of EFS recovery agent key	PKI
12	Database replication across WAN links	IPSec; VPN

14.2 The solution to item 2 in Exercise 14.2 is presented in Figure 14.24.

Answers to Review Questions

1. You cannot assume anything other than if your firewall is set correctly, traffic that passes through it is probably okay. You may be vulnerable to attacks from other quarters. Look for remote access servers, dial-up modems, and even disgruntled employees.

2. NAT and Proxy Server do not send out internal addresses in packets destined for the public network. They use different addresses. No one can learn of your private addressing scheme.

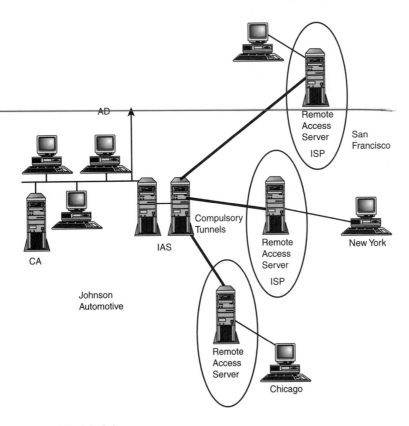

FIGURE 14.24
Johnson Automotive remote access solution.

APPLY YOUR KNOWLEDGE

3. You can delegate authority to user-level accounts to do some administrative tasks. This way you can limit the number of necessary administrator accounts. Having many administrator accounts, especially if they are assigned to do simple chores, is not a good idea. Administrator accounts give a log of authority and privilege, and should be reserved strictly for those activities.

4. With Windows 2000, you can delegate authority over an OU that contains either computers, users, or both users and computers. You can be very specific and granular. Accounts can be normal user-level accounts. You give them only the privileges that they need, where they need them.

5. Office politics can prevent the implementation of sound security solutions. They can also block sanctions for those who do not follow policy. On the other hand, if you figure out the unwritten rules and the centers of power, you will have an easier time.

6. A screened subnet is a subnet allocated to hold computers that must have connectivity to the external network. These may be mail servers, Web servers, and the like. You place this subnet so that it has access to the external world. You place a firewall in between the external world and your internal network. You filter inbound traffic and direct appropriate traffic to this subnet and these servers, while preventing its passage to the rest of your network. You then allow appropriate traffic (of a much more narrowly defined nature) to and from other computers on your network.

7. Certificates from other PKI may be used in Windows 2000 if the following steps are taken:

   1. Add the CA for the PKI to your Certificate Trust List.

   2. Create user account(s) for your partner to use.

   3. Import foreign certificates and map them to the user accounts you have created.

   4. Control these user accounts by specifying what the certificates can be used for, and by protecting resources and user rights in the normal manner.

8. A VPN can be established. The endpoint at headquarters is a remote access server. Each salesperson can have the client VPN endpoint configured on his or her laptops. If possible, an ISP can be contracted with to provide local numbers in as many cities as possible. To reach headquarters, the VPN is established across the Internet.

9. Install Services for UNIX, Services for Macintosh, Configure appropriate protocols. Configure services appropriately. Provide Windows client software as necessary. Control file resource access. Create users for UNIX, Macintosh, and Novell users to use. Add File and Print Services for NetWare.

10. Telnet generally uses clear text. To remove this risk and protect the Telnet server in Windows, you can configure it to require an NTLM authentication. You can use IPSec to encrypt all Telnet communications.

APPLY YOUR KNOWLEDGE

Answers to Exam Questions

1. **D.** No restrictions have been set on any of the volumes. (For more information, see the section "Providing secure Access for Macintosh Clients.")

2. **C.** Volume size is as big as it can be. By placing a password on the volume and giving it to the ArtDept users, only they will be allowed to access it; thus it is reserved for their use. The Microsoft UAM will allow Macintosh users to create a 14-character password. No attempt is made to restrict printer access. (For more information, see the section "Providing Secure Access for Macintosh Clients.")

3. **A, B.** Remote access servers alone will not give them centralized authentication and accounting. By adding IAS, they will have this feature and can control policies from a central location. (For more information, see the section "Windows 2000 Security for Remote Access Users.")

4. **A, B, C.** Certificates are a good choice for authentication when providing access to business partners. They provide a more secure way to control access. A VPN protects data as it travels across any network. Even if you have a private line between the partners, establishing a VPN directly from the client to your server protects data from end to end. Routing and Remote Access can be used to provide the endpoint for the VPN. Policies on the remote access server can assist you in controlling access. (For more information, see the sections "E-Commerce Solutions" and "Secure Access Between Private Networks.")

5. **C, D.** Although you may be using IAS for your RADIUS server, the choices in the GUI specify Windows Authentication or RADIUS. IAS is the Microsoft service that provides RADIUS authentication. (For more information, see the section "Windows 2000 Security for Remote Access Users.")

6. **A, C, D.** IPSec is not an authentication choice. You can configure IPSec to be used for all communications, but it is not an authentication choice. (For more information, see the section "Security and the LAN.")

7. **B.** After Routing and Remote Access Servers are configured to use RADIUS for authentication, the Remote Access Policies on the IAS server are used. Any Remote Access Policies configured on the Routing and Remote Access Servers arc ignored. (For more information, see the section "Windows 2000 Security for Remote Access Users.")

8. **D.** Everything looks good here, but there is no remote access configured—that is, no modems and no Internet connection mentioned. (For more information, see the section "Securing Resources.")

9. **B.** Clients can now remotely access the server and run the application; however, the users will still have to find the application and run it. It will not start automatically. (For more information, see the section "Securing Resources.")

10. **A, B, D, E.** You should do all these things to secure access to resources in a LAN. You do not need to install Routing and Remote Access. (For more information, see the section "Security and the LAN.")

APPLY YOUR KNOWLEDGE

Suggested Readings and Resources

1. *Microsoft Resource Kit 2000.* Microsoft Press, 2000.

   Internetworking Guide:

   - Chapter 11: Services for UNIX

   - Chapter 12: Interoperability with Novell

   - Chapter 13: Services for Macintosh

   - Appendix B: UNIX Interoperability Concepts

   Deployment Planning Guide:

   - Chapter 7: Determining Network Connectivity Strategies

   - Chapter 11: Planning Distributed Security

   - Chapter 16: Deploying Terminal Services

   - Chapter 17: Determining Windows 2000 Network Security Strategies

2. Atkins, Derek (ed.). *Internet Security, Professional Reference, Second Edition,* New Riders, 1997.

   - Part II: Gaining Access and Securing the Gateway

3. Chapman, D. Brent and Elizabeth D. Zwicky. *Building Internet Firewalls.* O'Reilly, (1995).

4. Kaeo, Merike. *Designing Network Security,* Cisco Press (1999).

   - Part III: Practical Implementation

This chapter covers the following Microsoft-specified objectives for the "Designing Security for Communication Channels" section of the Designing Security for a Microsoft Windows 2000 Network exam:

Design an SMB-signing solution.

Design an IPSec solution.

- Design an IPSec encryption scheme.
- Design an IPSec management strategy.
- Design negotiation policies.
- Design security policies.
- Design IP filters.
- Define security levels.

▶ Securing resources at the client and server level is not enough. Communications must also be secured. Every communication will not require the same level of attention; you need to refer to your list of analyzed risks and considerations on especially sensitive servers. If all computers, clients, and servers are grouped into security levels, you can then determine the policies you want to set for communications between them.

▶ When dealing with LANs, WANs, and communications that take you to and across public networks, two methods can help you: SMB signing and IPSec. SMB signing refers to the digital signing of each packet in a Server Message Block (SMB) communication between two computers. You can use SMB signing to help protect network communications with downlevel clients. IPSec, or IP Security, is a protocol that you can use to provide integrity, confidentiality, and authentication of network communications. You can use IPSec to protect communications between Windows 2000 computers.

▶ You can use Group Policy to enable and enforce both of these methods.

CHAPTER **15**

Designing Security for Communication Channels

OUTLINE

▶ SMB signing is not widely used and is less understood than IPSec. It is really very simple. Review the definitions and uses of this method, and then concentrate your efforts on IPSec.

▶ Effectively conquering the intricacies of IPSec is no small task. Because it is an emerging protocol, it is difficult to keep up with the RFCs. Fortunately, to understand and use the Microsoft implementation you have less to study. I suggest you plan to spend some time with the RFCs, but do use them to obtain your initial understanding. Your study efforts should give you the understanding necessary to design an IPSec implementation for a Windows 2000 network. To obtain that understanding, you should do the following:

- Identify the Windows 2000 IPSec components and what they do.

- Examine the flow of communication processing that IPSec inserts into the normal IP communication structure.

- Examine default policies, rules, filters, and filter actions. What are they supposed to do? What happens if you implement them? What happens if you implement them on a DHCP server or on a DNS server?

- Set up and use a default policy for IPSec communications between computers. Does it work as expected? Can a non-IPSec–enabled computer communicate with the IPSec–enabled computers? (Does the policy work as expected?)

- Read and think about the information provided about reasons for design choices. Do you agree? How would these decisions play in your environment? What choices would you make?

- Imagine your network and its systems. How would you design an IPSec solution for them?

INTRODUCTION

Network communications can be secured. How much of this process you need to secure, and how much is desirable, is matter of policy. This chapter shows you how to design a strategy using SMB signing and/or IPSec. The chapter examines the procedural implementation of each and discusses your available design choices.

Because each method can be enabled and enforced through Group Policy, this chapter also shows you where and how to do this.

SMB SIGNING

Design an SMB-signing solution.

SMB is the file-sharing protocol used by Windows computers. It is also known as the Common Internet File System (CIFS). A newer version of this protocol has been available for Windows NT 4.0 since Service Pack 3. This version added two features: the support for mutual authentication and the support for message authentication.

Mutual authentication can prevent a "man-in-the-middle" attack. Mutual authentication requires both the client and the server to identify themselves. In the classic man-in-the-middle attack pattern, a computer sits between a client and server and participates in their conversation; it intercepts their messages and may change them before passing them on. When authentication is required, the attacker may be able to pretend to be either the client or the server, but he has a hard time proving it. Requiring digital signatures on all SMB packets also prevents the attacker from changing packet information before sending it on.

SMB signing prevents the data in packets from being changed during transit.

On Windows NT 4.0 and Windows 98 clients, two registry key entries must be made to implement SMB signing. One key is used to "enable" signing, the other to "require" signing. Both keys must be configured. If servers are configured to enable signing and not configured to require it, unconfigured clients may still communicate in the normal manner. Clients configured to enable SMB signing will communicate in the secure manner. If servers are configured to require signing, communication with nonenabled clients cannot take place.

By default, installing the service pack does not enable or require SMB signing when installed on a server. It is enabled by default when you install it on a Windows NT 4.0 Workstation.

SMB signing does not work with direct host IPX protocol because the direct host IPX protocol modifies SMBs and makes them incompatible with SMB signing.

CPU performance is reduced (10–15%) when SMB signing is enabled and required.

SMB message signing capabilities are provided in Windows 2000 so that you may secure communications with downlevel computers. You should design your communications security using IPSec otherwise.

Registry Key Modifications

To enable SMB message signing on the server, add the value `EnableSecuritySignature` to the following key:

HKEY_LOCAL_MACHINE\SYSTEM\CurrentControlSet\
Services\LanManServer\Parameters

The value should have data of type `REG_DWORD`. A value of `0` disables SMB signing; a value of `1` enables it.

To require message signing, add the following value:

`RequireSecuritySignature`

Make it type `REG_DWORD`, with a value of `1`. As with SMB enable, a value of `0` disables the requirement.

Settings are made on the workstation as follows:

Windows 2000 Professional:

MACHINE\System\CurrentControlSet\Services\
LanmanWorkstation\Parameters\ EnableSecuritySignature

MACHINE\System\CurrentControlSet\Services\
LanmanWorkstation\Parameters\RequireSecuritySignature

Windows NT Workstation 4.0:

HKLM\SYSTEM\CurrentControlSet\Services\RDr\Parameters

Windows 98 (which includes the updated version of the SMB protocol; make changes to the registry key):

HKLM\system\CurrentControlSet\Services\VxD\Vnetsup

In all cases, you should close the Registry Editor and reboot the systems.

In all cases, for all systems, make sure to include both keys if requiring signing. If you require but do not enable, no client can connect to the server.

Windows 2000 SMB Message Signing

If you require message authentication between Windows NT or Windows 98 computers and Windows 2000 computers, you can enable SMB message signing in Windows 2000.

The Windows 2000 Server Service uses the same registry settings to enable and require SMB message signing. The Workstation Service uses the LanmanWorkstation key identified earlier. You can also control SMB signing through the Security Option Settings under Local Policy in the Security Settings container of Group Policy. You can set them in the local Group Policy or apply them to the site, domain, or OU Group Policy objects (GPOs).

By default, domain controllers have EnableSecuritySignature set to 1 (enabled). The Domain Controllers GPO has this option enabled. Additionally, this takes precedence over any local settings at a specific DC.

You have the following policy security options:

- ◆ Digitally sign server communications (When possible) – Enabled
- ◆ Digitally sign server communications (Always)
- ◆ Digitally sign client communications (When possible)
- ◆ Digitally sign client communications (Always)

If you modify security options to require SMB signing, make sure that you also enable them.

Group Policy settings are applied to the registry in the usual manner. Figure 15.1 shows SMB signing enabled, not required.

IPSEC

The IPSec protocol is used in two ways in Windows 2000: transport mode (used to secure communications between computers within your internal network) and with an L2TP tunnel (to secure, via a VPN and the use of L2TP, communications between networks). IPSec also has a tunnel mode, but the current recommendation is to use the tunnel mode of L2TP and use IPSec for encryption. In the first case, the computers involved are each configured to use IPSec when communicating between themselves; in the latter, Routing and Remote Access Service is configured to provide a tunnel endpoint for router-to-router or client-to-router communications. Both communications are controlled through Group Policy.

You can use IPSec to provide the following:

◆ **Access control**—Connection negotiation and filtering of inbound communications.

◆ **Integrity**—Checksums and message digest algorithms are used to allow detection of tampered packets.

◆ **Data origin authentication**—Ensuring source.

◆ **Outbound protocol filtering**—Management of data before it leaves the system.

The IPSec algorithm accomplishes this via crypto-algorithm independence, thus ensuring flexibility in its use, as well as the capability to change as new and possibly more secure algorithms are developed. Windows 2000, as must any implementation, specifies and limits the crypto-algorithms that may be used.

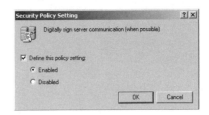

FIGURE 15.1
SMB signing enabled.

NOTE

VPNs Inside Your Network   There is no reason a VPN cannot be created within your internal network (to secure communications to and from sensitive servers, for example). It is, however, less typical.

IPSec Architecture

One of the strengths of IPSec is that it is implemented at the IP layer. Therefore, it affords protection to IP and upper-layer protocols such as TCP, UDP, ICMP, and so on, but does not require modification of applications to benefit from its use. IPSec protects the communication process and does not interfere with the local computers' processing of the application; it just protects that application's communications as they travel from one computer to another. To the user of the properly configured network, IPSec is transparent.

This means that if I, as a user, am using Microsoft Word and saving my documents on a file server, I will not be aware that IPSec is protecting that data as it travels across the network. It also means that if I attempt to FTP that same file to an FTP server, and my computer has an IPSec filter that does not allow outward-bound FTP packets, my attempt will fail.

How does this work?

The IPSec architecture consists of the following:

◆ Key management via Internet Key Exchange (IKE) formerly referred to as ISAKMP/Oakley

◆ A Security Policy database that defines the rules for the disposition of all traffic (inbound or outbound)

◆ The Authentication Header (AH) protocol, which provides integrity and data origin authentication

◆ The Encapsulating Security Payload (ESP), which provides packet encryption, integrity, and data origin authentication

◆ Native IP stack implementation

FIGURE 15.2
IPSec components.

Both the AH and ESP protocols have two modes: transport and tunnel. Many pundits do not currently recommend that the tunnel mode of these protocols be used. If you do need to tunnel IPSec packets, as in the deployment of a VPN, Windows 2000 can use the tunnel produced by L2TP.

Figure 15.2 presents a model of the IPSec components.

Key Management

Key management, the process of determining secret keys and managing their distribution and disposition, is a problem for many security protocols. Securing their distribution is one of the biggest problems. IPSec allows manual configuration and distribution of keys by an administrator. This is often not practical because IPSec can involve many computers and frequent key changes, including changes done during sessions.

Instead, IPSec uses IKE, an automated key management protocol. This protocol can use preshared signatures, public key encryption, or symmetric key encryption for authentication. To implement the use of public key encryption, you must have previously configured a public key infrastructure (PKI).

IPSec sessions are identified by the use of a Security Association (SA). SAs are further described in the following section. Each SA connection uses IKE to define the formats for exchanging keys and key-generation information.

Security Policy Database

A Security Policy database (SPD) defines what IPSec protects. In Windows 2000, this database is defined using Group Policy. An IPSec policy container lives in the Security Settings container of the Group Policy object.

When a connection is made, it is defined by an SA. The SPD also contains the collection of SAs.

IPSec policies spell out exactly what type of traffic may enter or leave the computer as well as how connections can be made. Like an internal firewall, IPSec establishes a boundary between the computer and the outside network. Each packet that seeks to cross the boundary must pass a test. A packet is either discarded or allowed to pass based on IP and transport layer header information. The information is matched against SPD entries or filters. Connection establishment and communications are likewise specified. Policies define what needs to be encrypted, authenticated, and decrypted and how that should be accomplished.

> **NOTE** **Tip** Remember that the SPD controls all traffic, including key management traffic. You need to account for IKE traffic in your SPD, or it may be discarded!

The Windows 2000 SPD resides in Active Directory, in the local Group Policy, and/or in the registry. If it is configured to control domain members, it should be defined in Active Directory. Nondomain members can have security policies defined in the local computer Group Policy database. Group Policy is applied to the registry in the normal manner. If no Group Policy is defined, settings can be manually made to the registry.

Authentication Header Protocol

The AH protocol provides data origination authentication, integrity, and an anti-replay service. It does not provide confidentiality—that is, it does not encrypt the data.

Origination authentication and integrity are provided at the packet level. They are accomplished via the use of Hash Message Authentication Code (HMAC) algorithms. An AH header is placed in the packet between the IP and the TCP/UDP headers (see Figure 15.3)

The header is comprised of information that can be used to authenticate and verify the integrity of the packet when it reaches its destination. The header is composed of the following:

◆ **Next header**—The nature of the next header (a TCP or UDP header, for example)

◆ **Length**—The length of the AH header

◆ **Security Parameters Index (SPI)**—Indicates which SA this packet is identified with

◆ **Sequence number**—A 32-bit number that identifies the sequence, or order, of this packet in the security association communication

◆ **Authentication data**—The check value, or hash value

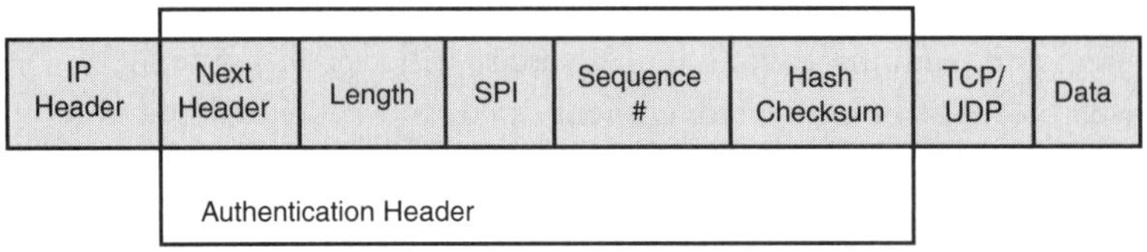

FIGURE 15.3
AH packet structure.

Authentication and integrity of the packet is determined when the receiver calculates the hash value and compares it with the one provided in the Authentication Data field of the AH header. If the values match, the packet is okay; if they do not match, it is discarded. The entire packet, with the exception of portions of the IP header that may change (for example, time-to-live), is signed. Figure 15.4 shows the arrangement of the packet and indicates the signed portions.

Anti-replay protection (the guarantee that the packet has not been just captured and re-sent as part of an attack) is provided by checking the sequence number in the header. The number is checked against a list of previously received packets for this SA connection. If the packet has previously been received, it is rejected.

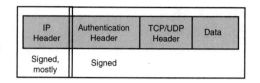

FIGURE 15.4
AH-protected packet.

Encapsulating Security Payload

The ESP provides authentication, integrity, confidentiality, and anti-replay. It can be used alone or with AH. ESP provides the encryption capability that AH does not. The main reason for combining the two is that ESP, unlike AH, does not normally sign the entire packet. Typically, ESP signs the IP data payload; no portion of the IP header is signed. If ESP is used in tunnel mode, it does sign the entire header.

ESP works by inserting an ESP header between the IP protocol and the TCP/UDP header as well as by including ESP trailers.

The ESP header includes the SPI and the ESP sequence number. The sequence number provides anti-replay protection. The SPI identifies the SA being used by this packet. Because many SAs can be used simultaneously, the capability to identify which SA a packet belongs to is necessary. The ESP trailers include the following:

◆ Padding—Used to adjust the block size to meet the block size of the block cipher

◆ Padding length

◆ Next header pointer

◆ Authentication Data—Hash checksum

The checksum is calculated over the ESP header, the ESP trailer, and the payload data. Figure 15.5 shows the encrypted portions of the packet and those that are signed.

FIGURE 15.5
ESP-protected packet.

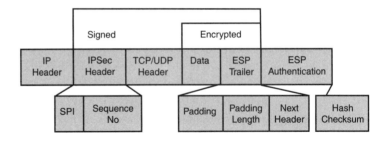

As with AH, ESP provides authentication and integrity via the hash checksum. It provides anti-replay protection via the sequence number. Encryption is provided via algorithms specified in the policy database for the SA being used. Note that no keys are sent with the packets.

IP Stack Implementation

The Windows 2000 IP stack differs completely from the one in Windows NT 4.0. In the new IP stack, IPSec is implemented between the transport and IP layers (see Figure 15.6). Notice in the figure that a small portion of IPSec is also indicated in the data link layer and labeled "offload." As you may be aware, IPSec adds additional processing overhead to the CPU when it prepares packets for data communications. The performance "hit" is often measured at a 10–15% increase. In Windows 2000, the encryption portion of IPSec can be offloaded to special cryptographic processors on network cards that have been developed for this purpose.

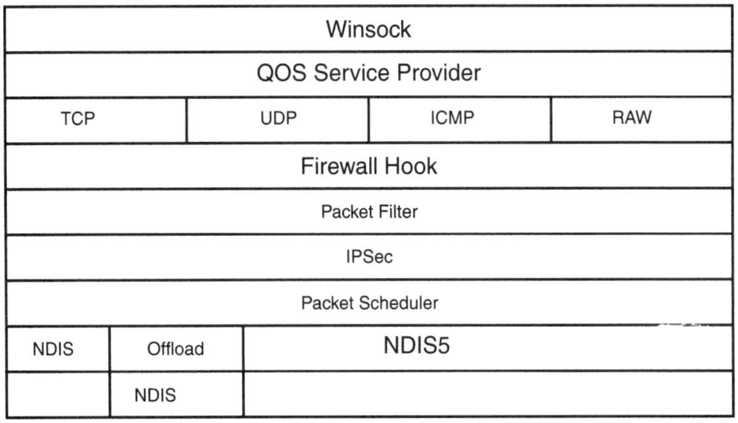

Winsock			
QOS Service Provider			
TCP	UDP	ICMP	RAW
Firewall Hook			
Packet Filter			
IPSec			
Packet Scheduler			
NDIS	Offload	NDIS5	
	NDIS		

FIGURE 15.6
IP stack.

Windows 2000 IPSec Implementation Components

Windows 2000 implements IPSec policy by using the following components (see Figure 15.7):

◆ IPSec Policy Agent Service

◆ Internet Key Exchange

◆ Security Associations

The IPSec Policy Agent Service retrieves IPSec policy from Active Directory, or in its absence from the registry, and passes it on to IKE and to the IPSec driver. The IPSec Policy Agent Service runs on each Windows 2000 computer. Policy retrieval occurs when the system starts and—if the computer is joined in a domain at intervals specified in IPSec policy for the domain—as a result of WinLogon polling. The WinLogon Service polls Active Directory for changes to the Group Policy. If the service discovers changes to IPSec policy, it notifies the IPSec Policy Agent, and then changes are applied to the client computer.

Internet Key Exchange manages Security Associations and generates and manages the authentication keys used to secure communications. IKE manages the connection negotiations in two phases. In the first, a secure, authenticated channel is established. In the second, SAs are negotiated. Two phases are used to ensure a more efficient operation.

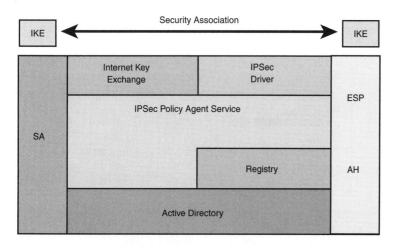

FIGURE 15.7
Windows 2000 IPSec components.

The steps in the phases are detailed in the later section "Designing Negotiation Policies and Encryption Schemes."

Security Associations specify the key to be used and the security protocol choice. They are uniquely identified by their SPI.

IPSec Communications on the Internal Network

You can configure IPSec settings in the registry or Active Directory. IPSec policies are applied to local computers, domain members, domains, organizational units, or other Group Policy objects in Active Directory. IPSec policies configured as part of Active Directory for domain use are applied to computers that are members of the domain when Group Policy is refreshed. If those computers are disconnected temporarily from the domain, the settings are stored temporarily in the local registry.

IPSec Group Policy Objects

IPSec can be implemented as part of Group Policy. IPSec Group Policy settings are placed in the Security Settings\IP Security Policies container (see Figure 15.8).

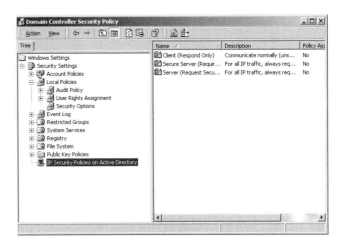

FIGURE 15.8
IPSec Group Policy objects.

Local IPSec settings are overridden by settings made at the site, domain, or OU level, as long as the computer is connected to the domain. Remember that the order of processing is local, site, domain, OU.

You can use the IPSecurity Policy Management console to create, edit, and delete security policies.

To create a new policy, you can use the IP Security Wizard. Right-click IP Security Policies. On the pop-up menu, click Create IP Security Policy. To use the wizard to write the policy you need, you must understand the choices you have.

Table 15.1 lists your choices.

TABLE 15.1

WIZARD PARAMETERS

Item	Description
Name	The policy name must be unique.
Description	Description of the policy.
Activate the default response rule	The default response rule responds if no other rule applies.
Set the initial authentication method for the default rule	Each rule requires an authentication method. Authentication methods are shared key, Kerberos, and certificates (see the section "Authentication Methods"). Rules may be modified to configure them for more than one. If you want to use certificates, you must already have a valid certificate. Preshared keys are left unencrypted in the policy.

After you have finished using the wizard, you may edit the policy to change these settings and to make further choices (see Table 15.2).

TABLE 15.2

POLICY PARAMETERS

Item	Description
General	
Check for policy changes every: *n* minute(s)	How often policy agent checks Group Policy for updates.
Advanced	
Master Key Perfect Forward Secrecy	If selected, the failure of Phase II negotiations requires a new negotiation of Phase I authentication (see the section "IPSec Encryption Scheme Design").
Authenticate and generate a new key after every *n* minute(s)	How often a new key should be generated.
Authenticate and generate a new key every *n* session(s)	How often a new key should be generated.
Protect identities with these security methods	Security methods include DES or 3DES for encryption, and SHA1 or MD5 for integrity. All four possibilities are defined by default. Diffie-Hellman base encryption material (key size) is also determined here. Both 3DES choices use Medium; both DES choices use Low. This, and the order of processing, can be changed. These methods are attempted during negotiation to determine which one the client and server can use.
Rules	
IP Security Rules	Create rules for policy. Rules are security actions that apply to particular computers. Policies can have multiple rules. If you elected to add the default rule, you can modify it here.

To add new rules, select the Add button. You may either use the rules wizard or not.

To edit rules, select the Edit button.

Rules have the following configurable components:

◆ Security methods

◆ Session Key Perfect Forward Secrecy

◆ Authentication methods

◆ Connection types (LAN, remote access, or all-network connections)

Predefined Policies

Predefined policies can be modified for particular needs and then activated. To activate a policy, perform the steps listed in Step By Step 15.1.

STEP BY STEP

15.1 Assign an IPSec Policy

1. Right-click the policy.

2. Click Properties.

3. Select the Rule to Activate option.

4. Click OK.

IPSec over L2TP

If you choose to use IPSec to establish a virtual private network (VPN), the recommended procedure is to utilize L2TP as the tunneling protocol. This is because the combination of L2TP and IPSec offers more advantages than IPSec in tunnel mode.

Computer certificates are required for L2TP over IPSec connections.

This is accomplished by configuring the properties of the external interface in the Routing and Remote Access console. You must set L2TP over IPSec input and output packet filters. Filters are configured for UDP ports 500 (IKE), protocol ID 50 (ESP), and possibly protocol ID 51 (AH).

You must configure all input and output filters to secure communications. If they are the only filters, only IPSec over L2TP is allowed to pass between the remote access client and the server.

Designing IPSec Management

Design an IPSec management strategy.

IPSec management is accomplished by specifying IPSec policies. Because IPSec policies affect communications between systems, IPSec policies are generally implemented at the site, domain, or OU level, not at the local computer policy level. Computers that store or manage extremely sensitive information can be grouped in an OU. Client systems allowed to communicate with them can also be placed in an OU.

Systems that, although they are joined in a domain, are temporarily out of communication with a domain controller have their policy information cached in their registry.

Systems not joined in a domain can have local policies defined.

Management may be delegated to OUs if the OUs represent groups of computers that need to communicate with each other. Domain-level polices can be implemented to cover broad applications such as a requirement to use 3DES as the encryption protocol for all IPSec communications.

IPSec management should be considered when designing OUs and the delegation of administrative responsibilities for those OUs. Three possible OUs might be for computers holding classified, sensitive, or normal information,

If computers have been administratively grouped to provide it, policies for these systems can be developed and applied with Group Policy to ensure its usage.

One point to keep in mind is that policies are not refreshed if these systems are not in contact with their domain controllers. If connectivity is removed, a local policy or registry entries could be used to change the policy. You should ensure that local Group Policy and the registry are secured.

Designing Negotiation Policies and Encryption Schemes

Design negotiation policies.

Negotiation of connections is managed by IKE. Two phases are used: one for ensuring a secure communications channel, and the other to negotiate the use of SAs. To design policies that stipulate these negotiations, you must understand their process. Design, then, consists of making the choices in each area negotiated, which will best fulfill the desired level of security for each IPSec connection. These choices can then be described in IPSec policies and applied to each computer desired by using Group Policy.

Phase I Negotiation

The first phase includes the negotiation of the following:

◆ The encryption algorithm

◆ The hash algorithm

◆ Authentication method

◆ Diffie-Hellman group to be used for base keying

◆ Identification of the SA(s) to be used

If the secure channel is completed, messages are sent by the sender-indicated desired SAs. The responder cannot modify this offer, but can accept it or reply back with a list of other SAs it has information on. Modified offers are rejected by the sender. Any number of SAs can be used. Realistically, the number is limited by system resources.

Phase I SA is cached, so multiple Phase II SA negotiations may be used. This caching and reuse of the master key may provide an opportunity for key compromise. You can protect the key by enabling Perfect Forward Secrecy (PFS). PFS determines how a new key is regenerated. When it is chosen on the master key, reauthentication is necessary and the Phase I SA is not reused.

The choice of encryption algorithms is between DES and 3DES.

You can choose either MD5 or SHA as the hash algorithm.

Authentication Methods

Authentication methods can be certificate, preshared key, and/or Kerberos v5. Certificates and preshared keys protect the computer identity. Kerberos v5 leaves the computer ID unencrypted until the entire payload is encrypted during authentication. Preshared key is the least secure. A key must be entered and is available in the interface.

Diffie-Hellman Group

Secure communications requires the establishment of the same, shared key, without sending the key across the network. IPSec uses the Diffie-Hellman (DH) algorithm for this purpose. Diffie-Hellman groups determine the length of the base prime number used for the DH exchange. DH groups are as follows:

◆ Group 1, 768 bits

◆ Group 2, 1024 bits

Using a larger base prime number should make the key harder to break.

No keys are exchanged in any IPSec communication. Instead, only the base information deed to generate the shared, secret key is exchanged. The base information is used to generate the master key that can then be used to authenticate the computers involved in the exchange.

The DH exchange must be authenticated; otherwise, communications will not continue. It works like this:

1. A negotiation connection is made between two computers.

2. Information on how to generate a master key is exchanged.

3. The master key is generated at each computer.

4. The master key is used to encrypt information that can be used to mutually authenticate the computers involved in the change.

New keys can be generated during the IPSec communication.

Phase II Negotiation

The second phase is used to negotiate the SAs to be used. In the first phase, the sender tells the receiver what it would like, and the receiver tells the sender whether that is available. In the second phase, the actual SA connection is negotiated. The following three steps occur:

1. Policy negotiation or choice of AH or ESP, hash algorithms, and encryption algorithms.

2. Frequency of session key material refresh/exchange keys are regenerated by each computer during the lifetime of the SA according to the scheduled exchange of new base information provided by IKE.

3. SAs, SPI, and generated keys are given to the IPSec driver.

In phase two, a pair of SAs is created for every SA negotiated. One is used for inbound traffic, and one for outbound traffic. Each is identified by an SPI, and each has its own key.

During negotiation, if time-out limits are exceeded, IPSec attempts to return to the negotiation of Phase I SA. The Phase I SA can expire as well; but, by keeping SA negotiation separated into two phases, a more efficient process is put into place because the initial negotiation and reauthentication do not have to be repeated.

You can set the number of Phase II SA negotiations by policy.

IPSec Encryption Scheme Design

Design an IPSec encryption scheme.

Determining the IPSec encryption scheme to be used depends on an evaluation of the available protocols for both negotiation phases against the issues of performance and cost. It also requires a decision about the reuse of keying material.

Protocols, Performance, and Cost

DES has come under attack as being insecure in today's environment. It was once postulated that the number of potential keys in DES was so broad that cracking a single key would take light-years.

Several successful attempts at cracking DES have been accomplished in much less time. Any decision on which algorithm to be used should consider that the times represented do not represent the decryption of messages in which keys were changed multiple times, however, nor of communications over a long period of time. Instead the solution to the question "what is the key used to encrypt this?" was answered. Furthermore, in making choices about encryption strength, it is often a balancing act between performance, cost, and the need to maintain the confidentiality of the data. If it takes an attacker longer than the lifetime of the value of the message to decrypt the message, this may be more than adequate.

Think, for example, of the value of information about changing stock market prices. How valuable is much of that information if received a day later? Hours later?

Performance is reduced by using most encryption algorithms. Stronger algorithms usually reduce performance more than less strong algorithms.

3DES, or triple DES, is considered more secure. 3DES places a larger burden on the CPU than DES does.

You can use hardware acceleration boards to offset the performance problem, but these increase the cost of the solution.

You should make your choice of encryption algorithms based on your needs and the tools available.

Perfect Forward Security

The use of PFS was identified earlier as a way to ensure that each Phase II negotiation required a new Phase I authentication negotiation. This prevented the reuse of cached authentication material and the reuse of keying material. It was also identified as a major hindrance to a snappy performance.

Using PFS for session keying does not impose near the penalty. It does require a new DH exchange so that new keys may be generated based on new base keying material. The reuse of keying material does provide a window of opportunity for attackers because it gives them more time to discover that information. With knowledge of a key, and the information used to generate new keys, an attacker could possibly discover the sum total of the information in the communication.

Key compromise may be inevitable. PFS ensures that a compromised key gets the attacker access only to data encrypted with that key, not to the entire communication.

PFS is not a negotiated property. It does not have to be enabled on the sender and the receiver to work. If it is enabled on the responder side of an SA, and a new key is required (the SA expires), any messages from the sender are rejected and a new negotiation is required. It is not the use of PFS that is being negotiated, however; it is the SA itself that includes the exchange of base keying material.

IPSec Policies

IPSec policies contain rules. Each rule has a list of IP filters used to determine which types of packets can cross the boundary between the local computer and the network. Designing security policies consists of determining which traffic patterns should be managed and how they are handled. The rule might state block, encrypt to pass, or pass in the clear.

Design security policies.

IPSec policies are composed of rules that determine how and when the policies are used. Rules are triggered by source, destination, and type of IP traffic. The rules consist of a list of filters and filter actions. A match between a filter and packet header information triggers the rule. What happens when the rule is triggered is determined by the filter actions. Each policy can have multiple rules, and the rules can all be active simultaneously or singly.

Figure 15.9 displays the default rules.

Policies may be designed for different computers or to specify different types of communications such as Internet and intranet communications. Devices other than computers, such as routers, can also have IPSec policies designed for them. How policies for non-Windows 2000 devices are determined is not part of this discussion.

Designing IPSec policies, then, consists of the following:

◆ Designing filters

◆ Designing rules by determining which filters belong in which rule

◆ Designing policies by determining which rules should be part of the policy

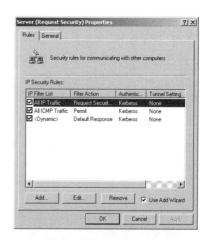

FIGURE 15.9
Default IPSec rules.

Managing IPSec policy is concerned with determining which policies are assigned to which computers and delegating authority to do so.

Before more closely inspecting the makeup of filters, you should take a look at the process in which they are used.

The IPSec driver watches outbound and inbound packets. Outbound packets must be secured and possibly encrypted; inbound packets need to be verified and possibly decrypted. The driver uses a filter list provided by the IPSec Policy Agent.

The IPSec driver outbound communication process looks like this:

1. Attempts to match all outbound packets against its filter list.

2. If there is no match, the packet is discarded.

3. When a match occurs, the driver initiates the negotiation by notifying IKE.

4. The driver receives the SA from IKE. The SA contains the session key.

5. Looks up the SA in its database.

6. Inserts the SPI into the IPSec header.

7. Signs and, if required, encrypts the packet.

8. Sends packet to IP to be forwarded.

The IPSec driver inbound communication process for these packets follows these steps:

1. Receives the session key, SA, and SPI from IKE.

2. Looks up the inbound SA in database by SPI and destination address.

3. Checks signature.

4. Decrypts if necessary.

5. Sends packet to the TCP/IP driver.

6. Driver sends to the application.

Filter Design

Rules specify filter actions. They also specify authentication methods, IP tunnel settings, and connection types.

Design IP filters.

Filters determine whether a rule is triggered. They determine this by specifying information that can be matched with complementary information in the packets being inspected. IP packet headers contain information on its source and destination address, and the type of traffic. Filters then are designed to indicate acceptance or rejection of each packet based on this information. The process by which they do so is called packet filtering.

Each filter contains the following:

- ◆ **Source and destination address**—Can be specific IP addresses, subnets, or networks.

- ◆ **Protocol**—The default covers all protocols in the TCP/IP suite. Individual protocols can be specified.

- ◆ **Source and destination ports (TCP and UDP)**—The default covers all ports, but can be configured to apply only to packets on a particular port.

Both inbound and outbound filters must exist. In both inbound and outbound communications, packets are matched with filters. Inbound filters respond to a request for secure communication or match the packets with an existing SA and process the packets. Outbound filters trigger a security negotiation.

There must be a filter for every possible packet type that is part of the communication to which an associated rule applies.

To design filters, you must first determine whether you require anything beyond the defaults. If you create a rule, the default filters apply unless changed. There are default policies and rules in place; perhaps one of them will do.

The most common filter to implement is to identify the IP address or range of addresses with which a computer or a group of computers would be allowed to communicate. This is how communications could be secured within a group of computers that consist of sensitive servers of a particular type and the clients that were allowed to communicate with them. The accounting processes of the case study company, Tremain Polson, can be examined to consider such a design. Tremain Polson uses an accounting database–based product to perform accounting functions. This accounting package runs on a Microsoft SQL server database and has specific client portions installed and run on Windows 2000 Professional machines. Approved individuals can use the client software and connect to the database to authorize checks, invoices, salary increases, and the like, as well as to make adjustments to accounts and print reports. Security is accomplished via authentication of the user and authorization of the use of the product as well as parts of the database. Normal communications between client and server systems are not encrypted. Further protection of session communications could be accomplished using IPSec.

In addition to specifying packet encryption and authentication, a filter can restrict communications to the subnet that encompasses all the approved client machines. If it is necessary to engage in communications with the servers for other purposes, filters can be added to specific individual IP addresses.

Filters could also be included for specific protocols. If these are implemented, however, care must be taken to include a filter for every protocol that might be used for the allowed communications between the systems.

Filter Lists

Filter lists can include more than one filter. If you are using a filter to cover all computers, use the generic Any IP Address instead of trying to specify all the computers.

Filter list order does not matter. All filters are simultaneously retrieved by the IPSec Policy Agent and are processed from most to least specific.

Filter Actions

Filter actions, or what happens if a match is found, is the other part of policy design. Each rule needs to specify what will happen. Filter actions often define the type of policy. They also indicate the connection type and authentication method. Figure 15.10 shows the default server (Request Security) rule. Default rules and policies are discussed in section "Predefined Policies."

The type of policy can be as follows:

◆ **Passthrough policy**—IPSec ignores the traffic.

◆ **Blocking policy**—This traffic will not be accepted or allowed to pass. This will help stop communication from a rogue computer; it can also prevent traffic from leaving a system.

◆ **Permit policy**—No traffic is allowed unless a filter for it is defined.

◆ **Negotiated policy**—The policy is negotiated with other IPSec-enabled computers, but allows communication with non-IPSec–enabled computers.

Passthrough policy is a good idea when communication is necessary with a computer that cannot be secured, the traffic is not considered sensitive enough, or the traffic provides it own protection (Kerberos, SSL, PPTP).

Blocking policy is used to prevent communications with rogue computers. You can also use it to prevent such traffic from leaving a computer.

A permit policy only "permits" traffic to pass that has been specifically identified.

Policy negotiations are necessary sometimes—this is a good idea in situations in which you need to control communications from sensitive computers, but allow it from nonsensitive computers. You must control communications with the nonsensitive computer in other ways. This policy is also put into place to ensure some communications if other policies are preventing it incorrectly, or as a default for all communication not specified in the policy.

This type of fallback policy is useful during testing, but can allow unprotected communication if policy negotiations for the more secure policies fail.

The connection type defines whether the rule applies to a particular interface such as dial-up adapter or network card. A use of connection type specificity enables you to relegate the use of policy (but only when you are on the road, not when connected to the local LAN).

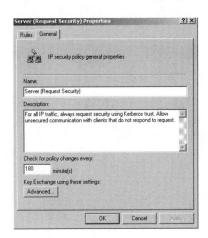

FIGURE 15.10
Server (Request Security) rule.

Authentication methods identify which method can be used for the connection. Because a match must be made with the other side of the connection, some policies specify multiple methods to ensure one can be agreed upon. Greater security can be ensured if smaller ranges are identified.

Authentication methods include the following:

◆ **Kerberos v5**—This is the default authentication protocol in Windows 2000. It can be used for any clients using Kerberos v5 that are members of a trusted domain. (Non-Windows 2000 systems that implement Kerberos v5 and members of a trusted domain can use this method.)

◆ **Public key certificates**—These are necessary for Internet communications, remote access, external partner access, L2TP communications, and computers that do not use Kerberos v5. To use certificates, at least one trusted Certificate Authority (CA) must be configured.

◆ **Preshared keys**—These are agreed upon by two users. Both must manually configure IPSec policies. The key is used for authentication, not encryption. The key is stored, unprotected, in IPSec policy.

Predefined Policies

Before you develop IPSec policies, you should examine the default policies to see whether they meet some or all of your needs. They are also a good source to examine to understand how GUI interfaces represent rules and filters and their corresponding actions. You can use them as templates in designing your own rules. Predefined default policies, rules, and filter actions are as follows:

◆ **Client (Respond Only)**—Does not secure communications most of the time. Can respond to requests for secure communications by using default response rule. Only requested port and protocol traffic is secured. This is a good policy to set on clients. When the client needs to access a secured server, it will respond; but otherwise, use normal communications.

NOTE

Certificate Tip Microsoft certificates with the Strong Private Key Protection advanced option do not work with IKE. Certificates from VeriSign, Netscape, and Entrust have been tested for compatibility. Check the compatibility list at http://www.microsoft.com/windows2000/upgrade/compat/search/software.asp for more information. Specific IKE or IPSec certificates are not required. When attempting to configure communications with others who are using IPSec, the certificate configuration must be agreed upon when attempting integration with third-party certificates. The administrators for both systems need to work together to ensure integration.

◆ **Server (Request Security)**—Secures communication most of the time. Allows unsecured communication from non-IPSec–enabled computers.

◆ **Server (Require Security)**—Always requires secured communications. Unsecured communications from any source are rejected.

Best Practices

Define security levels.

According to Microsoft, the following recommendations can assist you in determining the level of security you need to establish with IPSec policies and the best method for designing those policies:

◆ Evaluate type of information as to its sensitivity.

◆ Evaluate vulnerability to attacks that IPSec can prevent.

◆ Establish an IPSec security plan.

◆ Implement the plan using Group Policy.

In previous chapters, you learned to collect information on the nature of information contained in your organization's databases, who required access to that information, and the routes taken to obtain that information. Draw on that material to design the need for IPSec between groups of computers. If you have established administrative control groups (OUs) and have appropriately delegated authority for the administration of those groups, this is already done. If you do not think your initial design assists the design of IPSec policies, you may want to revisit it and design it with IPSec in mind.

You also evaluated your vulnerability to attack. Reconsider those vulnerabilities now in light of what IPSec can do to help prevent them.

Types of attacks and how they may be foiled by appropriate IPSec policies include those listed in Table 15.3.

TABLE 15.3

COMMON ATTACKS

Attack	Description	IPSec Protection
Eavesdropping	Using a sniffer or packet analyzer to capture and examine packets. Clear text can be read. The attacker may also obtain significant information about the network (such as IP addresses, names and addresses of domain controllers, database and file servers, and which services are on the network and where).	Data can be encrypted. Information about the packet can also be encrypted so that the only information available to a sniffer is the source and destination address.
Modification	Using these same tools, the attacker can modify data in the packet, and no one will be the wiser.	Because packets are signed, encrypted, and can be authenticated, modification of data can be detected and the packet rejected.
IP address spoofing	The attacker modifies packets coming from his computer to look like they are coming from a computer in your network. This can be as simple as changing the IP address on his machine to one of your computers that he has crashed, to modifying the packets through some tool.	IP spoofing alone will not get a packet past IIPSec filters.
Password attacks	The attacker obtains a valid user ID and password and uses that to access data or to compromise systems (delete data, reroute data, modify network configuration, for example).	Packets that contain information about passwords and program packets that might include clear-text passwords are encrypted making their obtainment by network attack less likely. Social engineering cannot be prevented by IPSec.
Denial of Service attack	Attacker prevents normal users from gaining access to a system and may crash the system. This may be done by sending invalid data, flooding a computer with too much traffic, or blocking traffic.	IPSec alone cannot prevent denial-of-service attacks, although they may contain them at security gateways.
Man-in-the-middle attack	The attacker monitors and captures and controls the communication between two other computers without the knowledge or permission of the users of these computers. The attacker may respond as the other party in the conversation to keep it going.	Packets can be encrypted and keys changed frequently. The attacker would find it quite difficult to obtain enough information to participate in a real-time attack of this type.
Compromised-key attack	The attacker obtains a key that has been used to encrypt data. The key can be used to decrypt the data. The attacker uses this without the knowledge of the sender or receiver. He may also use this key to attempt to discover other keys being used.	Perfect Forward Security can keep a compromised key from allowing the attacker anything more than the data that has been encrypted by the compromised key. Changing keys frequently keeps that to a minimum.
Application layer attack	A fault is caused in the application running on an application server or the OS of the server. This gives the attacker a way to bypass normal controls and perhaps gives him the ability to delete, modify data, crash the application, disable other security controls, introduce a virus, or load a sniffer program on the compromised machine and use it to further inspect data on your network.	If communications to and from the application server are protected by IPSec encryption, and filter lists and action allow only the necessary protocols and communication with a smaller pool of IP addresses, there is less chance of this.

Attack	*Description*	*IPSec Protection*
Replay attack	The attacker captures packets and uses them later to attempt access.	Anti-replay is accomplished by the sequence number included in the packet. The receiving computer checks for evidence of receiving this packet previously. If it has, the packet is rejected.

With this information in-hand, you should be able to classify the systems that require different levels of communication security and validate your collections of these computers into various OUs. To complete your IPSec security plan, identify these OUs and define policies for each OU. Remember that OUs can be granularized by nesting OUs and that IPSec policies may be granularized by designing appropriate filters.

When designing policies, remember that for many cases, at least, you must balance security levels by considering the efficiencies of the required access. Remember that in some cases, there will be levels at which efficiency is not a consideration. If you are protecting updates to salary levels or access to classified government information, for example, the wait required for processing the request is rarely considered important enough to reduce the security demands placed on that request.

Levels of computer security identified by Microsoft include the following:

◆ **Minimal**—No sensitive data, no IPSec.

◆ **Standard**—Balanced security using a range of policies including minimal policies (including polices such as enabled, but not required).

◆ **High security**—Highly sensitive data at risk of theft or disruption (that is, remote dial-up, public network communications). The predefined policy Secure Server (Require Security) can be used. It will require IPSec on all traffic inbound and outbound. It uses strong confidentiality and integrity algorithms, Perfect Forward Security, key lifetimes and limits, and strong Diffie-Hellman groups. Unsecured communication is blocked.

Use these groups to begin your placement of computers into security-level requirements. Refine them as you identify particular concerns in your organization. Possible refinements might include special handling for any remotely accessed servers, SNMP monitoring, and security gateways.

Remotely accessed servers have the following special requirements:

◆ Authentication methods must include certificates.

◆ At least one computer-level public key certificate must be configured on each remote client and remote access server.

Remote administration of internal computers can be configured if you are willing to write a rule to allow it. This rule needs to allow internal RPC traffic and specify the outgoing address of the subnet where an administrative console lies and the incoming IP address of the managed computer.

If you are using SNMP management tools, you must add a permit rule to allow SNMP messages to pass without encryption. Use the IP filter list to specify addresses of SNMP management systems and agents. SNMP uses UDP ports 161 and 162. You may recall that the permit rule blocks communications not specified in the filter list.

Security gateways (firewalls, proxy server, routers, or access points to the outside world) require special filters so that IPSec packets are not blocked. You need to write filters to allow the following inbound and outbound packets to pass:

◆ IP protocol 51 (IPSec AH)

◆ IP protocol 50 (IPSec ESP)

◆ UDP port 500 (IKE)

Make sure that all clients of DHCP, DNS, WINS, and domain controllers are IPSec–capable, or configure a fallback policy rule to deal with non-IPSec–capable clients. If you do not, these clients cannot use these network services.

CASE STUDY: TREMAIN POLSON PKI

BACKGROUND

Tremain Polson has a research division. Industrial spying has become a large concern of the research director. She wants to ensure that no unauthorized communication with research databases is allowed.

PROBLEM STATEMENT

The research group consists of 56 scientists and their staff. The risk of unauthorized individuals gaining information from research databases is considered to be strong. There is a desire to add network communication protection to ensure this does not happen.

Information Systems Manager

The research group is already isolated. No Internet or other public or private network connection is allowed.

Systems Administrator

The research group is on its own subnet and there is a policy against dial-up connections. Plans exist to place research computers in a single domain.

Research Director

I want every possible protection in place. We just cannot afford the risk that one of our competitors has infiltrated our workforce or has purchased their assistance. I can vouch for all of my group, but I have no control over other members of this company.

CURRENT SYSTEM

The research group uses complex passwords. Modems are not allowed. Internet access is via kiosk machines in the company library as is access to email. Email is protected by encryption.

ENVIRONMENT

Three database servers and three file servers are dedicated to the research department.

System Admin

In addition to the servers which were upgraded to Windows 2000 last week, 56 PCs that have just had Windows 2000 installed recently replaced older systems running Windows 98.

ENVISIONED SYSTEM

IPSec will be used for all communications.

Research Director

We don't have to worry about accidental access from outside the department. I don't have to worry that somebody decided he wasn't going to follow policy. Policy is implemented in the software.

Information Systems Manager

IPSec will be used for all communication within the research department.

continues

CASE STUDY: TREMAIN POLSON PKI

continued

Systems Admin

IPSec policies will be written to enforce the highest-strength encryption. The policies will require IPSec negotiation and there will be no "fallback" policy if negotiation fails. Inbound and outbound filters will require a match, or the communication fails. This is the only way to ensure that some communication from outside the research department can communicate with any computer in that subnet. Filters on some servers will vary because not all servers require the same protocols. Filters for workstations will be designed around their needs.

SECURITY

IPSec will provide secure communications. Group Policy will enforce it. Protection for Group Policy will be implemented by not delegating administration of the research OU. Policy will be changed only by systems administrators under the advice of the research director.

PERFORMANCE

By anticipating the processing requirements of IPSec, auxiliary processing can be provided.

Systems Admin

A decrease in performance is not expected because we will install special network cards on servers and on whichever client machines need them. The network cards will perform the encryption.

Information Technology Manager

Performance cannot suffer due to the use of IPSec.

MAINTAINABILITY

Group Policy will ensure the maintainability of the policies.

AVAILABILITY

The system must be available and protected 24×7.

ANALYSIS

The use of IPSec for network communications in the research department is a good one, but should not be envisioned as the end-all answer to protection from within (or without). What would prevent an employee with the appropriate access level from copying proprietary information from the servers or his desktop to removable media? Who or what controls access to the printer (and its output)?

A carefully designed IPSec policy prohibits connections from research department employees to resources for which they do not have clearance. Likewise, should an improper network connection, unauthorized modem, or other connection to the research department system occur, IPSec can protect access to the data. However, it relies on control of passwords. What good is IPSec if someone can learn the password of approved users and access his or her computer? In this case, the intruder could log on as the user and access data as if IPSec were not in place.

CHAPTER SUMMARY

Unsecured network communications results in vulnerability to many attacks. To secure network communications, you must have the requisite knowledge, the ability to design the correct policies, and the ability to implement them. You can maintain your policies by using Group Policy.

KEY TERMS

- Security Association (SA)
- Authentication Header (AH)
- Encapsulating Security Payload (ESP)
- Internet Key Exchange (IKE)
- Diffie-Hellman (DH) group
- Server Message Block (SMB) signing
- anti-replay
- Security Parameters Index (SPI)
- Perfect Forward Security (PFS)
- preshared keys

APPLY YOUR KNOWLEDGE

Exercises

15.1 Configure IPSec Communications

Estimated Time: 15 minutes

1. Check the Domain Controller Group Policy. Is a policy in place? What is it?

    To check the Domain Controller Group Policy, follow these steps:

    1. Open Active Directory Users and Computers.

    2. Right-click the Domain Controllers OU and click Properties.

    3. Click Group Policy.

    4. The Default Domain Controllers Policy should be the only policy.

    5. Click Edit. (Do *not* change anything! Use Cancel to back out of property pages.)

    6. Select the Windows Settings\Security Settings\IpSecurity Policies folder.

    7. Examine the three default policies. Are any assigned? (Policies must be assigned before they can be used.) For this exercise to work, no policies should be assigned at the Domain Controllers OU level because they would override your settings working at the Local Policy level.

    8. Examine the Secure Server (Require Security) policy by double-clicking on the policy and then double-clicking on the All IP Traffic rule.

    9. What is the filter action?

    10. What does this mean (double-click the filter action)?

    11. What is the connection type?

2. Configure the domain controller to require IPSec encryption for All IP Traffic.

    To do so, follow these steps:

    1. Open Local Computer Active Directory Users and Computers.

    2. Select the IP Security Policies folder.

    3. Are any policies assigned?

    4. Open the Secure Server policy.

    5. Is there a difference in the IP filter list between this and the default domain controller policy?

    6. Is there a difference in the IP filter list for all IP traffic?

    7. What does the filter action specify?

    8. Close the property pages by using the Cancel button on each.

    9. Right-click on the policy and click Assign to assign the policy for this domain controller.

    10. Open a command prompt.

    11. Type `secedit /refreshpolicy machine_policy`.

3. Use a nonenabled computer and attempt to contact the domain controller. Can you? Why?

    To make this attempt, follow these steps:

    1. Open Windows Explorer.

    2. Attempt to navigate to My Network Places\Entire Network\Microsoft Windows Network*domain name**computer name*.

    3. What happens?

APPLY YOUR KNOWLEDGE

4. Configure a client and attempt to connect to the domain controller. Use the configured client and attempt to connect with the domain controller. Can you? Why?

1. Open the client's local security policy.

2. Select the IPSec Policies folder.

3. Double-click on the client policy.

4. What does this policy specify?

5. Close the property pages by canceling out of them.

6. Right-click on the client policy and select Assign.

7. Open a command prompt.

8. Type `secedit /refreshpolicy machine policy`.

9. Open Windows Explorer.

10. Attempt to navigate to My Network Places\Entire Network\Microsoft Windows Network*domain name**computer name*.

11. What happens?

Review Questions

1. Why should the `EnableSecuritySignature` registry value be set to 1 if the `RequireSecuritySignature` registry value is set to 1?

2. You want to enable SMB signing between all computers capable of SMB signing. You do not want to allow any SMB communications from unsecured computers. Make a list of the settings to change and where on which OS. Do not assume that all computers have the same OS installed.

3. Why should you use IKE for IPSec key management?

4. Where are IPSec security policies defined?

5. What happens with respect to IPSec policy if a client computer joined in the domain can no longer connect to a domain controller?

6. How should you configure management of IPSec policy?

7. What is Perfect Forward Secrecy? Why is it used?

8. Why is negotiation divided into two phases?

9. What does the IPSec Policy Agent Service do?

10. When configuring a security gateway, what special filters must be included?

Exam Questions

1. BK Productions requires additional security for their Windows 2000 file server. They want to protect the file server by requiring SMB signing. All client computers are Windows NT Workstation 4.0 computers. All computers and the file server are joined in a domain.

Required Result:

SMB signing should be implemented so that Windows NT 4.0 computers can have secure communications with a Windows 2000 Server used as a file server.

Optional Desired Results:

Only computers configured for SMB signing will be able to communicate with the server.

APPLY YOUR KNOWLEDGE

Because files may be stored on the client systems, client computers will also require SMB signing for all communications.

Proposed Solution:

The following security option(s) is enabled in the local computer security policy.

- Digitally Sign Server Communications (Always)

- Digitally Sign Server Communications (When Possible)

In the registry of all Windows NT clients, the RequireSecuritySignature and EnableSecuritySignature values are set to 1.

Evaluation of Proposed Solution:

Which result(s) does the proposed solution produce?

A. The proposed solution produces the required result and both of the optional results.

B. The proposed solution produces the required result and one of the optional results.

C. The proposed solution produces the required result but neither of the optional results.

D. The proposed solution does not produce the required result.

2. BK Productions requires additional security for its Windows 2000 file server. The company wants to protect the file server by requiring SMB signing. All client computers are Windows NT Workstation 4.0 computers. All computers and the file server are joined in a domain.

Required Result:

SMB signing should be implemented so that Windows NT 4.0 computers can have secure communications with a Windows 2000 Server used as a file server.

Optional Desired Results:

Only computers configured for SMB signing will be able to communicate with the server.

Because files may be stored on the client systems, client computers will also require SMB signing for all communications.

Proposed Solution:

The following security option(s) is enabled in the GPO of the OU that contains the server:

- Digitally Sign Server Communications (Always)

- Digitally Sign Server Communications (When Possible)

In the registry of all Windows NT clients, the RequireSecuritySignature and EnableSecuritySignature values are set to 1.

Evaluation of Proposed Solution:

Which result(s) does the proposed solution produce?

A. The proposed solution produces the required result and both of the optional results.

B. The proposed solution produces the required result and one of the optional results.

C. The proposed solution produces the required result but neither of the optional results.

D. The proposed solution does not produce the required result.

APPLY YOUR KNOWLEDGE

3. The Tremain Polson systems administrator is setting up the research department's IPSec implementation. He wants to use the most secure authentication, but does not want to require the implementation of a PKI. What does he choose?

    A. Certificates

    B. Kerberos

    C. Preshared keys

    D. NTLMv2

4. Next he must design filters. What information in the following list will not be needed for implementation?

    A. Source address

    B. Destination address

    C. Application

    D. Name of the computer

    E. Protocol

    F. Source and destination ports.

5. He finds that he will have several filters for one policy. He wants to make sure that his filters are applied in the correct order. How can he ensure that?

    A. Because filter lists are processed top to bottom and the last processed wins, he puts his most important filter at the bottom.

    B. Because filters are processed bottom to top and the last processed wins, he puts his most important filter at the top.

    C. Because filters are processed in a priority order specified by the SPI number, he can order his filters by giving them appropriate SPI numbers.

    D. Because filters are processed in the order of most to least specific, he really can't control the order of processing by placement in the interface.

6. Davison, Weidermier, and West will be implementing IPSec for communications between their branch offices and the main office. The firm will use the Internet. You are asked to prepare information on the requirements for this. You are going to advise the firm to use certificates. What else will you determine the firm needs to implement this choice for authentication? (Choose the best answer.)

    A. The computer must have an IPSec certificate, which must be present.

    B. EFS certificates must be present.

    C. A trusted CA must be available.

    D. Server certificates must be purchased from a public certificate authority.

7. Once an IPSec policy is enabled:

    A. All communications to that computer must use IPSec.

    B. Communications with that computer will use IPSec if they can; if negotiations fail, unsecured communications will take place.

    C. If IPSec is required or merely suggested will be determined by the IPSec policy.

    D. The computer is invulnerable to attack.

8. Match the security level (alphabet) with the type of computer (Roman numeral) that fits in it.

APPLY YOUR KNOWLEDGE

Security Level	Type of Computer
A. Minimal	i. Remote access server
B. Standard	ii. Accounting database server
C. High security	iii. Hold no sensitive data
	iv. Domain controller
	v. DNS server

9. The AH protocol provides what?

   A. Authentication

   B. Confidentiality

   C. Integrity

   D. Anti-replay services

10. The ESP protocol provides what?

    A. Authentication

    B. Confidentiality

    C. Integrity

    D. Anti-replay services

Answers to Exercises

15.1 The solutions to Exercise 15.1 are as follows:

1.9. What is the filter action? Requires Security.

1.10. What does this mean (double-click the filter action)? It means that security is negotiated, and that unsecured communications are accepted, but only an IPSec response is sent.

1.11. What is the connection type? All network connections.

2.3. Are any policies assigned? No.

2.5. Is there a difference in the IP filter list between this and the default domain controller policy? Yes. There is a filter for ICMP traffic that is unchecked.

2.6. Is there a difference in the IP filter list for all IP traffic? Yes. It matches all IP packets from this computer to any other computer except broadcast, multicast, Kerberos, RSVP(resource reservation protocol), and ISAKMP.

2.7. What does the filter action specify? Accept unsecure but always respond using IPSec.

3.3. What happens? The error message `Not Accessible` displays.

4.4. What does this policy specify? Uses IPSec to respond to servers that require IPSec.

4.11 What happens? You can browse the domain controller. You can connect to any shares to which you have permission to connect.

Answers to Review Questions

1. If both keys are not set, no communications can occur.

2. Set the two values, `RequireSecuritySignature` and `EnableSecuritySignature`, to `1` in the following places:

   Windows NT:

   Server Service

   HKEY_LOCAL_MACHINE\SYSTEM\CurrentControlSet\Services\LanManServer\Parameters

   Workstation Service

   HKEY_LOCAL_MACHINE\SYSTEM\Services\Rdr\Parameters\

APPLY YOUR KNOWLEDGE

Windows 98:

HKEY_LOCAL_MACHINE\SYSTEM\
CurrentControlSet\Services\Vdr

Windows 2000:

Server Service

HKEY_LOCAL_MACHINE\SYSTEM\
CurrentControlSet\Services\LanManServer\
Parameters

Workstations Service

HKEY_LOCAL_MACHINE\SYSTEM\
CurrentControlSet\Services\
LanManlanmanworkstation\Parameters

3. IKE is automated. Configuring preshared keys would become an impossible task. Preshared keys remain in clear text in the policy and therefore make things more vulnerable.

4. IPSec security policies are defined in Group Policy (local, site, domain, OU).

5. The polices are cached in the registry.

6. Management of IPSec policy should be done through Group Policy. Authority can be delegated if policies are applied to domain or OUs.

7. Perfect Forward Security limits the use of keying material to one time. It is used to make sure a compromised key gets the attacker the information that was encrypted with that key only.

8. Two phases make things more efficient. If a Phase II times out, Phase I can be reused; this saves the initial authentication time.

9. The IPSec Policy Agent Service retrieves the policies from Active Directory and passes them to IKE and the IPSec driver.

10. Protocol ID 50 (IPSec ESP) and 51 (IPSec AH). UDP port 500 (IKE).

Answers to Exam Questions

1. **D.** The policy here is being implemented in the local Group Policy. The domain policy overrides this policy. The domain policy is by default set to digitally sign when possible. (For more information, see the section "Windows 2000 SMB Message Signing.")

2. **A.** The policy is placed in the proper location, and the server is appropriately configured for SMB signing. Workstation computers are configured as well. (For more information, see the section "Windows 2000 SMB Message Signing."

3. **B.** Although a preshared key could be used and does not require a PKI, it is the least-secure authentication method. NTLMv2 is not an option. (For more information, see the section "Authentication Methods.")

4. **C, D.** Filters do not contain the names of any computers or applications. Filters do contain the source address, destination address, protocol number, or source and destination ports. (For more information, see the section "Filter Design.")

5. **D.** Filter lists are simultaneously retrieved and processed in the order of most to least specific. (For more information, see the section "Filter Lists.")

6. **A, C.** If certificates are to be used as an authentication method, the PKI must be established prior to its attempt. The computer certificate must be present on both sides of the negotiation and the certificates must have been issued by the trusted CA. The CA does not have to be an external CA. EFS certificates are used for encrypting and decrypting files, not for IPSec communications. (For more information, see the section "Authentication Methods.")

APPLY YOUR KNOWLEDGE

7. **C.** IPSec policies can specify that IPSec must be used, or may be used. (For more information, see the section "IPSec.")

8. **A – iii; B – iv, v; C – i, ii.**

Security Level	Type of Computer
A. Minimal	iii. Hold no sensitive data
B. Standard	iv. Domain controller
C. High security	i. Remote access server
	ii. Accounting database server

Minimal defines computers that do not hold sensitive data. Better defining words might be "not considered especially sensitive, or sensitive enough." Standard is just about every computer. DNS servers and domain controllers are sensitive, but care must be taken not to block communications to them! Highly sensitive computers such as accounting databases and remote access servers should be well protected. (For more information, see the section "Best Practices.")

9. **A, C, D.** The AH protocol does not provide confidentiality; it does not encrypt. (For more information, see the section "IPSec.")

10. **A, B, C, D.** The ESP protocol provides all services. (For more information, see the section "IPSec.")

Suggested Readings and Resources

1. Q161372: How to Enable SMB Signing in Service Pack 3

2. Q230545: SMB Signing in Windows 98

3. Service Pack 3: README.TXT file

4. RFCs

   - 2411: The IPSec Document Roadmap

   - 2405: The ESP DES-CBC Cipher Algorithm with Explicit IV

   - 2451: The ESP CBC-Mode Cipher Algorithms

   - 2085: HMAC-MD5 IP Authentication with Replay Prevention

   - 2104: HMAC: Keyed Hashing for Message Authentication

   - 2403: The Use of HMAC-MD5-96 with ESP and AH

   - 2404: The Use of HMAC-SHA1-96 with ESP and AH

   - 2402: IP Authentication Header (AH)

   - 2406: IP Encapsulating Security Payload (ESP)

   - 2047: The Internet IP Security Domain of Interpretation for IKE

   - 2401: Security Architecture for the Internet Protocol

   - 2410: The NULL Encryption Algorithm and Its Use with IPSec

FINAL REVIEW

Fast Facts

Study and Exam Prep Tips

Practice Exam

To secure a Windows 2000 network, you must study two main topics: Windows 2000 and the company to whom the network belongs. If you understand the business model, culture, organization, and current infrastructure, you will better be able to protect its information systems. A good Windows 2000 security design is obtained by fully understanding the current system and any plans for the future.

A few quick facts about Windows 2000 are listed here:

◆ Windows 2000 enables two-way transitive trusts based on Kerberos V5.

◆ Trusts in Windows 2000 are automatically created between the forest root domain and the root domain of each domain tree added to the forest.

◆ Users and computers can be authenticated between any domains in the domain tree or in the forest.

◆ Organizational units (OU) are Active Directory containers. They can be used to organize users, groups, computers, and other OUs. They are the smallest scope to which a Group Policy can be defined and administrative authority can be delegated.

◆ Default security templates are available to assist in your development of security baselines for different types of Windows 2000 computers in your network.

◆ Operations masters are roles that involve single master replication.

Fast Facts

ANALYSIS AND SECURITY REQUIREMENTS

◆ The Global Catalog is composed of a partial replica of every object in Active Directory.

◆ Secedit is a command that enables you to configure and analyze computer security settings from the command line.

Some of these items need further discussion and are detailed in these sections.

SECURITY TEMPLATES

One way to ease the development and implementation of security policy for your Windows 2000 network is to develop security baselines. To do so, determine the types of servers and client systems that you have and the relative security structure that you want to impose upon them. Then you can either match these requirements with existing security templates or create your own. Default security templates are listed in Table 1.

Operations Masters

Five operation master roles exist:

◆ **Forest-wide operations master roles**—One of each is created during the promotion of the first domain in the forest.

- **Schema master**—Controls updates and modifications to the schema.

- **Domain Naming master**—In charge of additions and deletions of domains and sites in the forest.

SUMMARY TABLE 1
SECURITY TEMPLATES

Computer	Template	Definitions
Default workstation	basicwk.inf	Basic: Reverts to default setting applied. Does not modify user rights.
Default server	basicsv.inf	
Default domain controller	basicdc.inf	
Compatible workstation or server	compatws.inf	Compatible: Lowers security settings on common application access files, folders, and registry keys.
Secure workstation or server	securews.inf	Applies recommended security settings for all security areas except files, folders, and registry keys. Settings that impact the operating
Secure domain controller	securedc.inf	system are changed. This template also enables SMB packet signing. It does not change any DACLs, but it does warn of the installation of unsigned drivers.
Highly secure workstation or server	hisecws.inf	Applies Settings for network communications. This template provides maximum protection for network traffic protocols used between
Highly secure domain controller	hisecdc.inf	Windows 2000 computers. No communication with Windows 95 or Windows NT occurs. This template requires packet signing and signing of drivers.
Dedicated domain controller	dedicadc.inf	Can no longer run server-based applications on domain controllers. This template provides default settings for local users defined like that of workstations and servers.
Domain controller initial security	DC Security.inf	Same settings as applied during dcpromo.

◆ **Domain-wide operations master role**—One exists for each domain:

   • The **Relative ID (RID) master**—Allocates relative ID sequences to each domain controller in its domain.

   • The **PDC emulator**—Acts as a Windows NT PDC for non-Windows 2000 clients in the domain, or if Windows NT BDCs are present.

   • The **Infrastructure master**—Updates the group-to-user references when group members are renamed or changed.

Secedit

Syntax:

Secedit/analyze [/DB *filename*]/CFG filename] [/log *logpath*][/verbose][/quiet]

For a list of Secedit parameters, see Table 2.

To configure system security:

Secedit /configure [/DB *filename*][/overwrite] [/areas *area1 area2* . . .][/log *logpath*][/verbose] [/quiet]

SUMMARY TABLE 2
SECEDIT PARAMETERS

Parameter	Explanation
/DB *filename*	Path to security template database.
/CFG *filename*	Path of security template (without this, any configuration in the database is used).
/log path	Path to log.
/verbose	More detailed information provided during analysis.
/quiet	Parameter to suppress screen and log output. Analysis results will still be viewable in Security Configuration and Analysis.
/overwrite	Parameter to specify that the new security template should overwrite any template or composite template stored in the database instead of appending it.
/area *area1 area2* . . .	Security areas to be applied to the system. Default is all. Areas include: SECURITYPOLICY, GROUP_MGMT, USER_RIGHTS, REGKEYS, FILESTORE, and SERVICES.
Machine_policy	Settings for local computer.
User_policy	Settings for local user account currently logged on.
/enforce	Parameter to refresh, even if no changes have been made to the Group Policy object settings.
/mergedPolicy	Parameter to merge and export domain and local policy settings.
/analyze	Parameter to compare the current system with an identified template.

To refresh security settings:

Secedit /refreshpolicy {machine_policy|user_policy} [/enforce]

To export security settings:

Secedit /export[mergedPolicy][/DB *filename*] [/CFG *filename*][/areas *area1, area2* . . .] [/log *logpath*][/verbose][quiet]

Designing a Security Solution

To design a security solution, you must know the basics of Windows 2000 security structures. Basics to study include these:

◆ File and folder permissions

◆ Default access by basic groups

◆ Registry permissions

◆ Audit strategies

◆ Types of groups and group scope

◆ Group membership and privileges

◆ Group Policy

◆ Encrypting file system

◆ Authentication

◆ Public key infrastructure

File and Folder Permissions

Knowledge of file and folder permissions is important to protect data from access by unauthorized individuals and to allow only the desired access by those who are authorized.

◆ Basic file and folder permissions:

- **Modify**—A combination of List Folder Contents, Write, and Delete and Read Permissions

- **Read & Execute**—A combination of Traverse Folder/Execute File, Read Attributes, Read Extended Attributes, and Read Permissions

- **List Folder Contents**—A combination of Traverse Folder/Execute File, List Folder/Read Data, Read Attributes, Read Extended Attributes, and Read Permissions

- **Read**—A combination of List Folder/Read Data, Read Attributes, Read Extended Attributes, and Read Permissions

- **Write**—A combination of Create Files/Write Data, Create Folders/Append Data, Write Attributes, Write Extended Attributes, and Read Permissions

- **Full Control**—A combination of all of the above

◆ File and folder advanced permissions:

- **List Folder/Read Data**: List Folder—View file names and subfolder names in the folder. Read Data—View data in files.

- **Read Attributes**—View file or folder attributes. (Attributes are defined by NTFS and include Read-Only, Hidden, and so on.)

- **Read Extended Attributes**—View extended attribute. (Extended attributes are defined by programs.)

- **Create Files/Write Data**: Create Files— Create files in folders. Write Data—Change data in file.

- **Create Folders/Append Data:** Create Folders—Create folders within folders. Append Data—Make changes to the end of the file, but not change, delete, or overwrite existing data.

- **Write Attributes**—Change attributes of a file or folder.

- **Write Extended Attributes**—Change extended attributes of a file or folder.

- **Delete Subfolders**—Delete subfolder or file.

- **Delete**—Delete the file or folder.

- **Read Permissions**—Read file or folder permissions.

- **Change Permissions**—Change permissions of file or folder.

- **Take Ownership**—Take ownership of the file or folder.

Default File Access for Basic Groups and Basic Privileges

System file access and basic privileges are set for the following groups:

◆ **Power Users**—Privileges are backward compatible with Windows NT 4.0. Members of the Power Users group can install most applications and have modify access to %windir% and %windir%\system32.

Power Users have read-only access to files that were installed in these directories during setup. As a result, applications that they install can write new

files into system directories but cannot modify Windows 2000 system files. In addition, Power Users cannot install Windows 2000 services.

◆ **Administrators, System and Creator Owner**—These users have full control to file system and registry objects that exist at the beginning of GUI mode setup. Administrators have the same level of rights and permission as in NT 4.0.

◆ **Users**—Write access is given only as listed in Table 3.

SUMMARY TABLE 3
USER FILE ACCESS

File Path	What Is?	Permission
HKEY_Current_User	User part of registry	Full Control
%User Profile%	User's profile directory	Full Control
All Users\Documents	Shared documents location	Modify
All Users\Application Data	Shared application data Location	Modify
%Windir%Temp	Per-machine temp folder	Traverse, Synchronize, Add File, Add Subdir
\(Root Directory)	Root	Not configured during setup

Users may not even be able to read data on the rest of the system, by default.

◆ **Account Operators, Server Op and Print Operators**—These users have the same level of access and privileges as in NT 4.0.

Registry Permissions

Registry permissions include these:

- **Query Value**—Ask for and get the value of a key.

- **Set Value**—Change a key value.

- **Create Subkey**—Create a subkey.

- **Enumerate subkeys**—List the subkeys.

- **Notify Changes**—Set auditing.

- **Create Link**—Link this key to some other key.

- **Write DAC**—Change permissions.

- **Read Control**—Find the owner of the key.

Audit Strategies

Auditing access and the use of privileges is an important part of designing security. Deriving an audit policy has five parts:

- First, learn what can be audited and what useful information it will give you.

- Next, decide which objects you will need to audit on a regular basis and what you will be looking for.

- Derive strategies for gleaning information using periodic or fixed-frame audit techniques.

- Learn how to turn on auditing and how to establish each available facet.

- Determine how you are going to cope with the multitude of records produced.

The following basic categories can be audited.

- **Account Logon Events**—When a domain controller gets a logon request, this category will be activated. This includes the issuing of Kerberos tickets for resource access.

- **Account Management**—Security events are triggered if a user account is created, deleted, or changed.

- **Directory Service Access**—This category is activated when an Active Directory object is accessed. Like file and folder objects, Directory Service objects have multiple activities that can be audited. The number and kind of activities will depend on the type of object being audited. Setting this category will not automatically generate the thousands of events you might expect. You must visit the property pages of the Active Directory object and set auditing for specific users or groups.

- **Logon Events**—Events are recorded when a user logs on or logs off. Audit logon failure to find if someone is trying a random password hack. In high-security networks, you may want to audit logon success periodically during heavy vacation times, or at any time that you want to find out if passwords have been compromised.

- **Object Access**—When an object is accessed, this category will be activated. As you know, each object has a security descriptor attached to it that is composed in part by a Discretionary Access Control List (DACL). The DACL allows fine-grained control of object access. A second part to the security descriptor is the System Access

Control List (SACL). The SACL specifies when to record access or failed access to the object. You create entries in the SACL when you identify an object for auditing and indicate users and groups to watch for. File and folder access audit is set in Windows Explorer. When you select the file or folder to audit, you can audit success or failure of the access activities (refer to Figure 6.3 in Chapter 6).

◆ **Policy Change**—When a policy affecting security, user rights, or auditing is changed, an event is generated.

◆ **Privilege Use**—A user right is used to do something. Every privilege that a user has—even including the right to access a file—is recorded.

◆ **Process Tracking**—This is used to track what a program is doing while it is executing. It is valuable to the developer during testing. You can use this to verify that the activities of a supplied program are not doing anything that would compromise security.

◆ **System Events**—System events such as shutting down the computer are recorded.

Types of Groups and Group Scope

Unlike Windows NT 4.0, Windows 2000 computers and users can be combined into groups. Two types of groups exist: distribution groups (for email lists) and security groups. Security group types are these:

◆ **Computer Local**—Exists only on a single computer.

◆ **Domain Local**—Can be used to give broad access to resources on any Windows 2000-based computer in the domain.

◆ **Global**—Is a good choice for establishing a one-to-one relationship between groups of people and a job.

◆ **Universal**—Used to assign access to multiple, similar groups that exist in many domains. Membership is stored in the Global Catalog. Global groups can be members of Universal groups.

A number of built-in groups are provided. Standalone servers and Win2k Professional have Computer Local groups. They are listed here:

◆ Administrators

◆ Power Users

◆ Users

◆ Guests

Domain controllers have a slightly different set of user groups. These groups are Domain Local groups:

◆ Administrators

◆ Account Operators

◆ Backup Operators

◆ Guests

◆ Print Operators

◆ Replicator

◆ Server Operators

The following groups are global groups in mixed mode. The last three (Enterprise Admins, Group Policy Creator Owners, and Schema Admins) become Universal groups in native mode.

◆ **Domain Users**—Are automatic members of the Users group

◆ **Domain Admins**—Are automatic members of the Administrators group

◆ **Domain Guests**—Are automatic members of the Guests group

◆ **DNS Administrators**—Manage DNS servers

◆ **Cert Publishers**—Manage certification servers

◆ **Enterprise Admins**—Are automatic members of the Administrators group.

◆ **Group Policy Creator Owners**—Create and administer Group Policy.

◆ **Schema Admins**—Manage the schema.

By default, Enterprise Admins have full control over all objects in a forest. This account has administrative rights in all domains in the forest because it is has membership in the Administrators group for every domain in the forest.

Predefined computer groups are listed here:

◆ **RAS and IS Servers**—Can access remote access properties of users. (Domain Local Scope—no default membership.)

◆ **Domain controllers**—Manage Active Directory and other computers. (Global Scope—all domain controllers in domain.)

◆ **Domain computers**—Computers joined in the domain. (Global Scope—all member servers and workstations joined in the domain.)

◆ **DNS Update Proxy**—DNS clients are allowed to update DNS updates for other clients.

Implicit groups are as follows:

◆ **Everyone**—All security principals and anonymous users

◆ **Interactive**—Anyone logged on locally

◆ **Authenticated User**—Anyone who has been authenticated

◆ **Creator Owner**—The user who created an object or has taken ownership of an object

◆ **Network**—Anyone currently accessing resources across the network

◆ **Dialup**—Users using RAS

◆ **Anonymous Users**—Any user who is touching resources but who is not logged on as a user with a Windows 2000 account

Group Membership and Privileges

What groups can include is based on the domain mode: mixed mode vs. native mode.

Groups in native mode can contain the following:

◆ **Domain Local**—User accounts, Global groups, Universal groups from any domain in the forest, and Domain Local groups from the same domain

◆ **Global**—User accounts and global groups from the same domain only

◆ **Universal**—User accounts, Global groups, and other Universal groups from any domain in the forest

Groups in mixed mode can contain the following:

- **Domain Local**—User accounts and Global groups from any domain
- **Global**—User accounts from the same domain
- **Universal**—Not applicable

Administrator rights are listed in Table 4.

SUMMARY TABLE 4
ADMINISTRATORS ONLY

	Logon Right	Privilege	Information
Log on as a batch job	X		Log on using a batch facility.
Create page file		X	Create a page file.
Debug programs		X	Debug low-level objects such as threads.
Force shutdown from remote systems		X	Shut down a computer remotely.
Load and unload device drivers		X	Install and uninstall device drivers.
Manage auditing and security log		X	Specify resources to audit access to. View and clear security logs. This privilege does not include the privilege to set system audit policy.
Modify firmware environmental variables		X	Change system environmental variables stored in nonvolatile RAM.
Take ownership of files or other objects		X	Even if permissions do not include access for this user, ownership can be taken.

Groups privileges are listed in Table 5.

SUMMARY TABLE 5
ADMINISTRATORS AND OTHER GROUPS

	Right or Privilege	Admins Plus?	Definition
Access this computer from a network	Right	Everyone, Power User	Connect to computer across a network.
Log on locally	Right	Backup Operator, Power User, Everyone (client or standalone server)	Sit at console and log on interactively.
Back up files and file folders	Privilege	Backup Operator	File and folder permission cannot keep users from copying files to backup tapes using a backup program.
Bypass Traverse Checking	Privilege	Everyone	Even if no access to a folder is granted, a user can access files within the folder when given appropriate privileges.
Change System Time	Privilege	Power Users	Set computer time clock.
Increase scheduling priority	Privilege	Power Users	Boost the priority of a process.
Profile a single process	Privilege	Power Users	Sample a process, a useful tool for developers.
Restore files and file folders	Privilege	Backup Operators	Restore backed-up files and folders, even without specific permissions set.
Shut down the system	Privilege	Backup Operators, Everyone, Power Users, Users	Shut down the system interactively.

Group Policy

Group Policy can be used to set computer configuration options such as these:

◆ **Security**—Many security settings can be set using Group Policy for implementation across sites, domains, and OUs.

- Account policy settings

- User rights, audit policy, and security options

- Event log settings

- Restricted groups

- System services

- Registry and file system access

- Public key policies

- IP security policy

◆ **Administration**—.adm files are unicode text files that list categories that can be set in the Group Policy snap-in.

- Desktop appearance

- System service settings, such as automatic and manual

- Internet Explorer settings

- System settings such as logon, disk quotas, DNS, client, Group Policy, and Windows File Protection

- Network settings, such as whether a user can configure his offline file settings, and whether network connection sharing is enabled

- Printer settings, such as whether printers are automatically published in Active Directory

- Software settings

◆ **Scripts**—This includes logon, logoff, boot, and shutdown scripts.

◆ **Software Installation**—Installation, updates, and uninstalls can be arranged according to GPC.

◆ **Folder Redirection**—The user's folders can be stored on the network, but they appear to the user to be located on the current computer.

Group Policy is actually expressed in two parts: Group Policy templates and the local system policy.

Group Policy templates store group policy settings. They are stored as *.inf files in a domain controller's sysvol folder. Each template is placed in its own folder and can be found at

<system root>\sysvol\sysvol\<domain name>\ Policies \<GUID\

The local system policy is stored in the <system root>\ system32\GroupPolicy folder on the local machine.

The behavior of Group Policy inheritance is controlled by four configurations:

◆ Default Behavior

◆ Override

◆ Block Inheritance

◆ Loopback

Default behavior consists of the following:

◆ Computer Group Policies are applied when the computer is booted.

◆ User Group Policy is applied when a user logs on.

◆ Policies are reapplied throughout the day.

◆ Local computer policy is applied.

◆ Any site policy is applied.

◆ Any domain policies are applied.

◆ Organizational unit policy is applied.

◆ If OUs are nested, each inner nested OU Group Policy is applied.

◆ At each level, all applicable Group Policies are applied in the order specified by the administrator.

◆ Excluding the local computer policy, the policy closest to the user or group is applied.

Group Policy itself can be controlled using Group Policy. The available settings are defined in Table 6.

SUMMARY TABLE 6
GROUP POLICY SETTINGS

Policy	Explanation
Disable background refresh of Group Policy	Group Policy is not updated as long as a computer is in use (a user is logged on). When the user logs off, Group Policy is updated.
Apply Group Policy for computers asynchronously during startup.	The system can display the logon prompt before all policies have been applied. This makes it appear to the user as if logon time is reduced, but the user's interface may not be really ready for use.
Apply Group Policy for users asynchronously during logon	The system can display the desktop before updating Group Policy. If Group Policy affects the appearance of the desktop, its appearance may change as policy finishes applying.
Group Policy refresh interval for computers	The frequency for background updating (updating while the computer is being used) is specified here. By default, the setting is every 90 minutes, with an offset of 0 to 30 minutes, so that not all policies on all computers will attempt to update at the same time. The frequency can be set from 0 to 64,800 minutes (45 days). A setting of 0 will attempt to start the updating every 7 seconds. Short update times are not very useful because they may interfere with network usage and user work.
Group Policy refresh interval for domain controllers	Here you specify the background update policy for domain controllers. Group Policy is updated by default on domain controllers every 5 minutes. Any setting on this policy at the local computer policy setting level is ignored. Frequency and recommendations are the same as the settings described for the item above.
User Group Policy loopback processing mode	Alternate user policies are applied on this computer when a user logs on. A computer with this setting determines the application of policies. While usually a user's Group Policy settings are applied no matter which computer he logs on to, if this policy is set, the computer Policy Settings determine the settings that a user receives. Quite often this setting is used for kiosk computers in malls and airports, for classroom or library computers, and for any computer that needs to stabilize to one consistent configuration. There are two modes to select here: Replace, which indicates that user settings defined in the computer's Group Policy settings replace the user policies normally set by the user, and Merge, which means that the computer-defined user settings merge with the user-defined user settings. If conflicts occur, the computer's Group Policy user settings win.
Group Policy slow link detection	A rate of data transmission assigned here is compared with the actual rate of data transmission from the domain controller to the computer. If the domain transfer rate is slower than the policy rate, the link is considered slow, and an action can be specified by the program implementing the policy. The rate set is in kilobits per second.

By default, when a slow link is detected, the following processing occurs:

◆ Security settings and administrative templates will update, even over a slow link.

◆ Software installation, scripts, folder redirection, and Internet Explorer maintenance will not occur.

ENCRYPTED FILE SYSTEM

The following is true about the encrypted file system:

◆ Encrypted files that are moved will remain encrypted even if the destination folder is not encrypted.

◆ Files copied to an unencrypted folder on the same volume will remain encrypted.

◆ Moving files or folders to a volume that is not NTFS, such as one formatted FAT or FAT32, or a floppy disk formatted with FAT, can become decrypted.

◆ System files cannot be encrypted.

◆ Encrypted files can be deleted by any user who has delete permission in that folder.

◆ Encrypted files will remain encrypted if they are backed up using Microsoft Backup.

◆ The possibility exists that encrypted file information could be clear text in the paging file during reading and use by an application. To secure this information, set the policy to clear the pagefile at user logoff.

◆ A compressed file cannot be encrypted.

Cipher is a command-line tool used to encrypt and unencrypt files.

Authentication

Components of the security subsystem are used in the authentication process:

◆ **Security Reference Monitor (SRM)**—The SRM checks user permissions to access objects. It enforces access validation and audit policy. It is used by both kernel and user modes. The SRM generates the audit messages.

◆ **SAM**—In Windows NT 4.0, the SAM was the repository for all account information in a domain. It is still used to store local user accounts. Every Windows 2000 Server, Advanced Server, and Professional system has a SAM when installed. SAM is used to store the original installation Administrator account. When a server is promoted to domain controller, the SAM accounts are no longer accessible.

◆ **Local Security Authority (LSA)**—The LSA generates the access tokens, manages local security policy, provides interactive user authentication, and hands off authentication to the Kerberos client or NTLM protocols for network-based authentication.

Windows 2000 can utilize many methods of authentication. Determining which method is used and how to choose the appropriate authentication method consists of knowing how each authentication method works and where it may be applied. In some cases, you do not have choices; in others, you can strengthen or adjust parameters to manage the security of the process. Authentication methods include Kerberos, NTLM, RADIUS, smart cards, and certificates. Certificates are explored under the heading of public key infrastructure. Information on the other authentication methods follows.

Another aspect of authentication concerns its integration with other systems. Information on Kerberos integration follows the general discussion of methods.

Kerberos

Components of Kerberos are listed here:

◆ **Authentication Server**—This server performs authentication of the client against the KDC.

◆ **Ticket-Granting Server**—This server grants tickets for resource servers to authenticated clients.

◆ **Kerberos Distribution Center (KDC)**—The KDC provides key storage. In Kerberos classic, a database, the KDB stores keys. Windows 2000 uses Active Directory for key storage.

◆ **Kerberos Administration Server (KADM)**—All modification of the KDC is done from the KADM. Windows 2000 domain controllers are responsible here.

◆ **Kerberos realm**—This is a logical organization of Kerberos servers and clients. Windows 2000 uses the word *domain* instead of *realm*.

Default Kerberos policy in Windows 2000 and that of the RFC recommendations is listed in Table 7.

SUMMARY TABLE 7
DEFAULT POLICY SETTINGS IN WINDOWS 2000

Policy	Win2K default	Kerberos RFC Recommendation
Are tickets renewable?	Yes	Yes
Are tickets proxiable?	Yes	Yes
Are tickets forwardable?	Yes	Yes
Maximum ticket lifetime (MaxTicketAge)	10 hours	1 day
Maximum renewable ticket age (MaxRenewAge	7 days	1 week
Maximum service ticket lifetime (MaxServceAge)	10 hours	No recommendation in RFC 1510
Maximum skew time (difference in computer clocks, MaxClockSkew)	5 minutes	No recommendation in RFC 1510
Enforce user logon restrictions (look at user rights policy on target computer first, TicketValidateClient)	Enabled (a 1 means enabled)	No recommendation in RFC 1510

NTLM

NTLMv2 supports session security and 128-bit encryption for message confidentiality, but it must be configured.

> Registry key:
>
> HKLM\System\CurrentControlSet\control\LSA
>
> Value: LMCompatibilityLevel
>
> Value TYPE: REG_DWORD – number
>
> Range: 0-5
>
> Default 0

To determine the setting for this value, see Table 8.

SUMMARY TABLE 8
MAXIMIZING AUTHENTICATION USING LMCOMPATIBILITYLEVEL

	Definition	*Notes*
Level 0	Use LM response and NTLM response; never use NTLMv2 session security	Default. SP4 clients can connect to SP3 servers but will use LM and NTLM.
Level 1	Use NTLMv2 session security, if negotiated	See Chapter 12, "Designing Windows 2000 Network Services Security." SP4 clients connecting to SP3 servers will use LM and NTLM.
Level 2	Send NTLM authentication only	A client configured this way will not be capable of connecting to Windows 9x and below.
Level 3	Send NTLMv2 authentication only	Only NTLMv2 will be used.
Level 4	DC refuses LM authentication	Windows 9x clients can't connect.
Level 5	DC refuses LM and NTLM authentication (accepts only NTLMv2)	Windows 9x clients can't connect. Windows NT clients without service pack 4 cannot connect.

Smart Cards

The smart card can be used to authenticate to Windows 2000 using the PKINIT extension to the Kerberos standard.

The private key/public key management is via Windows 2000 Certificate Services. PIN management is via the smart card itself, not Windows 2000.

RADIUS Authentication

RADIUS authentication is a choice when designing authentication for remote access users. It involves the use of Routing and Remote Access Servers and the Internet Authentication Service (IAS). Steps to RADIUS authentication are listed here:

1. The client system creates an Access Request packet, which includes the username, password (as a message digest using RSA MD5), client ID, and port ID.

2. The Access Request packet is submitted to the RADIUS server via the network.

3. The RADIUS server receives and validates the shared secret.

4. If an Access-Accept message is returned, it will have the configuration data needed by the client to access services on the network. (For example, IP address, subnet mask, and so on.)

Internet Authentication Service (IAS) is Microsoft's implementation of RADIUS. IAS uses Windows 2000 Active Directory for authentication.

IAS can be used to authenticate a variety of users and/or computers using a variety of authentication protocols:

◆ PAP

◆ CHAP

◆ MSCHAP

◆ Extensible Authentication Protocol (EAP)

◆ Dialed Number Identification Service (DNIS)

◆ Automatic Number Identification Service (ANI)

◆ Guest Authentication

Kerberos Integration Issues

Can Windows 2000 clients participate in a classic Kerberos realm? Yes, if they are configured to do so. UNIX clients also can be configured to use the services of the Windows 2000 KDC. In some scenarios, access of both UNIX and Windows clients to UNIX resources and Windows resources can be configured. Table 9 lists the arrangements.

Management utilities for configuring interoperability are listed here:

◆ **KSETUP**—To configure alternate KDCs

◆ **KTPASS**—To set the password, account name mappings, and keytab generation for UNIX services

◆ **TRUSTDOM**—To set up cross-realm trusts, Windows 2000 and MIT Kerberos classic realms

Authentication Givens/Best Practices

To make authentication choices, consider the following items in Table 10 and Table 11.

SUMMARY TABLE 9
KERBEROS MIXED SCENARIOS

Clients	KDC	Resources	K Logon	Notes
Windows 2000 Professional	Windows 2000 MIT realm	Windows 2000 and UNIX	Windows 2000 KDC	Establish one-way trust between Windows 2000 and UNIX realm. Windows 2000 clients can access UNIX resources.
Windows 2000 Professional and UNIX	MIT realm Windows 2000	Windows 2000 and UNIX	MIT KDC	Establish a two-way trust between Windows 2000 and MIT. Clients have access to Windows 2000 resources through the Windows domains, and access to Kerberized applications on the UNIX servers through the MIT realm logon. Account mapping is used. Accounts must be synchronized between the domain/realm.

SUMMARY TABLE 10
BASIC SECURITY CONSIDERATIONS

	Default	Current Configuration	Best practice	Long Term
Will you be retaining Windows NT?	NTLM, LM		NTLMv2	
Will you be retaining Windows 9x?	LM		NTLMv2	
Will you be retaining Macintosh?	UAM or AppleShare		UAM	
Will you be retaining Novell?	None		MSDSN	
Will you be retaining UNIX?	None		Kerberos	
Will you be retaining IBM mainframe or AS/400?	None		SNA Server	

SUMMARY TABLE 11
SUPER SECURITY CONSIDERATIONS

Yes/No	
Do you have interbusiness data sharing needs?	Consider RADIUS, PKI
Do you have problems securing passwords?	Consider smart cards
Do you need to secure sections of your network?	Consider RADIUS, VPNs, and PKI
Do you need to protect/restrict Internet or intranet Web access?	Consider digest authentication IIS 5.0
Do you need to set up or maintain an e-commerce site?	Consider SSL/TLS and other Certificate Services

PUBLIC KEY INFRASTRUCTURE

By enabling and configuring Windows 2000 Certificate Services, you can develop a public key infrastructure. This enables you to use certificates for IPSec, authentication, and smart cards, and to centrally manage the encrypting file system recovery agents. You may also use features of Windows 2000 and other PKI-enabled applications.

Windows 2000 provides the following PKI-enabled applications:

◆ Encrypting file system

◆ Smart card services

◆ Internet Explorer

◆ Internet Information Server

Other Microsoft applications that are PKI-enabled are these:

◆ Microsoft Money

◆ Microsoft Outlook

◆ Microsoft Outlook Express

To understand and use Certificate Services requires an understanding of Certificate Authorities, certificates, cryptographic service providers, certification authority policies, the certificate life cycle, and the location of the logical certificate stores. To integrate with other Certification Authorities, you will need to know the import and export formats available, the specifics of mapping certificates to users, and the types of features that may prevent integration. Finally, you should be aware of several useful utilities.

Certificates are used in Windows 2000 for the following purposes:

◆ Server authentication (e-commerce)

◆ Client authentication (remote access, smart cards)

◆ Encrypting file system

◆ IPSec (network traffic encryption)

◆ Code signing (active content)

◆ Secure email

Certificate Authority options are listed here:

◆ **Enterprise Root CA**—Most trusted CA in the enterprise; requires Active Directory

◆ **Enterprise subordinate CA**—Issues certificates and obtains a certificate from another CA

◆ **Standalone root CA**—Most trusted CA in hierarchy; doesn't require Active Directory

◆ **Standalone subordinate CA**—Issues certificates and obtains a certificate from another CA

Default CSPs for Certificate Services include the items in Table 12.

SUMMARY TABLE 12
DEFAULT AVAILABLE CSPs

CSP	Hash Algorithms Available
Microsoft Base Cryptographic Provider	MD4, MD5, SHA-1
Microsoft Base DSS Cryptographic Provider	SHA-1
Gemplus GEmSAFE Card CSP v 1.0	All of above
Schlumberger Cryptographic Service Provider	All of above plus SSL3 SHAMD5

Default templates are available as described in Table 13.

SUMMARY TABLE 13
DEFAULT CA POLICIES DESCRIBING AVAILABLE CERTIFICATE TEMPLATES USES

Policy	Certificate Purpose(s)
EFS recovery agent	File recovery
Basic EFS	Creating encrypting file system-protected files
Domain controller	Client and server authentication
Web Server	Server authentication
Computer	Client and server authentication
User	EFS, secure email, client authentication
Subordinate Certification Authority	All
Administrator	Code signing, Microsoft trust list signing, EFS, secure email, client authentication

Parts of the certificate life cycle are listed here:

◆ The CA is installed and CA certificates are issued.

◆ The CAs issue server and user certificates.

◆ If necessary, the certificates are revoked.

◆ Certificates are renewed or expire.

◆ A Certificate Revocation List is published.

◆ The CA's certificate is renewed before it expires.

◆ The CA is revoked or is retired.

Logical stores include those in Table 14.

SUMMARY TABLE 14
LOGICAL CERTIFICATE STORES

Logical Store	Purpose	Notes
Active Directory User Object	Certificates published in the AD for this user.	Shown only in console for user.
Enterprise Trust	CTLs	If a certificate has a path to a CTK, it is trusted by the computer as specified in the CTL.
Intermediate Certification Authorities	Certificates for CAs that are not trusted roots	Subordinate CAs.
Personal	Individual certificates	Your user certificate.
Request	Pending or rejected requests	A list of any requests that are pending or rejected.
SPC	Certificates of software publishers trusted by this computer	Software is downloaded without prompting. By default, this is empty.
Trusted Root Certification Authorities	Certificates for root CAs	If a certificate has a certification path to a root CA here, it is trusted.

Certificates may be revoked before their expiration. Revoked certificates are listed in the Certificate Revocation List (CRL). The CRL must be available at all times and is checked before a certificate is allowed to be used. Certificates are revoked for following reasons:

- Unspecified
- Key compromise
- CA compromise
- Change of affiliation
- Suspension
- Cease of operation
- Certificate hold

Export and import formats for certificates are shown in Table 15.

SUMMARY TABLE 15
CERTIFICATE EXPORT AND IMPORT FORMATS

Format	Description
Personal information exchange (PKCS#12)	Transfer of keys from one computer to another, or from a computer to removable media
Cryptographic message syntax standard (PKCS #7)	Transfer of certificate and all certificates in its path: computer to computer, or computer to removable media
DER-encoded binary X.509	Used for interoperability with non-Windows 2000 CAs (uses the .cer extension)
Base64-encoded X.509	Interoperability with non-Windows 2000 CAs (uses .cer extension)

Utilities for use with certificate services are these:

- **CertUtil**—This utility verifies keys and dumps configuration information.
- **CertReq**—This utility can be used to request certificates from the command prompt.

- **Certserv**—Diagnostics mode starts Certificate Services as a standalone application rather than a service.

One method of integrating PKIs is to allow users with certificates from other CAs to access Windows 2000 resources. One step in this process is the mapping of these certificates to Windows 2000 user accounts. Mapping certificates to users works in three ways, which are explained in Table 16.

SUMMARY TABLE 16
DETERMINING MAPPING TYPE

Mapping Type	Use Issuer for Alternate Security Identity	Use Subject of Alternate Security Identity	
One-to-one	Selected	Selected	Map certificate to one account.
Many-to-one	Clear	Selected	Any certificate with the same subject is mapped to the user account, regardless of the issuer.
Many-one	Clear	Selected	Any certificate that has to the same issuer to the user account, regardless of the subject of the certificate.

Microsoft standards for PKI include the support of ITU X.509 version 3 and version 1 certificate formats, and a number of standard cryptographic algorithms.

- RSA
- DSA
- DH
- RC2, RC4, RC5

◆ DES40

◆ DES56

◆ 3DES

The public key standards are supported:

◆ **PKIX**—Internet drafts, including RFC 2459, from the public key infrastructure working group

◆ **X.509**—ITU specification that describes certificate format

◆ **PKCS**—Public key cryptography standards specifications

◆ **TLS**—Drafts from the IETF Transport Layer Security working group

◆ **S/MIME**—Drafts from the IETF S/MIME Mail Security working group

◆ **Kerberos**—RFC 1510 and PKINIT from IETF Common Authentication Technology (CAT) working group

◆ **PC/SC**—Personal computer/smart card specifications

These features do not work with third-party PKIs:

◆ Auto enrollment and renewal of machine certificates is not supported.

◆ Windows 2000 PKI management tools are not supported.

◆ Applications that do not use CryptoAPI cannot use roaming profiles to store user certificates.

◆ If the third-party PKI replaces the Windows 2000 GINA, support for smart card logon is removed.

◆ The smart card logon certificate must be issued by a Windows 2000 Enterprise CA published in Active Directory for the domain. (Thus, a foreign CA can't use a name-spoof attack and gain entry into your network.)

◆ The issuing CA for smart card logon must be Windows 2000, but the parent or root CA can be a third-party CA.

◆ EFS automatic enrollment is not supported.

Certificate chain building for Windows 2000 chain building is a bottom-up process. The steps followed are listed here:

1. The trusted certificate chain delivered with the certificate is examined for possible links to the trusted CA.

2. If the path is not complete, the Authority Key Identifier (AKI) field on the certificate is used to find the parent certificate(s) on the local computer.

3. If the path is not complete, the Authority Info Access (AIA) field in the certificate is checked for location information to obtain parent certificates from the location specified.

4. If the path is not complete, the issuer name information in a certificate is used to find a parent certificate.

NETWORK SERVICES SECURITY

To secure networks, you must be aware of the network services in place on your network and what can be done to secure them. Network services to secure in Windows 2000 include DNS and its dynamic updating by DNCP, RIS, SNMP, and Terminal Services.

DNS

Securing DNS involves an understanding of zone types and a discussion of dynamic updating of DNS by DHCP.

DNS zones are listed here:

◆ **Standard primary**—A read/write zone file. Changes to records are recorded in this standard text file.

◆ **Standard secondary**—A read-only zone file. Changes recorded to the primary are replicated to secondary. Secondary zone files are used to distribute the workload across computers and to provide backup.

◆ **Active Directory-integrated**—New in Windows 2000. This zone file exists only in Active Directory, not in a text file. Updates occur during Active Directory replication.

By default, the DHCP server registers and updates Windows 2000 clients with DNS based on the request made by the DHCP client. Other options for DHCP are these:

◆ For Windows 2000 clients:

  • **ALWAYS**—DHCP always registers and updates the client information, both the A and the PTR resource records. DHCP examines the FQDN option of the DHCPRE-QUEST message to get the client name and IP address, and uses this information to update the DNS server.

  • **NEVER**—DHCP will never update the record.

◆ Windows NT and 9X computers cannot request DHCP registration or dynamically update DNS on their own. DHCP can be configured to update both records.

DNS updates occur as follows:

◆ Every 24 hours

◆ If the TCP/IP changes

◆ If the DHCP address is renewed or a new lease is obtained

◆ If a plug-and-play event occurs

◆ If an IP address is added or removed from computer for static adapter, with no restart needed

◆ If the user types `IPCONFIG/registerdns` at the command prompt

Advantages of Active Directory Integrated zones include these:

◆ Protection for the DNS server from unauthorized updating by configuring secure dynamic updates

◆ No single point of failure

◆ Fault tolerances; all records are replicated in Active Directory

◆ Single replication topology, with no separate zone transfer—all is done in Active Directory replication

◆ Secure dynamic updates; permissions can be set on zones and records within those zones

The algorithm used by Windows 2000 is defined in the Internet draft "GSS Algorithm for TSIG (GSS-TSIG)," which uses Kerberos version 5 as the underlying security. Resource records used are listed here:

◆ **TKEY**—Transfers security tokens from client to server and server to client, and establishes secret keys

◆ **TSIG**—Send and verifies digitally signed messages

The secure update process is composed of the following steps:

1. The client queries the local name server to find the authoritative server for the name to update.

2. An insecure update is attempted.

3. The insecure update is refused.

4. TKEY negotiation occurs. (What security do client and server both use?)

5. TKEY tells the client to use Kerberos.

6. Mutual authentication takes place.

7. Security context is established, including the TSIG key.

8. The client attempts to update with TSIG.

9. The server uses security context and TSIG to verify the update.

10. The server attempts to add, delete, or modify the resource record in Active Directory if the client has the proper permissions.

11. A reply from the server to the client indicates success or failure.

RIS

To utilize RIS, you must have the following:

◆ RIS installed on a Windows 2000 Server.

◆ A DNS server present on the network that supports service records SRV RR (RFC 2052) and the dynamic update protocol (RFC 2136).

◆ A DHCP server present on the network. Remote boot clients will obtain an IP address from the DHCP server.

◆ Access to Active Directory (membership in an Active Directory domain). RIS uses Active Directory to locate clients and other RIS servers.

◆ Client machines that meet hardware requirements.

RIS clients hardware requirements are as follows:

◆ P-166 or better Net PC PXE-based, remote boot-enabled

◆ 32MB RAM

◆ 800MB or larger disk drive

◆ DHCP PXE-based boot ROM version l99c or later, or network adapter supported by RIS boot floppy disk

To restrict which computers can update or install the OS, you configure the RIS administrative option: Do not respond to unknown client computers. When this is checked, only computers that exist in or that have been prestaged (that have a computer account created in Active Directory) can access the RIS server. The RIS server checks Active Directory to verify that a computer account exists.

To prestage computer accounts, you create them in Active Directory in the normal manner, or you create the computer account using the computer GUID. The GUID is in the system BIOS of the computer; you may find it also listed on the outside of the computer case.

SNMP

SNMP is a management system that can request information and make configuration requests such as the following:

◆ Protocol ID and stats

◆ Hardware/software configuration

◆ Device performance stats

◆ Device errors

◆ Other statistics

SNMP messages are listed as follows:

◆ **GET**—Report information.

◆ **GET-NEXT**—Browse the hierarchy of objects.

◆ **SET**—Configure.

◆ **GET-BULK**—Get as much information as possible so that I don't have to keep asking.

◆ **NOTIFY**—Trap message.

Configuring security for SNMP may include any of the following:

◆ Configure traps to do security checking.

◆ Join hosts and agents to SNMP communities, and use these to authenticate SNMP messages.

◆ Secure SNMP messages with IP security.

SNMP community traps are listed as follows:

◆ None or Notify causes the agent to discard requests and send an authentication trap.

◆ Read Only does not allow the processing of SET requests. The requests are discarded, and a trap is entreated.

◆ Read Create and Read Write allows processing of all requests, including SET.

Other options include setting which hosts' packets will be accepted from the following:

◆ **Accept SNMP packets from any host**—This is the default.

◆ **Accept SNMP packets from these hosts**—A list of acceptable hosts represents acceptable management systems.

Terminal Services

To secure terminal services, you should do the following:

◆ Not require smart cards. Smart cards cannot be used for Windows 2000 Terminal Services authentication.

◆ Disable FTP service to prevent access to the file system.

◆ Terminal services can be accessed using L2TP or PPTP over the Internet.

◆ Remove OS/2 and POSIX subsystems.

PROVIDING SECURE ACCESS BETWEEN NETWORKS

Securing access between networks is accomplished by understanding the ways in which networks connect, and then implementing checks and balances to control these access points.

The paths into your network that use Routing and Remote Access Services include demand-dial routing, remote access (dial-up), and virtual private networks. These services can be protected by using the authentication methods outlined in Table 17.

SUMMARY TABLE 17
REMOTE ACCESS AUTHENTICATION METHODS

Protocol	Notes
Extensible Authentication (EAP)	May include smart card, MD5-Challenge, TLS, or RADIUS.
Microsoft Encrypted Authentication Version 2 (MS-CHAP v2)	Mutual authentication is required. Separate keys are used for transmitted and received date.
Microsoft Encrypted Authentication (MS-CHAP)	Remote access server requires only MD4 hash of the password to validate.
Encrypted Authentication (CHAP)	Password is never sent over the link. MD5 is used for challenge hash.
Shiva Password Authentication Protocol (SPAP)	Used by remote access client to authenticate itself to a Shiva remote access server. More secure than PAP, but less than CHAP or MS-CHAP.
Unencrypted Password (PAP)	Plain-text authentication.
Unauthenticated access	No authentication required.

In addition, when implementing a VPN tunnel, you have the encryption choices in Table 18.

SUMMARY TABLE 18
REMOTE ACCESS PROFILE ENCRYPTION CHOICES

Connection	Basic	Strong	Strongest
Dial-up and PPTP	MPPE/40-bit	MPPE/56-bit	MPPE/128-bit
L2TP over IPSec	56-bit DES	56-bit DES	3DES

Demand-Dial Connections

Demand-dial connections are implemented using one way or two-way connections. Table 19 and Table 20 identify these possibilities.

SUMMARY TABLE 19
ONE-WAY INITIATED CONNECTION CONFIGURATION

Router	Name of Local Interface	Dial-In User Account	Name of Remote Router Interface	Dial-Out User Account
Head-quarters	NewYork	NewYork		
New York Branch Office	HeadQTRS		NewYork	NewYork

SUMMARY TABLE 20
TWO-WAY INITIATED CONNECTION CONFIGURATION

Router	Interface	Dial-In User Account	Remote Router Interface	Dial-Out User Account
Head-quarters	NewYork	NewYork	HeadQTRS	HeadQTRS
New York Branch Office	HeadQTRS	HeadQTRS	NewYork	NewYork

Routing and Remote Access Servers Authentication

Routing and Remote Access Servers can choose an authentication provider, either Windows Integrated or RADIUS. If they choose Windows Integrated, additional policies for authorization are configured on the RRAS server. If RADIUS is selected, centralized policies are configured on the IAS server. IAS authentication still involves the lookup of a user account within Active Directory.

Virtual Private Networks

Virtual Private Networks (VPN) are configured through RRAS. Two possibilities exist: PPTP, or L2TP over IPSec.

Four encapsulation processes are used by PPTP:

1. The data payload is encrypted and encapsulated with a PPP header.

2. The PPP frame is encapsulated with a modified GRE header.

3. The GRE–PPP-encapsulated payload is encapsulated with an IP header that includes source and destination addresses of the PPTP client and PPTP server.

4. The IP datagram is encapsulated with a header and a trailer for the data link-layer technology of the physical interface.

L2TP encapsulation has five parts:

1. PPP payload is encapsulated with a PPP header and an L2TP header.

2. The L2TP-encapsulated packet is encapsulated with a UDP header, with source and destination ports set to 1701.

3. Depending on policy, UDP message is encrypted and encapsulated with an IPSec Encapsulation Security Payload (ESP) header and trailer, and an IPSec Authentication (AH) trailer (see Chapter 15, "Designing Security for Communication Channels").

4. The IPSec-encapsulated packet is encapsulated with an IP header containing the source and destination IP address of the VPN client and VPN server.

5. The IP datagram is encapsulated with the header and trailer for the data-link physical interface.

L2TP over IPSec is also defined by the following:

◆ Authentication with IPSec over L2TP is two–fold: Both computer and user authentication is performed.

◆ Encryption is provided by IPSec. Both DES with a 56-bit key and Triple DES (3DES) are available. New DES encryption keys are generated after every five minutes or 250MB of data transferred. New 3DES keys are generated every hour or every 2GB of data transferred. AH connections use new hash keys after every hour or 2GB of data transferred.

◆ Data authentication and integrity uses either Hash Message Authentication Code (HMAC) Message Digest 5 (MD5), which produces a 128-bit hash of the payload, or by the HMAC Secure Hash Algorithm (SHA), which produces a 160-bit hash.

◆ Packet filtering can be configured to make sure that the VPN server performs routing only between the VPN clients and the intranet, not between others.

DESIGNING SECURITY FOR COMMUNICATION CHANNELS

Securing resources at the client and server level is not enough. Communications must also be secured. Every communication will not require the same level of attention, so you need to refer to your list of analyzed risks and considerations on especially sensitive servers. If on all computers, client and server are grouped into security levels, you then can determine the policies you want to set for communications between them.

Two methods are available to help you across the LAN and the WAN, and also when communications take you to and across public networks. These methods are SMB signing and IPSec. SMB signing refers to the digital signing of each packet in a server message block communication between two computers. SMB signing can be used to help protect network communications with downlevel clients. IPSec, or IP Security, is a protocol that can be used to provide integrity, confidentiality, and authentication of network communications. IPSec can be used to protect communications between Windows 2000 computers.

Both of these methods can be enabled and enforced by using Group Policy.

SMB Signing

SMB signing can be configured for Windows 9x, Windows NT 4.0, and Windows 2000. SMB signing for downlevel clients is configured through their registries. SMB signing for Windows 2000 is done using Group Policy.

To secure downlevel clients and servers, registry settings are used. To enable SMB message signing on the server:

Add the value EnableSecuritySignature to the key:

HKEY_LOCAL_MACHINE\SYSTEM\
CurrentControlSet\Services\LanManServer\Parameters

The value should have data of type REG_DWORD. A value of 0 disables SMB signing; a value of 1 enables it.

To require message signing:

Add the value RequireSecuritySignature, type REG_DWORD, with a value of 1. As with SMB enable, a value of 0 will disable the requirement.

Settings are made on the workstation at:

HKLM\SYSTEM\CurrentControlSet\Services\
RDr\Parameters

Windows 98 also includes the updated version of the SMB protocol. Make changes to the registry key:

HKLM\system\CurrentControlSet\Services\
VxD\Vnetsup

In all cases, you should close the Registry Editor and reboot the systems.

In all cases for Windows NT and for Windows 98, make sure to include both keys if requiring signing. If you require but do not enable, then no client will be capable of connecting to the server.

SMB message signing on Windows 2000 is enabled or disabled in Group Policy. The following security settings can be set:

◆ Digitally Sign Server Communications (Always)

◆ Digitally Sign Client Communications (When Possible)

◆ Digitally Sign Client Communications (Always)

If you modify security options to require SMB signing, make sure that you also enable them.

IPSec

IPSec can be used for encryption of a L2TP VPN. IPSec also can be used without L2TP to provide the following:

◆ **Access control**—Connection negotiation and filtering of inward-bound communications occur.

◆ **Integrity**—Checksums and message digest algorithms are used to allow detection of tampered packets.

◆ **Data origin authentication**—Assurance of the source takes place.

◆ **Outward-bound protocol filtering**—Data is managed before it leaves the system.

The IPSec architecture consists of the following components:

◆ Key management via Internet Key Exchange (IKE), formerly referred to as ISAKMP/Oakley

◆ A security policy database that defines the rules for the disposition of all traffic, inbound or outbound

◆ The Authentication Header (AH) protocol, which provides integrity and data origin authentication

◆ The encapsulating security payload (ESP), which provides packet encryption, integrity, and data origin authentication

◆ Native IP stack implementation

When configuring IPSec policy, you have a number of options to consider. Table 21 lists and explains these options.

SUMMARY TABLE 21
IPSec POLICY PARAMETERS

TAB/Item	*Description*
General	
Check for policy changes every *number* minute(s)	How often will policy agent check Group Policy for updates?
Advanced	
Master Key Perfect Forward Secrecy	If selected, the failure of Phase II negotiations will require a new negotiation of Phase I authentication.
Authenticate and generate a new key after every *number* minutes	How often should a new key be generated?
Authenticate and generate a new key every session(s)	How often should a new key be generated?
Protect identities with these security methods	Security methods include: DES or 3DES for encryption, and SHA1 or MD5 for integrity. All four possibilities are defined by default. Diffie-Hellman base encryption material (key size) is also determined here. Both 3DES choices use medium; both DES choices use low. This and the order of processing can be changed. These methods will be attempted during negotiation to determine which one the client and server will be capable of using.
Rules tab	Create rules for policy. Rules are security actions that apply to particular computers. Policies can have multiple rules. If you elected to add the default rule, you can modify it here.

Two phases exist to IPSec negotiation, Phase I and Phase II.

The first phase includes the negotiation of the following:

◆ The encryption algorithm

◆ The hash algorithm

◆ The authentication method

◆ Diffie-Hellman (DH) group to be used for base keying (Group 1: 768 bits; Group 2: 1024 bits)

◆ Identification of the SA(s) to be used

The second phase is used to negotiate the SAs:

1. Policy negotiation or choice of AH or ESP, hash algorithms, and encryption algorithms

2. Frequency of session key material refresh/exchange

3. SAs, SPI, and generated keys given to the IPSec driver

IPSec policies can be of many types:

◆ **Pass-through policy**—IPSec ignores the traffic.

◆ **Blocking policy**—This traffic will not be accepted or allowed to pass.

◆ **Permit policy**—No traffic is allowed unless a filter for it is defined.

◆ The policy is negotiated with other IPSec-enabled computers, but it allows communication with non-IPSec-enabled computers.

Authentication methods are these:

◆ Kerberos v5, the default authentication protocol in Windows 2000

◆ Public key certificates

◆ Pre-shared keys

Predefined IPSec policies are defined but must be assigned to be used. These policies are listed here:

◆ **Client (Respond Only)**—Doesn't secure communications most of the time. Can respond to requests for secure communications by using default response rule. Only requested port and protocol traffic is secured.

◆ **Server (Request Security)**—Secures communication most of the time. Allows unsecured communication from non-IPSec-enabled computers.

◆ **Secure Server (Require Security)**—Requires IPSec at all times.

The specific port and protocols IDs used by IPSec are listed here:

◆ IP Protocol 51 (IPSec AH)

◆ IP Protocol 50 (IPSec ESP)

◆ UDP port 500 (IKE)

This element of the book provides you with some general guidelines for preparing for a certification exam. It is organized into four sections. The first section addresses your learning style and how it affects your preparation for the exam. The second section covers your exam preparation activities and general study tips. This is followed by an extended look at the Microsoft Certification exams, including a number of specific tips that apply to the various Microsoft exam formats and question types. Finally, changes in Microsoft's testing policies, and how these might affect you, are discussed.

LEARNING STYLES

To better understand the nature of preparation for the test, it is important to understand learning as a process. You probably are aware of how you best learn new material. You may find that outlining works best for you, or, as a visual learner, you may need to "see" things. Whatever your learning style, test preparation takes place over time. Obviously, you shouldn't start studying for these exams the night before you take them; it is very important to understand that learning is a developmental process. Understanding it as a process helps you focus on what you know and what you have yet to learn.

Thinking about how you learn should help you recognize that learning takes place when you are able to match new information to old. You have some previous experience with computers and networking. Now you are preparing for this certification exam. Using this book, software, and supplementary materials will not just add incrementally to what you know; as you study, the organization of your knowledge actually restructures as you integrate new information into your existing knowledge base. This will lead you to a more comprehensive understanding of the tasks and concepts

Study and Exam Prep Tips

outlined in the objectives and of computing in general. Again, this happens as a result of a repetitive process rather than a singular event. Keep this model of learning in mind as you prepare for the exam, and you will make better decisions concerning what to study and how much more studying you need to do.

STUDY TIPS

There are many ways to approach studying just as there are many different types of material to study. However, the tips that follow should work well for the type of material covered on the certification exams.

Study Strategies

Although individuals vary in the ways they learn information, some basic principles of learning apply to everyone. You should adopt some study strategies that take advantage of these principles. One of these principles is that learning can be broken into various depths. Recognition (of terms, for example) exemplifies a more surface level of learning in which you rely on a prompt of some sort to elicit recall. Comprehension or understanding (of the concepts behind the terms, for example) represents a deeper level of learning. The ability to analyze a concept and apply your understanding of it in a new way represents a further depth of learning.

Your learning strategy should enable you to know the material at a level or two deeper than mere recognition. This will help you perform well on the exams. You will know the material so thoroughly that you can easily handle the recognition-level types of questions used in multiple-choice testing. You will also be able to apply your knowledge to solve new problems.

Macro and Micro Study Strategies

One strategy that can lead to this deeper learning includes preparing an outline that covers all the objectives and subobjectives for the particular exam you are working on. You should delve a bit further into the material and include a level or two of detail beyond the stated objectives and subobjectives for the exam. Then expand the outline by coming up with a statement of definition or a summary for each point in the outline.

An outline provides two approaches to studying. First, you can study the outline by focusing on the organization of the material. Work your way through the points and sub-points of your outline with the goal of learning how they relate to one another. For example, be sure you understand how each of the main objective areas is similar to and different from another. Then, do the same thing with the subobjectives; be sure you know which subobjectives pertain to each objective area and how they relate to one another.

Next, you can work through the outline, focusing on learning the details. Memorize and understand terms and their definitions, facts, rules and strategies, advantages and disadvantages, and so on. In this pass through the outline, attempt to learn detail rather than the big picture (the organizational information that you worked on in the first pass through the outline).

Research has shown that attempting to assimilate both types of information at the same time seems to interfere with the overall learning process. Separate your studying into these two approaches, and you will perform better on the exam.

Active Study Strategies

The process of writing down and defining objectives, subobjectives, terms, facts, and definitions promotes a more active learning strategy than merely reading the material. In human information-processing terms, writing forces you to engage in more active encoding of the information. Simply reading over it exemplifies more passive processing.

Next, determine whether you can apply the information you have learned by attempting to create examples and scenarios on your own. Think about how or where you could apply the concepts you are learning. Again, write down this information to process the facts and concepts in a more active fashion.

The hands-on nature of the step-by-step tutorials and exercises at the ends of the chapters provide further active learning opportunities that will reinforce concepts as well.

Common-Sense Strategies

Finally, you should also follow common-sense practices when studying. Study when you are alert, reduce or eliminate distractions, and take breaks when you become fatigued.

Pre-Testing Yourself

Pre-testing allows you to assess how well you are learning. One of the most important aspects of learning is what has been called "meta-learning." Meta-learning has to do with realizing when you know something well or when you need to study some more. In other words, you recognize how well or how poorly you have learned the material you are studying.

For most people, this can be difficult to assess objectively on their own. Practice tests are useful in that they reveal more objectively what you have learned and what you have not learned. You should use this information to guide review and further studying. Developmental learning takes place as you cycle through studying, assessing how well you have learned,

then reviewing, and then assessing again until you feel you are ready to take the exam.

You may have noticed the Practice Exam included in this book. Use it as part of the learning process. The *ExamGear, Training Guide Edition* test simulation software included on the CD also provides you with an excellent opportunity to assess your knowledge.

You should set a goal for your pre-testing. A reasonable goal would be to score consistently in the 90-percent range.

See Appendix D, "Using the ExamGear, Training Guide Edition Software," for more explanation of the test simulation software.

EXAM PREP TIPS

Having mastered the subject matter, the final preparatory step is to understand how the exam will be presented. Make no mistake: A Microsoft Certified Professional (MCP) exam will challenge both your knowledge and your test-taking skills. This section starts with the basics of exam design, reviews a new type of exam format, and concludes with hints targeted to each of the exam formats.

The MCP Exam

Every MCP exam is released in one of three basic formats. What's being called exam format here is really little more than a combination of the overall exam structure and the presentation method for exam questions.

Understanding the exam formats is key to good preparation because the format determines the number of questions presented, the difficulty of those questions, and the amount of time allowed to complete the exam.

Each exam format uses many of the same types of questions. These types or styles of questions include several types of traditional multiple-choice questions, multiple-rating (or scenario-based) questions, and simulation-based questions. Some exams include other types of questions that ask you to drag and drop objects on the screen, reorder a list, or categorize things. Still other exams ask you to answer these types of questions in response to a case study you have read. It's important that you understand the types of questions you will be asked and the actions required to properly answer them.

The rest of this section addresses the exam formats and then tackles the question types. Understanding the formats and question types will help you feel much more comfortable when you take the exam.

Exam Format

As mentioned above, there are three basic formats for the MCP exams: the traditional fixed-form exam, the adaptive form, and the case study form. As its name implies, the fixed-form exam presents a fixed set of questions during the exam session. The adaptive form, however, uses only a subset of questions drawn from a larger pool during any given exam session. The case study form includes case studies that serve as the basis for answering the various types of questions.

Fixed-Form

A fixed-form computerized exam is based on a fixed set of exam questions. The individual questions are presented in random order during a test session. If you take the same exam more than once, you won't necessarily see the exact same questions. This is because two or three final forms are typically assembled for every fixed-form exam Microsoft releases. These are usually labeled Forms A, B, and C.

The final forms of a fixed-form exam are identical in terms of content coverage, number of questions, and allotted time, but the questions are different. You may notice, however, that some of the same questions appear on, or rather are shared among, different final forms. When questions are shared among multiple final forms of an exam, the percentage of sharing is generally small. Many final forms share no questions, but some older exams may have a 10–15 percent duplication of exam questions on the final exam forms.

Fixed-form exams also have a fixed time limit in which you must complete the exam. The *ExamGear, Training Guide Edition* software on the CD-ROM that accompanies this book provides fixed-form exams.

Finally, the score you achieve on a fixed-form exam, which is always reported for MCP exams on a scale of 0 to 1,000, is based on the number of questions you answer correctly. The passing score is the same for all final forms of a given fixed-form exam.

The typical format for the fixed-form exam is as follows:

◆ 50–60 questions.

◆ 75–90 minute testing time.

◆ Question review is allowed, including the opportunity to change your answers.

Adaptive Form

An adaptive-form exam has the same appearance as a fixed-form exam, but its questions differ in quantity and process of selection. Although the statistics of adaptive testing are fairly complex, the process is concerned with determining your level of skill or ability with the exam subject matter. This ability assessment begins with the presentation of questions of varying levels of difficulty and ascertaining at what difficulty level you can reliably answer them. Finally, the ability assessment determines whether that ability level is above or below the level required to pass that exam.

Examinees at different levels of ability will see quite different sets of questions. Examinees who demonstrate little expertise with the subject matter will continue to be presented with relatively easy questions. Examinees who demonstrate a high level of expertise will be presented progressively more difficult questions. Individuals of both levels of expertise may answer the same number of questions correctly, but because the higher-expertise examinee can correctly answer more difficult questions, he or she will receive a higher score and is more likely to pass the exam.

The typical design for the adaptive form exam is as follows:

◆ 20–25 questions.

◆ 90 minute testing time (although this is likely to be reduced to 45–60 minutes in the near future).

◆ Question review is not allowed, providing no opportunity for you to change your answers.

The Adaptive-Exam Process

Your first adaptive exam will be unlike any other testing experience you have had. In fact, many examinees have difficulty accepting the adaptive testing process because they feel that they were not provided the opportunity to adequately demonstrate their full expertise.

You can take consolation in the fact that adaptive exams are painstakingly put together after months of data gathering and analysis and that adaptive exams are just as valid as fixed-form exams. The rigor introduced through the adaptive testing methodology means that there is nothing arbitrary about the exam items you'll see. It is also a more efficient means of testing, requiring less time to conduct and complete than traditional fixed-form exams.

As you can see in Figure 1, a number of statistical measures drive the adaptive examination process. The measure most immediately relevant to you is the ability estimate. Accompanying this test statistic are the standard error of measurement, the item characteristic curve, and the test information curve.

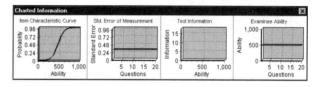

FIGURE 1
Microsoft's adaptive testing demonstration program.

The standard error, which is the key factor in determining when an adaptive exam will terminate, reflects the degree of error in the exam ability estimate. The item characteristic curve reflects the probability of a correct response relative to examinee ability. Finally, the test information statistic provides a measure of the information contained in the set of questions the examinee has answered, again relative to the ability level of the individual examinee.

When you begin an adaptive exam, the standard error has already been assigned a target value below which it must drop for the exam to conclude. This target value reflects a particular level of statistical confidence in the process. The examinee ability is initially set to the mean possible exam score (500 for MCP exams).

As the adaptive exam progresses, questions of varying difficulty are presented. Based on your pattern of responses to these questions, the ability estimate is recalculated. At the same time, the standard error estimate is refined from its first estimated value of one toward the target value. When the standard error reaches its target value, the exam is terminated. Thus, the more consistently you answer questions of the same degree of difficulty, the more quickly the standard error estimate drops, and the fewer questions you will end up seeing during the exam session. This situation is depicted in Figure 2.

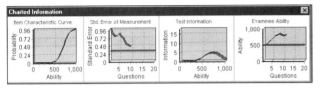

FIGURE 2
The changing statistics in an adaptive exam.

As you might suspect, one good piece of advice for taking an adaptive exam is to treat every exam question as if it were the most important. The adaptive scoring algorithm attempts to discover a pattern of responses that reflects some level of proficiency with the subject matter. Incorrect responses almost guarantee that additional questions must be answered (unless, of course, you get every question wrong). This is because the scoring algorithm must adjust to information that is not consistent with the emerging pattern.

Case Study Form

The case study-based format first appeared with the advent of the 70-100 exam (Solution Architectures). The questions in the case study format are not the independent entities that they are in the fixed and adaptive formats. Instead, questions are tied to a case study, a long scenario-like description of an information technology situation. As the test taker, your job is to extract from the case study the information that needs to be integrated with your understanding of Microsoft technology. The idea is that a case study will provide you with a situation that is more like a "real life" problem situation than the other formats provide.

The case studies are presented as "testlets." These are sections within the exam in which you read the case study, then answer 10 to 15 questions that apply to the case study. When you finish that section, you move onto another testlet with another case study and its associated questions. There may be as many as five of these testlets that compose the overall exam. You will be given more time to complete such an exam because it takes time to read through the cases and analyze them. You may have as much as three hours to complete the exam—and you may need all of it. The case studies are always available through a linking button while you are in a testlet. However, once you leave a testlet, you cannot come back to it.

Figure 3 provides an illustration of part of a case study.

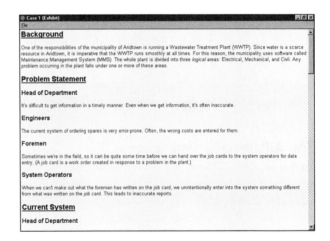

FIGURE 3
An example of a case study

Question Types

A variety of question types can appear on MCP exams. Examples of many of the various types appear in this book and the *ExamGear, Training Guide Edition* software. We have attempted to cover all the types that were available at the time of this writing. Most of the question types discussed in the following sections can appear in each of the three exam formats.

The typical MCP exam question is based on the idea of measuring skills or the ability to complete tasks. Therefore, most of the questions are written so as to present you with a situation that includes a role (such as a system administrator or technician), a technology environment (100 computers running Windows 98 on a Windows 2000 Server network), and a problem to be solved (the user can connect to services on the LAN, but not the intranet). The answers indicate actions that you might take to solve the problem or create setups or environments that would function correctly from the start. Keep this in mind as you read the questions on the exam. You may encounter some questions that just call for you to regurgitate facts, but these will be relatively few and far between.

In the following sections we will look at the different question types.

Multiple-Choice Questions

Despite the variety of question types that now appear in various MCP exams, the multiple-choice question is still the basic building block of the exams. The multiple-choice question comes in three varieties:

◆ **Regular multiple-choice.** Also referred to as an alphabetic question, it asks you to choose one answer as correct.

◆ **Multiple-answer multiple-choice.** Also referred to as a multi-alphabetic question, this version of a multiple-choice question requires you to choose two or more answers as correct. Typically, you are told precisely the number of correct answers to choose.

◆ **Enhanced multiple-choice.** This is simply a regular or multiple-answer question that includes a graphic or table to which you must refer to answer the question correctly.

Examples of such questions appear at the end of each chapter.

Multiple-Rating Questions

These questions are often referred to as scenario questions. Similar to multiple-choice questions, they offer more extended descriptions of the computing environment and a problem that needs to be solved. Required and desired optional results of the problem-solving are specified, as well as a solution. You are then asked to judge whether the actions taken in the solution are likely to bring about all or part of the required and desired optional results. There is, typically, only one correct answer.

You may be asking yourself, "What is multiple about multiple-rating questions?" The answer is that rather than having multiple answers, the question itself may be repeated in the exam with only minor variations in the required results, optional results, or solution introduced to create "new" questions. Read these different versions very carefully; the differences can be subtle.

Examples of these types of questions appear at the end of the chapters.

Simulation Questions

Simulation-based questions reproduce the look and feel of key Microsoft product features for the purpose of testing. The simulation software used in MCP exams has been designed to look and act, as much as possible, just like the actual product. Consequently, answering simulation questions in an MCP exam entails completing one or more tasks just as if you were using the product itself.

The format of a typical Microsoft simulation question consists of a brief scenario or problem statement, along with one or more tasks that you must complete to solve the problem. An example of a simulation question for MCP exams is shown in the following section.

A Typical Simulation Question

It sounds obvious, but your first step when you encounter a simulation question is to carefully read the question (see Figure 4). Do not go straight to the simulation application! You must assess the problem that's presented and identify the conditions that make up the problem scenario. Note the tasks that must be performed or outcomes that must be achieved to answer the question, and then review any instructions you're given on how to proceed.

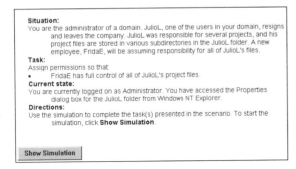

FIGURE 4
A typical MCP exam simulation question with directions.

The next step is to launch the simulator by using the button provided. After clicking the Show Simulation button, you will see a feature of the product, as shown in the dialog box in Figure 5. The simulation application will partially obscure the question text on many test center machines. Feel free to reposition the simulator and to move between the question text screen and

the simulator by using hotkeys or point-and-click navigation, or even by clicking the simulator's launch button again.

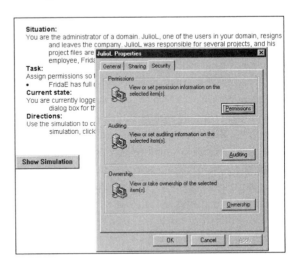

FIGURE 5
Launching the simulation application.

It is important for you to understand that your answer to the simulation question will not be recorded until you move on to the next exam question. This gives you the added capability of closing and reopening the simulation application (using the launch button) on the same question without losing any partial answer you may have made.

The third step is to use the simulator as you would the actual product to solve the problem or perform the defined tasks. Again, the simulation software is designed to function—within reason—just as the product does. But don't expect the simulator to reproduce product behavior perfectly. Most importantly, do not allow yourself to become flustered if the simulator does not look or act exactly like the product.

Figure 6 shows the solution to the example simulation problem.

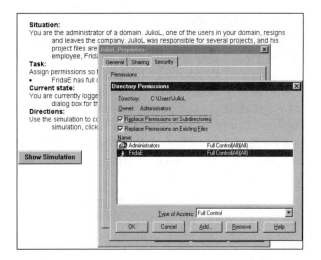

FIGURE 6
The solution to the simulation example.

Two final points will help you tackle simulation questions. First, respond only to what is being asked in the question; do not solve problems that you are not asked to solve. Second, accept what is being asked of you. You may not entirely agree with conditions in the problem statement, the quality of the desired solution, or the sufficiency of defined tasks to adequately solve the problem. Always remember that you are being tested on your ability to solve the problem as it is presented.

The solution to the simulation problem shown in Figure 6 perfectly illustrates both of those points. As you'll recall from the question scenario (refer to Figure 4), you were asked to assign appropriate permissions to a new user, Frida E. You were not instructed to make any other changes in permissions. Thus, if you were to modify or remove the administrator's permissions, this item would be scored wrong on an MCP exam.

Hot Area Question

Hot area questions call for you to click on a graphic or diagram in order to complete some task. You are asked a question that is similar to any other, but rather than clicking an option button or check box next to an answer, you click the relevant item in a screen shot or on a part of a diagram. An example of such an item is shown in Figure 7.

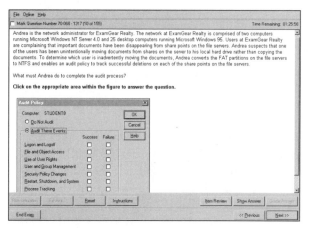

FIGURE 7
A typical hot area question.

Drag and Drop Style Questions

Microsoft has utilized two different types of drag and drop questions in exams. The first is a Select and Place question. The other is a Drop and Connect question. Both are covered in the following sections.

Select and Place

Select and Place questions typically require you to drag and drop labels on images in a diagram so as to correctly label or identify some portion of a network. Figure 8 shows you the actual question portion of a Select and Place item.

FIGURE 8
A Select and Place question.

Figure 9 shows the window you would see after you chose Select and Place. It contains the actual diagram in which you would select and drag the various server roles and match them with the appropriate computers.

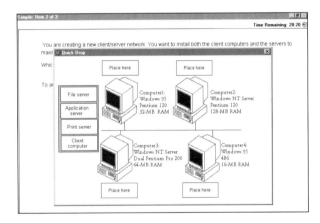

FIGURE 9
The window containing the diagram.

Drop and Connect

Drop and Connect questions provide a different spin on the drag and drop question. The question provides you with the opportunity to create boxes that you can label, as well as connectors of various types with which to link them. In essence, you are creating a model or diagram in order to answer the question. You might have to create a network diagram or a data model for a database system. Figure 10 illustrates the idea of a Drop and Connect question.

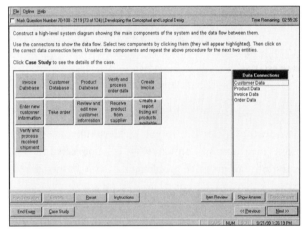

FIGURE 10
A Drop and Connect question.

Ordered List Questions

Ordered list questions simply require you to consider a list of items and place them in the proper order. You select items and then use a button to add them to a new list in the correct order. You have another button that you can use to remove the items in the new list in case you change your mind and want to reorder things. Figure 11 shows an ordered list item.

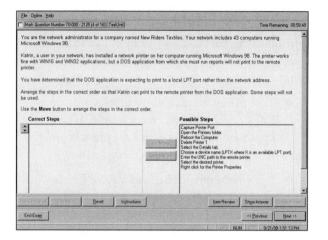

FIGURE 11
An ordered list question.

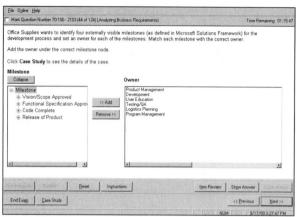

FIGURE 12
A tree question.

Tree Questions

Tree questions require you to think hierarchically and categorically. You are asked to place items from a list into categories that are displayed as nodes in a tree structure. Such questions might ask you to identify parent-child relationships in processes or the structure of keys in a database. You might also be required to show order within the categories, much as you would in an ordered list question. Figure 12 shows a typical tree question.

As you can see, Microsoft is making an effort to utilize question types that go beyond asking you to simply memorize facts. These question types force you to know how to accomplish tasks and understand concepts and relationships. Study so that you can answer these types of questions rather than those that simply ask you to recall facts.

Putting It All Together

Given all these different pieces of information, the task now is to assemble a set of tips that will help you successfully tackle the different types of MCP exams.

More Exam Preparation Tips

Generic exam-preparation advice is always useful. Tips include the following:

◆ Become familiar with the product. Hands-on experience is one of the keys to success on any MCP exam. Review the exercises and the Step by Steps in the book.

◆ Review the current exam-preparation guide on the Microsoft MCP Web site (www.microsoft.com/mcp/examinfo/exams.htm). The documentation Microsoft makes available over the Web identifies the skills every exam is intended to test.

◆ Memorize foundational technical detail, but remember that MCP exams are generally heavier on problem solving and application of knowledge than on questions that require only rote memorization.

◆ Take any of the available practice tests. We recommend the one included in this book and the ones you can create using the *ExamGear* software on the CD-ROM. As a supplement to the material bound with this book, try the free practice tests available on the Microsoft MCP Web site.

◆ Look on the Microsoft MCP Web site for samples and demonstration items. These tend to be particularly valuable for one significant reason: They help you become familiar with new testing technologies before you encounter them on MCP exams.

During the Exam Session

The following generic exam-taking advice that you've heard for years also applies when you're taking an MCP exam:

◆ Take a deep breath and try to relax when you first sit down for your exam session. It is very important that you control the pressure you may (naturally) feel when taking exams.

◆ You will be provided scratch paper. Take a moment to write down any factual information and technical detail that you committed to short-term memory.

◆ Carefully read all information and instruction screens. These displays have been put together to give you information relevant to the exam you are taking.

◆ Accept the non-disclosure agreement and preliminary survey as part of the examination process. Complete them accurately and quickly move on.

◆ Read the exam questions carefully. Reread each question to identify all relevant detail.

◆ Tackle the questions in the order in which they are presented. Skipping around won't build your confidence; the clock is always counting down (at least in the fixed form exams).

◆ Don't rush, but also don't linger on difficult questions. The questions vary in degree of difficulty. Don't let yourself be flustered by a particularly difficult or wordy question.

Fixed-Form Exams

Building from this basic preparation and test-taking advice, you also need to consider the challenges presented by the different exam designs. Because a fixed-form exam is composed of a fixed, finite set of questions, add these tips to your strategy for taking a fixed-form exam:

◆ Note the time allotted and the number of questions on the exam you are taking. Make a rough calculation of how many minutes you can spend on each question, and use this figure to pace yourself through the exam.

◆ Take advantage of the fact that you can return to and review skipped or previously answered questions. Record the questions you can't answer confidently on the scratch paper provided, noting the relative difficulty of each question. When you reach the end of the exam, return to the more difficult questions.

◆ If you have session time remaining after you complete all the questions (and if you aren't too fatigued!), review your answers. Pay particular attention to questions that seem to have a lot of detail or that require graphics.

◆ As for changing your answers, the general rule of thumb here is *don't*! If you read the question carefully and completely and you felt like you knew the right answer, you probably did. Don't second-guess yourself. If, as you check your answers, one clearly stands out as incorrect, however, of course you should change it. But if you are at all unsure, go with your first impression.

Adaptive Exams

If you are planning to take an adaptive exam, keep these additional tips in mind:

◆ Read and answer every question with great care. When you're reading a question, identify every relevant detail, requirement, or task you must perform and double-check your answer to be sure you have addressed every one of them.

◆ If you cannot answer a question, use the process of elimination to reduce the set of potential answers, and then take your best guess. Stupid mistakes invariably mean that additional questions will be presented.

◆ You cannot review questions and change answers. When you leave a question, whether you've answered it or not, you cannot return to it. Do not skip any question, either; if you do, it's counted as incorrect.

Case Study Exams

This new exam format calls for unique study and exam-taking strategies. When you take this type of exam, remember that you have more time than in a typical exam. Take your time and read the case study thoroughly. Use the scrap paper or whatever medium is provided to you to take notes, diagram processes, and actively seek out the important information. Work through each testlet as if each were an independent exam. Remember, you cannot go back after you have left a testlet. Refer to the case study as often as you need to, but do not use that as a substitute for reading it carefully initially and for taking notes.

FINAL CONSIDERATIONS

Finally, a number of changes in the MCP program will impact how frequently you can repeat an exam and what you will see when you do.

◆ Microsoft has instituted a new exam retake policy. The new rule is "two and two, then one and two." That is, you can attempt any exam twice with no restrictions on the time between attempts. But after the second attempt, you must wait two weeks before you can attempt that exam again. After that, you will be required to wait two weeks between subsequent attempts. Plan to pass the exam in two attempts or plan to increase your time horizon for receiving the MCP credential.

◆ New questions are being seeded into the MCP exams. After performance data is gathered on new questions, the examiners will replace older questions on all exam forms. This means that the questions appearing on exams will regularly change.

◆ Many of the current MCP exams will be republished in adaptive form. Prepare yourself for this significant change in testing; it is entirely likely that this will become the preferred MCP exam format for most exams. The exception to this may be the case study exams because the adaptive approach may not work with that format.

These changes mean that the brute-force strategies for passing MCP exams may soon completely lose their viability. So if you don't pass an exam on the first or second attempt, it is likely that the exam's form will change significantly by the next time you take it. It could be updated from fixed-form to adaptive, or it could have a different set of questions or question types.

Microsoft's intention is not to make the exams more difficult by introducing unwanted change, but to create and maintain valid measures of the technical skills and knowledge associated with the different MCP credentials. Preparing for an MCP exam has always involved not only studying the subject matter, but also planning for the testing experience itself. With the recent changes, this is now more true than ever.

This exam consists of 64 questions that reflect the material you have covered in the chapters and that are representative of the types that you should expect to see on the actual exam.

The answers to all questions appear in their own section following the exam. It is strongly suggested that when you take this exam, you treat it just as you would the actual exam at the test center. Time yourself, read carefully, and answer all the questions to the best of your ability.

Most of the questions do not simply require you to recall facts, but require deduction on your part to come up with the best answer. Most questions require you to identify the best course of action to take in a given situation. Many of the questions are verbose, requiring you to read them carefully and thoroughly before you attempt to answer them. Run through the exam; for questions you miss, review any material associated with them.

Practice Exam

Exam Questions

1. You have been hired as a consultant to implement security for a Windows 2000 network. Your network consists of 1 domain and 211 Windows 2000 workstations. Of the following, which is the most important in regard to physical security of servers?

   A. The amount of users in the network

   B. The protocols to be used in the network

   C. The amount of bandwidth between network sites

   D. The location of each server

2. You are creating a plan for security for your company, an international manufacturer. Your network consists of 2 domains, 3 member servers, and 876 Windows 2000 workstations. Your supervisor, Nancy, is concerned about the conceptual parts of the company that will be covered by your security plan. Of the following, which business aspects should be included in your security plan? Choose all that apply:

   A. Information flow

   B. Flow chart of the company

   C. Communication flow

   D. Product life cycle

3. Pierre, your supervisor, is unclear on why you need to know so much information about how his company works to set up adequate security measures for your Windows 2000 network. Of the following, which is the most viable answer to Pierre's question?

   A. Security is based on the size of the business.

   B. Security is based on the financial structure of the business.

   C. Security should help, not hinder, the business.

   D. Security should be built around the existing business flow.

4. You are designing Windows 2000 security for a large accounting firm. Currently, the firm consists of 1 Windows NT 4.0 domain with 3 domain controllers, 2 member servers, 456 Microsoft Windows NT workstations, and a few Macintosh clients. While you are interviewing a manager, he informs you that his company will be purchasing several smaller accounting firms in the next year. How does this affect your plan for security? Choose two:

   A. Make considerations for adding additional protocols.

   B. Make considerations for adding additional network cables.

   C. Make considerations for adding additional users.

   D. Make considerations for adding additional operating systems.

5. Arrange the following items in order from a user's first access to the network to accessing a resource on a Windows 2000 server:

   A. Password

   B. DACL

   C. Access token

   D. Username

   E. Security provider

6. You are proposing an intense security plan for an international company's new Windows 2000 network. The company's current network consists of a Microsoft Windows NT 4.0 domain with three domain controllers. All the users currently are using Microsoft Windows 98. The CIO and the

CFO would like to know how the company can become accountable for the security measures proposed in your plan. Of the following, which two are viable solutions for incurring the expense of your plan?

A. Raise fees for clients to generate income to cover the plan.

B. Include security as a budgeted expense.

C. Charge-back each department for the plan.

D. Implement the plan as funds become available.

7. You have been hired as a consultant for an international finance firm to evaluate its security model and to make recommendations for its existing network. The company currently has a Windows 2000 domain, a Microsoft Windows NT 4.0 domain, four NetWare Servers, and a Mac zone. One of the firm's chief concerns is that as it has acquired several other businesses, it also has acquired several network operating systems. The company wants you to propose a secure, affordable plan for sharing information throughout the world with these different operating systems. Which is a viable proposal?

A. Convert the entire network to Windows 2000.

B. Create several smaller networks, and share information via an email server.

C. Create an intranet environment, and share information through Web access.

D. Create a central server to which all users connect. Install SQL Server, and create a central database for sharing information. All data is entered via Access.

8. You are a consultant for an accounting software company. The company would like to implement a very secure Windows 2000 network. You pro-

pose using the C2 guidelines. The CIO is not familiar with C2 attributes. Of the following, which are C2 attributes?

A. Mandatory logon and authentication by a network operating system

B. Discretionary access control to resources

C. Guest account enabled, but with limited access to network resources

D. Accountability and auditing of users' activities and resource access

9. What is authentication?

A. The access of a resource in a Windows 2000 environment

B. The correct combination of a username and a password in a Windows 2000 environment

C. The capability to log on to a Windows 2000 network

D. The capability for a server to communicate with other servers in different domains

10. You are the team leader for the Windows 2000 security team. Your network consists of 1 Windows 2000 domain, 3 member servers, and 876 Windows 2000 workstations in seven different locations throughout North America. You need a way to easily locate resources and security access to them to help plan your security implementation. Of the following, which will help you to develop your plan the most?

A. Network design map

B. Database of IP addresses of all servers

C. List of all resources in the network

D. Names of all shared printers, applications, and data

11. You are the consultant for a small manufacturing company with headquarters in Boston and a plant located in Woburn. The network currently is comprised of a Windows NT 4.0 domain in Boston and a Windows 98 workgroup in the Woburn plant. The owner informs you that he needs a way for the plant in Woburn to supply daily reports to the headquarters in Boston. He stresses that the reports are pretty small, that this must be cost-effective, and above all, that this must be secure. Of the following, which is a good recommendation for this need?

   A. Connect the Boston and Woburn offices with a T1 line.

   B. Connect the Boston and Woburn offices with a VPN.

   C. Have the Woburn office email the report each evening.

   D. Have the Woburn office dial into the Boston office each evening and complete the report through a dial-up connection.

12. You are the team leader for a Windows 2000 security design. You must create a network that is secure and cost-effective. Your company has offices in 25 different cities throughout the Northeast, and each office currently connects to the headquarters in New York. Arrange the following list of possible network design types in order of most expensive to least expensive:

   A. Logical star

   B. Partial mesh

   C. Full mesh

   D. Physical star

13. What is bandwidth?

   A. The number of bits that can be transmitted per second over a network medium

   B. The number of bits that can be transmitted per millisecond over a network medium

   C. The number of megabits that can be transmitted per second over a network medium

   D. The number of megabits that can be transmitted per minute over a network medium

14. You are a consultant for a medium-size manufacturing plant that has 14 sites throughout North America. Each site connects to the headquarters in Atlanta and has access to databases, applications, and resources in each of the other sites. Maria, the CIO of the company, would like to implement IPSec and encryption for each WAN connection. Of the following, which should you examine first before implementing this security?

   A. DHCP-assigned IP addresses versus manual IP addresses

   B. The location of the domain controllers

   C. The types of resources accessed in each site

   D. The available bandwidth of each WAN connection

15. You have been hired by a medium-size financial company to evaluate its network security. The company has just recently upgraded to a Windows 2000 domain, 4 member servers, and 89 Windows 2000 workstations. The CEO is very concerned about the safety and security of the data on the network. Of the following issues, arrange from most to least important issues for any network:

   A. Usernames and passwords

   B. Access to backup media

C. Physical access to servers

D. Permissions to resources

16. You are the network administrator for a Windows 2000 network. Your network consists of 1 Windows 2000 domain, 2 member servers, and 138 Windows 2000 workstations. One of your assistants, Sam, reports to you that he will store a copy of the ERD at his home in case one of the existing disks goes bad. Is this a good idea? Why or why not?

A. This is a good idea because ERDs can go bad.

B. This is a good idea because off-site storage ensures protection against fire or damage to the existing ERD.

C. This is not a good idea because Sam may lose the ERD.

D. This is not a good idea because Sam may use a brute force attack on the ERD to gain the administrator's password.

17. You are the network administrator for a Windows 2000 domain that consists of 3 domain controllers, 2 Windows 2000 Advanced Servers, and 498 Windows 2000 Workstations. You and Sally, an assistant, are configuring various services on your servers. Some services use a local account, while others must have a user account associated with them. Explain to Sally why some services require a user account associated with them:

A. Services that use a user account can be audited.

B. Services that use a user account are using the SID to access resources and do activities.

C. Services that use a user account are local to that machine and cannot be logged on through the logon screen.

D. Services that use a user account are hidden from the LSA so that they can complete the activity required by the service.

18. What is a transitive trust?

A. A transitive trust allows users to log on to any Windows 2000 server.

B. A transitive trust allows users to access resources in remote servers.

C. A transitive trust restricts users from accessing resources in domains other than where your user account is located.

D. A transitive trust is created automatically to all NT servers, regardless of their location.

19. You have been hired as a Windows 2000 security consultant for a large finance company. The network consists of 1 domain, 4 member servers, and 741 Windows 2000 workstations. The company has sites in 23 states. Users from each site access resources in all of the other sites and had no trouble accessing resources under Windows NT 4.0. Mark, the administrator of the network, reports that everything worked great until he upgraded to 2000, and now connections seem to be much slower than before. He shares information about the changes he has made. Of the following changes, which two would have an impact on the slower connection of the sites now?

A. IPSec

B. DHCP server in each location

C. Encryption of data

D. Router IP filtering

20. Maria is network administrator for a medium-size insurance company. She has recently upgraded the company's network to Windows 2000 and is now starting to create a security baseline for each server in the environment. Her boss, the CIO, does not understand why Maria needs a baseline for each server. Of the following, which are valid reasons to create a security baseline for each server? Choose all that apply:

    A. A security baseline will serve as a marker against which to compare future changes.

    B. A security baseline will allow Maria to establish how busy a server is.

    C. A security baseline will allow Maria to expose any weakness on a server.

    D. A security baseline will allow Maria to develop a more comprehensive plan on how to secure current and future servers.

21. You have been hired as a consultant for a medium-size insurance company. The company has installed Windows 2000 Servers on eight computers but is uncertain of some of the terminology encountered. Specifically, Fred is very confused on what a domain controller does under Windows 2000. Of the following, what are attributes of a Windows 2000 domain controller? Choose all that apply:

    A. User logon processing

    B. Authentication of users

    C. Directory searches

    D. Storage of directory data

22. James, the CIO of Harberson Tractor Equipment, is considering applying a domain template for his Windows 2000 domain controllers. He is considering the securedc template because it offers

account lockout features set to just 30 minutes. He has hired you to help him with some of the other features of this template. Of the following, which are also attributes of the securedc template?

    A. Enforce password history: 24 passwords remembered

    B. Minimum password length: 6 characters

    C. Maximum password age: 42 days

    D. Minimum password age: 2 days

23. You are the security consultant for a financial company. The network consists of 4 domain controllers and 88 Microsoft Windows 2000 Professional workstations. The company recently upgraded all computers to Windows 2000 and now is interested in applying a security template to the domain controllers. The company's primary concern is security versus ease of use. The financial information must not be jeopardized by intruders. Which security template should you suggest?

    A. securedc

    B. basicdc

    C. hisecdc

    D. nosecdc

24. What is the schema?

    A. A visual representation of a network

    B. A visual representation of a Windows 2000 forest

    C. A definition of the kinds of objects and type of information about those objects included in Active Directory

    D. A definition of the kinds of objects and type of information about those objects included in the Global Catalog

25. Your company has just upgraded four of its seven Windows NT 4.0 domain controllers to Windows 2000 servers. One of your servers has been configured as a PDC emulator. Why?

    A. The PDC emulator is required whenever a 4.0 PDC has been upgraded to Windows 2000.

    B. The PDC emulator is required whenever a Windows NT 4.0 PDC is still active on the network.

    C. The PDC emulator is required whenever a 4.0 BDC has been upgraded to Windows 2000.

    D. The PDC emulator is required whenever a 4.0 BDC is still active on the network.

26. How many PDC emulators can be on a Windows 2000 network at once?

    A. 1

    B. 4

    C. 8

    D. Depends on the number of existing BDCs

27. You have been hired by an insurance company to configure security for its Windows 2000 RAS servers. The company has 40 sales reps who dial in to the RAS server throughout the day and night to access resources throughout the network. Your primary goal is to establish security for the internal network from the RAS server and to allow access for authorized users only. Of the following activities, which would help meet your goal?

    A. Establish Remote Access Policy.

    B. Disconnect these RAS servers from the internal network.

    C. Create a standard template to apply to all RAS servers.

    D. Implement smart card authentication.

28. You have been hired as a Windows 2000 security consultant to establish security settings for the laptops using Windows 2000 Professional at Boston Importers Corporation. Jerri, the CEO, informs you that her salespeople often use the laptops in the field and are not always on the network in the office. She is concerned about users' laptops being lost and stolen. The data on the laptop is very secure and could jeopardize her clients' interests. Which desktop template for security should you apply to the laptops?

    A. basicwk

    B. securews

    C. hisecws

    D. compatws

29. You have been hired as a Windows 2000 security consultant for Jameson Industries. The network consists of 2 domain controllers and 786 Windows 2000 workstations, all located in one building. Mr. Jameson, the owner, would like to create an employee directory that users could access in the lobby to call employees without having to disturb the receptionist each time. His concern, however, is that some users could steal the machine or compromise the data. What suggestions could you make for Mr. Jameson?

    A. Use a Windows 2000 kiosk with strict policies.

    B. Create a kiosk that uses a mouse only.

    C. Create a kiosk that uses a touch screen only.

    D. Create a kiosk with strict policies that uses a touch screen only and is housed inside a secure cabinet to prevent theft or damage.

30. You are the network administrator for a Windows 2000 network. Your network consists of 4 domain controllers, 2 member servers, and 381 Windows 2000 workstations. Your staff on the help desk has been complaining that users are deleting files from the WINNT folder, causing various errors and headaches. Ben, your assistant, says that users can't delete files from the WINNT folder because 2000 will not allow them to delete files from this folder by default. Is Ben correct? Why or why not?

    A. Ben is correct. Windows 2000 warns users that they cannot delete files from the directory.

    B. Ben is correct. Windows 2000 uses Windows File Protection to halt users from deleting Windows files.

    C. Ben is incorrect. Windows does not offer any warning to users who try to delete system files.

    D. Ben is incorrect. Windows 2000 will hinder users from deleting files only if the Windows File Protection is installed.

31. You have been hired as a Windows 2000 security expert for Data Management Systems. The company's Windows 2000 network contains very secure data that cannot be jeopardized. One of its primary concerns deals with backing up and restoring its four servers' data. The company has asked you to propose a plan that would ensure security throughout the backup and restore process. Of the following, which are two secure proposals?

    A. Add only one user to the Backup Operators group. Only this user may back up and restore data.

    B. Assign one user the rights to back up, and assign another user the rights to restore.

    C. Create two groups, Backup and Restore, and add the same user account to each group.

    D. Assign at least two users the rights to back up data. Allow only the administrator the right to restore data.

32. You are the administrator for a Windows 2000 network. Your network is comprised of 3 domain controllers and 987 Windows 2000 workstations. Jonathon reports that two of his staff members, Dave and Rex, should be able to access and create folders and files in the folder named Sales on the server Orion, but they should not be able to delete any files or folders that they create. What combination of permissions will you assign for the users Dave and Rex on the folder Sales? Choose all that apply:

    A. List folder/read data

    B. Read attributes

    C. Create files/write data

    D. Create folders/append data

33. Frances is the network administrator for a large textile mill. His network consists of 4 Windows 2000 domain controllers and 78 Windows 2000 workstations. He would like to implement auditing as part of his security design and network design. What should be two primary goals of any audit design?

    A. Watch for possible intruders

    B. Watch for network downtimes

    C. Watch for congested servers

    D. Watch for access problems

34. You are a Windows 2000 security consultant. You have been contracted by Dian Mechanics to help design a valid audit policy. The network consists of 8 Windows 2000 servers, 3 of which are domain controllers and 44 of which Windows 2000 workstations. Of the following, what are valid choices of things that can be audited? Choose all that apply:

    A. Account logon

    B. Account logoffs

    C. Object access

    D. Changing the system time

35. Your company, HardWare International, has 7 Windows 2000 servers and 49 Windows 2000 workstations. You suspect that a few users are trying to hack into your network as Diana, the CFO. What entries should you add to your audit policy specifically to attempt to catch these users?

    A. System events

    B. Logon events

    C. Account management

    D. Object access

36. You are the Windows 2000 security consultant for a large retail company in Illinois. The company's network consists of 21 Windows 2000 servers and 356 Windows 2000 workstations. Jerry, the CEO, has concerns that users may be trying to break into the network. He has had you establish an audit policy but is still worried that the security log is not capturing the events. He wants you to set the security log so that it will capture all events. What setting should you choose in the security log?

    A. Log size 512; Overwrite Events As Needed

    B. Log size 1024; Do Not Overwrite Events; clear log manually

    C. Log size 1024; Overwrite Events Older Than Seven Days

    D. Log size 10240; Do Not Overwrite Events; clear log manually

37. You are the network administrator for a Windows 2000 network. Your network consists of 8 Windows 2000 domain controllers and 166 Windows 2000 workstations. Your boss, Tracey, is concerned that the Guest account may be allowing users to log on to the network. She asks you to take all measures necessary to restrict the Guest account from ever being capable of logging on to the network. You assure her that this Guest account is disabled, but that you can still take some measures to prevent the Guest account from logging on if someone makes it active. Of the following, which are settings that could keep the Guest account from logging on to your network? Choose all that apply:

    A. Delete the Guest account.

    B. Set all logon hours to Deny.

    C. Set the logon properties to the name of a workstation that does not exist.

    D. Set the password to an alphanumeric setting.

38. You are the Windows 2000 network administrator for the Quality Distributors Company. Your network is comprised of eight different domains throughout the United States. Vesla, your assistant, would like to create a domain local group in her domain in Wisconsin. She calls you and asks who can be a member of this Domain Local group. Of the following, who can be a member of this local group? Choose all that apply:

    A. User accounts

    B. Universal groups

    C. Global groups

    D. Domain Local groups from her domain

39. What is a Universal group used for?

    A. To organize users throughout a single domain

    B. To organize users throughout multiple domains

    C. To organize groups throughout a single domain

    D. To organize global groups throughout multiple domains

40. You are the network security consultant for a medium-size printing company. The network consists of 4 Windows 2000 domain controllers and 245 Windows 2000 workstations. Jerry, the network administrator, informs you that currently every member of his IT team is an administrator. He reasons that this is needed because he wants all of his staff to be able to change user passwords as needed. You recommend that he remove some of his users from the Administrator role and add the users to the Account Operators role. Jerry is not convinced this is what he needs. What can members of the Account Operators group do? Choose all that apply:

    A. Create accounts

    B. Delete accounts

    C. Add users to the Server operators group

    D. Change users passwords

41. You are the network administrator for a large bakery. The network consists of 4 Windows 2000 domains, named North, South, East, and West, throughout the United States, and 899 Windows 2000 workstations. Sales reps from each domain need access to a database located within the South domain. You have decided to create groups to control access to the database. Which group scheme would be appropriate so that users from each domain can access the database in the South domain?

    A. Create a Universal group, and place all the Sales users in the Universal group. Grant the Universal group access to the database in the South domain.

    B. Create four Sales Domain Global groups, and grant access to each group to the database.

    C. Create a Sales Global group in each domain. Add the four Sales Global groups to a Universal group. Grant the Universal group rights to the database.

    D. Create a local group, and add all the Sales users to the local group. Grant the local group rights to the database.

42. You are the Windows 2000 network consultant for a small construction company. The network consists of 2 domain controllers and 47 Windows 2000 workstations. John, the owner of the construction company, would like to log on to the server, install Microsoft Office, and work at the server as if it were a workstation. He is not an administrator. He reports to you that he cannot log on to the server. What is the problem?

    A. John's account does not have rights to log on to the server. You must allow the Users group to log on locally at the server.

    B. John's account does not have rights to log on to the server. You must add John's account to the Administrators group.

    C. John's account does not have rights to log on to the server. You cannot assign the Users group to log on locally to the server.

    D. John's account does not have rights to log on to the server. You must add John's account to the Server Operators group.

43. You are the network administrator for a medium-size publishing company in Charlotte. The company is comprised of 1 Windows 2000 domain, 2 domain controllers, and 101 Windows 2000 workstations. The company is comprised of several different magazines and departments within each magazine entity. You have been asked to create a scheme that would allow one individual to manage users within the magazine, but not users in other magazines. How would you accomplish this task?

    A. Assign one individual Administrator rights over his own domain.

    B. Create several groups for each magazine entity, and allow one user from each magazine to the respective groups.

    C. You will have to create four different domains. One user from each domain will be an administrator of that domain only. You will be the administrator for each domain.

    D. Create four different organizational units. Designate one individual in each OU, and then delegate the necessary rights for that OU only.

44. You have been contracted as a Windows 2000 security consultant to help a large manufacturing company upgrade its domains to a Windows 2000 network. Currently, the network consists of four Windows NT 4.0 domains throughout North America. Each domain trusts all other domains. The Global Domain Admins group is a member of all other domains' local Administrators group. The company would like to flatten its domains, yet still be able to delegate control to each geographical section of the country. Of the following, which is a viable solution?

    A. Create four different domains, and use transitive trusts to establish a relationship among the domains.

    B. Create one domain, with four different OUs. Each OU would be responsible for its users and resources.

    C. Create four domains, with four different OUs. Each OU would be a subset of the existing domain, with transitive trusts between each of the four domains.

    D. Create four domains and assign an administrator of each domain to be responsible for only that domain. A forest administrator could be created that has rights to resources in all domains.

45. The International Finance and Trust Company has hired you as a Windows 2000 network security consultant. The company consists of 8 different domains, 14 domain controllers, and 654 Windows 2000 workstations. When the company developed its domains, it created Global groups in each domain, such as Sales, Marketing, Finance, and Managers. The company now has resources throughout its domains to which users from each domain would need access. How can you organize their groups even further?

    A. You should create local groups and add the Global groups to the local ones.

    B. You should create Global groups in each domain and add the other Global groups to the new Global groups.

    C. You should create Universal groups.

    D. You should merge the domains together.

46. You have been hired as a Windows 2000 security consultant for the Myriad Developers Company. The network consists of 1 domain, made up of 3 domain controllers, 82 clients using Windows 2000 Professional, and 136 clients using Windows NT 4.0 Workstation. The company has developed Group Policy for its domain, and this seems to be working when clients log on from the Windows 2000-based computers but not from the others. What do you suspect is the problem?

    A. You must create a PDC emulator.

    B. Group policies work only with Windows 2000-based computers.

    C. Group policies cannot co-exist with .pol files; you should delete any existing .pol files.

    D. Group policies must be stored on a PDC emulator's Netlogon share for non-Windows 2000 computers to have the policies enforced.

47. You have been contracted by a large insurance company as a Windows 2000 security expert. The network consists of 1 domain made up of 2 Windows 2000 domain controllers and 84 Windows 2000 Professional workstations. You are explaining the concept of using group policies for their environment. Janet, the CEO, does not understand all the features that Group Policy can do for her company. Of the following, which are features of group policies?

    A. Software deployment

    B. Software policies

    C. Scripts

    D. File and folder management

48. Virginia is the network administrator of a Windows 2000 domain. Her domain consists of 2 domain controllers and 99 Windows 2000 workstations. She has created group policies to

manage many different facets of security. She would like to make changes to the existing policy but is uncertain when the changes would take effect. She decides to call you, the Windows 2000 expert, to ask when group policies are enforced against the client workstations. When are they enforced?

    A. At logon only

    B. At logoff only

    C. Throughout the day in 5-minute intervals

    D. Throughout the day in 90-minute intervals

49. You have been hired as a Windows 2000 security consultant by the North America Developers Company. The network consists of 8 Windows 2000 servers (3 of which are domain controllers) and 88 laptops running Windows 2000 Professional. Henry, the owner of the company, is concerned that the laptops may be lost or stolen as his employees travel throughout the world. If the data on these laptops was compromised, it could be disastrous. What additional security could you implement on these laptops?

    A. Mandatory logons

    B. File and folder encryption

    C. Data storage at the server only

    D. Only administrator access to the data

50. You are the network administrator for an insurance company. Your network consists of 1 Windows 2000 domain consisting of 2 domain controllers and 84 Windows 2000 Professional workstations. Your manager, Shirley, would like to implement another layer of security to your Windows 2000 network. She asks to propose a few suggestions. The two requirements she asks is that the security measure include both a physical device and a unique key or combination of keys unique to each individual user. Of the following,

which are secure measures that you could include in your proposal to Shirley?

A. Username and strong password

B. Fingerprint reader

C. Smart card reader

D. Hand geometry reader

51. You are the Windows 2000 security consultant for a financial institution in the Southeast. The network consists of 4 domain controllers, 8 member servers, and 211 Windows 2000 Professional workstations. The manager has requested a security device to increase security on the network. You have proposed to add smart cards to each workstation and server. Part of your proposal includes valid consideration for installing the smart cards with Windows 2000. Of the following, which are issues to be considered when adding the smart cards?

A. The need to install Microsoft Certificate Service

B. The number of users affected by the cards and card readers

C. Timings for installing the card readers

D. A plan for replacing lost cards

52. You are the administrator of a Windows 2000 network. Your network consists of 2 domain controllers, 1 member server, and 88 Windows 2000 workstations. You have been tasked with creating a dial-up server; for security, you would like to create a RADIUS server. Your boss, Stephen, would like to know what the advantages of RADIUS server is. Of the following, what are advantages to using a RADIUS Server?

A. Allows remote access for a large number of users

B. Allows control of Internet access through the server

C. Allows security over tunneled users

D. Allows users to access the network using any protocol

53. You are the network administrator for a Windows 2000 domain. Your environment consists of 2 domain controllers, a member server, and 95 Windows 2000 workstations. You decide that you need to change your Windows 2000 member server's name but find that you cannot. You are logged on as Administrator. What do you suspect is the problem?

A. You cannot change the name of a Windows 2000 server.

B. You cannot change the name of a Windows 2000 server if Certificate Services are installed.

C. You cannot change the name of a Windows 2000 server if users are connected to the server.

D. You cannot change the name of a Windows 2000 server if WINS is installed.

54. Why should you back up the entire server, not just the CA?

A. The CA is dependent on the entire structure of the server.

B. The CA is dependent on the Active Directory of the domain.

C. If the IIS metabase is damaged and is not backed up with the CA, the CA will fail to start.

D. If the IIS metabase is not backed up with the CA, the CA will not start when restored.

55. You are the network administrator for a large food cannery in central Arkansas. Your network consists of 8 Windows 2000 servers and 420 Windows 2000 Professional workstations. You are using certificates as part of your security design. A user leaves your company, and you would like to revoke the certificate for that user. Of the following, which are valid reasons that you could supply for revoking the certificate? Choose all that apply:

   A. Key compromise

   B. Change of affiliation

   C. Suspended

   D. Cease of operation

56. Why must the public key remain public?

   A. So that anyone may use it to encrypt a message

   B. So that anyone may use it to decrypt a message

   C. So that anyone may use it to encrypt or decrypt a message

   D. So that users of the User group may decrypt a message

57. You are a Windows 2000 security consultant for a midwestern financial institution. The network consists of 8 domain controllers, 4 member servers, and 211 Windows 2000 Professional workstations. The company has several offices throughout Illinois and Indiana, with headquarters located in Chicago. Users from each location tunnel through the Internet to access resources at the company's headquarters. The company has hired you to propose a security plan for these remote users and the data on the network. You have proposed IPSec. What advantages will IPSec offer to this institution?

   A. Access control of inward-bound traffic

   B. Integrity of packets between two hosts

   C. Outward-bound protocol filtering

   D. A record of all incoming IP addresses

58. You are the network administrator for a Windows 2000 network. Your network consists of 3 domain controllers and 88 workstations throughout Nevada. You have implemented IPSec and IPSec policies in your environment to increase security of traffic between network sites. You are monitoring outward-bound IPSec traffic. Arrange the following list in the correct order of outbound IPSec driver communication:

   A. Signs and encrypts the packet.

   B. Attempts to match all outbound packets against its filter list.

   C. Sends packet to IP to be forwarded.

   D. Discards packet if there is no match.

   E. Looks up the SA in the database.

   F. When a match occurs, initiates the negotiation by notifying the IKE.

   G. Receives the SA from IKE. The SA contains the session key P10.

   H. Inserts the SPI into the IPSec header.

59. You are a Windows 2000 security consultant for Cherry Lane Distributors. The network consists of 2 domain controllers and 123 Windows 2000 workstations. The company has contracted you to design a security plan for the users who often dial in to the network. You proposed a RADIUS server for secure dial-in sessions. Cheri, the owner, asks what makes RADIUS secure for dial-in accounts. What features are part of RADIUS' security measures?

   A. Data encryption

   B. NetBIOS gateway

   C. Callback security

   D. Caller ID

60. You are a Windows 2000 security consultant. A large accounting firm in the Southwest has hired you to help develop system policies. The network consists of 1 domain, 7 sites, 4 organizational units, 8 domain controllers, 3 member servers, and 987 Windows 2000 workstations. The accounting firm has hired you specifically to help them with group policies. The firm's biggest concern is the processing order of the policies. Arrange the following steps of group policy processing order, from first to last:

  A. If OUs are nested, each inner nest OU group policy is applied.

  B. Local Computer Policy is applied.

  C. User Group Policy is applied.

  D. Excluding Local Computer Policy, the policy closest to the user or group is applied.

  E. Any domain policies are applied.

  F. Organizational Unit Policy is applied.

  G. Computer Group Policy is applied.

  H. At each level, all applicable group policies are supplied in the order specified by the administrator.

  I. Any site policy is applied.

  J. Policies are applied throughout the day.

61. You are the network administrator for a large manufacturing firm. Your network consists of 1 Windows 2000 domain controlled by 3 domain controllers, 2 member servers, and 904 Windows 2000 workstations. You are presenting a new plan for security management and would like to create a visual to demonstrate three distinct areas of security: Physical, Network, and Data Security. Using your knowledge of security and Windows 2000, arrange the following attributes under the correct category:

  A. Card readers

  B. Certificate servers

  C. Kiosks

  D. IPSec

  E. NTFS

  F. Locked server rooms

  G. RADIUS

  H. Routers

  I. Encryption

62. You have been hired as a Windows 2000 security consultant by the Marshall Real Estate Company. The network consists of 3 Windows 2000 domains, 187 Windows 2000 Professional workstations that users use to dial in to the headquarters, and several smaller sites scattered throughout the states that are connected to the headquarters through leased lines. The company has tasked you with the job of creating security for its laptops, its WAN environment, and RAS security. Bob, the owner of the company, has asked you to create a visual representation of the security features of each of the three areas. Arrange the following topics under the correct category for him:

  A. Account lockouts

  B. RADIUS

  C. NTFS security

  D. Callback security

  E. Encryption

  F. VPN

  G. Bandwidth

  H. IPSec

  I. Caller ID

63. You are the network consultant for Wright Way Investors. The network consists of 1 domain, 7 domain controllers, 4 members servers, and 423 Windows 2000 workstations. Mary Ann, the owner of the investment company, has asked you to implement security for the network. You mention that you'd like to start with using security templates. She is interested and would like you to create a flowchart of the different templates that could be used. Arrange the following attributes under the correct template heading:

   A. Account Lockout Duration, set by the administrator

   B. Send NTLM response only

   C. Retain Security Log for 7 days

   D. Security log 10240K

   E. Account Lockout Duration 30 minutes

   F. Security log 512K

   G. Refuse NTLM and LM Authentication

   H. Disabled Guest Account access to application log

   I. Security log 5120K

64. You are the network administrator for a plastic molding company in New York. Your network consists of 1 Windows 2000 domain in native mode, 3 sites, 4 domain controllers, 1 member server, and 283 Windows 2000 Professional workstations. You are planning to create groups and have decided to create a visual of what group attributes are. Arrange the following group attributes under the correct heading:

   A. User accounts and Global groups from the same domain

   B. Can be a member of Domain Local groups in the same domain

   C. Can be a member of Global groups in the same domain

   D. Used to set access permissions in a domain

   E. Accessible by any server on the network

   F. Can be a member of Universal and Domain Local groups in any domain

   G. Can contain user accounts, Universal groups, and Global groups from any domain

   H. Can contain user accounts, Universal groups, and Global groups from any domain

   I. Used to assign permissions across domains

ANSWERS TO EXAM QUESTIONS

1. **D.**   The location of each server is paramount when it comes to security. All good security begins with physical security. For more information, see the section "Analyzing Existing and Planned Business Models," in Chapter 1, "General Business Analysis."

2. **A, C, D.**   To design an effective security model, you should be familiar with how the organization itself is designed. Specifically, this includes the information flow, the communication flow, and the product life cycle. For more information, see the section "Analyzing Existing and Planned Business Models," in Chapter 1, "General Business Analysis."

3. **C.**   When designing an effective security model, keep in mind that the model should help the existing business model, not hinder it. For more information, see the section "Analyzing Existing and Planned Business Models," in Chapter 1, "General Business Analysis."

4. **B, C.** When designing your security model, always consider acquisitions that your company may make because this can affect your plans for access to resources for managing the number of users currently in your environment. For more information, see the section "Analyzing Existing and Planned Business Models," in Chapter 1, "General Business Analysis."

5. **D, A, E, C, B.** When a user logs on, a valid username and password are required. The security provider confirms that this is a valid username and password and offers the user an access token. The access token is then compared against the resource's DACL to allow or deny user access to a given resource. For more information, see the section "End-User Requirements," in Chapter 2, "Analyzing IT."

6. **B, C.** When reporting to IT management on how to cover expenses, two common methods are including security as a budgeted expense, and creating a security charge-back for internal departments. For more information, see the section "IT Management," in Chapter 2, "Analyzing IT."

7. **C.** By creating an intranet, you can share data with users from different operating systems and network operating systems. For more information, see the section "Physical and Information Security Models," in Chapter 2, "Analyzing IT."

8. **A, B, D.** The guest account should not be enabled as part of C2 security. For more information, see the section "Physical and Information Security Models," in Chapter 2, "Analyzing IT."

9. **B.** Authentication is the approval of a username and a password in a Windows 2000 environment. If the username and password are not correct, then logon to the network is denied. For more information, see the section "Physical and Information Security Models," in Chapter 2, "Analyzing IT."

10. **A.** A network design map will give you a visual of where potential weakness or attacks could originate. For more information, see the section "Analyze Company Size and User and Resource Distribution," in Chapter 3, "Analyzing Technical Environments."

11. **B.** By connecting the Boston and Woburn locations via a VPN, you can implement a secure, cost-effective means of gathering the daily reports. For more information, see the section "Assess Available Connectivity," in Chapter 3, "Analyzing Technical Environments."

12. **C, D, B, A.** The full mesh is rarely used today because it is the most expensive. The logical star is one of the most common topologies with VPNs. For more information, see the section "Assess Available Connectivity," in Chapter 3, "Analyzing Technical Environments."

13. **A.** Bandwidth is the number of bits that can be transmitted per second over a network medium. This is also referred to as the "throughput." For more information, see the section "Assess Net Available Bandwidth," in Chapter 3, "Analyzing Technical Environments."

14. **D.** When implementing accounting and security features to any network, always consider the available bandwidth and then consider what impact the proposed changes will have on the bandwidth. For more information, see the section "Assess Net Available Bandwidth," in Chapter 3, "Analyzing Technical Environments."

15. **C, A, D, B.** Physical access to servers is always a top priority. Servers should be in a physically secure environment to reduce the threat of theft or vandalism. Usernames and passwords are a virtual key to the network resources. Incorrect permissions to resources can be disastrous. Finally, access to backup media could allow company secrets to be carried off the premises. For more

information, see the section "Analyze Data and Systems Access Method," in Chapter 3, "Analyzing Technical Environments."

16. **D.**   This is not a good idea! Secure your ERDs because several programs can exploit the SAM on the disk to hack in as user accounts. For more information, see the section "Analyze Data and Systems Access Method," in Chapter 3, "Analyzing Technical Environments."

17. **B.**   Some services in Windows 2000 require a SID to be associated with the service so that the service may complete a process or access data. For more information, see the section "Analyze Data and Systems Access Method," in Chapter 3, "Analyzing Technical Environments."

18. **B.**   A transitive trust allows users to access resources in remote domains. For more information, see the section "Analyze Data and Systems Access Method," in Chapter 3, "Analyzing Technical Environments."

19. **A, C.**   When Mark enforced IPSec and encryption of data, he increased the amount of overhead required to move the same amount of data on Windows NT 4.0. For more information, see the section "Assess Net Available Bandwidth," in Chapter 3, "Analyzing Technical Environments."

20. **A, C, D.**   A security baseline allows you to predict security changes, expose existing weaknesses, and develop a more comprehensive security plan. For more information, see the section "Domain Controllers Baseline," in Chapter 4, "Designing a Security Baseline."

21. **A, B, C, D.**   A domain controller manages user logons, authentication, directory searches, and directory storage. For more information, see the section "Domain Controllers Baseline," in Chapter 4, "Designing a Security Baseline."

22. **A, C, D.**   The securedc template does offer a minimum password length, but it is set to eight characters rather than six characters. For more information, see the section "Domain Controllers Baseline," in Chapter 4, "Designing a Security Baseline."

23. **C.**   Servers that require a very high amount of security should use the hisecdc template. For more information, see the section "Domain Controllers Baseline," in Chapter 4, "Designing a Security Baseline."

24. **C.**   A schema defines the kinds of objects and the type of information about those objects that can be stored in Active Directory. For more information, see the section "Active Directory Introduction," in Chapter 4, "Designing a Security Baseline."

25. **D.**   The PDC emulator is required whenever a BDC is still active on the network, or if non-Windows 2000 clients are in the domain. For more information, see the section "Domain Controllers Baseline," in Chapter 4, "Designing a Security Baseline."

26. **A.**   You are allowed only one PDC emulator per domain. For more information, see the section "Operations Master," in Chapter 4, "Designing a Security Baseline."

27. **A, C, D.**   Answer B is not a valid answer because simply disconnecting the RAS servers from the internal network would defeat the point of remote users dialing into the network to access resources. For more information, see the section "Servers," in Chapter 4, "Designing a Security Baseline."

28. **C.**   The security template you should use is hisecws. For more information, see the section "Desktop Computers," in Chapter 4, "Designing a Security Baseline."

29. **D.**   By creating a Windows 2000 kiosk with a touch screen, and by housing the equipment in a secure cabinet, vandalism and theft are kept to a minimum. For more information, see the section "Kiosks," in Chapter 4, "Designing a Security Baseline."

30. **D.**   Ben is incorrect. Windows 2000 will warn users that they should not delete the files in the WINNT directory, but users can (and will) delete files from this directory if Windows File Protection is not installed. For more information, see the section "Applying Security to File Systems," in Chapter 5, "Securing Resources."

31. **B, D.**   By assigning one user backup permissions and another user restore permissions, each user can do only half of the backup and restore procedure. This makes the backup media more secure. The second option is to allow only an administrator to restore the backups. For more information, see the section "Analyzing Registry Keys Access," in Chapter 5, "Securing Resources."

32. **A, C, D.**   To allow Dave and Rex to access and create folders and files in the Sales share, but not allow them to delete any contents of the Sales share, these users would need these permissions: list folder/read data, create files/write data, and create folders/append data. In addition, we would deny Dave and Rex the ability to delete subfolders and files in this share. For more information, see the section "Applying Security to File Systems," in Chapter 5, "Securing Resources."

33. **A, D.**   A good audit design not only catches potential intruders, but it also helps users access the data to which they need access. If several users are constantly accessing a particular resource and are getting denied, then there is a good chance that the users actually may need access to the resource. For more information, see the section "What Can Be Audited?" in Chapter 6, "Designing an Audit Policy."

34. **A, C, D.**   Account logons are useful to see when users are attempting to log on to the network. Object Access reports when a resource was attempted to be accessed. Changing the system time is a user right, which is recorded. Logoffs are not recorded. For more information, see the section "What Can Be Audited?" in Chapter 6, "Designing an Audit Policy."

35. **A, B, C.**   If you suspect that users are attempting to hack into the network as other users, you should audit system events, such a server reboots; logon successes, to see if users are logging on to the network at odd hours; and the use of user rights because another administrator or account operator may be changing a user's password and then logging on as that user. For more information, see the section "What Can Be Audited?" in Chapter 6, "Designing an Audit Policy."

36. **D.**   By setting the log size to 10240 (or larger), you have a pretty good guarantee that the log size will continue to record security events. If the log size is set too low and the option of Do Not Overwrite Events is set, then when the log size is full, no more events will be recorded. For more information, see the section, "Determine How You Are Going to Cope with the Multitude of Records Produced," in Chapter 6, "Designing an Audit Policy."

37. **B, C.**   You cannot delete the Guest account because it is a built-in account. You may set all logon hours to Deny, and you can force the Guest account to only log on to a workstation that does not exist. For more information, see the section "Built-In Users," in Chapter 7, "Designing a Security Group Strategy."

38. **A, B, C, D.**   User accounts, Universal groups, Global groups, and Domain Local groups from Vesla's domain can be included in her Domain Local account. For more information, see the

section "Types of Groups and Group Scope," in Chapter 7, "Designing a Security Group Strategy."

39. **D.** A Universal group is used to organize users throughout multiple domains. For more information, see the section "Types of Groups and Group Scope," in Chapter 7, "Designing a Security Group Strategy."

40. **A, C, D.** Account Operators are powerful users; they can create accounts, delete accounts, and change user passwords. They cannot, however, add users to the Administrator's group or any operator group. For more information, see the section "Default Groups," in Chapter 7, "Designing a Security Group Strategy."

41. **C.** To grant all the Sales users rights to the Sales database, create four Global groups, one per domain, to organize each domain's sales users. Then add the four Global Sales groups to a Universal group that has rights to the Sales database. As new Sales users are hired, they must be added to only the appropriate Global Sales group to have access to the database. For more information, see the section "Using Security Groups to Provide Resource Access," in Chapter 7, "Designing a Security Group Strategy."

42. **C.** The Users group cannot be assigned the permission to log on locally in Windows 2000. For more information, see the section "Using Security Groups to Provide Resource Access" in Chapter 7, "Designing a Security Group Strategy."

43. **D.** By creating one domain and four different OUs in the domain, you can delegate administrative duties to one (or more) individual(s) in the OU to manage users. For more information, see the section "Delegation of Authority," in Chapter 7, "Designing a Security Group Strategy."

44. **B.** Create one domain, with four different OUs. Then assign one or more persons in each OU to administer each unit's users and resources. For more information, see the section "User Rights and Privileges," in Chapter 7, "Designing a Security Group Strategy."

45. **C.** You should create Universal groups to organize users and groups throughout several domains, and to grant those users permissions to resources. For more information, see the section "User Rights and Privileges," in Chapter 7, "Designing a Security Group Strategy."

46. **B.** Group policies work only with Windows 2000-based computers. For computers using an older version of NT or Windows 95/98, you must create .pol files through the System Policy Editor. For more information, see the section "Policies for Windows NT and Windows 9x Computers in a Windows 2000 Domain," in Chapter 8, "Designing a Security Policy Inheritance."

47. **A, B, C, D.** Group policies in Windows 2000 are much more powerful than system policies in Windows NT 4.0 and Windows 9x. Group policies can be created to deploy software, implement software restrictions, call scripts, and manage file and folders for users. For more information, see the section "Creating, Editing, and Applying Group Policies," in Chapter 8, "Designing a Security Policy Inheritance."

48. **D.** By default, policies are updated throughout the day in 90-minute intervals. This is a change from Windows NT and Windows 9x, in which policies were applied at logon. For more information, see the section "Creating, Editing, and Applying Group Policies," in Chapter 8, "Designing a Security Policy Inheritance."

49. **B.**   Users of the laptops can encrypt their files and folders to ensure that their data remains private if the laptop becomes lost. For more information, see the section "Encrypting Files—User Processes," in Chapter 9, "Designing an Encrypting File System Strategy."

50. **B, C, D.**   Shirley can implement fingerprint readers, hand geometry readers, and most likely, smart cards. Each of these security devices requires the users to supply a key of some type—whether the key is a fingerprint, a handprint, or a pin number based on the type of intermediary security device in place. For more information, see the section "Windows 2000 Security Model," in Chapter 10, "Designing an Authentication Strategy."

51. **A, B, C, D.**   If you'd like to use smart cards as part of your security design, you also must include the Microsoft Certificate Service, consider the number of users in your network, allot timings for installing the card readers, and implement a plan for replacing lost or stolen smart cards. For more information, see the section "Smart Cards," in Chapter 10, "Designing an Authentication Strategy."

52. **A, B, C.**   RADIUS allows you to control remote access for a large number of users, allows you to control Internet access through the server, and provides security for tunneled users. For more information, see the section "RADIUS: Internet Authentication Service," in Chapter 10, "Designing an Authentication Strategy."

53. **B.**   After you have installed Certificate Services, you cannot change the name of your server or add it to or remove it from a domain. For more information, see the section "Installing Certificate Services," in Chapter 11, "Designing a Public Key Infrastructure."

54. **C.**   If you were to restore the CA to a server whose IIS metabase has been damaged or lost, the IIS will fail to start, and thus Certificate Services will fail to start. Always back up the IIS metabase. For more information, see the section "Configuring a CA," in Chapter 11, "Designing a Public Key Infrastructure."

55. **A, B, D.**   When a user leaves your company, you may revoke a certificate. When revoking the certificate, you may provide a reason why the certificate is being revoked. Of the many reasons why, key compromise, change of affiliation, and cease of operation are three. For more information, see the section "Certificate Lifecycle—Managing Certificates," in Chapter 11, "Designing a Public Key Infrastructure."

56. **A.**   The public key remains public so that users may use it to encrypt a message. The key to decrypt the message remains private. For more information, see the section "Certificate Lifecycle—Managing Certificates," in Chapter 11, "Designing a Public Key Infrastructure."

57. **A, B, C.**   IPSec offers control of inward- and outbound-packets through filtering, and integrity of packets between two hosts through checksums to detect packet tampering. You should be aware of the available bandwidth, however, before implementing IPSec because the additional overhead may slow connections. For more information, see the section "IPSec," in Chapter 15, "Designing Security for Communication Channels."

58. **B, D, F, G, E, H, A, C.**   The IPSec driver first attempts to match all outbound packets against its filter list. If there is no match, the packet is discarded. If there is a match, the driver initiates the negotiation by notifying IKE. IKE sends the driver the SA, which contains the session key. The driver looks up the SA in its database and inserts the SPI into the IPSec header. The driver then signs and encrypts the packet. Finally, the packet is released to IP to be forwarded to the

host. For more information, see the section "IPSec" in Chapter 15, "Designing Security for Communication Channels."

59. **A, C, D.**   RADIUS includes features for data encryption, callback security, and caller ID. For more information, see the section "RADIUS: Internet Authentication Service," in Chapter 10, "Designing an Authentication Strategy."

60. **G, C, J, B, I, E, F, A, H, D.**   Computer group policies are applied when the computer is turned on. User group policies are applied when the user logs on. Policies are reapplied throughout the day. The local computer policy is applied. Any site policy is applied. Domain polices then are applied. OU policies are applied. If OUs are

nested, each inner nest OU group policy is applied. At each level, all applicable group policies are applied in the order specified by the administrator. Finally, the policy closest to the user or group is applied. For more information, see the section "Group Policy Inheritance," in Chapter 8, "Designing Security Policy Inheritance."

61. See Figure PE.1.

   For more information, see the sections "Examining Dial-In Access" and "Applying Security to File Systems," in Chapter 5, "Securing Resources."

62. See Figure PE.2.

   For more information, see the section "Examining Dial-In Access," in Chapter 5, "Securing Resources."

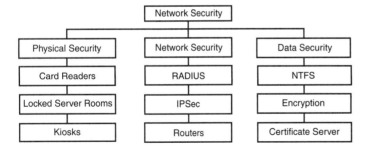

FIGURE PE.1
Figure for question 61.

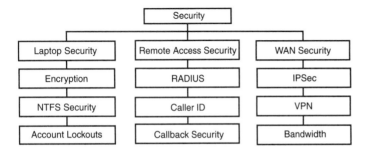

FIGURE PE.2
Figure for question 62.

63. See Figure PE.3.

 For more information, see the section "Domain Controllers Baseline," in Chapter 4, "Designing a Security Baseline."

64. See Figure PE.4.

 For more information, see the section "Using Security Groups to Provide Resource Access," in Chapter 7, "Designing A Security Group Strategy."

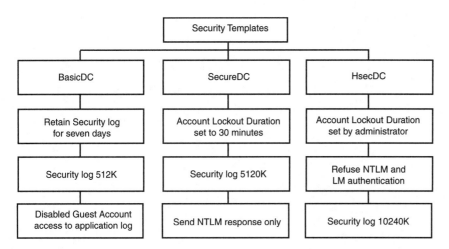

FIGURE PE.3
Figure for question 63.

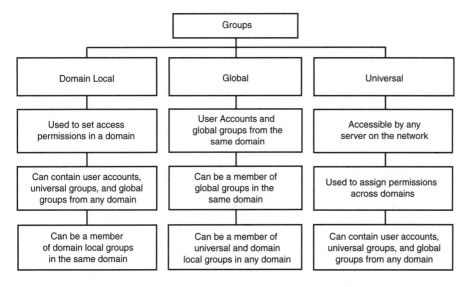

FIGURE PE.4
Figure for question 64.

APPENDIXES

Glossary

3DES (Triple DES)   An offshoot of the Data Encryption Standard. 3DES encrypts data three times.

x.509.v3 certificate   An ITU standard certificate format for PKI.

A

Access Control List (ACL)   A list of users, groups, and the permissions they have to access the resource, referred to as a DACL in Windows 2000.

Active Directory   Microsoft's directory services for Windows 2000.

antireplay   Preventing the use of a captured packet in a replay attack.

AppleTalk   Apple networking system.

Apply Group Policy   A Group Policy is applied to a security group that is within its container if this permission is set in the Group Policy Object for the security group. For example, the Administrators group default security permissions do not include the Apply Group Policy permission. If an administrator's account falls within the scope of the Group Policy, the policy is not applied.

asymmetric cryptography   Cryptography that uses two keys. These keys are referred to as a public key and a private key.

asymmetric encryption   A process of encryption in which two unique keys are used. A public key is used to encrypt, and a private key is used to decrypt.

attributes   The specific characteristics that describe an object.

Audit Policy   On a Windows 2000 computer, this simply is a collection of settings that indicate what should be recorded when something happens.

authentication   The process of making sure that an individual is who he says he is. This process of proving identity is often accomplished by using a user ID and a password.

Authentication Header (AH)   Protocol that provides integrity, antireplay, and authentication. Used by IPSec.

Authentication Server   A component of the Kerberos protocol that handles the initial communication with the Kerberos client. In Windows 2000, this service issues TGTs to the Kerberos clients.

authenticator   A component of Kerberos used to prove that a ticket is valid and is being sent from a valid client.

authorization   The process of approving access to data.

authorization   The process of determining what access is allowed to resources. It is often referred to as access control.

B

B channel   Primary channel in ISDN.

B2B   Business-to-business has always meant the purchase of products by one business from another (the commercial market), verses the purchase of products by the consumer market. B2B has come to mean a type of business that specializes in doing this over the Internet. The B2B business becomes a portal for commercial enterprise on the Internet.

bandwidth   The amount of data that can be transmitted in a period of time over a network link.

Berkeley Internet Name Domain (BIND)   A DNS service.

built-in groups   When a server is promoted to a domain controller, the built-in groups have installed in them Domain Local groups that are already defined. Predefined default user accounts and Global groups are installed in the User folder. Other Domain Local groups may be created in the User folder when optional services such as DHCP and DNS are installed on the domain controller.

business process   A method for accomplishing a business task.

C

C2   One of many security designations established by the U.S. Security Agency. A C2-level system meets requirements set for discretional access control, object reuse, identification and authentication, and auditing as defined in the U.S. Department of Defenses' National Computer Security Center (NCSC) publication "Trusted Computer Systems Evaluation Criteria."

CA hierarchy   A structure that arranges CAs in the order of most trust to least trust. Each CA, except the root CA, receives its certificate from another CA and traces its authority back to the root. Each CA can operate independently of the other CAs unless it needs to renew its certificate or check a CRL to validate another CA in the hierarchy.

certificate   A digital structure that includes identifying information and a public key to be used in a PKI. The certificate is issued and signed by a CA.

Certificate Authority (CA)   A software service, or server charged with creating, assigning, and managing certificates.

certificate chain   A list of certificates that link the end-entity certificate to the CA root.

certificate enrollment   The process of obtaining a certificate.

certificate mapping   The process of binding an imported certificate to a Windows 2000 Active Directory user account.

certificate repository   A storage vehicle for certificates.

Certificate Revocation List (CRL)   A list of certificates that have been revoked by the CA.

Certificate Services   The services provided by the PKI. In Windows 2000, Certificate Services is the mechanism by which a CA is established and operates.

certificate templates   Certificates used for different purposes may require different information and format. Certificate templates are used with information provided through a wizard or a Web page to produce the correct type of certificate.

Certreq A command-line utility that can be used to request certificate from the command prompt.

Certsrv A command-line utility that is used to start Certificate Services as a standalone application rather than a Windows 2000 service.

Certutil A command-line utility used to manage, upgrade, and diagnose a CA.

Challenge Handshake Authentication Protocol (CHAP) An authentication protocol used to authenticate remote access via PPP.

channel A communications path between two computers or devices.

Cipher A command-line utility that can be used to encrypt and decrypt EFS-protected files and folders.

class A logical object in the schema of the Active Directory.

Client/Server Service Exchange A communication of the Kerberos protocol that exchanges a service ticket for access to a server.

committed information rate (CIR) The amount of bandwidth that is guaranteed on a Frame Relay service.

community In SNMP, a community is a rudimentary attempt at security. Agents will respond only to a management program that is in the community.

compulsory tunneling A compulsory tunnel is a path between two computers across a network or networks. When packets travel from one computer to the other, they must follow the tunnel.

Computer groups These groups contain computers. They are used to identify computer with special roles and privileges.

Computer Local group Exists only on a single computer.

Creator Owner An implicit group. You create it, you own it. CREATOR OWNER is used to assign permissions to the object to the user who first created the object.

cross-certification The process of two CAs accepting the certificate of each other as trusted.

CryptoAPI Microsoft's programming interface that provides functions for encryption, decryption, and digital signing. CryptoAPI may be used to implement a particular CSP that has been written to CryptoAPI. The CSP does the actual encryption and decryption.

cryptographic service provider (CSP) An element used to provide the cryptographic interface between a program and Microsoft Windows operating systems. Several exist natively. Third-party products may need to provide their own CSPs. The CSP performs the encryption/decryption.

cyclic redundancy check A technique for detecting errors in data transmission.

D

Data Decryption Field (DDF) The field attached to an encrypted file that includes an copy of the session key encrypted with the user's public key.

Data Recovery Field (DRF) The field attached to an encrypted file that includes a copy of the session key encrypted with the recovery agent's public key.

decrypt To unscramble the encrypted text back into its original format.

delegation of authority The ability to give only the privileges necessary to ordinary users so that they perform management tasks.

Delegation of Control Wizard   A wizard that makes it easy to delegate authority to users.

demand-dial routing   Creates a dial-up connection between two networks. The connection can be configured to be persistent.

demilitarized zone (DMZ)   The area of a network that is set aside for high-risk computers that may be accessed from untrusted networks. The DMZ resides between the private network and the public network. This is also known as a screened subnet.

Diffie-Hellman (DH) group   Group that specifies the length of the initial prime number used in creating the key.

digest   A product created by applying a cryptographic hashing algorithm over some data.

digest authentication   A system of providing authentication of the Internet to a Web server without sending a clear–text password.

digital subscriber line (DSL)   A transmission technology that allows more data to be carried over existing copper telephone wire. It is commonly used for fast Internet connections and is used for lines between the home or office and the telephone switching stations, not between switching stations.

Discretionary Access Control List (DACL)   A list of objects (users, groups) that have access to files, folders, printers, and other objects, and what kind of access they have. *See also* security descriptor.

distribution group   A mailing list. In the Active Directory, this is a group of users. This type of group can be used by Exchange Server as a distribution list. The group cannot be assigned to DACLs or SACLs, and thus no distribution membership SID is included in the access token created during logon.

domain   A logical collection of computers; a security boundary in Active Directory.

domain controller   A server in an Windows 2000 network that provides the Active Directory service to network users and computers. It stores directory data, and manages user logon, authentication, and directory searches.

Domain Controller Security Policy console   This console is used for setting Group Policy for the domain controllers OU in Active Directory.

Domain Local group   A group that can be used to give access to any computer in the domain. It can contain members from the local domain and other domains in the forest. In a native mode domain, Universal groups, Global groups, user accounts, and other Domain Local groups can be members.

domain naming master   The operations master that is in charge of additions and deletions of domains and sites in the forest.

Domain Security Policy console   This console is used to set Group Policy for all the computers in the domain.

E

Effective Settings   Local policy settings can be overridden by domain or OU Group Policy settings. The Effective Settings column of the Local Computer Policy indicates the combined Local and Group Policy in effect for the computer.

electronic data interchange (EDI)   Transfer of information from one company to another.

emergency repair disk (ERD)   As disk made to assist in the recovery of Windows 2000 systems. It is created using the Windows 2000 backup utility. It can be used to help you repair problems with system files, the startup environment, your boot volume, and the partition boot section. It does not contain a copy of the registry.

Encapsulating Security Payload Protocol (ESP)
Provides integrity, authentication, antireplay, and encryption. It is a part of IPSec.

encrypt   To scramble or make meaningless clear text. In data communications, cryptographic algorithms are used to encrypt data that might be otherwise read by unauthorized people. The data can be decrypted at its destination.

Enterprise Admins   A group in the root forest domain that is a member of all Administrator groups in the forest. By default, only those in the Enterprise Admins group can authorize DHCP servers and add Enterprise CAs.

Enterprise CA   A Microsoft CA that uses the Active Directory as its store.

Everyone   The Everyone group contains anyone who can gain access to the system, including anonymous users.

Extensible Authentication Protocol (EAP)   This protocol allows the negotiation of a specific authentication schema at the time the remote access client attempts to connect to either the remote access server or the IAS server.

F

File Encryption Key (FEK)   The key used to encrypt the file. It is a symmetric key used in EFS.

firewall   A product (program or device) that blocks all but approved traffic between the networks connected to the firewall.

forest   Composed of domains that share the same schema, configuration, and Global Catalog. All domains in the forest are connected by Kerberos v5 transitive trusts.

G

generic routing encapsulation (GRE)   A process used in PPTP VPN. They are the PPP packets used by PPTP for transport.

Global group   Can be used throughout the forest. Can contain members only from the domain where the Global group is created.

group ID (GID)   In UNIX, groups are represented by GIDs.

Group Policy   A collection of computer and user settings, including desktop settings, password policy, audit settings, security options, and so on, that can be configured centrally and applied to groups of users or computers. Users and computers can be grouped into organizational units (OUs). Group Policy can be applied to sites, domains, and OUs.

Group Policy Container (GPC)   An Active Directory container that can have a Group Policy Object applied. Each container can have multiple Group Policy Objects.

Group Policy filtering   Group Policies are not applied to security groups. Group Policies are applied to Group Policy containers such as OUs, sites, or domains. However, you can determine which Group Policy gets applied to a security group by using the Security tab to filter, or remove, security groups. Because a user must have the Read and Apply Group Policy rights before Group Policy can be applied, you add a group to the Security page and make sure that the user does not have these permissions.

Group Policy Object (GPO)   A particular Group Policy. It can be linked to a GPC.

group scope   Where a group can be used in the domain tree. Three scopes exist: Universal, Global, and Domain Local.

H

hash algorithm   An algorithm used to scramble data. Many cryptographic hash algorithms are one-way.

hierarchical trust model   A trust model in which each CA traces its authority directly back to a single root. Each CA can operate independently of another.

I

IAS Service (Internet Authentication Service)   Can be used to control and document authentication and authorization of external users.

IIS metabase   A database of information critical to the operation of IIS. Without this database, the IIS services will not start.

implicit groups   You are a member of implicit groups depending on what you are doing. For example, you are a member of the Interactive group if you are logged on locally.

infrastructure master   The Windows 2000 operations master that updates group to user references when usernames or group names are changed.

interdomain   Kerberos communications and activities between realms.

Internet Authentication Server (IAS)   Microsoft implementation of RADIUS.

Internet Connection Sharing   A part of dial-up connections that allows a Windows 2000 computer to share its Internet connection with other computers in a home network.

Internet Key Exchange (IKE)   Manages the keys used in IPSec communications.

IPSec   A protocol that is used to secure communications between computers. IPSec is an extension of the TCP/IP protocol.

K

kerberized application   An application written to take advantage of the underlying systems implementation of Kerberos.

Kerberos   An authentication protocol that consists of a database of users and keys. Rules are strictly defined to determine how the process of authentication is handled between clients and servers, and servers and servers. A large number of checks and balances exist to protect against possible attacks.

Kerberos database (KDB)   In classic Kerberos, the database of users and keys.

Kerberos Distribution Center (KDC)   In Windows 2000, the two services, Authentication Service and Ticket Granting Service, that manages the access to the user database and issue TGTs and service tickets.

Kerberos ticket   A document used in the Kerberos protocol for authentication.

kiosks   A special type of computer that is set up and used by multiple people usually without logon.

L

LAN Manager (LM)   An authentication protocol used by Windows 9x, and considered to be less secure than NTLM.

Layer 2 Tunneling Protocol (L2TP)   A tunneling protocol used to create a VPN. It is commonly secured with IPSec.

latency   In general, the time one component is delayed as it is waiting on another. In networking, the time it takes data to travel from one place to another.

Lightweight Directory Access Protocol (LDAP)   A standard for querying LDAP directories.

Line Printer Daemon (LPD)   A service that allows the printing of files to Windows 2000-controlled printers from TCP/IP hosts.

line print remote (LPR)   A command used with an LPD print server to print files.

linking   A Group Policy object is said to be linked to a Group Policy container. Although you can link the same policy to multiple containers, this is not a good practice.

Local Security Authority (LSA)   Component of the security subsystem that manages authentication.

Local Security Policy console   This console is used to set security policy for the local computer. Settings made to site, domain, and OUs the computer is a member of will override any policy set locally.

LocalTalk   A component of the Apple networking system that is reduced in functionality. For example, LocalTalk networks can have only 254 nodes.

M

Manage Documents   A permission on the printer that allows users to pause, delete, and resume documents on a printer.

Manage Printer   A permission that allows users to make setting changes on the printer, but not share it or delete it.

Message Exchange   A subprotocol of the Kerberos protocol that groups messages used in communications between Kerberos clients and the Kerberos server.

mixed mode   A Windows 2000 domain that contains Windows NT 4.0 backup domain controllers.

MS-CHAP   Microsoft CHAP. Unlike CHAP, MS-CHAP does not send the password in the clear.

MSGINA   The process that produces the familiar logon screen. When smart card services are installed, it produces the request for the PIN number screen instead.

N

name cracking   The process of adding a domain name to a username submitted to an IAS server.

native mode   A Windows 2000 domain that includes only Windows 2000 domain controllers.

nested groups   Groups within groups. In a native mode domain, Global groups can be nested within other Global groups. Universal groups may be nested within Global groups.

net available bandwidth   The bandwidth left after other bandwidth consumption by applications and services.

Network Access Server (NAS)   The NAS receives connections from clients from other networks. A Microsoft Routing and Remote Access server can be a NAS.

Network Address Translation (NAT)   NAT replaces the source address of the source computer on packets traveling from the private network to the public network. When the response is returned, the address is mapped to the original source address. Port mapping may also be included.

network file system (NFS)   A file system used by UNIX systems that allows clients to mount server volumes and logically represent them as local drives.

Network Trust Model   A trust model in which each CA essentially trusts the other. A directory is required to be present so that the validity of any certificate can be traced back; which every trust path is necessary until some common trust is discovered.

NTFS   A file system with many features that assist hardening the system, including granular access permissions down to the file level and the Encrypting File System.

NT LAN Manager (NTLM)   Authentication protocol used by Windows NT. Windows 2000 can also use this protocol to authenticate Window NT computers and can use it if Kerberos authentication fails.

NTLMv2   NT LAN Manager authentication Protocol version 2, a more secure version of NTLM that is supported by Windows 2000, Windows NT 4.0 SP3 or higher, and Windows 9x with the DS Client software.

NWLink   Microsoft's implementation of Novell's IPX/SPX protocol.

O

object   In the Active Directory, a schema defines the particular classes and attributes that can exist. A class defines a structure composed of attributes. The class describes possible directory objects that can be created. An object is the physical expression of a class. Possible objects include users, computers, OUs, and so on.

operations master   Replication in Windows 2000 is primarily multimaster. Some Active Directory data cannot be replication in this fashion and requires single-master replication. Each type of single-master replication required is handled by a specific operations master. Some operations masters, such as the domain naming master and the schema master, exist only once in a forest. Other operations masters, such as the relative identifier master, the PDC emulator, and the infrastructure master, exist in every domain in the forest. Each operations master is hosted by a domain controller.

organizational unit (OU)   A way to group computers and users within a domain for delegation of administrative duties or the application of Group Policy.

P

perfect forward security (PFS)   Assures that a compromised key gets the attacker only the information that was encrypted by that key. When PFS is required, the base information used to generate keys is never reused.

permanent virtual circuit flapping   The defined routing circuit selection keeps changing because problems on the network are periodically making one path not available. This is a symptom of intermittent failure across dedicated lines.

permanent virtual circuits   Circuits put into place that do not change for a long time. Permanent virtual circuits are possible with both ATM and Frame Relay.

Point-to-Point Tunneling Protocol (PPTP)   Used to create a VPN. It is supported by Win9x, Windows NT, and Windows 2000. PPP can use NAT, and it uses TCP 1723 and Protocol ID 47.

Power User   A group of users on standalone Windows 2000 servers and Windows 2000 Professional workstations. These users have special rights and privileges.

preauthentication   The process of validation of client credentials by the Authentication Server.

Pre-Boot Execution Environment (PXE)   An architecture for bootstrapping a client computer. The first time it boots, a PXE-compliant computer uses DHCP to request an IP address from a Remote Installation Services server. It sends its globally unique identifier

(GUID) as part of this request. The client receives an IP address and that of the RIS server. An installation of an OS follows.

preshared keys   Keys are written down in the IPSec policy. They must match on each side of an IPSec communication.

Primary Domain Controller (PDC) emulator   Acts as a Windows NT PDC if needed by non-Windows 2000 clients in the domain or if any Windows NT BDCs are present. In a Windows 2000 native-mode domain, the PDC emulator has password changes replicated preferentially and is the focus for Group Policy object modification by default.

product life cycle   Descriptions of the stages in a product's life, from its conception through its maturity and beyond.

propagational delay   Another way of referring to latency.

proxy server   A server that forwards requests for Web and WinSock services from an internal client. The IP address is usually changed to an external address, and the Web pages returned are usually cached for use by others.

public key infrastructure (PKI)   Technology, hardware, and software that supports the use of public/private key pairs for authentication between computers and/or users of those computers.

public/private key pair   A cryptographic method in which two asymmetric keys are used to encrypt and decrypt messages.

R

RAS server   A remote access server is used to control external access to internal resources.

realm   A logical grouping of Kerberos client and server computers. In Windows 2000, the term *domain* is used instead.

realm stripping   The process of removing a realm name from a username submitted to a RADIUS server.

Recovery Agent   A user with the privilege of having a key that can be used to decrypt the DRF, and thus gain the session key that can be used to recover the EFS encrypted file. This user is the local administrator, by default.

relative ID (RID) master   The operations master that is responsible for allocating relative ID sequences to each domain controller. This ensures that domain controllers in a domain do not issue duplicate SIDs (the SID is composed of a domain component and a RID).

Remote Access Policy   A policy that can be written to impact any user that accesses the network through this service. It can be centralized by configuring a RAS server as a RADIUS client.

Remote Authentication Dial-In User Service (RADIUS)   A service that provides authentication, authorization, and accounting for dial-up accounts. It is often used by ISPs and others to control access to a network from dial-up accounts.

Remote Installation Services (RIS)   A program that allows the remote installation of an operating system on new computers. The Microsoft Windows 2000 server includes a RIS program for installing Windows 2000 Professional.

Remote Procedure Call (RPC)   A method of splitting code between computers on a network. Part of the code runs on a client, and part runs on a server. The RPC is the part of the code that is aware of the network and knows how to communicate across it.

Request for Comment (RFC)   A tool of the IETF used to reach consensus on various Internet activities and protocols.

Restricted groups   Groups identified as restricted can have their membership controlled externally to the domain or computer by Group Policy.

RID   The unique portion of a SID. The nonunique portion of a SID is that part which represents the domain. Because there are multiple domain controllers in an operations master, the RID master allocates blocks of RIDs to the domain controllers.

root CA   The first CA, the CA that does not require authorization from another CA to operate. It issues its own certificate.

Routing and Remote Access   A service that has components for routing and controlling remote access to the server.

Routing Information Protocol (RIP)   A specification for how IP or IPX is routed. Routers use this protocol to communicate their networks to one another.

S

S/MAIL   Secure email. This Can be either S/MIME, or some other form of secure mail. Secure email is usually encrypted.

Scard COM   A noncryptographic API used to write interfaces for smart card applications.

schema   Defines the classes and attributes available within a directory. It defines the attributes that make up each class.

schema master   The operations master that is responsible for modification of schema data.

screened subnet   Another name for a demilitarized zone.

Secedit   A command-line tool for analyzing and applying security templates.

Secure Sockets Layer (SSL)   A protocol used to provide authentication and encrypted communications between Web browsers and Web servers.

Security Accounts Manager (SAM)   The repository for local machine accounts in Windows 2000, and local and network (domain) accounts in Windows NT.

Security Association (SA)   An SA defines the connection for IPSec connections.

Security Configuration and Analysis console   An MMC snap-in that allows the configuration and analysis of computers.

security descriptor   A data structure that includes lists of SIDs and their access privileges (DACL), as well as lists of SIDS and the need to record their access or attempts at access (SACL).

Security groups   Groups of users that are used to assign access and user rights (as opposed to distribution groups, which cannot be assigned permissions or rights).

Security Parameters Index (SPI)   An IPSec component that identifies the SA to which a packet belongs.

security principal   A user, group, computer, or service account that can be given rights, privileges, and permissions within the domain. A security principal can initialize activity.

Security Reference Monitor (SRM)   Part of the security subsystem that manages authorization and auditing details.

security support provider (SSP)   A dynamic link library that makes a security package available via an SSPI. A security package maps the SSPI functions to an implementation of the security protocol used by the package, such as NTLM, Kerberos, or SSL.

Security Support Provider Interface (SSPI)   An API that insulates programmers from the details of security programming for different protocols.

security templates   Configuration settings in a script file that can be used to apply, analyze, or modify computer security policy

service   In Windows 2000, a process that runs in the background to perform some tasks. It may run at all times or respond to some activity.

service account   An account that is used by a service to authenticate and authorize server processes.

Service Advertising Protocol (SAP)   A NetWare process for identifying services on a network.

service level agreement (SLA)   A contract that specifies the performance levels a communications provider must guarantee. It often spells out the penalty for not providing that service.

service ticket   A Kerberos ticket that can be used for access to a particular server.

Services for Macintosh (SFM)   The utility that provides file and print services for Macintosh computers.

Services for UNIX (SFU)   A product available for Windows 2000 that provides UNIX access to Windows servers and UNIX utilities.

session key   A cryptographic key shared between two parties and used to encrypt and decrypt messages.

skew time   The allowed difference between client and server time in a Kerberos system.

smart cards   Small, credit card-sized cards that hold information. Some of them have small integrated circuits (IC). They are often used for alternative authentication purposes.

SMB signing   The process of digitally signing SMB packets for mutual authentication.

SNMP Agent   A program that runs on a device and responds to requests for information and possible action from an SNMP management program.

SNMP Management System   Simple Network Management Protocol system is one that can control devices on a network. The SNMP agent is installed on each device, and the management program can query the agent for information about its status. The program may also be capable of changing settings on these devices.

soft costs   Those costs that cannot easily be attributable to a particular product or action.

ssod   A synchronization daemon that must run on a UNIX server to provide encrypted password synchronization with Windows 2000 services for UNIX systems.

standalone CA   A Microsoft CA that does not use Active Directory.

standalone server   A server that is not a member of a domain.

subordinate CA   A CA that is reliant on another CA for its authorization to function. Its certificate is issued by another CA.

switched virtual circuit   A temporary virtual circuit that is set up as the needs arises. SVCs can be used by ATM or Frame Relay.

symmetric cryptography   Cryptography that uses a shared, single key.

System Access Control List (SACL)   A listing of users or group SIDS, including what should be audited when they access the object to which the SACL is attached.

T

Telnet   A TCP/IP communications protocol that allows remote administrative control of a server. The Telnet server component must be running on the server, and the Telnet client must be running on the client.

Terminal Services   A Windows 2000 service that allows the connection of non-Windows clients to a multiuser version of Windows 2000. Keystrokes and mouse clicks travel from the client to the server. The server returns display screens.

Ticket Granting Service Exchange   A communication of the Kerberos protocol that exchanges the TGT for a service ticket.

ticket-granting ticket (TGT)   A Kerberos ticket that can be used to obtain service tickets.

transitive trust   Trust that, although only established between two computers, implies trust to any other computers each of these has.

trap   In SNMP, a trap is a setting that, when triggered, sends an alarm or message from an SNMP-enabled device to the SNMP management program.

tree   A number of domains that share the same contiguous DNS name space in a forest.

Trojan virus   A program that masquerades as a benign application but, when run, is malignant.

tunneling   Network data is carried over another network's structure. The data is encapsulated, and the external address is of the tunnel endpoint, not the final destination.

U

Universal Authentication Module (UAM)   A component that, when added to a Macintosh computer, can provide network authentication with Windows networks. A Microsoft version of this module increases security by adding longer password capability.

Universal group   This group can contain members from other domains. It is used to collect multiple groups from many domains, and it reduces replication traffic. Universal groups exist only in native-mode domains. They store their membership in the Global Catalog.

user id (UID)   In UNIX, users are represented by UIDs.

Users   A group that includes all users except the Guest Account in the domain.

V

virtual circuit   A connection that acts as if it is a direct connection between two hosts, when it actually may be routed in a roundabout way.

virtual private network (VPN)   A network composed of connections, usually across a public network. Private data is tunneled and encrypted. Connections are made as needed; they are not permanent.

W

Windows File Protection (WFP)   Keeps folks from overwriting or deleting system files.

X

external data representation (XDR)   An open source method for providing data translation that may be necessary as to use across data networks.

APPENDIX B

Overview of the Certification Process

You must pass rigorous certification exams to become a Microsoft Certified Professional. These closed-book exams provide a valid and reliable measure of your technical proficiency and expertise. Developed in consultation with computer industry professionals who have experience with Microsoft products in the workplace, the exams are conducted by two independent organizations. Sylvan Prometric offers the exams at more than 2,000 authorized Prometric Testing Centers around the world. Virtual University Enterprises (VUE) testing centers offer exams at more than 1,400 locations as well.

To schedule an exam, call Sylvan Prometric Testing Centers at 800-755-EXAM (3926) (or register online at http://www.2test.com/register) or VUE at 888-837-8734 (or register online at http://www.vue.com/ms/msexam.html). At the time of this writing, Microsoft offered eight types of certification, each based on a specific area of expertise. Please check the Microsoft Certified Professional Web site for the most up-to-date information (www.microsoft.com/mcp/).

TYPES OF CERTIFICATION

◆ **Microsoft Certified Professional (MCP).** Persons with this credential are qualified to support at least one Microsoft product. Candidates can take elective exams to develop areas of specialization. MCP is the base level of expertise.

◆ **Microsoft Certified Professional+Internet (MCP+Internet).** Persons with this credential are qualified to plan security, install and configure server products, manage server resources, extend service to run CGI scripts or ISAPI scripts, monitor and analyze performance, and troubleshoot problems. Expertise is similar to that of an MCP but with a focus on the Internet.

◆ **Microsoft Certified Professional+Site Building (MCP+Site Building).** Persons with this credential are qualified to plan, build, maintain, and manage Web sites using Microsoft technologies and products. The credential is appropriate for people who manage sophisticated, interactive Web sites that include database connectivity, multimedia, and searchable content.

◆ **Microsoft Certified Database Administrator (MCDBA).** Qualified individuals can derive physical database designs, develop logical data models, create physical databases, create data services by using Transact-SQL, manage and maintain databases, configure and manage security, monitor and optimize databases, and install and configure Microsoft SQL Server.

◆ **Microsoft Certified Systems Engineer (MCSE).** These individuals are qualified to analyze the business requirements for a system architecture; design solutions; deploy, install, and configure architecture components; and troubleshoot system problems.

◆ **Microsoft Certified Systems Engineer+Internet (MCSE+Internet).** Persons with this credential are qualified in the core MCSE areas and also are qualified to enhance, deploy, and manage sophisticated intranet and Internet solutions that include a browser, proxy server, host servers, database, and messaging and commerce components. An MCSE+Internet-certified professional is able to manage and analyze Web sites.

◆ **Microsoft Certified Solution Developer (MCSD).** These individuals are qualified to design and develop custom business solutions by using Microsoft development tools, technologies, and platforms. The new track includes certification exams that test the user's ability to build Web-based, distributed, and commerce applications by using Microsoft products such as Microsoft SQL Server, Microsoft Visual Studio, and Microsoft Component Services.

◆ **Microsoft Certified Trainer (MCT).** Persons with this credential are instructionally and technically qualified by Microsoft to deliver Microsoft Education Courses at Microsoft-authorized sites. An MCT must be employed by a Microsoft Solution Provider Authorized Technical Education Center or a Microsoft Authorized Academic Training site.

NOTE For up-to-date information about each type of certification, visit the Microsoft Training and Certification Web site at http://www.microsoft.com/mcp. You can also contact Microsoft through the following sources:

- Microsoft Certified Professional Program: 800-636-7544

- mcp@msource.com

- Microsoft Online Institute

CERTIFICATION REQUIREMENTS

The following sections describe the requirements for the various types of Microsoft certifications.

NOTE An asterisk following an exam in any of the following lists means that it is slated for retirement.

How to Become a Microsoft Certified Professional

To become certified as an MCP, you need only pass any Microsoft exam (with the exceptions of Networking Essentials, #70-058* and Microsoft Windows 2000 Accelerated Exam for MCPs Certified on Microsoft Windows NT 4.0, #70-240).

How to Become a Microsoft Certified Professional+Internet

To become an MCP specializing in Internet technology, you must pass the following exams:

◆ Internetworking with Microsoft TCP/IP on Microsoft Windows NT 4.0, #70-059*

◆ Implementing and Supporting Microsoft Windows NT Server 4.0, #70-067*

◆ Implementing and Supporting Microsoft Internet Information Server 3.0 and Microsoft Index Server 1.1, #70-077*

   OR Implementing and Supporting Microsoft Internet Information Server 4.0, #70-087*

How to Become a Microsoft Certified Professional+Site Building

To be certified as an MCP+Site Building, you need to pass two of the following exams:

◆ Designing and Implementing Web Sites with Microsoft FrontPage 98, #70-055

◆ Designing and Implementing Commerce Solutions with Microsoft Site Server 3.0, Commerce Edition, #70-057

◆ Designing and Implementing Web Solutions with Microsoft Visual InterDev 6.0, #70-152

How to Become a Microsoft Certified Database Administrator

There are two MCDBA tracks, one tied to Windows 2000, the other based on Windows NT 4.0.

Windows 2000 Track

To become an MCDBA in the Windows 2000 track, you must pass three core exams and one elective exam.

Core Exams

The core exams required to become an MCDBA in the Windows 2000 track are as follows:

◆ Installing, Configuring, and Administering Microsoft Windows 2000 Server, #70-215

   OR Microsoft Windows 2000 Accelerated Exam for MCPs Certified on Microsoft Windows NT 4.0, #70-240 (only for those who have passed exams #70-067*, #70-068*, and #70-073*)

◆ Administering Microsoft SQL Server 7.0, #70-028

◆ Designing and Implementing Databases with Microsoft SQL Server 7.0, #70-029

Elective Exams

You must also pass one elective exam from the following list:

◆ Implementing and Administering a Microsoft Windows 2000 Network Infrastructure, #70-216 (only for those who have *not* already passed #70-067*, #70-068*, and #70-073*)

OR Microsoft Windows 2000 Accelerated Exam for MCPs Certified on Microsoft Windows NT 4.0, #70-240 (only for those who have passed exams #70-067*, #70-068*, and #70-073*)

◆ Designing and Implementing Distributed Applications with Microsoft Visual C++ 6.0, #70-015

◆ Designing and Implementing Data Warehouses with Microsoft SQL Server 7.0 and Microsoft Decision Support Services 1.0, #70-019

◆ Implementing and Supporting Microsoft Internet Information Server 4.0, #70-087*

◆ Designing and Implementing Distributed Applications with Microsoft Visual FoxPro 6.0, #70-155

◆ Designing and Implementing Distributed Applications with Microsoft Visual Basic 6.0, #70-175

Windows NT 4.0 Track

To become an MCDBA in the Windows NT 4.0 track, you must pass four core exams and one elective exam.

Core Exams

The core exams required to become an MCDBA in the Windows NT 4.0 track are as follows:

◆ Administering Microsoft SQL Server 7.0, #70-028

◆ Designing and Implementing Databases with Microsoft SQL Server 7.0, #70-029

◆ Implementing and Supporting Microsoft Windows NT Server 4.0, #70-067*

◆ Implementing and Supporting Microsoft Windows NT Server 4.0 in the Enterprise, #70-068*

Elective Exams

You must also pass one elective exam from the following list:

◆ Designing and Implementing Distributed Applications with Microsoft Visual C++ 6.0, #70-015

◆ Designing and Implementing Data Warehouses with Microsoft SQL Server 7.0 and Microsoft Decision Support Services 1.0, #70-019

◆ Internetworking with Microsoft TCP/IP on Microsoft Windows NT 4.0, #70-059*

◆ Implementing and Supporting Microsoft Internet Information Server 4.0, #70-087*

◆ Designing and Implementing Distributed Applications with Microsoft Visual FoxPro 6.0, #70-155

◆ Designing and Implementing Distributed Applications with Microsoft Visual Basic 6.0, #70-175

How to Become a Microsoft Certified Systems Engineer

You must pass operating system exams and two elective exams to become an MCSE. The MCSE certification path is divided into two tracks: Windows 2000 and Windows NT 4.0.

The following lists show the core requirements for the Windows 2000 and Windows NT 4.0 tracks and the electives.

Windows 2000 Track

The Windows 2000 track requires you to pass five core exams (or an accelerated exam and another core exam). You must also pass two elective exams.

Core Exams

The Windows 2000 track core requirements for MCSE certification include the following for those who have *not* passed #70-067, #70-068, and #70-073:

◆ Installing, Configuring, and Administering Microsoft Windows 2000 Professional, #70-210

◆ Installing, Configuring, and Administering Microsoft Windows 2000 Server, #70-215

◆ Implementing and Administering a Microsoft Windows 2000 Network Infrastructure, #70-216

◆ Implementing and Administering a Microsoft Windows 2000 Directory Services Infrastructure, #70-217

The Windows 2000 Track core requirements for MCSE certification include the following for those who have passed #70-067*, #70-068*, and #70-073*:

◆ Microsoft Windows 2000 Accelerated Exam for MCPs Certified on Microsoft Windows NT 4.0, #70-240

All candidates must pass one of these three additional core exams:

◆ Designing a Microsoft Windows 2000 Directory Services Infrastructure, #70-219

   OR Designing Security for a Microsoft Windows 2000 Network, #70-220

   OR Designing a Microsoft Windows 2000 Infrastructure, #70-221

Elective Exams

Any MCSE elective exams that are current (not slated for retirement) when the Windows 2000 core exams are released can be used to fulfill the requirement of two elective exams. In addition, core exams #70-219,

#70-220, and #70-221 can be used as elective exams, as long as they are not already being used to fulfill the "additional core exams" requirement outlined previously. Exam #70-222 (Upgrading from Microsoft Windows NT 4.0 to Microsoft Windows 2000) can also be used to fulfill this requirement. Finally, selected third-party certifications that focus on interoperability may count for this requirement. Watch the Microsoft MCP Web site (www.microsoft.com/mcp) for more information on these third-party certifications.

Windows NT 4.0 Track

The Windows NT 4.0 track is also organized around core and elective exams.

Core Exams

The four Windows NT 4.0 track core requirements for MCSE certification are as follows:

◆ Implementing and Supporting Microsoft Windows NT Server 4.0, #70-067*

◆ Implementing and Supporting Microsoft Windows NT Server 4.0 in the Enterprise, #70-068*

◆ Microsoft Windows 3.1, #70-030*

   OR Microsoft Windows for Workgroups 3.11, #70-048*

   OR Implementing and Supporting Microsoft Windows 95, #70-064*

   OR Implementing and Supporting Microsoft Windows NT Workstation 4.0, #70-073*

   OR Implementing and Supporting Microsoft Windows 98, #70-098

◆ Networking Essentials, #70-058*

Elective Exams

For the Windows NT 4.0 track, you must pass two of the following elective exams for MCSE certification:

◆ Implementing and Supporting Microsoft SNA Server 3.0, #70-013

   OR Implementing and Supporting Microsoft SNA Server 4.0, #70-085

◆ Implementing and Supporting Microsoft Systems Management Server 1.2, #70-018

   OR Implementing and Supporting Microsoft Systems Management Server 2.0, #70-086

◆ Designing and Implementing Data Warehouse with Microsoft SQL Server 7.0, #70-019

◆ Microsoft SQL Server 4.2 Database Implementation, #70-021*

   OR Implementing a Database Design on Microsoft SQL Server 6.5, #70-027

   OR Implementing a Database Design on Microsoft SQL Server 7.0, #70-029

◆ Microsoft SQL Server 4.2 Database Administration for Microsoft Windows NT, #70-022*

   OR System Administration for Microsoft SQL Server 6.5 (or 6.0), #70-026

   OR System Administration for Microsoft SQL Server 7.0, #70-028

◆ Microsoft Mail for PC Networks 3.2-Enterprise, #70-037*

◆ Internetworking with Microsoft TCP/IP on Microsoft Windows NT (3.5–3.51), #70-053*

   OR Internetworking with Microsoft TCP/IP on Microsoft Windows NT 4.0, #70-059*

◆ Implementing and Supporting Web Sites Using Microsoft Site Server 3.0, #70-056

◆ Implementing and Supporting Microsoft Exchange Server 4.0, #70-075*

   OR Implementing and Supporting Microsoft Exchange Server 5.0, #70-076

   OR Implementing and Supporting Microsoft Exchange Server 5.5, #70-081

◆ Implementing and Supporting Microsoft Internet Information Server 3.0 and Microsoft Index Server 1.1, #70-077*

   OR Implementing and Supporting Microsoft Internet Information Server 4.0, #70-087*

◆ Implementing and Supporting Microsoft Proxy Server 1.0, #70-078

   OR Implementing and Supporting Microsoft Proxy Server 2.0, #70-088

◆ Implementing and Supporting Microsoft Internet Explorer 4.0 by Using the Internet Explorer Resource Kit, #70-079

   OR Implementing and Supporting Microsoft Internet Explorer 5.0 by Using the Internet Explorer Resource Kit, #70-080

◆ Designing a Microsoft Windows 2000 Directory Services Infrastructure, #70-219

◆ Designing Security for a Microsoft Windows 2000 Network, #70-220

◆ Designing a Microsoft Windows 2000 Infrastructure, #70-221

◆ Upgrading from Microsoft Windows NT 4.0 to Microsoft Windows 2000, #70-222

How to Become a Microsoft Certified Systems Engineer+Internet

You must pass seven operating system exams and two elective exams to become an MCSE specializing in Internet technology.

Core Exams

The following seven core exams are required for MCSE+Internet certification:

◆ Networking Essentials, #70-058*

◆ Internetworking with Microsoft TCP/IP on Microsoft Windows NT 4.0, #70-059*

◆ Implementing and Supporting Microsoft Windows 95, #70-064*

  OR Implementing and Supporting Microsoft Windows NT Workstation 4.0, #70-073*

  OR Implementing and Supporting Microsoft Windows 98, #70-098

◆ Implementing and Supporting Microsoft Windows NT Server 4.0, #70-067*

◆ Implementing and Supporting Microsoft Windows NT Server 4.0 in the Enterprise, #70-068*

◆ Implementing and Supporting Microsoft Internet Information Server 3.0 and Microsoft Index Server 1.1, #70-077*

  OR Implementing and Supporting Microsoft Internet Information Server 4.0, #70-087*

◆ Implementing and Supporting Microsoft Internet Explorer 4.0 by Using the Internet Explorer Resource Kit, #70-079

  OR Implementing and Supporting Microsoft Internet Explorer 5.0 by Using the Internet Explorer Resource Kit, #70-080

Elective Exams

You must also pass two of the following elective exams for MCSE+Internet certification:

◆ System Administration for Microsoft SQL Server 6.5, #70-026

  OR Administering Microsoft SQL Server 7.0, #70-028

◆ Implementing a Database Design on Microsoft SQL Server 6.5, #70-027

  OR Designing and Implementing Databases with Microsoft SQL Server 7.0, #70-029

◆ Implementing and Supporting Web Sites Using Microsoft Site Server 3.0, # 70-056

◆ Implementing and Supporting Microsoft Exchange Server 5.0, #70-076

  OR Implementing and Supporting Microsoft Exchange Server 5.5, #70-081

◆ Implementing and Supporting Microsoft Proxy Server 1.0, #70-078

  OR Implementing and Supporting Microsoft Proxy Server 2.0, #70-088

◆ Implementing and Supporting Microsoft SNA Server 4.0, #70-085

How to Become a Microsoft Certified Solution Developer

The MCSD certification has undergone substantial revision. Listed below are the requirements for the new track as well as the old.

New Track

For the new track, you must pass three core exams and one elective exam.

Core Exams

The core exams are as follows. You must pass one exam in each of the following groups:

Desktop Applications Development (one required)

◆ Designing and Implementing Desktop Applications with Microsoft Visual C++ 6.0, #70-016

    OR Designing and Implementing Desktop Applications with Microsoft Visual FoxPro 6.0, #70-156

    OR Designing and Implementing Desktop Applications with Microsoft Visual Basic 6.0, #70-176

Distributed Applications Development (one required)

◆ Designing and Implementing Distributed Applications with Microsoft Visual C++ 6.0, #70-015

    OR Designing and Implementing Distributed Applications with Microsoft Visual FoxPro 6.0, #70-155

    OR Designing and Implementing Distributed Applications with Microsoft Visual Basic 6.0, #70-175

Solution Architecture (required)

◆ Analyzing Requirements and Defining Solution Architectures, #70-100

Elective Exam

You must pass one of the following elective exams:

◆ Designing and Implementing Distributed Applications with Microsoft Visual C++ 6.0, #70-015

◆ Designing and Implementing Desktop Applications with Microsoft Visual C++ 6.0, #70-016

◆ Designing and Implementing Data Warehouses with Microsoft SQL Server 7.0, #70-019

◆ Developing Applications with C++ Using the Microsoft Foundation Class Library, #70-024

◆ Implementing OLE in Microsoft Foundation Class Applications, #70-025

◆ Implementing a Database Design on Microsoft SQL Server 6.5, #70-027

◆ Implementing a Database Design on Microsoft SQL Server 7.0, #70-029

◆ Designing and Implementing Web Sites with Microsoft FrontPage 98, #70-055

◆ Designing and Implementing Commerce Solutions with Microsoft Site Server 3.0, Commerce Edition, #70-057

◆ Programming with Microsoft Visual Basic 4.0, #70-065*

◆ Application Development with Microsoft Access for Windows 95 and the Microsoft Access Developer's Toolkit, #70-069

◆ Designing and Implementing Solutions with Microsoft Office 2000 and Microsoft Visual Basic for Applications, #70-091

◆ Designing and Implementing Database Applications with Microsoft Access 2000, #70-097

◆ Designing and Implementing Collaborative Solutions with Microsoft Outlook 2000 and Microsoft Exchange Server 5.5, #70-105

◆ Designing and Implementing Web Solutions with Microsoft Visual InterDev 6.0, #70-152

◆ Designing and Implementing Distributed Applications with Microsoft Visual FoxPro 6.0, #70-155

◆ Designing and Implementing Desktop Applications with Microsoft Visual FoxPro 6.0, #70-156

◆ Developing Applications with Microsoft Visual Basic 5.0, #70-165

◆ Designing and Implementing Distributed Applications with Microsoft Visual Basic 6.0, #70-175

◆ Designing and Implementing Desktop Applications with Microsoft Visual Basic 6.0, #70-176

Old Track

For the old track, you must pass two core technology exams and two elective exams for MCSD certification. The following lists show the required technology exams and elective exams needed for MCSD certification.

Core Exams

You must pass the following two core technology exams to qualify for MCSD certification:

◆ Microsoft Windows Architecture I, #70-160*

◆ Microsoft Windows Architecture II, #70-161*

Elective Exams

You must also pass two of the following elective exams to become an MSCD:

◆ Designing and Implementing Distributed Applications with Microsoft Visual C++ 6.0, #70-015

◆ Designing and Implementing Desktop Applications with Microsoft Visual C++ 6.0, #70-016

◆ Designing and Implementing Data Warehouses with Microsoft SQL Server 7.0, #70-019

◆ Microsoft SQL Server 4.2 Database Implementation, #70-021*

  OR Implementing a Database Design on Microsoft SQL Server 6.5, #70-027

  OR Implementing a Database Design on Microsoft SQL Server 7.0, #70-029

◆ Developing Applications with C++ Using the Microsoft Foundation Class Library, #70-024

◆ Implementing OLE in Microsoft Foundation Class Applications, #70-025

◆ Programming with Microsoft Visual Basic 4.0, #70-065

  OR Developing Applications with Microsoft Visual Basic 5.0, #70-165

  OR Designing and Implementing Distributed Applications with Microsoft Visual Basic 6.0, #70-175

◆ Designing and Implementing Desktop Applications with Microsoft Visual Basic 6.0, #70-176

◆ Microsoft Access 2.0 for Windows-Application Development, #70-051*

   OR Microsoft Access for Windows 95 and the Microsoft Access Development Toolkit, #70-069

   OR Designing and Implementing Database Applications with Microsoft Access 2000, #70-097

◆ Developing Applications with Microsoft Excel 5.0 Using Visual Basic for Applications, #70-052*

◆ Programming in Microsoft Visual FoxPro 3.0 for Windows, #70-054*

   OR Designing and Implementing Distributed Applications with Microsoft Visual FoxPro 6.0, #70-155

   OR Designing and Implementing Desktop Applications with Microsoft Visual FoxPro 6.0, #70-156

◆ Designing and Implementing Web Sites with Microsoft FrontPage 98, #70-055

◆ Designing and Implementing Commerce Solutions with Microsoft Site Server 3.0, Commerce Edition, #70-057

◆ Designing and Implementing Solutions with Microsoft Office (code-named Office 9) and Microsoft Visual Basic for Applications, #70-091

◆ Designing and Implementing Collaborative Solutions with Microsoft Outlook 2000 and Microsoft Exchange Server 5.5, #70-105

◆ Designing and Implementing Web Solutions with Microsoft Visual InterDev 6.0, #70-152

Becoming a Microsoft Certified Trainer

To fully understand the requirements and process for becoming an MCT, you need to obtain the Microsoft Certified Trainer Guide document from the following WWW site:

```
http://www.microsoft.com/mcp/certstep/mct.htm
```

At this site, you can read the document as a Web page or display and download it as a Word file. The MCT Guide explains the process for becoming an MCT. The general steps for the MCT certification are as follows:

1. Complete and mail a Microsoft Certified Trainer application to Microsoft. You must include proof of your skills for presenting instructional material. The options for doing so are described in the MCT Guide.

2. Obtain and study the Microsoft Trainer Kit for the Microsoft Official Curricula (MOC) courses for which you want to be certified. Microsoft Trainer Kits can be ordered by calling 800-688-0496 in North America. Those of you in other regions should review the MCT Guide for information on how to order a Trainer Kit.

3. Take and pass any required prerequisite MCP exam(s) to measure your current technical knowledge.

4. Prepare to teach a MOC course. Begin by attending the MOC course for which you want to be certified. This is required so that you understand how the course is structured, how labs are completed, and how the course flows.

5. Pass any additional exam requirement(s) to measure any additional product knowledge that pertains to the course.

6. Submit your course preparation checklist to Microsoft so that your additional accreditation may be processed and reflect on your transcript.

> **WARNING**
>
> You should consider the preceding steps a general overview of the MCT certification process. The precise steps that you need to take are described in detail on the Web site mentioned earlier. Do not misinterpret the preceding steps as the exact process you must

If you are interested in becoming an MCT, you can obtain more information by visiting the Microsoft Certified Training WWW site at `http://www.microsoft.com/train_cert/mct/` or by calling 800-688-0496.

What's on the CD-ROM

This appendix is a brief rundown of what you'll find on the CD-ROM that comes with this book. For a more detailed description of the newly developed *ExamGear, Training Guide Edition* exam simulation software, see Appendix D, "Using the ExamGear, Training Guide Edition Software." All items on the CD-ROM are easily accessible from the simple interface. In addition to *ExamGear, Training Guide Edition*, the CD-ROM includes the electronic version of the book in Portable Document Format (PDF), several utility and application programs, and a complete listing of the test objectives and where they are covered in the book.

EXAMGEAR, TRAINING GUIDE EDITION

ExamGear is an exam environment developed exclusively for New Riders Publishing. It is, we believe, the best exam software available. In addition to providing a means of evaluating your knowledge of the *Training Guide* material, *ExamGear, Training Guide Edition* features several innovations that help you to improve your mastery of the subject matter.

For example, the practice tests allow you to check your score by exam area or category to determine which topics you need to study more. In another mode, *ExamGear, Training Guide Edition* allows you to obtain immediate feedback on your responses in the form of explanations for the correct and incorrect answers.

Although *ExamGear, Training Guide Edition* exhibits most of the full functionality of the retail version of *ExamGear*, including the exam format and question types, this special version is written to the Training Guide content. It is designed to aid you in assessing how well you understand the Training Guide material and enable you to experience most of the question formats you will see on the actual exam. It is not as complete a simulation of the exam as the full *ExamGear* retail product. It also does not include some of the features of the full retail product, such as access to the mentored discussion groups. However, it serves as an excellent method for assessing your knowledge of the Training Guide content and gives you the experience of taking an electronic exam.

Again, for a more complete description of *ExamGear, Training Guide Edition* features, see Appendix D, "Using the ExamGear, Training Guide Edition Software."

EXCLUSIVE ELECTRONIC VERSION OF TEXT

The CD-ROM also contains the electronic version of this book in Portable Document Format (PDF). The electronic version comes complete with all figures as they appear in the book. You will find that the search capabilities of the reader come in handy for study and review purposes.

Copyright Information and Disclaimer

New Riders Publishing's *ExamGear* test simulator: Copyright © 2000 by New Riders Publishing. All rights reserved. Made in U.S.A.

Using the ExamGear, Training Guide Edition Software

This training guide includes a special version of *ExamGear*—a revolutionary new test engine that is designed to give you the best in certification exam preparation. *ExamGear* offers sample and practice exams for many of today's most in-demand technical certifications. This special Training Guide edition is included with this book as a tool to utilize in assessing your knowledge of the Training Guide material while also providing you with the experience of taking an electronic exam.

In the rest of this appendix, we describe in detail what *ExamGear, Training Guide Edition* is, how it works, and what it can do to help you prepare for the exam. Note that although the Training Guide edition includes nearly all the test simulation functions of the complete, retail version, the questions focus on the Training Guide content rather than on simulating the actual Microsoft exam. Also, this version does not offer the same degree of online support that the full product does.

EXAM SIMULATION

One of the main functions of *ExamGear, Training Guide Edition* is exam simulation. To prepare you to take the actual vendor certification exam, the Training Guide edition of this test engine is designed to offer the most effective exam simulation available.

Question Quality

The questions provided in the *ExamGear, Training Guide Edition* simulations are written to high standards of technical accuracy. The questions tap the content of the Training Guide chapters and help you review and assess your knowledge before you take the actual exam.

Interface Design

The *ExamGear, Training Guide Edition* exam simulation interface provides you with the experience of taking an electronic exam. This enables you to effectively prepare for taking the actual exam by making the test experience a familiar one. Using this test simulation can help eliminate the sense of surprise or anxiety that you might experience in the testing center, because you will already be acquainted with computerized testing.

STUDY TOOLS

ExamGear provides you with several learning tools to help prepare you for the actual certification exam.

Effective Learning Environment

The *ExamGear, Training Guide Edition* interface provides a learning environment that not only tests you through the computer, but also teaches the material you need to know to pass the certification exam. Each question comes with a detailed explanation of the correct answer and provides reasons why the other options were incorrect. This information helps to reinforce the knowledge you have already and also provides practical information you can use on the job.

Automatic Progress Tracking

ExamGear, Training Guide Edition automatically tracks your progress as you work through the test questions. From the Item Review tab (discussed in detail later in this appendix), you can see at a glance how well you are scoring by objective, by unit, or on a question-by-question basis (see Figure D.1). You can also configure *ExamGear* to drill you on the skills you need to work on most.

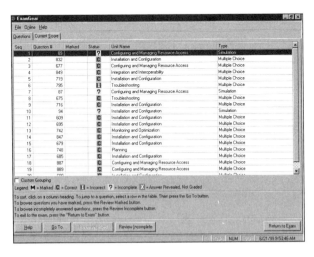

FIGURE D.1
Item review.

How ExamGear, Training Guide Edition Works

ExamGear comprises two main elements: the interface and the database. The *interface* is the part of the program that you use to study and to run practice tests. The *database* stores all the question-and-answer data.

Interface

The *ExamGear, Training Guide Edition* interface is designed to be easy to use and provides the most effective study method available. The interface enables you to select from the following modes:

◆ **Study Mode.** In this mode, you can select the number of questions you want to see and the time you want to allow for the test. You can select questions from all the chapters or from specific chapters. This enables you to reinforce your knowledge in a specific area or strengthen your knowledge in areas pertaining to a specific objective. During the exam, you can display the correct answer to each question along with an explanation of why it is correct.

◆ **Practice Exam.** In this mode, you take an exam that is designed to simulate the actual certification exam. Questions are selected from all test-objective groups. The number of questions selected and the time allowed are set to match those parameters of the actual certification exam.

◆ **Adaptive Exam.** In this mode, you take an exam simulation using the adaptive testing technique. Questions are taken from all test-objective groups. The questions are presented in a way that ensures your mastery of all the test objectives. After you have a passing score or if you reach a point where it is statistically impossible for you to pass, the exam is ended. This method provides a rapid assessment of your readiness for the actual exam.

Database

The *ExamGear, Training Guide Edition* database stores a group of test questions along with answers and explanations. At least three databases are included for each Training Guide edition product. One includes the questions from the ends of the chapters. Another includes the questions from the Practice Exam. The third is a database of new questions that have not appeared in the book. Additional exam databases may also be available for purchase online and are simple to download. Look ahead to the section "Obtaining Updates" in this appendix to find out how to download and activate additional databases.

INSTALLING AND REGISTERING EXAMGEAR, TRAINING GUIDE EDITION

This section provides instructions for *ExamGear, Training Guide Edition* installation and describes the process and benefits of registering your Training Guide edition product.

Requirements

ExamGear requires a computer with the following:

◆ Microsoft Windows 95, Windows 98, Windows NT 4.0, or Windows 2000.

A Pentium or later processor is recommended.

◆ Microsoft's Internet Explorer 4.01 or later version.

Internet Explorer 4.01 (or a later version) must be installed. (Even if you use a different browser, you still need to have Internet Explorer 4.01 or later installed.)

◆ A minimum of 16MB of RAM.

As with any Windows application, the more memory, the better your performance.

◆ A connection to the Internet.

An Internet connection is not required for the software to work, but it is required for online registration, product updates, downloading bonus question sets, and for unlocking other exams. These processes are described in more detail later.

Installing ExamGear, Training Guide Edition

Install *ExamGear, Training Guide Edition* by running the setup program that you found on the *ExamGear, Training Guide Edition* CD. Follow these instructions to install the Training Guide edition on your computer:

1. Insert the CD in your CD-ROM drive. The Autorun feature of Windows should launch the software. If you have Autorun disabled, click Start, and choose Run. Go to the root directory of the CD and choose START.EXE. Click Open and OK.

2. Click the button in the circle, and you see the welcome screen. From here you can install *ExamGear*. Click the ExamGear button to begin installation.

3. The Installation Wizard appears onscreen and prompts you with instructions to complete the installation. Select a directory on which to install *ExamGear, Training Guide Edition* (the Installation Wizard defaults to `C:\Program Files\ExamGear`).

4. The Installation Wizard copies the *ExamGear, Training Guide Edition* files to your hard drive, adds ExamGear, Training Guide Edition to your Program menu, adds values to your Registry, and installs test engine's DLLs to the appropriate system folders. To ensure that the process was successful, the Setup program finishes by running *ExamGear, Training Guide Edition.*

5. The Installation Wizard logs the installation process and stores this information in a file named `INSTALL.LOG`. This log file is used by the uninstall process in the event that you choose to remove *ExamGear, Training Guide Edition* from your computer. Because the *ExamGear* installation adds Registry keys and DLL files to your computer, it is important to uninstall the program appropriately (see the section "Removing *ExamGear, Training Guide Edition* from Your Computer").

Registering ExamGear, Training Guide Edition

The Product Registration Wizard appears when *ExamGear, Training Guide Edition* is started for the first time, and *ExamGear* checks at startup to see whether you are registered. If you are not registered, the main menu is hidden, and a Product Registration Wizard appears. Remember that your computer must have an Internet connection to complete the Product Registration Wizard.

The first page of the Product Registration Wizard details the benefits of registration; however, you can always elect not to register. The Show This Message at Startup Until I Register option enables you to decide whether the registration screen should appear every time *ExamGear, Training Guide Edition* is started. If you click the Cancel button, you return to the main menu. You can register at any time by selecting Online, Registration from the main menu.

The registration process is composed of a simple form for entering your personal information, including your name and address. You are asked for your level of experience with the product you are testing on and whether you purchased *ExamGear, Training Guide Edition* from a retail store or over the Internet. The information will be used by our software designers and marketing department to provide us with feedback about the usability and usefulness of this product. It takes only a few seconds to fill out and transmit the registration data. A confirmation dialog box appears when registration is complete.

After you have registered and transmitted this information to New Riders, the registration option is removed from the pull-down menus.

Registration Benefits

Remember that registration allows you access to download updates from our FTP site using *ExamGear, Training Guide Edition* (see the later section "Obtaining Updates").

Removing ExamGear, Training Guide Edition from Your Computer

In the event that you elect to remove the *ExamGear, Training Guide Edition* product from your computer, an uninstall process has been included to ensure that it is removed from your system safely and completely. Follow these instructions to remove *ExamGear* from your computer:

1. Click Start, Settings, Control Panel.

2. Double-click the Add/Remove Programs icon.

3. You are presented with a list of software that is installed on your computer. Select ExamGear, Training Guide Edition from the list and click the Add/Remove button. The *ExamGear, Training Guide Edition* software is then removed from your computer.

It is important that the INSTALL.LOG file be present in the directory where you have installed *ExamGear, Training Guide Edition* should you ever choose to uninstall the product. Do not delete this file. The INSTALL.LOG file is used by the uninstall process to safely remove the files and Registry settings that were added to your computer by the installation process.

USING EXAMGEAR, TRAINING GUIDE EDITION

ExamGear is designed to be user friendly and very intuitive, eliminating the need for you to learn some confusing piece of software just to practice answering questions. Because the software has a smooth learning curve, your time is maximized because you start practicing almost immediately.

General Description of How the Software Works

ExamGear has three modes of operation: Study Mode, Practice Exam, and Adaptive Exam (see Figure D.2).

All three sections have the same easy-to-use interface. Using Study Mode, you can hone your knowledge as well as your test-taking abilities through the use of the Show Answers option. While you are taking the test, you can expose the answers along with a brief description of why the given answers are right or wrong. This gives you the ability to better understand the material presented.

The Practice Exam section has many of the same options as Study Mode, but you cannot reveal the answers. This way, you have a more traditional testing environment with which to practice.

The Adaptive Exam questions continuously monitor your expertise in each tested topic area. If you reach a point at which you either pass or fail, the software ends the examination. As in the Practice Exam, you cannot reveal the answers.

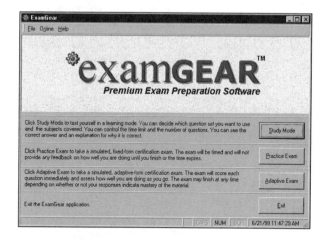

FIGURE D.2
The opening screen offers three testing modes.

Menu Options

The *ExamGear, Training Guide Edition* interface has an easy-to-use menu that provides the following options:

Menu	Command	Description
File	Print	Prints the current screen.
	Print Setup	Allows you to select the printer.
	Exit ExamGear	Exits the program.
Online	Registration	Starts the Registration Wizard and allows you to register online. This menu option is removed after you have successfully registered the product.
	Check for Product Updates	Downloads product catalog for Web-based updates.
	Web Browser	Opens the Web browser. It appears like this on the main menu, but more options appear after the browser is opened.
Help	Contents	Opens *ExamGear, Training Guide Edition*'s help file.
	About	Displays information about *ExamGear, Training Guide Edition*, including serial number, registered owner, and so on.

File

The File menu allows you to exit the program and configure print options.

Online

In the Online menu, you can register *ExamGear, Training Guide Edition*, check for product updates (update the *ExamGear* executable as well as check for free, updated question sets), and surf Web pages. The Online menu is always available, except when you are taking a test.

Registration

Registration is free and allows you access updates. Registration is the first task that *ExamGear, Training Guide Edition* asks you to perform. You will not have access to the free product updates if you do not register.

Check for Product Updates

This option takes you to *ExamGear, Training Guide Edition*'s Web site, where you can update the software. Registration is required for this option to be available. You must also be connected to the Internet to use this option. The *ExamGear* Web site lists the options that have been made available since your version of *ExamGear* was installed on your computer.

Web Browser

This option provides a convenient way to start your Web browser and connect to the New Riders Web site while you are working in *ExamGear, Training Guide Edition*. Click the Exit button to leave the Web browser and return to the *ExamGear* interface.

Help

As it suggests, this menu option gives you access to *ExamGear's* help system. It also provides important information like your serial number, software version, and so on.

Starting a Study Mode Session

Study Mode enables you to control the test in ways that actual certification exams do not allow:

◆ You can set your own time limits.

◆ You can concentrate on selected skill areas (units).

◆ You can reveal answers or have each response graded immediately with feedback.

◆ You can restrict the questions you see again to those missed or those answered correctly a given number of times.

◆ You can control the order in which questions are presented—random order or in order by skill area (unit).

To begin testing in Study Mode, click the Study Mode button from the main Interface screen. You are presented with the Study Mode configuration page (see Figure D.3).

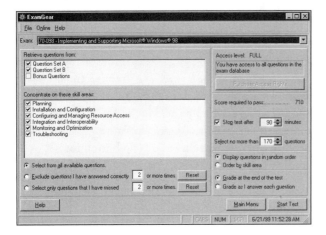

FIGURE D.3
The Study Mode configuration page.

At the top of the Study Mode configuration screen, you see the Exam drop-down list. This list shows the activated exam that you have purchased with your *ExamGear, Training Guide Edition* product, as well as any other exams you may have downloaded or any Preview exams that were shipped with your version of *ExamGear*. Select the exam with which you want to practice from the drop-down list.

Below the Exam drop-down list, you see the questions that are available for the selected exam. Each exam has at least one question set. You can select the individual

question set or any combination of the question sets if there is more than one available for the selected exam.

Below the Question Set list is a list of skill areas or chapters on which you can concentrate. These skill areas or chapters reflect the units of exam objectives defined by Microsoft for the exam. Within each skill area you will find several exam objectives. You can select a single skill area or chapter to focus on, or you can select any combination of the available skill areas/chapters to customize the exam to your individual needs.

In addition to specifying which question sets and skill areas you want to test yourself on, you can also define which questions are included in the test based on your previous progress working with the test. *ExamGear, Training Guide Edition* automatically tracks your progress with the available questions. When configuring the Study Mode options, you can opt to view all the questions available within the question sets and skill areas you have selected, or you can limit the questions presented. Choose from the following options:

◆ **Select from All Available Questions.** This option causes *ExamGear, Training Guide Edition* to present all available questions from the selected question sets and skill areas.

◆ **Exclude Questions I Have Answered Correctly X or More Times.** *ExamGear* offers you the option to exclude questions that you have previously answered correctly. You can specify how many times you want to answer a question correctly before *ExamGear* considers you to have mastered it (the default is two times).

◆ **Select Only Questions That I Have Missed X or More Times.** This option configures *ExamGear, Training Guide Edition* to drill you only on questions that you have missed repeatedly. You may specify how many times you must miss a question before *ExamGear* determines that you have not mastered it (the default is two times).

At any time, you can reset *ExamGear, Training Guide Edition*'s tracking information by clicking the Reset button for the feature you want to clear.

At the top-right side of the Study Mode configuration sheet, you can see your access level to the question sets for the selected exam. Access levels are either Full or Preview. For a detailed explanation of each of these access levels, see the section "Obtaining Updates" in this appendix.

Under your access level, you see the score required to pass the selected exam. Below the required score, you can select whether the test will be timed and how much time will be allowed to complete the exam. Select the Stop Test After 90 Minutes check box to set a time limit for the exam. Enter the number of minutes you want to allow for the test (the default is 90 minutes). Deselecting this check box allows you to take an exam with no time limit.

You can also configure the number of questions included in the exam. The default number of questions changes with the specific exam you have selected. Enter the number of questions you want to include in the exam in the Select No More than *X* Questions option.

You can configure the order in which *ExamGear, Training Guide Edition* presents the exam questions. Select from the following options:

◆ **Display Questions in Random Order.** This option is the default option. When selected, it causes *ExamGear, Training Guide Edition* to present the questions in random order throughout the exam.

◆ **Order by Skill Area.** This option causes *ExamGear* to group the questions presented in the exam by skill area. All questions for each selected skill area are presented in succession. The test progresses from one selected skill area to the next, until all the questions from each selected skill area have been presented.

ExamGear offers two options for scoring your exams. Select one of the following options:

◆ **Grade at the End of the Test.** This option configures *ExamGear, Training Guide Edition* to score your test after you have been presented with all the selected exam questions. You can reveal correct answers to a question, but if you do, that question is not scored.

◆ **Grade as I Answer Each Question.** This option configures *ExamGear* to grade each question as you answer it, providing you with instant feedback as you take the test. All questions are scored unless you click the Show Answer button before completing the question.

You can return to the *ExamGear, Training Guide Edition* main startup screen from the Study Mode configuration screen by clicking the Main Menu button. If you need assistance configuring the Study Mode exam options, click the Help button for configuration instructions.

When you have finished configuring all the exam options, click the Start Test button to begin the exam.

Starting Practice Exams and Adaptive Exams

This section describes the Practice and Adaptive Exams, defines the differences between these exam options and the Study Mode option, and provides instructions for starting them.

Differences Between the Practice and Adaptive Exams and Study Modes

Question screens in the Practice and Adaptive Exams are identical to those found in Study Mode, except that the Show Answer, Grade Answer, and Item Review buttons are not available while you are in the process of taking a practice or adaptive exam. The Practice Exam provides you with a report screen at the end of the exam. The Adaptive Exam gives you a brief message indicating whether you've passed or failed the exam.

When taking a practice exam, the Item Review screen is not available until you have answered all the questions. This is consistent with the behavior of most vendors' current certification exams. In Study Mode, Item Review is available at any time.

When the exam timer expires, or if you click the End Exam button, the Examination Score Report screen comes up.

Starting an Exam

From the *ExamGear, Training Guide Edition* main menu screen, select the type of exam you want to run. Click the Practice Exam or Adaptive Exam button to begin the corresponding exam type.

What Is an Adaptive Exam?

To make the certification testing process more efficient and valid and therefore make the certification itself more valuable, some vendors in the industry are using a testing technique called *adaptive testing*. In an adaptive exam, the exam "adapts" to your abilities by varying the difficulty level of the questions presented to you.

The first question in an adaptive exam is typically an easy one. If you answer it correctly, you are presented with a slightly more difficult question. If you answer that question correctly, the next question you see is even more difficult. If you answer the question incorrectly, however, the exam "adapts" to your skill level by presenting you with another question of equal or

lesser difficulty on the same subject. If you answer that question correctly, the test begins to increase the difficulty level again. You must correctly answer several questions at a predetermined difficulty level to pass the exam. After you have done this successfully, the exam is ended and scored. If you do not reach the required level of difficulty within a predetermined time (typically 30 minutes) the exam is ended and scored.

Why Do Vendors Use Adaptive Exams?

Many vendors who offer technical certifications have adopted the adaptive testing technique. They have found that it is an effective way to measure a candidate's mastery of the test material in as little time as necessary. This reduces the scheduling demands on the test taker and allows the testing center to offer more tests per test station than they could with longer, more traditional exams. In addition, test security is greater, and this increases the validity of the exam process.

Studying for Adaptive Exams

Studying for adaptive exams is no different from studying for traditional exams. You should make sure that you have thoroughly covered all the material for each of the test objectives specified by the certification exam vendor. As with any other exam, when you take an adaptive exam, either you know the material or you don't. If you are well prepared, you will be able to pass the exam. *ExamGear, Training Guide Edition* allows you to familiarize yourself with the adaptive exam testing technique. This will help eliminate any anxiety you might experience from this testing technique and allow you to focus on learning the actual exam material.

ExamGear's Adaptive Exam

The method used to score the Adaptive Exam requires a large pool of questions. For this reason, you cannot use this exam in Preview mode. The Adaptive Exam is presented in much the same way as the Practice Exam. When you click the Start Test button, you begin answering questions. The Adaptive Exam does not allow item review, and it does not allow you to mark questions to skip and answer later. You must answer each question when it is presented.

Assumptions

This section describes the assumptions made when designing the behavior of the *ExamGear, Training Guide Edition* adaptive exam.

◆ You fail the test if you fail any chapter or unit, earn a failing overall score, or reach a threshold at which it is statistically impossible for you to pass the exam.

◆ You can fail or pass a test without cycling through all the questions.

◆ The overall score for the adaptive exam is Pass or Fail. However, to evaluate user responses dynamically, percentage scores are recorded for units and the overall score.

Algorithm Assumptions

This section describes the assumptions used in designing the *ExamGear, Training Guide Edition* Adaptive Exam scoring algorithm.

Unit Scores

You fail a unit (and the exam) if any unit score falls below 66%.

Overall Scores

To pass the exam, you must pass all units and achieve an overall score of 86% or higher.

You fail if the overall score percentage is less than or equal to 85% or if any unit score is less than 66%.

Inconclusive Scores

If your overall score is between 67 and 85%, it is considered to be *inconclusive*. Additional questions will be asked until you pass or fail or until it becomes statistically impossible to pass without asking more than the maximum number of questions allowed.

Question Types and How to Answer Them

Because certification exams from different vendors vary, you will face many types of questions on any given exam. *ExamGear, Training Guide Edition* presents you with different question types to allow you to become familiar with the various ways an actual exam may test your knowledge. The Solution Architectures exam, in particular, offers a unique exam format and utilizes question types other than multiple choice. This version of *ExamGear* includes cases—extensive problem descriptions running several pages in length, followed by a number of questions specific to that case. Microsoft refers to these case/question collections as *testlets*. This version of *ExamGear, Training Guide Edition* also includes regular questions that are not attached to a case study. We include these question types to make taking the actual exam easier because you will already be familiar with the steps required to answer each question type. This section describes each of the question types presented by *ExamGear* and provides instructions for answering each type.

Multiple Choice

Most of the questions you see on a certification exam are multiple choice (see Figure D.4). This question type asks you to select an answer from the list provided. Sometimes you must select only one answer, often indicated by answers preceded by option buttons (round selection buttons). At other times, multiple correct answers are possible, indicated by check boxes preceding the possible answer combinations.

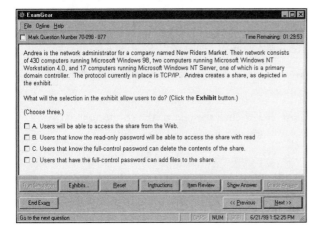

FIGURE D.4
A typical multiple-choice question.

You can use three methods to select an answer:

◆ Click the option button or check box next to the answer. If more than one correct answer to a question is possible, the answers will have check boxes next to them. If only one correct answer to a question is possible, each answer will have an option button next to it. *ExamGear, Training Guide Edition* prompts you with the number of answers you must select.

◆ Click the text of the answer.

◆ Press the alphabetic key that corresponds to the answer.

You can use any one of three methods to clear an option button:

◆ Click another option button.

◆ Click the text of another answer.

◆ Press the alphabetic key that corresponds to another answer.

You can use any one of three methods to clear a check box:

◆ Click the check box next to the selected answer.

◆ Click the text of the selected answer.

◆ Press the alphabetic key that corresponds to the selected answer.

To clear all answers, click the Reset button.

Remember that some of the questions have multiple answers that are correct. Do not let this throw you off. The *multiple correct* questions do not have one answer that is more correct than another. In the *single correct* format, only one answer is correct. *ExamGear, Training Guide Edition* prompts you with the number of answers you must select.

Drag and Drop

One form of drag and drop question is called a *Drop and Connect* question. These questions present you with a number of objects and connectors. The question prompts you to create relationships between the objects by using the connectors. The gray squares on the left side of the question window are the objects you can select. The connectors are listed on the right side of the question window in the Connectors box. An example is shown in Figure D.5.

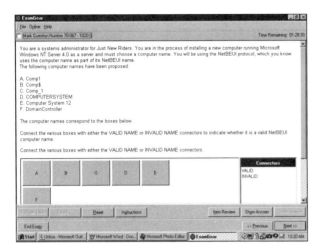

FIGURE D.5
A typical Drop and Connect question.

To select an object, click it with the mouse. When an object is selected, it changes color from a gray box to a white box. To drag an object, select it by clicking it with the left mouse button and holding the left mouse button down. You can move (or drag) the object to another area on the screen by moving the mouse while holding the left mouse button down.

To create a relationship between two objects, take the following actions:

1. Select an object and drag it to an available area on the screen.

2. Select another object and drag it to a location near where you dragged the first object.

3. Select the connector that you want to place between the two objects. The relationship should now appear complete. Note that to create a relationship, you must have two objects selected. If you try to select a connector without first selecting two objects, you are presented with an error message like that illustrated in Figure D.6.

FIGURE D.6
The error message.

Initially, the direction of the relationship established by the connector is from the first object selected to the second object selected. To change the direction of the connector, right-click the connector and choose Reverse Connection.

You can use either of two methods to remove the connector:

◆ Right-click the text of the connector that you want to remove, and then choose Delete.

◆ Select the text of the connector that you want to remove, and then press the Delete key.

To remove from the screen all the relationships you have created, click the Reset button.

Keep in mind that connectors can be used multiple times. If you move connected objects, it will not change the relationship between the objects; to remove the relationship between objects, you must remove the connector that joins them. When *ExamGear, Training Guide Edition* scores a drag-and-drop question, only objects with connectors to other objects are scored.

Another form of drag and drop question is called the *Select and Place* question. Instead of creating a diagram as you do with the Drop and Connect question, you are asked a question about a diagram. You then drag and drop labels onto the diagram in order to correctly answer the question.

Ordered-List Questions

In the *ordered-list* question type (see Figure D.7), you are presented with a number of items and are asked to perform two tasks:

1. Build an answer list from items on the list of choices.

2. Put the items in a particular order.

FIGURE D.7
A typical ordered-list question.

You can use any one of the following three methods to add an item to the answer list:

◆ Drag the item from the list of choices on the right side of the screen to the answer list on the left side of the screen.

◆ From the available items on the right side of the screen, double-click the item you want to add.

◆ From the available items on the right side of the screen, select the item you want to add; then click the Move button.

To remove an item from the answer list, you can use any one of the following four methods:

◆ Drag the item you want to remove from the answer list on the left side of the screen back to the list of choices on the right side of the screen.

◆ On the left side of the screen, double-click the item you want to remove from the answer list.

◆ On the left side of the screen, select the item you want to remove from the answer list, and then click the Remove button.

◆ On the left side of the screen, select the item you want to remove from the answer list, and then press the Delete key.

To remove all items from the answer list, click the Reset button.

If you need to change the order of the items in the answer list, you can do so using either of the following two methods:

◆ Drag each item to the appropriate location in the answer list.

◆ In the answer list, select the item that you want to move, and then click the up or down arrow button to move the item.

Keep in mind that items in the list can be selected twice. You may find that an ordered-list question will ask you to list in the correct order the steps required to perform a certain task. Certain steps may need to be performed more than once during the process. Don't think that after you have selected a list item, it is no longer available. If you need to select a list item more than once, you can simply select that item at each appropriate place as you construct your list.

Ordered-Tree Questions

The *ordered-tree* question type (see Figure D.8) presents you with a number of items and prompts you to create a tree structure from those items. The tree structure includes two or three levels of nodes.

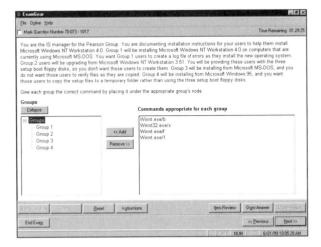

FIGURE D.8
A typical ordered-tree question.

An item in the list of choices can be added only to the appropriate node level. If you attempt to add one of the list choices to an inappropriate node level, you are presented with the error message shown in Figure D.9

FIGURE D.9
The Invalid Destination Node error message.

Like the ordered-list question, realize that any item in the list can be selected twice. If you need to select a list item more than once, you can simply select that item for the appropriate node as you construct your tree.

Also realize that not every tree question actually requires order to the lists under each node. Think of them as simply tree questions rather than ordered-tree questions. Such questions are just asking you to categorize hierarchically. Order is not an issue.

You can use either of the following two methods to add an item to the tree:

◆ Drag the item from the list of choices on the right side of the screen to the appropriate node of the tree on the left side of the screen.

◆ Select the appropriate node of the tree on the left side of the screen. Select the appropriate item from the list of choices on the right side of the screen. Click the Add button.

You can use either of the following two methods to remove an item from the tree:

◆ Drag an item from the tree to the list of choices.

◆ Select the item and click the Remove button.

To remove from the tree structure all the items you have added, click the Reset button.

Simulations

Simulation questions (see Figure D.10) require you to actually perform a task.

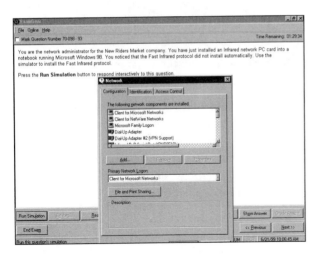

FIGURE D.10
A typical simulation question.

The main screen describes a situation and prompts you to provide a solution. When you are ready to proceed, you click the Run Simulation button in the lower-left corner. A screen or window appears on which you perform the solution. This window simulates the actual software that you would use to perform the required task in the real world. When a task requires several steps to complete, the simulator displays all the necessary screens to allow you to complete the task. When you have provided your answer by completing all the steps necessary to perform the required task, you can click the OK button to proceed to the next question.

You can return to any simulation to modify your answer. Your actions in the simulation are recorded, and the simulation appears exactly as you left it.

Simulation questions can be reset to their original state by clicking the Reset button.

Hot Spot Questions

Hot spot questions (see Figure D.11) ask you to correctly identify an item by clicking an area of the graphic or diagram displayed. To respond to the question, position the mouse cursor over a graphic. Then press the right mouse button to indicate your selection. To select another area on the graphic, you do not need to deselect the first one. Just click another region in the image.

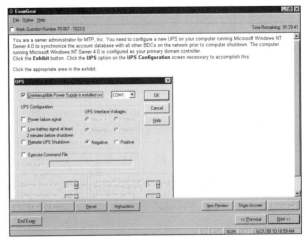

FIGURE D.11
A typical hot spot question.

Standard ExamGear, Training Guide Edition Options

Regardless of question type, a consistent set of clickable buttons enables you to navigate and interact with questions. The following list describes the function of each of the buttons you may see. Depending on the question type, some of the buttons will be grayed out and will be inaccessible. Buttons that are appropriate to the question type are active.

◆ **Run Simulation.** This button is enabled if the question supports a simulation. Clicking this button begins the simulation process.

◆ **Exhibits.** This button is enabled if exhibits are provided to support the question. An *exhibit* is an image, video, sound, or text file that provides supplemental information needed to answer the question. If a question has more than one exhibit, a dialog box appears, listing exhibits by name. If only one exhibit exists, the file is opened immediately when you click the Exhibits button.

◆ **Reset.** This button clears any selections you have made and returns the question window to the state in which it appeared when it was first displayed.

◆ **Instructions.** This button displays instructions for interacting with the current question type.

◆ **Item Review.** This button leaves the question window and opens the Item Review screen. For a detailed explanation of the Item Review screen, see the "Item Review" section later in this appendix.

◆ **Show Answer.** This option displays the correct answer with an explanation of why it is correct. If you choose this option, the current question will not be scored.

◆ **Grade Answer.** If Grade at the End of the Test is selected as a configuration option, this button is disabled. It is enabled when Grade as I Answer Each Question is selected as a configuration option. Clicking this button grades the current question immediately. An explanation of the correct answer is provided, just as if the Show Answer button were pressed. The question is graded, however.

◆ **End Exam.** This button ends the exam and displays the Examination Score Report screen.

◆ **<< Previous.** This button displays the previous question on the exam.

◆ **Next >>.** This button displays the next question on the exam.

◆ **<< Previous Marked.** This button is displayed if you have opted to review questions that you have marked using the Item Review screen. This button displays the previous marked question. Marking questions is discussed in more detail later in this appendix.

◆ **<< Previous Incomplete.** This button is displayed if you have opted to review questions that you have not answered using the Item Review screen. This button displays the previous unanswered question.

◆ **Next Marked >>.** This button is displayed if you have opted to review questions that you have marked using the Item Review screen. This button displays the next marked question. Marking questions is discussed in more detail later in this appendix.

◆ **Next Incomplete>>.** This button is displayed if you have opted to review questions, using the Item Review screen, that you have not answered. This button displays the next unanswered question.

Mark Question and Time Remaining

ExamGear provides you with two methods to aid in dealing with the time limit of the testing process. If you find that you need to skip a question or if you want to check the time remaining to complete the test, use one of the options discussed in the following sections.

Mark Question

Check this box to mark a question so that you can return to it later using the Item Review feature. The adaptive exam does not allow questions to be marked because it does not support item review.

Time Remaining

If the test is timed, the Time Remaining indicator is enabled. It counts down minutes remaining to complete the test. The adaptive exam does not offer this feature because it is not timed.

Item Review

The Item Review screen allows you to jump to any question. *ExamGear, Training Guide Edition* considers an *incomplete* question to be any unanswered question or any multiple-choice question for which the total number of required responses has not been selected. For example, if the question prompts for three answers and you selected only A and C, *ExamGear* considers the question to be incomplete.

The Item Review screen enables you to review the exam questions in different ways. You can enter one of two *browse sequences* (series of similar records): Browse Marked Questions or Browse Incomplete Questions. You can also create a custom grouping of the exam questions for review based on a number of criteria.

When using Item Review, if Show Answer was selected for a question while you were taking the exam, the question is grayed out in item review. The question can be answered again if you use the Reset button to reset the question status.

The Item Review screen contains two tabs. The Questions tab lists questions and question information in columns. The Current Score tab provides your exam score information, presented as a percentage for each unit and as a bar graph for your overall score.

The Item Review Questions Tab

The Questions tab on the Item Review screen (see Figure D.12) presents the exam questions and question information in a table. You can select any row you want by clicking in the grid. The Go To button is enabled whenever a row is selected. Clicking the Go To button displays the question on the selected row. You can also display a question by double-clicking that row.

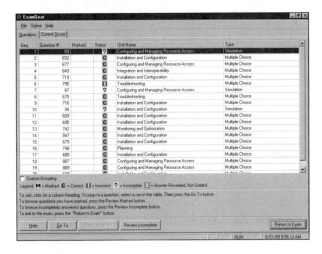

FIGURE D.12
The Questions tab on the Item Review screen.

Columns

The Questions tab contains the following six columns of information:

- ◆ **Seq.** Indicates the sequence number of the question as it was displayed in the exam.

- ◆ **Question Number.** Displays the question's identification number for easy reference.

- ◆ **Marked.** Indicates a question that you have marked using the Mark Question check box.

- ◆ **Status.** The status can be M for Marked, ? for Incomplete, C for Correct, I for Incorrect, or X for Answer Shown.

◆ **Unit Name.** The unit associated with each question.

◆ **Type.** The question type, which can be Multiple Choice, Drag and Drop, Simulation, Hot Spot, Ordered List, or Ordered Tree.

To resize a column, place the mouse pointer over the vertical line between column headings. When the mouse pointer changes to a set of right and left arrows, you can drag the column border to the left or right to make the column more or less wide. Simply click with the left mouse button and hold that button down while you move the column border in the desired direction.

The Item Review screen enables you to sort the questions on any of the column headings. Initially, the list of questions is sorted in descending order on the sequence number column. To sort on a different column heading, click that heading. You will see an arrow appear on the column heading indicating the direction of the sort (ascending or descending). To change the direction of the sort, click the column heading again.

The Item Review screen also allows you to create a *custom grouping*. This feature enables you to sort the questions based on any combination of criteria you prefer. For instance, you might want to review the question items sorted first by whether they were marked, then by the unit name, then by sequence number. The Custom Grouping feature allows you to do this. Start by checking the Custom Grouping check box (see Figure D.13). When you do so, the entire questions table shifts down a bit onscreen, and a message appear at the top of the table that reads `Drag a column header here to group by that column`.

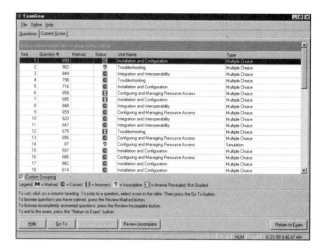

FIGURE D.13
The Custom Grouping check box allows you to create your own question sort order.

Simply click the column heading you want with the left mouse button, hold that button down, and move the mouse into the area directly above the questions table (the custom grouping area). Release the left mouse button to drop the column heading into the custom grouping area. To accomplish the custom grouping previously described, first check the Custom Grouping check box. Then drag the Marked column heading into the custom grouping area above the question table. Next, drag the Unit Name column heading into the custom grouping area. You will see the two column headings joined together by a line that indicates the order of the custom grouping. Finally, drag the Seq column heading into the custom grouping area. This heading will be joined to the Unit Name heading by another line indicating the direction of the custom grouping.

Notice that each column heading in the custom grouping area has an arrow indicating the direction in which items are sorted under that column heading. You can reverse the direction of the sort on an individual column-heading basis using these arrows. Click the column heading in the custom grouping area to change the direction of the sort for that column heading only. For example, using the custom grouping created previously, you can display the question list sorted first in descending order by whether the question was marked, in descending order by unit name, and then in ascending order by sequence number.

The custom grouping feature of the Item Review screen gives you enormous flexibility in how you choose to review the exam questions. To remove a custom grouping and return the Item Review display to its default setting (sorted in descending order by sequence number), simply uncheck the Custom Grouping check box.

The Current Score Tab

The Current Score tab of the Item Review screen (see Figure D.14) provides a real-time snapshot of your score. The top half of the screen is an expandable grid. When the grid is collapsed, scores are displayed for each unit. Units can be expanded to show percentage scores for objectives and subobjectives. Information about your exam progress is presented in the following columns:

◆ **Unit Name.** This column shows the unit name for each objective group.

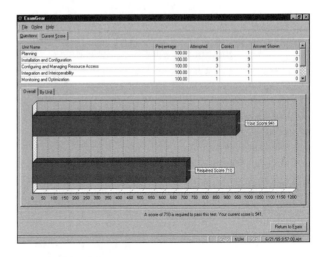

FIGURE D.14
The Current Score tab on the item review screen.

◆ **Percentage.** This column shows the percentage of questions for each objective group that you answered correctly.

◆ **Attempted.** This column lists the number of questions you answered either completely or partially for each objective group.

◆ **Correct.** This column lists the actual number of questions you answered correctly for each objective group.

◆ **Answer Shown.** This column lists the number of questions for each objective group that you chose to display the answer to using the Show Answer button.

The columns in the scoring table are resized and sorted in the same way as those in the questions table on the Item Review Questions tab. Refer to the earlier section "The Item Review Questions Tab" for more details.

A graphical overview of the score is presented below the grid. The graph depicts two red bars: The top bar represents your current exam score, and the bottom bar represents the required passing score. To the right of the bars in the graph is a legend that lists the required score and your score. Below the bar graph is a statement that describes the required passing score and your current score.

In addition, the information can be presented on an overall basis or by exam unit. The Overall tab shows the overall score. The By Unit tab shows the score by unit.

Clicking the End Exam button terminates the exam and passes control to the Examination Score Report screen.

The Return to Exam button returns to the exam at the question from which the Item Review button was clicked.

Review Marked Items

The Item Review screen allows you to enter a browse sequence for marked questions. When you click the Review Marked button, questions that you have previously marked using the Mark Question check box are presented for your review. While browsing the marked questions, you will see the following changes to the buttons available:

◆ The caption of the Next button becomes Next Marked.

◆ The caption of the Previous button becomes Previous Marked.

Review Incomplete

The Item Review screen allows you to enter a browse sequence for incomplete questions. When you click the Review Incomplete button, the questions you did not answer or did not completely answer are displayed for your review. While browsing the incomplete questions, you will see the following changes to the buttons:

◆ The caption of the Next button becomes Next Incomplete.

◆ The caption of the Previous button becomes Previous Incomplete.

Examination Score Report Screen

The Examination Score Report screen (see Figure D.15) appears when the Study Mode, Practice Exam, or Adaptive Exam ends—as the result of timer expiration, completion of all questions, or your decision to terminate early.

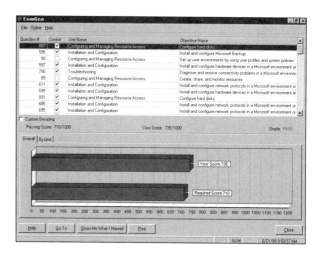

FIGURE D.15
The Examination Score Report screen.

This screen provides you with a graphical display of your test score, along with a tabular breakdown of scores by unit. The graphical display at the top of the screen compares your overall score with the score required to pass the exam. Buttons below the graphical display allow you to open the Show Me What I Missed browse sequence, print the screen, or return to the main menu.

Show Me What I Missed Browse Sequence

The Show Me What I Missed browse sequence is invoked by clicking the Show Me What I Missed button from the Examination Score Report or from the configuration screen of an adaptive exam.

Note that the window caption is modified to indicate that you are in the Show Me What I Missed browse sequence mode. Question IDs and position within the browse sequence appear at the top of the screen, in place of the Mark Question and Time Remaining indicators. Main window contents vary, depending on the question type. The following list describes the buttons available within the Show Me What I Missed browse sequence and the functions they perform:

◆ **Return to Score Report.** Returns control to the Examination Score Report screen. In the case of an adaptive exam, this button's caption is Exit, and control returns to the adaptive exam configuration screen.

◆ **Run Simulation.** Opens a simulation in Grade mode, causing the simulation to open displaying your response and the correct answer. If the current question does not offer a simulation, this button is disabled.

◆ **Exhibits.** Opens the Exhibits window. This button is enabled if one or more exhibits are available for the question.

◆ **Instructions.** Shows how to answer the current question type.

◆ **Print.** Prints the current screen.

◆ **Previous or Next.** Displays missed questions.

Checking the Web Site

To check the New Riders Home Page or the *ExamGear, Training Guide Edition* Home Page for updates or other product information, choose the desired Web site from the Web Sites option of the Online menu. You must be connected to the Internet to reach these Web sites. When you select a Web site, the Internet Explorer browser opens inside the *ExamGear, Training Guide Edition* window and displays the Web site.

OBTAINING UPDATES

The procedures for obtaining updates are outlined in this section.

The Catalog Web Site for Updates

Selecting the Check for Product Updates option from the Online menu shows you the full range of products you can either download for free or purchase. You can download additional items only if you have registered the software.

Product Updates Dialog Box

This dialog box appears when you select Check for Product Updates from the Online menu. *ExamGear, Training Guide Edition* checks for product updates from the New Riders Internet site and displays a list of products available for download. Some items, such as *ExamGear* program updates or bonus question sets for exam databases you have activated, are available for download free of charge.

Types of Updates

Several types of updates may be available for download, including various free updates and additional items available for purchase.

Free Program Updates

Free program updates include changes to the *ExamGear, Training Guide Edition* executables and runtime libraries (DLLs). When any of these items are downloaded, *ExamGear* automatically installs the upgrades. *ExamGear, Training Guide Edition* will be reopened after the installation is complete.

Free Database Updates

Free database updates include updates to the exam or exams that you have registered. Exam updates are contained in compressed, encrypted files and include exam databases, simulations, and exhibits. *ExamGear, Training Guide Edition* automatically decompresses these files to their proper location and updates the *ExamGear* software to record version changes and import new question sets.

CONTACTING NEW RIDERS PUBLISHING

At New Riders, we strive to meet and exceed the needs of our customers. We have developed *ExamGear, Training Guide Edition* to surpass the demands and expectations of network professionals seeking technical certifications, and we think it shows. What do you think?

If you need to contact New Riders regarding any aspect of the *ExamGear, Training Guide Edition* product line, feel free to do so. We look forward to hearing from you. Contact us at the following address or phone number:

New Riders Publishing
201 West 103 Street
Indianapolis, IN 46290
800-545-5914

You can also reach us on the World Wide Web:

`http://www.newriders.com`

Technical Support

Technical support is available at the following phone number during the hours specified:

317-581-3833

Monday through Friday, 10:00 a.m.–3:00 p.m. Central Standard Time.

Customer Service

If you have a damaged product and need a replacement or refund, please call the following phone number:

800-858-7674

Product Updates

Product updates can be obtained by choosing *ExamGear, Training Guide Edition*'s Online pull-down menu and selecting Products Updates. You'll be taken to a private Web site with full details.

Product Suggestions and Comments

We value your input! Please email your suggestions and comments to the following address:

`certification@mcp.com`

LICENSE AGREEMENT

YOU SHOULD CAREFULLY READ THE FOLLOWING TERMS AND CONDITIONS BEFORE BREAKING THE SEAL ON THE PACKAGE. AMONG OTHER THINGS, THIS AGREEMENT LICENSES THE ENCLOSED SOFTWARE TO YOU AND CONTAINS WARRANTY AND LIABILITY DISCLAIMERS. BY BREAKING THE SEAL ON THE PACKAGE, YOU ARE ACCEPTING AND AGREEING TO THE TERMS AND CONDITIONS OF THIS AGREEMENT. IF YOU DO NOT AGREE TO THE TERMS OF THIS AGREEMENT, DO NOT BREAK THE SEAL. YOU SHOULD PROMPTLY RETURN THE PACKAGE UNOPENED.

LICENSE

Subject to the provisions contained herein, New Riders Publishing (NRP) hereby grants to you a nonexclusive, nontransferable license to use the object-code version of the computer software product (Software) contained in the package on a single computer of the type identified on the package.

SOFTWARE AND DOCUMENTATION

NRP shall furnish the Software to you on media in machine-readable object-code form and may also provide the standard documentation (Documentation) containing instructions for operation and use of the Software.

LICENSE TERM AND CHARGES

The term of this license commences upon delivery of the Software to you and is perpetual unless earlier terminated upon default or as otherwise set forth herein.

TITLE

Title, ownership right, and intellectual property rights in and to the Software and Documentation shall remain in NRP and/or in suppliers to NRP of programs contained in the Software. The Software is provided for your own internal use under this license. This license does not include the right to sublicense and is personal to you and therefore may not be assigned (by operation of law or otherwise) or transferred without the prior written consent of NRP. You acknowledge that the Software in source code form remains a confidential trade secret of NRP and/or its suppliers and therefore you agree not to attempt to decipher or decompile, modify, disassemble, reverse engineer, or prepare derivative works of the Software or develop source code for the Software or knowingly allow others to do so. Further, you may not copy the Documentation or other written materials accompanying the Software.

UPDATES

This license does not grant you any right, license, or interest in and to any improvements, modifications, enhancements, or updates to the Software and Documentation. Updates, if available, may be obtained by you at NRP's then-current standard pricing, terms, and conditions.

LIMITED WARRANTY AND DISCLAIMER

NRP warrants that the media containing the Software, if provided by NRP, is free from defects in material and workmanship under normal use for a period of sixty (60) days from the date you purchased a license to it.

THIS IS A LIMITED WARRANTY AND IT IS THE ONLY WARRANTY MADE BY NRP. THE SOFTWARE IS PROVIDED "AS IS" AND NRP SPECIFICALLY DISCLAIMS ALL WARRANTIES OF ANY KIND, EITHER EXPRESS OR IMPLIED, INCLUDING, BUT NOT LIMITED TO, THE IMPLIED WARRANTY OF MERCHANTABILITY AND FITNESS FOR A PARTICULAR PURPOSE. FURTHER, COMPANY DOES NOT WARRANT, GUARANTEE, OR MAKE ANY REPRESENTA-TIONS REGARDING THE USE, OR THE RESULTS OF THE USE, OF THE SOFTWARE IN TERMS OR CORRECTNESS, ACCURACY, RELIABILITY, CURRENTNESS, OR OTHERWISE AND DOES NOT WARRANT THAT THE OPERATION OF ANY SOFTWARE WILL BE UNINTERRUPTED OR ERROR FREE. NRP EXPRESSLY DISCLAIMS ANY WARRANTIES NOT STATED HEREIN. NO ORAL OR WRITTEN INFORMATION OR ADVICE GIVEN BY NRP, OR ANY NRP DEALER, AGENT, EMPLOYEE, OR OTHERS SHALL CREATE,

MODIFY, OR EXTEND A WARRANTY OR IN ANY WAY INCREASE THE SCOPE OF THE FOREGOING WARRANTY, AND NEITHER SUBLICENSEE OR PURCHASER MAY RELY ON ANY SUCH INFORMATION OR ADVICE. If the media is subjected to accident, abuse, or improper use, or if you violate the terms of this Agreement, then this warranty shall immediately be terminated. This warranty shall not apply if the Software is used on or in conjunction with hardware or programs other than the unmodified version of hardware and programs with which the Software was designed to be used as described in the Documentation.

LIMITATION OF LIABILITY

Your sole and exclusive remedies for any damage or loss in any way connected with the Software are set forth below.

UNDER NO CIRCUMSTANCES AND UNDER NO LEGAL THEORY, TORT, CONTRACT, OR OTHERWISE, SHALL NRP BE LIABLE TO YOU OR ANY OTHER PERSON FOR ANY INDIRECT, SPECIAL, INCIDENTAL, OR CONSEQUENTIAL DAMAGES OF ANY CHARACTER INCLUDING, WITHOUT LIMITATION, DAMAGES FOR LOSS OF GOODWILL, LOSS OF PROFIT, WORK STOPPAGE, COMPUTER FAILURE OR MALFUNCTION, OR ANY AND ALL OTHER COMMERCIAL DAMAGES OR LOSSES, OR FOR ANY OTHER DAMAGES EVEN IF NRP SHALL HAVE BEEN INFORMED OF THE POSSIBILITY OF SUCH DAMAGES, OR FOR ANY CLAIM BY ANOTHER PARTY. NRP'S THIRD-PARTY PROGRAM SUPPLIERS MAKE NO WARRANTY, AND HAVE NO LIABILITY WHATSOEVER, TO YOU. NRP's sole and exclusive obligation and liability and your exclusive remedy shall be: upon NRP's election, (i) the replacement of our defective media; or (ii) the repair or correction of your defective media if NRP is able, so that it will conform to the above warranty; or (iii) if NRP is unable to replace or repair, you may terminate this license by returning the Software. Only if you inform NRP of your problem during the applicable warranty period will NRP be obligated to honor this warranty. SOME STATES OR JURISDICTIONS DO NOT ALLOW THE EXCLUSION OF IMPLIED WARRANTIES OR LIMITATION OR EXCLUSION OF CONSE-QUENTIAL DAMAGES, SO THE ABOVE LIMITATIONS OR EXCLUSIONS MAY NOT APPLY TO YOU. THIS WARRANTY GIVES YOU SPECIFIC LEGAL RIGHTS AND YOU MAY ALSO HAVE OTHER RIGHTS WHICH VARY BY STATE OR JURISDICTION.

MISCELLANEOUS

If any provision of the Agreement is held to be ineffective, unenforceable, or illegal under certain circumstances for any reason, such decision shall not affect the validity or enforceability (i) of such provision under other circumstances or (ii) of the remaining provisions hereof under all circumstances, and such provision shall be reformed to and only to the extent necessary to make it effective, enforceable, and legal under such circumstances. All headings are solely for convenience and shall not be considered in interpreting this Agreement. This Agreement shall be governed by and construed under New York law as such law applies to agreements between New York residents entered into and to be performed entirely within New York, except as required by U.S. Government rules and regulations to be governed by Federal law.

YOU ACKNOWLEDGE THAT YOU HAVE READ THIS AGREEMENT, UNDERSTAND IT, AND AGREE TO BE BOUND BY ITS TERMS AND CONDITIONS. YOU FURTHER AGREE THAT IT IS THE COMPLETE AND EXCLUSIVE STATE-MENT OF THE AGREEMENT BETWEEN US THAT SUPERSEDES ANY PROPOSAL OR PRIOR AGREEMENT, ORAL OR WRITTEN, AND ANY OTHER COMMUNICATIONS BETWEEN US RELATING TO THE SUBJECT MATTER OF THIS AGREEMENT.

U.S. GOVERNMENT RESTRICTED RIGHTS

Use, duplication, or disclosure by the Government is subject to restrictions set forth in subparagraphs (a) through (d) of the Commercial Computer-Restricted Rights clause at FAR 52.227-19 when applicable, or in subparagraph (c) (1) (ii) of the Rights in Technical Data and Computer Software clause at DFARS 252.227-7013, and in similar clauses in the NASA FAR Supplement.

Index

A

access
  local network resource access (end-user requirement analysis), 61-62
  public networks, 663-664
    hiding internal network addresses, 665-666
  remote network resource access (end-user requirement analysis), 62
access control. *See also* **authorization**
  local access, 676
  public network access, 663-664
    blocking protocol traffic, 667-669
    client-side configuration, 667
    hiding internal network addresses, 665
    limiting portals, 669
    NAT, 665-666
    office policies, 669
    server-side configuration, 666-667
  over WANs, 688
    screened subnets, 689
access method analysis, 112
  authentication, 113-114
  authorization, 114-115
  backup data, 115-116
  external access, 116
  physical access, 113
access permissions. *See* **permissions**
account logon events (audit policy design), 262
account management events (audit policy design), 262
Account Operators group
  privileges, 761
  security group design strategy, 296

Account Policies (security templates), 172
Account Policy Settings
  desktop computer security templates, 195-196
  domain controller security templates, 175-176
  server security templates, 188
accounts. *See* **user accounts**
acquisition plans (organizational structure analysis), 31
Active Directory
  components, 162-163
  directory service access events (audit policy design), 262-264
  domains, 163-164, 167
  features, 161-162
  forests, 163-164
  Global Catalog, 185
  OUs (organizational units), 166
  relationship with Kerberos, 427, 429
  schema (security), 242-244
  security features, 163
  sites, 166-167
  trees, 163-164
  trusts, 165-166
  Windows 2000 PKI, 511
Active Directory Integrated zones (DNS), advantages, 776
Active Directory-integrated zone files, 570-572
active study strategies, 786
adaptive exams
  described, 788-789
  process, 789-790
  tips for, 797
addressing schemes, hiding, 665
  NAT, 665-666

D

H

M

N

Q-R

T

U

X-Z

Additional Tools for Certification Preparation

Selected titles for networking professionals on the road to certification

Taking the author-driven, no-nonsense approach that we pioneered with our *Landmark* books, New Riders proudly offers something unique for Windows 2000 administrators—an interesting and discriminating book on Windows 2000 Server, written by someone in the trenches who can anticipate your situation and provide answers you can trust.

INSIDE
Windows 2000
Server

New Riders

William Boswell

ISBN: 1-56205-929-7

Windows 2000
ESSENTIAL REFERENCE

Includes coverage of Server, Workstation, and Professional

New Riders

Steven Tate, et al.

Architected to be the most navigable, useful, and value-packed reference for Windows 2000, this book uses a creative "telescoping" design that you can adapt to your style of learning. It's a concise, focused, and quick reference for Windows 2000, providing the kind of practical advice, tips, procedures, and additional resources that every administrator will need.

ISBN: 0-7357-0869-X

Understanding the Network is just one of several new titles from New Riders' acclaimed *Landmark Series*. This book addresses the audience in practical terminology, and describes the most essential information and tools required to build high-availability networks in a step-by-step implementation format. Each chapter could be read as a stand-alone, but the book builds progressively toward a summary of the essential concepts needed to put together a wide area network.

Understanding
the Network
A Practical Guide to
Internetworking

New Riders

Michael J. Martin

ISBN: 0-7357-0977-7

New Riders
Windows 2000 Resources

Advice and Experience for the Windows 2000 Networker

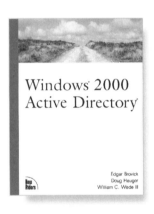

LANDMARK SERIES

We know how important it is to have access to detailed, solution-oriented information on core technologies. *Landmark* books contain the essential information you need to solve technical problems. Written by experts and subjected to rigorous peer and technical reviews, our *Landmark* books are hard-core resources for practitioners like you.

ESSENTIAL REFERENCE SERIES

The *Essential Reference* series from New Riders provides answers when you know what you want to do but need to know how to do it. Each title skips extraneous material and assumes a strong base of knowledge. These are indispensable books for the practitioner who wants to find specific features of a technology quickly and efficiently. Avoiding fluff and basic material, these books present solutions in an innovative, clean format—and at a great value.

CIRCLE SERIES

The *Circle Series* is a set of reference guides that meet the needs of the growing community of advanced, technical-level networkers who must architect, develop, and administer Windows NT/2000 systems. These books provide network designers and programmers with detailed, proven solutions to their problems.

The Road to MCSE Windows 2000

The new Microsoft Windows 2000 track is designed for information technology professionals working in a typically complex computing environment of medium to large organizations. A Windows 2000 MCSE candidate should have at least one year of experience implementing and administering a network operating system.

MCSEs in the Windows 2000 track are required to pass **five core exams and two elective exams** that provide a valid and reliable measure of technical proficiency and expertise.

See below for the exam information and the relevant New Riders title that covers that exam.

Core Exams

MCSE Candidates (Who Have Not Already Passed Windows NT 4.0 Exams) st Take All 4 of the Following Core Exams:

m 70-210: Installing, Configuring Administering Microsoft® dows® 2000 Professional

m 70-215: Installing, Configuring Administering Microsoft dows 2000 Server

m 70-216: Implementing Administering a Microsoft dows 2000 Network structure

m 70-217: Implementing Administering a Microsoft dows 2000 Directory ices Infrastructure

 ISBN 0-7357-0965-3
 ISBN 0-7357-0968-8

 ISBN 0-7357-0966-1
 ISBN 0-7357-0976-9

or

MCPs Who Have Passed 3 Windows NT 4.0 Exams (Exams 70-067, 70-068, and 70-073) Instead of the 4 Core Exams at Left, May Take:

Exam 70-240: Microsoft Windows 2000 Accelerated Exam for MCPs Certified on Microsoft Windows NT 4.0.

(This accelerated, intensive exam, which will be available until December 31, 2001, covers the core competencies of exams 70-210, 70-215, 70-216, and 70-217.)

 ISBN 0-7357-0979-3

 ISBN 0-7357-0976-9

MCSE Training Guide: Core Exams (Bundle)

PLUS - All Candidates - 1 of the Following Core Elective Exams Required:

am 70-219: Designing a Microsoft Windows 2000 Directory ices Infrastructure

am 70-220: Designing Security for a Microsoft Windows 2000 Network

am 70-221: Designing a Microsoft Windows 2000 vork Infrastructure

 ISBN 0-7357-0983-1
 ISBN 0-7357-0984-X
 ISBN 0-7357-0982-3

US - All Candidates - 2 of the Following Elective Exams Required:

current MCSE electives (visit www.microsoft.com for a list of current electives)

cted third-party certifications that focus on interoperability will be accepted as an alternative to one ive exam. Please watch for more information on the third-party certifications that will be acceptable.)

am 70-219: Designing a Microsoft Windows 2000 Directory Services Infrastructure

am 70-220: Designing Security for a Microsoft Windows 2000 Network

am 70-221: Designing a Microsoft Windows 2000 Network Infrastructure

m 70-222: Upgrading from Microsoft Windows NT 4.0 to Microsoft Windows 2000

 ISBN 0-7357-0983-1
 ISBN 0-7357-0984-X
 ISBN 0-7357-0982-3

e exams that can also be used as elective exams may only be counted once toward a certification; that is, if a candidate receives for an exam as a core in one track, that candidate will not receive credit for that same exam as an elective in that same track.

New Riders

WWW.NEWRIDERS.COM

Books for Networking Professionals

Windows NT/2000 Titles

Windows 2000 TCP/IP
By Karanjit Siyan, Ph.D.
2nd Edition
700 pages, $34.99
ISBN: 0-7357-0992-0
Available August 2000

Windows 2000 TCP/IP cuts through the complexities and provides the most informative and complex reference book on Windows 2000-based TCP/IP topics. The book is a tutorial-reference hybrid, focusing on how Microsoft TCP/IP works, using hands-on tutorials and practical examples. Concepts essential to TCP/IP administration are explained thoroughly, and are then related to the practical use of Microsoft TCP/IP in a serious networking environment.

Windows 2000 DNS
By Roger Abell, Herman Knief, Andrew Daniels, and Jeffrey Graham
2nd Edition
450 pages, $39.99
ISBN: 0-7357-0973-4

The Domain Name System is a directory of registered computer names and IP addresses that can be instantly located. Without proper design and administration of DNS, computers wouldn't be able to locate each other on the network, and applications like email and Web browsing wouldn't be feasible. Administrators need this information to make their networks work. *Windows 2000 DNS* provides a technical overview of DNS and WINS, and how to design and administer them for optimal performance in a Windows 2000 environment.

Windows 2000 Registry
By Sandra Osborrne
2nd Edition
550 pages, $34.99
ISBN: 0-7357-0944-0
Available August 2000

Windows 2000 Registry is a powerful tool for accomplishing many important administration tasks, but little information is available on registry settings and how they can be edited to accomplish these tasks. This title offers unique insight into using registry settings to software or configure client systems in a Windows 2000 environment. The approach of the book is that of revealing the GUI through the registry, allowing system administrators to edit the registry settings to efficiently accomplish critical tasks such as configuration, installation, and management.

Windows 2000 Server Professional Reference
By Karanjit Siyan, Ph.D.
3rd Edition
1800 pages, $75.00
ISBN: 0-7357-0952-1

Windows 2000 Server Professional Reference is the benchmark of references available for Windows 2000. Although other titles take you through the setup and implementation phase of the product, no other book provides the user with detailed answers to day-to-day administration problems and tasks. Real-world implementations are key to help administrators discover the most viable solutions for their particular environments. Solid content shows administrators how to manage, troubleshoot, and fix problems that are specific to heterogeneous Windows networks, as well as Internet features and functionality.

Windows 2000 Professional
By Jerry Honeycutt
350 pages, $34.99 US
ISBN: 0-7357-0950-5

Windows 2000 Professional explores the power available to the Windows workstation user on the corporate network and Internet. The book is aimed directly at the power user who values the security, stability, and networking capabilities of NT alongside the ease and familiarity of the Windows 95/98 user interface. This book covers both user and administration topics, with a dose of networking content added for connectivity.

Windows NT Power Toolkit
By Stu Sjouwerman and Ed Tittel
1st Edition
800 pages, $49.99
ISBN: 0-7357-0922-X

This book covers the analysis, tuning, optimization, automation, enhancement, maintenance, and troubleshooting of Windows NT Server 4.0 and Windows NT Workstation 4.0. In most cases, the two operating systems overlap completely. Where the two systems diverge, each platform is covered separately. This advanced title comprises a task-oriented treatment of the Windows NT 4.0 environment. By concentrating on the use of operating system tools and utilities, resource kit elements, and selected third-

party tuning, analysis, optimization, and productivity tools, this book will show you how to carry out everyday and advanced tasks.

Windows 2000 User Management
By Lori Sanders
300 pages, $34.99
ISBN: 1-56205-886-X

With the dawn of Windows 2000, it has become even more difficult to draw a clear line between managing the user and managing the user's environment and desktop. This book, written by a noted trainer and consultant, provides comprehensive, practical advice to managing users and their desktop environments with Windows 2000.

Windows 2000 Deployment & Desktop Management
By Jeffrey A. Ferris, MCSE
1st Edition
400 pages, $34.99
ISBN: 0-7357-0975-0

More than a simple overview of new features and tools, *Windows 2000 Deployment & Desktop Management* is a thorough reference to deploying Windows 2000 Professional to corporate workstations. Incorporating real-world advice and detailed exercises, this book is a one-stop resource for any system administrator, integrator, engineer, or other IT professional.

Planning for Windows 2000

By Eric K. Cone, Jon Boggs, and Sergio Perez
1st Edition
400 pages, $29.99
ISBN: 0-7357-0048-6

Windows 2000 is poised to be one of the largest and most important software releases of the next decade, and you are charged with planning, testing, and deploying it in your enterprise. Are you ready? With this book, you will be. *Planning for Windows 2000* lets you know what the upgrade hurdles will be, informs you of how to clear them, guides you through effective Active Directory design, and presents you with detailed rollout procedures. Eric K. Cone, Jon Boggs, and Sergio Perez give you the benefit of their extensive experiences as Windows 2000 Rapid Deployment Program members by sharing problems and solutions they've encountered on the job.

Inside Windows 2000 Server

By William Boswell
2nd Edition
1533 pages, $49.99
ISBN: 1-56205-929-7

Finally, a totally new edition of New Riders' best-selling *Inside Windows NT Server 4.* Taking the author-driven, nononsense approach pioneered with the *Landmark* books, New Riders proudly offers something unique for Windows 2000 administrators—an interesting, discriminating book on Windows 2000 Server written by someone who can anticipate your situation and give you workarounds that won't leave a system unstable or sluggish.

BackOffice Titles

Implementing Exchange Server

By Doug Hauger, Marywynne Leon, and William C. Wade III
1st Edition
400 pages, $29.99
ISBN: 1-56205-931-9

If you're interested in connectivity and maintenance issues for Exchange Server, this book is for you. Exchange's power lies in its capability to be connected to multiple email subsystems to create a "universal email backbone." It's not unusual to have several different and complex systems all connected via email gateways, including Lotus Notes or cc:Mail, Microsoft Mail, legacy mainframe systems, and Internet mail. This book covers all of the problems and issues associated with getting an integrated system running smoothly, and it addresses troubleshooting and diagnosis of email problems with an eye toward prevention and best practices.

Exchange System Administration

By Janice Rice Howd
1st Edition
300 pages, $34.99
ISBN: 0-7357-0081-8

Your Exchange server is installed and connected—now what? Email administration is one of the most critical networking jobs, and Exchange can be particularly troublesome in large, heterogeneous environments. Janice Howd, a noted consultant and teacher with more than a decade of email administration experience, has put together this advanced, concise handbook for daily, periodic, and emergency administration. With in-depth coverage of topics like managing disk resources, replication, and disaster recovery, this is the one reference every Exchange administrator needs.

SQL Server System Administration

By Sean Baird,
Chris Miller, et al.
1st Edition
352 pages, $29.99
ISBN: 1-56205-955-6

How often does your SQL Server go down during the day when everyone wants to access the data? Do you spend most of your time being a "report monkey" for your coworkers and bosses? *SQL Server System Administration* helps you keep data consistently available to your users. This book omits introductory information. The authors don't spend time explaining queries and how they work. Instead, they focus on the information you can't get anywhere else, like how to choose the correct replication topology and achieve high availability of information.

Internet Information Services Administration

By Kelli Adam
1st Edition,
200 pages, $29.99
ISBN: 0-7357-0022-2

Are the new Internet technologies in Internet Information Services giving you headaches? Does protecting security on the Web take up all of your time? Then this is the book for you. With hands-on configuration training, advanced study of the new protocols, the most recent version of IIS, and detailed instructions on authenticating users with the new Certificate Server and implementing and managing the new e-commerce features, *Internet Information Services Administration* gives you the real-life solutions you need. This definitive resource prepares you for upgrading to Windows 2000 by giving you detailed advice on working with Microsoft Management Console, which was first used by IIS.

SMS 2 Administration

By Michael Lubanski
and Darshan Doshi
1st Edition
350 pages, $39.99
ISBN: 0-7357-0082-6

Microsoft's new version of its Systems Management Server (SMS) is starting to turn heads. Although complex, it allows administrators to lower their total cost of ownership and more efficiently manage clients, applications, and support operations. If your organization is using or implementing SMS, you'll need some expert advice. Michael Lubanski and Darshan Doshi can help you get the most bang for your buck with insight, expert tips, and real-world examples. Michael and Darshan are consultants specializing in SMS and have worked with Microsoft on one of the most complex SMS rollouts in the world, involving 32 countries, 15 languages, and thousands of clients.

SQL Server Essential Reference

By Sharon Dooley
1st Edition
500 pages, $35.00 US
ISBN: 0-7357-0864-9

SQL Server Essential Reference is a comprehensive reference of advanced how-tos and techniques for SQL Server 7 administrators. This book provides solid grounding in fundamental SQL Server 7 administrative tasks to help you tame your SQL Server environment. With coverage ranging from installation, monitoring, troubleshooting security, and backup and recovery plans, this book breaks down SQL Server into its key conceptual areas and functions. This easy-to-use reference is a must-have for any SQL Server administrator.

UNIX/Linux Titles

Solaris Essential Reference
By John P. Mulligan
1st Edition
300 pages, $24.95
ISBN: 0-7357-0023-0

Looking for the fastest and easiest way to find the Solaris command you need? Need a few pointers on shell scripting? How about advanced administration tips and sound, practical expertise on security issues? Are you looking for trustworthy information about available third-party software packages that will enhance your operating system? Author John Mulligan—creator of the popular "Unofficial Guide to The Solaris™ Operating Environment" Web site (sun.icsnet.com)—delivers all that and more in one attractive, easy-to-use reference book. With clear and concise instructions on how to perform important administration and management tasks, and key information on powerful commands and advanced topics, *Solaris Essential Reference* is the book you need when you know what you want to do and only need to know how.

Linux System Administration
By M. Carling, Stephen Degler, and James Dennis
1st Edition
450 pages, $29.99
ISBN: 1-56205-934-3

As an administrator, you probably feel that most of your time and energy is spent in endless firefighting. If your network has become a fragile quilt of temporary patches and work-arounds, this book is for you. Have you had trouble sending or receiving email lately? Are you looking for a way to keep your network running smoothly with enhanced performance? Are your users always hankering for more storage, services, and speed? *Linux System Administration* advises you on the many intricacies of maintaining a secure, stable system. In this definitive work, the authors address all the issues related to system administration, from adding users and managing file permissions, to Internet services and Web hosting, to recovery planning and security. This book fulfills the need for expert advice that will ensure a trouble-free Linux environment.

GTK+/Gnome Application Development
By Havoc Pennington
1st Edition
492 pages, $39.99
ISBN: 0-7357-0078-8

This title is for the reader who is conversant with the C programming language and UNIX/Linux development. It provides detailed and solution-oriented information designed to meet the needs of programmers and application developers using the GTK+/Gnome libraries. Coverage complements existing GTK+/Gnome documentation, going into more depth on pivotal issues such as uncovering the GTK+ object system, working with the event loop, managing the Gdk substrate, writing custom widgets, and mastering GnomeCanvas.

Developing Linux Applications with GTK+ and GDK
By Eric Harlow
1st Edition
490 pages, $34.99
ISBN: 0-7357-0021-4

We all know that Linux is one of the most powerful and solid operating systems in existence. And as the success of Linux grows, there is an increasing interest in developing applications with graphical user interfaces that take advantage of the power of Linux. In this book, software developer Eric Harlow gives you an indispensable development handbook focusing on the GTK+ toolkit. More than an overview of the elements of application or GUI design, this is a hands-on book that delves into the technology. With in-depth material on the various GUI programming tools and loads of examples, this book's unique focus will give you the information you need to design and launch professional-quality applications.

Linux Essential Reference
By Ed Petron
1st Edition
350 pages, $24.95
ISBN: 0-7357-0852-5

This book is all about getting things done as quickly and efficiently as possible by providing a structured organization for the plethora of available Linux information. We can sum it up in one word—value. This book has it all: concise instructions

on how to perform key administration tasks, advanced information on configuration, shell scripting, hardware management, systems management, data tasks, automation, and tons of other useful information. This book truly provides groundbreaking information for the growing community of advanced Linux professionals.

Lotus Notes and Domino Titles

Domino System Administration
By Rob Kirkland, CLP, CLI
1st Edition
850 pages, $49.99
ISBN: 1-56205-948-3

Your boss has just announced that you will be upgrading to the newest version of Notes and Domino when it ships. How are you supposed to get this new system installed, configured, and rolled out to all of your end users? You understand how Lotus Notes works—you've been administering it for years. What you need is a concise, practical explanation of the new features and how to make some of the advanced stuff work smoothly by someone like you, who has worked with the product for years and understands what you need to know. *Domino System Administration* is the answer—the first book on Domino that attacks the technology at the professional level with practical, hands-on assistance to get Domino running in your organization.

Lotus Notes & Domino Essential Reference

By Tim Bankes, CLP
and Dave Hatter, CLP, MCP
1st Edition
650 pages, $45.00
ISBN: 0-7357-0007-9

You're in a bind because you've been asked to design and program a new database in Notes for an important client who will keep track of and itemize myriad inventory and shipping data. The client wants a user-friendly interface that won't sacrifice speed or functionality. You are experienced (and could develop this application in your sleep), but feel you need something to facilitate your creative and technical abilities—something to perfect your programming skills. The answer is waiting for you: *Lotus Notes & Domino Essential Reference*. It's compact and simply designed. It's loaded with information. All of the objects, classes, functions, and methods are listed. It shows you the object hierarchy and the relationship between each one. It's perfect for you. Problem solved.

Networking Titles

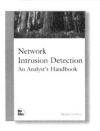

Network Intrusion Detection: An Analyst's Handbook

By Stephen Northcutt
1st Edition
267 pages, $39.99
ISBN: 0-7357-0868-1

Get answers and solutions from someone who has been in the trenches. The author, Stephen Northcutt, original developer of the Shadow intrusion detection system and former director of the United States Navy's Information System Security Office at the Naval Security Warfare Center, gives his expertise to intrusion detection specialists, security analysts, and consultants responsible for setting up and maintaining an effective defense against network security attacks.

Understanding Data Communications, Sixth Edition

By Gilbert Held
Sixth Edition
600 pages, $39.99
ISBN: 0-7357-0036-2

Updated from the highly successful fifth edition, this book explains how data communications systems and their various hardware and software components work. More than an entry-level book, it approaches the material in textbook format, addressing the complex issues involved in internetworking today. A great reference book for the experienced networking professional that is written by the noted networking authority, Gilbert Held.

Other Books By New Riders

Microsoft Technologies

ADMINISTRATION

Inside Windows 2000 Server
1-56205-929-7 • $49.99 US / $74.95 CAN
Windows 2000 Essential Reference
0-7357-0869-X • $35.00 US / $52.95 CAN
Windows 2000 Active Directory
0-7357-0870-3 • $29.99 US / $44.95 CAN
Windows 2000 Routing and Remote Access
Service
0-7357-0951-3 • $34.99 US / $52.95 CAN
Windows 2000 Deployment & Desktop
Management
0-7357-0975-0 • $34.99 US / $52.95 CAN
Windows 2000 DNS
0-7357-0973-4 • $39.99 US / $59.95 CAN
Windows 2000 User Management
1-56205-886-X • $34.99 US / $52.95 CAN
Windows 2000 Professional
0-7357-0950-5 • $34.99 US / $52.95 CAN
Planning for Windows 2000
0-7357-0048-6 • $29.99 US / $44.95 CAN
Windows 2000 Server Professional Reference
0-7357-0952-1 • $75.00 US / $111.95 CAN
Windows 2000 Security
0-7357-0991-2 • $39.99 US / $59.95 CAN
Available September 2000
Windows 2000 TCP/IP
0-7357-0992-0 • $34.99 US / $52.95 CAN
Available August 2000
Windows 2000 Registry
0-7357-0944-0 • $34.99 US / $52.95 CAN
Available August 2000
Windows 2000 Terminal Services and Citrix
MetaFrame
0-7357-1005-8 • $39.99 US / $59.95 CAN
Available October 2000
Windows NT/2000 Network Security
1-57870-253-4 • $45.00 US / $67.95 CAN
Available August 2000
Windows NT/2000 Thin Client Solutions
1-57870-239-9 • $45.00 US / $67.95 CAN
Windows 2000 Virtual Private Networking
1-57870-246-1 • $45.00 US / $67.95 CAN
Available September 2000
Windows 2000 Active Directory Design &
Migration
1-57870-242-9 • $45.00 US / $67.95 CAN
Available September 2000
Windows 2000 and Mainframe Integration
1-57870-200-3 • $40.00 US / $59.95 CAN
Windows 2000 Server: Planning and Migration
1-57870-023-X • $40.00 US / $59.95 CAN
Windows 2000 Quality of Service
1-57870-115-5 • $45.00 US / $67.95 CAN
Windows NT Power Toolkit
0-7357-0922-X • $49.99 US / $74.95 CAN
Windows NT Terminal Server and Citrix
MetaFrame
1-56205-944-0 • $29.99 US / $44.95 CAN
Windows NT Performance: Monitoring,

Benchmarking, and Tuning
1-56205-942-4 • $29.99 US / $44.95 CAN
Windows NT Registry: A Settings Reference
1-56205-941-6 • $29.99 US / $44.95 CAN
Windows NT Domain Architecture
1-57870-112-0 • $38.00 US / $56.95 CAN

SYSTEMS PROGRAMMING

Windows NT/2000 Native API Reference
1-57870-199-6 • $50.00 US / $74.95 CAN
Windows NT Device Driver Development
1-57870-058-2 • $50.00 US / $74.95 CAN
DCE/RPC over SMB: Samba and Windows NT
Domain Internals
1-57870-150-3 • $45.00 US / $67.95 CAN

APPLICATION PROGRAMMING

Delphi COM Programming
1-57870-221-6 • $45.00 US / $67.95 CAN
Windows NT Applications: Measuring and
Optimizing Performance
1-57870-176-7 • $40.00 US / $59.95 CAN
Applying COM+
ISBN 0-7357-0978-5 • $49.99 US / $74.95 CAN
Available August 2000

WEB PROGRAMMING

Exchange & Outlook: Constructing Collaborative
Solutions
ISBN 1-57870-252-6 • $40.00 US / $59.95 CAN

SCRIPTING

Windows Script Host
1-57870-139-2 • $35.00 US / $52.95 CAN
Windows NT Shell Scripting
1-57870-047-7 • $32.00 US / $45.95 CAN
Windows NT Win32 Perl Programming:
The Standard Extensions
1-57870-067-1 • $40.00 US / $59.95 CAN
Windows NT/2000 ADSI Scripting for System
Administration
1-57870-219-4 • $45.00 US / $67.95 CAN
Windows NT Automated Deployment and
Customization
1-57870-045-0 • $32.00 US / $45.95 CAN

BACK OFFICE

SMS 2 Administration
0-7357-0082-6 • $39.99 US / $59.95 CAN
Internet Information Services Administration
0-7357-0022-2 • $29.99 US / $44.95 CAN
SQL Server System Administration
1-56205-955-6 • $29.99 US / $44.95 CAN
SQL Server Essential Reference
0-7357-0864-9 • $35.00 US / $52.95 CAN

Open Source

MySQL
0-7357-0921-1 • $49.99 US / $74.95 CAN
Web Application Development with PHP
0-7357-0997-1 • $45.00 US / $67.95 CAN
Available June 2000
PHP Functions Essential Reference

0-7357-0970-X • $35.00 US / $52.95 CAN
Available August 2000
Python Essential Reference
0-7357-0901-7 • $34.95 US / $52.95 CAN
Autoconf, Automake, and Libtool
1-57870-190-2 • $35.00 US / $52.95 CAN
Available August 2000

Linux/Unix

ADMINISTRATION

Linux System Administration
1-56205-934-3 • $29.99 US / $44.95 CAN
Linux Firewalls
0-7357-0900-9 • $39.99 US / $59.95 CAN
Linux Essential Reference
0-7357-0852-5 • $24.95 US / $37.95 CAN
UnixWare 7 System Administration
1-57870-080-9 • $40.00 US / $59.99 CAN

DEVELOPMENT

Developing Linux Applications with GTK+ and
GDK
0-7357-0021-4 • $34.99 US / $52.95 CAN
GTK+/Gnome Application Development
0-7357-0078-8 • $39.99 US / $59.95 CAN
KDE Application Development
1-57870-201-1 • $39.99 US / $59.95 CAN

GIMP

Grokking the GIMP
0-7357-0924-6 • $39.99 US / $59.95 CAN
GIMP Essential Reference
0-7357-0911-4 • $24.95 US / $37.95 CAN

SOLARIS

Solaris Advanced System Administrator's Guide,
Second Edition
1-57870-039-6 • $39.99 US / $59.95 CAN
Solaris System Administrator's Guide, Second
Edition
1-57870-040-X • $34.99 US / $52.95 CAN
Solaris Essential Reference
0-7357-0023-0 • $24.95 US / $37.95 CAN

Networking

STANDARDS & PROTOCOLS

Cisco Router Configuration & Troubleshooting,
Second Edition
0-7357-0999-8 • $34.99 US / $52.95 CAN
Understanding Directory Services
0-7357-0910-6 • $39.99 US / $59.95 CAN

Understanding the Network: A Practical Guide to
Internetworking
0-7357-0977-7 • $39.99 US / $59.95 CAN
Understanding Data Communications, Sixth
Edition
0-7357-0036-2 • $39.99 US / $59.95 CAN
LDAP: Programming Directory Enabled

Applications
1-57870-000-0 • $44.99 US / $67.95 CAN
Gigabit Ethernet Networking
1-57870-062-0 • $50.00 US / $74.95 CAN
Supporting Service Level Agreements
on IP Networks
1-57870-146-5 • $50.00 US / $74.95 CAN
Directory Enabled Networks
1-57870-140-6 • $50.00 US / $74.95 CAN
Differentiated Services for the Internet
1-57870-132-5 • $50.00 US / $74.95 CAN
Quality of Service on IP Networks
1-57870-189-9 • $50.00 US / $74.95 CAN
Designing Addressing Architectures for
Routing and Switching
1-57870-059-0 • $45.00 US / $69.95 CAN
Understanding & Deploying LDAP Directory
Services
1-57870-070-1 • $50.00 US / $74.95 CAN
Switched, Fast and Gigabit Ethernet, Third
Edition
1-57870-073-6 • $50.00 US / $74.95 CAN
Wireless LANs: Implementing Interoperable
Networks
1-57870-081-7 • $40.00 US / $59.95 CAN
Wide Area High Speed Networks
1-57870-114-7 • $50.00 US / $74.95 CAN
The DHCP Handbook
1-57870-137-6 • $55.00 US / $81.95 CAN
Designing Routing and Switching Architectures for
Enterprise Networks
1-57870-060-4 • $55.00 US / $81.95 CAN
Local Area High Speed Networks
1-57870-113-9 • $50.00 US / $74.95 CAN
Available June 2000
Network Performance Baselining
1-57870-240-2 • $50.00 US / $74.95 CAN
Economics of Electronic Commerce
1-57870-014-0 • $49.99 US / $74.95 CAN

SECURITY

Intrusion Detection
1-57870-185-6 • $50.00 US / $74.95 CAN
Understanding Public-Key Infrastructure
1-57870-166-X • $50.00 US / $74.95 CAN
Network Intrusion Detection: An Analyst's
Handbook
0-7357-0868-1 • $39.99 US / $59.95 CAN
Linux Firewalls
0-7357-0900-9 • $39.99 US / $59.95 CAN

LOTUS NOTES/DOMINO

Domino System Administration
1-56205-948-3 • $49.99 US / $74.95 CAN
Lotus Notes & Domino Essential Reference
0-7357-0007-9 • $45.00 US / $67.95 CAN

Software Architecture & Engineering

Designing for the User with OVID
1-57870-101-5 • $40.00 US / $59.95 CAN
Designing Flexible Object-Oriented Systems with
UML
1-57870-098-1 • $40.00 US / $59.95 CAN
Constructing Superior Software
1-57870-147-3 • $40.00 US / $59.95 CAN
A UML Pattern Language
1-57870-118-X • $45.00 US / $67.95 CAN

Professional Certification

TRAINING GUIDES

MCSE Training Guide: Networking Essentials,
2nd Ed.
156205919X • $49.99 US / $74.95 CAN
MCSE Training Guide: Windows NT Server 4,
2nd Ed.
1562059165 • $49.99 US / $74.95 CAN
MCSE Training Guide: Windows NT
Workstation 4, 2nd Ed.
1562059181 • $49.99 US / $74.95 CAN
MCSE Training Guide: Windows NT Server 4
Enterprise, 2nd Ed.
1562059173 • $49.99 US / $74.95 CAN
MCSE Training Guide: Core Exams Bundle, 2nd
Ed.
1562059262 • $149.99 US / $223.95 CAN
MCSE Training Guide: TCP/IP, 2nd Ed.
1562059203 • $49.99 US / $74.95 CAN
MCSE Training Guide: IIS 4, 2nd Ed.
0735708657 • $49.99 US / $74.95 CAN
MCSE Training Guide: SQL Server 7
Administration
0735700036 • $49.99 US / $74.95 CAN
MCSE Training Guide: SQL Server 7
Database Design
0735700044 • $49.99 US / $74.95 CAN
CLP Training Guide: Lotus Notes 4
0789715058 • $59.99 US / $84.95 CAN
MCSD Training Guide: Visual Basic 6 Exams
0735700028 • $69.99 US / $104.95 CAN
MCSD Training Guide: Solution Architectures
0735700265 • $49.99 US / $74.95 CAN
MCSD Training Guide: 4-in-1 Bundle
0735709122 • $149.99 US / $223.95 CAN
CCNA Training Guide
0735700516 • $49.99 US / $74.95 CAN
A+ Certification Training Guide, 2nd Ed.
0735709076 • $49.99 US / $74.95 CAN
Network+ Certification Guide
073570077X • $49.99 US / $74.95 CAN
Solaris 2.6 Administrator Certification Training
Guide, Part I
157870085X • $40.00 US / $59.95 CAN
Solaris 2.6 Administrator Certification Training
Guide, Part II
1578700868 • $40.00 US / $59.95 CAN
MCSE Training Guide: Windows 2000
Professional
0735709653 • $49.99 US / $74.95 CAN •
MCSE Training Guide: Windows 2000 Server
0735709688 • $49.99 US / $74.95 CAN •
MCSE Training Guide: Windows 2000 Network
Infrastructure
0735709661 • $49.99 US / $74.95 CAN
MCSE Training Guide: Windows 2000 Network

Security Design
073570984X • $49.99 US / $74.95 CAN
MCSE Training Guide: Windows 2000 Network
Infrastructure Design
0735709823 • $49.99 US / $74.95 CAN
MCSE Training Guide: Windows 2000 Directory
Svcs. Infrastructure
0735709769 • $49.99 US / $74.95 CAN
MCSE Training Guide: Windows 2000 Directory
Services Design
0735709831 • $49.99 US / $74.95 CAN
MCSE Training Guide: Windows 2000
Accelerated Exam
0735709793 • $59.99 US / $89.95 CAN
MCSE Training Guide: Windows 2000 Core
Exams Bundle
0735709882 • $149.99 US / $223.95 CAN

HOW TO CONTACT US

IF YOU NEED THE LATEST UPDATES ON A TITLE THAT YOU'VE PURCHASED:

1) Visit our Web site at www.newriders.com.

2) Enter the book ISBN number, which is located on the back cover in the bottom right-hand corner, in the site search box on the left navigation bar.

3) Select your book title from the list of search results. On the book page, you'll find available updates and downloads for your title.

IF YOU ARE HAVING TECHNICAL PROBLEMS WITH THE BOOK OR THE CD THAT IS INCLUDED:

1) Check the book's information page on our Web site according to the instructions listed above, or

2) Email us at nrfeedback@newriders.com, or

3) Fax us at 317-581-4663 ATTN: Tech Support.

IF YOU HAVE COMMENTS ABOUT ANY OF OUR CERTIFICATION PRODUCTS THAT ARE NON-SUPPORT RELATED:

1) Email us at nrfeedback@newriders.com, or

2) Write to us at New Riders, 201 W. 103rd St., Indianapolis, IN 46290-1097, or

3) Fax us at 317-581-4663.

IF YOU ARE OUTSIDE THE UNITED STATES AND NEED TO FIND A DISTRIBUTOR IN YOUR AREA:

Please contact our international department at international@mcp.com.

IF YOU ARE INTERESTED IN BEING AN AUTHOR OR TECHNICAL REVIEWER:

Email us at opportunities@newriders.com. Include your name, email address, phone number, and area of technical expertise.

IF YOU WISH TO PREVIEW ANY OF OUR CERTIFICATION BOOKS FOR CLASSROOM USE:

Email us at nrmedia@newriders.com. Your message should include your name, title, training company or school, department, address, phone number, office days/hours, text in use, and enrollment. Send these details along with your request for desk/examination copies and/or additional information.

IF YOU ARE A MEMBER OF THE PRESS AND WOULD LIKE TO REVIEW ONE OF OUR BOOKS:

Email us at nrmedia@newriders.com. Your message should include your name, title, publication or website you work for, mailing address, and email address.

WE WANT TO KNOW WHAT YOU THINK

To better serve you, we would like your opinion on the content and quality of this book. Please complete this card and mail it to us or fax it to 317-581-4663.

Name _____

Address _____

City _____ State _____ Zip _____

Phone _____ Email Address _____

Occupation _____

Which certification exams have you already passed? _____
_____
_____
_____

Which certification exams do you plan to take? _____
_____
_____
_____

What influenced your purchase of this book?
❑ Recommendation   ❑ Cover Design
❑ Table of Contents   ❑ Index
❑ Magazine Review   ❑ Advertisement
❑ Reputation of New Riders ❑ Author Name

How would you rate the contents of this book?
❑ Excellent   ❑ Very Good
❑ Good   ❑ Fair
❑ Below Average   ❑ Poor

What other types of certification products will you buy/have you bought to help you prepare for the exam?
❑ Quick reference books   ❑ Testing software
❑ Study guides   ❑ Other

What do you like most about this book? Check all that apply.
❑ Content   ❑ Writing Style
❑ Accuracy   ❑ Examples
❑ Listings   ❑ Design
❑ Index   ❑ Page Count
❑ Price   ❑ Illustrations

What do you like least about this book? Check all that apply.
❑ Content   ❑ Writing Style
❑ Accuracy   ❑ Examples
❑ Listings   ❑ Design
❑ Index   ❑ Page Count
❑ Price   ❑ Illustrations

What would be a useful follow-up book to this one for you? _____
Where did you purchase this book? _____
Can you name a similar book that you like better than this one, or one that is as good? Why? _____
_____
_____

How many New Riders books do you own? _____
What are your favorite certification or general computer book titles? _____
_____

What other titles would you like to see us develop? _____
_____

Any comments for us? _____
_____
_____

MCSE TRAINING GUIDE: WINDOWS 2000 PROFESSIONAL   0-7357-0956-3

Fold here and tape to mail

- -

Place
Stamp
Here

New Riders Publishing
201 W. 103rd St.
Indianapolis, IN 46290